POLITICS, PARTIES, AND PRESSURE GROUPS

V. O. KEY, Jr.

Professor of Political Science
Johns Hopkins University

SECOND EDITION

1948

THOMAS Y. CROWELL COMPANY, New York

TO

F. M. S. and W. C. H.

Preface to the Second Edition

THE preparation of a second edition is an inconvenience that a person brings upon himself by writing a textbook. Yet that inconvenience is offset by the opportunity that a new edition gives an author to alter views that, on more sober reflection or in the light of later research and developments, appear to have been not well advised. In this edition I have taken advantage of the opportunity to revise my judgment on various points.

The new edition continues the basic assumption of the earlier book that a student cannot gain an adequate comprehension of politics by the concentration of attention narrowly on political parties. Hence, although all the customary data of texts designed for courses in political parties are included, there is also provided an extensive treatment of pressure groups, as well as a discussion of violence and education as political techniques, matters not usually dealt with in texts. Incidentally, the conception of political science as the study of political power, its acquisition and retention, is used to lend unity to the diverse materials included in this volume.

Those acquainted with the first edition will find that substantial parts of the original text have been redrafted to take into account recent events, to give place to new additions to the literature of politics, and to improve the presentation. Some rearrangements of chapter sequence suggested by teaching experience have been made and a new chapter, "Recent Party History," included. A liberal use of maps, charts, and graphs constitutes still another added feature of the new edition.

I am indebted to teachers who have used the first edition in their classes for valuable suggestions for improvements that have been incorporated into the present edition. A few students who have read the book through no choice of their own have also offered useful observations. Their comments have convinced me that textbooks would be better if students exercised more freely their right to bring authors to task for muddy passages and other infelicitous features that are bound to creep into books. I have also the usual obligations to record to those who aid in the making of a book. Miss Margaret E. Lough and Miss

Beatrice Blakslee of the Johns Hopkins University Library helped mightily in the search for materials. Mrs. Amelia Baier, in the midst of her duties as departmental secretary, managed to find time to type the manuscript. In expressing my gratitude to these and other persons, I have no desire to saddle them with responsibility for any of the imperfections of this book. The blemishes are to be attributed solely to me.

August 30, 1947 V. O. KEY, JR.

Contents

Contents

Part Five

THE PARTY AND THE GOVERNMENT

APPENDIX

Tables

xiii

Figures

Chapter 1

POLITICS

In its campaign literature in 1944 the CIO-PAC asserted: "Politics is the science of how who gets what, when and why." From this proposition it follows that self-interest alone obliges the citizen to study the issues, to inform himself of the views of the candidates, to vote, and to carry his own weight in politics generally. Critics and opponents of the CIO-PAC zestfully attacked its definition of politics as crassly materialistic, indicative of a corrosive cynicism, neglectful of the nobler sentiments of man, and as evidence that no candidate supported by the CIO-PAC merited public office. Yet in this campaign oratory these same opponents were validating the definition by doing their utmost to influence the determination of who gets what.

For bringing into open discussion a realistic conception of politics the CIO-PAC perhaps deserves some slight token of gratitude of the republic. Politics is not, like marbles, a game played for sport. It is a game played for keeps, a game in which the stakes are high. The way the game is played and who wins affect every citizen and perhaps even his children and grandchildren.

Whether the CIO-PAC definition is suitable for academic use is another matter. Insistence upon this conception of politics could set off a merry jurisdictional dispute among the academic disciplines. The economist would contend that his science deals with who gets what how; the political scientist might retort that the entire mechanism of production and exchange operates within the limits of an environment of protection and control fixed by government. The sociologist might assert that his science of society encompasses both politics and economics, and the historian could enter like claims of universality.

Broadly, the study of politics is concerned with the institutions and processes of governance. The study of the structure of government, of constitutions, of administration, of international relations, of the legislative process, of the dynamics of the political struggle, all revolve around the problem of the governing of men. Books on political parties deal with only a small segment of the entire field of politics. They treat the dynamics that make the wheels of government turn, the pressures, interests, and forces that animate the skeletal structure of government.

1. NATURE AND SCOPE OF POLITICS

A single thread runs through all the areas into which political scientists divide their subject for study. That thread is power. International politics concerns itself fundamentally with power relations between states. Constitutions may be considered as more or less rigid crystallizations of the balance of power among different classes and interests within a society. Legislation is patently a process in which groups, sections, parties, individuals contend for power. Administration partakes at times of the nature of legislation; at other times it carries into execution the verdict of the struggle for power within the legislature. Political parties and pressure groups are active elements within society seeking governmental power and influence. The element common to all these aspects of politics is power. Political power is exercised within an organized society. Political institutions and practices, it follows, must be studied in relation to their social context. The economic system, the ecclesiastical organization, the educational arrangements, the customs and traditions, and many other factors condition and influence the structure of power broadly considered.[1]

What is Power? If the essential character of political behavior is found in power relations, it becomes pertinent to inquire what is meant by the term "power." The word has connotations in popular usage that detract from its utility as a term for exact discussion. The word itself carries by implication its own adjectives and suggests overwhelming power or unlimited authority. But power may shade off by degrees from the autocratic to the opposite extreme of the most gentle influence. Power in all these degrees of meaning involves relations among human beings. The study of politics, then, encompasses only one of many types of relations among human beings. "The social sciences," says the sociologist, W. I. Thomas, "are fundamentally concerned with relationships between either individuals and individuals, individuals and groups, or groups and other groups." If politics is one of the social sciences—and there is nothing to be gained by entering into the controversy whether the social sciences are really "sciences"—the problem immediately arises of determining which of these human relations are to be considered as "political." George E. G. Catlin, a leading English political theorist, defines politics "as a study of the act of control, or

[1] See C. E. Merriam, *Political Power* (New York: McGraw-Hill, 1934).

as the act of human or social control." [2]   In a similar vein Harold D.
Lasswell, an American political scientist, says, "The study of politics
is the study of influence and the influential." [3]   Politics is, then, concerned with relationships of control or of influence.   To phrase the idea
differently, politics deals with human relationships of superordination
and subordination, of dominance and submission, of the governors
and the governed.   The study of politics is the study of these relationships of political power; the concern of practicing politicians is the
acquisition and retention of political power.

To think of these human relationships in terms of political power
may lead to an initial misinterpretation that should be avoided.   The
power relationship is not unilateral: it is a reciprocal relationship, and
the subject may affect the ruler more profoundly than the ruler affects
the subject.   Thus, observation, not of the rulers alone, but of the
relationships of ruler and ruled constitutes the essence of the study of
politics.

The relationship of ruler and ruled is a universal phenomenon.
Only anarchists and Communists are sufficiently endowed with imagination to envisage a society without governance; yet the sloughing off of the
state is hardly perceptible under communism in Soviet Russia.   Gaetano Mosca, a provocative Italian political thinker, observed: [4]

In all societies—from societies that are very meagerly developed and have
barely attained the dawnings of civilization, down to the most advanced and
powerful societies—two classes of people appear—a class that rules and a class
that is ruled.   The first class, always the less numerous, performs all political
functions, monopolizes power, and enjoys the advantages that power brings,
whereas the second, the more numerous class, is directed and controlled by the
first, in a manner that is now more or less legal, now more or less arbitrary and
violent. . . .

Mosca's notion of a ruling class falls hard on democratic ears, yet in
democracies there are certainly those who rule and those who are ruled.
However, the credentials of membership in a democratic "ruling class"
are neither explicit nor formalized; the lines delimiting the group are
not sharply drawn; and admission to the circle of the influential is
barred mainly to those without the wit or the will to compel their
acceptance.

What power relations are political?   To say that the study of politics

[2] *A Study of the Principles of Politics* (New York, 1930), pp. 68–69. Quoted by
permission of the Macmillan Company, publishers.
[3] *Politics, Who Gets What, When, How* (New York: Whittlesey House, 1936), p. 1.
[4] Gaetano Mosca, *The Ruling Class* (New York: McGraw-Hill, 1939), p. 50. See
also G. Ferrero, *The Principles of Power* (New York: Putnam's, 1942).

is the study of control, or of influence and the influential, states a characteristic of the nature of the human relationships involved, but does
not fix the outer boundaries of the subject. Does the study of politics
include all relationships of influence, control, power? A manufacturer,
advised by an astute advertising agency, persuades millions of people
to purchase his product in fear of halitosis. Are these relationships
of influence "political" in nature? A trade-union leader becomes a czar
of the bricklayers. Is he a politician exercising political power?
Through diligent self-promotion, a clubwoman becomes a leader of
clubwomen with great power in the organization. Is this relationship
of control "political"? A clergyman becomes a bishop and a power in
ecclesiastical matters. Are the process by which he reaches that position
and the power he exercises over subordinate clergy and laity political?

A substantial body of opinion holds these and other like control
relationships to be within the sphere of politics. However, in order
that this book may be kept within manageable limits it is restricted
primarily to an examination of those power or control relationships
having to do with the machinery of government. This working distinction has been made by A. Gordon Dewey: [5]

> With the activities of the New York State Medical Society, or the Actors'
> Equity Association, the political scientist is not ordinarily concerned; he
> would speak of them as professional, not political associations; indeed, he
> might be quite unaware of their existence. When, however, the chiropractors
> seek legislation favorable to their interests, and the physicians decide to
> oppose them, or the actors meet with Mr. Gompers and officials of allied or-
> ganizations with a view to curbing the influx of competing English artists, these
> organizations may be said to be engaging in "politics." And so on up the
> scale—from the efforts of the East Harlem Storekeepers' Association, Inc., to
> compel New York City by peremptory mandamus to remove pushcart peddlers
> from Park Avenue between 111th and 116th Streets, to slavery, secession, free
> silver, world democracy and Darwinism—no matter how the question may be
> obfuscated, whenever it tends to involve a utilization of the machinery of
> government, then it becomes a "political issue"; those concerned with it are
> involved in "political activity," and the phenomenon becomes one of these
> which it is the function of the political scientist to observe.

Statics and dynamics of power relations. The foregoing observations suggest the nature or character of human relations regarded as
political, and select for study those relations of power involving, directly or indirectly, a utilization of the machinery of government. In
speculation about these relations of political power a further distinction

[5] "On Methods in the Study of Politics," *Political Science Quarterly,* 38 (1923),
pp. 637–638.

can be made; namely, the differentiation between politics as status and as process. By analysis of the relations of political power prevailing at any particular time one could build up a picture of the status or position of the persons and classes of persons involved in a political system. Obviously political power is something more than an end in itself, although for many practitioners of the art of politics the deference that accompanies power may be an adequately satisfying end in itself. The examination of politics in terms of status might lead to a study of the distribution of the products of political power: "Who Gets What, When, How," as Lasswell has pungently expressed the matter in the subtitle to his *Politics*. What positions of power are held by whom? How is the distribution of income affected by political power? How does the system of taxation, for example, influence the distribution of income? What is the value of franchises, privileges, and perquisites dispensed by the government, and by whom are these privileges enjoyed? What values in the form of safety—of life, property, income— are enjoyed by whom?

A study of politics as status would furnish for a given moment a picture of the pattern of power and of the distribution of those ends or objectives that are gained through political power. An adequate textbook centered solely on a description of political status in the broad sense could hardly be written now. Textbook writers tend to lean on scholarship: they base their works on a mass of special studies already made by others. The pattern of the allocation of values through politics has not been explored thoroughly enough to permit ready collation, within textbook limits, of material that would present a comprehensive picture of politics as status in the United States.

In American writings on politics, the emphasis has been by and large on politics as process. The relations of political power are not static. They are constantly being readjusted and their maintenance in a fairly stable form requires never-ending effort by the possessors of power. New groups arise frequently to challenge the dominance of the old, and existing groups seek always to enlarge or defend the power and influence—the status—that they enjoy. It is this dynamic aspect of power relations that constitutes the process that eventuates in the pattern of political power prevailing at any particular time. For example, how and what persons and groups acquire political power; how pressure groups bring their strength to bear on legislative bodies; how individuals rise to positions of ascendancy in the political organization; how parties and other groups manipulate public opinion to attain a given end; how candidates gain the support of the electorate; these and other like matters have been the primary concern of students of politics in

the United States and it is from their writings that the textbook
writer must draw.[6]

2. DEMOCRATIC THEORY AND POLITICS

The notion of politics as the relationships between governor and
governed, or as the pattern of balance or equilibrium between groups
of diverse interests struggling for ascendancy, runs counter to traditional American ideology. The doctrine of "popular self-government,"
the idea that government reflects only the "general will," the belief in
government "of the people, by the people, and for the people," popular
conceptions of "public opinion" and its functions—all these conspire
to create a climate of attitudes hostile to the observation of the real
nature of the relationships of the leaders and the led. The belief is
engendered that the government is identical with the mass of the
population and that by some mysterious process the "will of the people"
is translated into governmental decision and thereby the people "rule
themselves." Faith in the idea of self-government has a profound
political effect. A general belief in such doctrines creates throughout
the masses of people a sense of security, of satisfaction with the established order, and of hope of eventual improvement of their lot by the
exertion of their own strength.

Yet the assertion that people "rule themselves" does not constitute a
satisfactory description of the political process as any man may observe
it for himself. An "inner circle" of leaders or competing "inner circles" perform the function of leadership and of governance. The mass
of citizens may choose from among competing "inner circles," a state of
affairs profoundly different from that prevailing in pre-democratic
times. Yet the initiative, the leadership, the power rest, not in the mass,
but in whatever group of leaders it tolerates.

Compatibility of idea of "self-rule" with power theory. If the
"inner circle" tends to make the decisions, to govern, to hold the political power, how are we to reconcile this state of affairs with the ideas of
democracy? The use of such phrases as the "ruling class" or the "relationships of the governor and governed" may convey an impression of
unlimited power to issue commands that must be obeyed. And in some
political situations these conditions exist, but in American politics
there has tended to be a great amount of give and take between the
"inner circle" and its followers. A leader must make his decisions and
plan his campaign after considering the probable effect of a proposed
line of action on his followers. "He must consider his decision not only

---

[6] For another analysis of the scope and nature of politics, see Roy V. Peel and
J. S. Roucek, *Introduction to Politics* (New York: Crowell, 1941), chaps. 1 and 5.

on 'the merits,' but also in its effect on any part of his following whose continued support he requires." [7] Furthermore, the position of the leading or ruling individuals may involve, not the imposition of will from above, but an attempt to control through persuasion. "Government," said Franklin D. Roosevelt in 1932, "includes the art of formulating a policy and using the political technique to attain to so much of that policy as will receive general support; persuading, leading, sacrificing, teaching always because the greatest duty of the statesman is to educate."

Occasionally ruling groups are overthrown. Is such an occurrence an act of the masses? Robert Michels asserts that it would be "an error to accuse the crowd of rising against its leaders, and to make the masses responsible for their fall. It is not the masses which have devoured the leaders: the chiefs have devoured one another with the aid of the masses." [8] He believes that "every great class-movement in history has arisen upon the instigation, with the co-operation, and under the leadership of men sprung from the very class against which the movement was directed." [9] If these generalizations are correct, popular revolutions owe their origin to splits or cleavages within the dominant elements of a society; each faction of the ruling group appeals for popular support and the one most successful in this endeavor carries the day.

A characteristic that differentiates democracies and dictatorships is that in a democracy antagonistic interests have the right of presenting their demands, of protesting decisions that they deem injurious to themselves, and of advancing their cause by all means short of actual violence—and often a bit of violence is tolerated. Although a dictator may consider the probable reaction by affected groups before making a decision, he is usually prepared to suppress dissent by force if necessary; indeed, he must anticipate the effect of a decision, for even in a dictatorship there are subtle means of expressing dissatisfaction, such as the withdrawal of popular applause, sabotage, and non-cooperation.

The general will: A product of competition for power. The problem of the politician or the statesman in a democracy is to maintain a working balance between the demands of competing interests and values. His task is not necessarily the expression of the "general will" or the "popular will." As John Dickinson has said: [10]

[7] Walter Lippman, *Public Opinion* (New York: Macmillan, 1922), p. 239.

[8] Robert Michels, *Political Parties, A Sociological Study of the Oligarchical Tendencies of Modern Democracy* (New York: Hearst's International Library Co., 1915), p. 165.

[9] *Ibid.*, p. 238.

[10] "Democratic Realities and Democratic Dogma," *American Political Science Review*, 25 (1930), pp. 291–292.

The task of government, and hence of democracy as a form of government, is not to express an imaginary popular will, but to effect adjustments among the various special wills and purposes which at any given time are pressing for realization.

Almost the whole range of political problems are problems of what may be called adjustment—of devising ways and means to curb particular "wills" or "interests," and thus clear the track for the realization of other wills and interests in fuller measure. This is the task of governmental decisions ranging in importance from where to locate a new street or sewage-disposal plant to whether or not to go to war. Government, from this point of view, is primarily an arbitrator, and since practically every arbitration must result in giving to one side more of what it thinks it ought to have than the other side is willing to admit, every governmental act can be viewed as favoring in some degree some particular and partial "will," or special interest. It is therefore meaningless to criticize government, whether democratic or not, merely because it allows special interests to attain some measure of what they think themselves entitled to. The question is rather whether it allows the "right" side, or the "right" special interest, to win; and the "right" special interest means only the one whose will is most compatible with what we, as critics, conceive to be the right direction for the society's development to take.

Within limits these special interests in a democracy are free to express their demands and their disagreements. This freedom of discussion makes especially difficult the role of the politician in a democracy: he must be able to hold together enough of these special interests to retain power; he must yield here, stand firm there, delay at the next point, and again act vigorously in a confusing complex of competing forces and interests. Here we have a clue to the function of the politician and to the reason for his generally low repute in our culture. He cannot give everybody everything he wants; at times he cannot be forthright; he must play the part of arbitrator and mediator, subject to the criticism of all. To avoid or mitigate conflict, he compromises or, as the stern moralist would say, "straddles the issue."

The presentation of these views on the nature of the political process makes occasion for the dispelling of another erroneous notion about politics, that is, that the process of politics operates only during political campaigns and elections. It is continuous, and elections are only recurring episodes in a never-ending process. Pulling and hauling between conflicting interests, the resolution of these conflicts, and maneuvering for position occur between elections as well as during campaigns. Actions by Congress, state legislatures, and city councils, and by executives and administrators are a part of the political process. The decisions taken, the laws made, the questions sidestepped and those straddled affect the relationships between special and partial interests, and these relationships make up the pattern of political power at any particular time.

The romantic political theory of early democratic thinkers had no place for class, for privilege, or for power other than that of "the people." This view that finds the mandate of government in "the general will" at first blush may seem to deny the validity of an analysis of political behavior based on the assumption that the essence of politics rests in relations of power. But only the most casual acquaintance with the workings of politics suggests the inadequacy of the copybook maxims of democracy as a description of the process of governing, no matter how powerful they may be in commanding the loyalty and faith of the citizen. As may be inferred from the preceding paragraphs, a realistic analysis of the struggle for power within a great democracy need not destroy the faith of the democrat. Such an analysis may merely furnish a more sophisticated defense of the tenets of the democratic order for those who live by political faith.

3. POLITICS AND ETHICS

A factor that often constitutes an intellectual block to the detached observation and analysis of political behavior comes from a deep-seated confusion of politics and ethics. The study of politics is often approached with the hope, not so much of seeing and understanding what occurs, but of learning what "ought to be." The observation, analysis, and description of conditions and processes are very different from the justification of values or preferences. The evaluation of the outcome of a political conflict—a decision made by law, by administrative act, or by the electorate—differs from an understanding of the contending forces, the stakes at issue, and the process of arriving at a reconciliation of conflict. Evaluation (or concluding whether a given course of action is "right" or "wrong") necessitates the possession of a standard or a yardstick for judgment; students—and professors, too,—are prone to arrive at dogmatic conclusions on the "merits" of a proposition without making explicit the standard of value, or the ethical norm, against which a particular proposition is measured.

Mingling of issues of fact and of questions of right and wrong. In political practice questions of right and wrong inevitably and invariably involve themselves in the competition for power. The separation of the evaluation of the moral issues—the questions of right and wrong —from the analysis of power relations—which, of course, may be influenced by moral considerations—raises serious difficulties. For example, in a given political dispute the interests of labor and of employers may be at issue   Employers may successfully appeal to political parties, to "public opinion," and bring adequate "pressure" to win the dispute. One observer may say that the "right" decision was made; another may assert vociferously that the decision was "wrong" or even iniquitous.   Both often make their evaluations without disclosing what general standard of right or wrong they are applying to the particular situation.   And those abstract standards must, in the nature of things, be subjective assumptions of value.   The analysis and understanding of the course of the dispute and of the matters at issue lie on a different plane from the justification of its outcome.   Ultimately, science has no answer to questions of "right" and "wrong"; it may merely facilitate informed choices by predicting the probable effects of different courses of action.   Once choices of public policy are made, the data of science may be mobilized to implement those choices.

Issues of political power tend to be stated in terms of conflicts of values, of standards of "right" and "wrong."   Political conflict is fought out within a context of moral values.   F. S. Oliver, an acute political thinker, concludes that [11]

In a thousand ways the art of politics is directly affected by moral considerations.   Nevertheless, politics cannot properly be regarded as a branch of virtuous conduct; for though the two things are often intertwined, each has its own separate root and stem.   The prime motive of the politician is not to do good to humanity or even to his own country, but simply to gain power for himself.   Yet he will inevitably fail if he refuses homage to the moral standards of his particular age.   And moreover—though this is a different matter—the great majority of politicians are to some extent restrained and impelled by their own consciences.   In taking stock of a politician, however, the first question is not whether he was a good man who used righteous means, but whether he was successful in gaining power, in keeping it, and in governing; whether, in short, he was skilful at his particular craft or a bungler.

If a politician would keep his followers loyal to him, he must be careful not to outrage their feelings of right and wrong.   His course of action is therefore determined from the beginning by the morals of other people.   Unless he can persuade his own party that his intentions are consistent with its standards of public conduct, he may as well go out of business.

The confusion of politics and ethics comes in part from the fact that every segment of society in seeking to advance its interests identifies its own advantage with the public good; hence, political discussion is filled with moral cant.   And in the process of political friction, competing interests put their claims into words that give their dispute the

[11] *Politics and Politicians* (London, 1934), p. 25.   Quoted by permission of The Macmillan Company, publishers.

appearance, and often the reality, of a head-on collision between two sets of moral values. And individuals tend to believe that their own interests and views coincide with the "right" or the "general welfare."

The Association of American Railroads, the Edison Electric Institute, the Congress of Industrial Organizations, the American Federation of Labor, the Anti-Saloon League, the Democratic party, or any other group seeking power or seeking to influence the course of public action rationalizes its own interests with the public good; and through the necessity for this process of moral justification groups may be brought to modify their more extreme demands. Similarly, Michels remarks, on the basis of his analysis of European parties: [12]

Political parties, however much they may be founded upon narrow class interests and however evidently they may work against the interests of the majority, love to identify themselves with the universe, or at least to present themselves as cooperating with all the citizens of the state, and to proclaim that they are fighting in the name of all and for the good of all. It is only the socialist orators who are sometimes found to proclaim that their party is specifically a class party. But they tone down this assertion by adding that in ultimate analysis the interests of their party coincide with those of the entire people.

Conditions differentiated from preferences. Enough has been said to indicate that politics is not a branch of moral philosophy. The matter is put succinctly by Lasswell: "The study of politics states conditions; the philosophy of politics justifies preferences." [13] In the present volume the attempt is, in the main, to state conditions. Considerable attention is given incidentally to methods or ways of arriving at conclusions about conditions. If the student will try to separate his moral evaluations of political acts from his observation and analysis of political conditions, he will be able better to understand and per-

---

[12] *Op. cit.*, p. 160.

[13] Political scientists dispute among themselves whether they should limit themselves to the objective analysis and description of political behavior. The broader, and perhaps more important, field of political philosophy, as defined by Lasswell, has its adherents who contend that the discovery of right courses of public policy, of what is best for the nation under given circumstances, is within the province of the political scientist. The controversy points up sharply the difference between the task of analyzing and describing conditions and that of arriving at moral judgments on political issues. The conclusions of a tract in defense of democracy, for example, rest on a very different basis from the findings of an analysis of the way voters respond to specified types of campaign appeals. See J. H. Hallowell, "Politics and Ethics," *American Political Science Review,* 38 (1944), pp. 639–655; W. F. Whyte, "A Challenge to Political Scientists," *idem,* 37 (1943), pp. 692–697; G. A. Almond, "Politics, Science, and Ethics," *idem,* 40 (1946), pp. 283–293; L. A. Dexter, "Political Processes and Judgments of Value," *idem,* pp. 294–301; W. F. Whyte, "Politics and Ethics: A Reply to John H. Hallowell," *idem,* pp. 301–307; J. H. Hallowell, "Politics and Ethics: A Rejoinder to William F. Whyte," *idem,* pp. 307–312.

ceive the nature of political behavior.[14] This injunction does not imply that political preferences or values are not important. It merely emphasizes that the methods of arriving at judgments and the judgments themselves on "conditions," to use Lasswell's term, are quite different from the processes used to reach conclusions on "preferences."

Methods of study can be used to arrive at statements of "conditions," methods the application of which by any student to the same data will yield about the same results. The intuitive processes used to arrive at "preferences" produce no such standard results. Thus a plutocrat and a democrat may set out to define the "good life" and arrive at quite different statements based on their preferences. Even in the devising of methods for the analysis of "conditions," the study of politics is a comparatively undeveloped science. One approach to the study of politics—used in the main in this book—is to center attention on the theme of power relations among individuals and groups and to identify recurring situations in those relations. For pedagogical reasons any text must be liberally supplied with concrete facts and events, but to take on greater meaning these facts and events must be related to or illustrative of general concepts or recurring situations. Knowledge of an isolated "fact" may be quite useless erudition; the isolated "fact" must be related to a larger theory of political behavior before the significance of the "fact" may be perceived. "Facts" and "events" are stated in this book usually, not for their own importance, but for their value in illustrating some general idea or proposition of politics. All of which is equivalent to saying that one needs to know something about trees to understand a forest, but that a myopic examination of trees furnishes no conception of the nature of the forest.

In summary, the study of politics concerns itself with the analysis of relations of power among human beings, with emphasis on those power relations that touch in one way or another the machinery of government. Democratic doctrines of self-government appear to deny the existence of some groups possessing power over others, but such relations of control appear in all societies. The study of relations of power —of control and of influence—must be differentiated from the justification of preferences in public policy or the defense and promotion of political ends. Yet those who seek power must take into account the moral standards or value preferences of the culture in which they operate. In the study of politics it is soon discovered that like or similar situations recur; and it is useful in teaching to relate specific cases and examples to these recurrent patterns of behavior. In a sense, the main concern of the political scientist is the discovery of these uniformities in political behavior.

[14] See J. T. Salter, *The Pattern of Politics* (New York: Macmillan, 1940), chap. 1, "Ethics and the Voter."

Part One

PRESSURE GROUPS

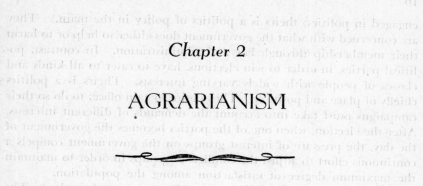

Chapter 2

AGRARIANISM

In the preceding general description of political behavior the struggle for power was suggested as the differentiating characteristic of those relationships deemed political. Power is seldom sought for its own sake. With power or with influence one may determine or at least sway the course of public policy. Who seeks to guide public policy? In the United States the most conspicuous contenders for power are the major political parties. Yet parties fight for power not so much in their own right as they do in their capacity as spokesmen for other interests in society. The party machine has an interest of its own to advance, but it gains power only to the extent that it can organize in its support sectors of society with objectives quite independent of those of the party machine. An understanding of political parties must be built on a foundation of knowledge about the principal social interests and their objectives with regard to public policy. In order to suggest the outlines of that knowledge Part I is devoted to a consideration of agriculture, labor, business, and other interest groups important in the American political scene. Political parties have to reckon with these groups, but these groups may and often do act to defend their objectives through nonparty associations.

A striking feature of American politics is the extent to which the political party is supplemented by private associations formed to influence public policy. These organizations, commonly called pressure groups, promote particular interests of their memberships by attempting to influence the government rather than by campaigning for public office and accepting responsibility for the management of the government. The political interests of labor, for example, may be advanced through lobbying and propaganda activities of pressure groups, such as the American Federation of Labor. The cause of business may be promoted in like fashion by the Chamber of Commerce of the United States. Such groups, while they may call themselves nonpolitical, are

engaged in politics; theirs is a politics of policy in the main.[1] They
are concerned with what the government does either to help or to harm
their membership through law and administration.   In contrast, political parties, in order to win elections, have to cater to all kinds and
classes of people with widely varying interests.   Theirs is a politics
chiefly of place and position.   They desire to gain office; to do so their
campaigns must take into account the demands of different interests.
After the election, when one of the parties becomes the government of
the day, the pressure of interest groups on the government compels a
continuous effort to adjust the conflicts of groups in order to maintain
the maximum degree of satisfaction among the population.

Pressure groups advance their causes by a variety of methods. The
larger groups carry on from year to year campaigns of propaganda to
develop public attitudes favorable to their interests.   Others conduct
intensive educational campaigns intermittently.[2] Creation of a generally favorable public opinion lays the basis for group success in coping
with governmental officials on particular issues.   Most of the larger
pressure groups maintain headquarters in Washington staffed by persons whose job is to keep close watch on legislative developments of
concern to the group; in addition, they present the group's viewpoint
to congressional committees, as well as to individual Congressmen.
These persons purport to speak for or to represent the membership of
their group; sometimes they are collectively referred to as a "third
house" of the legislative body.   Likewise they appear for the group
before administrative bodies and officials.   In state capitals the general arrangement is duplicated on a smaller scale.   Pressure-group
spokesmen importune the platform committees of party conventions
to include planks favorable to the interests of the group.   Furthermore
they sometimes endorse candidates, make campaign contributions, and
even canvass the voters for the election of party candidates sympathetic
to their cause.   In all these endeavors, the objectives of the pressure
group may be good or bad; the group may be animated by the highest

---

[1] For general surveys of pressure-group activity, see Pendleton Herring, *Group
Representation before Congress* (Baltimore: Johns Hopkins Press, 1929); D. C. Blais-
dell, *Economic Power and Political Pressures* (Monograph No. 26, Temporary Na-
tional Economic Committee, 1941); K. G. Crawford, *The Pressure Boys* (New York:
Messner, 1939); Stuart Chase, *Democracy Under Pressure* (New York: Twentieth
Century Fund, 1945.

[2] Dr. Mary E. Dillon differentiates between "pressure group" and "lobby," with the
attempt to influence public opinion as the differentiating characteristic of the pressure group.   Such a definition is useful in placing emphasis on the propaganda activities of the pressure group in contrast with the undercover techniques of the old-
style lobby.   See her "Pressure Groups," *American Political Science Review*, 36 (1942),
pp. 471–481.

moral purpose or it may be driving for the narrowest kind of class gain. Yet pressure-group operations constitute a significant supplement to the traditional type of representation under democratic government.

Basic to an understanding of American politics is a knowledge of the interests, desires, and ambitions of different classes and groups of citizens, for, in one sense, the principal function of the process of politics is the ironing out of friction that occurs when the desires of different groups clash. Review of the activities of pressure groups in the chapters that immediately follow furnishes an opportunity also to outline the composition of the principal interests in American society, to show how the more important of these classes and groups seek their objectives through political methods, and to indicate the general nature of these objectives. A further and valuable feature of each of these chapters is the illustration of a broad characteristic of political behavior that may apply to many situations other than that in which it is discussed. The chapter on labor, for example, illustrates the tendencies toward oligarchy and toward traditionalism in political behavior. Obviously these tendencies are not limited to labor organizations, but they may be illustrated in that context.

1. AGRICULTURE IN AMERICAN LIFE

Agrarian influence in American life has extended far beyond the sphere of politics. And in politics, although by 1940 the proportion of farm population in our total population had declined to 23.2 per cent, the influence of agriculture is far greater than might be expected from its relative numerical strength. Its influence has been felt in more pervasive and more subtle ways than through voting and lobbying. A nation once predominantly rural and still drawing a large proportion of its new population from the excess of rural over urban births has been deeply influenced by the moral values of farm people. The nature of the development and exploitation of farm land in the United States encouraged resourcefulness, independence, self-reliance, freedom. The same influences encouraged a mobility of population unknown to European peasantry, a trait of profound significance in the functioning of the American economy.[3] Rural attitudes and rural people, so the belief has been, constitute the reality and the strength of America. Thomas Jefferson asserted that people engaged in agriculture were "the chosen people of God, if ever He had a chosen

[3] See Ralph Turner, "The Cultural Setting of American Agricultural Problems," *1940 Yearbook of Agriculture;* C. Arnold Anderson, "Agrarianism in Politics" in J. S. Roucek, *Twentieth Century Political Thought* (New York: Philosophical Library, 1946), chap. 10.

people;" cities were "essentially evil" and "ulcers on the body politic."
These ideas did not die with Jefferson, and partly from the strength of
such notions agriculture has enjoyed a strategic advantage in politics.[4]
Moreover, rural attitudes, projected into urban problems both by
simple historical persistence and by rural-urban migration, have created
difficult problems of political adjustment of institutions and practices
to meet new situations.

Contraction of farm markets. The free and independent rural
yeomanry, however, has long since lost its position of dominance. Adverse trends have reduced the relative position of agriculture in the
American economy and brought about conditions within agriculture
requiring extensive political action. Contraction in the market for
agricultural products has necessitated painful adjustments in the farm
plant and in the farm labor force. The export market for farm products has declined since 1900 except for the temporary spurts in foreign
demand in World Wars I and II. In the period 1925–1929 it required
the product of about 50 million acres to meet annual export demands.
An annual average of only 23 million acres was required for this purpose
in the years 1935–1939.[5] Certain long-term dietary changes have operated to the disadvantage of some classes of farmers and to the advantage of others. The decline in wheat-flour consumption has been
notable. It was estimated in 1934 that had the 1900 level of cereal
consumption continued to prevail, over 20,000,000 more acres of
cereals would have been needed to feed the American people.[6] Another market for farm products diminished with the decline of the
horse and mule population by about 14 million from 1910 to 1940.
Fifty million acres formerly used to produce animal food thereby became available for other uses.

Technological change bringing higher productivity per farm worker
has compounded the effects of market contractions. In 1787 the surplus food produced by nineteen farmers went to "feed one city person."

[4] Gaus and Wolcott note the significance in American politics of the "moral importance" of "farmers in American society as a whole, and, consequently, of their
rightful claim upon that society for their fair share of its production, power, and
prestige. We have used the term 'moral importance' because this assumption, while
obviously related to and reflective of economic claims, has its more intangible, yet
equally important, implication that the essential nature of American society at its
best derives from the rural community of free, independent, land-owning, God-
fearing farmers."—*Public Administration and the United States Department of
Agriculture,* pp. 17–18.

[5] J. M. Brewster, "Farm Technological Advance and Total Population Growth,"
Journal of Farm Economics, 27 (1945), 509–525.

[6] National Resources Board, *A Report on National Planning, Part II, Report of
the Land Planning Committee* (Washington, 1934), p. 114.

In average years just before 1937, nineteen people on farms produced enough food for 56 nonfarm people, plus ten living abroad.[7]   So long as population increased rapidly enough to offset loss of foreign markets, market contractions through other causes, and increases in productivity, farming was an expanding business although it was becoming proportionately less important in the total economy.   In the 1920's, however, increase in the productivity was four times the rate of population increase.   In 1940, 79 workers could produce the quantity of farm products that had required the labor of 100 in 1930.[8]

Commercialization of agriculture.   Technological innovation has been accompanied by changes in the economic organization of agriculture, which have had far-reaching political consequences.   Agriculture has become a business instead of a way of life.   A farm is a factory instead of a place where one lives, rears his family, produces much of his food, and sells enough to buy only a few items in the market.   A statistical insight into the trend of events may be had from Table 1, which shows the sharp increase from 1910 to 1940 of the proportion of farm income attributed to capital and management.   In commercial farming it may be more accurate to say that the farmer invests, hires, and manages rather than to say that the farmer toils.   In some areas,

TABLE 1

Estimated Relative Share of Gross Income in Agriculture Imputed to Land, Labor, and Capital and Management [a]

Period	Labor	Land	Capital and Management	Total
1910–14	53.5	30.3	16.4	100.0
1924–28	47.4	30.2	22.4	100.0
1936–40	41.8	26.9	31.3	100.0

[a] E. O. Heady, "Changes in Income Distribution in Agriculture with Special Reference to Technological Progress," *Journal of Farm Economics,* 36 (1944), p. 440.

such as California, the economic organization of agriculture makes it not inaccurate to speak of "industrialized farming." [9]   Commercial farming brings a sharp differentiation between proprietor and laborer as well as a distinction between commercial farmer and family farmer. The social and economic differentiation between farm proprietor and

[7] National Resources Committee, *Technological Trends and National Policy* (Washington, 1937), Part III, Section I.

[8] Brewster, *op. cit.,* p. 515. See also J. A. Hopkins, *Changing Technology and Employment in Agriculture* (Washington: Government Printing Office, 1941).

[9] See Senate Committee on Education and Labor, Violations of Free Speech and Labor, Report pursuant to S. Res. 266 (Sen. Rep. No. 1150, Pt. 3, 77th Cong.).   Also, Carey McWilliams, *Factories in the Field* (Boston: Little, Brown, 1939).

farm laborer has introduced a class cleavage into agriculture that has had its repercussions in conflict of which government has had to take notice. Further, the rise of the commercial farmer—the agricultural businessman—has laid the basis for a greater community of interest between farmer and businessman. The farm-manager with his account books, his payrolls, and his capital accounts tends to replace the free and independent tiller of the soil who could afford to be radical and breathe fire.

Commercial farming produces a fundamental change in the economic status of the farmer. By devoting his efforts more exclusively to the raising of crops to be sold in the market, the farmer makes himself subject to all the storms of the economic system generally. Indeed, the key to the understanding of farm politics in the United States in the first half of the twentieth century lies in the practical unavailability to farmers of the weapons of economic defense used by industrial and financial interests. When overproduction and lower prices threaten, business groups may with some success act together to curtail production and safeguard themselves against the economic storm without the interposition of government. Millions of independent agricultural producers find concerted action impossible; hence they enter politics to seek through government a way to collective action by which they can be assured of their "fair" share of the national income.

The rise of commercial farming has also generated a conflict between the commercial farmer and the family farmer. About 50 per cent of the farms, it was estimated in 1942, produce about 90 per cent of the farm produce sold in the open market. The operators of these farms could readily grow all the crops needed for market and make 3 million other farmers excess and available for other employment.[10] When the farm population is divided into "big" farmers and "little" farmers, the basis exists for dispute between these two great groups about the nature of governmental agricultural policy, which can favor one or the other class but can hardly favor both classes.

Decline of proportion of population on farms. Another background fact of importance in examining the political role of agriculture is that during the past 50 years agriculture has diminished in importance in the American economy and in the total American population. By 1870 agricultural output, both in value and in quantity, had been exceeded by the product of manufacturing. From 1870 to 1940 farm workers decreased from over 50 per cent to less than 20 per cent of all workers. Agriculture, once the dominant interest in American society,

[10] M. R. Benedict, "Agriculture as a Commercial Industry Comparable to Other Branches of the Economy," *Journal of Farm Economics,* 24 (1942), pp. 476–496.

has had to share its power with the younger and lustier giants of industry and labor. Yet in politics agriculture has retained an enormous influence on those public policies of interest to agriculture. Any interest, once it gains power, is difficult to dislodge. Institutions adjust themselves only slowly to changed power relationships. For example, persistence of agrarian strength is aided by the disproportionate legislative representation which rural areas have managed to retain.[11]

2. CYCLES OF AGRARIAN DISCONTENT

Agriculture has not adjusted itself quietly to the changed conditions affecting it. Agrarian parties and pressure groups have risen to promote and defend the real or presumed interests of the agricultural sector of society. Agrarian agitation, at times a bit boisterous and disturbing to the conservative elements of society, has not occurred at a uniform pitch but has had its dull periods and its shrill points varying in intensity somewhat with the adversities of the farmers. Although the entire story of agrarian discontent need not be recounted here, episodes from it can be used to illustrate graphically a recurring pattern of political behavior. The nature of that recurring pattern may be indicated by noting that the structure of political power at any given time represents an equilibrium among the elements struggling for power and influence. The balance of power within international politics has its parallel in domestic affairs. At times the structure of power has remained in a state of static equilibrium over long periods, with a stratified social structure perpetuating itself through time. In modern times, however, a highly unstable equilibrium tends to be the general rule; new groups continually rise to challenge the power of the old; far-reaching readjustments of the relative status of the component groups in the pattern of political power occur; one new equilibrium is established only to be replaced by another.

The observer is faced by the paradox of depressed groups living quietly under conditions of the most bitter injustice for long periods and of other groups rising to demand retribution on the slightest pretext. What sets in motion these movements leading toward a new equilibrium of power? A "consciousness of need," as Lindeman calls it, must arise. If the circumstances of a particular segment of society become rapidly worse, a keen awareness of the change may be expected. Agitators come on the scene and spread the sentiment of injustice. A diagnosis explaining plausibly the origin of misfortune and generally placing responsibility somewhere—the railroads, the Jews, Wall Street,

---

[11] For a treatment of this matter, see pages 687–698.

the monopolists—is propagated. A formula to remedy the situation
and provide relief is devised. The movement encounters opposition
from the beneficiaries of the status quo. The formula is modified; compromise results. The movement perhaps achieves some success; it
gains a vested interest and stays to defend the new status quo against
subsequent assaults on the citadel of power by a new generation of
radicals.[12] The durability of a constitutional system depends to a high
degree upon its capacity to adjust itself to the demands of political
movements. Institutional inflexibility may lead to revolutionary movements on a grand scale.

Although the "farm problem," with the accompanying manifestations
of political discontent, has been with us almost continually since the
Civil War, farmers' movements have risen and fallen during this time
in something of a cyclical pattern reflecting, in part, changes in the
economic status of agriculture. The Granger movement, the Farmers'
Alliance, the Populist party, the Non-Partisan League, and the American Farm Bureau Federation constitute some of the manifestations of
farm discontent. It has been suggested that the peaks of a curve of
farm organization membership since the Civil War would correspond
with the troughs of a curve of farm prices over the same period.[13] The
detailed data on this point are not available, but obviously farm movements have been highly vocal at times of severe economic distress.

Granger movement. The Granger movement furnishes a concrete
example of the natural history of political movements generally. The
Grange reached its peak strength in the 1870's and served as a vehicle
for the expression of agrarian discontent in the northwestern corn-
and wheat-growing region embracing the upper Mississippi Valley from
Ohio to the western rim of settlement in Kansas and Nebraska. In
the late 'sixties and early 'seventies falling prices, caused mainly by
the changed demand situation following the Civil War, brought a
harvest of distress among farmers. The farmers, seeking out those
who had caused their misfortunes, blamed the railroads, the bankers,
and monopolies for their plight. Of these misdoers, the railroads bore
the brunt of Granger protest. Early methods of railroad finance were
not always in accordance with the soundest canons of investment.
Many farmers had invested in railroad stocks and many farm communities had voted bonds to subsidize railroad construction. Mis-
management frequently forced railroads into bankruptcy, in the process

---

[12] The above analysis follows in a general way E. C. Lindeman, *The Community*
(New York: Association Press, 1921), chap. 9, "The Process of Community Action."

[13] C. C. Taylor, "Farmers' Movements as Psychosocial Phenomena," *Publications,*
American Sociological Society, 23 (1929), pp. 153–162.

of which some of the water was squeezed from their capital structures. Thus farmers became disillusioned investors in railroad stocks at the same time that they had to pay taxes to retire railroad-subsidy bonds and high freight rates to ship their produce to market.

Discrimination in transportation rates caused as much resentment as did the absolute height of rates. Discrimination existed between persons and places. At junction points and other places where competition between lines occurred, rates were generally lower than at intermediate points where the railroads—the farmers felt—took advantage of the absence of competition arbitrarily to raise rates. Discrimination between persons consisted of giving a lower rate to one shipper than to another, often through secret rebates. Furthermore, the railroads quite often held the state legislatures in the palms of their hands. The railroads, however, were not left with the entire blame for the state of agriculture. Agrarian demonology reserved a prominent place for the commission man and other middlemen, who were accused of taking an unfairly large slice of the farmer's dollar. Also, high rates of interest and the difficulties of meeting interest and principal payments on heavy mortgages directed antagonism toward holders of mortgages.

The Patrons of Husbandry, or the Grange, proved a ready vehicle for the expression of farm discontent arising from the foregoing and other reasons. Founded in 1867 for the social and intellectual advancement of farmers, it originated as a secret order equipped with appropriate ritual and a hierarchy of officers with sonorous titles. It had only a slow growth until the early 'seventies when the pinch of economic adversity gave it momentum. The total number of Granges, or local chapters, increased from 11 in 1868 to 7,325 in 1873. During 1873, the panic year, and 1874 the organization spread like a prairie fire, and by the end of 1874 about 21,000 local Granges had been organized. At the peak about three-quarters of a million individuals were affiliated with the organization. Although the Grange extended into most of the states, the most highly organized region was the quadrilateral from Ohio to Dakota Territory, to Kansas, to Kentucky, to Ohio.

The Grange declared itself to be a nonpartisan organization. "No Grange," it was asserted in the Declaration of Purposes of the National Grange, "if true to its obligations, can discuss political or religious questions, nor call political conventions, nor nominate candidates, nor even discuss their merits in its meetings." Instead of attempting to nominate and elect candidates under its own banner, the Grange employed those methods now known as pressure-group techniques. Both the state Granges and the National Grange adopted resolutions concerning their stand on proposed legislation; petitions were used; delegations were sent to present to legislatures the Grange's views on pending legislation; candidates for public office were asked during campaigns to indicate their stand on proposed measures of interest to farmers.

Although the Grange was concerned with various types of legislation to alleviate the situation of the farmer, first place in its program was occupied by the proposal to regulate railroad corporations—at the time a radical suggestion characterized, by those who would be affected by the action, as communistic and subversive of our institutions. In several states the Grange was instrumental in inducing legislatures to enact laws regulatory of railroads. The immediate efficacy of these laws was not always great, yet many of the guiding principles of American railroad regulation ultimately established were of Granger origin. From another angle the Grange attacked the transportation problem by seeking the improvement of inland waterways; and its resolutions and agitation were doubtless a factor in causing Congress, in the decade from 1870 to 1880, to quadruple appropriations for river and harbor improvements over any prior decade.

During 1875–1880 the Grange suffered a sharp decline in membership. For various reasons it came to be discredited, and other organizations became more important spokesmen for agriculture. Yet the movement left behind a liberal education in pressure-group procedures for the farm population on which succeeding agricultural crusades could build; the once radical Grange persists to the present, having been transformed into a conservative and dignified farmers' organization not without power in dealing with Congress and the legislatures of those states in which its strength is concentrated.[14]

An analysis of the Granger movement serves to illustrate something of the genesis and evolution of a political movement; further data of an illustrative character may be drawn from the political activities of farmers after World War I. It was noted that before a "political movement" is inaugurated a "consciousness of need" is requisite. That consciousness may be brought about by a change in status for the worse or perhaps by some messiah holding out hopes for group betterment through proposed governmental action.

Farmer agitation, 1919–1933. The political activities of farmers following World War I were in the first instance set off by a sharp drop in

14 The information on the Grange is drawn primarily from S. J. Buck, *The Granger Movement* (Cambridge: Harvard University Press, 1913). For another significant interpretation, see Viva Belle Boothe, *The Political Party as a Social Process* (Philadelphia, 1923). See also F. A. Shannon, *The Farmer's Last Frontier* (New York: Farrar & Rinehart, 1945), chap. 13.

the prices of farm products. The nature of the precipitous decline in the economic position of agriculture can best be seen by reference to the graph in Figure 1. During the war the economic condition of agriculture had been one of prosperity because of the great demand for farm products, but in the depression of 1920–1921 farm prices fell farther and faster than the prices of goods purchased by the farmer. The agricultural producer thereby suffered a severe reduction in his real income, or purchasing power.

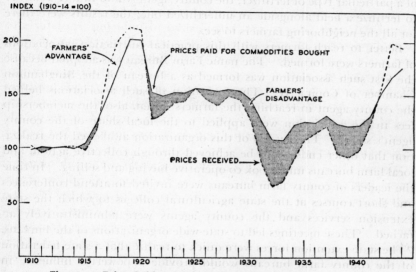

Figure 1.   Prices Paid and Prices Received by Farmers, 1910–1944

The collapse of farm prices in 1920–1921 was attributable to the convergence of a number of factors. To meet temporary wartime needs new land was put under the plow; existing farms were cultivated more intensively. The return of foreign lands to cultivation and the general economic aftermath of war struck the farmer with special force. The abnormal wartime demands for agricultural products had also postponed the full effects of long-term trends, such as the decline in the export market for American agricultural products and the increasing efficiency of agricultural production.

The principal channel for the expression of discontent from the resulting agricultural depression was the American Farm Bureau Federation. Its formation had been closely associated with the county-agent system, which originated in the decade 1900 to 1910. This system was developed to disseminate among farmers the findings of agricultural research carried on by the land-grant colleges, the state agricultural experiment stations, and the Federal Department of Agriculture. It took on its present administrative form in 1914 through the passage of the Smith-Hughes Act providing federal grants to state extension services, under the supervision of the land-grant colleges, which, in turn, made arrangements with county authorities to employ county agricultural agents. The county agents employed the "demonstration method" of teaching; if it was desired to show the effect of the use of a particular type of fertilizer, the county agent would induce a farmer to fertilize a field alongside an unfertilized one; the results were there for all the neighboring farmers to see.

Better to reach farmers with this practical instruction, associations of farmers were formed. The name Farm Bureau was adopted because the first such association was formed as a bureau of the Binghamton Chamber of Commerce. The formation of such associations helped the county agent in reaching the farmers; often, also, the membership fees in the association were applied to the local share of the county agent's salary. The success of this organization awakened the realization that other ends could be achieved through collective action, and local farm bureaus undertook co-operative buying and selling. In time the leaders of county farm bureaus were invited to attend conferences and short courses at the state agricultural colleges to which the state extension services and the county agents were administratively attached. These meetings led to state-wide organizations of the bureaus. "The state extension forces were quick to realize that a state federation of the county farm bureaus would provide a powerful influence in securing liberal appropriations from the legislatures for further extension work. The more active officers of the county farm bureaus, on the other hand, saw the possibilities of united action in getting financial support from the state for the furtherance of county farm bureau work." [15] In 1917 the New York State Farm Bureau Federation was formed; in 1918 a state federation for West Virginia came into existence; and similar federations were organized in other states.

In 1919 delegates from thirty-one states met at Chicago to create a national federation of state organizations. The union of the state federations into the American Farm Bureau Federation was not accomplished without difficulty; the more conservative farm states hesitated to join with the politically energetic Midwestern farmers; yet common ground was found. The national organization rested on a firm foundation of local Farm Bureaus, eventually organized in nearly all the agri-

[15] O. M. Kile, *The Farm Bureau Movement* (New York, 1921), p. 111. Quoted by permission of The Macmillan Company, publishers.

cultural counties, nurtured by the county agricultural agents. Presently the close collaboration between the county agent and the Farm Bureau proved embarrassing. Commercial interests objected to what was virtually a government subsidy to co-operatives through county-agent assistance, and formal connections between the extension services and the county agents and local Farm Bureaus were severed. But by this time the Farm Bureau Federation was established on a solid footing.

The Federation established a legislative office in Washington with its functions defined as follows: "First, to ascertain definitely, by referendum or otherwise, the farmers' attitude on pending legislation affecting agriculture; second, to thoroughly inform members of Congress concerning the farmers' legislative needs and requests; and, third, to report to the membership fully concerning the support or lack of support of individual congressmen." In 1921 and 1922 control of Congress was virtually wrested from the party leaders by the agricultural bloc, a coalition of Senators and Representatives of both parties from agricultural districts, formed "as a result of a series of helpful conferences at Farm Bureau legislative headquarters." [16] In each house an agricultural bloc was formed to study measures of interest to agriculture and to promote their passage by concerted action. A series of measures was agreed upon and passed. Bills to control grain exchanges, to regulate packers and stockyards, to enlarge appropriations for the construction of rural highways, and other measures of interest to farmers were adopted. The farm bloc entered into the log-rolling game and won tariff increases on many farm products.[17]

The Farm Bureau Federation and the agricultural bloc were not the only channels through which agricultural discontent found expression. Reference again to the graph in Figure 1 will indicate that the disadvantageous position of the farmer in terms of the relationship between agricultural and industrial prices continued during 1922 and 1924. In 1922 in Kansas a " 'dirt farmer' with radical leanings" won the governorship; in Minnesota a Farmer-Labor candidate polled 43 per cent of the votes for governor; in Iowa Smith W. Brookhart, an agrarian "radical" of the day, won the senatorship. Dissatisfaction with the major parties came to a head in 1924 when LaFollette and Wheeler entered the lists for the Presidency and Vice-Presidency under the Progressive and Farmer-Labor banners. Though they carried only

---

[16] *Ibid.*, p. 188.
[17] For a complete account of the activities of the agricultural bloc by one of its leading members, see Arthur Capper, *The Agricultural Bloc* (New York: Harcourt, Brace, 1922).

Wisconsin, they made an impressive showing, especially in the farm belt.[18]

Although measures adopted by Congress under the spur of the farm bloc's early activities were helpful, the status of agriculture remained fundamentally unchanged in 1925 and 1926. The disadvantage of the farmer, in terms of the relationship between agricultural and industrial prices, continued; as an attempt to close or reduce the gap between these prices, the McNary-Haugen bill was brought forward in several versions. The original bill was rejected in the House in June, 1924. Another version was defeated in 1926. Although backed with enthusiasm by the corn-belt states, the bill fell before the combined opposition of the Northeast and the South. "The vote was sectional, and neither party nor vocational lines held. Of the Republicans who voted, 55.6 per cent were opposed; of the Democrats, 56.7 per cent." [19] In 1927 the bill passed, in part because southern farmers had become less prosperous and southern legislators more favorably disposed toward farm relief, but it was vetoed by President Coolidge. It had passed by a vote in which party discipline had completely broken.[20] Again, in 1928 another version of the bill was passed, only to meet with presidential rejection.

The midwestern farm states carried their battle into the 1928 Republican convention and threatened rebellion against domination of the party by "industry and finance." Although they failed to persuade the Republican convention to commit itself to the McNary-Haugen plan, Hoover, triumphant in 1928, came into office thoroughly committed to "do something" about the farm problem. A special session of Congress in 1929 created the Federal Farm Board with a mandate to "promote the effective merchandising of agricultural commodities in interstate and foreign commerce, so that the industry of agriculture will be placed on a basis of economic equality with other industries." The object, in other words, was to close the gap between agricultural and industrial prices shown in Figure 1. From an appropriation of $500,000,000 the board made loans to farmers' cooperative marketing associations on the assumption that better prices might be obtained by controlled marketing. The board engaged in

18 F. E. Haynes, "The Collapse of the Farmer-Labor Bloc," *Social Forces*, 4 (1925), pp. 148–156. The percentages of the total presidential vote polled by the Farmer-Labor candidates in 1924 in the following states were: Wisconsin, 53.9; North Dakota, 45.1; Minnesota, 41.2; Montana, 37.7; Iowa, 27.8; Nebraska, 23.0; Ohio, 17.7; Illinois, 17.5; Michigan, 10.5.

19 A. W. Macmahon, "First Session of the Sixty-Ninth Congress," *American Political Science Review*, 20 (1926), pp. 604–622.

20 The Senate passed the bill by 47 (24 Republicans, 22 Democrats, 1 Farmer-Labor) to 39 (22 Republicans, 17 Democrats).

"stabilization operations"; that is, it purchased surpluses and held them from the market to maintain a higher price level. Quite apart from the effects of the 1929 economic crash on agriculture, the efforts of the Farm Board were doomed to failure. The board itself recognized "control of excessive production as absolutely essential" to improving the status of the farmer. The act it administered had the effect of maintaining prices to a degree, but such success merely compounded the difficulty in the long run, for better prices stimulated still more production. The Farm Board urged voluntary restraint—it could do no more—but that was inadequate to hold production to the limits necessary to maintain higher prices.[21]

During the presidential campaign of 1932 Franklin D. Roosevelt said, in effect, to Edward O'Neal, president of the American Farm Bureau Federation: "One of the first things I am going to do is to take steps to restore farm prices. I am going to call farmers' leaders together, lock them in a room, and tell them not to come out until they have agreed on a plan." [22] Western farmers, along with nearly everyone else, went Democratic, and immediately after his inauguration in 1933 Roosevelt called the promised meeting of leaders of farmers' organizations. Meanwhile, the plight of the farmers was becoming steadily worse. "Even among farmers, normally one of the most stable elements in American society, there were strikes, forcible interventions with legal processes such as mortgage sales, mob formation and violence, and even violence to constituted law officers such as sheriffs and judges." [23]

The measure agreed upon by the farm leaders and speedily enacted by Congress in 1933 came to be known as the Agricultural Adjustment Act. The act declared "the present acute economic emergency" to be "in part the consequence of a severe and increasing disparity between the prices of agricultural and other commodities, which disparity has largely destroyed the purchasing power of farmers for industrial products." The policy of Congress was declared to be to "re-establish prices to farmers at a level that will give agricultural commodities a purchasing power with respect to articles that farmers buy, equivalent to the purchasing power of agricultural commodities in" the prewar period. In other words, the object was to eliminate, in so far as practicable, the gap in our graph. The means of achieving this end was primarily by control of production, which involved ultimately the determination by public authority of the amount of each of the major commodities

[21] See Federal Farm Board, *First Annual Report* (1930).

[22] C. V. Gregory, "The American Farm Bureau Federation and the AAA," *Annals of the American Academy of Political and Social Sciences*, 179 (1935), pp. 152–157.

[23] Mordecai Ezekiel and Louis H. Bean, *Economic Bases for the Agricultural Adjustment Act* (Washington: Government Printing Office, 1933), p. 6.

that should be produced by each farmer. By this means it was hoped
to adjust agricultural production and thereby raise prices. The original Agricultural Adjustment Act was held unconstitutional in 1936,
but it was succeeded by other legislation with substantially the same
objectives. The period after 1933 marked the enactment of a variety
of other types of legislation calculated to alleviate the lot of the farmer.[24]

From spontaneous movement to crystallized interest group. The
rapid rise and spread of the Granger movement in the 'seventies and
the similar growth of the Farm Bureau Federation after World War I
were closely associated with economic disaster affecting large segments
of the farm population. The slow incubation of these movements,
their sudden gain in momentum, and their effectiveness in obtaining
governmental action are characteristics by no means limited to farmers'
movements. Nor does economic deprivation generate all political
movements. The prohibition movement and the agitation for woman
suffrage suggest themselves as examples not solely economic in origin.
But about farmers' movements a word of caution is in order. It is not
improbable that the period is over in which continuous ups and downs
occur in the organization of farmers, with one sweeping movement
replacing another as new crises arise. Membership in farm societies
will fluctuate and great economic upheavals may bring spurts of pressure activity by farmers, but farm organizations appear to have acquired
a stability that makes for continuous political activity in behalf of
agrarian interests. Fundamental changes in the status of agriculture
since the Civil War, referred to earlier in this chapter, have transformed
farmers (or a large percentage of them) into a new kind of economic class
more akin to industry than to the old-fashioned family farmer. Moreover, present types of public policy affecting agriculture require that
farm organizations—like tariff lobbyists and public utility legislative
representatives—give unremitting attention to the actions of government. Instead of a slumbering, rustic giant roused only by depression
and adversity, farmers have become a well-organized and competently
led group, with interest in public policy as keen and continuous as
that of any business or labor group.

These changes have converted agriculture from an amorphous sector of the population, stimulated to political rebellion by economic
adversity and lulled into content by prosperity, into a hardboiled,
crystallized pressure bloc constantly alert to its interests. For years

[24] For a useful survey of government policy relating to agriculture, see D. C. Blaisdell, *Government and Agriculture* (New York: Farrar and Rinehart, 1940). For an
informed analysis of general economic trends and tendencies affecting agriculture, see
T. W. Schultz, *Agriculture in an Unstable Economy* (New York: McGraw-Hill, 1945).

the object of farm agitation was to achieve parity in farm prices, that is, to raise farm prices to a point where one bushel of wheat would buy as much of what the farmer needed as it would in the base-period years just before World War I. As this level was approached, farm groups sought new definitions of parity. Perhaps by changing the base period for a particular commodity the parity goal would become higher, or by changing the method of computing parity the parity level for all products could be upped. From pressure for a principle that had an appearance of fairness the fight came to have the odor of the machinations of an old-style tariff lobby. In the midst of World War II, with farmers enjoying a high price for their products and paying a low price for their needs in comparison with their experience in World War I, the Farm Bureau Federation and the Grange unremittingly fought for a redefinition of parity, even at the risk of inducing an inflationary movement.

3. CLEAVAGES WITHIN AGRICULTURE

Discussion of agriculture as a single entity creates a false impression of likeness of interests among farmers. In fact, divergence of interests among different groups of farmers necessitates compromise and coalition in order to present a united front; and, at times, splits among farming groups lead to the defeat of agriculture as a whole. In the work of the agricultural bloc in the early 'twenties it was necessary to promote only those matters on which most farmers could agree. Senator Capper, in recounting the operations of the agricultural bloc, said: [25]

There are numerous subjects upon which farmers from different parts of the country do not agree, not because they differ in political faith but because of natural competition. Such questions were omitted from the bloc's program. One illustration of such a case is reclamation measures. . . . Many eastern farmers will agree with those from the west regarding the need for better rural credit, improved marketing and lower freight rates, but they disagree when it comes to a question of federal aid in the reclamation of new land which will bring products into competition with those from older farms.

O. M. Kile, a former official of the American Farm Bureau Federation, has noted the fact that these divergencies of interest among farmers create problems in the maintenance of unity in a national organization of farmers.[26]

[25] *The Agricultural Bloc* (New York: Harcourt, Brace, 1922), pp. 148–149.
[26] *Op. cit.,* p. 208. Quoted by permission of The Macmillan Company, publishers.

The South is interested in cotton; the North in corn and wheat. The New Englander wants the price of dairy feeds kept down; the Iowa producers want them put up. The Kansas farmer wants cheap freight rates on wheat; the Virginia farmer is not so much interested, since he gets Chicago prices plus freight. The South has the Negro problem; the Pacific Coast has the Japanese problem, and Texas has the Mexican problem.[27]

The relative significance of various types of farming in the national economy and in national politics may be suggested by figures on the value of the annual production of the more important commodities. In 1944 the total cash income from farm marketings in the United States was slightly more than 20½ billion dollars including government payments. Sixteen commodities each brought in more than 200 million dollars, as shown in Table 2. The value of the crop does not, of course, determine the political strength of its producers. The degree to which production has been commercialized may influence

TABLE 2

Cash Receipts from Major Farm Products, 1944 [a]

Commodity	Receipts in millions
Dairy products	$2,969
Hogs	2,796
Cattle and calves	2,607
Cotton and cottonseed	1,490
Eggs	1,336
Wheat	1,070
Truck crops and farm gardens	917
Tobacco	717
Corn	612
Chickens	541
Potatoes	396
Oranges	321
Sheep and lambs	302
Apples	265
Soybeans	245
Grapes	202

a *Crops and Markets*, July, 1945, p. 131.

27 The general remarks are illustrated by a comment in the congressional debate on the McNary-Haugen bill in 1926: "The state of Mississippi last year imported into her borders nearly $3,000,000 of feed and food. Increase that on the average of 50 per cent and the Haugen bill would cost the people of Mississippi more than a million dollars. . . ." The durability of the cleavage of interest is shown by the plea in 1942 of the managing director of the Northeastern Poultry Producers Council to his Congressman to do everything in his power to prevent the passage of legislation to raise the price of wheat and corn sold for poultry and dairy feed by the Surplus Marketing Administration.—*Congressional Record* (daily edition), March 9, 1942, pp. A979–980.

the extent to which the producers of a crop are organized. Wide geographical distribution of a comparatively unimportant crop economically may enable its producers to rely on the support of Senators from many states when issues affecting the crop arise.[28] Nevertheless, the figures in the table convey a rough notion of the relative political importance of the producers of the larger items in our agricultural output.

The political and economic interests of different types of farmers vary. These differences in interest are reflected to some extent in competing organizations of farmers; nevertheless, many factors other than cool calculation of interest are influential in conditioning the structure of farm organizations. The great general organizations of farmers, ranging from the extreme right to the left, are the National Grange, the American Farm Bureau Federation, and the National Farmers' Union. Each of these organizations attempts to cover the nation, although none is entirely successful. Each is equipped with all the customary organizational paraphernalia—annual national meetings designed to be representative of membership together with the necessary executive and administrative staffs—to determine the wishes and aspirations of the membership and to direct their strength, at the appropriate times, upon Congress and other national governmental agencies. Although each of the organizations attempts to increase its membership and to speak for "the farmer," there are differences in the interests of their memberships and in their attitudes on public policy.[29]

National grange. In its earlier days the National Grange, with its radical belligerency, aroused fear in the heart of Wall Street, but it has become the most conservative farm organization. It pictures itself as "the oldest and largest farm organization in America and the only Farm Fraternity in the World." It is a "social, educational and economic force, plus a neighborly and community building agency." It

---

[28] "The states producing sugar beets are, in the main, in the thinly settled western part of the United States. By virtue of the constitutional provisions with respect to the membership of Congress, these states, of course, have equal representation in the Senate with the heavily populated industrial states of the East. At any one time, therefore, the sugar beet bloc in the Senate can exert substantial legislative influence. In addition to this, the three industrial states which produce beets, Ohio, Michigan, and Indiana, are a pillar of strength in the Lower House although their production, as compared with that of Colorado or Utah, is of limited sectional importance."— J. E. Dalton, *Sugar, A Case Study of Government Control* (New York, 1937), p. 149. Quoted by permission of The Macmillan Company, publishers.

[29] The best recent survey of farmers' organizations is by Wesley McCune, *The Farm Bloc* (Garden City: Doubleday, Doran, 1943). For a useful brief description of these associations, see D. C. Wing, "Trends in National Farm Organizations," *1940 Yearbook of Agriculture* (Washington: Government Printing Office, 1941), pp. 941–979.

places emphasis, according to its literature, "on moral and spiritual idealism. It is a fraternity with a beautiful ritual." The latter refers to its master, overseer, steward, assistant steward, Ceres, Pomona, Flora, seventh degree initiates, and various strangely named functionaries. On the political front the Grange speaks in Washington through its able Washington representative, Fred Brenckman.

Grange membership is heavily concentrated in the states east of the Mississippi and north of the Mason and Dixon Line, with special strength in the northeastern states. The result is that the policies reflect the rural conservatism of these states and the interests of farmers advantageously situated with reference to rich domestic markets. This factor, as well as the heavy reliance in these states on products with primarily a domestic market (which to some extent removes these farmers from the serious effects of fluctuating prices fixed on a world market), lays the basis for a farm class that is more able to take care of itself than are growers of cotton, corn, and wheat.

The resolutions and literature of the Grange have a timbre not unlike Republican campaign speeches. In 1939 its Washington representative reported that the congressional session of that year "was characterized by a commendable effort . . . to restore a proper balance or equilibrium between the legislative and executive departments of the Government." In 1943 he reported that the current session of Congress had been "making a commendable effort to recapture the rights and prerogatives with which the legislative branch of the Government is vested under the Constitution." At its annual session in 1944 the National Grange resolved that the "exigencies of war furnish no excuse for evading or nullifying the letter or spirit of the Constitution." In 1939 the Grange reaffirmed "its stand against over-centralization of Government, which violates the wholesome American principle of home rule in local affairs." In 1943 it declared that the "phenomenal growth of our Federal bureaucracy constitutes a menace to our dual system of government and the liberties of the people." At the same session it favored "continued research to find new industrial uses for farm products." It suggested "proper appropriations" for agricultural education and "heartily" approved the efforts of the government to promote rural electrification.

The Grange is usually aligned with manufacturing on the tariff; it has demanded the repeal of the Reciprocal Trade Agreement Act with great vigor. Trade unions find no favor with the Grange, which opposes "all efforts of labor unions to organize farmers or farm workers." From time to time it has advocated adoption of legislation limiting activities of unions although it expresses "accord with the legitimate aims and objectives of organized labor."   Protest is expressed regularly against extensions of the reclamation program, as might be expected from a predominantly eastern organization.   The Grange early manifested lukewarmness toward New Deal programs to control agricultural production, primarily, it may be supposed, because Grange members did not have so much to gain thereby as do farmers of other sections. As federal agricultural programs evolved, however, the Grange veered to support of price-supporting policies.   Conservative though it may be, the Grange appears to retain more of the old-fashioned rural virtues of family farming than do organizations of more highly commercialized farmers.

Stripped of its froth and of its moral overtone—such as references in its literature to "the evils of strong drink"—the Grange, like a labor or business organization, has its eye on the main chance.   The Grange, like other farm organizations, has the advantage over such groups in that it can claim for its demands a pseudo-holy status: the farmer is the backbone of American society; virtue is rural.   Forces influencing the Grange make it more conservative than other farm organizations. Its strength, save for its branches in the Pacific Northwest, is concentrated in areas of traditional rural Republicanism.   Perhaps more important is the probability that conservative policies reflect the interests of its membership.

American Farm Bureau Federation.   The circumstances surrounding the establishment and early activities of the American Farm Bureau Federation have been noted.   The Federation more nearly blankets the country than does the Grange, but the Federation's greatest strength is in the Midwest, in the area from Ohio to Kansas to Minnesota.   Almost half of its membership is to be found in that section.   Membership in the southern states bulks smaller in the national picture, but the Federation is the strongest farm organization in that region. Energetic membership drives following 1940 strengthened the Federation in sections outside its original midwestern stronghold.   Membership by regions in 1944 was: midwestern, 408,478; southern, 252,626; northeastern, 119,703; western, 47,679.

Although comparative measurements of political strength are hazardous, the Farm Bureau is certainly the most powerful of the general farm organizations.   While it is regarded as a reactionary body by left-wing farm leaders, it is less conservative than the Grange.   It simply promotes the cause of the more prosperous farming classes with great zeal and ability.   Its national organization receives an annual income of over $250,000, and it employs able leaders and pays them well. It maintains a research staff to aid it in reaching its decisions; through its "department of information" it educates the general public as well as its own membership.

In presenting the views of the farmer to Congress, Federation officials are guided by resolutions and instructions voted by the annual convention. In making its wishes known, the Federation follows the usual methods of testifying before congressional committees, interviewing Congressmen, and stirring up pressure on statesmen in their home districts. By enlisting the support of its affiliated state and county organizations the Federation can turn enormous pressure on Congress.[30] The Washington representatives of the Federation watch the legislative process and guide the strategy of battle.[31] The general technique is well described by the following statement from a Federation report on congressional events in 1939:

> The preservation of the Agricultural Adjustment program, and the host of bills introduced affecting farmers, required the presence of President O'Neal in Washington almost continuously during the session of Congress. The members of our national Board of Directors rendered able assistance by coming to the national capital and helping to carry the legislative program to the members of Congress. The Federation also appreciates the valiant aid and support given by county Farm Bureau leaders and individual members. There has probably never been a year when Farm Bureau leaders were called upon so frequently for support, and, moreover, never a time when response was so generous, and so effective in accomplishing legislative results. With this loyal support, President O'Neal was able to lead these united forces to the victories so important to agriculture and to the Federation.[32]

[30] Note the following extract from a telegram in March, 1942, from the President of the Federation to all state federations: "The Agricultural Appropriations Committee did not carry out our recommendations for economy in the enormous cost of administration of Farm Security Administration and other agricultural agencies. . . . I appeal to you to give us your aggressive support in this crucial struggle by contacting all your Congressmen immediately in every way possible, including a heavy barrage from your counties and from those interested in any phase of agriculture." —*Congressional Record* (daily edition), March 9, 1942, p. 2183.

[31] In the course of the debate on appropriations for the Farm Security Administration, referred to in the preceding note, Representative Hook asserted: "One of the most revolting things that has come to my attention since I have been a Member of Congress was the fact that Edward O'Neal, head of the Farm Bureau Federation, sat in the gallery yesterday afternoon signaling and directing the efforts of those on the floor of the House to sabotage one of the finest Government agencies that this Government has had in the interest of the small farmer and the war program. I say this advisedly because I saw it with my own eyes, and I refer to many others, including my good friend Jed Johnson of Oklahoma, who observed the same tactics."— *Congressional Record* (daily edition), March 13, 1942, p. 2502.

[32] *Twenty Years with the American Farm Bureau Federation*, p. 26.

With its center of gravity in the corn-hog-wheat Midwest, the Federation, although in agreement with the Grange on many issues, has differed sharply with it on other important questions. Cotton also plays a part in its policies. Growers of corn, hogs, wheat, and cotton are aided only slightly, if at all, by tariff legislation. In 1940 the Farm Bureau supported the extension of the reciprocal trade agreements program.[33] It has been more favorable than the Grange toward compulsory production control. Presumably this attitude arises from the different positions of the bulk of the membership of the two groups respecting the world market. The early activity of the Federation relating to the McNary-Haugen bills has been noted. The Federation says that it "secured passage of the first Agricultural Adjustment Act"; that it "secured passage of the second Agricultural Adjustment Act providing for production control of basic commodities." As agricultural policy evolved, the Federation supported other measures calculated to assure parity prices for farmers.

Although the Farm Bureau Federation has been divorced formally from the state agricultural extension services, a close informal connection continues to prevail.[34] That relationship is reflected in the policies of the Federation. Like the state extension services, it has an upper-class farmer orientation, and both groups share a restrained enthusiasm for national agricultural programs calculated to benefit the lower third of the farm population. Moreover, the Federation tends to ally itself with the state extension services in their jurisdic-

---

[33] The following extract from the 1938 Annual Report of the Federation indicates further its attitude on the tariff. It had been proposed that pressure be brought to ascertain the advisability of seeking removal of tapioca and other starches from the free list under the Netherlands Trade Agreement. An investigation was made and the facts disclosed "indicated that little or nothing could be gained to aid the corn growers through the opening of this agreement with respect to tapioca imports and that such action might seriously jeopardize important gains in our exports of corn, wheat and many other farm products which we are now enjoying."

[34] Of interest is an item in the 1940 resolutions of the Grange: "Extension workers should be paid entirely from public funds, leaving them free to serve the people without favoritism or discrimination. Under no circumstances should any farm organization be allowed to graft itself upon the extension service, nor dominate it to serve its own ends." The close affiliation between the Farm Bureau Federation, county extension workers, and Federal agricultural programs has led in some places to something approaching the check-off in the solicitation of Farm Bureau members. Thus, at the Coahoma County, Mississippi, office of the Agricultural Adjustment Administration a large sign read: "Pay Your Farm Bureau Dues Here—The Farm Bureau Federation Is Responsible for Getting Your Agricultural Adjustment Administration Payments." An Alabama county agent in 1939 sent letters to farmers notifying them that government conservation checks were to be distributed and at the time a representative of the Farm Bureau would be on hand "to give you an opportunity to join your community farm bureau."—See Joint Committee on Reduction of Nonessential Federal Expenditures, *Hearings,* pt. 3, pp. 766–774, 903–905 (February, 1942).

tional disputes with the United States Department of Agriculture. In its 1940 convention, for example, the Federation proposed to divest the existing departmental hierarchy of its authority over the more important farm programs and to place control in state committees "appointed anually . . . from nominations by the State director of extension after consulting with State-wide farm organizations." In a number of states, such a policy would constitute, in effect, a delegation of administrative authority to the Farm Bureau Federation.

The Farm Bureau Federation has taken generally a hostile attitude toward the work of the Farm Security Administration, a unit of the Department of Agriculture that originated in the early days of the New Deal as an agency to rehabilitate low-income farmers. It initiated rural relief operations and administered programs to combat tenancy. From the nature of its policies it reached a class of farmers not served by the principal programs of farm credit and production management. Early in 1942 the Federation launched a barrage against the Farm Security Administration,[35] which was vulnerable to charges of inefficiency and ill-advised action. The Federation action was interpreted, however, as the effort of an organization representative of large-scale, commercialized farming, which did not "want any governmental agency to help restore tenants, sharecroppers, and farm laborers to ownership and operation of their own farms" and thus to check the growth of the type of farming in which the Federation was concerned.[36] Federation attitudes probably reflect in part a class cleavage within agriculture, especially in the South where the co-existence of large-scale farm operations with widespread rural poverty, all mixed with race antagonisms, diverges sharply from stereotypes of bucolic contentment and pastoral beauty.

National Farmers' Union. The Farmers' Educational and Co-operative Union of America, commonly known as the National Farmers' Union, speaks for a mildly left-wing segment of American agriculture. In some respects the Union is the surviving remnant of the old-fashioned, western agrarian radicalism; its views stand in sharp contrast to those of the Farm Bureau Federation, which reflect the modern commercialization of farming. The strength of the Union is centered principally in Oklahoma, Kansas, Nebraska, Iowa, the Dakotas, and Colorado on the western margin of tillable lands. In much of this

[35] See statements by Edward A. O'Neal, President of the American Farm Bureau Federation, Hearings, Joint Committee on Reduction of Nonessential Federal Expenditures, Pt. 3 (February 6, 10, 13, and 27, 1942).

[36] Representative Dingell in *Congressional Record* (daily ed.), March 13, 1942, p. 2505. See Oren Stephens, "FSA Fights For Its Life," *Harper's*, April, 1943, pp. 479–487.

region agriculture is on a precarious footing, and this fact perhaps accounts for the more drastic policies advocated by the union. It is often found in sharp conflict with the Farm Bureau Federation, which consists, in the main, of the more prosperous farmers. The Farmers' Union in the 'twenties and 'thirties placed great emphasis on legislative plans to bring to the farmer a guaranteed return equal to his cost of production—a policy that suggests the hypothesis that the center of gravity of its membership lies with the marginal agricultural producers. The Union advocates an economic reconstruction in which co-operative business, "owned by producers and consumers," will replace private enterprise. This method, the union averred in its 1940 legislative program, "is the only means by which the potential abundance of this Nation may be made available to all its people and by which true democracy may be maintained and safeguarded." In keeping with its doctrines, the Union has sponsored and promoted co-operative terminals, insurance companies, creameries, and agencies for the purchase of farm supplies and the sale of farm products.[37] The Union believes that "American agricultural policy should be built on the solid foundation of the family-type farm, operated by its owner." It asserts that existing "large-scale, factory-type, farming units must be required to cease exploitation of human beings and the sacrifice of human welfare and security by which they make a fictitious claim to 'efficiency'; they must be required to meet wage and working conditions that will permit the workers they employ to live at decent, American levels." From this general viewpoint the Union has defended the Farm Security Administration against the attacks of the Farm Bureau Federation. Moreover, the Union maintains more friendly relations with urban labor than does the Farm Bureau, which is not infrequently allied with commerce and industry on questions of labor policy.

Other farm groups. In addition to these general farm organizations, there are other groups organized along commodity lines. One of the more important of these is the National Co-operative Milk Producers' Federation, which, as its name implies, is a federation of about 70 milk producers' co-operative associations. The membership of the Federation's affiliates is concentrated mainly north of the Ohio, in the states of Wisconsin, Iowa, Nebraska, Colorado, and Wyoming, and around the metropolitan centers of the Pacific coast. The Milk Producers' Federation has a unity of interest and objective that makes it one of the most aggressive of the farm organizations. The spirit of the dairyman, in fact, is more akin to that of the manufacturer than that of the

---

[37] See W. P. Tucker, "The Farmers Union, The Social Thought of a Current Agrarian Movement," *Southwestern Social Science Quarterly*, 17 (1946), pp. 45–53.

farmer; the dairyman is, after all, something of a manufacturer who processes cow feed into milk and butter. In the achievement of its objectives the Federation disburses about $75,000 annually including the cost of the maintenance of its ably staffed Washington headquarters. It seeks legislation to assure the maximum possible return to dairymen and to this end has supported the enactment of laws authorizing agreements by which the marketing of milk is controlled and the price fixed at a higher level than would exist under free competition. During World War II the Federation bitterly opposed governmental subsidization of milk prices and contended that the retail price of milk should have been allowed to rise.

Co-operatives enjoy certain exemptions from taxation, and the Federation resists proposals to subject them to taxation on the plausible ground that they occupy a status different from that of corporations. The dairymen, producers for a domestic market, are violently opposed to reciprocal trade agreements. "We object," said the Federation in 1939, "to being traded down the river for the benefit of a few large industries, such as the automotive and chemical industries, in order to enable such industries to increase their exports a little." The Federation believes that "the best way to approach prosperity is to increase the farmers' purchasing power instead of the present misguided method of trying to increase the purchasing power of urban labor and reduce the possible income of agriculturists." The dairymen stand firmly opposed to legislation governing the wages and hours of labor employed in the processing of dairy products in creameries and other such plants. The tendency of nondairy farmers to use land taken out of cultivation under the various agricultural programs for dairying brought vigorous protests from the Federation.

The Federation and allied dairy organizations exert their best efforts to obtain legislation restricting competition by substitutes for dairy products. Long before the Federation was formed, dairy farmers had brought about the passage of state and federal legislation restricting the marketing of oleomargarine by taxation and other means.[38] The Federation defends this legislation against proposals for repeal that are supported by oleomargarine manufacturers allied with Southern farmers, whose cottonseed oil is one of the vegetable oils usable in making oleomargarine. "We condemn," the Federation resolved in 1943, "the selfish, deceptive tactics of the oleomargarine interests to use the war emergency as their means, and the United States Senate as their foil, to wipe out consumer protective legislation of nearly 60 years'

[38] See W. T. Mickle, "Margarine Legislation," *Journal of Farm Economics,* 23 (1941), pp. 567–583.

standing against the fraud of colored oleomargarine." The oleo interests and their allies, on the other hand, contended that in time of emergency public policy should permit the free manufacture and marketing of a distinctive product of high nutritive value. Both parties, of course, produced scientists to verify their claims about their products. The Federation urges better enforcement of anti-filled-milk statutes, that is, statutes prohibiting the sale of skim milk spiked with vegetable oils, the sale of which, it is not unfair to suggest, may be a fraud on the customer as well as unfair competition with dairy products. In some instances the demands of private groups may coincide with the welfare of the general public. When oleomargarine is palmed off as butter or when filled milk is sold as natural milk, the consumer is defrauded. The enthusiasm of the dairymen for the prevention of fraud and the suppression of foods harmful to the public health easily passes over into a determination to use the government to restrain competition when no question of deception or of public health exists.[39]

Organization of agriculture has been limited mainly to farm owners and managers. Agricultural labor and farm tenants have not found their political voice through organization. The oldest organization that sought to recruit farm labor was the Industrial Workers of the World, which at its peak in the years 1916–1918 claimed a membership of 18,000 in its Agricultural Workers Organization. This membership consisted mostly of casual workers in the corn and wheat belts, but the I.W.W. within a few years practically disappeared. Since 1930 a few agricultural workers, principally migratory workers in fruits and vegetables, have been organized. Also since 1930 the Southern Tenant Farmers' Union has made some progress in bringing together the tenant farmers of that area.[40] In the few instances in which farm laborers have effectively organized, they have been suppressed with a ferocity that would make even some reactionary industrialists blush with shame. In addition, farm organizations have generally succeeded in excluding farm labor from the benefits of labor legislation, such as unemployment insurance, workman's compensation, wage and hour rules, and old-age insurance. These exceptions have been partly attributable to technical problems of administration, but farm organizations have generally favored the exclusions and have in some instances fought for and obtained exemptions in the application of this legislation to such processes as canning, packing, and the operation of creameries, matters

[39] The data concerning the Federation have been obtained from the excellent annual reports of its secretary and from the resolutions adopted by the annual conventions.

[40] For a comprehensive survey, see "Labor Unionism in American Agriculture," Bulletin No. 836, Bureau of Labor Statistics (1945).

essentially industrial in nature.[41]   In such lobbying endeavors, leaders
of the food-processing industry occasionally adorn their ears with wisps
of straw and attempt, with some success, to camouflage themselves as
farmers to gain legislative advantages.

This review of farm organizations omits consideration of a large
number of specialized farm organizations that make themselves felt in
the political process.   One of the more potent organizations is the
National Council of Farmer Co-operatives, made up of farmers' producer and consumer co-operatives.   Many other groups are organized
along commodity lines, such as the National Beet Growers Association,
the Co-operative Fruit and Vegetable Association, and the American
National Livestock Association.

Although differences of interest exist both among farmers and among
farm organizations, at times they find common ground and unite to
gain their legislative ends.   A striking example of unity among farm
organizations may be found in the history of price-control legislation
during World War II.   For a period of several years farm organizations had been seeking "parity" prices, that is, prices for farm products
that bore the same relationship to prices paid by farmers in a base
period—for most commodities a period before World War I.   As World
War II progressed, farm prices began to reach "parity" and farm organizations began to shift their ground and to seek new definitions of
"parity" that would permit even higher prices.[42]   As these things occurred, general inflation threatened and pressure mounted for wage
increases to meet the increasing cost of living.   In September, 1942,
the President sought legislation to stabilize farm prices, and a coalition
of farm organizations was formed to resist the presidential request.
The Farm Bureau Federation, the National Grange, the National Co-
operative Milk Producers' Federation, and the National Council of
Farm Co-operatives joined in an impressive lobbying campaign to gain
special treatment for agricultural commodities.   The Farm Bureau,
the National Grange, and others also joined together from time to time
in lobbying activities on questions of labor policy.   The National
Farmers' Union, however, ordinarily remained outside these coalitions.

These wartime maneuvers of farm organizations represented a continuation of intense interest of farmers in governmental decisions that
since 1929 have determined to some extent the size of the slice of the
national income received by agriculture.   When governmental deci-

41 See Harry Schwartz, "Organizational Problems of Agricultural Labor Unions,"
Journal of Farm Economics, 23 (1941), pp. 456–466.
42 See John D. Black, *Parity, Parity, Parity* (Cambridge: Harvard Committee on
Research in the Social Sciences, 1942).

·sions have such consequences, the farmer gains a tangible stake in national policy. Such circumstances have stimulated a strengthening of farmers' organizations and created a higher degree of political alertness among farmers. The agricultural population has begun to exert its strength more effectively and with more determination.

Incidentally, the intensified exertion of political influence by agriculture points to one of the grave political problems of the semiplanned economy into which we are moving. A great virtue of the competitive order has been that it compelled producers to try to use resources in the most economical fashion. When decisions on the use of the factors of production are made by public authority, as they are to a degree in agriculture, inefficient producers try to use their political strength to influence those decisions in order that they may remain in business. Inefficient agricultural producers are not alone in trying to stay in production through obtaining public subsidy. The history of the tariff is replete with instances of industrial producers actuated by the same motives. One of the serious problems of the politics of planning is how to bring about readjustments in the use of resources or, to state it negatively, how to avoid freezing the economic order.

4. THE GENESIS AND COURSE OF POLITICAL MOVEMENTS

The object of this chapter has been twofold: (1) to indicate the character of the political objectives of American agriculture; (2) to suggest the nature of political movements in general by the use of agrarian movements as illustrations. It may be well to recapitulate the argument covering the second point and to add certain general comments and further illustrative material. What is it that sets off political agitation, that brings about demands for governmental action? In the examples chosen agriculture, particularly certain segments of it,[43] had suffered keen economic injury, deprivation of income, in comparison with the immediately earlier status of the farmer. This change in circumstances generated discontent among the agricultural sections

---

[43] Benton H. Wilcox has shown in detail how the agrarian radicalism of the northwestern states has been associated with agricultural conditions considerably different from those in surrounding states. Thus, the radical movements tended to be concentrated in those farming areas suffering special economic distress. See his "An Historical Definition of Northwestern Radicalism," *Mississippi Valley Historical Review,* 26 (1939), pp. 377–394. The close association of agrarian radicalism with urban movements should also be pointed out. See C. M. Destler, "Western Radicalism: Concepts and Origins," *Mississippi Valley Historical Review,* 31 (1944), pp. 335–368. For a suggestive analysis of early English radical agitation, see W. W. Rostow, "Business Cycles, Harvests, and Politics: 1790–1850," *Journal of Economic History,* 1 (1941), pp. 206–221.

of the population, and that discontent found expression in political demands.

It would be absurd to generalize from these agricultural movements and contend that all political movements are set in motion by a change in the external conditions affecting a group of people. Yet some new element must be introduced into a situation to stimulate resort to political action. That new element may be an economic change, as in agriculture, dislocating pre-existing relationships; or it may be a threat to a status already enjoyed. The ubiquity of changed economic situations as a factor in starting political movements give rise to the theory that economic factors underlie all political activity.

It seems clear, however, that other factors may be influential in setting into motion movements leading to a new political equilibrium.[44] New ideas and scientific discoveries, for example, may direct attention to conditions hitherto unperceived, or point to possibilities previously unknown, and be instrumental in stimulating political action. The discovery of the possibility of immunization against certain diseases by vaccination and other methods, for example, laid the basis for political crusades for compulsory, universal vaccination in which many battles between the vaccinators and antivaccinators were fought. On the other hand, an idea, or ideal, may be a factor of great force in movements leading to the reshaping of public policy. How is one, for example, to explain the movements for the expansion of manhood suffrage? The woman suffrage movement? Or what single factor was at the bottom of the prohibition movement? Or why does a movement begin at any particular time rather than at an earlier time? A concrete condition may exist over long periods, and at some particular moment unrest flares up to redress a long-standing wrong.

Simple explanations of the origins of movements must be accepted with reserve. In the example discussed at length, agrarian agitation, there is no certain means of knowing whether the collapse of farm prices in 1920 and 1921 was the causal factor in the political movement. In other words, if the collapse in prices had not occurred, would agitation have taken place anyway? Probably not, but there is no means of knowing absolutely.[45]

---

[44] For an analysis of the relationship between rainfall and farmers' political attitudes, see J. D. Barnhart, "Rainfall and the Populist Party in Nebraska," *American Political Science Review*, 19 (1925), pp. 527–540.

[45] The relation between the incidence of strikes and of economic fluctuations suggests some of the limitations of the theory of deprivation as a stimulant of social movements. Low levels in strikes come in years of declining business activity and when business is below normal. When the business curve begins to go upward, strikes tend to increase. In depression years the number of strikes remains at low levels. A

The introduction of a new element requiring readjustment in the entire social situation does not inevitably lead to political action. A thin line separates the political and nonpolitical. In postwar American agriculture, certain leaders, such as President Coolidge, counseled the farmers to abide by the operation of beneficent economic laws. By that, they meant that farmers producing at high cost should reduce their costs, produce something else on their lands, or seek a livelihood in industry; that agriculture should adjust itself to the changed situation by the inexorable process of bankruptcy for high-cost producers. The farmers refused to or could not take that course of action, and governmental remedies were sought. Harold Lasswell says: "Although political movements begin in unrest, all social unrest does not find expression in political movements. Under some conditions, a community which is visited by plague may pray; under other conditions, the community will demand the retirement of the health commissioner." [46] To use a less remote example: at one time when unemployment increased, a citizens' committee would solicit funds to maintain a soup line for those in distress; now pressure is brought on public authorities to increase th. appropriation for unemployment relief. In one culture drought-stricken farmers may pray for rain; in another they may petition Congress to appropriate for the installation of an irrigation works. Thus, the content of the governmental sphere changes. Unrest may work itself out by expression through religious channels. The Negro, for example, kept in subordination by "white supremacy" may seek satisfaction in ecclesiastical activity.[47] Additional examples could be cited, but these suffice to indicate that social discontent finds expression, and social adjustments are made, through many channels and mechanisms other than governmental.

When conditions are ripe for the rise of a political movement, a leader may come on the scene with a remedy. It is essential that the real functions of leadership, agitation and education in political movements, be perceived. Before there can be a political movement, the persons making up the movement must be conscious of a common cause, a common injury, a common goal. How is this consciousness

---

wave of strikes, however, may differ from a widespread movement of almost spontaneous origin in that cool calculations of strategy and timing may be governing. Union leaders, though, are not free from pressure of the mass of union membership in determining strike strategy. See Dale Yoder, "Economic Changes and Industrial Unrest in the United States," *Journal of Political Economy*, 48 (1940), pp. 222–237.

[46] H. D. Lasswell, "The Measurement of Public Opinion," *American Political Science Review*, 25 (1931), pp. 311–336.

[47] See B. E. Mays and J. W. Nicholson, *The Negro's Church* (New York, 1933), p. 281.

created? Fundamentally by the sharing of experience; and leaders, agitators, propagandists furnish the channels for the communication of a consciousness of common interest. The agitator thus serves as a medium both for cementing together those with a common concern and for externally expressing that common concern. The leader converts the mutterings at the cross-roads, in the taverns, and wherever men gather, into a movement, that is, a joint effort by a considerable number of persons to influence the course of events. Often would-be leaders misjudge the timeliness of their actions and there is no response to their offer to lead. In such instances the time is not at hand to convert the discontent of scattered individuals into a cohesive movement.

As a sense of common cause grows, a remedy is evolved. For the agrarian unrest after World War I the McNary-Haugen bill served as a goal. As a rallying cry for his movement, Dr. Townsend evolved the "Townsend Plan"; Henry George, the "single tax"; William Jennings Bryan, free coinage of silver at 16 to 1. As movements become more complex, a wide range of individual measures may be brought under the canopy of a single slogan: the "New Deal"; the "full dinner pail"; the "return to normalcy." For effective agitation, the most complex measures must be reducible to simple slogans. For effectiveness, the remedy around which a political movement is rallied need not be workable. In fact, the remedies advocated by messiahs often are, as the saying goes, "snares and delusions." Yet the expression of discontent is symptomatic of need for readjustment; even if the proposed therapy is futile, the pressure may compel the government to devise a substitute treatment. For example, the Townsend Plan, which proposed $200 a month for every person over 60, was claimed by all the experts to be unworkable, but the pressure of Dr. Townsend's movement was significant in bringing about the enactment of the Social Security Act with a different method of caring for the aged. At times movements operate to dissipate frustrations by the mere expression of discontent, or they are worn down by the resistances of existing institutional patterns. In some instances—notably American municipal reform movements—discontent is blotted out by the enactment of an ordinance that symbolizes success for the movement but has no perceptible effect on the course of events.

In the course of their growth movements usually acquire an organizational apparatus and recruit a secretariat or a bureaucracy. Once the movement achieves its immediate objective, it may disappear, but often its institutional machinery gains virtual immortality. The movement may evolve into an organization that grasps new issues and new causes to keep itself alive. Most of the farmers' movements analyzed in this chapter have reached this stage in the life cycle of a movement. Most pressure groups, in fact, originate in an effort to cope with some immediate problem and then persist as an organization to deal with new matters of common concern to the membership.[48]

The foregoing discussion of the natural history of political movements suggests that one of the principal tasks of those who govern is to identify and deal with maladjustments that give rise to social discontent and political movements. The skill and insight with which a politics of prevention is followed will determine whether those who govern will continue to govern. The identification of social maladjustments generally tends to be neglected until they give rise to strong movements in demand of action; in rare instances all the techniques of social research are brought into play to observe, foresee, and plan thoroughly to meet rising problems. Those who govern may choose to wear down by delay and obstruction rather than to appease movements of discontent. They may deem it desirable to ignore, deny, or suppress. More often they do not have the wit to see that something should be done; otherwise the personnel of governments would not change so frequently.

[48] For general discussions of the nature of social movements, see: J. S. Burgess, "The Study of Modern Social Movements as a Means for Clarifying the Process of Social Action," *Social Forces*, 22 (1944), pp. 269–275; R. C. Fuller and R. R. Myers, "The Natural History of a Social Problem," *American Sociological Review*, 6 (1941), pp. 320–339; R. M. MacIver, *Society, A Textbook of Sociology* (New York: Farrar & Rinehart, 1937), chaps. 21–28; R. M. MacIver, *Social Causation* (Boston: Ginn, 1942); Hadley Cantril, *The Psychology of Social Movements* (New York: Wiley, 1941).

Chapter 3

WORKERS

INDUSTRIALIZATION has been at the roots of most of the great domestic political issues in the United States since the War between the States. The rise of manufacturing and the development of associated financial, transport, and distributive organizations generated changes of profound political significance. The expansion of new economic interests brought struggles for a redistribution of political power, and the erection of mighty structures of private industrial power brought demands from disadvantaged groups for governmental redress of grievances. Agrarian protest movements that swept the country in the latter part of the nineteenth century failed to stay the hand of the new colossus of finance and industry. After the turn of the century in the Progressive movement and in Woodrow Wilson's crusade for the "new freedom" the middle classes and the small entrepreneur fought only a delaying action against the same antagonist.

In the battle for power in the state the worker has proved to be, at least potentially, the strongest force loosed by the process of industrialization. The growth of industry in the United States thrust into numerical preponderance a working class sharply distinguishable in status and condition from the farmer and the small entrepreneur. In the main without property, this class found itself arrayed against those possessing title to this world's goods. With its resources limited to skills of mind and of muscle, it occupied a situation of great insecurity. Without cash reserves, its very food and shelter were dependent on the vagaries of business conditions that determined the regularity of the pay envelope. This new class enjoyed many of the disadvantages of serfdom, with few of the rights which that status entailed. Individually almost powerless, the only mode for defense and offense open to the industrial worker was collective action.

The American industrial laboring class emerged in an ideological climate superficially hospitable to political action. Doctrines of political equality, of the right of self-government, of liberty of expression seemed to pave the way for the new toiling masses to grasp power and to mold the state to suit their wishes. Moreover, while American workers were increasing in number, socialist ideas were blossoming around the globe. Heady doctrines were proclaimed: Workers of the world should unite and take what was justly theirs. By merging socialism and democracy, the workers did not have to take what they wanted. All they had to do was to vote for it. He who would understand politics in the large may ponder well the status of labor: a great force numerically in a society adhering to the doctrine of the rule of numbers, yet a group lacking proportionate durable political power as a class.

1. INCOHESIVENESS OF LABOR

Shifts in the occupational composition of a people may have far-reaching political consequences. Transfer of large segments of the population into the wage-earning class may have especially notable effects on political behavior. Well over half our people are wage-earners and might be classified as "workers" or "laborers," yet "workers" as a class have been unable to exert effectively their potential political power. Organized labor has attracted to its ranks only a small proportion of "workers." Organized labor itself has been beset by internal splits and disputes. In politics labor as a class has been divided. Why this state of affairs exists needs to be explored, but first it is advisable to examine the extent to which the occupational pattern has been altered in recent decades.

To show the changes wrought in the nature of our society by the process of industrialization is difficult because of the nature of the available statistics. Presumably the change of greatest political significance comes from the decline in the proportion of farmers, independent artisans, and business proprietors in the total population and from the enormous increase in the proportion of the population that gets its living from wages and salaries. Such trends reflect the creation of a new class likely to act in new ways in the struggle for political power. Census operations, however, do not yield data showing whether people derive their living from wages, from interest and dividends, from entrepreneurial income, from managerial salaries, or from other sources. Such data would offer suggestive inferences in the study of political behavior. The general trends, however, are indicated by the data presented in Figure 2. The proportion of the population engaged in manufacturing and mechanical pursuits did not change markedly between 1870 and 1940, but the proportion engaged in trade and in clerical or "white-collar" occupations increased sharply. Thus, although factory or industrial workers are a minority of all gainful workers, wage earners of all kinds undoubtedly make up a majority. The relative strength of various groups in the population—and it is relative strength that is politically significant—changed considerably between 1870 and 1940. Note in Figure 2 the changing relationship between those in agriculture and in manufacturing and related occupations.[1]

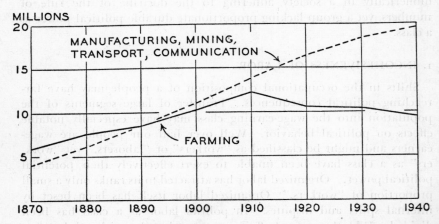

Figure 2. Growth of Occupational Groups Attached to Manufacturing, Mining, Transportation, and Communication Contrasted with Trend in Occupational Category of Farming, 1870–1940

Extent of unionization. Wage earners constitute by far the largest block of the adult population of the United States. Yet they are by no means a homogeneous group. Nor do most wage earners consider themselves as members of a "class" with common interests or common political objectives. Within the "laboring class" the widest kinds of diversities in income, in skills, in ways of living, and in political views prevail. One index of the amorphous nature of the "working class" is the small proportion affiliated with labor organizations. The degree to which workers are organized furnishes a crude notion of the effective strength of the group as a whole. In 1930 there were about 35,000,000 "organizable" employees engaged in nonagricultural pursuits, accord-

[1] Occupational data of the censuses from 1870, rearranged to obtain comparable figures from census to census, are conveniently available in Dewey Anderson and P. E. Davidson, *Occupational Trends in the United States* (Stanford: Stanford University Press, 1940).

ing to estimates by Leo Wolman.[2] Several million would now have to be added to such an estimate to account for growth in population and in industry. Thirty-five or forty million persons effectively organized could exert great power, but only a minority of the "organizable" is organized. Wolman estimated that in 1937 only about 10 per cent of the workers belonged to unions.[3] This proportion grew rapidly during World War II. Estimated membership of unions in 1940 was 8.5 million; in 1944, 13.7 million. The American Federation of Labor in 1944 reported a membership of 6.5 millions; in 1943 the Congress of Industrial Organizations, which does not regularly publish membership figures, claimed 5.3 millions; and in 1943 independent unions claimed an affiliation of 1.5 million. For strategic reasons unions ordinarily exaggerate their strength. Union membership at its wartime peak probably did not exceed one third of all "organizable" workers.

Not only do labor organizations attract only a part of all "organizable" workers, but their membership also fluctuates within a broad range. At times, particularly in the early history of the American labor movement, unions seemed fragile institutions, which were formed and re-formed as different leaders and ideologies gained ascendancy. Membership in labor organizations seems to vary roughly with the ups and downs of business conditions, but the major upward swings in membership have come at times when the government looked benignly on the labor movement. In World War I the strength of the American Federation of Labor rose rapidly, only to fall to a low point in 1933 and then begin to rise again in the halcyon days of the New Deal. In World War II total union membership shot upward and began to sag as return to civilian production got under way. The vicissitudes in the maintenance of labor organization led Selig Perlman to observe that a main feature of the American labor movement has been "a perpetual struggle to keep the organization from going to pieces for want of inner cohesiveness." [4] A reflection of that lack of "inner cohesiveness" is to be found in the internal government of the A.F.L., a confederation whose central governing body has only limited powers over the constituent units of the federation. The split of the C.I.O. away from the A.F.L. was a further evidence of the divisions within labor. Why this lack of "inner cohesiveness" within labor?

[2] Leo Wolman, "The Turning Point in American Labor Policy," *Political Science Quarterly,* 55 (1940), pp. 161–175.

[3] "Union Membership in Great Britain and the United States," National Bureau of Economic Research, *Bulletin 68,* December 27, 1937.

[4] Perlman, *A Theory of the Labor Movement* (New York: Macmillan, 1928), p. 154. See especially chap. 5, "Labor and Capitalism in America."

Heterogeneity of workers. In explanation of the weakness of the ties that bind labor together, it needs first to be said that workers are not all alike nor are their interests identical, at least not identical in the short run. College students, especially those with an upper middle-class background, are likely to consider labor a homogeneous mass; but within labor there are multifarious cleavages, both obvious and subtle. There is economic competition among different types of labor. Jurisdictional disputes among trade unions are manifestations of competition among different groups for the jobs in question. Battles among unions in such situations often are quite as bitter as conflict between employers and employees. Every union attempts to gain a monopoly of the labor supply in a given craft or industry; the resulting monopoly power is used in bargaining with the employer. But it must be remembered that monopoly over a particular labor market must be maintained by the union against threatened encroachments by competing laborers who would break the monopoly and work perhaps for lower wages or under different conditions.

Apart from economic competition, a variety of other differences contributes to conflicts in attitude and to labor disunity. Occupational and skill differences among workers create variations in attitude and in belief. Between the great mass of "white-collar" workers and factory workers a broad gulf exists. Railroad clerks, for example, although paid less than engine and shop workers, in some situations tend to identify themselves with the railroad executives.[5] Occupational and skill stratifications are reflected in voting. Estimates, by the American Institute of Public Opinion, of the percentage of classes of workers voting Democratic in the presidential elections of 1936, 1940, and 1944 suggest the significance of skill differences for political behavior:

	1936	*1940*	*1944*
Skilled workers	67	59	59
Semi-skilled workers	74	67	62
Unskilled workers	81	69	65

These broad categories, however, mask much wider political differences among workers. What would be expected, for example, of the private tutor of children of wealthy parents in contrast with public school teachers in a poor neighborhood? Of the executive's secretary and the typist in the stenographic pool? The range of variations among different types of workers generally is perhaps indicated by the data in

5 David Rodnick, "Status Values Among Railroadmen," *Social Forces*, 20 (1941), pp. 89–96. For other illustrative material, see H. J. Lahne, *The Cotton Mill Worker* (New York: Farrar & Rinehart, 1944).

Table 3, which show the party affiliations declared at registration by selected occupational groups in Santa Clara County, California, in 1934. The figures reflect peculiarities of the time and place, but the spread in partisan affiliation between different occupational groups would almost certainly appear in a study of broader coverage.

TABLE 3

Percentage of Selected Occupational Groups Registered as Republican in Santa Clara County, California, in 1934 [a]

Skilled		Semi-Skilled		Unskilled	
Policemen	66.0	Telephone employees	67.0	Houseworkers	71.0
Foremen, shop	65.0	Dressmakers	60.0	Custodians	62.0
Shoemakers	56.0	Railroad employees	54.0	Janitors	57.0
Engineers	55.0	Pressers	50.0	Gardeners	52.0
Carpenters	53.0	Watchmen	48.0	Teamsters	50.0
Firemen	50.0	Truck drivers	43.0	Cement workers	49.0
Printers	49.0	Bakers	41.5	Fruit workers	43.0
Mechanics	48.0	Linemen	39.0	Laborers	37.0
Plasterers	38.0	Cooks	35.0	Cannery workers	35.0
Tailors	34.0	Box makers	31.0	Waiters	28.0
All skilled	51.6	All semi-skilled	46.8	All unskilled	41.3
All electorate	57.0		57.0		57.0

[a] This table is constructed from more inclusive listings by Dewey Anderson and P. E. Davidson, *Ballots and the Democratic Class Struggle* (Stanford: Stanford University Press, 1943), pp. 129, 132, 134.

National, religious, and racial differences also introduce cleavages into the labor movement. Rivalries between workers of different national origins are not uncommon. The same skills are sometimes divided among Jewish and Gentile unions, while Catholics as a matter of religious principle oppose socialist tendencies within unions. A special problem is presented by the Negro; traditionally unions have discriminated against the Negro, at times excluding him from membership, at other times giving him the privilege of paying initiation fees and dues but not allowing him to participate in the management of union affairs. Non-discriminatory policies, however, have been adopted since 1935 by some unions, mainly by those affiliated with the C.I.O.[6]

Absence of class consciousness. The foregoing and other factors contribute to the lack of a labor "class consciousness," which is an essential prerequisite to concerted action in the political field and, perhaps to a

[6] H. R. Northrup, *Organized Labor and the Negro* (New York: Harper, 1944); H. R. Cayton and G. S. Mitchell, *Black Workers and the New Unions* (Chapel Hill: University of North Carolina Press, 1939).

lesser extent, in the area of economic warfare.[7]   It may be contended
with the Marxian rationale that the interests of all laborers are the
same, but until workers as individuals believe that to be so there can
be no crystallized consciousness of common cause and common goal
and, hence, no labor solidarity in action.   The fact is that few laborers
even consider themselves to be members of an industrial proletariat;
American laborers consider themselves middle class.   The American
Institute of Public Opinion reported in 1939 that only one of every sixteen Americans polled identified himself as belonging to the "lower
classes," while about 87 per cent thought of themselves as middle-class.
American society thus in a sense is a "classless" society, at least psychologically, and this condition militates against unity among workers.
The existence of a considerable degree of vertical occupational mobility
and the absence of a general attitude of acceptance and resignation to
an inherited class status create an environment for the American labor
movement quite different from that in a nation with a tradition of class
differentiation.

Hostility toward organized labor.   Attempts to unify the American
working classes also have met determined and powerful opposition,
not only from employers but from other sections of society.   Powerful
established ideologies and interests have met labor in head-on collision, and time and again labor has suffered reverses.   Perlman, in his
interpretation of the American labor movement, places great emphasis
on the strength of the institution of private property and the incom-
patibility of the objectives of organized labor with private property.
Whether labor seeks its ends by political means, by legislation, or by
economic means—the strike and bargaining—its objective is to restrict
the control of the employer over his productive property.   Perlman
holds that the lesson of the American labor movement "is that under
no circumstances can labor here afford to arouse the fears of the great
middle class for the safety of private property as a basic institution.
Labor needs the support of public opinion, meaning the middle class,
both rural and urban, in order to make headway with its program of
curtailing, by legislation and by trade unionism, the abuses which
attend the employer's unrestricted exercise of his property rights."[8]
The claims of labor have, to a considerable degree, been on matters
that employers have been unwilling to yield.   The principle of collective bargaining has been a basic point of dispute; it infringes, as Perlman
pointed out, on the privileges associated with private ownership and

[7] See C. C. North, "Class Structure, Class Consciousness, and Party Alignment,"
American Sociological Review, 2 (1937), pp. 365–371.

[8] *Op. cit.*, pp. 160–161.

management of property. The demand for collective bargaining and for union "recognition" has been met by private employers' armies, amply provisioned and munitioned, sometimes supported by police and troops. This resort to violence has been a factor of no mean importance in the prevention of the rise of a strong labor movement.[9] When the right of collective bargaining became guaranteed by the National Labor Relations Act, employer resistance to the application of the principle did not evaporate overnight. Sabotage of the law was widespread. To many employers, the fundamental principle of the act was inacceptable. Consequently some observers concluded that the law came too early, on the assumption that, in our society at any rate, law is workable only when it is generally acceptable to those most immediately affected.

All the influences operating on labor result in a labor movement that embraces only a small proportion of all workers and is a minority group within the entire population. Throughout their entire history American labor unions have had to fight an uphill battle even for the right to exist. The early unions were assaulted as anarchist or socialist. Eventually they became accepted, only to have the cry of communism raised against them. Even yet, organized labor has obtained only limited public acceptance of its objectives and methods, and large segments of the population are hostile to unions as such. Almost half the farmers, in polls during World War II, were not "in favor of" labor unions; they were more hostile toward unions than employers were. Moreover, union practices considered basic by labor leaders have gained even less public acceptance. About seven out of ten persons adhere to the open shop principle, that is, that a worker who takes a job should be free to join a union or not. The check-off, that is, the deduction of union dues by the employer from the worker's pay, finds little favor among the public generally. Union make-work or restrictive policies, such as limitations on the width of the brush to be used by a painter, arouse public animosity. On more important matters, such as when a union becomes a bit radical, the middle class screeches; and it is to be remembered that a large proportion of Americans is ideologically middle class.[10]

Hostility toward organized labor may point a moral. Labor movements in liberal-democratic states are animated by a faith that the status of the wage-earning classes may be improved by parliamentary means. This commonplace assumption carries with it some startling implications. If the assumption is correct, the laboring masses, by the

[9] For a summary of the use of violence vis-à-vis labor, see Chapter 20.
[10] See W. A. Lydgate, *What America Thinks* (New York: Crowell, 1944), chap. ii.

exertion of their political power, may remake the state or accomplish veritable revolution without violence. In practice, however, there are likely to be limits to the degree to which labor may improve its status within the framework of the liberal-democratic state. The rising strength of labor seems nearly always to be met by a unification of the employer groups and of others who might be injured by a further increase in labor's power. Expansion of the power of labor generates countervailing action by the dominant groups who possess vast resources to defend their status. As a result, the structure of the liberal-democratic state may be severely strained by internal struggles. Its maintenance, with its freedom for group advancement through peaceful political action, depends in no small measure on the self-restraint of the groups contending for power and influence. If the advantage of numerical strength is pushed too far, a labor movement may be wiped out by reaction.

The incohesiveness of the American labor movement projects itself into the government of labor organizations, into the political ideology of the labor movement, and into the political tactics employed by labor organizations. The governmental machinery of national labor organizations functions, and even persists, to a large degree by compromise thereby manifesting the influence of the inner contradictions of labor. The dominant political ideology of American labor adjusts itself to the limitations imposed by the middle-class orientation of most workers and by the strength of resistant capitalist ideology. On the whole, the political tactics of labor narrow down to those usable by any pressure group with negligible voting strength. They do not make up the strategy of a group large enough and confident of its ability to grasp control of the state.

2. GOVERNMENT OF TRADE UNIONS

Government of private groups generally. Examination of the government of the American Federation of Labor offers opportunity to suggest observations of general relevance for pressure societies, all of which are equipped with governmental apparatus for the management of their affairs. Groups of persons interested in improving their political status or in gaining influence in the state do not commonly rise spontaneously as one man and in unison shout their demands. From time to time, to be sure, intolerable circumstances generate virtually spontaneous movements that operate through the most rudimentary group machinery. Generally, however, a segment of society that seeks to improve or defend its status works through a relatively elaborate organization, which formulates and expresses its wishes. This machinery for group action constitutes a group government strikingly similar to that of the state itself.

Before the wishes of a group can be expressed, they must be ascertained. Although it may be supposed that the interests and needs of private associations vis-à-vis the state are perfectly clear, they seldom are. Generally, within the group there are conflicts of interest, of ideology, of aims. These must be settled in order that the group may go forth united to fight its battles. In reconciling internal differences and arriving at a policy reflecting the group interest, the workings of the government of private associations are almost as complex as the state's governmental apparatus. The private group, too, has its executive agencies and its courts, as well as its policy-determining bodies. It has its taxes and its crimes. It often has its own system of education, its heroes and patriots. It has sanctions to maintain group discipline and star chambers to purge dissentient elements.

Similarity between private associations and the state is not confined to the matter of governmental machinery: significant similarities also exist with respect to subtle characteristics of institutional behavior. Governments often are slow in adapting their institutional machinery to meet the requirements of new and changing circumstances; the same institutional lag may be observed in private associations. The relative simplicity of the government of private societies provides less friction to institutional evolution than does the highly complex and specialized machinery of the formal government; yet, as the government of private groups becomes more highly developed, its pains of adaptation come to be more nearly equivalent to those of the state.

Moreover, within private societies an oligarchical government may also exist, which is likely to reflect more faithfully the interests of the ruling bureaucracy or clique than those of the mass of its membership or "citizenry." The inevitable tendency toward oligarchy is present no less in private groups than in society as a whole. Furthermore, the professional leaders and bureaucrats of the private society, as the specialists in verbalization for the group, are apt to become so thoroughly and completely attached to a set of doctrines or ideologies that they lose their intellectual nimbleness. In such an instance, unreflecting attachment to a rigid ideology by the leadership of private groups may endanger survival.

Constitution of A.F.L. These general remarks, which are equally applicable to organizations of farmers, of businessmen, of veterans, and of other types of persons, may be given concreteness by an outline of the governmental structure of the American Federation of Labor. The

A.F.L., in terms of its constitution, is an "association . . . of such trade and labor unions as shall conform to its rules and regulations." Thus its constituent parts are not individual workers but unions or associations of workers federated together, again quoting the constitution, "to aid and assist each other; to aid and encourage the sale of union label goods; and to secure legislation in the interest of the working people, and influence public opinion, by peaceful and legal methods, in favor of organized labor." The creators of the A.F.L., like the founders of other federal systems, had to overcome the jealousies of the organizations being brought together. The necessity for unity was great enough to bring existing unions together to act in concert to promote common interests, but as for the internal affairs of each union the federation is "based upon a strict recognition of the autonomy of each trade."

The constituent units that enjoy "states' rights" within labor's federal system are about a hundred national and international unions, each of which is based on local unions of workers and has its own elaborate governmental machinery.[11] Among the more important of the affiliated unions are the United Brotherhood of Carpenters and Joiners; the International Association of Machinists; the Bricklayers, Masons, and Plasterers' International Union; the Brotherhood of Electrical Workers; and the Brotherhood of Teamsters and Chauffeurs, Stablemen and Helpers. Each of these national and international unions is built on a base of local trade unions, of which there are some 28,000. Each local has its president, secretary, and business agent. In the smaller locals only the business agent is a full-time employee, while in the larger locals the president or secretary may be a full-time employee, and several business agents may be employed. The presidents of most international unions with less than 100,000 members receive less than $7,500 annually; the presidents of larger internationals usually receive a more liberal compensation.[12]

It is the national and international unions, each dominated chiefly by a group of specialized labor leaders,[13] that designate the majority

11 There are city centrals, state federations, and other structural features of interest to the specialist, but the centers of power within the federation are the national and international unions. See Lewis L. Lorwin, *The American Federation of Labor* (Washington: Brookings, 1933), chap. 12.

12 Florence Peterson, *American Labor Unions* (New York: Harper, 1945), p. 115; *Economic Outlook* (published by C.I.O. Department of Research and Education), Vol. VII, No. 2, February, 1946.

13 "The technical specialization that inevitably results from all extensive organization renders necessary what is called expert leadership. Consequently the power of determination comes to be considered one of the specific attributes of leadership, and is gradually withdrawn from the masses to be concentrated in the hands of the leaders

of the delegates to the annual convention of the A.F.L. The convention, which meets for ten days or two weeks, constitutes the policy-determining or—to follow our governmental analogy—the legislative body of the Federation. The convention usually must deal with more than a hundred resolutions proposing new or altered policies; it handles these in the first instance through committees, of which there are fourteen, appointed by the president of the A.F.L. Recommendations of the committees may be debated on the floor of the convention, but the most heated discussions generally take place in the closed committee sessions. Convention proceedings tend to be smoothly staged by the controlling oligarchy.[14] Said the late Charles P. Howard, president of the International Typographical Union, at the 1936 convention: "During the years I have been a delegate to conventions of the American Federation of Labor I have observed the strongest cohesion in a controlling group for the purpose of determining every question from election of officers to selection of the city in which the convention is to meet the following year."[15]

The executive council, consisting of the president, fifteen vice-presidents, and the secretary-treasurer, elected annually by the convention, has the duty of carrying out the convention's decisions. It corresponds roughly to the cabinet of a parliamentary government, with the president in the position of prime minister. Like the cabinets of most parliamentary governments, it exercises wide discretion. It can interpret the convention resolutions in varying ways, and on many questions it is, of course. granted wide discretion by the constitution and the convention. The effectiveness of the executive council in governing the Federation is reflected in the fact that changes in its mem-

---

alone. Thus the leaders, who were at first no more than the executive organs of the collective will, soon emancipate themselves from the mass and become independent of its control."—Robert Michels, *Political Parties* (New York: International, 1915), pp. 31–32.

[14] "One cannot observe many of the conventions of the Federation without becoming impressed with the degree of control over policies exercised by the leaders. To the outsider these leaders appear as a coterie, set off from the rank and file of delegates, deciding major questions at issue, and supporting or opposing them as a body rather than as individuals. In spite of the democratic form of the convention procedure, therefore, the very loyalty of the lower for the higher officials, the very power exercised by these higher officials discourage real expressions of opinion on the part of the mass of delegates."—H. L. Childs, *Labor and Capital in National Politics* (Columbus: Ohio State University Press, 1930), p. 134.

[15] A.F.L., *Annual Convention, 1936, Proceedings*, p. 72. An interesting sidelight on the attitude of the controlling groups within the Federation is furnished by its championship of the initiative and referendum as a means of democratic control within the state; yet in 1912 when the socialist factions of the Federation attempted to bring about the adoption of the initiative and referendum for the affairs of the Federation itself the proposal was successfully resisted by the controlling clique.

bership usually follow death or resignation rather than refusal by the convention to re-elect.

The Federation, although managed by a cohesive ruling clique, exercises its power only within narrow limits. The unity and solidarity of the A.F.L. exist only so long as there is no encroachment upon the jealously guarded autonomy of the constituent national and international unions. "To hold together and to lead the medley of organization which formed the A.F. of L., with their different trade interests, industrial experiences, methods of procedure, and attitudes of mind, called for shrewd and flexible leadership. Gompers supplied that leadership by following the line of least resistance. He insisted on uniformity of policy and centralized authority only when absolutely essential. He bent to the will of the strong international unions when inevitable. By assuring trade autonomy, he won the support of the majority of the union leaders, who thus were made secure in their own domains. . . ." [16]

Indicative of the Federation's weakness and of the strength of the constituent national and international unions was the consideration by the 1940 annual convention of the problem of cleansing some of the constituent unions of racketeers. David Dubinsky, of the International Ladies Garment Workers Union, proposed that the executive council of the Federation be given authority to remove officials of constituent unions found guilty of racketeering. The council thus would have been authorized to deal effectively with malodorous situations in some of the unions that have given the entire labor movement a bad name. But the leadership of the A.F.L. as a whole was not prepared to go this far. So great was the power of "states' rights" in the A.F.L. that the convention limited itself to an expression of condemnation of racketeering union leaders and to a direction to the executive council to use its "influence" to bring about a house cleaning in the unions concerned. The 1941 convention again called upon the affiliated unions "to take prompt action whenever racketeering, wrongdoing or other crime is engaged in by any of their officers or members, which tends to bring dishonor on the trade union movement." [17] The same convention, however, defeated for re-election as eleventh vice-president of the Federation, George E. Browne, President of the International Alliance of Theatrical Stage Employees, who was under indictment for extortion of over $1,000,000 from the movie industry. Another illustration of the autonomy of the constituent unions is furnished by a debate in the 1944 convention on the question of their discrimination against Ne-

16 Lorwin. *op. cit.*, p. 75.
17 A.F.L., *Proceedings*, 1941, pp. 541–43.

groes. What could the Federation do about it? The answer was that each national and international union was "clothed with autonomous authority to formulate, shape, and administer its own affairs." [18]

In its early days the Congress of Industrial Organizations possessed a government more unitary than federal. Many of its unions depended on subsidies from the central headquarters and naturally central policies prevailed. As the C.I.O. unions succeeded in their organizing campaigns and developed their own revenues they became financially autonomous. With financial independence they gained freedom in other directions. The general constitutional trend moves toward the federalism of the A.F.L., but a more militant leadership maintains a higher degree of uniformity of policy.

Further parallels between public and union government. The foregoing brief description of the governmental structure of one union makes it clear that the student of political institutions deals with familiar materials when he examines the mechanisms of labor organizations. Further parallels between private and public government may be found. Observers of political parties have noted, for example, that the power of management and leadership of party affairs tends to gravitate into the hands of a relatively small coterie. Similarly, in labor organizations the interplay between leadership and mass seems to result in the transfer of authority to an oligarchy. In their formative stages unions function somewhat on the order of town meetings and their officials are nonprofessionals who devote only their spare time to group affairs. Gradually, as the union assumes additional functions, specialized or professional, labor leaders arise and the power of decision moves to the paid officials ("the office") of the union. Self-government within the union becomes a fiction.[19] Union affairs come to be managed by a self-perpetuating leadership. Illustrative of this tendency is the fact that opposition to the "organization" slate in the election of union officers is exceptional. Professor Taft finds from a study of seven unions over the period from 1910 to 1944 that 764 officers had been chosen and of these 634 ran unopposed. In only the International Typographical Union was the choice of officers ordinarily accompanied by opposition.[20] Of course, the absence of opposition to the official slate might indicate a high degree of mass satisfaction with union leader-

[18] A.F.L., *Proceedings*, 1944, pp. 504–507.
[19] Will Herberg, "Bureaucracy and Democracy in Labor Unions," *Antioch Review*, 2 (1943), pp. 405–417.
[20] Philip Taft, "Opposition to Union Officers in Elections," *Quarterly Journal of Economics*, 58 (1944), pp. 246–264. See also his "Democracy in Trade Unions," *Papers and Proceedings*, 58th Annual Meeting, American Economic Association (1946), pp. 359–369.

ship as well as oligarchical control. But the latter characterization is more apt, which is not to deny the advantages to labor of fairly strong leadership in its battle to improve its status. Nor is it to be forgotten that similar tendencies are found in business, professional, agricultural, and other private organizations. Yet it is hard to match some of the examples of abuse of power within labor organizations. In some instances, for example, union leaders have, in effect, "dissolved parliament" for long periods. The officers of the tobacco workers called no convention from 1900 to 1939 when a court order forced action.

Development of extensive organizational structure manned by professional or paid personnel introduces elements of inflexibility into labor organization, a characteristic certainly recurrent in public government. Once union structure is established, union oligarchies gain a vested interest in the established structure; adjustment to meet new conditions may alter the distribution of prestige, power, and revenues. Hence, proposals for such adjustments encounter resistance. The process is well illustrated by the creaking and groaning of the A.F.L. in dealing with the question of industrial unionism, which involved issues and behavior not unlike those arising in the adjustment of any federal governmental system to meet new requirements.

Craft *v*. industrial unionism: Institutional inadaptability. When a new industry develops, shall all the workers of the industry be organized into one big union or shall each craft union have "jurisdiction" over persons in the industry in its craft? This sort of issue continually arises to plague the A.F.L. and to absorb its energies. Illustrative is the jurisdictional issue raised by the growth of the neon sign industry. The executive council of the A.F.L. reported in 1936 that it had appointed a committee consisting of representatives of the Electrical Workers, the Painters, the Flint Glass Workers, and the Glass Bottle Blowers' Association to settle a jurisdictional controversy in the industry. The proposal of the executive council was not sufficiently inclusive, for when the report was acted upon by the convention, Delegate Moriarity, of the Sheet Metal Workers, pointed out that a representative of his organization should be added to the group.[21]

In mass-production industries using assembly-line methods it is often difficult to differentiate among the crafts involved, and craft unionism has appeared at its weakest in the attempt to organize these industries. How the jurisdictional jealousies of union bureaucracies and the inertia of the prevailing organizational structure hamper action is vividly illustrated by an effort of the A.F.L. to organize the automobile industry. A move to organize the workers of this industry in the years 1925–1927

[21] A.F.L. Convention, 1936, *Proceedings,* pp. 100, 432.

bogged down completely in the jurisdictional rivalry of the A.F.L. craft unions. In 1925 a committee of the Metal Trades Department of the A.F.L. suggested organization of this industry along industrial lines. The craft unions opposed this as well as a second suggestion that the workers be organized and later divided among the international and national unions. In the 1926 A.F.L. convention the Metal Trades Department introduced a resolution calling for organization of the auto workers, and the convention voted that questions of jurisdiction be dropped during the organization. In 1926 seventeen international unions with jurisdictional claims in the industry met to agree on a plan of campaign. William Green presided and declared that the basic question before the conference was "the question of suspension of jurisdiction." He said that if the unions would waive their claims, the A.F.L. would undertake to organize the industry, and later a plan could be worked out for the transfer of workers to the appropriate unions.

The international unions did not receive the proposal with enthusiasm, one reason for their attitude being that there were within the industry small numbers of skilled workers belonging to existing unions. The 1926 conference adjourned without agreement; in 1927 another conference, attended by representatives of only nine unions, adopted a plan to organize the industry and later to transfer the unionists to the appropriate international unions. Later in the year another conference was convened to determine the immediate steps to be taken. The campaign of organization made no headway, in part because of the lukewarm support of existing unions.[22] The mighty labor movement was stymied by its organizational rigidity and by the vested interest of the leaders of its constituent unions in the status quo.

In the A.F.L. conventions of 1934, 1935, and 1936 the issue of craft unionism versus industrial unionism came to a head. In 1934 the convention saw as its duty the formulation of "policies which will fully protect the jurisdictional rights of all trade unions organized upon craft lines and afford them every opportunity for development and accession of those workers engaged upon work over which these organizations exercise jurisdiction." In 1935 a heated battle in the convention culminated in the adoption of a resolution reaffirming the stand of the prior year. The resolution placed great emphasis upon the rights of existing organizations in the prevailing union structure. The minority, led by John L. Lewis of the United Mine Workers of America, argued that "common sense" required a molding of organization policies to "meet present-day needs." "In those industries where the work performed by a majority of the workers is of such nature that it might

[22] Lorwin, *op. cit.*, pp. 244–248.

fall within the jurisdictional claim of more than one craft union, or no established craft union, it is declared that industrial organization is the only form that will be acceptable to the workers or adequately meet their needs. . . ."

Birth of the C.I.O.   In November, 1935, the unions that had supported the minority view at the 1935 A.F.L. convention established the Committee for Industrial Organization to encourage the organization of workers in mass production and other industries "upon an industrial basis" and "to bring them under the banner and in affiliation with the American Federation of Labor as industrial organizations." The committee consisted of the presidents of the United Mine Workers of America; the International Typographical Union; the Amalgamated Clothing Workers of America; the International Ladies Garment Workers' Union; the United Textile Workers of America; the Oil Field, Gas Well, and Refinery Workers of America; the Cap and Millinery Department of the United Hatters, Cap, and Millinery Workers' International Union; and the International Union of Mine, Mill, and Smelter Workers.

Thus was set in course a chain of events that led to the split of the labor movement.   Sniping back and forth among the leaders of the A.F.L. continued until the 1936 annual convention.   The C.I.O. offered the A.F.L. $500,000 to undertake an organizing campaign among the steel workers if the A.F.L. would contribute $1,000,000, organize the workers along industrial lines, and place the campaign in the hands of leadership "such as to inspire confidence of success."   The executive council could not accept conditional contributions or surrender its right to exercise its best judgment and act in accordance with "the traditional organizing policies of the American Federation of Labor." Lewis urged the Amalgamated Association of Iron, Steel, and Tin Workers to accept the aid of the C.I.O. in organizing steel.   He argued that the policy of the executive council would immediately fill the "industry with a horde of organizers attached to craft unions, fiercely competing with each other for the new members who might be organized and for the few dollars which might be taken in as initiation fees and dues collections. . . ."   The C.I.O. then proceeded, by organizing steel, to demonstrate the soundness of its general strategy.

The executive council of the A.F.L. in August, 1936, found that twelve unions associated with the C.I.O. "had violated the constitution and laws of the American Federation of Labor by setting up a dual union called the Committee for Industrial Organization and by inaugurating a state of rebellion against the American Federation of

Labor. . . ." The council ordered these unions to withdraw from the C.I.O. on pain of suspension from the A.F.L. The council order, however, had no effect, and in 1938 the Committee for Industrial Organization became the Congress of Industrial Organizations.

In the 1936 convention there was debate whether the executive council had exceeded its authority in ordering the suspension of the C.I.O. unions; it was not unlike a constitutional argument before the Supreme Court, as well as an argument on the merits of the industrial form of organization. Delegate Zaritsky of the United Hatters, Cap, and Millinery Workers declared that experience with craft organization had been "unfortunate and unsatisfactory." He pleaded for a modernization of policies. William Green, president of the Federation, spoke for the old guard in defense of the "economic philosophy of the American Federation of Labor, a philosophy evolved out of a half century of varied experiences. It is not academic. It is practical. . . . That economic philosophy was sound forty years ago, it was sound thirty years ago, it was sound yesterday, it is sound now. . . ." Such fundamentalistic remarks have their parallels in religion and in the state; and, like other fundamentalism, they constitute by and large a rationalization of a vested interest in terms of the virtues of tradition.[23]

It would be an error to ascribe the split within organized labor solely to the issue of industrial versus craft unionism. The Federation had no special objection to industrial unionism; it included within its membership industrial unions; it had made some efforts to organize new industrial unions; and it was committed in 1934 to further efforts to form industrial unions in the mass-production industries. The opposition to industrial unionism became active only when there was danger of encroachment on the jurisdiction of existing organizations. Moreover, for several years a serious breach had existed between the old-guard oligarchy of the A.F.L. and the more militant "progressive" group which demanded the infusion of new blood into the governing body of the A.F.L. The craft-industrial issue was not untinged by the conflicting ambitions of union leaders.[24]

Nevertheless, the net effect of the inadaptability of the A.F.L. was the rise of a new labor organization, the Congress of Industrial Organizations, with its strength concentrated in the great industries that the A.F.L. had been unable to organize, such as the steel and automotive

[23] For a statement by the executive council reviewing the action with reference to the C.I.O., see Annual Convention, 1936, *Proceedings*, pp. 65–98.
[24] See Jack Barbash, "Ideology and the Unions," *American Economic Review*, 33 (1943), pp. 858–876.

industries. The division weakens labor both in political struggles and in the exertion of economic power.[25] The debilitating effect of disunion comes not only from the division of command of labor. In state and local political campaigns occasionally the two organizations are in direct opposition, as in the California gubernatorial campaign of 1946 and the Detroit mayoralty election of 1945. In other instances they often collaborate grudgingly and ineffectively. This sort of situation appeals to antilabor groups, who find it a ready and easy way to win elections as a consequence of a divided opposition.

3. POLITICAL IDEOLOGY OF THE A.F.L.

The dogma, no less than the organization, of a private society is likely to become so deeply rooted that it outlives its usefulness. The strain of adjusting the doctrine of the A.F.L. respecting the state's relation to labor parallels the difficulties of that organization in remodeling its governmental machinery to maintain solidarity.

Over a long period the policies of the A.F.L. regarding the role of government were astonishingly similar to those of business. Labor insisted as vociferously as business that the true doctrine was that of laissez faire: let the state leave labor alone; it would care for itself through organization, collective bargaining, and the strike. Governmental intervention through social legislation was frowned upon, since it might deprive labor of its freedom to employ the economic weapons at its command. The laissez-faire policy of the Federation was modified when employers made effective use of the state to combat labor unions. In 1906 the Federation enunciated "Labor's Bill of Grievances," which demanded, among other things, the exemption of labor unions from the application of the antitrust laws and the prevention of the use of the injunction in labor disputes. But even here the Federation was not seeking the positive aid of the state; it merely desired that it be freed from coercion by the state so that it might fight out its battle with employers on more even terms.

In other legislative demands of the Federation the general tendency was to bring only negative governmental assistance to the side of labor. Labor might ask that immigration be restricted, that the Chinese be excluded, that convict-labor not be used in competition with free men; but it wanted to be left free to determine the essential items of the labor contract—wages and hours—through collective bargaining directly with the employer. In situations in which collective bargaining was not a suitable method, the Federation asked for positive legislation

[25] For an informed account of the division within American labor, see Herbert Harris, *Labor's Civil War* (New York: Knopf, 1940).

for the benefit of certain classes of employees. It sought wage-and-hour legislation for government employees, a matter which could be dealt with in no other way. In addition, the Federation urged legislation for women, children, and seamen. In each of these groups, as Dr. Carroll has pointed out, "the workers are under some particular legal or political handicap." [26]

Labor thus placed great faith in collective bargaining: it sought legislation only to deal with matters beyond the scope of collective bargaining. The factors that caused a growing demand and need for industrial unionism likewise undermined the practical basis of the doctrine of laissez faire. Giant corporations with tens of thousands of employees replaced small concerns more susceptible to coercion by the strike. Employers developed more effective means of combating unionism, such as the company union, employee representation, employee stock ownership, private armies, and like devices. Outright migration of industry or transfer of production by a company from one plant to another in a nonunion section could be resisted only unsuccessfully by collective bargaining.

A marked change in union political philosophy first appeared in the railroad brotherhoods, not affiliated with the A.F.L., and the railroad unions of the Federation. When the Government undertook to regulate railroad rates and thereby to determine the income from which wages could be paid, it was inevitable that the railroad unions would need to exert their political strength to advance their cause. The strategic importance of the railroads in national economic life made railroad strikes matters which the Government could not consider as mere private disputes of no public importance. The Government must take a hand in the prevention and settlement of railroad strikes. Moreover, the strike was more effective in dealing with small employers in competitive industries than in bargaining with great railroad corporations with ample resources for their own defense. The aggressive hostility of the railroads after the World War made it difficult even for labor to maintain the right to organize without governmental assistance.[27] Simple reliance on "economic power" was inadequate for the railroad employees. Their political strength and activity have been reflected in a long series of legislative acts, including the Railway Labor Act of 1926 which guaranteed to them the right to organize.

It would be far too simple an interpretation to attribute the resistance

[26] See Mollie Ray Carroll, *Labor and Politics* (Boston: Houghton Mifflin, 1923), chap. 2, "History of the Federation's Attitude Toward Legislation and Politics."

[27] Philip Taft, "Labor's Changing Political Line," *Journal of Political Economy*, 45 (1937), pp. 636–637.

of the Federation to policy change solely to the force of the idea of laissez faire.   Yet that has been an element in the situation.   Philosophies and ideas have a strength of their own; and, through propagation by unreflecting apostles, they may be perpetuated beyond their time.[28]   Factors other than ideological faith contribute to the comparative conservatism of the A.F.L.   Professor Taft points out that the building trades have played a significant part in forming the policies of the Federation and these unions not being faced by large aggregations of capital "felt they had nothing to gain from government intervention in economic matters." [29]   A deeper consideration may be that during its history the American labor movement has had to resist attempts by single-taxers, anarchists, socialists, communists, and others to capture it.   Sometimes results disastrous for labor came from such alliances, and labor leaders adopted as protective coloration a fervent affirmation of the dominant ideologies of the society.[30]

The persistence of the doctrine of laissez faire appears vividly in the hesitance of the Federation in endorsing the principle of unemployment insurance.   In the 1930 convention the proposal was voted down. "The issue presented," the resolution stated, "is one of vital importance. It involves the question of whether the American Federation of Labor shall continue to hew to the line in demanding greater freedom for the working people of America, or whether liberty shall be sacrificed in a degree sufficient to enable the workers to obtain a measure of unemployment relief under government supervision and control."   The convention decided in favor of freedom.   In 1931 the executive council, after further consideration, again recommended against unemployment insurance.   The workers, the resolution stated, "are being asked by the promoters of compulsory unemployment insurance in the United States to yield up their birthright, to practically surrender in their struggle for liberty, by enactment of legislation deliberately calculated to give the employers increased power of control over the workers."

28 See Paul K. Crosser, *Ideologies and American Labor* (New York: Oxford University Press, 1941).

29 *Op. cit.,* 637–638.   Point is given to Professor Taft's remarks by a statement of W. L. Hutcheson, President of the United Brotherhood of Carpenters and Joiners, in 1944.   He opined that in "many respects our accepted American free enterprise system has been in sad and constant retreat throughout the eleven years of New Deal rule."   He concluded that labor demanded of both parties "the preservation of free enterprise," "the abatement of bureaucracy," "the halt of paternalism," "the creation of postwar jobs through private industry," "the maintenance of labor's social gains," and "the protection of our national interest."—"Labor and the Presidential Election," *American Federationist,* March, 1944, pp. 7–9.

30 Evidence on this point may be found in the fascinating biography of Samuel Gompers by Rowland Hill Harvey, *Samuel Gompers, Champion of the Toiling Masses* (Stanford University Press, 1935).

In the discussion of the question in the 1931 convention, a minority enthusiastically assaulted the doctrines of the executive council, but the Federation again went on record in favor of liberty and adopted the suggestion of the executive council that "a national conference of employers and labor be called by the President of the United States to deal directly and constructively with the unemployment problem. . . ." At that time the Federation's statisticians estimated the unemployed at 5,415,000, excluding from the count unemployed agricultural laborers. In 1932 the Federation finally endorsed the principle of unemployment insurance in response "to the combined pressure from its own local unions, from the radical elements in and outside its ranks, and from middle-class organizations." [31] It is of interest, as additional indication of the strength of the governing oligarchy, that the executive council was not reversed by the convention in 1932; its about-face preceded that of the convention.

The laissez-faire doctrine limited the role of organized labor in advancing the status of workers. The theory in essence was that labor would take care of itself by collective bargaining and by strikes. It would thus raise wages, improve working conditions, and lower hours. But workers are concerned about a great many things other than wages, working conditions, and hours of labor. Public schools, housing, health, foreign policy and a great range of other matters are of interest to labor. Should labor exert its political strength in such matters? The laissez-faire doctrine has pretty well gone by the boards. On some points labor voices its traditional doctrine, as in 1945 when it opposed President Truman's plan for a greater degree of governmental intervention in the settlement of employer-employee disputes. It wants to retain freedom to exert its economic powers. Yet it demands political action on a broader and broader front. William Green, president of the A.F.L., in 1939 summed up the shift in philosophy:

The labor movement has had to adapt itself to changed conditions. For many years its chief emphasis was on the use of its economic power, the united efforts of the workers, to add to the sum of human happiness. But as we observed the changed conditions of industry our philosophy broadened. We

---

[31] Lorwin, *op. cit.*, p. 294. The action on unemployment insurance, says William Green, was the first break in the Federation's opposition to social insurance. In 1916 Gompers appeared before a congressional committee to argue against a bill to create a special commission to study the question of compulsory social insurance. An A.F.L. committee, appointed in 1918, recommended against compulsory health insurance "as likely to injure unions by permitting too much control by the government and as interfering with the development of union insurance systems." Even at that time, however, opinion was divided. Green, then the spokesman for the United Mine Workers, was in favor of compulsory health insurance. See William Green, *Labor and Democracy* (Princeton: Princeton University Press, 1939), pp. 33–39.

now seek benefit for the workers and all our fellow men by the use of either direct economic strength or legislation as the situation demands. Neither alone can suffice. This is not a selfish struggle. . . . In battling as we are for the achievement of economic justice and social righteousness, we are also fighting the battle of the republic.[32]

4. POLITICAL TACTICS OF LABOR

The political tactics and strategy of the American Federation of Labor have been designed to fit its politico-economic philosophy. If the principal mode of advancing the cause of labor is through the strike and collective bargaining, political action will occupy only a subordinate role.

Opposition to a labor party. In the Federation, Samuel Gompers succeeded in firmly establishing the doctrine that it was inexpedient for labor to attempt to form an independent political party and seek control of the government, although the proposal to follow an independent political line on the pattern of European socialist and labor parties has been before the Federation almost continually. In 1888 Gompers said to the Federation convention: "Many delegates may feel the desirability of forming a third, or what is known as an independent, political party; but in view of recent experience I can only say that such action, for the present at least, would be in the extreme unwise." [33] In 1894 he reminded the convention that in the preceding year many local unions had "plunged into the political arena by nominating their candidates for public office" and that "in each one of these localities politically they were defeated and the trade union movement more or less divided and disrupted." The consequences of political action on a national scale, he said, were "too portentous for contemplation." [34] In 1906 he pointed out that to advance through a labor party would require waiting "until labor elects a majority of the legislature and a governor and then a President of the United States, who shall appoint the justices of the Supreme Court. I am afraid we are going to wait a long time! Trade unionists don't propose to wait so long to secure material improvement in their conditions." [35] In 1917 he repeated his doctrine: ". . . the wage-earners have been united to one or the other of the two strong, political parties and they are bound to these parties by ties of

[32] *Labor and Democracy*, as cited, p. 67. See also G. G. Higgins, *Voluntarism* in *Organized Labor in the United States, 1930–1940* (Washington: Catholic University Press, 1944).

[33] Samuel Gompers, *Labor and the Common Welfare* (New York, 1919), p. 123. Quoted by permission of E. P. Dutton & Co., Inc., copyright owner.

[34] *Ibid.*, p. 125.

[35] *Ibid.*, p. 128.

fealty and of tradition. It would take years ever to separate any considerable number of workers from their fealty to the old party." [36]

Gompers' position on the feasibility of a labor party was correct, but in the absence of a labor party how was labor to pursue its originally limited political aims? The Federation adopted essentially the same tactics that business had used so effectively: the policy of working within both the established parties. "We must be partisan for a principle and not for a party," said Gompers in 1909. "Labor must learn to use parties to advance our principles, and not allow political parties to manipulate us for their own achievement." [37] This is still the official line of the A.F.L. In 1944 William Green, A.F.L. president, reiterated the nonpartisan doctrine and declared that labor refused to tie itself "as the tail to the kite of any political party." [38] Instead the Federation lobbies for the enactment of favorable legislation and for the defeat of unfavorable proposals, addressing its appeals and demands without discrimination to legislators of both parties.

Types of legislation sought. The types of legislation that labor has fought for and against have been determined to a large extent by the prevailing philosophy of labor. As already indicated, the A.F.L., until recently at any rate, has been committed to a doctrine of taking care of the interests of its membership principally through the economic weapons of bargaining and strikes rather than through appeal for the positive exercise of governmental power. In keeping with this ideology it manifested perhaps the keenest interest in legislation to prevent the employer's use of the power of the state to crush labor. The limitation of the power of the courts to issue injunctions restraining labor activity in industrial disputes was urged in the 1906 "Bill of Grievances" of the A.F.L. In 1914 the Clayton Act prohibited the issuance of injunctions by federal courts in labor disputes "unless necessary to prevent irreparable injury to property or to property right . . . , for which injury there is no adequate remedy at law." The act was hailed by labor leaders as the "Magna Carta of Labor," yet as interpreted by the courts the act improved the status of labor but little. In 1932 more sweeping limitations on the power of the federal courts to issue injunctions in labor disputes were laid down by the Norris-LaGuardia Act. This legislation has greatly reduced the range of situations in which employers may appeal for injunctions to restrain unions in the exercise of their economic power.

The most recent legislation of importance in the field of collective

---

[36] *Ibid.,* p. 142.

[37] *Ibid.,* pp. 138–139.

[38] "Labor and Politics," *American Federationist,* June, 1944, p. 1.

bargaining is the National Labor Relations Act, guaranteeing to employees "the right to self-organization, to form, join, or assist labor organizations, to bargain collectively through representatives of their own choosing, and to engage in concerted activities, for the purpose of collective bargaining or other mutual aid or protection." This act, passed in 1935 to succeed parts of the invalidated National Industrial Recovery Act, established administrative machinery to assure the right of collective bargaining, and prohibited a number of specified "unfair practices" by employers calculated to discourage or prevent collective bargaining.

The legislation already mentioned was designed primarily to facilitate collective bargaining, to permit labor to help itself. The change of policy of the A.F.L. on unemployment compensation has been cited. In 1935 the Federal Social Security Act was passed, including, among other sections, provision for a system of unemployment compensation. Another far-reaching change in public policy occurred in 1938 with the passage of the Fair Labor Standards Act to fix minimum wages and maximum hours in those industries within the reach of the federal commerce power. The C.I.O. actively supported the bill; the A.F.L. in 1937 hesitated on questions of method of establishing these standards. The Roosevelt administration leaders were pressing for the passage of the bill. Although amendments were adopted to meet most of the objections of the A.F.L., the situation was such as to lend some color to the view that the administration had to force the bill down the throat of the A.F.L.[39]

These illustrations of legislation that labor organizations have lobbied for furnish only a meager notion of the variety of laws of interest to labor. Labor organizations assert themselves on everything from federal tax policy to the nature of the retirement system for firemen in Podunk, but they exert themselves most energetically on matters affecting labor unions as such and their methods of operation. Labor fought tooth and nail to outlaw the use of the injunction against itself in disputes with employers. It conducted a long campaign to make illegal the "yellow-dog" contract, a contract under which a worker would

[39] In 1937 William Green, president of the A.F.L., expressed approval of a version of the bill then pending; opposite views were expressed by John P. Frey, head of the Metal Trades Department of the A.F.L., and by the heads of the Union Label Department and the Building Trades Department. At the 1937 convention President Green was instructed to confer with the department heads of the A.F.L. before making any further statements on the wage-hour issue. This action gave credibility to the view in some quarters that Mr. Green was a forward-looking man held captive by a reactionary clique of leaders. For a complete discussion of the passage of the wage-hour bill, see Paul H. Douglas and Joseph Hackman, "The Fair Labor Standards Act of 1938," *Political Science Quarterly*, 43 (1938), pp. 491–515.

agree not to join a union as a condition of getting a job. In World War II labor lobbyists attempted, but failed, to prevent the passage of the Smith-Connally Act, a law calculated to prevent strikes by requiring a vote of workers precedent to the calling of a strike. In World War II unions also resisted, unsuccessfully in a number of states, the passage of laws to control union operations by requiring licenses of union officers, by prohibiting strikes except when authorized by majority vote, and by regulating union dues and fees and the system of internal government of unions.

On such questions, which go to the heart of union existence and operation, all labor organizations flay right and left with might and main. As one moves out into the field of legislation for the general betterment of labor the C.I.O., it is probably not unfair to say, has had a broader interest and a more forceful policy than the A.F.L. The difference stems in part from the A.F.L. idea that if labor organizes it can look out for itself through bargaining, in part from the liberal sprinkling of intellectuals in the C.I.O. leadership in contrast with the old-time walking-delegate leadership of the A.F.L., and in part from other factors. The enthusiastic collaboration of the C.I.O. with the New Deal and the measured restraint of the A.F.L. typify the difference in spirit of the two organizations. In their lobbying activities trade unions can, if they wish, interest themselves in almost every policy of concern to the mass of citizens, for workers are the mass of citizens. In this respect they are in marked contrast with pressure groups speaking for relatively small numbers of persons. The absence of pressure organizations to speak for the interests of the average man leaves a void which conceivably might be occupied to a greater degree by labor unions.

A.F.L. in campaigns. Lobbying for legislation—and the needling of administrative officials to obtain or to prevent action—presumably carries more weight if it is backed up by a considerable group of alert and informed voters. The crucial problem of labor's political tactics is posed by the issue in what manner and to what degree labor's votes shall be mobilized. On this matter the A.F.L. has followed its "non-partisan" policy of aiding its friends and opposing its enemies. In exploring the "non-partisan" policy of the A.F.L. in electoral campaigns one enters a never-never land where one cannot be sure that things are what they seem. The Federation officially takes no stand in presidential campaigns (although it did endorse La Follette, the Progressive candidate, in 1924), yet its president and other officials may in their personal capacities endorse a candidate.[40] These same persons, in their

40 In the 1940 presidential campaign the A.F.L. executive council announced: ". . . the executive council of the A.F. of L. is of the opinion that the membership of the

capacities as leaders of national or international unions may "officially" support one of the presidential candidates.[41] The tenuosity of the unity of the Federation, noted earlier, permits some of the constituent unions, or at least their leaders, to lean toward one party, others toward another, without disrupting the organization. The unionist may be confounded or outraged by the spectacle of his leaders arrayed on opposite sides of the political fence. William Hutcheson, of the Carpenters, has occupied a high place in Republican councils for many years; Dan Tobin, of the Teamsters, has been equally highly placed among the Democrats. In 1944 eleven of the fifteen members of the A.F.L. executive council were prominent supporters of Roosevelt; A.F.L. officials, present at the Democratic convention as regularly chosen delegates, played an important part in bringing about the nomination of Truman as the vice-presidential candidate. Several of the larger unions, such as the Machinists, Garment Workers, and Teamsters, campaigned vigorously for the Democratic ticket.[42] Yet the A.F.L. maintained its "nonpartisan" policy and some of its high officials published essays about the hazards of partisan activity, the duty of labor unions to limit themselves to organizing and bargaining, and the danger that labor might lose an election and with it all its gains.[43] The spectator finds himself confused by the tangled situation. In presidential campaigns the A.F.L declines to stand up and be counted. It leaves open a route for strategic retreat by keeping a foot in both camps. Yet it likes to see a friend of labor win and undoubtedly in so far as the A.F.L. has exerted influence in presidential campaigns since 1930 that influence has been in support of the Democratic candidates.

The "nonpartisan" doctrine makes more sense in its application to campaigns for the choice of legislators. Here the Federation can separate the sheep from the goats and endorse candidates who have a "good" record on labor issues regardless of their party affiliation. During every campaign the Federation publishes and circulates a list of con-

---

A.F. of L. should continue to adhere to its non-partisan political policy during the ensuing political campaign

"All information regarding platforms, candidates and their records will be compiled by the executive council and submitted to the officers and members of the A.F. of L. so that they may exercise their political judgment in a way which will be to the individual and collective interest of all working men and women."—*The New York Times,* October 3, 1940.

[41] See, for example, the resolution by the General Executive Board of the International Brotherhood of Teamsters, Chauffeurs, Warehousemen and Helpers endorsing Franklin Roosevelt in 1944, *American Federationist,* October, 1944, pp. 7–8.

[42] Alfred Braunthal, "American Labor in Politics," *Social Research,* 12 (1945), 1–21.

[43] See R. J. Watt, "Labor and Politics," *American Federationist,* September, 1944, pp. 5–7.

gressional candidates together with data indicating their record on labor questions. The intensity of the campaign which the Federation may actually make in support of its friends or against its enemies varies a great deal with circumstances. Occasionally a special effort is made to defeat persons particularly obnoxious to the A.F.L. The efficacy of Federation efforts to punish its enemies and reward its friends, however, rarely equals the claims of labor leaders. After the Senate rejection of Judge J. J. Parker's nomination to be a member of the Supreme Court, for example, the Federation sought to punish those Senators who had supported the confirmation of a man deemed by the Federation to be antilabor. "In the state primaries which followed, several Senators who had voted for confirmation were defeated for renomination. In the ensuing election, several Senators who had been successful in the primary were defeated on election day. Some of these were Republicans, others Democrats." [44] But the data showing how much influence the A.F.L. has in determining the outcome of such primaries and elections are of dubious validity. One of the difficulties is that state and local A.F.L. leaders may or may not choose to follow the lead of their national officers in exerting such influence as the state federation may have. Thus in 1944 when the national headquarters endorsed Stephen Day, of Illinois, Martin Dies, of Texas, Gerald Nye, of North Dakota, and several other notorious isolationists with good records on narrow labor issues, local unions in these states rebelled against national leadership. This sort of incident suggests the tendency of pressure organizations to look at one aspect of a candidate's record to the exclusion of all others. It used to be said, for example, that the Anti-Saloon League would support a scoundrel so long as he was sober enough to vote dry when the roll calls came around. Decentralization within the A.F.L. permits considerable autonomy to state and local leaders who often have their connections with state and local machines and who also have local or personal axes to grind.[45]

C.I.O. the same but different. The C.I.O. manifests less temerity about electoral activity than the A.F.L., yet the policies of both organizations are fundamentally the same, that is, "nonpartisan." Sidney Hillman, of the C.I.O., spoke the language of William Green, of the A.F.L., in 1944 when he said: "We will neither attempt to capture nor submit to capturing by either of the political parties." [46] Nevertheless, the

[44] John P. Frey, "Labor in Politics," *American Federationist*, 39 (1932), pp. 1012–1021.
[45] See Joel Seidman, "Organized Labor in Political Campaigns," *Public Opinion Quarterly*, 3 (1939), p. 650.
[46] C.I.O., *Proceedings, Seventh Constitutional Convention*, November 20–24, 1944, p. 208.

C.I.O. expresses itself more forthrightly and expends greater effort in supporting its friends than does the A.F.L. The political program of the C.I.O. began in the 1936 campaign with the formation of Labor's Nonpartisan League. The League followed a policy of active and large-scale campaigning, in contrast with the earlier relatively weak efforts of the A.F.L. The League spent several hundred thousand dollars and carried its organizing and speaking campaign down into the states and cities in support of the re-election of Roosevelt. After the campaign the League remained to lobby before Congress in support of New Deal measures, such as Roosevelt's program for the "rejuvenation" of the Supreme Court. In 1938 the League participated, without brilliant success, in the congressional campaigns. Of the forty-three Congressmen on its "blacklist," only three were defeated. Of the House candidates who received its support, ninety-eight won and one hundred lost.

The League eventually languished, but in 1943 the C.I.O. initiated another political effort. The sharp reverses suffered by the Democrats in the congressional elections of 1942 aroused fears that perhaps a rightist candidate might win the Presidency in 1944. In July, 1943 the C.I.O. established its Political Action Committee which campaigned for the renomination of Roosevelt and Wallace by the Democratic party. The PAC failed to bring about the renomination of Wallace, but did succeed in vetoing the nomination of persons unacceptable to them. The PAC also supported and opposed candidates in the party primaries and claimed, with some color of credibility, to have defeated a goodly number of anti-Administration Democrats in the primaries. Although the PAC claimed to be "nonpartisan" in the traditional style of American labor, its operations differed enormously in degree from those of the A.F.L. With its more centralized organization, the C.I.O. could mobilize a nation-wide vote getting machine of its own as it drew on the personnel of its headquarters and its affiliated unions. In some cities it erected canvassing machines from the precinct up which operated with more zeal and more efficiency than the regular Democratic organizations whose leaders viewed this upstart movement with some alarm. The PAC in the 1944 campaign did not limit itself to the consideration of the record of the candidate on labor issues narrowly defined. It made the test of its support the attitude of congressional candidates toward the New Deal generally, although it did find opportunity to support at least one liberal Republican. In its propaganda work the PAC distributed millions of pamphlets and leaflets, which were smartly written and designed and showed up the regular party literature for what it was,

stodgy and amateurish.[47]   The work of the CIO-PAC evoked cries of
dictatorship, communism—and some Communists were to be found in
its ranks—, threats to the American way of life, and other imprecations
characteristic of campaigns.   It is doubtful that the influence of the
PAC was great enough to warrant the charges by Republican campaigners.   Nevertheless, PAC campaigns in some close states probably
turned the tide for the Democratic candidate.[48]   In November, 1944,
the C.I.O. voted to continue the PAC, but it is foolhardy to predict
whether the PAC will continue as a formidable campaigning organization in the forthcoming campaigns.

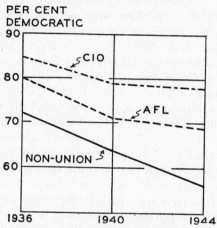

**Figure 3.   AIPO Estimates of Democratic
Percentage of Members of C.I.O. and
A.F.L. and Nonunion Workers in Presi-
dential Elections of 1936, 1940, and 1944**

The activities of labor organizations generally produce a higher degree of political homogeneity among union members than exists among
workers generally.   Examination of the data in Figure 3 indicates the
degree to which members of C.I.O. and A.F.L. unions tended to be

[47] A number of the pamphlets are reproduced in Joseph Gaer's *First Round, The
Story of the CIO Political Action Committee* (New York: Duell, Sloan and Pearce,
1944).

[48] See R. H. Rovere, "Labor's Political Machine," Harper's, 190 (June, 1945), pp.
592–601; Sidney Hillman, "The Truth About the PAC," *New Republic*, 111 (August
11, 1944), pp. 209–211; "Report on the C.I.O. Political Action Committee," House
Special Committee on Un-American Activities, H. Rep. No. 1311, 78th Cong., 2d sess.,
March 29, 1944; Beulah Amidon, "Labor in Politics," *Survey Graphic*, 33 (1944), pp.
390–393.

Democratic in the presidential elections of 1936, 1940, and 1944. The chart, based on polls by the American Institute of Public Opinion, should be discounted somewhat to allow for the normal margin of error in opinion samples. Nevertheless, the persistent divergence in the behavior of union and nonunion workers is significant, although this difference is probably a phenomenon common to all social classes. It has been found, for example, that persons of economic classes predisposed toward Republicanism who participate in organizations such as chambers of commerce and other sorts of social groups are actually more nearly unanimous in their political views than persons of like interests and predispositions who do not participate in the activities of such groups.[49] Similarly workers who meet together, talk together, and share experiences in union work would in the normal course be expected to manifest a higher degree of political homogeneity than workers of like condition who did not participate in such group activities. Given this tendency toward similarity of views, the real test of the political strength of labor organizations is the degree to which the leaders of an organization can shift the votes of the members in one direction or another. A relatively small controllable vote can be the balance of power. The probable truth is that leaders of labor organizations can swing relatively few votes from one party to another.[50] A leader is a leader in no small part because he senses the wishes of his followers and expresses them. The probability, however, is that in campaigns for Democratic nominations for state, local, and congressional office, labor organizations, if they work at it, can exert much influence on the selection of nominees, a different matter than swinging votes from party to party.

Labor in state and local politics. A word needs to be said about the role of labor in state and local politics. Naturally the situation differs greatly from locality to locality, but in general the degree of labor's political activation in state and local affairs is probably less than in national affairs. In municipalities labor organizations are generally to be found either against or lukewarm toward so-called "good government" and "reform" movements. Those movements usually seek lower taxes, are often under the leadership of business groups, and not in-

[49] See Paul F. Lazarsfeld, *The People's Choice* (New York: Duell, Sloan and Pearce, 1944), chap. xv, "The Political Homogeneity of Social Groups."

[50] In 1940, John L. Lewis attempted to swing the labor vote to Willkie. Irving Bernstein finds "little evidence that John L. Lewis' action moved any appreciable number of C.I.O. workers, their families, or their sympathizers to vote for Willkie." His conclusion is based on an analysis of the vote in areas in which C.I.O. membership was concentrated. The decline in Democratic vote in these areas, from 1936 to 1940, did not differ materially from the decline elsewhere. See "John L. Lewis and the Voting Behavior of the C.I.O.," *Public Opinion Quarterly*, 5 (1941), pp. 233–249.

frequently desire to lower levels of municipal services of particular concern to workers. Local labor leaders often are meshed into the local machine, and the charge often can be justly made that they are kept in leash by the machine through the acceptance of patronage. In state politics labor occasionally manages to exert considerable strength —as in Minnesota, Wisconsin, New York—but on the whole it plays a fairly ineffectual role. The long history of the use of state troops in industrial disputes indicates negatively labor's influence in state politics. In most states labor participation in politics has not gone beyond the A.F.L. "nonpartisan" policy applied to a comparatively narrow range of issues. Yet the application of this policy has produced a respectable body of labor legislation in a goodly number of states.

5. OLIGARCHY, TRADITIONALISM, AND POLITICAL CHANGE

Selected aspects of the American Federation of Labor have been given emphasis in this chapter for the purpose of furnishing a concrete example of certain characteristics of political behavior. (1) It was pointed out that before an interest group can give effective expression to its demands it must possess an organization or government to determine what its interests are and how they may be promoted. (2) The hardening of the governmental structure of the private association into a well-knit machine may be accompanied by the development of an inadaptability in which the leadership is not truly representative of the interests of the mass of the membership of the society concerned. (3) The doctrines and faith, the ideas that dominate the thought and action of the leadership, may likewise become inflexible and prevail beyond their applicability. Two factors, however, should be borne in mind: it is not to be supposed that these characteristics are limited to the A.F.L., and it is freely conceded that these phases of the Federation have perhaps been exaggerated in this discussion. To make plain the more general implications, it is perhaps necessary to carry the discussion a step further.

The first proposition—that private associations possess governments of their own—is so obvious as to require no elaboration. Trade associations, labor organizations, churches, political parties, all possess a rudimentary internal governmental machinery; and the process of politics and governance within these groups has an intimate kinship with the politics of the state as a whole. The political process within the private association or pressure group has as one of its main functions the reconciliation of internal differences within the group. The success with which the politicians of the American Federation of Labor or of the

Chamber of Commerce of the United States unite the divergent factions of their respective organizations determines both the effectiveness with which the strength of the group as a whole is brought to bear on Congress and other political authorities, as well as the nature of the demands made on public agencies.   A private association with a diversified membership may be able to act unitedly only on a few items; a more homogeneous private society may be able to act with great strength on a long series of policy items.   Moreover, on many matters of no fundamental importance, Congress and state legislatures are inclined to grant whatever request the pressure group makes if the affected interests are united and if no other group seriously opposes.   Time and again legislative committees tell competing agricultural groups, or labor groups, or business groups to get together and settle their differences, and then the law they desire will be forthcoming without serious question.[51] Public issues, thus, are pushed back for settlement by private negotiation.

The average American looks on bossism in party organizations as an abnormal and undesirable practice, but the examination of a single private association, the American Federation of Labor, indicates the development within that organization of an oligarchical control not basically unlike that in the party.   A tendency toward control by an oligarchy seems inevitable in group behavior.   The term "oligarchy" carries a distasteful connotation, yet it may be perfectly normal or "natural" for group leadership to tend toward long tenure and toward self-perpetuation.   This state of affairs does not mean that the interests of the mass of the group are neglected by its leaders.   A person is not repeatedly re-elected to the presidency of the A.F.L. (or the Farm Bureau Federation or the Tenth Ward Municipal Reform League) by disregarding the interests of the group.   In fact, a group may gain in stability and in strength by continuity of leadership.   Students of American political institutions, in which rotation in office and instability are the general rule, perhaps go too far in concluding that oligarchical continuity in private associations must produce unrepresentative leadership.   To be sure, in labor unions (and in corporations and in churches) from time to time leadership maintains its power by means not entirely fair, with results injurious to the group.

Oligarchical leadership (both in elective positions and in the staff or "bureaucracy") of an organization, however, undoubtedly in most in-

<hr />

[51] To illustrate the proposition further: A publication of the National Lumber Manufacturers' Association declares that public officials prefer to have "the view of an industry, rather than to listen *ad infinitum* to the variant views of countless individuals."—Quoted by Donald Blaisdell, *Economic Power and Political Pressures* (Monograph No. 26, Temporary National Economic Committee, 1941), p. 3.

stances contributes to inadaptability of an organization's program and policy. Perhaps the more tightly knit the oligarchy, the greater is its. inadaptability. In large-scale hierarchies, admission to the circle of leadership and domination is co-optative. When advancement depends on the decision of those already in the charmed circle, a premium is likely to be placed on conformity and orthodoxy. The "elder statesmen" with ideas of another day hold onto their power and make life difficult for the "young Turks." The prevailing attitudes tend to be perpetuated. Thus in armies, navies, the hierarchies of labor organizations, civil services, universities, and learned societies, co-option to the top often accentuates inadaptability. Yet hierarchical structure does. not absolutely preclude change; the eternal character of the Roman Catholic Church, for example, rests in considerable measure on a hierarchical resilience, toughness, and adjustability. The citation of a case in the history of the A.F.L. to illustrate the recurring pattern of resistance and inner conflict of associations when faced by new necessities contains an ironic note. Pressure groups are commonly supposed to ascertain their objectives rationally and pursue them with decisiveness, but the force of custom and of precedent is felt there as elsewhere. Habitual courses of action persist, and before a group can move effectively toward political action there is the initial task of overcoming the brake of inertia.

These observations about the behavior of private associations have an applicability to society generally. The preceding chapter included observations on the factors associated with the initiation of movements to bring about political change. Equally important are elements that retard change, that preserve the status quo, and that discourage innovation. The radical and the conservative struggle incessantly. The sociologists have a word for the hesitancy to alter practices to meet new conditions; Professor Ogburn, the originator of the concept, calls it "social lag." [52] Perhaps thus christening the phenomenon does not illuminate the situation. For the student of politics it is necessary only to call attention to the widespread prevalence of hesitancy to meet changed conditions and situations even among interest groups vitally affected. It is certainly not to be thought, however, that all hesitancy to embrace new ideas reflects stupidity; conservatism and resistance to change in the status quo may rest on a real and substantial interest that is at stake; on the other hand, conservatism may rest on unreflecting habit, tradition, failure to re-examine experience.[53] Those who view political ac-

[52] On the general problem, see W. F. Ogburn, *Social Change* (New York: Huebsch, 1922), especially Part III, "Cultural Inertia and Conservatism," and Part IV, "Social Maladjustments."

[53] Some time ago Machiavelli observed similar tendencies: "And it ought to be remembered that there is nothing more difficult to take in hand, more perilous to

tion as solely a rational expression of self-interest may well ponder the numerous instances in which innovations opposed by groups following traditional modes of thought later turn out to be helpful to the opponents, or at least not harmful.

Mention was made of the tendency toward rigidity of ideas and doctrines and its effect on adaptability of political attitudes. It is perhaps erroneous to invest doctrine with a personality; it is perhaps more accurate to say that individuals become intellectually imprisoned within the bounds of more or less finely wrought, logical systems. Perception is clouded and behavior conditioned by a body of verities that once possessed an experiential basis. The A.F.L., attached to a laissez-faire doctrine, gravely and bitterly debated the principle of unemployment insurance when millions were unemployed. The Social Democrats, deeply attached to the doctrine of parliamentarianism, found themselves unable to crush a rising Hitlerism. The American business community, indoctrinated with the notion of the sacredness of a "favorable balance of trade," became intellectually paralyzed after World War I and did not adapt itself and its government to the requirements of a creditor nation. Even within industry, the management experts complain, old processes and old methods are often clung to even unto bankruptcy. It must be concluded that thought, the throwing off of old patterns of ideals, the re-examination of experience, is one of the most burdensome and painful of human endeavors. The tendency of traditional modes of thought to persist is present in politics as elsewhere and profoundly conditions political behavior.

Traditionalism really amounts to habitual ways of doing things and to habitual ways of thinking about them. And traditionalism is likely to become decorated with a frosting of rationalization and justification. But it is important to note that these habitual ways of doing things constitute a powerful element in social and political stability. And the running of the business of society, governmental and otherwise, requires a high degree of stability and continuity. As political and social relationships become customary and habitual, they persist through more or less unconscious or unwilled conformity. The political equilibrium is threatened when the consequences of the customary and habitual are recognized and questioned. The process of establishing

---

conduct, or more uncertain in its success, than to take the lead in the introduction of a new order of things. Because the innovator has for enemies all those who have done well under the old conditions, and lukewarm defenders in those who may do well under the new. This coolness arises partly from fear of the opponents, who have the laws on their side, and partly from the incredulity of men, who do not readily believe in new things until they have had a long experience in them"—*The Prince,* chap. 6.

new ways of doing and looking at things is accompanied by political friction. Once established, these new ways soon become traditional and are relegated to the habitual. But the recognition of the function of tradition in governing thousands of social and political relationships of human beings should not bring a blindness to the need for departing from the traditional when it endangers group survival.[54]

[54] The following observations by F. H. Allport are suggestive: "The social or political order rests fundamentally upon stable, common and reciprocal ways of behaving in the stock situations and relationships of life. All citizens react in practically the same manner with reference to a policeman, a traffic signal, a tax collector, or the exchange in labor or commodities which they expect for a dollar bill. Not only does each respond in a regular and predictable manner toward such objects; but each knows that others may be depended upon to behave in the same way. Social organization and the rise of political and economic institutions are thus made possible. It might even be said that these common habits of response underlying ordered relationships, considered together with their appropriate stimuli, are the institutions of society. Political structure resolves itself psychologically into predictable political behavior."—"The Psychological Nature of Political Structure," *American Political Science Review*, 21 (1927), pp. 611–618.

Chapter 4

BUSINESS

BUSINESSMEN are a heterogeneous lot. The president of a life insurance company seeks safety in investment. The wildcat operator bets his fortune that oil will flow from a hole in the ground. Both are businessmen. The corporate bureaucrat managing a railroad organization encrusted with traditional practices and the management expert guiding an automobile manufacturing company with an experimental spirit in production methods are both businessmen. The steel magnate who espouses the inflexible views typical of heavy industry and the clothing-maker who has anxieties about the drift of public opinion call themselves businessmen. The barber shop proprietor, the manager of far-flung chain-store enterprises, the corner grocer, the broker, the banker, the gadget maker, the shoe manufacturer, the undertaker, the tulip-bulb importer—all these and many others are covered by the term "businessman."

The variety of interests suggested by the foregoing enumeration of a few categories of enterprisers might indicate that discussion of "the businessman" in the political process would be a futile undertaking. Perhaps one might better treat the activities of particular classes or groups of businessmen for their interests are diverse and sometimes in conflict. Perhaps easy generalizations that "businessmen" believe this or that or that "businessmen" want this or that conceal a more complex reality in which a gradation of opinions prevails among different groups. Differences of interest among business groups are commonplace, yet "businessmen" maintain a remarkable solidarity on basic political issues. A network of common interests pulls the business community together on major issues where its security is threatened despite minor rifts in its ranks from time to time. Party lines, sectional lines, religious lines rarely divide businessmen when their common interests are involved. Within the business community powerful factors operate to discipline the dissident and to bring conformity to the predominant views. Unanimity is rare, but a predominant business sentiment usually crystallizes and makes itself heard on major issues threatening the group as a whole. Dissenting voices are neither numerous nor loud.

With the decline in the importance of agriculture, the preponderance of American wealth came to be controlled by businessmen, and the power of wealth in politics is an age-old phenomenon. The holders of wealth have great stakes in the outcome of the political struggle; they have the time to devote to political maneuver or the money to employ others to do so. The power wielded by business in American politics may puzzle the person of democratic predilections. A comparatively small minority exercises enormous power. Agriculture, a relatively declining "industry" in the entire economy, occasionally fights a rearguard action against business but more often allies itself with industry. Labor occasionally makes an assault on the business citadel. Yet, withal, business retains great influence and a position of potent leadership in the affairs of nation, state, and city. Perhaps fundamentally the power of business depends on its success in obtaining a general public acquiescence in the exercise of that power. An adequate comprehension of that process would require an examination of the entire problem of the maintenance of a capitalistic civilization, an inquiry that would lead beyond the borders of formal politics. Within the narrower political sphere, business consciously and systematically cultivates public opinion.

1. THE RISE OF INDUSTRY AND TRADE

The power of business has been manifest from the beginnings of America. Charles A. Beard has demonstrated that the forces of wealth —money, trade, personalty of various forms—well organized along the seaboard were chiefly influential in the adoption of the Constitution.[1] Yet business did not attain its full flowering until after the Civil War. The southern planter aristocracy, built on a foundation of slave labor and the cotton gin, was to hold sway until definitely put to rout by the alliance of northeastern business and northwestern free agriculture in the Civil War, the outcome of which Miriam Beard calls "the victory of American business over plantocracy." [2]

Expansion of business in the national economy. Business had been a lusty infant before the Civil War, and afterward the trend toward a more highly industrialized society continued unabated and without significant hindrance. In 1870 slightly over one half of the gainfully employed were engaged in agriculture, fishing, and forestry; about one

---

[1] *The Economic Interpretation of the Constitution* (New York: Macmillan, 1913).
[2] *A History of the Business Man* (New York: Macmillan, 1938), chap. 24.

third, in manufacturing, mining, and commerce. The large proportion of the population then engaged in agriculture, particularly in the Northwest, probably accounts for the belief and hope of agrarian groups that they might gain control of the government through the election of candidates of their own choosing. By 1930, however, the proportions were reversed; slightly more than 50 per cent of all gainfully employed workers were engaged in industry, mining, and commerce and only about 20 per cent in agriculture and related pursuits.

The statistics thus show that since the Civil War the number of persons engaged in manufacture and commerce has grown much more rapidly than the number engaged in agriculture. The predominance of business may likewise be demonstrated by indication of the proportion of the national income produced by various segments of the economy. In 1943 slightly less than one tenth of the national income produced could be credited to agriculture while manufacturing could claim almost one third. When transportation, mining, public utilities, finance and trade are taken into account in income calculations, the proportion of the national income attributable to business activity overshadows all other elements. One can agree with Calvin Coolidge that "The business of America is business." The figures are presented in Table 4.

TABLE 4

Income Produced by Important Segments of the American Economy (in millions)

	1935	1943
Total	$55,719	$149,392
Agriculture	4,983	13,158
Manufacturing	12,790	48,591
Transport	4,084	9,685
Power and gas	1,153	1,667
Communications	724	1,176
Trade	8,153	17,551
Finance	5,680	9,165
Services	5,596	10,362

Trend toward consolidation within industry. Not only has business grown more rapidly than other pursuits and become a larger and larger part of the national economy, but also within most lines of business endeavor a trend has occurred toward the concentration of a larger and larger proportion of activity into fewer and fewer individual concerns. In almost every type of economic endeavor the small corporation and the individual entrepreneur have lost ground to the giant corporation. Control over larger and larger segments of our industrial life has been gained by trusts, monopolies, holding companies, combinations, and various other mechanisms for the concentration of economic power. In fact, American politics since the Civil War may be said to have been largely occupied with the problem of big business and its relationships to other elements in the population. Thus, in the earlier discussion of agrarian politics reference was made to the presumed relationship of the economic ills of agriculture to the advantageous position enjoyed by industry under tariff legislation and in other ways; the growth of big business has obviously also been connected with the labor movement and labor demands.

Standard Oil has been called the "first great American trust." During the Civil War the petroleum industry developed rapidly in Pennsylvania; at the outset it was carried on by a large number of producers and refiners. John D. Rockefeller, exceedingly able and resourceful, was to change all this. Within a few years, as the result of purchase, lease, amalgamation, and more or less peaceful conquest, most of the refineries passed into the hands of his companies, and pipe lines were gradually brought under Standard control. Standard became a symbol for "big" business and bore the brunt of attacks on monopolies and trusts for a time.

Another spectacular achievement in business consolidation was the formation of the American Tobacco Company, one of the moving spirits in which was J. B. Duke. In steel, the United States Steel Corporation was created in 1901 to control over half the steel production of the nation under the leadership of Judge Elbert Gary. In agricultural implements, the International Harvester Company was formed by a combination of implement manufacturers under the guidance of J. P. Morgan. Behind each of these and other great movements toward industrial consolidation and combination was a long and involved struggle for supremacy.

Although the trend toward concentration has proceeded year in and year out, it moved with special rapidity in the years from 1897 to 1903 and from 1925 to 1929. The earlier period saw the emergence of such noted corporate names as International Silver, United Shoe Machinery, American Can, Eastman Kodak, Corn Products, International Nickel, and International Harvester. The peak of activity in the later period came in the frenzied spring quarter of 1929, when more mergers occurred than in any full year of the decade, 1920–1929. In both periods of peak concentration rates the investment markets readily absorbed the paper issued as a result of consolidations and mergers. The typical pattern was the purchase of existing firms and the formation of a new corporation whose capital structure liberally reflected the supposed increment of value through the merger over the total cost of the individual firms consolidated. The handsome rewards of the promoters came from the margin between the market value of the new securities and the cost of the merged enterprises.[3]

Profits for promoters were not the only incentive driving toward combination and consolidation. In some instances the object was simply to gain a monopolistic position and monopolistic profits. In other instances the organizers of combinations asserted that consolidation was essential to establish "order" in a highly competitive industry, rent by price wars and violent price fluctuations. Often the economies of large-scale production were instrumental in bringing about consolidation, but sometimes consolidation brought large-scale production. Whatever the motivation, a condition of concentration of control has been brought about.

Degree of concentration. The degree to which the movement toward concentration has gone may be indicated by the fact that the two hundred largest nonfinancial corporations "controlled in 1933 approximately 19 to 21 per cent of the national wealth, between 46 to 51 per cent of the Nations' industrial wealth, and approximately 60 per cent of the physical assets of all non-financial corporations." [4] Whatever measure is used, the degree of concentration is striking. A study of the hundred largest manufacturing companies gave the following results: [5]

With size measured by employment:
  100 companies employed 20.7 per cent of all the manpower engaged in manufacturing;
With size measured by value added by manufacture:
  100 companies contributed 24.7 per cent of all the value added in manufacturing activity;
With size measured by value of product:
  100 companies accounted for 32.4 per cent of the value of products reported by all manufacturing plants.

Still another measure of corporate concentration reveals factors not shown by figures on production and employment. Concentration of profits appears to be more marked than the concentration of production, since many concerns show a deficit, break even, or earn a very low return. In 1929 the net income of all corporations was $8,740,000,000,

[3] W. L. Thorp, "The Merger Movement" in Temporary National Economic Committee, Monograph No. 27, *The Structure of Industry* (1941), pp. 231–234.
[4] National Resources Committee, *Structure of the American Economy*, Part 1, p. 105.
[5] *Ibid.*, p. 102.

10 per cent of which was earned by five corporations.[6]   Mr. E. D. Kennedy concludes that "out of $100 of profits made by American companies in 1929, five made $10 and the other 455,995 made $90." [7] The top thirteen companies in that year chalked up about 16 per cent of the net income of all corporations.   The data indicate that by 1937 there was an even greater concentration of profits among a few corporations.

Great blocs of economic power thus have come to be concentrated in a relatively few giant concerns.   These companies spend large sums of their stockholders' money publicizing the fact that ownership is distributed among huge numbers of stockholders.   In fact, however, corporate concentration of ownership is paralleled by a concentration of dividend-paying stock in a comparatively small number of individuals. At the end of 1937 from 8,000,000 to 9,000,000 persons in the United States owned stock in at least one corporation, yet the division of stock among these millions of persons was such that in 1937:

> The largest 1,000 recipients of dividends received 10.4 per cent of all cash dividends;
> The largest 25,000 recipients received 37.6 per cent of all cash dividends; and
> The largest 100,000 recipients received 57.5 per cent of all cash dividends.

Thus slightly over 10 per cent of the stockholders received more than 50 per cent of all cash dividends.[8]

As a consequence of the movement toward consolidation and concentration an income and power pyramid has been erected within the industrial system, concentrating economic power and income within a comparatively few hands.   This system, like all economic systems, constitutes an arrangement for the control of the flow of income and non economic rewards.   Concentration of economic power, however, is peculiarly susceptible to political attack; bigness in our culture invites assault.   Moreover, governmental control of a few industrial giants is in many ways administratively simpler than governmental control of many units in an atomized economy.   Thus the maintenance of a concentration of economic power becomes in many ways dependent upon the success of political strategy for obtaining general acquiescence in its existence.   The rewards of the system, of course, encourage its most stubborn and able defense.   Any economic system maintains itself to a considerable degree from its own momentum; success breeds longevity

[6] General Motors. A. T. &. T., U.S. Steel, Standard of New Jersey, and Pennsylvania Railroad.
[7] E. D. Kennedy, *Dividends to Pay* (New York: Reynal and Hitchcock, 1939), p. 27.
[8] Temporary National Economic Committee, Monograph No. 29, *The Distribution of Ownership in the 200 Nonfinancial Corporations* (1941), pp. 10–18.

in social systems.   But businessmen do not leave it all to chance: they organize to look out for their interests, just as do farmers, workers, and others.

2. ORGANS OF BUSINESS

Businessmen are highly organized to deal collectively with matters of mutual concern and among those matters is that of influencing public opinion and public policy.   The roster of business organizations reflects both the diversity of American business and the joining habits of the American businessman.   The Department of Commerce in 1941 listed 1,900 trade associations that were national or interstate in scope; its directory included 300 other business associations with a broader membership than that of a trade association, which usually admits only business competitors in a single line of activity.   The Department estimated that at least 3,000 local business groups, such as chambers of commerce, existed.

Every conceivable line of industrial and commercial activity has formed a more or less elaborate association.   The enumeration of a few organizations will suggest their variety: the American Petroleum Institute, the National Coal Association, the Associated General Contractors of America, the National Canners Association, the American Cotton Manufacturers Association, the National Lumber Manufacturers Association, the American Newspaper Publishers Association, the National Fertilizer Association, the American Iron and Steel Institute, the Automobile Manufacturers Association, the Pin Manufacturers Institute, the National Retail Dry Goods Association, the American Federation of Retail Kosher Butchers, and the American Bankers Association.

Obviously these and hundreds of other business associations differ widely in size, resources, and objectives.   Some associations attempt to speak for the business community as a whole, such as the Chamber of Commerce of the United States in national affairs and state and local chambers of commerce in their respective spheres; others have homogeneous industrial membership, such as the National Terra Cotta Manufacturers Association.   Some of the organizations have staffs and budgets of considerable size while in other instances a single man manages a stable of associations: Mr. Joseph Gooch, for example, has served simultaneously as the secretary of the Amusement Ticket Manufacturers Association, the Association of Coupon Book Manufacturers, the Clothing Ticket Manufacturers Association, the Transit Ticket Manufacturers Association.   Some of the organizations are short-lived affairs;

others have had a continuous existence of over 75 years. Nearly every organization claims to represent and to speak for its industry, yet in almost half of the associations over 40 per cent of the costs of operation are borne by the four largest contributors.[9]

In addition to public education and political activity most business associations have other objectives. Trade associations, in a sense, represent an extension of the movement toward consolidation: by association of independent firms, with the advice of a lawyer skilled in antitrust matters, some of the advantages of consolidation may be gained without actual merger. Some trade associations appear to have been formed solely for the purpose of fixing prices or of limiting competition in one way or another.[10] Others, such as the National Canners' Association, perform research for the industry as a whole. Most of the associations serve as channels for the interchange of technical information, for the discussion of problems common to all members of the industry, and for other like purposes. Nearly all business associations, however, have, at least incidentally, the function of representing the industry before legislative committees and other public authorities when public action is desired or when public action impinges or threatens to impinge unfavorably on the membership of the association.

Chamber of Commerce of the United States. The largest and most conspicuous spokesman for business is the Chamber of Commerce of the United States. It is essentially a federation of other business organizations—state and local chambers of commerce, trade associations, and societies of businessmen not organized for private purposes—almost 2,000 in all. The chamber thus consists of a cross section of all types of American business with widely diverse interests. This varied composition of the organization is responsible for the types of views expressed by the Chamber. It speaks with great forthrightness and explicitness chiefly on those few issues on which business as a whole has a common interest and a common view. On other issues it often takes a vague and general position, not unlike many planks in party platforms. On some issues it is silent. The generalities, like the planks of party platforms, represent an effort to find a formula on which all concerned can agree. In the Chamber's official pronouncements there is sometimes a tendency toward statesmanship—that is, a consideration of the interests of the nation as a whole—in sharp contrast with the

[9] For a listing of associations and other relevant data, see Department of Commerce, *Trade and Professional Associations of the United States* (Industrial Series No. 3, 1942).

[10] For a thoroughgoing analysis of the fundamental significance of business associations, see R. A. Brady, *Business as a System of Power* (New York: Columbia University Press, 1943).

attitudes of narrower business organizations designed to promote the
interests of a compact and homogeneous industrial group.

The resolutions of the Chamber's 1946 annual meeting illustrate the
foregoing remarks. The Chamber resolved in favor of the "proven
American System of voluntary, competitive private enterprise." Nevertheless, it conceded some limitations on freedom of enterprise, for example, that electrical utilities should be "properly regulated." It was
willing that price control remain in effect a few months longer and
saw "temporary modified export control" as a "practical necessity."
Its more general view was that government controls of business enterprise should be reduced in scope.

In many of the resolutions of the Chamber a plaintive plea for
states' rights made itself heard. The "dual system" of banking involving the preservation of state-chartered banks, the Chamber argued
in 1946, should be preserved. More education was thought desirable,
but the states should find the money for this "wise investment." Forest
control should not be made a sole federal responsibility. The success
of the labor-relations laws of some states merited "serious consideration
by other states." State, rather than federal, control of petroleum
should be encouraged. Extensions of national parks should be made
only with the consent "of the legislatures of the states concerned."
States should be free to fix certain policies regarding unemployment
compensation. In stream pollution control state control and local
"initiative and responsibility should be preserved."

On labor policies the Chamber advocated a reconsideration of the
National Labor Relations Act. It sought equality for the employer
under the act and the requirement that employees be under an obligation to bargain with the employer. It opposed mass picketing, the
unionization of supervisory employees, monopolistic practices by labor,
discrimination by labor in the use of materials made by non-union
labor, and sympathetic strikes. The Chamber resolved that unions
should be placed under a legal obligation to abide by their contracts.

The Chamber was against high taxes and for a reduction of the public debt. Corporate taxation should be reduced; the rates on capital
gains should be reduced. Congress should surrender the field of estate
and gift taxation to the states. The principle of charging off for depletion against federal taxes should be expanded to cover other types of
mines, quarries, and other natural resources. On the tariff, the Chamber spoke like a politician: "a constructive and realistic tariff policy
which will encourage the maximum flow of international trade but
which at the same time will afford reasonable protection for American

producers against destructive or otherwise unfair competition from abroad."

The Chamber supported various types of agricultural measures in much the same tone as the Farm Bureau Federation or the Grange, an indication of the coalition between conservative farm organizations and business. The Chamber "emphasized" the principle of tariff protection for agriculture subject to "destructive competition from abroad." It commended "new provisions made for research by the Department of Agriculture." It favored concentration of all farm credit operations of the federal government in one agency.[11]

Although the annual meetings of the Chamber serve as sounding boards for views of business, its work is not limited to these sessions. It maintains a staff at its headquarters in Washington to conduct research and to make known the views of organized business to Congress and to administrative agencies. Its committees analyze issues as they arise and disseminate information to the membership and to the interested public outside. Its publicity staff prepares for release to the daily press and to specialized journals news about the Chamber and its views. Its official organ, *Nation's Business,* presents the Chamber's views to the membership and to the public. During congressional sessions its staff follows closely the work of Congress and keeps the membership informed on legislative developments relevant to their interests.[12]

An interesting adaptation of the referendum has been used by the Chamber to ascertain the sentiment of its membership on issues "national in character, timely in importance, and general in application to business and industry." When the Chamber's board of directors determines to submit such an issue to the membership for a vote, it refers the matter to a special committee for study and recommendations. The ballot and the committee's recommendations, together with a statement presenting the arguments against the views of the special committee, are transmitted to the members, which it will be remembered, are organizations, such as local chambers of commerce, and not individuals. Each member organization may cast as many votes on a referred question as it is entitled to delegates at the annual meeting of the Chamber. The casting of the votes of the member organization is determined in various ways: by special meetings, by a referendum, by executive committees, by executive officers. The members voting usually approve the recommendations of the Chamber

[11] See Chamber of Commerce of the United States, *Policy Declarations, 34th Annual Meeting, April 30–May 2, 1946.*

[12] For a valuable analysis of the work of the Chamber, see H. L. Childs, *Labor and Capital in National Politics* (Columbus: Ohio State University Press, 1930).

committees by large majorities.   It is doubtful whether the referendum
serves the creative function of facilitating participation in policy
formulation by the membership, but the voting procedure, in a culture
devoted to voting, undoubtedly lends greater moral authority to the
Chamber's legislative recommendations.   The extent of the use of the
referendum is indicated by the fact that the referendum on the National
Labor Relations Act in 1940 was the Chamber's seventy-fourth referendum.

National Association of Manufacturers.   One of the most articulate
organs of business is the National Association of Manufacturers, formed
in 1895 for the purpose of promoting the cause of trade and commerce
by aiding in the passage of legislation and by other means.   Like the
Chamber of Commerce, this association has a heterogeneous membership and must concentrate its attention only on those matters in which
its membership has a common cause.   But because the N.A.M. has a
much narrower membership than the Chamber, it is a more zealous
and harder-hitting organization.   Probably the greatest source of cohesion for the association is an antipathy to organized labor apparently
shared by all its membership.

Since 1932, when the question of the place of organized labor became much more prominent, the N.A.M. has been reorganized and
reactivated.   Prior to 1933 it had been led mainly by smaller manufacturers, but after that time larger corporations took over the leadership and, to a large degree, the financing of the organization and used
it as a vehicle to fight legislative proposals favoring organized labor.
The association's membership increased from 1,469 firms in 1933 to
2,912 in 1937 and to about 15,000 in 1946.   These 15,000 firms, the
Association asserted, produced about 85 per cent of all goods manufactured by about 150,000 firms eligible to membership in the Association.   Furthermore, a very large proportion of its three million annual
budget comes from a very small proportion of its membership.

With the growth of its membership, a small number of large concerns
has assumed a greater and greater importance in the management of
the affairs of the Association.   Although the Association claims that
the policies it advocates represent accurately the views of its members
and of manufacturers generally, such assertions are open to doubt. The
usual apparatus of committees and representative machinery formulates
and promulgates the policies of the Association; yet, as practicing
politicians have long been aware, the filtering of the views of the membership through several layers of organizational mechanism can readily
produce a spurious appearance of unanimity.   In its 1946 fight against
the renewal of price-control legislation, the Association asserted that

its 141-man board of directors unanimously agreed. Whether this represented the views of the members of the Association was doubtful. Nevertheless, the Association spent around $400,000 in newspaper and other advertising to make its views known. At about the same time sampling polls of businessmen indicated that a substantial sector of the business community differed from the Association's spokesmen. Like many other interest groups, the Association appears to be fairly rigidly controlled by a comparatively small number of its members.[13]

Since 1934 the N.A.M. has devoted great effort to a campaign of "public education" aimed primarily toward the creation of attitudes hostile to the New Deal. The objective of the Association's propaganda was explained in a resolution adopted in 1934:

Public policies in our democracy are eventually a reflection of public opinion. If we are to avoid disaster, it is essential that this public opinion be informed and able to discriminate between the sound and the unsound; between the true and the untrue or the half true. Today, the achievements of a hundred and fifty years and continued progress in the future are in serious jeopardy because the facts concerning past accomplishments and how they have been attained are being ignored or distorted.

For the purpose of taking the truth to the American public, a national industrial information committee and subsidiary state and local committees were formed, and money was raised to pay the cost. For the public information work of the N.A.M. alone the following sums were received:

1934	$ 36,500.00
1935	112,659.58
1936	467,759.98
1937	793,043.06

Outlays for "public information," made principally through the Association's subsidiary, the National Industrial Information Committee, continued to grow and in 1943 reached $1,037,000 and in 1944 about $1,385,000.[14]

A major objective of the propaganda program was to create anti-labor sentiment, especially against the C.I.O.[15] The necessity for public education was stated in an Association document:

[13] See David A. Munro, "The NAM Juggles the Facts," *New Republic*, 114 (1946), pp. 757–761. For observations on the potency of minority control of the NAM in wartime, see Bruce Minton, "The duPont Conspiracy," *The New Masses*, November 17, 1942, pp. 5–10.

[14] Hearings, House Committee to Investigate Campaign Expenditures, 78th Cong., 2d sess. pt. 2 (1944), p. 118.

[15] On the history of N.A.M. labor policies, see A. G. Taylor, *Labor Policies of the National Association of Manufacturers* (Urbana: University of Illinois, 1928).

Now, more than ever before, strikes are being won or lost in the newspapers and over the radio. The swing of public opinion has always been a major factor in labor disputes, but with the settlement of strikes being thrown more and more into the laps of public officials, the question of public opinion becomes of greater importance. For it is public opinion—what the voters think—that moves those elected to action along one course or another.

The Association used all the channels of education in an "effort to bring about a more sympathetic understanding of manufacturing industry by the American public." Newspapers were furnished releases explaining "industry's viewpoint"; through the newspapers a daily comic feature, "Uncle Abner Says," was distributed. Full-page advertisements were placed in the newspapers to promote "community harmony." To radio stations were furnished electrical transcriptions of "The American Family Robinson," a program "combining entertainment with simple facts about the American industrial system," according to a statement by the N.A.M. Motion pictures were prepared and offered to schools and other institutions. In many instances the persons subjected to the propaganda of the N.A.M. were unaware of the source. "The National Association of Manufacturers," the La Follette committee found, "has blanketed the country with a propaganda which in technique has relied upon indirection of meaning, and in presentation upon secrecy and deception. Radio speeches, public meetings, news, cartoons, editorials, advertising, motion pictures and many other artifices of propaganda have not in most instances disclosed to the public their origin with the association." [16]

In its lobbying work the N.A.M. has generally been one of the most reactionary of business associations. One of the recent measures to which it offered strenuous opposition was the National Labor Relations Act. The methods of the Association in combating this measure resembled the mine-run of lobbying techniques. One feature of their campaign that is difficult for the less-prosperous groups to use was the extensive reliance on visits by delegations of businessmen to Washington. The following letter by an executive of the N.A.M. to local employer associations describes the technique:

Don't overlook the oft-repeated suggestion that the bringing of delegations to Washington is effective. One of the most representative groups of this character that has yet been brought down was engineered by Elmer Donnell of the Associated Industries of Missouri, who brought in a special train of 48

[16] Senate Report No. 6, Part 6, Report of the Committee on Education and Labor, pursuant to S. Res. 266, 76th Congress, 1st Session (1939), p. 218. See also "The Public Is Not Damned," *Fortune,* March, 1939.

Missouri business leaders on Sunday, April 7, and held meetings with the Missouri delegation in Congress.

The next 3 or 4 weeks are going to be propitious times for such visits to Washington and the N.A.M. will be glad to co-operate with you in any fashion in arranging such a visit.

It would be a good idea if the executives of those associations who have conducted groups to Washington would write a letter to all the other State association executives telling just their experiences and the benefits that came out of this trip.

The idea of holding the meetings in Washington on Sunday is a pretty good one, since the Members of the Senate and the House are not required to be on the floor that day, and it gives the delegation an opportunity to get them to a meeting.[17]

Association of Life Insurance Presidents. In contrast with the broader membership and interests of the Chamber of Commerce, the Association of Life Insurance Presidents represents a type of business association concerned with only one sort of business. The Association was formed in 1906 shortly after the revelations of the Armstrong Committee of the New York State Legislature respecting the lobbying activities of life insurance companies. One of the Association's objectives is "to consider carefully measures that may be introduced from time to time in legislative bodies, with a view to ascertaining and publicly presenting the grounds which may exist for opposing or advocating the proposed legislation." The policies of the Association are determined at annual gatherings of its membership, and in the interim an executive committee makes detailed decisions. A staff of over 60 persons carries on the work of the Association in accordance with the decisions and instructions of the responsible leaders.

The Association's legislative work is given an unusual character by the fact that insurance companies, although doing business throughout the nation, are subject to regulation by each of the forty-eight states rather than by the national government. The Association, then, must keep in touch with the course of legislative action in all the states. The ramifications of the life insurance business are so extensive that the companies may be affected by a wide range of measures concerned with such matters as regulation, taxation, real-estate law. The mere examination of bills to ascertain whether they are of concern to the insurance companies is a huge task. The numbers of bills examined by the staff of the Association in the odd years when most state legislatures are in session have been:

[17] *Ibid.*, p. 116.

1925	....	2,626
1927	....	3,045
1929	....	4,336
1931	....	5,739
1933	....	10,427
1935	....	10,876
1937	....	11,047

Not all these measures affected the companies seriously or even at all, but it was necessary to sift through all of them to identify the proposals impinging on the companies.

The methods employed by the Association in presenting the viewpoint of the insurance business to state legislatures do not differ in any material aspect from the general run of lobbying. The Association, however, has special facilities for making its wishes felt. Each of the larger companies has an elaborate agency organization reaching into almost every state. These nation-wide organizations are supplemented by the agency systems of companies operating in more limited areas. When the Association desires pressure to be brought on a legislature, it gets in touch with the home offices of the companies, which in turn stimulate their local agents in the state concerned to make known to their representatives the attitudes of the insurance agents. Moreover, life insurance agents frequently become members of legislatures and are in a position to aid the cause.[18] The Association's organization of insurance people in the state concerned brings the insurance views to bear in an effective way. The work of watching legislation, organizing opposition, educating legislators, and employing local law firms to represent the Association before the legislature involves considerable outlay. Its expenditures for representation before legislatures and before other departments of government in recent years have been as follows:

1934	....	$29,158.72
1935	....	90,239.49
1936	....	27,846.65
1937	....	74,056.15
1938	....	23,501.41

18 For example, in a report to the association on a legislative proposal for savings bank insurance in Rhode Island, it was said: "This Bill, I feel, is a serious one to life insurance interests and is taking considerable time. From all I can ascertain the following is the situation: The Bill still rests in the House Finance Committee. Fortunately a member of this Committee is Mr. Charles Brown, General Agent of the Columbian National and he naturally is opposed to the Bill. . . ."—Temporary National Economic Committee, Hearings, Part 10, p. 4804.

These figures do not include allowance for the time spent by agents of individual companies on legislative work; as the figures stand, the outlays by the Association appear to be modest if the magnitude of the legislative task is kept in mind.

The types of legislative proposals in which the Association of Life Insurance Presidents is interested may be indicated by excerpts from a report to the membership by the general manager of the Association on 1937 legislation:

> Ten premium tax increase bills on foreign companies failed in 8 states— California, Colorado, Florida, Georgia, Minnesota, Nevada, Oklahoma, Washington. None enacted. Such proposals so far failed this year would have increased the annual tax by $3,300,000. . . .
>
> Nine savings bank life insurance bills failed in 7 states—Colorado, Connecticut, Missouri, New York, Ohio, Pennsylvania, Rhode Island. None enacted.
>
> Seven bills specifically to restrict policy loan interest failed in 5 states— 4½% in Minnesota and New York; 4% in Colorado and Pennsylvania, and prohibition of any interest in California. None enacted.
>
> A large number of net- and gross-income and sales-tax measures, broad enough to include insurance were proposed. Numerous inheritance, intangible, gifts, stamp, capital-stock, mortgage- and municipal-tax bills, would have imposed additional taxes on life insurance.
>
> A new Georgia law requires deposits by life insurance companies. In Alabama, Arkansas, Delaware, and Nebraska, proposals to require bonds or deposits in the state were unsuccessful.
>
> Forty measures of interest from a mortgage loan viewpoint were enacted. Nearly half extend emergency laws permitting stays of foreclosures, extensions of redemption periods, or modifications of deficiency-judgment rights. . . .[19]

3. BUSINESS, LEGISLATION, AND PUBLIC OPINION

Associations of businessmen are conspicuous in the promotion of the cause of business; their methods and activities in the long-run are aimed toward the building of a favorable public opinion. In this endeavor they are not alone, but neither labor nor agriculture cultivates public favor with equal success or with the same sense of urgent necessity. Even after the depression and the New Deal, business leaders, according to the polls, enjoyed higher public prestige than labor leaders.[20] Businessmen, a small minority highly vulnerable to political attack, labor under a greater necessity of gaining public favor than do

---

[19] For further information on the work of the association, see Temporary National Economic Committee, *Hearings*, 76th Congress, 1st Session, pursuant to Public Resolution No. 113, Part 10 (Washington: Government Printing Office, 1940).

[20] Elmo Roper, "The Public Looks at Labor Unions," *Harvard Business Review*, 21 (1942–43), pp. 425–431.

groups whose memberships comprise substantial blocs of the public.
Business has not always been sensitive to public opinion. While the
attitude of "the-public-be-damned" is not dead, business now deliberately attempts to gain public favor. Whether this alteration of appearance reflects a real change of attitude may be questioned. At any
rate business associations and corporations employ in large numbers
public-relations experts, those masters of the verbal magic that trans-
mutes private advantage into the public good. The assiduous dedica-
tion of effort to the capture of public favor in general is not unrelated
to the efforts of business to cope with the most concrete issues of public
policy. A reservoir of public good-will enables the business association or concern better to gain its end in any particular situation.

Early disregard of public opinion. It has not been so long since the
principal business leaders felt no concern about what the public thought
of them or of their industries. The men who built up great corporate
concerns were often ruthless. The process of combination and suppression of competition required men of that character—men who in
another day perhaps might have been the barons, chieftains, and war
lords. Moreover, they were engagingly frank. Witness the testimony
of Henry Havemeyer, sugar refiner, in the 'nineties:

Senator Allen. . . . If you fix the price at 4 cents for granulated throughout
the United States the others obtain it, don't they? And in that way the price
is controlled.

Mr. Havemeyer. We undertake to control the price of refined sugar in the
United States. That must be distinctly understood.

Senator Allen. And the price of refined sugar in the United States is higher
to the American people in consequence of the existence of the American Sugar
Refining Company than it would be if the different companies in your organization were distinct and independent companies?

Mr. Havemeyer. For a short time it is.

Senator Allen. And what difference does it make for the consumers in this
country in a year, in your judgment?

Mr. Havemeyer. It has been in three years past three-eights of a cent more
on every pound they ate, as against doing business at a loss.

Senator Allen. And that would be about how much in round numbers?

Mr. Havemeyer. It is a large sum in the aggregate.

Senator Allen. How many millions?

Mr. Havemeyer. I should say it was close to $25,000,000 in three years.

Senator Allen. And you intend to keep your hold upon the American people as long as you can?

Mr. Havemeyer. As long as the McKinley bill is there we will exact the
profit.

Senator Allen. Is that the result of the McKinley bills?

Mr. Havemeyer. We should not have achieved it without the McKinley bill; but a great deal of the profit is due to these men in consequence of combining the different interest and the skill and labor attending it.[21]

The spirit of the builders of big business, in an extreme form, is manifested by a letter from the president of one of the railroads controlling the anthracite mines. It was written at the time of the coal strike of 1902 in reply to a letter pleading that, as a Christian, the railroad president should grant a concession to the strikers, end the strike, and thereby earn the blessing of God and the thanks of the nation.

I have your letter of the 16th instant.

I do not know who you are. I see that you are a religious man; but you are evidently biased in favor of the right of the working man to control a business in which he has no other interest than to secure fair wages for the work he does.

I beg of you not to be discouraged. The rights and interests of the laboring man will be protected and cared for—not by the labor agitators, but by the Christian men to whom God in His infinite wisdom has given control of the property interests of the country, and upon the successful management of which so much depends.

Do not be discouraged. Pray earnestly that right may triumph, always remembering that the Lord God Omnipotent still reigns, and that His reign is one of law and order, and not of violence and crime.[22]

Concern for public attitudes. The "divine right" theory of industrial power began to be displaced by a different business attitude after 1900.[23] Public resentment of the "trusts" and concrete action in the form of prosecutions for conspiracy in restraint of trade forced a recognition of the need for a different policy if business hoped to maintain its status. Ivy Lee, the first of the great public-relations counselors, opened shop in 1903. He and his imitators found clients aware of the new trend of events, and the public-relations industry flourished. At crucial periods, such as the years 1936–1940, businessmen became acutely aware of the problem of building favorable public sentiment and business propaganda experts prospered.[24]

The public utility executives were among the first to see the advisability of educating public opinion as a form of insurance against exten-

---

21 Senate Report No. 606, 53rd Congress, 2nd Session (1894), pp. 337–338.

22 Quoted by George S. Counts, *The Prospects of American Democracy*, p. 61.

23 N. S. B. Gras, "Shifts in Public Relations," *Bulletin of the Business Historical Society*, 19 (1945), pp 97–148.

24 "The Public Is Not Damned," *Fortune*, March, 1939.

sive governmental intervention in response to demands from sections of the public affected by corporate policy. President Vail, of the Bell System, in 1913 expressed the new viewpoint:

All industrials, particularly utilities, are face to face with problems, the solution of which will largely determine the future of the business; they are, in the last resort, subject to a control and regulation far stronger than that exercised by commissions or by legislators, that influence and power that makes and unmakes legislators and judges; the influence and power of public desire and public selfishness, which if not regulated or controlled will lead to chaos and disaster. The only regulation or control for this is that common sense which, directed by education and observation, and rightfully administered and regulated, will conserve the interests of all.[25]

The practice of the A.T. & T. of devoting careful attention to its public relations paid off handsomely in the long run. It became our largest nonfinancial corporation, a natural target for political attack, and virtually a national monopoly. Yet it weathered the New Deal without ill results; its store of public good-will make it an unlikely object of attack by crusaders.[26]

The public-relations specialist did not come into his own until after World War I, during which governmental propaganda agencies impressively demonstrated what could be done with public opinion through skillful propaganda. As a result of that example, industry more generally undertook to create a favorable context of public attitudes within which to operate. Business associations planned and executed large-scale programs of public education. One of the largest efforts was by the National Electric Light Association, a group that later dissolved when the full magnitude of its propaganda program became generally known. The rationale of its program, and indeed of most organized efforts to mold public opinion, was stated in 1925 by B. J. Mullaney, a utility leader: [27]

I am fairly familiar with legislative practice and procedure and have not many illusions in that quarter. Sometimes the political road has to be traveled. When a destructive bill is pending in a legislature it has to be dealt

25 N. E. Long, "Public Relations Policies of the Bell System," *Public Opinion Quarterly*, October, 1937, p. 18.

26 Richardson Wood, "The Corporation Goes into Politics," *Harvard Business Review*, 21 (1942–43), pp. 60–70.

27 Federal Trade Commission, Summary Report . . . on Efforts by Associations and Agencies of Electric and Gas Utilities to Influence Public Opinion, Sen. Document No. 92, Part 71A, 70th Congress, 1st Session, 1934, p. 17. This report contains a comprehensive account of the efforts by a pressure group to manipulate public attitudes; it may well be scanned by the student to obtain a notion of the methods used, which are similar to those employed by other groups.

with in a way to get results. I am not debating that. But to depend, year after year, upon the usual political expedients for stopping hostile legislation is shortsightedness. . . . In the long run isn't it better to lay a groundwork with the people back home who have the votes, so that proposals of this character are not popular with them, rather than to depend upon stopping such proposals when they get up to the legislature or commission? . . . I am not suggesting in any sense that we can ignore the political angle; we live under a political form of government. Everything that we do focuses at one time or another in legislative action, whether it be in local city councils, in State legislatures, or in the National Congress.

In the intensification of business' wooing of the public after World War I, business associations, such as the National Association of Manufacturers, were active, but the giant corporations also undertook independently to create a more favorable set of public attitudes. Every conceivable medium through which the public might be reached was utilized. Corporate officials came to be publicized to dramatize the work of business; they expressed views on all sorts of public questions. Henry Ford, for example, became one of the major public oracles. Through advertisements on a country-wide scale with only a slight function in the attraction of patronage, attempts were made to mold public attitudes. Advertisements were used to tell of the scientific achievements of industrial laboratories, of the heroic work of public-utility maintenance men in time of disaster, of the long service that particular families have given to companies, of the great contributions of this or that corporation to scores of communities, of the services of the sugar-refining industry to farmers and laborers, of the remarkable facilities provided by the corporation in its company towns, of the achievements of industry, and of the "American way." Examination of almost any periodical furnished examples of advertisements that appeared to be designed, not primarily to sell goods, but to create a favorable public attitude toward industry either in general or regarding particular industries or situations. Furthermore the press, a big business in its own right, could be depended on to propagate sound doctrines, and, as every successful regime attracts its courtiers, so also did business become the beneficiary of unplanned and unsought adulation.

The great political triumph of large-scale enterprise has been the manufacture of a public opinion favorably disposed toward, or at least tolerant of, gigantic corporations. In a social milieu originally hostile toward monopolies and trusts, business has succeeded in building up great prestige and power; and it should be remembered that power depends in considerable measure on acquiescence. Businessmen, of course, deny that they possess power; but great corporations, operating under semi-monopolistic conditions, exert great authority over laborers, consumers, and the communities in which they operate.[28] The sheer magnitude of their operations, however, also makes them especially sensitive to public policies. A tax measure, for example, that takes $100 from a small enterprise may take $10,000,000 from the great corporation. It will probably be resisted with much greater vigor by the latter than by the former.

As industrial power grew and the conscious policy of manipulating public attitudes to retain that power came to be adopted, big business-men underwent a curious metamorphosis. They came to act like politicians; or, as they termed it, they became industrial statesmen. Similarly, they became sensitive to public criticism and they planned their major policies and decisions with a sharp eye on the anticipated public reaction. And, like politicians, their decisions have come to be influenced, within limits, by the anticipated public reaction. The doctrine that corporate office is a public trust came to be promulgated; and to it lip service, at least, was paid.

General and continuing campaigns of public information merely prepare the ground for intensive battles for or against particular legislative proposals or administrative actions. A review of a few specific legislative battles will illustrate the general types of public policy in which business manifests the keenest interest. These cases will incidentally throw some light on the methods employed by business groups to attain objectives in particular situations.

Resistance to regulation. On occasion business welcomes public regulation—such as regulation guaranteeing quasi-monopolistic rights. Taxi companies, for example, are usually glad to be regulated when the regulation limits the rise of competition. More frequently the "better element" of an industry does not oppose regulation because it may hamper only those who give the trade a bad name. Generally, however, business opposes with might and main the extension of public control.

The fight against the enactment of the Public Utility Holding Company Act of 1935 constitutes a sample of industry at its worst in the resistance to regulation. A series of investigations had revealed nu-

[28] In opening an antitrust case against the motion picture industry in June, 1940, Thurman Arnold, chief of the Antitrust Division of the Department of Justice, said: "The danger in this country is private seizure of power. It is subject to no checks and balances; it is subject to no elections every four years; it is subject to no criticism and no attacks because no other knows about it. It is private seizure of industrial power which the Sherman Act prevents."—*The New York Times,* June 4, 1940.

merous abuses in connection with the operation of utility holding companies, and the losses suffered by thousands of investors in what proved to be worthless stock set the stage for the campaign for the bill. Although there were many variations on the main theme, the principal type of abuse in connection with the holding company was the acquisition of control of a number of operating companies by a single holding company. Through the exercise of this control, the holding company proceeded to milk the subordinate operating companies of funds that otherwise could have gone into dividends to stockholders of the operating companies or into reductions in rates to consumers. An investment of $23,000 in one holding company, for example, controlled over a billion dollars worth of assets.[29] By exorbitant charges to the subordinate operating companies for management and other services, the cream was drawn off to the holding company or was divided among those controlling the holding company.

In the unsuccessful fight against the bill to regulate and break up certain types of holding companies, the lead was taken by the Committee of Utility Executives. It spent over $150,000 in its agitation against the bill. Among its expenditures was an item of $5,000 a month to the firm of Ivy Lee & T. J. Rose, public-relations counselors. Conducting an independent campaign was the Associated Gas & Electric Company, a concern looked down on even by other utility companies. Associated spent in the neighborhood of $800,000 to create sentiment against the bill. The movement against the legislation was characterized by a campaign calculated to instill fear and panic in the minds of investors. For the purpose of translating this fear into effective political pressure, a barrage of telegrams was aimed at Congress. The workers throughout the country soliciting telegrams—the utility companies paid the tolls—let their enthusiasm run away with them and began to sign to the messages names selected at random from city directories. The revelation of these practices by a special investigating committee headed by Hugo Black took much of the wind out of the utility sails, but even then it required powerful persuasion by the White House to push the bill through Congress.[30]

Not infrequently when regulatory legislation is proposed, the wise leaders of the industry will support a moderate amount of regulation to eliminate abuses and forestall more serious regulation, as well as to

[29] Hearings before the Senate Committee on Interstate Commerce on S.1725, 74th Congress, 1st Session (1935).

[30] For material on the lobbying campaign, see Hearings before a Senate Special Committee to Investigate Lobbying Activities Pursuant to S. Res. 165, 74th Congress, 1st Session. For a summary of the testimony, see K. G. Crawford, *The Pressure Boys* (New York: Messner, 1939), chap. 4.

appease public opinion. But the fight against the holding-company bill was a battle to the bitter end by men defending an untenable position. Joseph P. Tumulty, once secretary to Woodrow Wilson and retained for the duration of the fight by one of the holding companies, advised his client: [31]

Frankly, I sometimes wonder at the lack of political judgment of some of the leaders of the utility world. It is obvious to the smallest mind in Washington that the utility business is in for readjustment. The wisest man in this business will recognize this and, if he has vision, will conduct himself accordingly. No man connected with the utilities business will lose sight of the fact that it is a quasi-public one. In this situation it is, therefore, foolish to approach the President with grand proclamations without first proving to him that, in good faith, the Augean Stables are being cleaned. Surely, your friend's poor sense of Washington psychology has made him appear like a babe-in-the-woods. Knowing you and believing that in the conduct of your company you have shown statesmanlike vision, I plead with you to try to bring that vision more and more into play lest the harassment from which you suffer may grow more serious with the passing days.

Often business groups can call on the press for substantial support in campaigns against regulatory legislation. The newspapers, as business enterprises of considerable magnitude themselves, enjoy a community of interest with business generally. Their reliance on advertising for revenue places them in a position of special susceptibility to pressure for their support. An example is furnished by the Food, Drug, and Cosmetic Act of 1938. The legislative history of this act began in 1933 when the late Senator Copeland of New York introduced a bill to revise, extend, and strengthen the Pure Food and Drug Act of 1906 in a manner, among other things, to penalize the more extravagant claims through advertising of the therapeutic efficacy of patent medicines. Among the steps recommended to its members by the United Medicine Manufacturers was that of securing "co-operation of newspapers in spreading favorable publicity, particularly papers now carrying advertising for members of the association." The press responded and the legislation was generally pictured as an assault on freedom of the press and as a step toward dictatorship. The nature of the tactics in enlisting press support may be suggested by a letter from the president of the Creomulsion Company, Inc., to editors of country newspapers: [32]

---

[31] Hearings, as cited, Part 2, p. 868.

[32] Hearings before a Subcommittee of the House Committee on Interstate and Foreign Commerce on H.R. 6906, H.R. 88055, H.R. 8941, and S. 5, 74th Cong., 1st sess. (1935), p. 680.

You are about to lose a substantial amount of advertising revenue from foods, cosmetics, and drug manufacturers. Your pocketbook is about to be filched, and you will see how if you personally study or have your lawyer study for you the enclosed copy of the Tugwell bill. . . . From a profit standpoint you will quickly see how you will be affected by this bill if it becomes law. . . . We ask you to take an active, aggressive stand against this bill, not as a matter of cooperation to us or other advertisers, but for your own business interests and the best interest of your community. . . . If this bill should become law, we will be forced to cancel immediately every line of Creomulsion advertising.

It is sometimes easy to suppose that all responsible proposals for public regulation are in the public interest. That is by no means necessarily the case. Public regulation strikes at the fundamental philosophy of businessmen, sometimes increases costs, and almost always adds to the complexities of the management of business enterprise. Business, however, like other groups generally attempts to make its case for or against particular public policies, whatever its merits may be, in terms of the public interest. It is better strategy, in the American political milieu, to contend for the general welfare rather than for a patently selfish interest. Thus in 1946 the National Association of Manufacturers made a bitter fight against the extension of price-control legislation. The following interchange between the Chairman of the House Committee on Banking and Currency and Mr. Robert Wason, President of the N.A.M., constitutes a recurring pattern of private-group rationalization of its objectives:

The Chairman. Now, we want to get the truth of the subject. When they put a witness on the stand, they usually ask him if he has any interest in the controversy, and I would like to ask you whether or not your organization has any interest in the rise of prices, whether or not it would benefit by the rise of prices.

Mr. Wason. We believe that there would be an improvement in the profit position of total industry.

The Chairman. Your organization goes much further [in opposing price control] than most of the organizations that have appeared before us.

Mr. Wason. We are aware of that, Mr. Spence.

The Chairman. Well, how do you account for that?

Mr. Wason. We are standing for a correct economic principle, and we want to go on record here and now against those controls and this particular control of our economy. We want the people to be freed.

We may lack numbers. We may be greatly outvoted. This may be extended, but in the future, we want to be on record as having taken our stand for the welfare of this Nation, and we do not want the responsibility on our shoulders, if it is extended.[33]

[33] House Committee on Banking and Currency, 79th Cong., 2d sess., Hearings on H.R. 5270, Vol. 1 (1946), pp. 814–815.

Mitigation of enforcement. If a regulatory law is adopted, business groups (and other groups) draw back to the next line of defense and attempt to assure that the legislation will be administered "reasonably." For example, administration of the Sherman Act of 1890, which makes illegal combinations in restraint of trade in interstate commerce, has been of interest to business, especially those concerns that felt themselves susceptible to prosecution under the act. The tactics against the Sherman Act have been, not to make a frontal assault for repeal, but to obtain an unenergetic enforcement of the act.

Under lax enforcement there may be increased concentration of corporate control as well as combinations restraining trade. "It is a well-known fact," said the Attorney General in 1938, "that the antitrust laws have been ineffective in preventing combinations in restraint of trade. There is probably no community, small or large, in America today, and no industry, which does not furnish some instances of such combinations." He explains the reasons: ". . . the disproportion between the magnitude of the task of administration and the size of the available staff throughout the history of the antitrust laws has been little short of staggering. . . . From 1914 to 1923, during which our system of mass production and vast corporate enterprise may almost be said to have become of age, the average number of attorneys in the Antitrust Division was only eighteen. With such a personnel, regardless of what the formula of the law might have been, no practical results were possible." [34] During Franklin D. Roosevelt's second term increases in staff were made, but the staff remained far from adequate. It must be remembered that prosecutions for antitrust violation do not try themselves. Extensive investigations of documents, records, and economic data must be carried on in advance of trial; witnesses must be interviewed and cases prepared for trial.

Defense of the right of combination. American business loudly proclaims the virtues of free, competitive enterprise, yet no more consistent thread runs through its lobbying activities than defense of the right of combination in restraint of trade. It cannot be argued that under modern industrial conditions the doctrines of free competition are indubitably correct public policy; antitrust prosecutions may in some instances correspond to the ceremony of exorcising evil spirits. Yet we have had the odd paradox of business passionately defending the doctrine of free competition and industriously opposing governmental action calculated to assure competition.

The Tydings-Miller Act of 1937 furnishes an example of business

[34] *Report of the Attorney General,* pp. 57–58.

pressure activities leading to legislation favorable to restraint of trade. Prior to the passage of this act in a series of decisions the courts had applied the Antitrust Act to agreements and other actions calculated to fix prices of articles sold at retail. Retailers, primarily druggists, had promoted the passage of state legislation legalizing contracts between manufacturers and retailers fixing re-sale prices of various commodities. In some instances retailers had boycotted manufacturers who did not attempt to compel all retailers to maintain high prices. These state laws, usually quietly lobbied through legislatures, were of limited efficacy as long as re-sale price maintenance was illegal for goods sold in interstate commerce. Retail druggists and others sought an exemption from the Sherman Act. In 1937 the Tydings-Miller Act legalized these contracts in restraint of trade in those states that had state legislation permitting re-sale price maintenance contracts. These state acts, incidentally, were known as "fair trade" laws, an obvious propaganda device: it is "unfair" to sell Ipana at a lower price than does your competitor around the corner.

Federal legislation legalizing re-sale price maintenance came only after a number of years of agitation. Prime leaders in the movement were the druggists represented by the National Association of Retail Druggists and state pharmaceutical associations. The druggists succeeded in bringing to their support the National Association of Retail Grocers, the American Book Sellers Association, the National Automobile Dealers Association, and the National Association of Manufacturers. Department stores, retail clothiers, and mail order concerns were unable to amass sufficient strength to defeat the druggists who pressured Congress through their "contact committees." The work of these committees was described in the journal of the drug association:

One of the outstanding achievements of the association through its Washington Office was the organization of the congressional contact committees. Under this plan, in 1935 and 1936, there were organized in each congressional district committees of pharmacists who were known to be friends of or intimately acquainted with Senators and Congressmen. These committeemen were the "minute men" upon whom the association relied to act, quickly and decisively, whenever the association's legislative program needed special attention. . . .

This year the congressional contact committees were reorganized on a county basis, nearly every county in the entire United States being represented on the contact committee lists in the Washington Office. These organizations, kept alive and enthused by the regular messages from the Capital, proved their effectiveness time and again this spring. Now, these committees are busy among the pharmacists and other independent businessmen of their counties, keeping a steady barrage of letters and telegrams directed upon the White House, in an effort to convince the President that he should reconsider his action in delaying the passage of the Tydings-Miller bill.[35]

One aspect of this pressure technique deserves special note. The National Association of Retail Druggists did not rely on its professional staff to sell the idea to Congress. It used its members over the country who had personal acquaintance with legislators. This custom prevails among pressure groups generally. The assumption is that if leading citizens from the home city descend on Washington and see their Congressman, a man with whom they play golf and poker and whom they perhaps call "Joe," the day may be saved.[36]

The effects of the Tydings-Miller Act are of some interest to show what the excitement was about. The retail druggists' association advocated that under the law a minimum mark-up of 50 per cent over cost be fixed by manufacturers; the various associations attempted to coerce manufacturers to place their products under re-sale price maintenance and to fix the prices to the satisfaction of retailers. The effects on prices were most marked in large cities where on many drugs and related products, such as cosmetics and baby foods, prices charged by chain and department stores (who had opposed the legislation) rose while prices in independent stores declined by a lesser amount.[37]

Following the institution of antitrust suits against certain railroads, the Association of American Railroads in 1945 began a campaign to bring about the adoption of legislation exempting railroads from the Antitrust Act if their agreements to fix rates had received the approval of the Interstate Commerce Commission. The movement for the adoption of this legislation presents an excellent example of one interest rallying to its support a wide variety of related and unrelated inter-

[35] Quoted in *Report of the Federal Trade Commission on Resale Price Maintenance* (1945), p. 65.
[36] Concerning the work of the Association of Railway Executives the following report covering a meeting of the Law Committee of the Association in 1934 is of interest: "Judge Fletcher contemplates asking the executives to approve a plan of selecting a number of railroad men who have extensive personal acquaintance with members of this Congress to be assigned to the work of following the progress of the various bills. . . . In his judgment, the effective work in opposition to bills harmful to railroads can only be done through personal interviews with Congressmen conducted by men personally acquainted with the Congressmen they interview, and for whom the interviewed Congressmen would have a feeling of respect and confidence."— Hearings before a Subcommittee of the Senate Committee on Interstate Commerce, pursuant to S. Res. 71, 75th Congress, 2nd Session (1940), Part 23, p. 10,087.
[37] For the details see *Report of the Federal Trade Commission on Retail Price Maintenance* (1945).

ests within the nation. Officials of the Association, mainly persons who were railroad executives, presented the technical case for the bill to the House committee. The necessity of legalizing longstanding practices of conferring in the fixing of rates was defended on the ground, among others, of the extreme complexity of the problem. It was pointed out, for example, that between New York and Chicago traffic could be moved over 884 routes comprised of various combinations of 55 railroads and 6 water lines. To maintain fair rates, it was necessary, so the argument ran, to have rate conferences and other cooperative arrangements among the carriers. The effects of the practices of combination were not analyzed, but the probabilities are that they tend to freeze the prevailing geographical distribution of trade and industry and to prevent shippers receiving the full advantage in rates of the most economical routes. At any rate the railroads did not depend solely on the merits of their case. They organized a most impressive show of political force.

A mere listing of the organizations that either appeared before the House committee or submitted statements endorsing the railroad bill filled fifteen pages in small print. About fifty governmental authorities were recorded in support of the bill. This group included principally state regulatory commissions ranging from the Arizona Corporation Commission to the Maine Public Utilities Commission. About twenty carrier organizations joined in support of the bill, including such organizations as the American Merchant Marine Institute, Inc., the Freight Forwarders Institute, and the Intercoastal Steamship Freight Association. About 85 shippers', traffic, and transportation organizations endorsed the bill, among which were the Atlantic States Shippers Advisory Board, the Industrial Traffic Association of San Francisco, the Junior Traffic Club of Seattle and the Texas Industrial Traffic League. About 125 agricultural and livestock organizations accommodated their railroad friends by approving the bill. This category included the American Farm Bureau Federation, the California Lima Bean Growers Association, the Idaho Farmers' Union, and the Wyoming Wool Growers' Association. About one hundred business organizations made statements in support of the measure. They ranged from the Alabama Cotton Manufacturers Association to the Oregon State Pharmaceutical Association. Approximately 550 chambers of commerce, civic, and other organizations allowed their names to be used in support of the measure. In the roster were the Abilene (Texas) Chamber of Commerce, the Anaheim (California) Chamber of Commerce, the Azusa (California) Chamber of Commerce, the Crete (Nebraska) Chamber of Commerce, the Lansing (Michigan) Chamber of Commerce, the Providence (Rhode Island) Chamber of Commerce, and several hundred others.[38]

Obviously such a demonstration does not organize itself. The railroad associations nurtured the grass-roots movement with both care and thoroughness. But this instance is only illustrative of a general practice of pressure groups to attempt to bring to their support in particular legislative battles all groups that have even the most remote interest in the matter. The more witnesses in support of a particular position, the greater the appearance of universality of demand becomes and the more insignificant the opposition may be made to appear.[39]

Minimization and shifting of taxation. Business groups, as well as others, watch the development of tax policy constantly and make such efforts as they can to bring about tax reductions or the adoption of legislation transferring the burden of taxation to others. Probably organized pressure on tax matters is most importunate on special types of taxation and on special provisions of tax laws applying to small groups or classes rather than in connection with tax principles of general applicability. The following extracts from a 1944 presidential veto of a tax bill, a veto that was overridden, illustrate the types of special tax provisions that occur. The student with a bit of native shrewdness can guess with fair accuracy the types of lobbying pressure that produced each of the items mentioned. The extracts from the veto message follow:

The bill is replete with provisions which not only afford indefensible special privileges to favored groups but set dangerous precedents for the future. . . .

Among these special privileges are:

(a) Permission for corporations reorganized in bankruptcy to retain the high excess-profits credit and depreciation basis attributable to the contributions of stockholders who are usually eliminated in the reorganization. This privilege inures to the benefit of bondholders who, in many cases, have purchased their bonds in the speculative market for far less than their face value. It may open the door to further windfall profits in this market because of the undeserved benefit received by reorganized corporations.

38 Consult Hearings, Subcommittee of the Committee on Interstate and Foreign Commerce, House, 79th Cong., 1st sess., on H.R. 2536 (1945).

39 To illustrate further the effort to bring related associations into legislative alliances, the following statement by the general manager of the Association of Life Insurance Presidents may be quoted: "When the Wheeler-Rayburn bill was pending affecting the utilities, we were importuned—our association was importuned—to take part in it on the theory that it would affect the securities of our companies. As a matter of fact, the utilities securities for our companies are in the underlying operating companies, and we took no part in that, even though it might in some instances have affected us, because we felt that was out of our field."—Temporary National Economic Committee, Hearings, Part 10, p. 4441.

(b) Percentage depletion allowances, questionable in any case, are now extended to such minerals as vermiculite, potash, feldspar, mica, talc, lepidolite, barite, and spodumene. In the case of some of these minerals the War Production Board refused to certify that current output was inadequate for war needs.

(c) The lumber industry is permitted to treat income from the cutting of timber, including selective logging, as a capital gain rather than annual income. As a grower and seller of timber, I think that timber should be treated as a crop and therefore as income when it is sold. This would encourage reforestation.

(d) Natural gas pipe lines are exempted from the excess-profits tax without justification and in a manner which might well lead oil companies to request similar treatment for their pipe lines.

(e) Commercial air lines are granted an unjustifiable extension of the tax subsidy on their air-mail contracts.[40]

Seekers of subsidy. From what has been said about organized business and legislation it may be inferred that the role of business has been principally to oppose legislative proposals thought to be inimical to its interests. And probably business has been more concerned with opposing than in proposing legislation. The reason is simple. The great economic revolution in which business took the place of agriculture as the dominant factor in economic life profoundly altered the old order, but the old order could be altered outside the framework of government. Business could take care of itself; others, injured by the power of business, sought legislation to control business. It needs perhaps to be noted that the structure of government (and perhaps the nature of human behavior) is such that business in its role of obstructor of legislation has enjoyed an advantageous strategic position. It is much easier for a minority (and those immediately concerned with proposed legislation are nearly always a minority) to block legislation than for an equally powerful minority to bring about its passage. The burden of the proof is on those who seek to change the prevailing order, and the steps in the legislative procedure at which bills may be quietly buried are numerous. If defeated at one point, the defenders may withdraw to the next line of defense, and to the next and the next.

Yet certain types of business organizations seek positive legislation. Manufacturing industry has been avid to obtain tariff favors, and during most of the time since the Civil War, manufacturing has been able to write its own tariff acts. The tariff is an indirect kind of subsidy to business; other businesses seek subsidies directly from the Treasury. One of the more important of such groups is the shipping industry, which claims that it cannot compete with foreign shipping, often sub-

[40] *Congressional Record*, vol. 90, pt. 2, p. 1959. (1944).

sidized, without government support.[41]   The claim is probably correct
but subsidy smothers managerial ingenuity in the reduction of costs.
Moreover, shipping subsidy programs have in practice often smelled
to the high heavens; subventions to the shipping industry have at times
been siphoned off into excessive managerial charges rather than used
to make American shipping strong.

Occasionally business groups oppose subsidies, but there are subsidies and subsidies.   Thus in 1946 the Producers' Council, an organization of 80 manufacturers of building materials and 20 trade associations
of manufacturers of building materials and equipment, strenuously fought the subsidy feature of a program for expediting the construction of housing for veterans.   This subsidy proposal, however,
was associated with a proposal to maintain ceiling prices and to swell
production of building materials by government subsidies to high-cost
producers and to other producers whose output could be increased
by subsidies.   This two-point program was proposed as an alternative
to a general increase of prices of building materials.   The Producers'
Council, as do all groups, attempted to defend its position, not as a
means of gaining selfish advantage, but as a method for better attaining the public objective: "We therefore feel fully justified in saying that
those who insist on the subsidy plan and oppose ceiling price adjustments are themselves working against the best interests of the veterans,
though they may not realize that fact."   The Council recommended
"judicious increases in the ceiling prices on scarce building materials
and equipment." [42]

Business regards with a cold eye that which it considers a subsidy
for a competitor.   The railroads, for example, manifest no ardor for
river-and-harbor appropriations.   Their attitude is perhaps slightly
exaggerated in a memorial to Congress by the Trinity Improvement
Association, a group dedicated to making navigable the Trinity River,
a Texas stream without a formidable flow: "Most respectfully the attention of the Congress of the United States is called to the disloyal
pernicious activities of the Association of American Railroads whose
subversive tactics in wartime are imperiling the freedom of our Nation and aiding our country's foes."   These comments were called
forth by the opposition of the A.A.R. to a measure authorizing emergency river-and-harbor improvements.   The Improvement Association

41 For an account of pressure for shipping subsidies, see Paul M. Zeis, *American
Shipping Policy* (Princeton: Princeton University Press, 1938).   See also Allen Bernard,
"The Ship-Charter Scandal," *New Republic,* 114 (1946), pp. 761–765.

42 Hearings before Subcommittee of the Senate Committee on Banking and Currency
on H.R. 4761, 79th Cong., 2d sess. (1946), pp. 173–174.

went on to say: "The million-dollar rail lobby in Washington could gracefully receive, in gratitude for the services of their organization, the Iron Cross from the Nazis or from the Mikado the Order of the Chrysanthemum with its scummy yellow ribbon." Further, it was predicted: "The Hun, the Dago, and the Jap newspapers will hail the sabotage of transportation development in America if those unnatural political pals, the railroads and the CIO, wreck this wartime measure." [43] Similarly the electrical utilities oppose appropriations for public power projects.[44]

States' rights. Business has in general stood for state power and against national power. The reason for this constitutional position is easy to see; it is no matter of devotion to principle. In many instances legislation regulatory of business can be effective only if it is national in application. To stand for a narrow construction of national power, as business has usually done, is to stand against effective governmental action in situations requiring national action. But there is a further reason for the position of business on the division of power between the national government and the states. The relations of business with state and local machines have been so intimate that business could block much legislation in the sphere of state power, or at least prevent its effective administration. A characteristic of the federal system seems to be that entrenched interests in the long run can better protect themselves in dealings with state legislatures than with Congress or with federal administrators.

Business lobbyists have shed tears in the name of states' rights on many occasions, but a notable instance occurred in 1943 and 1944 when insurance companies rallied in support of a "bill to affirm the intent of the Congress that the regulation of the business of insurance remain within the control of the several States." The business of insurance had long been considered not to be interstate commerce and, hence, not within the range of federal power. The Sherman Antitrust Act of 1890 prohibited combinations in restraint of trade in interstate commerce. On suit instituted by the Department of Justice in 1942, the federal courts were called upon to reconsider whether fire insurance could be brought under the interstate commerce power. The case against the South-Eastern Underwriters Association charged conspiracy to restrain trade by fixing rates and conspiracy to monopolize trade in insurance, all in contravention of the Sherman Act. The Department of Justice argued for a reconsideration of past precedent on

[43] *Congressional Record* (daily edition), February 28, 1942, p. A848.
[44] See Carroll Kilpatrick, "The Power Lobby Is Back," *New Republic*, 114 (1946), pp. 650–651.

various grounds, including the argument that authoritative opinion contemporary with the formation of the Constitution, viz., that of Alexander Hamilton, held insurance to be within the commerce power. The position of the government in the case ultimately persuaded the Supreme Court.[45]

Even before the Supreme Court gave its opinion, the insurance companies and associations hastened to their friends in Congress to bring about the adoption of the bill mentioned above. In the hearings on the bill it appeared that state control of fire insurance was generally extremely ineffective and that the insurance companies were trying to play both ends against the middle by defeating restraints by either state or federal government. That combination and monopoly existed was undenied. The sole issue became one of states' rights.

Insurance companies possessed excellent facilities to promote the bill. Their cause was pictured as a battle to the death against the encroachments of the federal government; hearts bled and tears were shed. More practically, local agents of insurance companies scattered throughout the length and breadth of the land brought their influence to bear upon their representatives. State governors and insurance departments rushed in to support the companies. Associations of insurance companies presented evidence and urged Congressmen to pass the bill. The Insurance Executives Association, an association of the presidents of fire-insurance companies, presented evidence. The strategy apparently was to conduct a whirlwind campaign for the passage of the bill before potential opposition could be aroused.

The strategy of jamming through or slipping through a bill before the opposition awakes and before the evidence is all in is common. In this instance, it happened to fail. Senator Joseph C. O'Mahoney, of Wyoming, a zealous anti-monopolist, began to organize the opposition to the bill. It turned out that not all persons associated with the insurance business were happy about the bill: many of them had been injured by the monopolistic practices of insurance groups. Although most state officials concerned with insurance did the bidding of the insurance companies and supported the legislation, a few here and there arose to plead for a bit of federal assistance in the control of huge enterprises clothed with a public interest. The American Federation of Labor appeared against the legislation: if insurance were considered as interstate commerce, company agents and employees could claim the benefits of the National Labor Relations Act and the Wage and Hour Act. Shortly after the Supreme Court decision holding fire

[45] *United States* v. *South-Eastern Underwriters Assn.*, 332 U.S. 533 (1944).

insurance subject to the Antitrust Act, the House passed the bill, 283–54, but the Senate allowed it to die.[46]

States as industrial fiefs. In the lobbies of the state capitols business associations are, on the whole, more powerful than in Washington, and, in addition, some types of groups exert considerable influence in state affairs but have less or no concern with national policy. This greater power of business in state government grows from several factors. The groups that habitually oppose the demands of business are often more powerful on the national scene than at individual state capitols. In most agricultural states, for example, labor organizations can muster relatively little strength in comparison with their national strength while business in such states is comparatively much stronger than on the national scene. Further, the tie between business leaders and political leaders is more intimate in many states than in the national government. The dominance of the lawyer and the businessman in the membership of state legislatures, coupled with the fact that most state legislators must make a livelihood from something other than public office, produces virtually an identity between business and legislature in a great many states. Local machines also tend to rely heavily on business for financial support and business tends to ally itself with the stronger machine in the state, whatever label it may bear.[47]

Almost all the types of business concerned with national policies are represented at state capitols, but their interests differ in importance at the state and federal levels; then, too, some types of business are concerned more with state than federal matters. In almost every state electrical utilities constitute an important lobby; they are deeply concerned with state regulatory policies. To some extent they replace the railroads, which at an earlier time played a much more important part in state politics than now. Truck and bus groups have substantial stakes in the actions of state legislatures and regulatory bodies. Insurance companies, state-chartered banks, and savings and loan associations, small-loan companies, and other financial interests subject to state regulation have their representatives on hand when state legislatures

[46] See Joint Hearing before the Subcommittees of the Committees on the Judiciary, 78th Cong., 1st sess., on S. 1362, H.R. 3269, and H.R. 3270 (1943–1944).

[47] The following testimony by a former president of the New York, New Haven & Hartford Railroad Company is of interest:

"*Mr. Folk.* The New Haven Railroad was not very partisan, anyway, was it? It was Republican in Republican States and Democratic in Democratic States, and it endeavored to get near those having power and influence, no matter what their politics might be. Is not that the case?

"*Mr. Mellen.* We always liked to get under the best umbrella in case of a storm." —Senate Document No. 543, 63rd Congress, 2nd Session, Evidence Taken by the Interstate Commerce Commission, p. 940.

are in session. Race-track gambling interests, often disguised as associations for the improvement of the breed of the horse, are important in many states; and the liquor industry pays close attention to state matters of interest to it. Natural-resource industries—petroleum, mining, forestry—probably on the whole play a bigger role in state politics than in national affairs. Contractors, organized and individually, have a keen interest in state public-works policy.

Occasionally one or two great business concerns either dominate or play an extremely significant role in the politics of a state. At an earlier time the leading railroad corporation in a state often occupied a position of leadership in a business coalition with the party machine. Latterly the railroads have shared or abdicated their leadership to others. In Montana it is said that the Anaconda Copper Company and the Montana Power Company have exerted great strength in the politics of the state.[48] In California the Pacific Gas and Electric Company, while not dominating the affairs of the state, represents an instance of a single corporation with not inconsiderable power. In other instances an industry composed of many units wields a determining influence at least on questions of concern to it, such as the associations of coal mine owners in Kentucky, who for long years succeeded in blocking legislation calculated to enforce safety standards. In other states tightly organized business groups, such as the Illinois Manufacturers Association, play a leading role in the state legislative process.

4. THE WEB OF PECUNIARY RELATIONS

The business community maintains a remarkable solidarity of opinion on major public issues. This internal solidarity increases its power in maintaining its position in society as a whole. Although in the nature of a competitive system, keen and deep conflict of interest exists within the business class, these differences tend on the whole to be composed when questions of common concern to most elements of business arise.

A highly specialized society with the accompanying system of exchange is bound together by a webwork of pecuniary relations that profoundly affects the structure of political power. The traditional analysis of these relations in terms of a market, by hypothesis without friction, deflects attention from their political effects. A capitalistic class, by this sort of analysis, consists of persons at war with each other and animated by the doctrine of letting the devil take the hindmost. The economists' analysis of economic behavior often conveys the im-

[48] See Joseph Kinsey Howard, "The Montana Twins in Trouble," *Harper's*, September, 1944.

pression of a perfectly fluid social structure. That impression is, of course, erroneous. The pecuniary relations existing in an economy of extensive division of labor often have secondary effects of a political character not ordinarily covered by economic analysis.

Consider the remarkable unanimity of the business and financial community on many public questions. To a high degree this cohesion comes from the sharing of common interests, but not infrequently sections of the business and financial community are kept in line through pecuniary leverage. Interlocking directorates are sometimes cited as a concrete mechanism for achieving business and financial unity, yet probably other relationships are in the large more significant. In the relationships of client and counsel, manufacturer and customer, distributor and customer, banker and debtor, employer and employee, investor and broker, there exist powerful mechanisms for disciplining those whose conduct deviates from that demanded by group opinion. These relationships are not determined solely on an economic calculus, and, even if they were, one can always find another source of supply for a material or a service. Let a manufacturer espouse views unacceptable to the business and financial community generally, and he may discover that he has become an undesirable credit risk and his customers may seek other sources of supply. Such instances are, to be sure, rare, but their rarity is a tribute to the effectiveness of the threat of economic coercion in the maintenance of conformity to group mores.

Lurid portrayals of men of wealth conspiring to exert their economic power to maintain the position of business as a whole are, of course, generally absurd. Without design the system as a whole tends to produce conformity to its values, a striking feature of the behavior of the business community that is not commonly noted. A powerful discipline makes it difficult for a businessman to call his soul his own, that is, if he wants to stay in business.[49] He must have regard for his customers,[50] his suppliers, his bankers, his stockholders, his brokers, his lawyers, and all others with whom he deals. The net result is a power-

[49] This need not be true of a person who has truly enormous wealth, who lives from investments, or who is not particularly concerned that he remain in business. See Gabriel Almond, "The Political Attitudes of Wealth," *Journal of Politics,* 7 (1945), pp. 213–255.

[50] The realities are suggested by a letter to the members of the National Association of Manufacturers by its president with reference to the Wagner labor relations bill pending in 1935:

"We suggest that you consider the following steps:

"1. Advising your suppliers and dealers of the importance of this bill to your company. (A special letter on this has been sent to a few companies, so it is possible that this letter may be a duplication on this particular point.)"—Senate Report No. 6, Part 6, 76th Congress. 1st Session. p. 103.

ful restraint, which keeps business minorities small and makes those businessmen who oppose the majority of their fellows likely prospects for the bankruptcy courts.

In specific businesses that are compelled to pay considerable attention to their governmental relations, private economic relations sometimes run perilously close to bribery. The old-time railroad custom of "retaining" the leading attorney (who usually had precious little legal work to do) in each county seat along the line was designed to influence persons of great importance in each community. Some electric utilities have followed the same practice. A similar relationship is suggested by the remarks in the 'twenties by the president of a large utility concerning the desirability of maintaining deposits in country banks. He reported: [51]

> The bankers, as a rule, are economically minded about as we are, but, nevertheless, we came to the conclusion about 15 years ago that as a practical incentive to get them to work with us, there is no substitute for deposits. . . . I may add, in passing, that we have at this time accounts with 230 country banks scattered all over our territory; and while our policy keeps an average of around a million and a half dollars tied up in balances in these country depositaries, we believe it is well worth while—first, because the service they render to us as a banker is worth something, and, secondly, because it cements their friendship and cooperation. Incidentally, we require no interest on these deposits.

In some instances power is gained through the ability to influence the course of individual careers, although this is perhaps an euphemistic way to describe what sometimes happens.[52]

Another secondary effect of the power of money is the control of centers for the diffusion of ideas and for opinion manipulation. The tendency of newspapers to follow in general the point of view of the dominant economic groups in their respective communities is evident. In some instances this parallelism has been brought about by corrupt

[51] Federal Trade Commission, Summary Report . . . on Efforts by Associations and Agencies of Electric and Gas Utilities to Influence Public Opinion, Sen. Document No. 92, Part 71A, 70th Congress, 1st Session, 1934, p. 235.

[52] Donald Richberg says: "The individual public servant cannot fight the machine for long. He is forced out, or scared out, or bought out, or starved out, or tired out, or—in a host of cases—he is absorbed into the machine. Either he is given a better public job, with the understanding that he will be 'good,' or he is given a private job where he must be good. During my long struggle with the gas company, I saw added to the company payroll a public utility commissioner, a corporation counsel, a United States senator, a justice of the state Supreme Court, a tax assessor and a host of other former public officials."—*The Tents of the Mighty* (New York: Clark, Willet & Colby, 1930), pp. 117–118.

means,[53] but more often it rests on the simple fact that newspaper publishers are the same sort of people with the same sorts of interests as other members of the economic elite. Pressures thought sinister are brought into play only as punitive and disciplinary measures when ideological insurrection occurs or is threatened.[54] In many instances the urge of those in subordinate positions to conform is so strong that those who control the purse do not have to take any deliberate steps to make their power felt.[55] Every regime has its sycophants.

The relation between moneyed interests and political parties, discussed fully in another connection,[56] reveals another type of opinion-forming center that is strongly influenced by pecuniary means. The bulk of campaign contributions come from business of one type or another; the impact on politicians, year after year, campaign after campaign, is not to be ignored. The etiquette of campaign contributions is also indicative of an aspect of pecuniary power that it is essential to understand—that the power is not in a broad sense a sordid matter. It is in many respects in accordance with the prevailing mores. To make a campaign contribution with the expectation of receiving a specific return in the form of public action is considered to be "bad" form. To contribute, however, to the support of a party that espouses

[53] The leader of the campaign against a prohibition amendment in Pennsylvania in 1889 said: "We bought them by paying down so much cash. I visited the editors in person or had some good man to do so and arranged to pay each paper for its support a certain amount of money. Throughout the state we paid weekly papers from $50 to $500 to publish such matters as we might furnish either news or editorial, but the city dailies we had to pay from $1000 to $4000. Other papers we could not buy straight out, consequently we had to pay from thirty to sixty cents per line for all matter published for us, according to the circulation and ability of the paper."—Quoted in Colvin, *Prohibition in the United States* (New York: Doubleday, Doran, 1926), p. 205.

[54] On the case of the Chattanooga News, see Gordon Gaskill, "A Newspaper Is Killed," *The New Republic*, January 15, 1940. A business committee in Iowa supporting a campaign for a "fair trade" law reported that one daily newspaper ran detrimental articles: "This," the committee stated, "was taken care of by having one very large and regular advertiser 'call' them on it." Federal Trade Commission, *Report on Resale Price Maintenance* (1945), p. 59.

[55] William Green has written: "I had been invited to address a mass meeting on Sunday afternoon, October 10, under the auspices of the Young Men's Christian Association in this 'open shop' town (Detroit). On October 5, the Detroit newspapers carried a statement that the invitation would be cancelled and next day I received an official call from the president and secretary of the Y.M.C.A. who advised me that the board of directors had decided to withdraw the invitation. They expressed sincere regret and explained that the Y.M.C.A. had under way a building program running into several million dollars and they were apprehensive that if this mass meeting were held the building program would be jeopardized."—*Labor and Democracy* (Princeton: Princeton University Press, 1939), p. 115.

[56] See below, chap. 15.

a general policy under which the contributor and others as well may benefit is morally approved. The relationship is more subtle than merely one of "buying" a policy; we tend to contribute to "our" crowd.

Consider the secondary effects of the relationship of employer and employee. In isolated company towns the power to hire and fire has served as the basis for dictatorial control of almost every phase of community life. Such communities present, the Commission on Industrial Relations declared in 1916, "every aspect of a state of feudalism except the recognition of specific duties on the part of the employer." [57] In many localities black-listing by employers has been used to maintain a subservient laboring class.[58] Quite apart from these more or less pathological situations, employers gain great power in many communities partly, but only partly, from the power to hire and fire.

The foregoing specific examples have no great importance in themselves, but they serve to illustrate the broad proposition that economic relations have an effect in the determination of the structure of social power. The dominant economic groups gain internal coherence by the network of pecuniary relations, and by the same means they gain loyalty and enforce submission from subordinate groups and individuals. In the analysis of the political effects of pecuniary relations it is necessary to differentiate between the short-term maneuvers for position by specific interests and the long-term effect of the entire economic system in the perpetuation of the political system. *In toto* the long-term political effects of these pecuniary relations in the cementing of the loyalty of retainers and beneficiaries is impressive. Contrariwise, maladroit exercise of economic power may stimulate revolt.

Some observers occasionally assert that pecuniary power is limited to capitalistic regimes, but that conclusion is only superficial. Broadly considered, the power under discussion is the power to allocate the flow of income. That power exists at some point or points under any regime. Its use to induce regional or class famines, to bring submission, to assure regional or class prosperity, to reward loyalty under dictatorial regimes far exceeds in scope and effectiveness the comparatively unsystematic control in private hands under a capitalistic order.

[57] Senate Document No. 415, 64th Congress, 1st Session (1916), Vol. 1, p. 78.

[58] Consider the following letter of November 7, 1919, from the Pittsburgh Steel Products Company to the Page Steel and Wire Company at the time of the great steel strike: "Attached hereto is list of former employees who have failed to return to work in our Plant. This list is forwarded to you so that proper action can be taken —should they apply for work at your Plant. We would ask that you kindly consider this as confidential."—Commission of Inquiry, The Interchurch World Movement, *Report on the Steel Strike of 1919* (New York: Harcourt, Brace and Howe, 1920), p. 219.

Chapter 5

OTHER INTEREST GROUPS

THE preceding chapters outlined the operations of a few important pressure groups with their membership drawn from the ranks of labor, business, and agriculture. Many other organizations of similar composition could also be mentioned, for common economic interest frequently brings men to unite to gain power for the improvement and protection of their status. Other common interests also bind men together, and one could list hundreds of groups, at least partially non-economic in nature that make themselves heard in the affairs of local, state, and national governments. While it is impracticable and pointless to catalog all such groups, it is in order to list a few examples to indicate the broad range of interests animating pressure activities.

Religious groups and reform groups—the line between the two categories is hazy—exert considerable influence on political decision. Pressure operations of churches are often carried on by lay organizations, subsidiary agencies, and closely related but not formally affiliated groups. Thus, legislators hear from the representatives of such Roman Catholic organizations as the National Catholic Welfare Conference, the National Council of Catholic Men, the Knights of Columbus, the Legion of Decency, and the Catholic Daughters of America. Legislation concerning sterilization of the feeble-minded, child labor, education, birth control, and broader issues of social welfare attract the attention of such groups.[1] Although Protestant denominations are less thoroughly organized, the Federal Council of Churches of Christ in America, the Methodist Board of Temperance, and the Council for Social Action of the Congregational Churches likewise make themselves felt in the legislative process.[2] While not formally affiliated with any

[1] See the excellent review by T. T. McAvoy, C.S.C., "The Catholic Church in the United States between Two Wars," *Review of Politics*, 4 (1942), pp. 409-431.
[2] Pressure on government to obtain or to prevent particular action is to be differentiated from the influence of "religion" in elections, a matter that has not been thoroughly studied in the United States. Individual clergymen wield no mean influence in elections in many localities. Moreover, nearly always the religious beliefs

Protestant church, the Anti-Saloon League, in its prime an extremely powerful group, had close relations with several Protestant denominations.[3]

Another category of pressure groups consists of nationalist and internationalist organizations. The American Association for the United Nations succeeded the League of Nations Association as spokesman for an internationalist point of view. In the days preceding American entry into World War II the Committee to Defend America by Aiding the Allies and the America First Committee vigorously presented opposing viewpoints.[4] The field of pressure in foreign policy is, of course, not monopolized by single-purpose groups; organizations ranging from the beet growers to the watch-makers union express views on this subject.

Although women's organizations are divergent in their objectives, it is feasible to include organized women as a special category of pressure groups. The League of Women Voters has a long and distinguished record of lobbying in support of governmental measures of general interest. The American Association of University Women has been active on some issues. The Daughters of the American Revolution might better be included among the nationalist organizations. The General Federation of Women's Clubs has exerted strong influence in support of such proposals as the elimination of roadside billboards. Women as a group have few common political interests, and, hence, women's organizations have difficulty finding issues on which they can unite. Women's groups with a multi-class membership maintain unity on only the most innocuous matters. Women's groups with class-segregated membership, however, can push sharply defined objectives without threatening internal unity. Witness the Daughters of the American Revolution and the Women's Trade Union League; both are militant organizations, but each is representative of a single class interest.

For almost whatever public purpose one can imagine, he can discover a group organized to promote that cause. The Society for the Preservation of New England Antiquities, the Society for the Prevention of

---

of candidates are a factor. Religion is not a matter of such political indifference that Protestant communities elect Catholics and Catholic communities Protestants; the tendency is that elected officials parallel in religion their constituencies. See M. M. McKinney, "Religion and Elections," *Public Opinion Quarterly*, 8 (1944), pp. 110–114. In constituencies of mixed religious composition party leaders give prayerful attention to balancing the ticket by including in positions of appropriate prominence Catholic, Protestant, and Jew.

[3] See Peter Odegard, *Pressure Politics, The Story of the Anti-Saloon League* (New York: Columbia University Press, 1928).

[4] See Walter Johnson, *The Battle Against Isolation* (Chicago: University of Chicago Press, 1944).

Cruelty to Animals, the Ohio Society of Old Age Pensioners, the Fifth Ward Neighborhood Improvement Association, the Southern Conference for Human Welfare, the American Foundation for the Blind, the Anti-Profanity League, the American League to Abolish Capital Punishment, the National Association for Universal Fingerprinting, the National United Italian Associations, the National Noise Abatement Council, the American Wildlife Institute—these suggest the range of organized groups that, among other activities, interest themselves in public policy.

Obviously examination in detail of these and scores of other groups is not feasible. It is sufficient to note that they leave their impress in the books of congressional statutes, state laws, and municipal ordinances. In this chapter it is proposed to concentrate attention on three types of groups—veterans, Negroes, and the professions—together with some of the general problems of politics relevant to their operations.

1. VETERANS' ORGANIZATIONS

"The American idea of war," said Thomas B. Reed, Speaker of the House, in 1897, "is to take the farmer from his plow, and to return him to his plow—with a pension!" [5] Every war has been followed by the establishment of a society of veterans to bring pressure for the creation of conduits from the Federal Treasury to the pockets of the veterans. It may fairly be questioned whether the pension objective is in reality the basic cohesive element in veterans' organizations. Deeply etched recollections of shared experiences that set the soldier apart from the civilian undoubtedly cement such groups together, but their preoccupation with bonuses, pensions, and like matters is certainly their most prominent characteristic.

Grand Army of the Republic. Of organizations of old soldiers, the greatest, until the American Legion, was the Grand Army of the Republic, which consisted of Union veterans of the Civil War. The G.A.R. played a peculiar role in American politics. About three million persons served in the Union armies in the Civil War. Normally they would be expected to be adherents of the Union, later known as the Republican, party. The political affiliations of the G.A.R. membership and its sectional concentration gave the pension issue an especial appeal to Republican politicians. Pension appropriations would in most instances reach Republican hands and, in turn, would cement the Civil War veteran more thoroughly to the Republican party. The

[5] Quoted by Nicholas Murray Butler, *Across the Busy Years* (New York: Scribners, 1939), Vol. 1, 298–299.

loyalties of northwestern war veterans, assured by pension legislation as well as by the Republican homestead policy, must be given a place among the factors holding together within the Republican party for many years the divergent interests of eastern finance and western agriculture.[6]

In the election of 1888 the influence of the pension issue was especially notable. The desire of the G.A.R. for pension legislation was cultivated and stimulated by its official organ, *The National Tribune*, published by the head of the largest firm of pension attorneys in Washington. Pension agents, who waxed prosperous by pressing the claims of the old soldiers for their just due, were desirous of increasing the sphere of their work. The election of 1888 presented the pension issue squarely. Cleveland had aroused the animosity of the veterans by vetoing certain pension legislation; the Republicans nominated Harrison, an old soldier. The Democrats favored reduction of the tariff as a means of reducing the Treasury surplus; the Republicans thought the surplus might well be disposed of by an increase in the payments to veterans. In the doubtful state of Indiana the pension issue was most strongly played up. Republican speakers went about "representing Cleveland as an inhuman monster and Benjamin Harrison as an angel of mercy carrying a purse hanging mouth downward." The victory for Harrison has been interpreted as a victory for the G.A.R. Cleveland lost both Indiana and New York, states in which pension agitation had been strong. Whether the vote of the soldiers decided the election, the Harrison administration proceeded to give the soldiers what they wanted to the accompaniment of considerable maladministration in the pension office.[7]

American Legion. The success of the G.A.R. in the extraction of money from the Federal Treasury has been greatly overshadowed in magnitude by the operations of the American Legion. Formed after World War I, the Legion soon achieved a membership of around one million, or about one third of those eligible for membership. It gave promise of eventually disappearing with the death of its generation of veterans, but a new crop of veterans came with World War II. The Legion's vigorous campaign to recruit younger veterans enabled it to claim a membership of over 3,000,000 in 1946.

[6] The Confederate veterans looked to their state governments for pensions and consequently southern Democrats viewed with a cool eye proposals for federal pension legislation.

[7] See D. L. McMurry, "The Political Significance of the Pension Question, 1885–1897," *Mississippi Valley Historical Review*, 9 (1922), pp. 19–36; McMurry, "The Bureau of Pensions during the Administration of President Harrison," *ibid.*, 13 (1926), pp. 343–364.

The Legion is organized in local posts, which are grouped in state legions, all capped by the national organization, led by the National Commander. Legion policies are formulated at annual conventions, colorful gatherings that became somewhat more sedate during the inter-war years with the advancing age of World War I veterans. During the interim between conventions the National Commander and the executive committee, with the aid of a staff of over 200 at national headquarters, carry out Legion policies. The Legion constitution provides:

> The American Legion shall be absolutely non-political and shall not be used for the dissemination of partisan principles nor for the promotion of the candidacy of any persons seeking public office or preferment. No candidate for or incumbent of a salaried elective public office shall hold any office in the American Legion or in any Department or Post thereof.

In the interpretation of this clause there is in practice no limitation on the Legion in the promotion of public policy. Like the Farm Bureau Federation or the National Association of Manufacturers, the Legion does not nominate or endorse candidates for public office; nevertheless, it reserves freedom of action in making its wishes known and in bringing its strength to bear on legislative bodies on questions of public policy. The nonpartisan policy serves the same function in the Legion that it does in other pressure groups: that is, it prevents division on questions of candidates for public office and at the same time permits the maintenance of unity on those issues in which Legion members possess a common interest.

Although the Legion has branched out and taken an interest in a wide range of public issues, its central concern and probably the magnet lending cohesion to the group has been the hope for additional compensation, perhaps ultimately a pension, from the Federal Treasury. In 1920 the Legion succeeded in persuading Congress to raise the monthly pensions for disabled veterans from $30 to $100 a month. In 1924 came its first great success when it induced Congress to grant adjusted service compensation, or the "bonus," which was, in effect, a bonus to be paid with accrued interest in 1945. In 1931 the Legion was back again asking, successfully, that veterans be permitted to borrow on their bonus certificates. In 1936 legislation providing for immediate payment of the bonus was passed. In its bonus campaigns the Legion has been able to drive through Congress bills over the vetoes of President Coolidge, Hoover, and Roosevelt.

How is the power of the Legion to be explained? Undoubtedly war veterans, especially those disabled in battle, have a special claim on their country.   The general sentiment supporting that claim creates a favorable atmosphere for the work of the Legion.   Moreover, from a political standpoint, a matter of no small importance is the fact that the Legion has no compact and active counter-pressure group against which to work.   If the A.F.L., for example, strikes out for legislation, its lobbyists will likely be met head on by the lobbyists and publicity experts of the National Association of Manufacturers.   The Legion, however, encounters no such opposition.   Apart from these favorable conditions, the Legion leaves nothing to chance.   Its Washington lobby is one of the most able.   It maintains complete records of the positions taken by each Congressman on matters of interest to the Legion; it is able, through its local Legion posts in every congressional district, to lay down a formidable bombardment of telegrams and letters on Congress. It is not clear that the leadership of the Legion always represents either the interests or desires of the rank and file of its membership.   A professionalized leadership or oligarchy has arisen that is able in an authoritarian manner to carry along the membership of local Legion posts, or at least prevent expression of serious disagreement with national headquarters policy.[8]

In the public mind the Legion is identified chiefly with the bonus, yet it has been interested in a broad range of legislation.   At a recent session of Congress the Legion legislative committee pressed for action on 124 pieces of legislation.   A matter of major interest to the Legion has been the question of adequate hospital facilities for veterans.   This service was originally limited to veterans disabled in the course of military duty, but under the pressure of the Legion eligibility for public hospital and medical care has been repeatedly broadened until it approaches socialized medical and hospital care for all who served in the armed forces, regardless of whether the need arises from service-connected causes.   Another important point in the veterans' program has been preference in public employment.   In this the Legion demands that preference be given to veterans regardless of their ability in comparison with other applicants.[9]

[8] In congressional debate on a bill backed by the Legion, Representative Simmons of Nebraska, a Legionnaire, said: "The statement is made that the passage of this bill has been persistently urged by the American Legion, but from that it does not follow that the rank and file of the membership of this great veterans' organization either know its provisions or approve of its passage.   Reluctantly I have reached the conclusion that in this matter the National Convention of the American Legion does not represent the sentiment of either its membership or of the service men of the nation."   Quoted by Marcus Duffield, *King Legion* (New York: Cape and Smith, 1931), p. 54.

[9] For the information on the measures in which the Legion interests itself, see the *Proceedings* of the annual convention in which reports of the Washington representa-

Another phase of the Legion and politics remains to be mentioned. Officially, in keeping with its nonpartisan policy, the Legion does not nominate or endorse candidates. Yet Legion politics is an avenue toward eminence in politics outside. By winning an election as Post Commander, Department Commander, or as National Commander, a man may achieve prominence and later gain support in party campaigns. A striking example is the political career of Paul V. McNutt, who gained sufficient renown in his Legion work eventually to become governor of Indiana and later a presidential possibility. Thus, Legion politics is a stepping stone toward political preferment. Moreover, candidates with Legion membership do not hesitate to recall that fact to their "buddies" and appeal for support on that ground. In turn, party leaders in making up slates usually try to see that there is a Legionnaire on the slate who has a strong appeal for the "Legion vote." In this respect the Legion, as Legion, perhaps has no special political significance. Party leaders usually compose their slates to make like appeals to the Catholics, the Irish, the Elks, or whatever other group seems to be of importance in their constituency.

Other veterans' groups. While the Legion has been the largest veterans' organization, other groups have maintained a separate existence. The Veterans of Foreign Wars, formed after the Spanish-American War, limits its membership to veterans who have had overseas service and thereby excludes the home-front soldier. The program of the VFW is a "bread-and-butter" program much like that of the Legion. Its 1945–1946 legislative program, for example, included 91 items, a large proportion of which related to the enlargement or maintenance of veterans' perquisites. The Disabled American Veterans is a veterans' group of long standing. Its small membership consists of persons with disability incurred in military service, a condition of affiliation which gives its legislative demands a special moral force.[10]

After World War II the older veterans' organizations campaigned vigorously to enlist the new generation of ex-soldiers. Their efforts promised to test the capacity of well-entrenched oligarchies to assimilate a new and younger group. In its past record the Legion had both an asset and a handicap in its membership campaigns. The Legion had consisted mainly of the more prosperous veterans of World War I. As a consequence its program on issues apart from narrow "bread-and-

---

tive appear. Veterans' organizations also concern themselves with a wide variety of state legislation. In 1946 a 300-page book was required to summarize state laws granting perquisites and privileges of one sort or another to veterans. House Committee on Pensions, 79th Cong., *State Veterans Laws* (1946).

[10] See Charles Hurd, "Who Speaks for the Veterans?" *Common Sense*, August, 1945, pp. 9–11.

butter" questions had been conservative, if not reactionary. It had shown little sympathy for labor unions. It had shouted for nationalistic measures and for national defense but had shown little awareness of the threat of fascism. This record stimulated those of contrary political inclinations to attempt to form new organizations to attract the veterans of World War II. Further factors stimulating new organizations were the absence of common experience between the veterans of the two wars and their differences in age and outlook.

The two principal new groups formed were the American Veterans of World War II (known as Amvets) and the American Veterans Committee (commonly called the AVC). Both groups are small, but Amvets, a cautious middle-of-the-road organization, has attracted less public attention than the AVC. The little but lusty AVC has had the temerity to challenge the old and mighty Legion on issues of public policy. The Legion, for example, regards the Dies Committee highly, whereas the AVC declares it to be an abomination. The AVC declares for "Citizens First, Veterans Second." The Legion and the VFW hint "Communism." The charge of Communism could not be established in 1946, but the AVC was generally to the left of the Legion. In 1946 it seemed doubtful that the new organizations could make much headway in recruitment of members against the entrenched veterans' groups which were utilizing their strength to the utmost to discredit and to freeze out the upstart societies. Yet the situation suggested that perhaps in the future veteran pressures would represent more of a cross-section of the entire veteran population than in the past.[11]

2. ELECTORAL EFFICACY OF PRESSURE GROUPS

The successful pressure operations of the American Legion raise a general question about the activities of pressure groups: To what extent can these societies threaten the continuance in office of the legislator who resists their demands? To what extent does the power of the pressure group rest on this electoral threat? Pressure organizations differ widely in the degree to which they attempt to sway the electorate. Some organizations, like the Anti-Saloon League in its hey-day,[12] openly and vigorously sought to influence voters for or against particular candidates according to their attitudes on the liquor question. Other groups, as the Legion, are avowedly nonpartisan and unconcerned with

11 See Willard Waller, *The Veteran Comes Back* (New York: Dryden, 1944); Charles G. Bolte, "The New Veteran," *Life*, December 10, 1945; L. G. Milner, "How American Is the Legion?" *New Republic*, 111 (1944), pp. 329–331; Sam Stavisky, "The Veterans Make Their Choice," *Harper's*, September, 1946, pp. 251–258.

12 See Odegard, *op. cit.*

elections, yet in their work there is present the suggestion of more or less spontaneous reprisal at the polls by their members against those who fail to support their program. Some groups depend on a general propaganda to influence the electorate toward their cause rather than on campaigns with respect to particular candidates. Nevertheless, the strength of all such groups is often supposed to rest ultimately on the probable action of their members at the polls. The late Frank Mondell, a prominent Republican congressional leader, concluded in 1923 that the political fortunes of Congressmen had come to depend "to a considerable extent upon the good will, the friendly attitude, the friendly reports of gentlemen who, as legislative representatives sit in the galleries, and, as the favored ones in old Roman days decreed life or death to the struggling gladiator in the arena by gesture of thumbs up or thumbs down, determine the political life and fortunes of members of Congress."

Are pressure groups stronger than parties? To what extent can organized minorities crack the electoral whip? No method of analysis is available to obtain the answer absolutely, but the limits of pressure-group electoral strength may be defined. The American Legion succeeded in persuading the House of Representatives to override presidential vetoes before the election of 1922, 1924, 1928, 1930, 1934, and 1936. If the membership of the Legion supported its friends and fought its enemies, regardless of their party affiliation, supposedly those members who had followed Legion leadership in the House would be returned to Congress in the next election in greater proportions than those members who had voted to uphold the presidential veto. If figures on all the elections following these vetoes are lumped together, the following ratios are obtained:

80.8 per cent of those who had voted to override the presidential vetoes were re-elected to the House;
77.4 per cent of those who had voted to sustain the presidential vetoes were re-elected to the House.

The difference between these two ratios suggests the outside limits of Legion influence over the entire period. Of course, it is not to be concluded that the slight advantage of Legion supporters was entirely attributable to the veteran vote. Many other variables entered into the outcome of these contests. One of those factors was party affiliation. At almost every congressional election there is a "trend" to one party or other. The question may be raised whether a Representative who followed the Legion line could overcome the trend against his party at the subsequent election. Or whether a representative who opposed the

Legion line would thereby lose sufficient strength to offset the advantage from the "trend" toward his party. The following computations, again lumping together all the elections in question, test these hypotheses:

85.4 per cent of the Representatives were re-elected who belonged to the party that gained seats and who had voted to override vetoes of Legion-sponsored measures;

84.3 per cent of the Representatives were re-elected who belonged to the party that gained seats and who had voted to sustain the presidential vetoes;

74.2 per cent of the Representatives were re-elected who belonged to the party that lost seats and who voted to override presidential vetoes of Legion-sponsored measures;

71.5 per cent of the Representatives were re-elected who belonged to the party that lost seats and who voted to sustain presidential vetoes.

Here again a presumption arises of an almost negligible advantage to supporters of the Legion, but note that a Representative belonging to the party reaping the advantage of the general trend is much more likely to be re-elected than persons of the opposite party regardless of their stand on Legion-sponsored measures.[13]   The figures suggest that votes are more apt to be influenced by the voters' evaluation of a party in general rather than by their evaluation of the voting record of a particular individual.   With striking exceptions, of course, a Congressman need not be greatly worried when a lobbyist says we "shall bear these voting records in mind election time," or "you will be sorry" come election day, or "we will certainly remember those who prove to be our friends and also those who are not."

Another indicator of the influence of the general trend toward a party in determining the outcome of congressional elections is furnished by the election of 1938.   In that year the Republicans did not lose a single district that they had carried in 1936; the trend from 1936 to 1938 was toward the Republicans, and Republican candidates in districts Republican in 1936 benefited from that trend to the extent that none of them lost.   The eighty seats that the Republicans gained in 1938 tended to come from among those districts that had been most narrowly won by the Democrats (or by Progressive candidates in a few instances) in 1936.   The general drift of sentiment was sufficient to pull these districts across the line into the Republican camp.   Of the 80 new seats won by the Republicans in 1938:

[13] The data on which the above is based are presented in more detail by Key, "The Veterans and the House of Representatives: A Study of a Pressure Group and Electoral Mortality." *Journal of Politics,* 5 (1943), pp. 27-40.

42 were from districts that had gone Democratic in 1936 by from 50.0 to 54.9 per cent of the major-party vote;

27 were from districts that had gone Democratic in 1936 by from 55.0 to 59.9 per cent of the major-party vote;

11 were from districts that had gone Democratic in 1936 by from 60.0 to 64.9 per cent of the major-party vote.

The conclusions from the foregoing data would have to be: (a) either that only Democrats antagonized pressure groups or (b) that Democrats suffered from the trend away from their party. That trend, of course, may have been helped along by operations of pressure societies that amazingly pushed in the same direction everywhere. There remains, of course, the possibility that pressure groups exerted their influence in the nominating primaries and conventions. In view of the low popular participation in most primaries they would presumably furnish organized minorities the best opportunity to wield the balance of power. Investigations on this point do not justify any general conclusions. It may be pointed out that the Republicans carried 90 congressional districts in both the election of 1936 and that of 1938. Of the ninety Republicans elected in 1936, eighty-three were returned in 1938. Of the seven who did not reappear in 1938, at least four died in office and one went to the Senate. Thus a maximum of two of ninety Republicans may have been the victims of organized minorities. Of the 264 seats carried by the Democrats in both elections, 224 were won by the same individuals. Of the 40 persons who did not return, nine died in office, three resigned before the end of their term, and three went to the Senate. The Democrats thus had a higher ratio of electoral mortality in the nominating process than did the Republicans.

Do voters "punish" individual Congressmen? Another factor that has some bearing on the theory of electoral penalization of legislators because of their vote on particular issues is the degree to which electors are familiar with their representative and with his voting record. Opinion polls indicate that a substantial proportion of the electorate is unfamiliar with the name of its representative. In a poll by the American Institute of Public Opinion in 1942, 50 per cent of the respondents were unable to give the name of the Representative from their district. Familiarity with the name of the representative was lowest in cities of over 500,000 and increased in each successive group of smaller cities reaching its highest point among farmers.[14] A poll by the National Opinion Research Center in 1944 revealed that only 31 per cent of the cross-section questioned could name both Senators correctly. Famili-

[14] Release of April 11, 1942.

arity with the names of Senators varied directly with education and economic status and was about twice as great among men as among women. Both polls included questions that revealed a high degree of unfamiliarity among the electorate with the attitudes of their Representatives and Senators on particular issues.

These findings are not startling; moreover both polls were taken at a time long in advance of the election before the information of the campaign could have made much impress on the voters. Nevertheless, they lend some support to the hypothesis that the voter tends to express a general approval or disapproval of the course of governmental policy as determined by the party in power. This postulate, if true, rebuts the assumption of a fine discrimination among individual candidates regardless of party, under the leadership of pressure groups, in so far as the great mass of the electorate is concerned.[15]

A plausible tentative conclusion may be that one must look, in the main, to factors other than their power to punish at the polls to explain the influence of pressure groups. They gain power in some instances merely from having representatives on hand to present their case to the legislator. In others their influence is founded on the simple fact that the legislator tends to go along with whatever interests are powerful in his district: a farmer from a corn-growing district is not apt to go counter to the American Farm Bureau Federation on an issue pertaining to corn. In still others the legislators' convictions may happen to coincide with the interest of particular groups. Yet a pervasive but unmeasurable influence may come from the legislator's fear of retaliation at the polls, by the fear, for example, not that he cannot be re-elected but that he may have to go to the trouble and expense of making a fight in the primary to win a renomination.

3. RACIAL AND NATIONALISTIC MINORITIES: THE SPECIAL CASE OF THE NEGRO

Among the cleavages that crisscross the population and give rise to opposing groups in politics are those between racial and nationalistic groups. The existence of such minorities adds immeasurably to the complexity of political life; and when nationalistic or racial drives are in the direction of disunity, they increase the difficulties of political leaders in holding together a combination powerful enough to govern.

---

[15] An odd illustration is furnished by the plaintive comment of Republican representatives supporting the extension of price control legislation in the spring of 1946. A great volume of critical mail arrived demanding that they support the Administration's price control program. The voter must swing with a broad ax and in swinging the ax it is much easier for him to differentiate between parties than between the voting records of individual representatives.

Yet probably nowhere else in the world has the problem of assimilating diverse peoples into a cultural and political system been so effectively accomplished as in the United States. It cannot be said that minority peoples have suffered no oppression; but the absence of formal legal restrictions has enabled them after a time to gain positions of political leadership, to acquire sophistication in the political ways of the new land, and to become in varying degrees culturally assimilated.

In this process of assimilation political parties have played an important role. Party leaders have sought the support of nationalistic groups and perhaps at times temporarily accentuated nationalistic feelings. Yet avenues of advancement in the party organization have been open to persons of foreign birth and extraction. Party activity has led to fairly rapid induction into public office and to responsibility and concern for a community broader than the national group. The party thus has been a significant instrument for the initiation of the new citizen into the life of American society. Germans, Poles, Italians, Irish, Swedes, Norwegians, and others have been amalgamated into the American community.[16]

The American political system has accommodated itself with fair success to immigrants of the white races regardless of their national origin. The Negro, however, has presented a far more difficult problem for a democratic political order. The normal political processes broke down at the time of the Civil War, a war fought between whites about the Negro. From the Civil War onward the status of the Negro was continuously an issue in American politics, an issue to which there seemed no solution. In this respect it was unlike other questions that seemed nearly always to be in process of settlement, given enough time and a modicum of good will among the disputants. With regard to the place of the Negro in American life, however, it has never appeared that working arrangements satisfactory to all concerned were emerging. The problem has been aptly characterised by a renowned Swedish scholar as "an American dilemma." [17]

To make this consideration of the Negro relevant to the subject of pressure groups, it is necessary to note the existence of the National Association for the Advancement of Colored People, which is an organization not solely of Negroes but, in considerable measure, of northern whites interested in the advancement of colored people. The NAACP operates after the fashion of pressure groups generally by lobbying for

[16] The first edition of this book (pp. 149–155) contains a brief account of nationality groups and American politics. For a more complete discussion, see P. H. Odegard and E. A. Helms, *American Politics* (New York: Harper, 1938).

[17] See the monumental treatise by Gunnar Myrdal, *An American Dilemma, The Negro Problem and Modern Democracy* (New York: Harper, 2 vol., 1944).

and against legislation of concern to its constituency. It has advocated federal anti-lynching legislation, the repeal of the poll tax, the adoption of measures against discrimination in employment, and the repeal of discriminatory statutes. It has participated actively in litigation to protect Negro rights and to test the constitutionality of legislation and practices affecting Negroes adversely. The story of the Negro in American politics, however, is much broader than the story of the NAACP.

In the United States the Negro as a group most nearly approximates the repressed minorities of minority-ridden European nations. Denial of easy access to participation in politics, denial of equal treatment in the administration of law and public services, frequent exclusion from trades and professions—these are but a few examples of the disabilities of the group. Translated into terms of dollars and cents—even if one excludes from calculation the psychological currency of security—the Negro is on the average much poorer than the white.

After the abolition of slavery, the theory was held by the dominant Republican leaders that the Negro could attain a status of equality and could protect himself against discrimination if he were given the ballot. As a basis for Negro participation in political life the Fourteenth Amendment, adopted in 1868, declared all persons born in the United States to be citizens and thereby unquestionably made Negroes citizens. The same amendment forbade any state to "make or enforce any law which shall abridge the privileges or immunities of citizens of the United States," to "deprive any citizen of life, liberty, or property without due process of law," or to "deny to any person within its jurisdiction the equal protection of the laws." Thus, the Negro was to receive the protection of the federal courts against discriminatory state action. The Fifteenth Amendment, which became effective in 1870, forbade the denial or abridgment by any state of the right of citizens to vote "on account of race, color, or previous conditions of servitude."

These constitutional guarantees have not brought about assimilation of the Negro into normal political life. During the period of Reconstruction, Negroes were able, with the assistance of white immigrants from the North known locally as "carpetbaggers," to control the governments of the southern states. When federal troops were withdrawn from the South, however, the Reconstruction governments collapsed and white supremacy was soon restored. Even now the Negro exercises the suffrage only to a very limited extent in these states.[18] But in some southern states Negroes have an opportunity to participate in national politics through their control of the Republican state organizations

---

[18] The question of Negro suffrage is discussed in ch. 16.

and, in turn, of the delegates to the Republican national conventions. In some southern states "lily-white" policies exclude Negroes from the Republican organizations. In the northern and border states the Negro has exercised the suffrage more freely; especially in the northern cities has he been able to exert his strength in politics. That strength is reflected in the election of Negroes to city councils, to state legislatures, and occasionally to the bench. In the complex factional politics of certain cities the Negro has gained significant influence in the selection of officers chosen at city-wide elections. In Chicago, for example, the Thompson faction of the Republican party leaned heavily upon the Negro vote, which constituted up to one fifth of the entire vote cast in the Republican primaries.[19] Seldom, however, does the Negro exert a strength commensurate with his numbers. If Harlem, for example, were filled with Irishmen instead of Negroes, New York City would probably resemble the Irish Free State, but the Negro influence is less pervasive.

In national politics the Negro has been traditionally allied with the Republican party from the historical association of that party with abolition and with the promotion of Negro rights. The Republican monopoly of the Negro vote, however, was broken by the Democrats under the leadership of Roosevelt. In the election of 1936 a large proportion of the Negro voters in the North swung to the support of the Democratic candidate. Following the election Negro sentiment, in common with that of all groups, veered away from the Democratic party. The American Institute of Public Opinion estimated that 76 per cent of Negroes in the northern states were Democratic in 1936; 66 per cent in June, 1940; and 64 per cent in August, 1940. In 1944 no estimate was published, but probably a slightly further disaffection of the colored vote occurred because of discrimination against Negroes in the Army, the unsatisfactory Democratic stand on the proposed Fair Employment Practices Act, and the inflammatory remarks of southern statesmen restive under a national policy hostile to southern beliefs. Despite these factors 60 per cent of Northern Negroes early in 1946 still regarded themselves as Democrats. The destruction of the blind loyalty of the Negroes to the Republicans has great significance. The concentration of the Negro vote in a few northern centers, with the consequence that a shift of the group one way or another may influence the electoral vote, gives the group potentially great influence.

[19] H. F. Gosnell, "How Negroes Vote in Chicago," *National Municipal Review,* 22 (1933), pp. 238–243. The only thorough analysis of the political behavior of the urban Negro is Gosnell, *Negro Politicians* (Chicago: University of Chicago Press, 1935).

To understand the nature of the equilibrium between white and black it is necessary to look beyond formal law and government. Interracial conflict in the United States has been settled, provisionally of course, by methods separate and apart from law. The relative status of the black and the white—and the Negro definitely occupies the subordinate status—is governed by folkways approaching in nature a caste system. These unwritten codes of behavior are most effective in the South, but they are not unfelt elsewhere. The Negro may live in certain areas and not in others. He may engage in certain occupations, but from others he is excluded. Toward whites he must maintain a respectful demeanor, but whites are not under a reciprocal obligation. Churches, school, labor unions are likely to be closed to him. And all these folkways are buttressed by a body of tradition, beliefs, and rationalizations.[20]

In a brilliant article, Guy B. Johnson has analyzed the process of interracial accommodation within the framework of the so-called caste system. Militant Negro leaders have sought interracial equality, but the door to equal participation has been closed and "the Negro has taken the only course left to him, namely, the building of a whole system of society on his side of the color line. The extent to which this process has gone is not appreciated by the average white man. In addition to the more visible separate schools, churches, and fraternal orders, there is a multiplicity of institutions and organizations which have grown up to answer the needs of the separate racial economy." [21] Booker T. Washington was the great expounder of the doctrine of submission and conciliation. In this, says Johnson, he relieved white tension and anxiety "on three points in particular: political participation, education, and social relations." To the Negro he preached that salvation would come, not through gaining "political participation or social status," but through "making a living, . . . becoming economically secure, . . . gaining competence and respectability." Johnson concludes that the effect of this social segregation of the Negro group is that "Negro life has become differentiated into social and economic classes in much the same way as white life. There is no real unity, no cohesion, in Negro life, and a truly race-wide leadership is virtually impossible." Leadership within the subordinate group, "particularly within the southern region, has rested on the approval of the dominant group as well as the following of the Negro group." Thus

[20] See the analysis by John Dollard, *Caste and Class in a Southern Town* (New Haven: Yale University Press, 1937).

[21] Guy B. Johnson, "Negro Racial Movements and Leadership in the United States," *American Journal of Sociology*, 43 (1937), pp. 57–71. See also Allison Davis and others, *Deep South* (Chicago: University of Chicago Press, 1941).

an interracial *modus vivendi* has been developed based to considerable degree on territorial, social, and economic segregation.[22]

It is not to be concluded that the existing relationship of superiority and subordination and the pattern of distribution of perquisites is morally "right," although it has worked over fairly long periods of time. Nevertheless, the *modus vivendi* represents an extremely unstable equilibrium characterized by considerable dissatisfaction on all sides. Its instability—and perhaps its transitory nature—is illustrated by events of World War II. To forestall a "march on Washington" the President in June, 1941, established a Fair Employment Practice Committee and a policy of nondiscrimination in employment in defense industries, to be enforced by clauses in government contracts. As the strain on productive resources became greater the need for more extensive use of Negro labor became pressing, and more energetic measures were taken. The resultant reaction of white workers and employers set off loud complaints, particularly by southern politicians, that the prevailing social system was threatened. Bitter speeches on "white supremacy" in Congress and elsewhere mirrored a widespread social tension not only in the South but also in other centers of Negro concentration. Even the Ku Klux Klan gave signs of revival. In the Democratic national convention of 1944 southern delegates successfully opposed endorsement of the establishment of the Fair Employment Practice Committee on a permanent statutory basis; some southern delegates appeared to regard this matter as the most important issue before the convention. Subsequently in the Senate the southern Democrats utilized the right of sectional veto—that is, the filibuster and threat of filibuster—to check bills to establish a permanent Fair Employment Practice Committee.[23]

The problem of the Negro has been commonly regarded as a problem of the South, but the migration of large numbers of Negroes to such northern cities as Chicago, Detroit, and New York is rapidly changing the geographical distribution of the Negro population. Perhaps the most critical problems of race relations are emerging in northern metropolitan centers. The changes in distribution of the Negro population since 1900 are suggested by the figures in Table 5. In the post-

---

[22] See Charles S. Johnson, *Patterns of Negro Segregation* (New York: Harper, 1943).

[23] For further data on the Negro, see C. S. Johnson, *The Negro in American Civilization* (New York: Henry Holt, 1930); C. S. Mangum, Jr., *The Legal Status of the Negro* (Chapel Hill: University of North Carolina Press, 1940); W. F. Nowlin, *The Negro in American National Politics* (Boston: Stratford, 1931); Roi Ottley, *'New World A-Coming'* (Boston: Houghton Mifflin, 1943); St. Clair Drake and H. R. Cayton, *Black Metropolis* (New York: Harcourt, 1945); S. O. Landry, *The Cult of Equality* (New Orleans: Pelican, 1945).

TABLE 5

Percentage of Total Population Negro in Selected States and Cities, 1900 and 1940

State	1900	1940
Mississippi	58.5	49.2
South Carolina	58.4	42.9
Louisiana	47.1	35.9
Georgia	46.7	34.7
Alabama	45.2	34.7
Florida	43.6	27.1
Arkansas	28.0	24.8
Michigan	0.6	4.0
Detroit	1.4	9.2
New York	1.4	4.2
New York City	1.8	6.1
Illinois	1.8	4.9
Chicago	1.8	8.2
Ohio	2.3	4.9
Cleveland	1.6	9.6

World War II era prospective technological developments in cotton production threatened to accelerate the movement of the Negro from southern agriculture to northern industry. The cotton-picking machine and the contrivance of chemical and mechanical means for the performance of other hand labor traditional to cotton culture promised to create agricultural unemployment and a resultant critical problem in population distribution and race relations.

4. THE PROFESSIONS

The prestige enjoyed by the professions has given their associations a political role of considerable importance. Within certain restricted spheres the professions are quite as powerful as the Farm Bureau or the American Federation of Labor. Yet when professional associations venture beyond these restricted areas their influence rapidly wanes. When their demands run counter to the interests of other well-organized groups, the conflict may end in compromise or defeat. Although it is commonly said that the public business is a matter of general concern, a great many legislative decisions and administrative acts have immediate interest and effect for only a small group. In those situations the affected group can often determine what the public policy shall be.

Of greatest concern to the professional associations is the control of entrance to the professions. Since the licensure of trades and professions is within the jurisdiction of the states, the chief political activities on this matter have been by the state associations, but the national professional associations have played a role of leadership. State medical societies and state bar associations have consistently fought for the establishment by law of higher qualifications for the right to practice these professions. In the continuous drive to raise the standards of admission, the medical societies and bar associations have been animated by mixed motives. The medical men have sought to drive out the incompetent and the quack in the name of the public interest. The lawyers have attempted to prevent the licensing of persons who would be unable competently to serve their clients. Further, both professions have, especially of late, been motivated by a desire to restrain competition.

One method of controlling entrance to a profession is by permitting its numbers to grow until professional fees are forced down by competition to the point at which economic considerations make entrance into the profession unattractive. Another is to raise the educational requirements and to make more difficult the entrance examinations. The lawyers and doctors have been adherents of the latter doctrine—a sort of "planned economy" for the professions. But it cannot be said that their attempts to ration the supply of lawyers and doctors have been based on any thoroughgoing analysis of public need for these services.[24]

Encouraged by the success of the lawyers and doctors, other groups have requested the intervention of the state in the matter of licensure. These groups, with more or less plausibility, justify their demands with the claim that they occupy a position analogous to that of the professions. Plumbers, accountants, engineers, electrical contractors, barbers, cosmetologists, pharmacists, architects, chiropractors, dentists, osteopaths, movie-projector operators, optometrists, real-estate salesman, insurance agents, morticians, nurses, naturopaths, and others have succeeded in persuading legislatures to create examining and licensing boards. In those trades connected with the building industry the power to license is notably abused; its control by the leaders of local unions, acting in combination with builders' associations, is often used to restrain competition.

A characteristic of the politics of the professional associations is the tendency toward the establishment of a guild system—that is, control over entrance to the profession by the profession itself.[25] In practice, a sort of pluralism has arisen in which the profession controls the standards of the profession in the name of the state. When legislative action is needed, the well-established professional societies can usually

[24] See E. C. Brown, *Lawyers and the Promotion of Justice* (New York: Russell Sage Foundation, 1938), pp. 164–195.

[25] See the thoughtful comments by Francis P. DeLancy, *The Licensing of Professions in West Virginia* (Chicago: Foundation Press, 1938).

bring about its passage. "Within its field," says McKean, the New Jersey "Medical Society is very influential. It can usually block such bills as it does not like, and it can secure the passage of the measures it approves." [26]   In the administration of licensing laws the organized profession usually has a strong voice. The governor will give heed to its recommendations in the appointment of members of the examining board. Not infrequently the statutes require the governor to appoint from the nominees of the professional society, and sometimes the law even delegates the power of appointment to the association. The trend toward the guild system has gone to the logical extreme in the establishment in some states of an "integrated" or "self-governing" bar to which all licensed lawyers must belong and which exercises, by delegation from the state, the power to admit to the profession and to discipline for unprofessional conduct. In some instances the state licensing and regulatory authority can act only with the formal consent of the regulated group. Thus, rules and regulations of the South Dakota state optometry board do not become effective until approved by the state association of optometrists.[27]

The profession attempts to protect its sphere from encroachments by new and competing groups. The orthodox medical practitioners have resisted efforts of chiropractors, osteopaths, and "drugless" healers to establish themselves. The first line of resistance has been on the question of licensure. Chiropractors, for example, have usually had to obtain positive legislation to permit practice before they could follow their calling without violating the state medical-practice acts. The medical men have usually been able to do no more than delay the chiropractors in their effort to obtain legislation. Then the battle shifts to other fronts. The unorthodox healers seek to obtain the right to practice in publicly supported hospitals and to serve the beneficiaries of workmen's compensation laws. The orthodox medical men fight in the name of the protection of the public against quacks; the newer groups demand the protection of the individual's right to choose his own physician. Similarly, the bar associations resist the practice of law by laymen. The encroachments of banks and trust companies in the field of estates and trusts have been fought by the lawyers, but large areas formerly exclusively in the province of the lawyer have been lost.[28]

[26] *Pressures on the Legislature of New Jersey* (New York: Columbia University Press, 1938), p. 71.

[27] For an interpretative survey of legislative and judicial tendencies, see J. A. C. Grant, "The Gild Returns to America," *Journal of Politics*, 4 (1942), pp. 303–336, 458–477.

[28] See M. L. Rutherford, *The Influence of the American Bar Association on Public Opinion and Legislation* (Philadelphia, 1937), pp. 93–99.

The political power of the professional group is likely to decline as the objectives of the profession encounter opposition from other interested groups. In some instances in defending their own status, the professions protect the general interest; at other times they delay readjustments that would promote the general welfare.

An interesting dispute has raged in recent years over the attitude of the American Medical Association toward the economic organization of medical practice. The national association and the state medical societies have generally opposed the introduction of health insurance under public authority, as well as the introduction of group practice under private auspices. To fight health insurance the association employs the ordinary methods of propaganda and lobbying; to deal with private group-practice plans it does not need to invoke the power of the state but can proceed by expulsion of the offending doctors from the medical societies and by other means. Although the majority opinion in the profession appears to be with the policy of the bureaucracy of the American Medical Association, certain leaders in the medical world have risen to challenge the orthodox view on health insurance.

The experience of the Medical Association suggests two important questions on the political role of the professions. At what point does the expert become a layman whose views perhaps deserve no special weight on the sole ground that authority should be conceded to competence? It may not be questioned, for example, that the wisest policy is to permit organized medicine to determine the amount of time the prospective doctor shall spend in studying anatomy. Perhaps when it comes to the question of the method of payment for medical service— by arrangements with individual practitioners at the time the service is required or by monthly deductions from the pay check under a system of health insurance—the attitudes of the profession may carry political weight but not the conclusiveness of expert opinion. Thus, Dr. Morris Fishbein, of the A.M.A., opined that the Wagner-Murray-Dingell social-security bill was "perhaps the most virulent scheme ever to be conjured out of the mind of man." This judgment should probably be placed on a different plane than Dr. Fishbein's opinion on the desirability of utilizing the cathartic qualities of Epsom salts under specified conditions.

The second point that the experience of the Medical Association suggests is that as a professional association expands its sphere of action beyond the narrow core of professional concern fissures are likely to develop. The A.M.A. is by no means rent internally with dissent, but there is important disagreement with the official policies. When the

experts engage in public disputes among themselves, their influence
is likely to diminish on all fronts.[29]

A striking indication of the projection of social and economic cleavage into a professional group is furnished by the organization of the
National Lawyers Guild. Dissatisfaction with the generally conservative attitude of the American Bar Association led to the forming of
another group to include

. . . all lawyers who regard adjustments to new conditions as more important
than the veneration of precedent, who recognize the importance of safeguarding and extending the rights of workers and farmers upon whom the welfare
of the entire nation depends, of maintaining our civil rights and liberties and
our democratic institutions, and who look upon the law as a living and flexible
instrument which must be adapted to the needs of the people.[30]

The Guild was organized mainly by lawyers of New Deal tendencies.
Even prior to the formation of the Guild, a few local groups had split
off from the established bar associations for reasons not unlike those
that motivated the founders of the Guild.

Professional associations commonly concern themselves with varying
sorts of public policy that do not immediately affect the narrow vocational interests of the group. In the promotion of these causes pe-
ripheral to their interests, the professional guilds are usually neither
so energetic nor so effective as they are in the protection of the core of
guild interest. In these larger undertakings, moreover, they are usually merely one of a larger number of groups interested.[31]

5. A TREND TOWARD A NEW GUILD SYSTEM?

The tendency of professional associations to gain virtual control of
the making and administering of laws vitally affecting their members
exemplifies a recurring and persistent drive by other sorts of groups
to gain similar positions of influence. The tendency is to seek to control those aspects of public policy of immediate concern to the group.
The traditional constitutional theory is that public power must be exercised by the government and may not be delegated to private groups.
This doctrine has been violated so frequently in the case of professional

[29] See the valuable article by Oliver Garceau, "Organized Medicine Enforces Its
'Party line,'" *Public Opinion Quarterly*, 4 (1940), pp. 408–428; also his *The Political
Life of the American Medical Association* (Cambridge: Harvard University Press,
1941).

[30] Quoted from the guild's constitution by Brown, *op. cit.*, p. 147.

[31] See H. F. Gosnell and M. J. Schmidt, "Professional Associations," *The Annals of
the American Academy of Political and Social Science*, 179 (1935), pp. 25–33; Rutherford, *op. cit.*; E. M. Martin, *The Role of the Bar in Electing the Bench in Chicago*
(Chicago: University of Chicago Press, 1936).

and semiprofessional groups that some observers raise the question whether we are not seeing a return of the guild system. Professional groups are not alone in attempting to gain control of phases of public power to be exercised by themselves without political accountability. In many areas the assertion is made that particular groups should be allowed a deciding voice in public policy determination and administration.

In searching for evidences of a trend toward "guildism" or "pluralism" in politics generally, the observer must differentiate sharply between the formal, or the legal, and the actual in governmental practice. The importance of this distinction may be inferred from a reconsideration of the role of professional groups. In the making of law, the professional group may be merely consulted; at the opposite extreme, the legislature may habitually enact into law without question the recommendations of the professional association. In both instances the form is the same; that is, the legislature makes the law. Yet the actual situations covered by the identical form differ greatly.

Similarly, form and practice in the administration of law may not, and often do not, coincide. The professional association may exert its influence by making representations to the agency regulating the profession; it may influence the governor to appoint its nominees to the regulatory body. The power of the professional association tends to become formalized when legislation provides that the governor must appoint its nominees to the regulatory agency. In all these forms, however, the formal authority of the state is preserved, but the power actually exercised by the private group may be great or little, whatever the form. The ascertainment of the precise degree to which a private association actually controls law and administration is a matter of no little difficulty; hence, attention is directed to the "tendency" toward guild autonomy, not to the "degree" of autonomy that actually prevails.

Nonprofessional associations infrequently win formal delegations of public power in the same manner as professional groups have. Yet examination of the actual relations of power indicates a similar effort by groups of many varieties to seize public power. In the examination of legislative practice it is exceedingly difficult to ascertain when representative bodies become rubber stamps for private interests, but the efforts from time to time of some private groups to take over the administration of law are readily perceptible. Administrators have broad discretion, and private groups often seek to influence, if not to control, the exercise of that discretion. In this endeavor private organizations use all the familiar devices of the pressure group: direct suasion, political threats, the stirring up of threats from "back home," the stimulation of editorial criticism, the manufacture of propaganda. On occasion the private group presumes in effect to issue orders to the government. In 1946 the Executive Committee of the American Legion had the effrontery virtually to summon General Omar Bradley, the Administrator of Veterans Affairs, to appear before it in Indianapolis to defend his policies. The General found it "impracticable" to attend and invited the Committee to appear in his Washington office at its convenience.

Relationships between private groups and administration go considerably further than aggressive pressure on the government. An intermingling of government and private instrumentalities sometimes goes so far as to make the line between public and private hazy indeed. In state governments, for example, it is often difficult to tell at what point the state banking department ends and the state bankers association begins. Professor Fesler, after an examination of the situation in several states, concludes: "State banking departments are typically dominated by the bankers' association of the state. . . ." He finds that the control of state departments concerned with insurance companies and building and loan associations is "roughly analogous to that of banking departments." [32]

This interweaving of the public and the private is often accomplished by influence, sometimes virtual control, over appointments to public office. In seeking to influence the selection of administrative officials, private groups almost invariably demand the designation of one of their own kind, of their own group, a person who "understands" their problems. The following resolution by the American Federation of Labor indicates the general spirit:

WHEREAS, The various Government agencies dealing with the problems of labor and labor relations are headed and staffed with executives who are not trained in the Labor Movement, therefore, be it

RESOLVED, That the American Federation of Labor make known by way of official communication to all such Government agencies and to the President of the United States, its opposition to the appointment in executive and/or administrative positions any person or persons who have not been trained in the Labor Movement and who are not themselves members of Organized Labor.[33]

Almost all groups try, either openly or covertly, to influence appointments to administrative positions in governmental agencies affecting

[32] "Independence of State Regulatory Agencies," *American Political Science Review*, 34 (1940), p. 943.

[33] American Federation of Labor, *Proceedings*, 1944, p. 534.

the group. In some instances this relationship is modified and formalized through the grant of permission to the association to designate boards advisory to those legally responsible for the administration of law. In the management of the range in the national forests, for example, the Forest Service consults with advisory boards representing local, state, and national livestock associations. In carrying out the Agricultural Adjustment Act, the Secretary of Agriculture was directed by Congress "to utilize the services" of state and local committees elected directly and indirectly by the farmers affected by the act. In these and other consultative relationships a close integration of public and private views may result, with the consequence that private groups positively contribute to the development of public policy in a spirit of comprehension of broad public needs in contrast with the typical narrow interest of the pressure group. The give-and-take between administrator and private spokesman may modify the views of the lobbyist, as well as those of the public official.[34]

Sometimes private associations are heard in open hearings by the administrative agency charged with the duty of issuing regulations. In the issuance or amendment of certain regulations under the Federal Food, Drug, and Cosmetic Act of 1938, for example, the Secretary of Agriculture is directed to hold a public hearing at which any interested person may be heard in person or by his representatives. Trade associations are the principal spokesmen for the industries to be affected by proposed regulations. Other agencies employ other devices to consult with the affected interests. Prior to the promulgation of new regulations in 1936 the Bureau of Marine Inspection and Navigation obtained criticism of the proposed regulations from such groups as the National Council of American Shipbuilders, the American Merchant Marine Institute, the Pacific Steamship Owners Association, and the Lake Carriers Association. During World War II the War Production Board build up an extensive system of industry advisory committees to aid in the framing of regulations and in the formulation of other policies concerning particular industries. These committees consisted of businessmen chosen by the Board in a manner to be representative of all segments of each industry: large and small, trade association and non-trade association, southern and northern.[35]

In some situations the relationship between the official agency and the affected interest is not carried on in a goldfish bowl. The Attorney

[34] See the discussion by John D. Lewis, "Democratic Planning in Agriculture," *American Political Science Review*, 35 (1941), pp. 232–249, 454–469.

[35] For a treatment of the practical and theoretical aspects of representation of interests, see Avery Leiserson, *Administrative Regulation, A Study in Representation of Interests* (Chicago: University of Chicago Press, 1942).

General's Committee on Administrative Procedure reported that the Federal Alcohol Administration, "not unlike other deliberative bodies, is not immune from the pressure of lobbying. Attempts to affect the agency's judgment are made *sub rosa* not only directly by the lobbies maintained by the industry, which are among the most potent in the country, but also indirectly through the legislative and executive branches of the Government. It is impossible, of course, to gauge the precise effect of these efforts upon the agency, but the pressure exerted through other official groups is said unquestionably to have some influence." [36]

In many instances executives and administrators seek informal consent or approval of leaders of pressure groups for contemplated courses of action. In some areas of federal administration the normal procedure is to advise these persons in advance of major decisions and to ask their approval. This type of relation does not prevail in quasi-judicial proceedings, but in other sorts of action it occurs frequently. In some instances consent is required by law as an antecedent to action, but such formal consent is ordinarily required of the persons to be affected rather than of their associations. The Department of Agriculture has made extensive use of referenda, both at its own option and under statutory requirement, as an antecedent to the initiation of administrative action. For example, a favorable vote of tobacco growers must occur before the Department can initiate a program of inspection and certification affecting a tobacco market. [37]

For administrative agencies to hear the views of private associations or to consult with them is quite different from the actual devolution of public power to the private group. From the examples that have been mentioned it may be inferred that the relationship between government and private association approaches the true guild form only rarely. Possibly the nearest approach, both in fact and in form, is a self-governing bar in which the association becomes a public agency vested with public power. Other professional associations tend toward true guilds in fact but not so often in form. Professional associations have a fairly homogeneous membership and a corporate sense. In other types of associations, however, the unity of interest and of objective is not usually so marked, and the group's domination of the governmental agency concerned is likely to be less complete. There may be, for example, a tendency for farm organizations to take over the operation of a state department of agriculture, but the fact that there

[36] Senate Document No. 185, Part 5, 76th Congress, 3d sess., p. 32.
[37] See L. V. Howard, "The Agricultural Referendum," *Public Administration Review*, 2 (1942) pp. 9–26.

may be several farm organizations leaves greater actual power in the hands of the state.   Probably the most vivid demonstration of the guild tendency in the non-professional fields of activity appeared in the National Recovery Administration when the directing groups of trade associations were assimilated into the governmental structure as code authorities to exercise governmental power over their respective industries.   The code authorities attempted to enforce as law in large degree the same kinds of rules that they had earlier sought, as private associations, to have their members follow.   This transition from the code of ethics of a private group to public law or rule illustrates the frequent tendency of law or rule to evolve from the workings of private groups that attempt to set up standards for the guidance of their own members.   In business endeavor these privately made rules are frequently, but not always, moves toward the restriction of competition.[38]

These examples of the interplay between government and private groups suggest the infinite variety of relationships that exist between ruler and ruled.   They range from private appropriation of state power to refined methods for obtaining the consent of the governed. They suggest the significance and difficulty of the problem in a highly differentiated society of arriving at the proper division of power between the state and the private association.

The tendency of power and influence to gravitate toward private associations has led some political theorists to advocate a reconstruction of the state in which formal power and authority would be vested in what are now private groups.   These doctrines of pluralism were influential in the theory of the Italian corporate state, although it seems doubtful whether the corporate nature of the Italian state ever advanced much farther than the theoretical stage.   A fundamental weakness of guild socialism and other pluralistic theories is that special interests cannot be depended on invariably to promote the public interest.   In one respect the chief problem of the sovereign state is to prevent private associations from injuring the general public.   And one method by which that end is achieved is through the compromise of conflicts between groups, which may, to be sure, involve a recognition at particular times that the public interest may be advanced by yielding to this or that private association.   Without the sovereign state, it is easy to imagine the anarchy of groups that would arise with the delegation of public authority to private associations.[39]

[38] See E. L. Heermance, "Self-Regulation and the Law," *Harvard Business Review,* 10 (1931–32), pp. 420–429.

[39] Consult Walter Gellhorn, *Federal Administrative Proceedings* (Baltimore: The Johns Hopkins Press, 1941), especially Part 4.

Chapter 6

SECTIONALISM AND URBANISM

THE GROUPS whose activities are described and analyzed in the preceding chapters are organized on non-geographical bases. Thus, the American Farm Bureau Federation presumes to speak for its farmer-members wherever they live. The National Association of Manufacturers considers itself to be the spokesman for manufacturers everywhere. The Congress of Industrial Organizations does not limit its membership to persons of a particular locality but to workers generally. Likewise the American Legion defines its constituency without the use of geographical criteria. All these interest groups whose basis of organization is non-geographical are often referred to as "functional" groups. This designation distinguishes them from groupings of persons defined geographically, such as sections, regions, states, cities, districts, wards.

Although regional, sectional, and other territorial interest groupings are not pressure groups in the usual sense of the term, it is desirable to consider these geographical political entities along with pressure groups. The political demands of the "functional" group often have the appearance of a sectional movement. Economic interests and functional groups are often segregated geographically. Senators and Representatives are elected from geographical areas rather than from "functional" constituencies, and when legislators speak for a functional group strong in their region the blocs within Congress take on a sectional form. Moreover, for many years it has been the custom to interpret American politics in large measure as a process of conflict and reconciliation between the great sections of the nation. It has been usual to speak of the North against the South, of combinations of the South and West against the Northeast, of the dominance of the North, of the conservative South, of the isolationist Midwest, and so forth. It is suggested in this chapter that the sectional interpretation of the cleavages of interest within American politics needs to be re-examined in the light of more recent developments, among which is the rise of powerful interest groups of non-geographical character.

In the study of politics one finds recurrent and persistent cleavages of interest along territorial lines: the people living in one area are arrayed against those living in another over one type of issue or another. An elementary example in municipal politics is a dispute between different sections of a city about the location of public facilities, such as parks, playgrounds, and schools. Similarly, disputes between the people of different areas occur frequently in state politics. At times issues of real substance are at stake. At other times no discernible issue of policy exists; a candidate from the northern section of a state, for example, may appeal to the people in his home territory to vote for him so that "we" may have one of "our" men as governor.[1] Such appeals to territorial interest and loyalty and such friction between the people of different areas are commonplace. Although the great conflicts between different sections of the nation in national politics are on a much larger scale, they are essentially of the same kind. On the international plane politics is almost purely conflict and adjustment between territorially defined groups of people.

To understand its real nature this phenomenon of intersectional conflict needs to be examined more closely. Does the mere fact that some people live in one part of the country and others in another generate sectional disputes for power? There may exist sectional and regional loyalties of people—to the South, to the West, to New England—that are not without strength. Differences in dialect, in social customs, in history set off the people in one area from those in another. Even without any other differences between the people of different areas, the mere fact of geographical segregation may furnish some basis for regional rivalries. More often, however, sectionalism is but a mask for some other interest. The concentration of cotton-growing in the South and of manufacturing in the Northeast is a better explanation of regional political differences than is the fact that some people are Southerners and others Northerners.

Is the mere fact that manufacturing is concentrated in one area, wheat cultivation in another, and cotton-growing in a third enough to create sectional disputes? Another factor must be present! When issues of governmental policy arise that affect different sections differently—one favorably, the other adversely—then sectional conflict

---

[1] The study of sectionalism in state politics has not been carried far, but for example of the possibilities in this sort of interpretation, see Paul Murray, "Economic Sectionalism in Georgia Politics, 1825–1855," *Journal of Southern History*, 10 (1944), pp. 293–307.

occurs. If issues arise between economic interests territorially segregated in sections of the nation, the intensity of conflict is increased by the fact that there are compounded with economic demands and interests the group strength and cohesion that come from loyalty to a particular region. In the United States the most significant basis of intersectional friction is undoubtedly to be found in the differing economic interests of the different sections; these, in turn, have developed in considerable measure from the varying geographic endowments of sections.[2]

If sectionalism has been to a large degree an expression of the economic interests of our great geographical regions, the inquiry may well be made why one need differentiate between these sectional cleavages and other conflicts over matters economic. Is not the conflict between agricultural and manufacturing populations, both of which are interspersed in the same area, identical with the same dispute between like populations territorially segregated? The issues may be identical, but their settlement may be more difficult. The differences may be more bitter and more persistent, for the way of life of a region may lead its citizens to look upon the "outsider" as an "alien"—a feeling not fundamentally unlike that of the people of one nation toward those of another in times of international dispute. In a nation of continental proportions in which geographic economic specialization finds expression in political sectionalism, the situation has potentialities of territorial disintegration that otherwise would not exist to the same extent. The factor of territorial differentiation and conflict in extreme form poses for the politician the problem of manufacturing a formula, a compromise, for the maintenance of national unity.

1. THE ADVANCING FRONTIER AND SECTIONALISM

Among great nations of modern times the United States has been unique in possessing a special type of sectional conflict growing out of the gradual spread of population over a continent. Long-established nations have sectional issues, but the westward movement in the United States caused the existence, over long periods of our history, of a special type of political conflict. The areas settled first along the Atlantic seaboard furnished capital for the development of the western

---

[2] This is not to suggest that all intersectional conflict has an economic basis. Intersectional rivalry may be founded on noneconomic territorial differentiation. In Canada, for example, the French-speaking, Catholic population is mainly concentrated in Quebec, while the remainder of the dominion is primarily Protestant and English-speaking. Issues between the two sections are by no means solely economic in nature.

wilderness and thereby created a relationship of creditor and debtor between geographically differentiated groups; and, as James Madison observed, the clashes of interest between debtor and creditor have always been a "durable" source of faction. In other ways the interests of the East and of the advancing frontier were in conflict. A thinly populated agricultural West had interests that often ran counter to those of the more densely populated financial and industrial East. And the dominance of the East in all matters was threatened by the development of the West.

Sectionalism and the Constitution. The early rise of sectional conflict in American politics is indicated by the fact that the debate over the adoption of the Constitution took the form of a dispute between the frontier and the seaboard. It has been observed earlier that conflict described or carried on in terms of sectionalism is often but a mask for underlying differences of interest of some other kind. In his classic study, *An Economic Interpretation of the Constitution*, Charles A. Beard has shown the importance of economic interests at stake in the adoption of the Constitution. In classifying the interests involved in the formulation and ratification of the document, Beard noted the existence of an important class of small farmers located mainly back from the seacoast, on the fringe of westward settlement, from New Hampshire to Georgia. This western inland section had interests antagonistic to those of the people of the seaboard. The small farmer was frequently in debt, often to a seaboard speculator, for his land; and he had to rely on the capital of the seaboard to develop the newly opened country. As a consequence of the difference of interests between the West and the East, there were to be found legislative proposals disquieting to the East, such as easy-money schemes to alleviate the lot of the debtor and laws postponing the collection of debt, an early parallel to the modern "mortgage moratorium."

Quite different were the economic interests of the owners of personal property, concentrated principally along the Atlantic seaboard. Property in the form of money was endangered by the demands for inflation emanating from the West. Public securities were selling at far below par, and ownership of the public debt was certainly not concentrated among the small farmers of the West. Manufacturing and shipping suffered from the tariff barriers between the individual states and from the absence of a strong central government to protect and promote their interests. Easterners owned large blocks of western lands that could not be profitably sold or developed in the absence of a strong central government.

In concluding an analysis of the vote on the ratification of the Constitution, Beard says: [3]

Inasmuch as the movement for the ratification of the Constitution centered particularly in the regions in which mercantile, manufacturing, security, and personalty interests generally had their greatest strength, it is impossible to escape the conclusion that holders of personalty saw in the new government a strength and defence to their advantage.

Inasmuch as so many leaders in the movement for ratification were large security holders, and inasmuch as securities constituted such a large proportion of personalty, this economic interest must have formed a very considerable dynamic element, if not the preponderating element, in bringing about the adoption of the new system.

. . . .

The opposition to the Constitution almost uniformly came from the agricultural regions, and from the areas in which debtors had been formulating paper money and other depreciatory schemes.

The cleavages in the battle over the adoption of the Constitution projected through into politics under the new federal government. Time was on the side of the growing West, which found its first great spokesman in Jefferson. The power of the Federalists depended primarily on the

. . . support of the wealthier classes of people and rested particularly on a combination of the commercial interests of the North Atlantic coast region, the tobacco planters of Virginia, and the rice planters of South Carolina. In 1801 Jefferson at the head of the Democratic-Republican party broke the power of this combination and obtained control of the federal government. There has been much discussion in recent years of the economic basis of Jeffersonian Republicanism. Out of the dust of controversy emerges the simple proposition that Jefferson succeeded in organizing the greater portion of the back-country grain growers from Maine to Georgia into a coherent "bloc," which formed the strongest element in his victorious combination.[4]

Jacksonian Democracy. Under the vigorous leadership of Jackson the Western forces were again united against those of the East, or at least against the moneyed parts of the eastern population. Jefferson and Jackson built their fences on the solid soil of unity of the sectional interest of the then West. Says Professor Woodburn: [5]

[3] *An Economic Interpretation of the Constitution of the United States* (New York, 1913), pp. 290–291. Quoted by permission of the Macmillan Company, publishers.

[4] A. N. Holcombe, *The Political Parties of To-day* (New York, 1924), p. 83. Quoted by permission of Harper and Brothers.

[5] J. A. Woodburn, "Western Radicalism in American Politics," *Mississippi Valley Historical Review*, 13 (1926), pp. 143–168.

For fifty years after Jefferson's triumph the democracy which he promulgated found its support not only in the western parts of the original thirteen states but in all the oncoming new states of the West. Omit the South and think only of the states of the Northwest, Ohio, Indiana, Michigan, Iowa, Wisconsin. The party of Jefferson and of Jackson was able to carry these states, as also Pennsylvania, until close to the days of the Civil War, until the restriction of slavery had become the dominant issue in American history and the Democratic party had come largely under the control of southern slaveholders.

The simple pattern of conflict between the seaboard and the frontier, however, was soon replaced by a more complex pattern of sectional interests. The issue of slavery and the Civil War split the western following of Jefferson and Jackson into northern and southern segments; the extension of settlement to the West formed additional regions with their own distinct interests. So long as there was a frontier, there was a frontier interest, but the regional or sectional interest of the frontier was only one part of a pattern of sectional division more complex than the simple cleavage of the East versus the West.

An interesting feature of the westward movement and of sectionalism was that party affiliations and attitudes of the East tended to be projected into the newly settled West. As the "solid West" disintegrated, "rival societies, free and slave, were marching side by side into the unoccupied lands of the West, each attempting to dominate the back country." [6] The process of colonization, in the later years at any rate, "largely followed the advance of the railroads. The result of this was that new settlers from the older sections tended to locate in groups with the further result that whatever sectional or political division may have existed in the older sections of the country tended to be reproduced in the areas where large groups of people from these sections assembled." [7] The Democratic and Republican parties, Dr. Boothe believes, "were able to extend their influence into the frontier sections of the country and to maintain their supremacy as political parties even though they were not adequately fostering the interests of the newer sections, the interests of which were becoming increasingly divergent from those of either the North or the South." [8]

In some respects the influence of economic motivation in the friction between the frontier and the older sections often has been overestimated. To some extent the complaints of the frontier were simply a demand

[6] Turner, *The Significance of Sections in American History* (New York: Holt, 1932), p. 27.
[7] Viva Belle Boothe, *The Political Party as a Social Process* (Philadelphia, 1923), p. 45.
[8] *Ibid.*, p. 29. See also J. K. Wright, "Voting Habits in the United States," *Geographical Review*, 22 (1932), pp. 666–672.

for a voice in the government, a concession that the East granted only grudgingly. Normally a lag occurs in the adjustment of governmental institutions in accordance with the territorial redistribution of population. The great westward movement will not be duplicated, but the relocation of population continues, and the adaptation of governmental institutions and the distribution of political power territorially are a recurring source of friction. The movement of population from the country to the cities—a movement equal in significance to the westward movement—has likewise been accompanied by friction and delay in institutional adjustment.

2. POLITICS OF SECTIONALISM

For the duration of the westward movement, the existence of a frontier created a tendency for conflict to take the shape of the frontier areas against the older settled parts of the country. As the frontier moved westward and more and more of the continent was developed, a more stable pattern of sectionalism developed. The newly settled areas acquired special economic interests, usually in accord with the nature of economic activity suitable to each, and the country became a checkerboard of natural territorial units each with its own political interest. We came to have, the late Professor Turner said, "unlike such countries as France and Germany, . . . the problem of the clash of economic interests closely associated with regional geography on a huge scale. Over areas equal to all France or to all Germany, either the agricultural or the manufacturing types are here in decided ascendency." [9] He likened the deliberations of party conventions and Congress and their outcome "to treaties between sections, suggestive of treaties between nations in diplomatic congresses."

The economic geography underlying some of these intersectional rivalries is suggested by Figures 4 and 5. Figure 4 shows the high degree of concentration of manufacturing in the states north of the Ohio and east of the Mississippi. Figure 5 shows the regional concentration of cotton production. Although these are only two of the many examples of regional differentiation and specialization, they have been extremely important in national politics. Northeastern manufacturing is always cohesive and influential in national politics, while cotton contributes to the unity of the South in the politics of the nation.

Intersectional combination and conflict. The existence of great sections with specialized economic interests creates the basis for conflict between these sections when issues arise on which their interests diverge.

[9] Turner, *op. cit.*, p. 36.

No single area, however, possesses enough power to control the nation. Intersectional combination, which inevitably carries with it some compromise of sectional differences, must occur before a majority can be formed. Political parties, in order to win elections and to govern, are compelled to unite sections with a total voting strength adequate to elect the President and a majority of Congress. And since the interests of those sections brought together under the same party manner may not be identical, there must be intersectional compromise within the party.

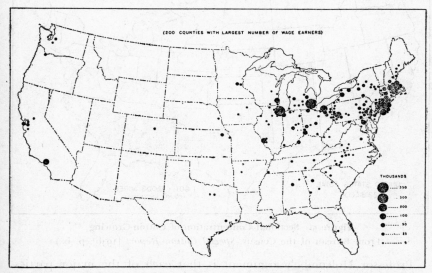

Figure 4. Regional Concentration of Wage Earners in Manufacturing Industries, 1935 (This figure shows the 200 counties having the largest number of wage earners. From National Resources Committee, *The Structure of the American Economy* [1939], Pt. I, p. 37.)

Professor Holcombe has made the most thorough analysis of American politics in terms of sectionalism. "National parties," he asserts, "as the history of national politics clearly demonstrates, can be formed only on the basis of durable combinations of sectional interests." [10] In an elaborate study, published in 1924, he attempted to trace the changing combinations of sectional interests making up both the major parties at various periods. Since American politics, up to that time at least, had been in the main agrarian politics, he sought to identify the principal sectional agricultural interests. By geography, for example, the South has been bound to cotton growing. The great

[10] *Op. cit.*, p. 355. Quoted by permission of Harper and Brothers.

corn belt stretches through Nebraska, Iowa, Illinois, Indiana, Ohio. The hay and pasture region, Wisconsin, Michigan, Pennsylvania, New York, and New England, constitutes another distinct agricultural section. The corn and winter-wheat belt includes most of Kansas, the southern half of Missouri, part of southern Illinois, Kentucky, part of Tennessee, western North Carolina, part of Virginia.

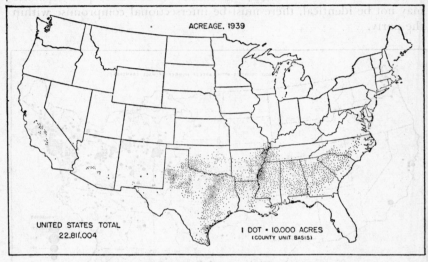

ACREAGE, 1939

UNITED STATES TOTAL
22,811,004

1 DOT = 10,000 ACRES
(COUNTY UNIT BASIS)

Figure 5.   Sectional Concentration of Cotton-Growing
(From Bureau of the Census, *Special Cotton Report* [1940], p. ix.)

Professor Holcombe's argument is that each of the major parties has been formed of a combination of sectional interests, that each party has had its most reliable and most faithful support centered in certain sections.   The Republican strength he found to be centered in rural and urban districts of the hay and pasture region, in the corn belt, and in the corn and winter-wheat region.   The most solidly Democratic sections he found to be the cotton belt, the subtropical coast region (an area on the fringe of the southern coast from Florida to southeastern Texas), and, in part, the corn and winter-wheat belts.   Each party, he shows, has had to reach out from its strongholds and annex the support of doubtful sections in order to win.[11]   The frequent

[11] The sectional interests that form the reliable and faithful core of each party gain a disproportionate influence in the party, and this assures that the economic interests of the section will be capably represented in the party councils.   The Democratic Senators and Representatives from the Solid South, for example, are re-elected term after term and gain positions of power in congressional committees under the seniority rules.   Similarly, in national conventions and in the informal party coun-

nomination by the Republicans of presidential candidates from Ohio, Indiana, and Illinois he interprets as a device to make the most "effective appeal to the farmers of the corn-growing regions," a doubtful area.

The formation of sectional combinations can be shown most clearly by analyses of elections of Representatives. However, in presidential elections from time to time the result is determined by the swing of a great section in one direction or the other. Compare, for example,

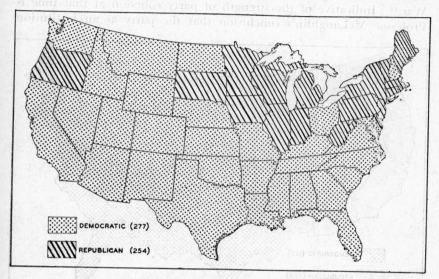

DEMOCRATIC (277)

REPUBLICAN (254)

Figure 6.   Electoral Vote by States in Presidential Election of 1916

the maps in Figures 6 and 7, which show the electoral vote by states in 1916 and 1920. In 1916 the Democratic South was joined by the West to overwhelm the North, while in 1920 the West moved over into the Republican column with the North to carry the election for Harding.

Maintenance of party unity necessitates compromise within the party between sectional interests.

The leaders of the Republican farmers of the Northwest are forced to favor a high tariff on cereals and a low tariff on manufactures, especially farm implements and supplies, while the leaders of the Republican manufacturers of the Northeast are forced to favor a low tariff on foodstuffs and raw materials and a high tariff on manufactured goods. . . . Likewise, the leaders of the Demo-

cils these persons, through long service in party affairs, gain positions of vantage from which to defend and promote the interests of their region. Likewise, Republican leaders from New England constituencies climb, through seniority, to positions of power in their party.

cratic cotton and tobacco planters of the South are forced to favor a tariff policy which is most objectionable to the Democratic sugar growers in the South and wool growers in the Far West.[12]

Although each party contains within itself sections with divergent interests, the party binds them together with bonds of great strength. The churches, for example, split into northern and southern branches earlier than the party ties broke in the friction leading to the Civil War.[13] Indicative of the strength of party cohesion at that time is Professor McLaughlin's conclusion that the party as an institution

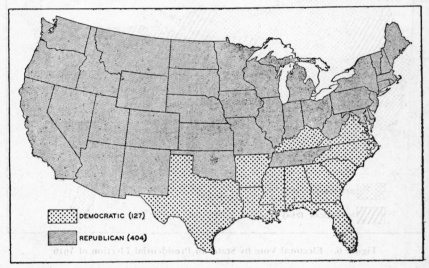

DEMOCRATIC (127)

REPUBLICAN (404)

Figure 7. Electoral Vote by States in Presidential Election of 1920

"was almost the last to yield to forces of disunion and disorganization; and, when it did yield, disunion was a fact." [14]

The politics of sectionalism is not solely a question of ironing out differences between sectional interests and uniting them to attain electoral victory. There remains the problem of relationships between the dominant sectional combination and the remainder of the country: the statesman must not carry his triumphant sectional combination too far in oppression of the interests of the losing areas. The

12 Holcombe, *op. cit.*, p. 352.   Quoted by permission of Harper and Brothers.

13 For a summarized presentation of Professor Holcombe's sectional interpretation of political behavior, see his essays in E. B. Logan (ed.), *The American Political Scene* (New York: Harper, rev. ed. 1938).

14 A. C. McLaughlin, *The Courts, The Constitution, and Parties* (Chicago: University of Chicago Press, 1912). p. 137.

success of our politicians in adjusting the interests of sections may be gauged by the fact that there has been only one Civil War. Prior to that struggle a series of compromises failed to yield a stable adjustment between sectional interests, and only military means could resolve the issue. Consideration of the Civil War illuminates the fundamental nature of all sectional disputes and highlights the importance of evolving workable balances between sectional interests. All other intersectional issues have been solved by the political technique of peaceful compromise; in all instances save the Civil War the issues were susceptible of settlement by means short of force. Professor Turner concluded: [15]

National party, then, has been in America a flexible bond, yielding in extreme cases to sectional insurgency, yielding often, in the construction of bills, to sectional demands and to sectional threats, but always tending to draw sections together toward national adjustments by compromise and bargain. A common language, law, and institutions, absence of sectional concentration of religions and races, absence of historical hatreds, have helped to prevent America from splitting apart and falling into European conditions; but regional geography, quasi-continental parties, and a national, that is intersectional (our equivalent of international), congressional organization by which sectionalism could express itself in voting instead of by war—these are important factors in the contrast between European and American ways of settling difficulties, and are important explanations of our continued unity.

Establishing intrasectional hegemony. Easy generalizations about sectionalism tacitly assume a homogeneity of interest within sections. If most of the people in an area possess like interests, presumably they will act alike in politics. The premise of homogeneity of interest, however, needs to be subjected to closer analysis. In fact, under present conditions, each region contains a diversity of interests that may or may not be conflicting. Before the section can exist and act as a political unit, these internal differences have to be ironed out. Unification of a section for its battles externally may be accomplished simply by the predominance of a single interest within the section: it is futile for lesser groups to protest that the majority voice of the section is in fact contrary to the will of minority elements. In other instances, the hatchet may be buried on some issues to attain sectional unity on others. For example, in the 'twenties a surprising similarity of view on the tariff issue prevailed between northern finance capital and northern organized labor. Or a sectional issue may have the happy faculty of cementing intrasectional groups. For example, in the free silver agitation of the latter part of the past century silver producers of the

[15] *Op. cit.,* p. 205.

mining states had a natural affinity for Bryanism but farmers for a different reason—the debtor's desire for a modicum of inflation—could join enthusiastically with silver producers and miners.[16]   In many instances apparent sectional solidarity, as manifested in congressional votes, does not reflect sectional homogeneity of interest; sharp intra-sectional differences may exist on some matters, but the indifference of some groups within the section to particular issues may allow other groups to make a show of sectional unity.

The South represents our most notable example of sectional solidarity.   That solidarity has rested not only on economic homogeneity but on a skillful maintenance of a dominant position within the South by a fairly small proportion of the population.   That condition is so marked that it suggests that sectional solidarity under present conditions must be mere façade concealing an oligarchical suppression or malrepresentation of substantial parts of the regional population.   Even prior to the Civil War, marked cleavages of interest existed within the South, and these differences in interest found expression in political parties. "The economic and political interests of the southern Whigs were the 'special interests' of the slavocracy.   During the early forties the Whig party was frequently denounced as the aristocratic party of the slave-holders."   Again: "Social distinctions served to confirm the lines which economic interests had already drawn.   The Whig planting aristocracy was a natural and an exclusive one."   The Democratic party "drew the opposite side of the social scale—especially upon the small farmer of the back hill-country who could always be reached by the party's appeal to the agrarian spirit." [17]   Before the South, as a section, could act as a unit it was necessary that the dominance of the slavocracy be established within the South.   In 1860, about 11,000 southern planters (about three fourths of one per cent of the total free population) owned fifty or more slaves each.   About 100,000 smaller planters owned from ten to fifty slaves each.[18]   The small, slaveholding segment of the population with almost a monopoly of wealth, talent, and leadership was able to impose its will on the South.[19]

16 See C. O. Johnson, "The Story of Silver Politics in Idaho, 1892–1902," *Pacific Northwest Quarterly*, 33 (1942), pp. 283–296.

17 A. C. Cole, *The Whig Party in the South* (Washington: American Historical Association, 1914), pp. 69–72.

18 Clement Eaton, *Freedom of Thought in the Old South* (Durham: Duke University Press, 1940), p. 35.

19 The strong position of the slaveholding class is vividly illustrated by the late Professor Dodd's statement that even "the Negroes knew a great war was beginning and that they were the objects of contention; but long discipline and curious pride in the prowess of their masters kept them at their lowly but important tasks.   They boasted that their masters could 'whip the world in arms.' "—*Expansion and Conflict* (Boston: Houghton Mifflin, 1915), p. 277.

After the Civil War another type of group succeeded in establishing its dominance in the South and maintained political solidarity over an extraordinarily long period. Oddly, the South's politics has been studied very little and the nature of its system of power has not been described in detail, but the main outlines are fairly clear. In the 1880's and 1890's the South was swept by the same type of agrarian radicalism that struck the Northwest. Conservatives in the South, representative of such indigenous enterprise as existed and of railroads and other enterprises owned outside the South, feared the radical movements as did conservatives elsewhere. From this point the documentation of conservative strategy becomes hazy, but the sequence of overt acts is plain. On the plea that the Negro must be kept in his place, state after state adopted poll taxes, literacy tests, and other requirements for voting. These suffrage limitations effectively disfranchised the Negro, but they also disfranchised a substantial element of the small, poor farming class, which furnished the core of agrarian radicalism.[20]

The use by Democratic leaders of the threat that the Negroes would hold the balance of power in the South if the whites divide plays an extremely significant part in the maintenance of the power of the ruling oligarchy. The anthropologists tell us that in primitive cultures the cohesion of social groups is mightily promoted by the proximity of unlike groups. The phenomenon of opposition stimulating unity exists also in nonprimitive cultures. Its strength is suggested by the data accumulated in Table 6. In 1928 several southern states broke

TABLE 6

Relationship between Percentage of Negro Population in Texas Counties and Presidential Vote by Counties in 1928

Per cent Negro at 1930 census	No. of counties	Number of counties in class that went —		Per cent of counties going Republican
		Democratic	*Republican*	
0.0–4.9	150	37	113	75.3
5.0–14.9	33	16	17	51.5
15.0–24.9	26	19	7	26.9
25.0–34.9	23	19	4	17.3
35.0 and over	22	21	1	4.5

away from the Democratic party because of the wetness and Catholicism of its candidate, Alfred E. Smith. The figures in the table show that

[20] See C. Vann Woodward, *Tom Watson, Agrarian Rebel* (New York: Macmillan, 1938); J. B. Clark, *Populism in Alabama* (Auburn, Ala., 1927); A. W. Moger, "The Origin of the Democratic Machine in Virginia," *Journal of Southern History,* 8 (1942), pp. 183–209.

attachment to the Democratic party was strongest in those Texas counties in which the proportion of Negro population was highest. In the counties with small percentages of Negro population the traditional partisan attachments were significantly weaker, but the Black Belt remained loyal to the Democratic party. It is, of course, quite probable that factors other than the Negro proportion of the population had influence in the correlation demonstrated by the table, but undoubtedly this factor played a major part in the pattern shown to exist.

The consequence of the factors entering into the southern political situation is that, by and large, southern politics has been dominated by machines in which were combined the wealthier farming classes, the local business interests, and the professional political group. A curious feature of the sectional structure of power has been that the southern governing oligarchy has allied itself in a considerable measure with economic interests external and often inimical to the interests of the mass of Southerners. The railroads, the petroleum industry, the utilities are in the main owned by outsiders. Moreover, other outsiders— northern manufacturing and finance—have a keen interest in keeping the South in a colonial status rather than in seeing it develop into a competitor.[21] In the years 1936–1946 no stancher defender of northern manufacturing and capitalism could be found than many southern statesmen in Congress. Conspicuous exceptions existed, to be sure, but the majority of southern senators and representatives recorded themselves on critical issues with fair consistency on the same side with Republican spokesmen for northern business. They tended to sacrifice the long-term interests of the South as a section for the short-term gains of the loose alliance of interests governing the South.

Yet another paradox of the South and its Democratic party is that the South must nurture liberalism. The only way in which it can win the Presidency is by allying itself with the West or with the laboring masses of the North. In periods of Republican ascendancy the Democrats retire to their southern strongholds and, as the party of the opposition, have no alternative but to speak as liberals against the conservative wing of the Republican party.[22] At propitious times the Democrats emerge from their southern hibernation with a Woodrow Wilson or a Franklin D. Roosevelt to challenge Republican domi-

[21] See B. B. Kendrick, "The Colonial Status of the South," *Journal of Southern History*, 8 (1942), pp. 1–22; A. B. Moore, "One Hundred Years of Reconstruction in the South," *Journal of Southern History*, 9 (1943), pp. 153–180; Marian D. Irish, "The Southern One-Party System and National Politics," *Journal of Politics*, 4 (1942), pp. 80–94; W. P. Webb, *Divided We Stand* (Austin: Acorn Press, 1944).

[22] See W. G. Carleton, "The Conservative South—A Political Myth," *Virginia Quarterly Review*, 22 (1946), pp. 179–192.

nance. Yet the conservative South in its alliances with the North or with the West does not wish to compromise on some issues to maintain Democratic unity. On the question of race relations, it stands adamant. On labor issues—wages and unionization, for example—it is willing to go so far and no farther. It has a dark streak of nativism, which manifests itself in the Ku Klux Klan and in anti-Semitic utterances. On these and other matters it threatened rebellion against the Democratic leadership in the presidential campaign of 1944 and was instrumental in defeating Wallace for the vice-presidential nomination. Moreover, by its stand on these questions, the South made a myth of the theory of party responsibility for legislation in the congressional sessions of 1945 and 1946.[23]

3. EXPRESSION OF SECTIONAL INTEREST

The mechanisms for the formulation and expression of regional demands are different from those employed to ascertain, formulate, and propagate the desires of nongeographical groups. Functional groups form associations outside the formal structure of government to state their desires. Thus, American business, or a substantial proportion of it, may speak through the Chamber of Commerce of the United States. Agriculture has its spokesmen in the Farm Bureau Federation, the Farmers' Union, the Grange, and various specialized organizations. Sectional interests do not rely on such nongovernmental associations to present their case. There is, for example, no Amalgamated Society of Southerners to carry on propaganda campaigns or to lobby in behalf of the cause of the South. Indeed, in a governmental system based on geographical representation no more suitable mechanisms for the expression of sectional aspirations can be found than spokesmen chosen by the voters in the districts composing the section.

Sectional blocs in representative bodies. Sectional interest, then, finds expression in all sorts of bodies and organizations based on geographical representation: Congress, state legislatures, party conventions, party committees. In the framing of platforms party conventions take into consideration sectional sensibilities and attempt to avoid jarring them. If the platform committee fails in this respect, an intersectional conflict may occur on the floor of the convention. Disputes over prohibition repeal in several Democratic national conventions tended to take the form of a sectional conflict. The debate over the farm plank in the Republican convention of 1928 arose because of

[23] See Carroll Kilpatrick, "Will the South Secede?" *Harper's Magazine*, March, 1943; H. C. Nixon, "The New Deal and the South," *Virginia Quarterly Review*, 19 (1943), pp. 321–333.

the platform committee's failure to conciliate leaders of the corn-hog areas in their recommendations.   In the selection of presidential candidates, sectionalism may play a part.   An important factor in the availability of an aspirant for the nomination is usually the apparent possession of capacity to draw voting support from all sections of the country —or at any rate the absence of a record that will hurt him as a candidate in any important section.   Occasionally minor parties arise on a foundation of sectional interest and dissatisfaction with the policies of the major parties.   The Populist party of the 'eighties and 'nineties was primarily a party of western agrarian unrest.   The later farmer-labor parties have tended to concentrate in the Middle West.   As for the post-Civil War Democratic party, we have one of the major political parties dominating and dominated by a region, the South.

In Congress, as questions arise that touch, either favorably or unfavorably, the status of the nation's great geographical regions, sectional groupings of Senators and Representatives occur.   On some issues fairly durable blocs persist from session to session and include in their membership Republicans and Democrats alike from the regions concerned.   Analysis of congressional votes would probably show considerable consistency of voting by spokesmen from the silver states, from the tobacco states, from the wheat states, from the cotton states. At times these groupings are so persistent that they gain a certain notoriety, but more frequently groupings on sectional lines are formed, dissolved, and reformed as occasion arises, so numerous are the divisive factors between sections and so varied are the sectional groupings into which a particular state may fall.[24]   Similarly, in state legislatures the members from one part of the state with a common sectional interest may band together to promote the shared cause.

Southern Governors' Conference.   The Southern Governors' Conference has functioned as a channel for the expression of sectional interest.   In 1941, in a memorial directed to the President, the governors called attention to "the dangerous and unwarranted centralization of national-defense production in the older and more congested industrial areas."   Of a total of "302 new plants, only 24 were located in the South."   The governors declared that the "best interests of the Nation can be served only if full use is made of the South's resources by industrial plants established in this area." [25]   The Conference has made a notable effort to reduce discrimination against the South in

[24] For an account of sectional cleavages in voting in Congress, see Hannah Grace Roach, "Sectionalism in Congress (1870–1890)," *American Political Science Review,* 19 (1925), pp. 500–526.

[25] *Congressional Record* (Daily edition), April 14, 1941, pp. 3139–3140.

the nation's freight-rate structure. Oddly enough the southern governors in their endeavor had little support from industry and business in their own region; they spoke more honestly for the long-run interests of their section than did southern business or the congressional delegations from southern states. Yet sectional unity through such groups as the Southern Governors' Conference tends to be transient, for there is a rapid turnover in the governors' chairs, and the mechanics of arranging co-operation among governors are not simple.[26]

These observations suggest that the federal system has been a factor of some importance in tempering the intensity of sectional feeling. With the division of each section into a number of states no effective machinery exists for the consolidation and expression of sectional demands. Unity of sectional action through cohesive action of combined state delegations in Congress is difficult to maintain. Division of sections into states weakens sectional drives that might come through the machinery of state government. The effect of the existence of a system of states dividing sectional interests into different political units can be better estimated by considering what would happen if there were, for example, a single cotton-belt state or a state of New England, with machinery for presenting its demands in national politics. By splintering and weakening the potential strength of sectional drives, the division of sectional interests into states contributes to national unity.

4. IS SECTIONALISM ON THE DECLINE?

An interpretation of American politics in terms of sectionalism has definite limitations. For sectionalism to exist in its most extreme form, it is essential that an economic interest, or some other interest, dominate a geographical region. Regional homogeneity of interest furnishes a durable basis for sectionalism. Thus, when there is sectional economic specialization with, say, agriculture dominant in one area and manufacturing in another, a sectional cleavage can be expected to arise. On the other hand, when sectional homogeneity declines—when a variety of interests exists in each region—and the differences between the various sections of the nation decline, political cleavages are not so likely to follow geographical lines. Perhaps that is the underlying reason why Professor Holcombe's sectional interpretation of our politics becomes somewhat strained today, as, indeed, he was one of the first to see. The tendency toward diversification of

[26] See H. C. Nixon, "The Southern Governors' Conference as a Pressure Group," *Journal of Politics*, 6 (1944), pp. 338–345.

economic interests within each of the great regions of the country weakens the fundamental basis of sectional unity.

Speculation on the likely course of sectionalism as a factor in American politics, then, must rest on an examination of underlying trends toward a continuation or a decline of sectional homogeneity of interest, the basic factor in sectional political unity. Factors of geography and of climate are constants that may condition the economic activity and, hence, the political attitudes of a region. So far as issues concerning silver are concerned, for example, the western silver-mining region is likely to remain a unit. The South, by geography and climate, is fitted for the production of cotton; the corn belt, for the production of corn and hogs. So long as we were predominantly an agrarian nation it could be assumed that the great crop regions, founded on climate and geography, would act as sectional units. But the dominance of cotton in the cotton belt and of corn in the corn belt is challenged. The economic basis for sectional unity tends to become weaker.

Diversification of interests dilutes sectionalism. How is the weakening of sectional solidarity to be explained? In large measure, the explanation lies in the diversification of interests within the traditional sections. In the South, for example, Professor Nixon says that as a result of the introduction of manufacturing it was "becoming rather respectable to be a Republican" in many manufacturing districts before 1928; furthermore, he attributes Hoover's southern vote in 1928 to "an interlocking of industrialism and Republicanism in the newer regions, where important interests sought insurance against upsetting the apple-cart of prosperity. That factor must be recognized with all due respect for the non-economic aspects of the religious and prohibition issues." He points out that the traditional southern attitude toward the tariff, conditioned by the dominance of the export crop of cotton, has been broken by the tariff attitudes of Florida and Louisiana on citrus fruits and sugar, of the Carolina manufacturers, of the Texas petroleum interests, and of the cottonseed oil and peanut industries in several southern states.[27] He also says that the South has an "urban proletariat" and a "rural peasantry" to be reckoned with, and that since 1930 a growing consciousness of group interest has arisen among southern tenant farmers, farm laborers, and industrial workers. All these factors have helped to weaken the unity of the sectional cotton empire.[28]

It does not necessarily follow that when manufacturing invades the South the southern manufacturer will make common cause with the

    [27] H. C. Nixon, "The Changing Political Philosophy of the South," *The Annals of the American Academy of Political and Social Science*, 153 (1931), pp. 246–250.
    [28] H. C. Nixon, "The Changing Background of Southern Politics," *Social Forces*, 11 (1932), pp. 14–18.

northern manufacturer, or that southern industrial labor will join with northern labor. As demonstrated by congressional debates over legislation fixing minimum wages and maximum hours of labor, the interests of the southern industrialist may be directly opposed to those of the northeastern manufacturer. The Southerner seeks to retain a lower rate than that prevailing in the Northeast; the Northeasterner fights as bitterly for a uniform wage rate so as to equalize that factor of cost between North and South. Yet on many other points of national policy they would be in agreement.

These remarks suggest that, paradoxically, sectional economic specialization may be a source of national cohesion as well as of division. The so-called "colonial areas," the South and the West, may fulminate picturesquely against the machinations of the manufacturing and money interests of the Northeast, but by virtue of geographical specialization itself the different sections are bound together by relationships of trade and mutual interdependence. It is only when maladjustments in these relationships give rise to a sense of discontent that sharp sectional conflict economically based is likely to take place.

It is easy to exaggerate the changes of the past forty years in the geographical distribution of industry. The movement of manufacturing away from the Northeast, for example, has been relatively slight. In 1899 the northeastern industrial area accounted for 86 per cent of the industrial jobs; in 1935, 82 per cent. Yet enough industry has developed in other sections to dilute the politics of former one-crop sections, both agriculturally and politically. Coupled with this tendency has been the decline in the relative importance of agriculture in the national economy. A dominantly agrarian economy is a remarkably good foundation for a politics of sectionalism since a sort of geographical and climatic determinism governs, within limits, the kinds of agricultural interests that will prevail in differentiated regions. The basis for agrarian sectionalism is weakened by the introduction of industry and other nonagricultural pursuits.[29]

Impact of urbanization. The great solvent of agrarian sectionalism is urbanism. A great area producing a major crop may be expected to carry along with it in national politics its small cities and villages that forage on the countryside, but a great industrial city is a different matter. It contains a variety of economic, racial, and social interests, often with little unity of purpose. It is possible to speak of wheat, say,

[29] For maps and analyses of the geographical distribution of production of different kinds—agricultural, industrial, and extractive—the student is referred to National Resources Committee, *The Structure of the American Economy, Part I, Basic Characteristics* (Washington, 1939), chap. 4, "The Structure of Production—Geographic Structure."

as the dominant concern of several millions of people scattered over several states. But, an equal number of people concentrated in the small area of a single city are not likely to be characterized by such unity of interest. The movement of a large proportion of the population to urban centers makes some of the older ways of thinking about our politics extremely unrealistic. Consider the maps in Figures 6 and 7 (pages 159–600), showing the electoral vote in 1916 and 1920. The

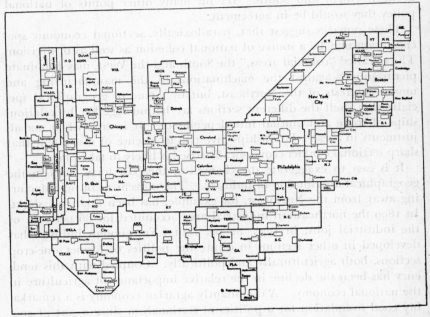

Figure 8. Picto-Map of the United States Showing States and Cities in Proportion to Population Rather than Area

(Copyright 1946 Erwin, Wasey & Company, Inc. Used by permission of the copyright owner and the United States Conference of Mayors.)

visual impression conveyed by such maps is of a population fairly evenly spread over a vast territory, with one section shifting from one side to the other in the two elections. A quite different impression of our politics is gained by thinking in terms of the map in Figure 8, which is, in a sense, no map at all. It shows the states in an area in ratio to their population, and within each state the boundaries of the major cities are drawn, not to geographical scale, but in proportion to the size of their population. Such a representation forcibly calls to attention the significance of cities in the total American population and, hence, in our national politics.

The general trend toward urbanism is, of course, well known, but a few specific facts are in order to nail down the proposition. In 1900, 39.7 per cent of our population lived in cities of over 2,500 population; by 1940, this proportion has grown to 56.5 per cent. More significant is the fact that by 1940, 140 metropolitan areas accounted for almost half (48 per cent) of the entire population of the country. The trend may be illustrated in another way. In 1900 we had 78 cities of over 50,000 population; in 1940, 199 such cities.

Political institutions lag in their adjustments to population changes, and the cities are generally underrepresented, in proportion to population, in state and national legislative bodies. Yet cities by virtue of the mere number of their inhabitants are coming to play a more and more significant role in national politics. Senators and Representatives from urban states constitute, after every census, a larger proportion of Congress. Similarly urban delegates to national conventions gradually become more numerous, and urban leaders occupy positions of greater importance in national politics since a larger and larger proportion of the votes in presidential elections are from the cities.

The growth of cities is not simply a matter of a quantitative increase in the proportion of the total vote in the cities. It involves also a qualitative change, at least in the cities of the North and West. The nature of that change is suggested by the figures in Table 7, showing the division of the major party vote in the presidential election of 1944 in counties containing cities of over 100,000 and in other counties. In the North and West the metropolitan counties gave Roosevelt a substantial majority, while Dewey led in other counties. The Democratic victory was in one sense a big-city victory. The cities could not have carried the election alone, but the Democratic majority there was sufficient to offset losses elsewhere.[30]

The qualitative change in politics wrought by urbanization consists chiefly in the introduction of class politics in substitution for or perhaps in supplementation of sectional politics. We still have sections, but something new has been added. Professor Holcombe points out that the old-time sectional struggles were primarily a "rustic politics." Parties were built mainly on a combination of agrarian and rural sections. The growth of cities introduced new interests into politics, and within the cities the primary political cleavage was inevitably along class lines.[31] The Democratic urban strength, as shown in Table 7,

[30] The American Institute of Public Opinion gives the following estimate of the Democratic percentage of the vote in 1944: Cities over 500,000, 61; cities under 500,000, 54; towns under 10,000, 49; farms, 48.—Release of March 3, 1945.

[31] A. N. Holcombe, *The New Party Politics* (New York: Norton, 1933), p. 11. Professor Holcombe develops his ideas further in *The Middle Classes in American*

came from its greater success in annexing the support of urban laboring classes.   In discussions of national politics it has been common to speak of the "balance-of-power" role of the West.   By alliance with the South it could throw an election one way; by alliance with the Northeast, the other way.   Perhaps since 1900 we have been moving into a new sort of condition in which the farm population holds the balance of power between the urban laboring classes and business and commercial groups.   By alliance with the workers, the farmers can elect a Democratic president; by moving across the line the farmers can boost the Republican vote.

TABLE 7

Division of Major-Party Vote in 1944 Presidential Election in Counties Containing Cities of over 100,000 Population and in Other Counties

Area	Total vote	Democratic	Per cent Democratic	Republican	Per cent Republican
South a					
Metropolitan					
Counties b	1,062,056	753,506	71.0	305,550	29.0
Other Counties	4,229,016	3,034,157	71.7	1,194,859	28.3
North and West					
Metropolitan					
Counties	19,998,762	11,104,536	55.5	8,894,226	44.5
Other Counties	22,319,834	10,710,953	48.0	11,608,881	52.0

a Texas, Oklahoma, Arkansas, Louisiana, Mississippi, Tennessee, Virginia, North Carolina, South Carolina, Georgia, Alabama, Florida.

b Counties including within their boundaries cities of 100,000 population or more.

Urbanization introduces class politics.   It also changes in other ways the character of the struggle for political power.   It cannot be said that students of politics have analyzed thoroughly the impact of urbanism on the nature and structure of political power, but one additional consequence of the growth of cities may be a reduction in reliance on tradition.   Such a hypothesis gains some support from the data in Figure 9.   The chart shows the Democratic percentage of the presidential vote in Chicago and in twenty rural Illinois counties over a period of fifty years.[32]   Note that the urban Democratic percentage

_____

Politics (Cambridge: Harvard University Press, 1940), pp. 65–123.   William Diamond has shown in detail how sectionalism had been diluted by urbanism as early as 1896.   See his "Urban and Rural Voting in 1896," *American Historical Review*, 46 (1941), pp. 281–305.

[32] The rural counties selected for analysis were those having no urban population according to the census definition in 1940.   They were Brown, Calhoun, Cumberland, Edwards, Gallatin, Hardin, Henderson, Jasper, Johnson, Kendall, Marshall, Monroe, Pope, Pulaski, Putnam, Schuyler, Scott, Stark, Washington, and Woodford.

fluctuates over a wider range than the percentage in the rural counties. The difference between metropolitan and rural political behavior is doubtless attributable to many factors and the relationship needs to be tested in other situations, but the chart suggests that a rural population may be more stable and less susceptible to appeals for change than an urban population. However, the partisan attachments of rural voters in agricultural areas less favored by nature than Illinois may be more tenuous.

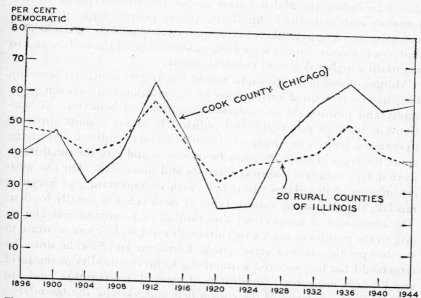

Figure 9. Democratic Percentage of Major-Party Presidential Vote in Cook County (Chicago), Illinois, and in Twenty Rural Illinois Counties

5. THE GEOGRAPHICAL CONDITIONING OF POLITICAL BEHAVIOR

From the discussion of sectionalism, it may have been inferred that sectional disputes in politics often arise from divergent economic interests of different sections of a nation and that these conflicting economic interests, in turn, rest fundamentally on differences in the nature of economic resources. The soil, climate, and crops of the Old South were suitable for employment of slaves; the soil and climate of the North were not. The two cultures clashed. The association of types of geographical environment with political attitudes has stimulated speculation about the geographical basis of politics, although most of this discussion has been centered on the geographical factor in international, rather than domestic, politics.[33]

In the writings of Montesquieu we find an early example of the geographical interpretation of politics. He placed emphasis on the influence of climate, temperature, and rainfall on human character and, in turn, on the nature of government. He believed, for example, that the colder climates produced a more restless and irritable people and a greater degree of political liberty; that the warmer climates produced an indifferent and lethargic people readily susceptible to subjugation and despotism. Similarly, plains people, without natural defensive barriers, were likely to live under a despot; those of the broken and mountainous country were better able to defend themselves and to maintain a higher degree of political liberty.

Montesquieu's generalizations would not receive much credence today, but more refined correlations of the relationship between geography and politics aid in understanding political behavior. A relationship between geography and political behavior is most apparent in agrarian politics in which geographical factors condition, over large areas, the types of crops that may be produced and give the inhabitants in that area common political interests and objectives. On the western margin of the plains wheat belt, with its uncertain and irregular rainfall, the clamor for various types of farm relief is usually loudest. The conditions of temperature and rainfall in Louisiana and Florida give us the politics of sugar cane, although it might be more accurate to say that politics gives us sugar cane in Louisiana and Florida, since the crop could not be produced without the indirect subsidies of the tariff and kindred measures. Conditions of rainfall, temperature, and soil delimit the boundaries of the cotton belt and likewise the boundaries of one of the more formidable sectional blocs in American politics. The seat of political activity of the extractive industries—mining and petroleum production—is determined by the geographical location of those resources. The juxtaposition of the raw materials for steel influences the location of the metal industries and, hence, the sectional locus of the manufacturers, who have been a most important element in national politics.

At times the notion of geographical influence has been pushed to the form of an extreme geographical determinism, but more recently students have pointed out that man may affect geography as well as

[33] See Samuel Van Valkenburg, *Elements of Political Geography* (New York: Prentice-Hall, 1939) ; Derwent Whittlesey, *The Earth and the State* (New York: Holt, 1939); Ellen C. Semple, *American History and Its Geographic Conditions* (Boston: Houghton Mifflin, 1903).

geography, man. The geography of the South did not predestine it to cotton culture and slavery; a complex of cultural factors—a demand for cotton, the availability of slaves, the existence of attitudes condoning slavery—brought about the utilization of southern soil by a slavocracy. Likewise, both the cotton and wheat belts have been pushed farther west by the breeding of plant strains that require less moisture and a shorter growing season; land geographically "destined" for grazing has been brought under cultivation. The textile industry, formerly concentrated in New England partially because of factors of climate and the availability of power, has moved southward with the development of new sources of power and new industrial techniques.

Man, however, cannot alter completely the geographical environment. "It has been said that the most foolish statement in the world is that man has harnessed nature. Equally indefensible is the statement that nature controls man." [34] Yet within the framework of a given culture and technology the geographical endowments of different regions undoubtedly determine to a considerable extent the kinds of economic enterprise in which people can engage and thereby color their interests and ambitions in national politics. When technology, industrial or agricultural, overcomes geographical factors influencing the kinds of occupations people follow, geography ceases to "condition" political behavior. Nevertheless, the effects of climate and the geographical distribution of natural resources are not easily overcome; and geographical factors may be found at the basis of many of the interests whose influence and activity have persisted in American politics over long periods of time.[35]

[34] Isaiah Bowman, *Geography in Relation to the Social Sciences* (New York: Scribner's, 1934), p. xiii.

[35] See H. M. McCarty, *The Geographic Basis of American Economic Life* (New York: Harper, 1940). For a useful, brief critique of the theories concerning the relationships of geography and society, the student is referred to R. M. MacIver, *Society* (New York: Farrar and Rinehart, 1937), chap. 5.

Chapter 7

ROLE AND TECHNIQUES
OF PRESSURE GROUPS

AT BOTTOM, the great complexity of modern politics rests upon the diversity of interests and consequent social cleavages generated by specialization in the production and distribution of goods and services, although divisions based on racial, religious, and regional differences are not without importance. A corollary of economic specialization is interdependence between the specialized segments of society. At these points of interdependence and interrelationship friction occurs and adjustments must be made. Often these accommodations are accomplished through the mediation of the politician, although to a degree not commonly realized they are achieved without the interposition of government.

Economic specialization creates conditions favorable to the development of an extremely large number and wide variety of organized groups interested in bringing their weight to bear on public policy. Although pressure groups are, of course, not new—the National Association of Cotton Manufacturers was formed in 1854, and other groups can claim a longer existence—the rapid proliferation of organized groups came in the present century. Their growth has been especially rapid since World War I. Since that time they have held themselves out as formulators, leaders, and propagators of group opinion, and have entered energetically into the work of educating the public concerning the justice of their cause. Perhaps the demonstration during World War I of opinion molding through large-scale propaganda gave a cue to the leaders of special-interest groups. Yet underlying this growth of organized interest groups has been the development of new and special economic interests that felt the need for some formal means of expressing their demands in the discussion of public policy.

Another element associated with the rise of interest groups has been the broadening scope of governmental control of private activity. If there is a real or threatened tax or regulatory act, the persons and corporations affected are spurred to organize to protect common interests.

The broader and more pervasive governmental control becomes, the greater is the likelihood that any particular group will have such an interest. To illustrate the point: In July, 1862, Congress levied a tax of one dollar per barrel on beer, and shortly thereafter the United States Brewers' Association was created. The preamble to its constitution stated: [1]

Cooperation is necessary. Owners of breweries, separately, are unable to exercise a proper influence in the legislative and public administration. It appears especially necessary for the brewing trade that its interests be vigorously and energetically prosecuted before the legislative and executive departments, as this branch of business is of considerable political and financial importance, exerting a direct as well as an indirect influence on political and social relations.

Other illustrations could be cited, but this incident illustrates a potent factor in the formation of pressure associations. When a law or proposed law impinges on scattered individuals, they are likely to be drawn together by a common interest in political offense or defense.[2] Strong and closely knit interests are likely to be found in those areas in which government control or government bounty is greatest.

In a negative way American political parties stimulate the formation of pressure groups. In our two-party system neither party can afford to commit itself completely to the views of any special interest in society since it would thereby alienate groups with opposing interests. The party cannot advocate wholeheartedly the views of particular interests. Hence, if these groups want to make themselves heard, it is almost necessary that they form themselves into special organizations with the function of arguing their case. In countries with multi-party systems pressure organizations exist, of course, but apparently they have a lesser role because some party is almost certain to be openly committed to the cause of almost every interest group of any consequence.

---

[1] Quoted by Peter Odegard, *Pressure Politics: The Story of the Anti-Saloon League* (New York: Columbia University Press, 1928), p. 245. Another example of the relationship between legislation and pressure organizations is furnished by the Manufacturers' Association of New Jersey which "was originally formed in 1905 to oppose the enactment of a workmen's compensation act."—D. D. McKean, *Pressures on the Legislature of New Jersey* (New York: Columbia University Press, 1938), p. 104.

[2] According to A. H. Kelly the "precipitating factor in the organization of a state manufacturers' association in Illinois came in 1893. The General Assembly, inspired by pressure from the State Federation of Labor, Jane Addams and Florence Kelly of Hull House, and various Chicago trade union groups, in June enacted a statute limiting the hours of labor for women to eight hours per day. The response was immediate." Leading industrialists "organized the Illinois Manufacturers' Association, for the specific purpose of destroying the law."—*A History of the Illinois Manufacturers' Association* (Chicago: University of Chicago Libraries, 1940), pp. 3-4.

However one may explain the rise of pressure groups, they exist in large number and a representative sample has been examined in preceding chapters.   These groups are constituted of diverse kinds of people with widely varying aims, yet they also possess common characteristics of interest to the student of the political process.   In this chapter the operations of these groups in general are analyzed with the object of indicating their similarities in function and method.

1. REPRESENTATIVE FUNCTION OF PRESSURE GROUPS

Pressure groups fill a gap in our formal political system by performing a function of representation beyond the capacities of representatives chosen by the voters in geographical districts.   If it is the duty of government in a democracy to reflect the wishes of the people, means have to be found to ascertain those wishes.   Formally elected representatives who sit in legislative bodies are chosen by the people residing in arbitrarily drawn geographical districts.   The constant increase of specialization in our society has made more and more difficult the task of the representative selected from a geographical area.   So long as the people of a particular congressional district, for example, are engaged in one type of farming and in occupations tributary to agriculture, the representative from the district can speak for their interests, but when the interests within his district become highly diversified he must tread warily lest he antagonize an important segment of his constituency. The result may be that important elements within his district do not have a voice in Congress or the state legislature.   Special interests came to be organized so that, in part, the cheese makers, the laborers, the drys, or others of like views and interests might have representatives who could state their attitudes authoritatively before the government and the public.

Formation of group opinion.   In order to determine and express its wishes, a segment of society composed of people with common interests has to develop a kind of government within the greater government of society as a whole.   It has been indicated that associations, such as the American Federation of Labor and the American Farm Bureau Federation, have their policy-forming conventions and congresses based on a system of representation of the organization's constituent units, and that these conventions adopt statements expressing the wishes and demands of the group as a whole.   By this process, internal differences within each interest group are ironed out and the association can approach the public and the government with a united front.   The reconciliation of differences within interest groups through the workings of their own governments facilitates the work of legislatures and of Congress by reducing the number of conflicts with which they have to deal, as well as by giving the formal government an authoritative statement of group attitudes. The formal governmental machinery is then left with the task of ironing out conflicting demands of groups with opposing interests. In a sense, then, the elaborate and extensive machinery of organization of private groups may be considered as a supplementation of the formal mechanisms of government as established by the Constitution and laws.

To say that pressure organizations have their representative assemblies that adopt resolutions stating their views by no means tells the entire story. According to some theories of political behavior it is fairly simple to forecast how persons of specified economic interests will view questions of public policy. Nothing could be further from the truth. Even if pure self-interest motivated political action, pressure groups would often be in a quandary about what position to take, for the determination of the direction in which one's interest lies is often fraught with difficulty. In fact, it could be persuasively argued that many groups often pursue courses of action directly opposite to their most selfish interest, so remarkable is the capacity of man for self-delusion. Hence, the interests of a group are not something to be easily discovered and stated. Furthermore pressure organizations are not only reflectors of group opinion; they are also to a considerable degree manufacturers of opinion. Their leaders play an important role in determining the views of the members of the group and in pointing out and persuading them wherein their interests lie. Oliver Garceau remarks that "it is in large, organized groups that opinion is manufactured. What they have to tell government was not there [within the group] independently, to be merely parroted by a group employee or officer." Of the American Medical Association, he says: "Official policy is evolved in the hierarchy of formal group institutions, and it is both a cause and a result of the group's total internal political process. But policy, when finally shaped, is regarded as a one-party line, to be put across to the membership by many techniques besides repetition and rational persuasion." [3] This comment could be applied generally to the operations of many other private associations.

This function of manufacturing opinion is closely related to the function of agitation. The leaders and permanent staffs of pressure groups are continually sounding the alarm of threatening dangers to arouse their members and prospective members. In fact, one sometimes sus-

[3] "Organized Medicine Enforces Its 'Party Line,'" *Public Opinion Quarterly*, 4 (1940), pp. 408, 428

pects that the paid staffs of pressure organizations thrive by attempts to panic their members by horrendous accounts of what is to come in the way of public regulation. The group bureaucracy, of course, prospers as it succeeds in arousing fears, but it is also true that individuals are likely to be much less well informed about what the legislative trend holds in store for them than are their professional lobbyists and leaders. This lack of information breeds an inertia difficult to overcome. Mc-Kean, after close observation of the lobby and the New Jersey legislature, reported that group secretaries often complained to him "that even when they explained to the members of their organizations how severely they would be affected by some legislation they could not arouse them sufficiently to induce them to write to legislators." [4]

Representative quality of group action. The representative qualities of the views of pressure organizations are limited by the fact that most of these groups do not include in their membership nearly all of the persons in the class that they purport to represent. The National Association of Manufacturers, for example, includes in its membership a very small proportion of the small manufacturers of the nation. Few trade associations include the entire industry in their membership. Probably two thirds of the farmers are not affiliated with any farm organization. Labor organizations have not succeeded in enrolling even a majority of the country's wage earners, although in some pursuits, as in railroading, a high proportion of the workers is unionized. The specific situation with regard to factory labor is shown in Table 8; the

TABLE 8

Fortune Survey Estimate of Union Membership of Factory Workers, 1943 [a]

	Men	Women
Nonunion	49.9%	54.5%
C.I.O.	21.3	21.7
A.F. of L.	18.7	13.0
Independent	7.6	7.9
Refused to say	2.5	2.9

a Reprinted from the January, 1943, *Fortune* Survey of Public Opinion, by special permission of the Editors.

data there suggests that union leaders could in 1943 claim to speak for only about half of all factory workers.

The fact that only a part of farmers, workers, and businessmen are affiliated with pressure organizations affects the representative character

4 McKean, *op. cit.*, p. 56.

of group action. A more significant limitation, however, flows from the fact that organization membership is usually not a typical sample of the class concerned as a whole. Thus, the more prosperous farmers affiliate with farm groups in a higher degree than do others. The farm organization thus speaks for a particular type of farmer whose interests and wishes may diverge from those of farmers generally. This higher degree of affiliation from the upper brackets appears to be common to nearly all organized groups. It severely limits the capacity of the group to speak for the class as a whole. Illustrative of the consequences is the fact that the War Production Board during World War II refused to recognize the executive committees or boards of directors of trade associations as spokesmen for industries; the Board designated its own committees with care to assure representation of unorganized business.

Even the views of the organized may be inaccurately represented. The official views of an association as stated in resolutions, programs, and platforms may reflect the views of the leaders and bureaucracy of the association rather than those of the mass of the membership. Oligarchy, as has been pointed out earlier, is not limited to the politics of the state: it thrives in private associations. The controlling oligarchy may speak for the interests of the group with varying degrees of accuracy. Of the American Legion, one of its members writes: "Resolutions which bear the weight of national destiny if carried out are droned off and passed with ringing flourish, and legislative agents hie off to deliver the total influence of the Legion on measures which have never been submitted for debate or study to any Legion post, and whose implications are understood by very few of the comrades." [5] These observations apply to other organizations as well. To a limited degree a check on the faithfulness with which pressure-group leaders reflect the views of their members is furnished by opinion polls. In a surprisingly large proportion of instances leaders take positions apparently diametrically opposite to the views of their members. Thus in 1942 in the midst of war, leaders of farm organizations steamrolled through the House of Representatives a measure to weaken inflation control while the polls showed an overwhelming proportion of farmers to be in favor of rigid

[5] Albion Roy King, quoted by William Gellermann, *The American Legion as Educator* (New York: Teachers College, 1938), p. 32. In connection with the consideration of a bill backed by the Legion lobby in 1940, Representative Miller of Connecticut said: "The same Legionnaire further writes me that after attending a district meeting representing all posts of the American Legion in the county, he was coming more and more to the conclusion that there were comparatively few members of the Legion who really knew what legislation the organization was pushing, even though their posts were bombarded with circulars urging them to have members write 'to your Congressman about this.'"—*Congressional Record* (daily edition), April 30, 1940, p. 8115.

price controls. Late in 1945 President Truman proposed a strike-prevention system that included a "cooling-off" period and fact-finding inquiries. Labor leaders almost unanimously opposed the plan, but according to the opinion polls, over two thirds of union members approved the proposal.

The representative quality of group leaders is sometimes warped by their unfaithfulness or poor judgment. Leaders of pressure groups, like other representatives, occupy something of an agency relationship to their constituencies, and agents are not always true to their principals. Every group leader comes to be subjected to external pressure to misrepresent the cause of his client; sometimes he yields to this pressure. Farm leaders, for example, receive the attention of business leaders, and at times the Farm Bureau and the Grange appear to be as much spokesmen for business as for farmers. It is contended by one observer, for example, that their positions in recent years "have coincided in all important respects with the actions and expressions of the National Association of Manufacturers and the United States Chamber of Commerce." [6] In some instances, labor leaders succumb to the same sort of pressure and use their influence as spokesmen for labor in a manner contrary at least to the long-run interests of labor generally. It needs to be kept in mind, however, that as spokesmen for antithetical interests confer over the conflicts in their views, they may modify their more extreme demands. Indeed, a quite general strategy is for one group to attempt to bring other groups to support its programs, but to do so it often needs to modify its views to take into account the opposing interests of others.

For other reasons also, one is not always certain for whom private groups speak. They are often not above a certain amount of deception. Not infrequently an organization with an impressive letterhead and name purports to speak for thousands or hundreds of thousands of people when it consists of nothing more than an energetic promoter who is financed by some interest group not anxious to make its identity known. These kinds of fly-by-night organizations are at least comparatively harmless since their insubstantial nature can readily be determined. Concealment of activity by more permanent groups, however, raises a more serious kind of problem. A recurring situation is illustrated by the remark of an official of the Association of American Railroads about a bill sponsored in the New Jersey legislature by the Chamber of Commerce of the State of New Jersey: "Mr. Russell thinks it inadvisable to let it be known . . . that this bill was prepared by railroad counsel or

[6] Russell Smith, "Big Business and the Farm Bloc," *Antioch Review,* 4 (1944), pp. 189–204.

is in any sense sponsored by any committee of the Association." [7] Again, a chain-store leader comments on a plan for the promotion of legislation: "The fact that the work is financed by chains must not be known, and will you please keep the contents of this letter strictly confidential." [8] Outright concealment of the source of pressure for or against particular measures is exceptional, but the practice is of sufficient frequency that the public official must keep alert to be informed of the parties at interest in any question.

Despite all the limitations on the representativeness of organized groups they are about the only organs for the determination of the wishes of important elements in society. In almost every country such groups have developed, and their widespread occurrence has led to suggestions that they should be given formal recognition in the governmental machinery. In certain European countries economic councils, paralleling the traditional parliaments have been created from time to time, in which associations of workers, bankers, steel manufacturers, farmers, and other interest groups are directly represented. In the democratic countries these bodies have generally been only advisory in nature and have made little headway, while in the dictatorial countries the chambers representative of economic interests were only adjuncts to the dictator. [9]

In the United States the notion of bodies representative of functional rather than of territorial interests has never been broached very seriously; [10] rather the idea has been advanced that the aggregate of interest groups with their spokesmen in Washington constitutes a sort of invisible representative machinery pulling the strings that guide the actions of Representatives and Senators.

Regulation of lobbying. Although proposals for the virtual incorporation of private associations into the formal governmental machinery for representation have won no support of consequence in the United States, a degree of regulation in recognition of the public in-

[7] Hearings before a Subcommittee of the Senate Committee on Interstate Commerce, pursuant to S. Res. 71, Investigation of Railroads, Holding Companies and Affiliated Companies, 75th Congress, 2nd Session, Part 23, p. 10,501.

[8] *Congressional Record,* Vol. 79, Pt. 8, p. 8992.

[9] Harwood L. Childs reports that in Germany the vocational organizations became after the dictatorship not channels "through which special interests made their influence felt upon government," but "instruments by which government exerted pressure upon these interests."—*An Introduction to Public Opinion* (New York: Wiley, 1940), pp. 103–104.

[10] The idea of functional representation, however, seems to have a special appeal to Catholic writers. See, for example, Michael O'Shaughnessy, *Economic Democracy and Private Enterprise* (New York: Harper, 1945).

terest in group operations has come about. In this development the tendency has been somewhat similar to the evolution of the regulation of political parties. Originally political parties were considered merely as private associations of citizens. Gradually their purely private character was modified by public regulation of their organization, of the methods of selection of their leaders, of the qualifications for membership, and of other matters. It came to be recognized that there was a public interest in party operations.

Sentiment has not developed to the same degree regarding pressure organizations, but regulation of lobbying before Congress and before some state legislatures constitutes a beginning toward regularization of the activities of pressure groups. In some states persons appearing before legislative committees are required to register with an appropriate official and indicate the name of their principal or the association they represent, the compensation they receive, the bills in which they are interested. Congress, in 1946, enacted similar legislation applicable to persons and groups that attempt to influence congressional action, directly or indirectly. The Federal Regulation of Lobbying Act [11] requires that individuals, associations, corporations, and others seeking to influence legislation register and file periodic reports of their receipts and expenditures.

Registration and financial reporting do not, of course, furnish information on the manner in which a group arrives at its legislative program, the representative or non-representative character of the group, or other data useful to the legislator in evaluating the statements of group spokesmen. Legislative committees have to take other steps to ascertain for whom the persons who appear before them are authorized to speak. Legislative representatives ("lobbyists") are sometimes asked in committee hearings how many members there are in the organization they represent; how the organization arrived at the view stated by its representative; and other questions designed to inform the legislators of the nature and character of the constituency represented before them. Such inquiries are well advised, for occasionally pressure groups exist that are little more than letterheads containing some impressive names; sometimes organizations of this kind exert considerable influence.

2. METHODS OF PRESSURE GROUPS

In the preceding chapters the methods used by pressure groups to attain their ends have been touched on in the treatment of particular situations, but it is worth while to bring together at one point a sum-

11 Public Law 601, 79th Congress, 1946.

mary treatment of group techniques. In general, it may be said that influence is brought to bear at whatever point in the political process that decisions are made affecting the group, which now means at about every decision-making point in the government. At an earlier time lobbying was confined chiefly to legislatures, but with the vast increase in the scope and range of administrative discretion the spokesmen of organized groups pay close attention to the work of administrative bodies as well.

Public education. Cultivation of public opinion occupies an important place in the programs of the larger and better-financed interest groups; only those organizations with substantial treasuries can hope to conduct a public-relations program of any significance. Probably the most ambitious effort of this sort was that carried on over a period of years by the National Electric Light Association, which sought by every conceivable channel to develop a set of public attitudes favorable to the electrical utilities. Over a longer period of time the National Association of Manufacturers has spent considerable sums annually in propaganda to create attitudes favorable to "free enterprise" and the "American way." These long-run campaigns calculated to create a reservoir of general good will or a general public opinion are to be differentiated from short-term campaigns designed to stir up public opinion on issues of the moment. All sorts of groups that are engaged in battles over public policy make appeals for public support on particular questions. Such rapid-fire campaigns cost less than a continuing effort, although sizeable sums can be spent in the purchase of advertising space to agitate for a national home for the Polynesians or against the duty-free importation of left-handed monkey wrenches.

Working within parties. Both major political parties receive impartially the attention of leaders of pressure organizations; these groups are not ordinarily partisan. They proclaim themselves to be "nonpartisan" or, as Samuel Gompers used to say, "partisan for principle." They attempt to infiltrate both parties to obtain support for the "principles" they advocate. This strategy is adopted as an alternative to the nomination of candidates in their own name, a futile endeavor in any case. The influence of private groups is felt in the drafting of platforms, the making of nominations, and in the election itself in some instances.

Political platforms usually reflect the demands of those groups that political leaders deem so powerful that it is imprudent to ignore their wishes. Often platform drafters are confronted by the necessity of making a choice between diametrically opposed interests, and the outcome may be an equivocal or vague platform pronouncement. As an organized group gradually convinces the public of the desirability of its cause, the successive party declarations may become firmer, with both parties progressing toward complete acceptance of the view of the organized groups at about the same rate. The leaders of organized groups may appear before the platform committees and urge that the party take a particular stand, but such lobbying is not always necessary. Platform drafters take into consideration the probable reaction of important interests to the position taken by the party. This anticipation of probable public reaction is a constant factor influencing decisions by politicians.

In conventions and primaries pressure groups often attempt to influence the choice of party nominees. In the nomination of candidates for the Presidency, important groups have, in effect, a veto. A national party must, if it hopes to win, draw its support from a cross-section of society. Its candidate should not have characteristics or a record that might offend any large element of the population. Likewise, aspirants for nominations for governor, for mayor, and for other offices made by the direct primary are more likely to be successful if they have not made an enemy of important elements of the population for whom organized pressure groups speak.

The policies of organized groups regarding their endorsement and campaigning for candidates differ as greatly as do their composition and objectives. At one extreme are those organizations that attempt to form effectively a solid bloc of voters that can be delivered to any candidate who takes the desired stand on the issue of interest to the group. Actually to deliver such a vote requires the existence of a well-disciplined group whose members are almost fanatical in their devotion to the cause. Historically the most impressive example of this type of group has been the Anti-Saloon League.[12] Rarely, except in limited areas, has any other group matched the League in capacity to deliver substantial blocs of voters. A more recent large-scale effort to muster private groups at the polls has been carried on by the CIO-PAC and the NC-PAC. Whether they make an intensive electoral campaign, most groups that have a numerically large membership analyze the voting records of candidates for Congress, state legislatures, and city councils. The membership is informed of the candidates' stand on issues of concern to the group and admonished to support their friends regardless of party affiliation. The Non-Partisan Political Campaign Committee of the American Federation of Labor, for example, circulates information about the congressional records of the candidates on issues of interest to labor; it occasionally makes a special effort to

[12] See Odegard, *op. cit.*

defeat for re-election candidates whose labor record is unusually objectionable.

It is common practice for groups to circulate questionnaires among candidates asking their stand on current issues. Thus the candidates are, in effect, asked to pledge themselves to a position on the question before election. The circulation of the statements of candidates among the voters is designed to serve the same purpose as the circulation of the legislative records of candidates seeking re-election.

As the composition of a pressure group becomes more heterogeneous and less well-disciplined, the difficulty of acting as a unit in elections becomes greater. Many organizations therefore do not endorse candidates but attempt to maintain friendly relationships with all candidates and all parties. Their objectives may be achieved by propaganda campaigns, by lobbying, by various methods. Often it is unwise to back either party; it is better to have friends in both camps, for the group must promote its objectives whatever party is in power.

The actual influence exerted by pressure groups in nominations and elections is a matter about which there is little precise knowledge. The professional politician, in a sense, makes it his business to estimate the strength of the various interests appealing to him for his support of particular policies. He risks his re-election—and his livelihood—on his ability to forecast the strength that can be mustered against him at the polls by the group that the lobbyist represents. Yet the politician acts on intuitive estimates of the situation. The chances are that the bark of most of the organized groups is more terrifying than their bite on election day, but there is little convincing evidence bearing on the question one way or the other.

Persuading legislators. Pressure groups are most conspicuous in their activities in support of and in opposition to legislative proposals. They have developed this work into a fine art, which can be reviewed at this point only in summary. Whether they work in Washington or in the state capitals, the methods of these groups are much alike. The association's staff is ordinarily in immediate charge of the legislative activities. The larger associations and interests maintain offices permanently in Washington, while the more common practice in the states is to assign men to the capital during legislative sessions. These men—lobbyists, legislative counsel—have often served in Congress or in the state legislatures. If they lack that experience, they are usually well informed on legislative procedure and tactics. Their tenure is likely to be longer than that of the legislator; and in the course of their long service they may come to gain the confidence and respect of the legislators.

The legislative staff of the association keeps close watch on the course of legislation in order that action may be taken when required. Typical is the procedure in the offices of the National Co-operative Milk Producers Federation:

. . . Each morning the Congressional Record is studied carefully both as to debates and the introduction of bills. Important statements are noted and copies are ordered of all bills having a direct or indirect bearing on dairy farmers' interests. These are studied, catalogued and their progress recorded by a card index system which includes data on amendments, conference reports, preliminary and final action, and the position of every Senator and Representative to the extent that these are of record.[13]

Continual watch over the proceedings of the legislative body is a part of association work; it thereby keeps posted on proposals detrimental to its interests and keeps track of bills that it is promoting. And it is important to note that a large proportion of legislation originates outside the legislature itself. The staff of the pressure group drafts bills for introduction into the legislative body, bills that, of course, reflect the policies of the association. The situation in Congress and in the state legislatures in general is suggested by studies of practices in Ohio. In 1929 Professor Harvey Walker analyzed the bills introduced in the Ohio Senate during the session of that year and found that 26 per cent of them were the brain children of the members of the Senate, while the remaining 74 per cent originated with, and were usually drafted by, outside groups and interests.[14] In 1939 Professor Walker examined the operation of the Ohio Senate session of that year and found substantially the same condition as had existed in 1929. In the 1939 session of the Senate 24 per cent of the bills introduced were represented to be of senatorial parentage and 76 per cent were introduced by senators at the request of agencies outside the legislature.[15] In the 1939 session of the Ohio House of Representatives about the same distribution of authorship of legislation was found to exist, with approximately three fourths of the bills originating outside the legislature.[16]

To learn that there is a bill to be defeated or to draft a bill to be introduced is merely the first step. The pressure group must have its friends within the legislative body who will either do its bidding or at

---

[13] *Activities of the National Cooperative Milk Producers Federation, Being a Description of Its Functional Organization Plus a Review of the 1944 Dairy Problems,* p. 13.

[14] Harvey Walker, "Where Does Legislation Originate?" *National Municipal Review,* 18 (1929), pp. 565–567.

[15] Walker, "Wellsprings of Our Laws," *National Municipal Review,* 28 (1939), pp. 689–693.

[16] Walker, "Who Writes the Laws," *State Government* 12 (1939), pp. 199–200.

least regard its views with sympathy.   Every pressure group of any importance has allies in the legislative body itself.   From the farming states will come Senators and Representatives who will aid the American Farm Bureau Federation in its legislative program.   The National Association of Manufacturers and the American Federation of Labor have their legislative allies from the industrial states.   Spokesmen for the American Legion may come from almost any part of the country.   Similarly in the state legislatures each group of importance generally has a member friendly to its interests on the floor.   Thus members of the legislative body friendly to the pressure group concerned take the lead in the introduction of legislation and in the obstruction of undesirable legislation.[17]

In the organization of the legislative body—that is, the appointment of committees and other functionaries of the body—pressure groups are likely to take a hand.   In some state legislatures it appears that membership on committees is determined to a large extent by pressure groups who are anxious to obtain appointment of their friends to committees that will handle their bills.   McKean says, for example, that in New Jersey the Manufacturers' Association has generally been successful in obtaining the appointment of members to the Senate labor committees who would be inclined to stop labor legislation.[18]   Endeavors to influence appointments to committees are not limited to state legislatures; the Association of American Railroads, for example, has an interest in the same matter in Washington.

Pressure groups are always represented before legislative committees when hearings open to interested parties are held on legislative proposals.   Some of the groups have effective research organizations that prepare factual data bearing on the proposals for presentation before the legislative committees; others are not strong on facts, but they make their position known.   In Washington the tendency seems more and more for the professional secretaries and counsel of pressure groups to depend on the officials of their organizations to appear before committees.   The full-time lobbyist is merely a "hired man"; he brings in the president and vice-presidents of the organization and coaches them on

[17] The type situation is indicated by the remarks of Clarence Cannon, Chairman of the House Appropriations Committee.   He took occasion to say a word of "appreciation" to Mr. Ed O'Neal of the Farm Bureau Federation and his staff for their "assistance" to him and other members of the House interested in farm legislation.   "We could not possibly have secured the enactment of appropriations to take care of the parity-payment checks or soil-conservation checks without the wise counsel and support of Mr. O'Neal and the actual votes he enlisted in our support."—Hearings before Subcommittee of House Appropriations Committee, 77th Congress, 2nd Session, on Agriculture Department Appropriation Bill, 1943, Part 2, p. 627.

[18] *Op. cit.*, p. 202.

the bill, and they appear before congressional committees. Since committees tend really to make legislation, the hearings before the committee assume great importance in the legislative process. Hearings enable Congress to ascertain the attitudes of all affected interests toward a particular piece of legislation, to acquire from those most intimately concerned a knowledge of its probable effect, and to arrive at some kind of workable compromise among those concerned.

Although great emphasis is placed on committttee deliberations, the pressure group does not ignore the other members of the legislative bodies. The more important groups maintain detailed records concerning the attitudes and interests of each member of the legislative body. These records aid them in informing their membership of the stand taken by particular members and also in directing pressure on the legislator when bills are approaching a vote. The pressure is brought in two ways: directly on the representative, at the seat of the government, by interviews, persuasion, buttonholing; and indirectly by the stirring up of interest in his home constituency and the directing of that pressure toward the legislator.

Pressure from home is broadly of two sorts: the "rifle" type and the "shot-gun" type. The first sort consists in enlisting the support of a very few persons known to have great influence with an individual legislator. The "shot-gun" approach is a general campaign in which all and sundry are asked to wire their Congressman. "Rifle" fire is an economical and simple method to influence a specific individual; its use requires that the pressure group know definitely who has influence with a faltering or recalcitrant legislator. These groups make it their business to acquire such information. The method is illustrated by the following letter from an insurance company legislative representative:

> The easiest way to handle this bill is to kill it. I think that has been done. The First National Bank, of Valdosta, Ga., is the financial backer of the Honorable Nelson, who introduced the bill. I hand you a copy of a telegram that was sent to Senator Nelson yesterday by this bank, at the instance of one of our agents, ex-Senator E. E. Dekle, to wit.
>
> I have an idea that the bill will now be withdrawn.[19]

The large-scale barrage of letters or telegrams to Congressmen has become commonplace. Groups differ in their ability to direct a stream of communications to Congressmen. The American Legion exhibits

[19] Temporary National Economic Committee, Hearings, Part 10, p. 4414. Dr. Zeller says that in New York the New York State Bankers Association relies on the "very personal" contact that local banks have with legislators and local party leaders.—*Pressure Politics in New York* (New York: Prentice-Hall, 1937), p. 47.

great virtuosity in this matter.   In times of stress its Washington representative can direct requests to key persons in each state who in turn forward the word to the local units of the organization.   The next day telegrams arrive in bales for the solons.   This sort of inspired campaign probably does not have so much weight with legislators as the random letter from constituents.   Legislators speak with tears in their voice of the influence of the letter written in pencil on a poor grade of paper without complete mastery of the rules of English composition.[20] They speak with disdain of a flood of communications, similar in phraseology and obviously stimulated by some interested party.   Yet the influence of telegrams and letters "from home" on the position taken by legislators remains unmeasured.   In a study of a selected group of Congressmen and their actions with reference to the repeal of the arms embargo late in 1939, it was concluded that they were "primarily motivated on this particular issue by personal conviction."   Party loyalty played an important role in determining their stand, and "probably more than half of the Congressmen voted against the expressed opinion of their constituents as judged by their mailbags." [21]

The structure and procedure of legislatures give great advantage to the group that seeks to prevent legislative action as against the group that wants to obtain positive legislation.   A bill has to go through many stages before it becomes a law, and at each of these steps it may be obstructed.   It may be killed in committee.   It may never come to a vote, if the committee reports it, provided that sufficient influence can be brought to bear on those controlling the legislative timetable.   If it comes to a vote, it may be defeated.   If it is passed by one house, the obstructionist then has a similar series of opportunities to check the bill in the other legislative chamber.   If all else fails, it may be possible to induce the executive to veto the bill.

To make this catalog of pressure-group concern more complete, it is necessary to mention the activities of organized groups in the field of direct legislation in those states that have adopted the initiative and referendum.   The initiative is a procedure by which a specified number of persons, through their signature to a petition, may bring a proposed statute or constitutional amendment to a vote of the people. The referendum is a related procedure by which a specified number of persons may by petition force a popular vote to be had on a measure

[20] See R. L. Neuberger, "I Go to the Legislature," *Survey Graphic,* 30 (1941), 373-376.

[21] E. Gleeck, "96 Congressmen Make Up Their Minds," *Public Opinion Quarterly,* 4 (1940), pp. 3-24.   See the significant study of congressional mail by Rowena Wyant and Herta Herzog, "Voting Via the Senate Mailbag," *Public Opinion Quarterly,* 5 (1941), pp. 359-382, 590-624.

enacted by the legislative body. These devices were calculated to furnish to the people methods by which they could both by-pass and check boss-controlled legislatures. In fact, the moving forces in the operation of the initiative and referendum are, of necessity, organized groups of citizens. Groups unable to obtain the passage of legislation by the representative body may resort to the initiative and take their case to the voters. Thus, when an initiative proposal appears on the ballot liberalizing the privileges of chiropractors, for example, one may be sure that an association of chiropractors has been the moving force in putting the measure on the ballot and in the campaign in its support. The referendum is ordinarily invoked by some group that has been unable to defeat a measure by legislative lobbying and hopes to win the battle before the electorate as a whole. Thus when a measure taxing oleomargarine is brought before the voters by referendum, one does not need to make much of an investigation to discover that the organized oleomargarine manufacturers furnished the money for the circulation of petitions and for the education of the voters concerning the iniquity of the legislation.[22]

Needling administrators. Pressure groups make their most spectacular appearances in supporting and opposing legislation, but perhaps equally important are their continuous relationships with the administrative agencies of government. Perhaps fifty years ago in the heyday of the lobbyist there were comparatively few occasions on which pressure groups needed to deal with administrative agencies; their interests could be adequately protected through legislation. With the growing complexity of government, legislative bodies have had more and more to delegate authority to administrative agencies to make rules and regulations. Administrators become legislators, and the agents of pressure groups inevitably direct their activities to the point in the governmental machinery at which authority to make decisions is lodged. Where power rests, there influence will be brought to bear. Even if the administrator possesses but slight rule-making power, he can enforce legislation vigorously or otherwise, and pressure may be brought to bear to influence the choice of policy.

An interest group may be instrumental in obtaining the passage of

[22] For detailed information on the use of the initiative and referendum, see H. F. Gosnell and M. J. Schmidt, "Popular Law Making in the United States, 1924–1936," New York State Constitutional Convention Committee, *Problems Relating to Legislative Organization and Powers* (1938), pp. 313–335. For detailed information on the initiative and referendum, see J. K. Pollock, *The Initiative and Referendum in Michigan* (Ann Arbor: University of Michigan Press, 1940); V. O. Key, Jr. and W. W. Crouch, *The Initiative and the Referendum in California* (Berkeley: University of California Press, 1939).

legislation. But to have it effectively administered it may be necessary to follow through with pressure, aid, and encouragement to the governmental agency charged with responsibility for enforcement of the legislation. A simple illustration is furnished by activities of railroad companies regarding laws fixing maximum weights for trucks, their chief competitors. The report of a representative of railroads in Iowa reads: [23]

Induced department to inaugurate statewide campaign to enforce all motor truck laws, assisted in the preparation of publicity in regard thereto and the circulation of such publicity through the Associated Press and other sources; assisted department in suggesting appropriate news releases in regard thereto throughout the year, and obtained state-wide publicity in regard to same.

Discovered that department did not understand most important part of law regarding truck weight limitations, to wit: gross load formula, and had not enforced same. Explained effect of same to inspectors; established personal acquaintanceship with them; worked with and personally trained them in the weighing of trucks, maintaining their good will throughout the year, and obtaining their activity at strategic points on request.

In the formulation of administrative rules and regulations there are frequent interchanges of opinion between administrative officials and representatives of the industries and interests to be affected by the administrative action. Some statutes prescribe that notice shall be given of contemplated regulations and that the interested parties shall be given an opportunity to be heard. In the absence of such statutory requirements it is common practice to ascertain the attitudes of the industry or other interests in advance of the promulgation of rules. Usually the most convenient way to find out how the affected interests feel about a particular course of action is to consult the officials of the organized group concerned. In a sense these formal hearings and informal conferences serve the same function as the hearings by congressional committees on proposed legislation.

Examples of the role of organized groups in furnishing information and points of view to those charged with the issuance of administrative legislation are to be found in almost every department of the government. The Secretary of Agriculture makes rules governing the use of national forest lands for grazing by stockmen, but in preparing and amending these rules stockmen's associations are solicited for suggestions from time to time. Furthermore, the local forestry officials often consult advisory committees from the associations about prob-

[23] Hearings before a Subcommittee of the Senate Committee on Interstate Commerce, pursuant to S. Res. 71, Investigation of Railroads, Holding Companies and Affiliated Companies, 75th Congress, 2nd Session, Part 23, p. 10,168.

lems of current administration of the grazing lands.[24]   When the Civil Aeronautics Authority proposes substantial changes in rules, drafts are submitted "to those organizations representing the affected portions of the industry.   Thus a proposed rule which applied only to airline pilots would not be submitted to the Private Pilots Association. Because the industry is so highly organized, the general practice is to send to the interested organizations enough copies of the proposed rule to distribute to their members." [25]

In the administration of the Fair Labor Standards Act the Wage and Hour Division was compelled to issue regulations dealing with the determination of the "reasonable cost" of facilities furnished to employees that might be included in computing the wages received.   A conference of the representatives of the principal industries to be affected by the proposed regulation was called.   Among the groups represented were the National Lumber Manufacturers Association, the Coal Association, the National Petroleum Association, the Textile Association, the American Mining Congress, and the National Sand and Gravel Association.   Copies of a tentative draft of the regulation served as a basis for discussion in which defects in the proposed rule were indicated.   A committee of the conference reformulated the rule, which was adopted by a vote of those present.   Subsequently the conference-approved draft was issued as a regulation by the administrator of the Wage and Hour Division.[26]   The administrator was, of course, under no compulsion to accept the recommendations of the conference, but there is great advantage in the formulation of regulations that both effectuate public policy and conform to the ideas of fairness and feasibility of those affected by the regulation.[27]

The relationships between the representatives of organized groups and administrative officials serve an important function.   The preparation of rules and regulations and the arrival at decisions on the details of complicated matters require knowledge that even the best-informed government official may not possess.   It is necessary to know as ac-

[24] See J. P. Comer, *Legislative Functions of National Administrative Authorities* (New York: Columbia University Press, 1927), chap. vii.

[25] Attorney General's Committee on Administrative Procedure, *The Administration of the Grain Standards Act* (mimeographed ed.), p. 7.

[26] Attorney General's Committee on Administrative Procedure, *Administration of the Fair Labor Standards Act of 1938* (mimeographed ed.), p. 147.

[27] In some instances the power to make regulations is, in effect, delegated to private associations.   Some state laws provide, for example, that there shall be admitted to practice medicine graduates only of those colleges that have met the requirements prescribed by the Association of American Medical Colleges.—See Lane W. Lancaster, "The Legal Status of 'Private' Organizations Exercising Governmental Powers," *Southwestern Social Science Quarterly*, 15 (1935), pp. 325–336.

curately as possible the probable effect of a proposed course of action; generally the best way to find out is to consult with the persons to be affected by it. Beyond this obvious function of obtaining information, consultation permits a more accurate estimate of the probable reception of the contemplated action. One of the most important elements of the art of governance is the ability to forecast reaction to a decision. Will it be hostile? Will it be critical? Will it be favorable? By consultation with the organs for group expression, tentative answers to these questions may be had. Even if it is necessary for the government in the general interest to issue a rule or make a decision that important groups may regard with horror, the mere fact that consultation has occurred may temper criticism.[28]

At times the organized group gains control of the governmental agency with which it is most concerned. That control may rest on the informal exertion of pressure on those legally responsible for the conduct of the agency, or it may be formally recognized by statute. Of the latter type the New Jersey State Department of Agriculture furnishes an excellent example. It is managed by a board selected by a convention of representatives of agricultural organizations designated by law. "Among the organizations named to send delegates are the Horticultural Society, the Grange, the Poultry Association, and several co-operative growers' associations." [29] Professional associations especially have been desirous of the inclusion in statutes of clauses providing that the professional examining boards should be appointed from among their nominees.

When several powerful groups among which friction exists are concerned in the administration of a law, it is essential that the appointing power be in the hands of public authority. Yet there is nearly always great pressure from private groups to influence appointments to the chief positions in administrative agencies of concern to them. Organized labor is deeply interested in appointments to the post of Secretary of Labor; organized business is likewise interested in appointments to the position of Secretary of Commerce and to membership on regulatory commissions. And the roll of other organized groups could be called, with similar results. Such groups, however, do not consistently have publicly proclaimed "candidates" for these appointments; generally they depend on informal consultation to obtain an acceptable appointment.

A well-worn channel by which private groups attempt to reach and

[28] See E. P. Herring *Public Administration and the Public Interest* (New York: McGraw-Hill, 1936).

[29] McKean, *op. cit.*, p. 147.

influence administrative agencies is through Representatives and Senators. Congressmen, so the reasoning goes, control appropriations and legislation, and their word will have something approaching an effect of intimidation on administrators. The possibilities are illustrated in a statement made by Chester Bowles, Price Administrator, in 1945:

It is conservatively estimated that more than 5,000 telegrams poured in upon Members of Congress on Wednesday and Thursday of last week, seeking exemption for automobile dealers from the cost absorption policy that has been applied to industries and trades ever since price control was established. It was the greatest single pressure group operation since OPA was established.

I was forewarned some months ago that if OPA did not give automobile dealers an exemption from our usual requirement of cost absorption that this would happen. I was told that their association claimed to be the most powerful organized group in the nation; that word had gone out to association members on this particular issue not to fire until they saw the whites of our eyes, but then to fire with super-force.

Obviously the order to fire went out. I can testify to the results from personal experience.

On last Tuesday night telegrams signed by automobile dealers began to trickle into my office downtown. On Wednesday morning the trickle increased to a steady stream. During the forenoon the stream became a flood. The crest of the flood was reached in mid-afternoon when between three and four o'clock my office received 52 telegrams—or nearly one a minute.[30]

3. PRESSURE GROUPS AND THE GENERAL WELFARE

In the nature of things pressure groups in large measure advocate action or inaction in conflict with the general welfare. This tendency is true *a fortiori* of the more powerful, adequately financed, and more ably staffed groups. They speak, on the whole, for people who are more aggressive, more privileged, and better off than the average of the citizenry. They eternally seek further advantage and more often than not get it. Their behavior is not often colored by any genuine concern for the common welfare, although they often claim to carry the burden of the general good.

Warfare between particular and general interest. These remarks ignore the numerous shades of gray that separate black and white, and the general proposition that pressure groups are inimical to the general welfare contains implicit assumptions about the nature of the common good. These assumptions ought to be made explicit. No definition of the general welfare universally acceptable could be formulated, but the doctrines of American democracy give weight to the

[30] Statement to the House Small Business Committee, November 13, 1945.

notion of the greatest good to the greatest number, and related ideas. It is much easier to define the general welfare negatively, that is, to identify proposals contrary to it. Proposals for the use of governmental powers to promote the narrow and selfish interests of small groups ordinarily at the expense of other groups or classes often conflict with the prevailing standards of the public good. From their very nature, pressure groups tend to promote such proposals. They are concerned not with the other fellow but with the interests of their own group, and quite frequently the controllers of the group use the group power to injure the interests of a substantial minority of their own members. Moreover, the professional bureaucrats of pressure groups are now the principal true demagogues in our politics in the sense that they appeal to the immediate selfish interests of their constituents to a far greater degree than do ordinary politicians. In fact, they often misrepresent their constituents, for public leaders can frequently obtain acceptance of a policy more nearly reflecting the general interest by going over the heads of pressure-group leaders to the workers, to businessmen, to farmers who have ordinarily a greater sense of community responsibility than do their hired men in the offices of pressure societies. Pressure-group bureaucracies, however, devote their efforts to the short-term, narrow interests of their principals; they constitute a large-scale institutionalization of social myopia.

On the basis of such conclusions, some naive souls propose that the commonwealth be cleansed of pressure groups. Let us cast the scoundrels into outer darkness and be done with it. The proponents of this method for the salvation of the republic are quite unaware of the nature of politics and of the functions of government. The principal driving forces in politics are class interests and group interests; they make themselves felt regardless of the kind of government or social organization that exists. It is a function of government to attempt to reconcile the interests of these groups, to devise policies that provide an accommodation among conflicting drives, to maintain social unity despite the inevitable diversity of interest of social groups and classes. Freedom of association and freedom of expression of interest facilitate the resolution of conflict through open discussion of divisive issues. If a citizen is dissatisfied, he is free to organize his own society to advance his own cause. Moreover, the promotion of the public good cannot be accomplished apart from class or special interest. The public good is, after all, a relative matter. It rarely consists in yielding completely to the demands of one class or group in society. It more often consists in the elaboration of compromise between conflicting groups, in the yielding to one class at one time and to another at another, and sometimes in the mobilization of the support of the great unorganized general public to batter down the demands of class interest.

Advantage goes to the organized. Inevitably pressure groups will exist and exert influence, but that fact need not blind us to the consequence of the nature of their work and organization. The evolution of a political milieu in which governmental officials habitually pay heed to organized groups gives great advantages to those classes of people who form themselves into associations and hire a lobbyist to stay in Washington and watch out for their interests. From the mere fact that they are always hearing from the spokesmen for these groups, public officials undoubtedly tend to yield to them. The tendency has been well described by Joseph R. Grundy, a lobbyist of note:

In Congress, from my experience, the fellow that makes the most noise, and the fellow that makes the most demands, that keeps his problems in front of them all the time, he gets service. If he doesn't; if he depends upon somebody else to do it for him, he is going to get what we all get when we don't go after the thing the way we ought to—nothing.[31]

Confronted by people of this kind, public officials sometimes mistake an executive secretary, a letterhead, and the output of a mimeograph for the general will.

The consequences of yielding to those groups with the most persistent spokesmen may vary under different situations. In many instances no significant opposition to a demand may be heard. The acceptance of the views of one group may injure the unheard side of a conflict of interest.[32] The side not heard may be the "general" public, consumers, or other like groups not formed into cohesive organizations. Yet when two more or less equally powerful groups are involved in a dispute over public policy, government may balance one off against the other and perhaps more easily arrive at a solution reflecting the general interest. But even in such situations, all the pressure and initiative is for action or inaction of benefit to particular groups. Few private groups advocate measures broader than their own interest, save when a broader interest fortuitously coincides with their own narrow interest. For example, organized business resisted the Public Utility Holding Company Act and the Food, Drug, and Cosmetic Act, but no cohesive organization of persons who would benefit by the legislation was on the scene. The investors who had been mulcted by holding-company promoters did not form societies with imposing

---

[31] Quoted by E. E. Schattschneider, *Politics, Pressures and the Tariff* (New York: Prentice-Hall, 1935), p. 219.

[32] See *ibid.*, for a revealing discussion of situations of this kind in congressional tariff-making.

titles and put on nation-wide campaigns of advertising; nor did they hire top-flight legal firms to speak for them before congressional committees. People who had been induced to purchase nostrums, extravagantly advertised in patently false and misleading fashion, did not send telegrams to Congress by the thousands asking that the bill be passed. Nor did they threaten to boycott their corner druggist if he did not exert his influence to aid in the passage of the measure. In the period of difficult adjustment after World War II the lobbyists for economic chaos were so numerous that the spokesmen for the general interest were lost in the crowd.

Strength of negativism. The power of pressure groups has been compounded by the historical accident that they arose in a period in which at least many of the more important groups could advance their interests by preventing governmental action. In the adjustment of government to meet the emerging problems of an industrial civilization positive governmental action is necessary, but the more powerful elements in American society on the whole conceive their interests to lie in the prevention of action. Thus, C. S. Mellen, one-time president of the New York, New Haven and Hartford Railroad Company once said: "We did not seek so much positive legislation. . . . We could get along very well if we were let alone—very well. . . . It is not so much the things we want to do to the other fellow, as to prevent what the other fellow wants to do to us." [33] In New York state legislation Dr. Zeller says that Associated Industries, an association of 1,500 manufacturing corporations, merchants, and other business corporations, has been concerned chiefly with "blocking rather than promoting legislation, in postponing or emasculating social legislation as long as possible to thus 'save as much money for industry as possible, even if it cannot be done indefinitely.' " [34] Preoccupation with the prevention of governmental action puts the leaders of private centers of power in the position of negation rather than of contriving and urging positive courses of governmental action. Thus the centers of initiative are weak, and the adverse influences working upon public officials are strong.

Coincidence of private and public interest. These remarks should not be allowed to blot out the fact that at times private interests furnish powerful drives in support of measures and actions in the public interest. This happens when private interest happens to parallel the public good. If it is assumed, for example, that the public welfare rests in energetic enforcement of the anti-trust laws, it could be pointed

[33] Senate Document No. 543, 53rd Congress. 2nd Session (1914), p. 924.
[34] Zeller, *op. cit.,* p. 55.

out that such enforcement as occurs is in large measure sparked by the demands of business interests that are being injured by or are in danger of injury from the monopolistic practices of other business interests. Often the drive for much needed public improvements comes from contractors' groups who hope to do the building although they may just as well urge unnecessary public improvements for the same reason. Medical associations are often in the background of movements to drive the quacks to cover. Taxpayers' associations usually are mainly concerned in keeping down the level of public services, but their demands for efficient operation of public services are unequivocally in the general welfare. On the other hand, private groups have a remarkable facility in the rationalization of private gain with the public interest. Thus, the Farm Bureau Federation and like groups exerted enormous influence in the adoption of our Philippine independence policy, on grounds of liberty for little peoples in accord with the American tradition and on the rather erroneous assumption that Philippine independence would be of great advantage to the American farmer by keeping out Philippine farm products.[35] An even better illustration comes from a letter to a Congressman in 1939 on the letterhead of the American Uniform Cap Company, "Military Caps Our Specialty": "I am writing to you as our Representative from Missouri to vote to repeal the Arms Embargo Act so that we may sell to foreign countries so as to protect our democracy and keep us out of war. Thank you very kindly." [36]

Contrasting objectives of party and pressure group. This consideration of the nature of influences exerted by private groups in the political process leads toward a review of the contrasting role of political parties. Pressure groups must fight for partial interests; from their nature political parties must seek to advance a program that will win the support of a majority of the people. Individual politicians, to be sure, may be and often are quite as narrow in their beliefs and endeavors as the most blatant advocate of private interest. Yet political parties as a whole must attempt to gain the support of a larger constituency; this endeavor requires a program at least ostensibly in the public interest. The leaders of pressure groups thrive by playing to group interest, by arousing anxieties and fears among their followers, by encouraging class and group cleavages. Political parties, on the other hand, must play down group interest by conciliating conflict, by compromising issues, by seeking formulae for the combination of many groups into a bloc

35 See Grayson L. Kirk, *Philippine Independence* (New York: Farrar & Rinehart, 1936), chaps. 4 and 5.
36 *Congressional Record* (daily edition), October 30, 1939, p. 1724.

strong enough to win. The political party must put forward a positive program rather than assume an attitude of complete negation; if it wins, it will be responsible for the management of the government and will be compelled to "do something." The pressure group must appeal to the partial interest; the political party, to the common interest. These remarks are given point by the following observations from a campaign speech by Franklin D. Roosevelt in Omaha in 1936:

Back of what we did was the conviction that the agricultural problem is not a problem for the farmer alone—that it is a problem for the Nation as a whole. This is the way we attacked it.

And the Nation is now going along with the farmer. Now for the first time in this industrial period of our history, the American people understand that there is a definite bond between agriculture and industry, that the money we have used for the restoration of American agriculture has been an investment in the restoration of American industry, an underwriting for the wages of American labor, a stimulus for profits in American business.

To put the discussion on a completely nonpartisan plane, it may be noted that in 1940 Mr. Wendell Willkie made his way to Omaha where in another speech on the farm question he implied that perhaps Mr. Roosevelt had fomented class conflict rather than reconciled differences. Yet Mr. Willkie's observations point to the concern of politicians with finding the common denominator among groups rather than in accentuating differences. He said:

Instead of working together, each group has found it necessary to fight for whatever advantage it can gain. The farmer, the worker, the investor and the businessman have been like four horses attached to the same evener, there in the hands of a reckless driver, and all horses plunging spasmodically in different directions. Those horses must pull together. We cannot hope to save this democracy of ours any other way.

From the foregoing analysis it is not to be concluded that all political leaders are angels and all pressure-group leaders rascals. Rather, both are in quest of "loaves and fishes," but from the nature of the circumstances in which they work they must operate in different ways. The pressure-group bureaucracy has to appeal to and promote group interest; the party leader must conciliate group differences and seek to form a large enough following from all classes of people to win an election.

4. DILEMMAS IN THE POLITICS OF ECONOMIC CONTROL

By placing the entire discussion of pressure organizations on a broader canvas, something may be grasped of the significance for American politics as a whole of the development of strong and crystallized private interest groups. The grand problems of domestic politics are associated with the rise of pressure organizations and with the underlying economic and social trends, which in turn furnish the basis for these organizations.

Specialization and differentiation of economic function characteristic of an industrial society place great economic power in the hands of private groups and individuals, power by action or inaction to affect, for good or for bad, other groups in society. Specialization of economic function creates a system of interdependence so delicate that maladjustments at any particular point are certain to have repercussions of widespread consequence. Writers on business monopoly have been fond of using the phrase "bottlenecks of business" to describe the control points at which power may be abused to the disadvantage of others within the economic system. Not only does business gain power from the process that creates these potential choke points. The power of labor too may be used at these strategic points in the economic system to levy tolls or to produce disruptions extending widely through the economic system. A small group of truck drivers, for example, may bring the life of a great city to a stand-still. Employees of a power company may do the same. The nation may be brought to its knees by a comparatively small number of railroad workers.

It should be noted also that the power of private groups becomes more potent in conditions of high level employment and production. When the economic system has within it considerable slack—unused or underutilized facilities, unemployed labor, unused transport capacity—a disruption at one control point in the economic system may be offset by the use of other facilities or resources. Thus, a strike in one bearing plant—or a demand for exorbitant prices by its operators—in a condition of low-level production may have little effect beyond the particular plant. But under circumstances of high level production users of bearings have no alternative source of supply to which they can turn, and the closing of a single plant may compel a shutdown in many other industries. In a sense, then, strikes under these conditions are in the same category as business monopolies. They are no longer merely private warfare between employer and employee that the community can tolerate; they are, in effect, strikes against the community.

Economic specialization places economic power in private hands. Although it does not automatically create politically powerful private groups, it does lay the basis for the activation and organization of the political power of such groups. Classes of persons with like interests and like objectives, interests and objectives different from those of others, arise and wait only to be aroused.

Traditionally the dominant American doctrine has been that the relationships among private economic groups be governed by the forces of the market. To this doctrine nearly all private groups even yet pay at least lip service. The pleas of the businessman for freedom of enterprise are matched by the demands of the union leader that he be allowed to bargain with employers rather than be subjected to compulsory arbitration in the fixing of wages, that his right to call a strike not be limited by law. Yet it is plain for all to see that economic "laws," and the forces of competition, and the "invisible hand" of the market are not adequate to integrate the efforts of all those involved in our economic system. The long-run trend has been toward more and more governmental interposition to compose conflicts within the economy, and the ineluctable logic of the nature of the economic system drives toward additional public control.

Now, the growth of governmental regulation seems to stimulate the growth of the organization of private interests and, by that means, to increase the political strength of private groups. The exercise of governmental power gives to all those affected a common interest in organizing to influence the way in which the power is exercised. The objective may be to prevent or to mitigate the severity of governmental action or it may be to promote governmental action. Labor groups organize to obtain legislation regulating employers; business competitors then find a common interest in organizing to obstruct such legislation. Agricultural groups organize to protect themselves against the power of industry and labor. Once it wins some legislative success, an agricultural group, like other groups, becomes stronger, more alert to its interests, and perhaps more avid in the pursuit of political advantage.

As interest groups become more strongly entrenched and gain in membership, their demands become more particularistic. Perhaps there is some inner logic of group formation and maintenance that brings concentration of attention on the short-term interests and ambitions of the persons composing the group. Probably the more cohesive the group becomes the more it tends to broaden the scope of its activities to encompass more and more of the attention and interest of its members. This monopolization of the right of representation of individuals focuses group effort on the promotion of the objectives of the group against all competing interests. At any rate, the probability is that to the degree that groups succeed in monopolizing the loyalty of

their members—in contrast with the situation in which individual
loyalties are divided among many groups—to that extent intergroup
cleavages are widened and deepened. Whatever the nature of the
process of group formation and differentiation may be, the growth of
stronger and stronger groups dedicated to the promotion of narrow
group claims places more and more strain on the social mechanisms for
the settlement of group and class conflict.

The dilemma of the politics of economic control comes from the
fact that governments must keep in check the pressures of particularism,
yet at the same time governments derive their power in no small degree
from the support of particularistic interests. Government—that is,
political parties, public agencies, the bureaucracy—has a social strength
within itself, but fundamentally its power comes from the support won
for its policies among the organized and unorganized private interests
of society. These are the groups whose activities the government must
control in the general interest.

The solution of the dilemma of controlling the controllers is not easy.
Government can play one group off against another. It can decide
that the public welfare requires favoring one interest over another at
one time and that later the balance of power must be redressed by a
shift of governmental policy in another direction. Government can
umpire disputes; it can ally itself with one combination of interests or
with another. Yet the question may well be raised whether this sort
of heroic juggling of huge power blocs produces adjustments of sufficient nicety to meet the necessities of the operation of the complex
modern economy. Skilled political leadership can at times cut through
the complex of loyalties and interests and reach the common denominator of citizen interest to mobilize mass support for programs in the
general welfare against the opposition of even the most powerful private group. Such deftness of political leadership, however, is not a
dependable quality of government. The problem of organizing public
power, adequate in strength yet responsibly exercised under public
control, for the reconciliation of group conflict and the imposition of
programs promotive of the general welfare will doubtless remain for
some time without a completely satisfactory solution.

Part Two

THE PARTY SYSTEM

Chapter 8

NATURE AND FUNCTION OF PARTY

GOVERNMENT derives its strength from the support or acquiescence of a combination of powerful elements in society. That support or acquiescence may be based on interest, fear, tradition, or a combination of these and other factors. The basis of governmental power differs with the traditions and nature of societies. In one instance a comparatively small group with control of instruments of violence may constitute the machinery of government and cow the populace into submission at least for a time. In other instances authority may rest to a far greater degree upon free consent of the governed. In one state those in the seats of power may claim the right to retain their places without challenge; in others provision may be made for periodic changes in the personnel of government by orderly processes.

A fundamental characteristic of democratic regimes is the existence of the right to compete for control of the government by peaceful appeal to the electorate. Equally basic is the right to seek to influence the temporary holders of power in the exercise of the duties vested in them. In turn, both of these rights—the right to compete for governmental control and the right to influence the government—depend on freedom of association. Neither of these rights can be utilized with great effect by individuals. Competition for control of the government must be carried on by and large by associations or groups, as must efforts to influence the holders of power.

The form and structure of associations competing for control of government depend somewhat on the nature of the society. In a highly specialized and differentiated society it is difficult for any single interest to compete successfully for the control of government. It is, for example, not probable that the Chamber of Commerce of the United States could put forward with any hope of success candidates for the Presidency, the Vice-Presidency, and Congress. Nor is it probable that the American Federation of Labor could do so. A combination of interests is necessary to win elections and to govern. Political parties attempt to form such a combination. They put forward candidates for public office. They compete by electoral means for control of the government apparatus. (This means, of course, that the "parties" of one-party states which brook no opposition are not parties in the western democratic sense.) Pressure groups, on the other hand, are mainly concerned with influencing the policies followed by the party after it gets into office.

Both pressure groups and political parties play important roles in American politics. The distinction often made between their functions is that pressure groups are interested in policy; political parties, in governmental personnel. That succinct differentiation is a bit too simple. Private associations are certainly concerned about the personnel of government; pressure groups constantly seek to influence appointments to public office. They are not indifferent to the selection of holders of elective office, but, unlike political parties, they do not take the responsibility of nominating and supporting candidates for such offices. Nor are political parties indifferent about public policy. Party leaders may have, and often do have, strong convictions on matters of public policy. But there is a fundamental difference in the motivation of the policy attitudes of parties and pressure groups. By the nature of the interests of their memberships, the attitudes of pressure groups toward public policy are fixed. Parties, on the other hand, are governed by no such rigid determination of their attitudes. They are apt to adhere to a doctrine of relativity of righteousness, and their stands on public policy may shift with the changing fortunes and influence of the various social groups to which they must appeal for electoral support.

1. THEORIES ABOUT THE NATURE OF PARTY

Both parties and pressure groups are associations, but it is much more difficult to grasp the real nature of political parties than it is to gain a comprehension of pressure groups. Pressure organizations have well-defined bodies of members, usually dues-paying, constitutions, duly constituted sets of officials, and other usual institutional apparatus. Political parties have the same characteristics—except that most of their "members" pay no dues and the fact of membership rests fairly lightly on their shoulders. These superficial similarities between the two types of association conceal more fundamental differences. The definition of the nature of political parties is attended by no little difficulty, and no pat definition contains a foundation for thorough comprehension of their nature.

Parties inherent in social groups. One approach toward an understanding of political parties is to consider the nature of the functioning of social groups of which the state is only one type. Within all sorts of associations or groups "political parties" exist, although they may not ordinarily be so designated. Affairs of a group, be it a nation, a church, a union, or a chamber of commerce, do not and cannot take care of themselves; small factions of men must advance proposals and must put themselves forward as willing to assume responsibility for handling the affairs of the group. Even in the smallest of societies a minority of "ring-leaders" or several minorities of such persons are almost invariably found. They propose ways of dealing with group problems and vie for public place; they exercise leadership. Parties are, it might be said, inherent in human society; these groups of leaders, of course, may or may not operate in every society as they do in a democratic society. They may simply be the strongest and best-armed men in a group. In a large and populous society the party group may become amorphous and ill-defined. Yet the function of public leadership is inherent in social existence; a society inherently has its leaders and followers and its would-be leaders. In a democratic society the principal leaders in political affairs are to be found in political parties.

These remarks, in essence, consist of the assertion that political parties are more or less axiomatic; they are inherent in social life although they are not always called "parties" and they operate in different ways in different cultures. Perhaps the validity of the foregoing interpretation of the nature of party may be suggested by a brief excursion into some phases of the development of parties in the United States. The early theory of democracy spoke of the "general will" and the "consent of the governed," but was not always explicit about how the "general will" was to be expressed or the "consent of the governed" granted. Speculators about democracy seemed to believe that by some mystic process the "will of the people" would be expressed and rulers would be selected. But a mass of people cannot act as a unit; a small inner circle has to narrow the choices for public office and to formulate questions of public policy. Or perhaps it would be more accurate to say that small groups of men by working together can control the mass. At any rate, early in our history small groups began to act in concert by agreeing on candidates and policies they would support before the electorate as a whole. An early example of this sort of activity was recorded in February, 1763, by John Adams in his diary:

This day I learned that the caucus club meets at certain times in the garret of Tom Dawes, the adjutant of the Boston regiment. He has a large house, and he has a movable partition of his garret, which he takes down, and the

whole club meets in one room.   There they smoke tobacco till you cannot see
from one end of the room to the other.   There they drink flip, I suppose, and
there they choose a moderator who puts questions to the vote regularly; and
selectmen, assessors, collectors, firewards, and representatives are regularly
chosen before they are chosen in the town.[1]

If planning and agreement by a caucus to work in concert was a
natural development in the town of Boston of 1763, it can readily be
seen that the work of some such extragovernmental group is much more
necessary to make representative government function over the entire
United States.   Yet the framers of the Constitution did not provide
any machinery analogous to the caucus or party to carry on these duties
in the formal mechanism of the national government; nor did they,
apparently, foresee the rise of political parties in their present form.
For the selection of the President, the framers devised the electoral
college to be appointed in each state "in such manner as the legislatures thereof" might direct.   The electors were to "meet in their respective states" and vote by ballot, and the ballots were to be forwarded
"to the seat of Government," where they would be opened and counted.
If there was a tie or if no person received a majority, the House of
Representatives was to choose the President.

In defending this system, Hamilton in *The Federalist* [2] explained
that it appeared best that the selection should be made by a "small
number of persons" chosen from the general mass who could be "most
capable of analysing the qualities adapted to the station."   Indirect
selection of the President through the electoral college was "peculiarly
desirable" since it afforded "as little opportunity as possible to tumult
and disorder."   Voting by the electors assembled in each state would
furnish an obstacle to "cabal, intrigue, and corruption."   "The business of corruption, when it is to embrace so considerable a number of
men, requires time as well as means.   Nor would it be found easy to
suddenly embark them, dispersed as they would be over thirteen states,
in any combinations founded upon motives which, though they could
not properly be denominated corrupt, might yet be of a nature to
mislead them from their duty."   Hamilton thought that the process
of election would afford a "moral certainty that the office of President"
would "never fall to the lot of any man . . . not in eminent degree
endowed with the requisite qualifications.   Talents for low intrigue
and the little arts of popularity" might "alone suffice to elevate a man
to the first honours in a single State"; but it would "require other

talents, and a different kind of merit, to establish him in the esteem and confidence of the whole Union, or of so considerable a portion of it as would be necessary to make him a successful candidate for the distinguished office of President of the United States."

As soon as the new government got well under way it became necessary to develop cabals and cliques outside the government to perform for the nation as a whole what the caucus club that met in Tom Dawes' garret did for Boston. That the electors in the several states would act independently and without concert was unlikely; in fact, prior to the first election under the Constitution, Hamilton himself "sent word into several States, advising that unanimous vote be given to Washington." [3] It was probably expected that the electors in the several states would represent the same interests and work together in the same manner as did the framers of the Constitution. "The constitutional history of the United States begins with the establishment of the government of the masses by the classes. It was expected as a matter of course that the gentry would control every branch of the government." [4]

The elaborate and cumbersome machinery provided by the Constitution for the election of the President perhaps, as some students contend, represented a deliberate effort to devise a scheme to be controlled by the "rich and well born." Probably there was an element of the sheer experimental in the plan. Theretofore rulers had been selected by and large by battle, birth, or marriage, or as representatives of cohesive and crystallized classes. What sort of substitute could be devised? At any rate, whether the "gentry" or the "people" governed, it was necessary to have some sort of machinery through which candidates could be agreed upon in advance. It was not likely that either the "gentry" or the "people" would leave the workings of the electors to chance, and with the broadening of the suffrage it became even more essential that there be means for consolidating forces on candidates and for making their merits and beliefs known. [5]

[3] Edward Stanwood, *A History of the Presidency* (Boston: Houghton Mifflin, 1926), Vol. I, p. 26.

[4] Ford, *Rise and Growth of American Politics* (New York: Macmillan, 1898), p. 59.

[5] It may be noted that even the threats of southern elements of the Democratic party in the campaign of 1944 not to instruct their electors for Roosevelt were in accord with the "rubber-stamp" tradition of the electoral college. The South Carolina convention, for example, declined to name its electors prior to the national convention; they wanted to await the action of the national convention on such matters as the "race" question, the poll tax, the vice-presidential nomination. The threat was that South Carolina Democratic electors might in November cast their vote for a candidate other than Roosevelt. However, the move in South Carolina and other states turned out to be a tempest in a teapot. Yet even had it been otherwise, the electors presumably would have voted in accord with the wishes of

Parties an element of governmental apparatus. Political parties are
ordinarily thought of as institutions separate and apart from the formal
apparatus of government, but the foregoing discussion suggests that
parties can be considered virtually as a part of the government, performing the vital function of leadership in the selection of governmental personnel and in the proposal of public policies. The conception of party as essentially an element in the governmental system is
given further color by the fact that political parties have come to be
closely regulated by law and thereby recognized as performing public
functions. The caucus club in Tom Dawes' garret in eighteenth-
century Boston operated without legal restriction or regulation. Presumably it could admit to its circle whom it wished and proceed as it
desired, but the present-day party is hedged about by legal restrictions
that grew out of abuses by the party when it was a purely voluntary
association of individuals.[6] As the party system developed, entrance
to public office came to be almost exclusively through party nomination. The cliques in control of parties named the candidates from
whom public elective officers were selected. The nominating system in
general use at the time regulation of parties began was particularly
susceptible to fraudulent manipulation. It was the convention system
based on the selection of delegates at "primary" meetings of voters in
each precinct—much on the order of the Boston caucus club. The
controlling clique might call the primary without adequate notice,
manage the meeting in an autocratic manner, intimidate the dissenting
members, and falsify the ballot count, all without penalty of law, for
the party was a voluntary and private association on the same legal plane
as the Ladies Wednesday Afternoon Sewing Circle.

The move toward the assimilation of American parties into the state
apparatus was gradual. The first laws governing parties were optional
in character; that is, if a party, under the pressure of public opinion,
elected to operate under them, a number of regulations governed the

_____

the party in the state, and the situation would have represented a party split rather
than a departure from the tradition that electors exercise no personal judgment but
merely record the wishes of the party.

6 In several southern states parties are yet considered to be private associations.
This legal fiction was maintained because as a private association the party could
exclude Negroes from its primaries, an exclusion which the state itself could not
accomplish because of the limitations of the Fourteenth Amendment of the Constitution. Although the parties have been deemed legally private associations, their
operations have been subjected to varying degrees of state control. The Supreme
Court, however, has interpreted this public regulation to constitute state acquiescence
in unconstitutional actions, and an effort has been made to remove all state control
and to return these parties to a purely private status. In 1944 South Carolina repealed all its legislation regulating parties and left to the party the entire management of its affairs.

conduct of its primaries.   Presently, mandatory laws were substituted for the optional, and detailed regulation of party activity was built up. Parties have generally lost the unlimited right to establish qualifications for membership; tests of membership are usually prescribed by law. Procedure to be followed in selecting candidates of the party is prescribed by law; generally the selection of party candidates is through a direct primary conducted by public officials under public regulation at public cost.   Where the convention system is retained, the membership of the convention is selected according to methods prescribed by statute, and the procedure of the convention itself is governed by law.[7]

The development of public regulation of party activities was resisted by those groups controlling the parties; they anticipated that the power they derived from control of the party would be weakened by public regulation.   The regulation of parties was urged as a means of wiping out abuses that had grown up around the party and of making the party less irresponsible and less independent of the wishes of the rank and file of the party membership.[8]   The culmination of the movement for regulation may be interpreted as an amalgamation of the machinery of private associations with the machinery of government itself; the party was found to perform an essential function in the governing process and it was appropriated by the state.   In practice, the regulation of parties is handled by the state legislatures; but the national conventions are not beyond state control in that delegates are often elected under procedures fixed by state law; and the national party organization is little more than a loose alliance of state organizations, each operating under the provisions of state law.[9]

Contestants for power.   Theories of the nature of political parties are sometimes phrased in terms of political power.   The customary definitions of party, although usually in other terms, agree essentially with the conception of parties as groups exercising leadership within the state; that is, they seek power in the community for the sake of varying objectives.   Yet whether the party is seen as inherent in social groupings, as a necessary extension of the apparatus of government, or as a contestant for power within the community, the essence is the same.   These are only different ways of looking at the same phenomenon.

[7] The rise of public control of parties is traced by C. E. Merriam and Louise Overacker, *Primary Elections* (Chicago: University of Chicago Press, 1928).

[8] For an early presentation of the case for party regulation, see Frank J. Goodnow, *Politics and Administration* (New York: Macmillan, 1900), pp. 206–250.

[9] The most thorough analysis of the legal status of parties is by Joseph R. Starr, "The Legal Status of American Political Parties," *American Political Science Review*, 34 (1940), pp. 439–455, 685–699.

Commentators on parties as contestants for power sometimes introduce confusion into the discussion by disputes about the "true" objective of party and by failure to indicate sharply the limits of the sub-
group within society that is said to be seeking power. What persons,
thus, are to be included within the "party" contesting for power?
Burke's often quoted definition of party is: "Party is a body of men
united, for promoting by their joint endeavors the national interest,
upon some particular principle in which they are all agreed." This
definition hardly fits all the facts in so far as American parties are concerned. American parties are not bodies of men "agreed" upon particular principles concerning the "national interest." Perhaps, as is
contended by Morse,[10] parties never promote the national interest; they
seek to advance something less than the national interest. Yet they
also seek to promote something more nearly the national interest than
do pressure groups. Burke's definition, however, in its implicit recognition of the party's function of leadership in promotion and of the
party's striving to gain power to advance particular objectives touches
on the reality of party.

The application of the criteria, "united" and "agreed" in Burke's
definition to the party groups within the American Congress leads to
a rejection of his definition, at least in part, and suggests the importance of delimiting the group included within the term party. Neither
the Republicans nor the Democrats within Congress can maintain unity
on many issues. Each party group finds many questions of principle
that render party leaders impotent and split the ranks of the party
group. On the other hand, the party machinery outside the government has less difficulty in maintaining unity during campaigns. The
parties, in a sense, are bodies of men united to get into office. Thus, in
May, 1946, at a time when the Democratic "parliamentary" party was
beset by internal dissension, Robert E. Hannegan, the Democratic
national chairman, stated: "After the primaries are over, we will support all the Democratic candidates vigorously. That has been our
policy and it will continue to be our policy." [11] Party unity in Congress might be weak, but the party outside Congress had to unite
to support for election each candidate bearing its label whether

[10] The late Professor Anson D. Morse said: "To sum up; the true end of party—the
end, I would repeat, of which it is itself conscious—is, in ordinary times, to promote
not the general interest, but the interest of a class, a section, or some one of the
many groups of citizens which are to be found in every state in which there is political life, an interest which is always something other—and generally, though not
always, something less—than the national interest." *Parties and Party Leaders* (Boston: Marshall Jones, 1923), p. 22.

[11] Washington *Post*, May 23, 1946.

he subscribed to the darkest conservatism or the pinkest liberalism.

The contrast in party emphasis on personnel and policy characterizes the definition of party by the late Professor Sait. "Party," he said, "may be defined as an organized group that seeks to control both the personnel and the policy of the government." [12] He adds that the "two characteristics of party—one having to do with the policy, the other with the personnel of the government—are not of equal significance. Politicians are far more preoccupied with getting offices than they are with proclaiming policies." [13] The emphasis in this conception of party on the objectives of the group differentiates party from other groups with political aims. In the analysis of pressure groups it was seen that a wide variety of organized groups, ranging from organized vice to organized religion, seeks to control, or at least to influence, the policy of government. But these associations do not ordinarily nominate candidates and campaign for their election to public office. Parties, on the other hand, attempt to place their nominees in elective office and fill those appointive offices included among the perquisites of the party that controls the government.

But what of the nature of the "group" that seeks to control the personnel and policies of the government? A useful working distinction to keep in mind is that between the inner core of party workers and leaders and the mass of partisans whose principal contribution to party activity is a vote on election day. Professor E. E. Robinson asserts that to comprehend the nature of a political party we must concentrate attention on the inner core or organization of the party which comes

into being for the purpose of fighting and governing. It is not concerned with matters of fact, or doctrine, or even of principle, except as they bear upon the great cause for existence: success at the polls. Such organizations not only contain men of divergent views; they must also appeal to voters of differing opinions, prejudices, and loyalties. It is folly to talk of finding an actual basis [for political parties] in any set of principles relating to public welfare.

He sees party as a "comparatively small and compact body of men. Real power rests with them. They formulate appeals, direct campaigns, discuss in advance, and decide the nature of programs to be submitted to the voters." [14] Professor Robinson's approach and his phraseology recall the theory that democratic politics is but a sublimation, perhaps temporary, of the use of force to gain control of govern-

[12] E. M. Sait, *American Parties and Elections* (New York: Century, 1927), p. 141.
[13] *Ibid.*, p. 143.
[14] E. E. Robinson, "The Place of Party in the Political History of the United States," *Annual Reports of the American Historical Association for the Years 1927 and 1928* (1929), p. 202.

ment. Whether this hypothesis correctly represents the evolutionary path followed in the development of the modern party is open to question; nevertheless, the theory gives a clue to the nature of the party struggle.

Emphasis on the importance of the inner group of leaders and workers in party activity serves to center attention on the main sources of party action, but the inner circle would amount to nothing without its following of faithful partisans. This is not to say that a more meaningful definition of party comes from defining party as a group consisting of those persons voting or registered as Democrats or Republicans. Party membership, however, may carry with it no strong sense of group attachment. In many states membership in either of the major parties is gained simply by a person's indicating the party with which he wishes to affiliate when he registers as a voter; affiliation is even less formal in other states. The process of gaining·membership in the party is a different matter from affiliation with more tightly organized groups. The party member does not go through an elaborate ritual of induction into the group; in most instances he neither is acquainted with nor knows the name of the ward or county chairman of his party; he probably never supports his party in any way financially; the various privileges and responsibilities of party membership rest lightly on his shoulders.[15]

Despite the informality of acquisition of legal membership in a party, the psychological attachment of the great mass of partisans to their party possesses remarkable durability. Even if the party member is an unfaithful attendant at party functions and an infrequent contributor to its finances, he is likely to have a strong attachment to the heroes of the party, to its principles as he interprets them, and to its candidates on election day. The mass of the membership thus conditions the attitudes of party leaders, who must act in a manner to retain its loyalty, and by its support gives strength to the leadership.[16] At later points detailed information on persistence of party attachment is presented. It is sufficient to note here that definition of party solely in terms of the inner core, the organization, serves to direct attention to an extremely important part of the party group, but party is considerably more than the inner ring of leaders and workers.

In the western democracies the competition for power implied in these definitions and excursions into the nature of party is, on the face

[15] See the analysis by C. A. Berdahl, "Party Membership in the United States," *American Political Science Review*, 36 (1942), pp. 16–50, 241–262.

[16] See the paper by J. W. Gannaway, "The Real Party Forces," *Iowa Journal of History and Politics*, 3 (1905), pp. 511–528.

of things at least, among rival parties.[17] Their contests, of course, often only reflect conflict between other interests in society. Freedom of formation of associations to seek to control the state prevails only in the western democracies and in states modeled after them. In this sense the Communist party of Russia is no party at all. Nor was the Nazi party of Germany or the Fascist party of Italy. These groups, at least after they gained control of the government, were not competitors for power in the way that the British Labor and Conservative parties battle for control of the government. Totalitarian parties have significant political functions, but they belong in a different category of institutions from parties of democratic states.[18]

2. THE TWO-PARTY PATTERN

Commentators on the American party system have long been perplexed by the fact that during most of our history power has alternated between two major parties. Although minor parties have risen from time to time and exerted some influence on governmental policy, the two major parties have been the only serious contenders for the Presidency. For relatively long periods, a single party has from time to time dominated on the national scene, but even during these eras the opposition has retained the loyalty of a substantial proportion of the electorate. Most of the voters consistently place their faith in one or the other of two parties and neither party has been able to wipe out the following of the other, as may be seen graphically from an examination of Figure 10, which depicts the division of the major-party vote since 1880.

From a knowledge of the divergent interests in American society one might expect numerous parties to be formed to represent interests with conflicting aims and objectives. It seems likely, in fact, that the framers of the Constitution expected the development of a multiplicity of parties, or, to use their terminology, factions. Madison, in the tenth

[17] The opinion of the late Senator John J. Ingalls, of Kansas, about the nature of party competition is of interest: "The purification of politics is an iridescent dream. Government is force. Politics is a battle of supremacy. Parties are the armies. The Decalogue and the golden rule have no place in a political campaign. The object is success. To defeat the antagonist and expel the party in power is the purpose. The commander who lost a battle through the activity of his moral nature would be the derision and jest of history. The modern cant about corruption in politics in fatiguing in the extreme. It proceeds from the tea-custard and syllabub dilettanteism, the frivolous and desultory sentimentalism, of epicenes." The editors of the *Nation* quoted this passage (Vol. 51, 1890, p. 371) on the occasion of the Senator's defeat which they regarded as an "incalculable gain."

[18] On the nature and function of parties generally, consult C. E. Merriam and H. F. Gosnell, *The American Party System* (New York: Macmillan, 1940), chap. 19.

essay of *The Federalist,* observed that those "who hold and those who are without property have ever formed distinct interests in society. Those who are creditors, and those who are debtors, fall under a like discrimination. A landed interest, a manufacturing interest, a mercantile interest, a moneyed interest, with many lesser interests, grow up of necessity in civilized nations, and divide them into different classes, actuated by different sentiments and views." Why not a different political party to represent each of these interests, which have, of course, grown in number and complexity since Madison wrote his sapient remarks?

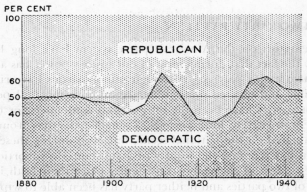

Figure 10. Division of Major-Party Popular Vote in Presidential Elections, 1880–1944

Influence of single-member districts and plurality elections. Mystics have occasionally sought to explain the biparty system on grounds of the genius of Anglo-Saxon peoples for self-government, but this proposition is about as specious as are most political theories resting on suppositions of peculiar racial or national characteristics. Among the influences leading the electorate to divide itself into only two major groups, great weight must be attributed to the system of choosing representatives from single-member districts by a plurality vote in contrast with systems of proportional representation which, of necessity, are based on multi-member districts. In a single-member district only two parties can contend for electoral victory with any hope of success; a third party is doomed to perpetual defeat unless it can manage to absorb the following of one of the major parties and thereby become one of the two parties itself. Parties do not thrive on the certainty of defeat. Faced by this prospect the only alternative is to support one or the other of two parties. The single-member district thus molds parties into the bipartisan pattern. Each of the contending groups in such a district must formulate its appeals with an eye to attracting a majority of the electors to its banner.[19]

The single-member district, it may be pointed out in rebuttal, has not prevented the rise of more than two parties in Great Britain. This assertion is quite true, but it can be contended that the single-member district system greatly handicaps any third party and perhaps tends to drive it to extinction. The Liberal party, thus, found its parliamentary representation reduced far below its proportion of the popular vote as the Labor party grew in strength. Liberal voters came under a powerful persuasion to move into the Conservative or Labor party to gain a voice in the choice of representatives.

The student of comparative government may also cite French experience as a limitation on the single-member district theory. The Third Republic used a variety of electoral arrangements, but during most of its life some type of single-member district prevailed. However, plurality-election in its pure form did not prevail. The significant influence of the practice of electing by pluralities may be isolated by comparing the party divisions in the first elections for the Chamber of Deputies and in the run-off or *ballottage* held one week later. The *ballottage* came one week after the first voting if no candidate received an absolute majority in the district, and at the second polling a plurality was adequate to elect. At the *ballottage* parties had a great incentive to combine in support of a single candidate in order to be behind the winning candidate. Party leaders of both the left and right before World War II attempted more and more to form these coalitions, which approached the bipartisan form, in the campaign before the *ballottage*. Through such combinations the final contest might be between only two or three candidates. This state of affairs prevailed in 90 per cent of the 424 districts in which *ballottage* was necessary in the 1936 election.[20]

The effect of the use of the single-member district is perhaps to encourage a two-party division within each representative district. Other influences federate the two principal party groups within each representative district into two great competing national organizations.

Centripetal influence of Presidency. One of these other influences that dispose parties toward a dual cleavage in the United States is the

[19] The single-member district interpretation is presented in a brilliant comparative study by F. A. Hermens, *Democracy or Anarchy?* (Notre Dame: The Review of Politics, 1941). See the penetrating analysis by E. E. Schattschneider, *Party Government* (New York: Farrar & Rinehart, 1942), Chap. 5.

[20] See W. R. Sharp, *The Government of the French Republic* (New York: Van Nostrand, 1938), chap. 3.

popular election of chief executives. If a party aspires to capture the Presidency, the governorship of a state, or the mayoralty of a city, it must attempt to consolidate under its banner a majority of the voters, and, in practice, no more than two parties may compete for a majority of the electorate. The Presidency, unlike a French cabinet, cannot be parceled out among minuscule parties. In essence, the centripetal influence on party machinery exerted by the election of the President is but the single-member district influence brought to bear on a larger scale. The President is, in effect, chosen by the electors in forty-eight single-member constituencies who designate their electors by a plurality vote. The necessity of uniting to have a chance of participating in a victory in a presidential campaign pulls the state party organizations together, and the state organizations, in turn, are based on other sets of single-member constituencies. In the election of governors and mayors the single-member constituency appears in a purer form.

Dualism of interest. Although the method of choosing the President exerts a powerful influence on party structure, Arthur Macmahon believes that in addition, the two-party division was "induced by the existence of two major complexes of interest in the country." [21] A cleavage between agriculture and the interests of the mercantile and financial community antedated even the adoption of the Constitution. That conflict of interest, with a growing industry allying itself with trade and finance, was fundamental in the debate on the adoption of the Constitution and remained the great issue in national politics afterwards. The Civil War, although it brought with it a realignment within national politics, re-enforced the dual division within national politics. Democrats recalled the heroes of the Confederacy, and the Republicans waved the "bloody shirt" to rally their followers.

The form in which institutions initially take shape has a potent and durable influence. The fact that something of a genuine dual cleavage of interest existed at the time of the adoption of the Constitution and at the time of the germination of political parties gave their bipartisan structure lasting momentum. Nothing emerges more clearly from a study of American politics than the conclusion that party attachments possess impressive persistence. This type of institutional behavior helps somewhat to fill in the gaps in any general theory of bipartisanism, as, for example, the existence of bipartisanism in Britain and its Dominions despite the lack of a unifying point, such as the American Presidency. In Great Britain the party system grew in a measure out of relatively well-defined class cleavages, as well as out of a struggle between the King and his supporters, on one hand, and those who were on the opposite side of the political fence. In this situation in Britain royal patronage and perquisites were used to form a king's party, whereas in France the monarchical custom was to divide and rule. These patterns once established have a life almost approaching immortality. The British system, in fact, could be exported bodily to the Dominions and there carry on the tradition.[22]

Uneven territorial distribution of party strength. An essential, although not necessarily a cause, for the existence of a two-party system is an uneven territorial distribution of the "complexes of interest" underlying parties or at least their popular following. Without this irregular distribution of voting strength, the majority party at any election would invariably win all the seats in the legislative body. The minority might have 49 per cent of the popular vote but none of the seats in the representative chamber. The election of Representatives in Kansas in 1944 illustrates the effect of a comparatively even distribution of strength. The vote in the congressional districts was as follows:

District	Democratic	Republican
1st	34,731	71,565
2nd	47,676	68,815
3rd	34,645	52,361
4th	63,843	90,186
5th	32,557	72,370
6th	32,408	63,035
Total	245,860	418,332

With 63 per cent of the popular vote in the state the Republicans won 100 per cent of the House seats; the Democrats polled 37 per cent of the popular vote, but won not a single seat. In other states a like advantage went to the Democrats.

In American politics the unequal territorial distribution of strength necessary for the maintenance of two parties has existed from the outset. Certain areas remain firm in their partisan loyalties even when the opposite party wins by a landslide in the nation as a whole. This state of affairs may be seen clearly in Figures 11 and 12. Figure 11 shows in black the Democratic counties in the presidential election of 1920. The Democratic candidate, James M. Cox, waged a hopeless campaign and polled only 36.1 per cent of the major-party popular vote, yet the sectional concentration of his strength was such that the Democratic counties make a sizeable dark spot on the map. Figure 12 presents

[22] See C. J. Friedrich, *Constitutional Government and Politics* (New York: Harper, 1937), chaps. 18 and 19.

similar data on the Republican vote in the presidential election of 1936. In that year the Republican candidate was a colorless Kansan named Landon, and the party's strength reached a new low of only 37.8 per cent of the major-party vote. Nevertheless, faithful partisans gave him a majority in counties concentrated mainly in the northeastern states but with a liberal sprinkling throughout the Middle West.[23] The strong

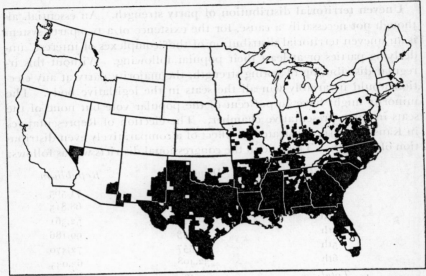

Figure 11. Democratic Counties in Presidential Election of 1920

tinge of sectionalism in American politics has always assured a majority in some areas to the minority party nationally. The unevenness of distribution of strength necessary to prevent disappearance of minority representation need not, of course, be sectional in character.

The uneven distribution of party strength plays an important part in the recruitment of party leaders and workers. A party with a majority in particular regions can always elect some Congressmen, who acquire experience and knowledge against the day when their party gains control nationally. In the same regions the minority party nationally may control state and local governments. The winning of these elections furnishes sustenance to the party workers, and these governments serve as training grounds for national service. The significance of this func-

23 In both maps most of the area shown in white went to the opposite party although in some instances counties shown in white were either unorganized or cast a plurality of their votes for minor-party candidates. For maps on another pair of campaigns, see Figures 6 and 7 on pages 159 and 160.

tion of recruitment and training of party timber appears vividly when one party sweeps the elections in areas where it has not enjoyed this advantage. The dearth of likely candidates in these regions is so great that, if the party wins unexpectedly, the persons who carry its label are often quite odd characters, with neither the aptitude nor the experience for statesmanship.

These observations point to an incidental consequence of the two-party system in the United States, viz., that over considerable areas we have in reality only a one-party system for purposes of state and local

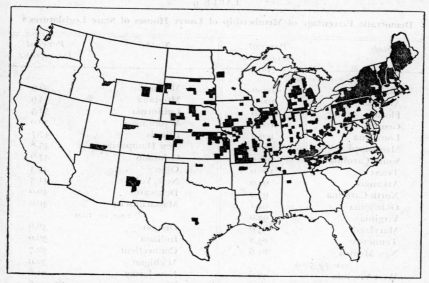

Figure 12. Republican Counties in Presidential Election of 1936

government. This condition has to be chalked up as a great failing of the biparty system. The tendency seems to be for those areas that are Democratic nationally to be even more Democratic locally and for areas Republican nationally to be even more Republican locally. In Table 9 the Democratic percentages of the lower houses of the state legislatures are shown. It may be seen from these data that in a considerable number of states the Republican minority is so small as to be negligible and that in a smaller number of states the Democratic minority approaches the vanishing point. The one-party system exists in its purest form in the southern states, but its incidence is not limited to that area. In one-party states factions, sometimes persistent, sometimes personal, sometimes transient, struggle for control of state and local government, but these groupings serve only to confuse the electorate and prevent clear-cut competition among well-defined groups for the control of state and local government.   General theories about parties have little relevance in description of the political battle in these areas.   "Intra-party battles in the South," Professor Powell concludes, "are not struggles between 'those who have' and 'those who have not,' in an economic sense, but rather are contests between 'some who have' and 'others who also have' to get more.   'Those who have not' are inarticulate and politically impotent." [24]

TABLE 9

Democratic Percentage of Membership of Lower Houses of State Legislatures [a]

State	Per cent Democratic	State	Per cent Democratic
80.0 to 100.0		Missouri	56.9
Alabama	100.0	Montana	53.9
Arizona	100.0	California	52.5
Florida	100.0	Wyoming	50.0
Georgia	100.0	Illinois	47.7
Louisiana	100.0	New Hampshire	45.8
Mississippi	100.0	Colorado	44.6
South Carolina	100.0	Ohio	43.4
Texas	100.0	New York	41.3
Arkansas	99.0	Delaware	40.0
North Carolina	95.0	Massachusetts	40.0
Oklahoma	94.1	*20.0 to 39.9*	
Virginia	93.0	Oregon	36.6
Maryland	85.0	Indiana	36.0
Tennessee	83.8	Connecticut	32.7
New Mexico	81.6	Michigan	32.0
60.0 to 79.9		New Jersey	31.6
West Virginia	78.6	Kansas	21.6
Utah	73.3	Iowa	20.3
Kentucky	72.0	*0.0 to 19.9*	
Washington	68.6	Wisconsin	15.0
Nevada	65.0	Vermont	15.0
Pennsylvania	60.5	Maine	14.5
40.0 to 59.9		South Dakota	13.3
Idaho	59.2	North Dakota	8.8
Rhode Island	59.0		

[a] Computed from data in Council of State Governments, *Book of the States*, 1941–42, p. 85.   Two states—Minnesota and Nebraska—choose legislators on nonpartisan ballots and, hence, cannot be included in the tabulation.

[24] A. L. Powell, "Politics and Political Parties: A Critique of Recent Literature." *Journal of Politics*, 4 (1942), pp. 95–106.   Professor Powell has proposed that the "factions" within the one-party state of Louisiana be formally recognized in the laws regulating party primaries creating, in effect, parties within a party to overcome some of the disadvantages of one-party dominance.   See his *Party Organization and Nominations in Louisiana* (University, La.: Bureau of Government Research, 1940), pp. 23–24.

Weakness of divisive influences. A factor of some importance, if not in preventing the rise of a multiparty system, at least in making the biparty system workable has been the practically complete absence from our politics of certain issues about which people may feel quite deeply. "Where economic, religious, or social groups are highly class conscious, there develops an insistence for the expression of their desires in the form of specially constituted class-parties." [25] Although there are racial minorities in the United States, they have either been politically repressed, as in the case of the Negro, or they have been, as in most instances, eager and able to earn a niche for themselves in the nation's social system. For example, the Germans of Milwaukee do not form a separatist party to return Milwaukee to the Fatherland as did the Germans of Alsace-Lorraine. Nor has there been a church with memories of earlier secular power and the habit of political action that would lead to the formation of religious political parties. The separation of church and state has in large measure kept from the political arena issues of a religious character. So far as economic classes are concerned, the feeling of class consciousness among workers has been weak in comparison with European countries, and labor parties have made little headway. The absence of religious, nationalistic, and economic sentiments on the European order has made it feasible for people of all these groups to work together in the same political parties rather than feel impelled to form splinter parties.

3. BIPARTISANISM AND POLITICAL ISSUES

The parties of a two-party system tend toward similarity in their views on public issues. They may and do have differences, but the points of agreement outnumber the points of disagreement. Their diffidence in taking clear-cut positions on issues of principle stand out sharply when American parties are compared with the parties of a multiparty system. Even in the British party system, Conservatives and Laborites find themselves in no fundamental disagreement on a considerable range of issues, and in Canada the American pattern is approached still more closely.

Similarities and differences in party composition. The tendency toward agreement between parties under a bipartisan system flows from the fact that party leaders must seek to build a majority of the electorate. In the nation as a whole a majority cannot be built upon the support of organized labor alone; the farmers cannot muster enough votes to form a majority; businessmen are decidedly in a minority. Given the traditional attachments of large blocs of voters in all these

[25] W. J. Shepard, "The Psychology of the Bi-Party System," *Social Forces*, 4 (1926), pp. 795–804.

classes to one party or another, about the only way in which a majority can be formed is to draw further support from voters of all classes and interests. To draw support from all classes and interests party leaders cannot afford to antagonize any major segment of the population. A convenient way to antagonize an element in the population is to take an unequivocal stand on an issue of importance. Similarities of composition, hence, contribute to two features of American parties: their similarity and their addiction to equivocation and ambiguity.

The data on party composition are limited in extent, but they support the foregoing general observations. From the extensive discussion of "class warfare" and "class hatreds and dissensions" in the early 'forties, it might be inferred that the fundamental pattern of division between the political parties has been altered. But that is not true. Each party continues to draw on all social classes for support. The data accumulated on this subject by the American Institute of Public Opinion are presented in Table 10. If the occupational groups are diagrammatically represented as horizontal bands in order of economic status, the line dividing Republicans and Democrats would be a diagonal, with more than half the highest economic classes on the Republican side and more than half the lower economic classes on the Democratic side of the line. Yet in each party are found substantial parts of every social class. Moreover, observation of the trends in

TABLE 10

Democratic Percentage of Major-Party Vote within Occupational Groups, 1936, 1940, and 1944 [a]

Occupational Groups	1936 Presidential Election	1940 Presidential Election	1944 Presidential Election
Professional	49	38	42
Businessmen	47	34	41
Farmers	59	54	48
White-collar workers	61	48	51
Skilled workers	67	59	59
Semiskilled workers	74	67	62
Unskilled workers	81	69	65

[a] E. G. Benson and Paul Perry, "Analysis of Democratic-Republican Strength by Population Groups," *Public Opinion Quarterly,* 4 (1940), pp. 464–473; AIPO Release, March 3, 1945.

Table 10 indicates that every class shifted its attitudes in the same direction between 1936 and 1940. Every class of the population, to some degree at least, responded to the same kind of appeals. In 1944 the Democrats regained some support among the business and professional classes in comparison with the 1940 vote, whereas the Republicans picked up strength among workers. This movement of labor toward the Republican party continued in the 1946 congressional election.

Similarities in the composition of the parties can be partially accounted for by the sectional distribution of the major strength of the two principal parties—resultant in considerable measure from the residue of attitudes and animosities left by the Civil War—coupled with the fact that through the federal system a great many issues are handled within the states. In other words, a sectional cleavage divides the parties nationally; but within each section the dominant interests, regardless of party, have had similar political philosophies on those matters handled by state governments. Those political philosophies, and the underlying interests, could be promoted through the state government without much concern about the particular party banner under which the political battle was fought. "In the South, where the most solid core of the party still rests, the Democrats are, by the very laws of their own being, the conservative political force. . . . The Democrats are indeed as much the representatives of property and business in the South as are the Republicans in the North." [26]

If the national party organizations are only loose alliances of state machines, it is to be expected that each party nationally will tend to take on the color of the most powerful of its state machines. And those state machines that are able to retain almost unbroken control of their state governments are likely to be highly influential in national party councils. If the most powerful Republican and Democratic state organizations are each dominated by a similar complex of interests, those views are likely to be projected into both national party organizations. To put the matter differently, there is no bloc of states each dominated by a well-established left-wing group that could form the basis for a national party organization.

Although the similarities in the composition of the two parties are significant, so are the differences. The data support Charles Beard's conclusion that "the center of gravity of wealth is on the Republican side while the center of gravity of poverty is on the Democratic side." [27] Democratic strength in the laboring groups is greater than that of the Republicans, a difference that gives the Democratic party an attractiveness to labor leaders and to others concerned with social reform. Furthermore, on some issues of public policy the ranks of the two parties hold contrasting attitudes. A clue to the inter-party clash in attitudes

[26] Paul H. Douglas, *The Coming of a New Party* (New York: Whittlesey House, 1932), p. 152.
[27] *National Municipal Review*, 6 (1917), p. 204.

comes from the February, 1944, *Fortune* Survey of Public Opinion (reprinted by special permission of the Editors). On polls of this sort evaluation of the significance of the findings is fraught with hazard, but the results may be presented for what they are worth. The question and the responses of the entire sample were as follows:

Which of these comes closest to expressing your ideas of what the government should do to avoid a period of unemployment after the war?
a. Let business and industry work out the problem without any government interference at all   14.7%
b. Depend mainly on business and industry to create enough employment normally, and just provide work at those times when industry cannot employ everyone   31.9
c. Carry on continuously a program of public works, enlarging it during periods of unemployment and reducing it when there are plenty of jobs   35.3
d. Carry on large government works all the time, even if business and industry find it hard to get enough workers in good times   7.1
e. Don't know   11.0

When the responses were classified according to party preference, fairly sharp differences of attitude appeared between adherents of the two parties. The responses classified according to party were:

	Those who expect to vote		Those who do not yet know
	Republican	Democratic	
a. Leave it all to business	22.1 ⎱	9.1 ⎱	12.8 ⎱
	⎰ 61.3	⎰ 37.3	⎰ 41.3
b. Let business lead	39.2 ⎰	28.3 ⎰	28.5 ⎰
c. Let government have a continous program	26.7 ⎱	44.4 ⎱	32.2 ⎱
d. Let government compete with business	5.6 ⎰ 32.3	9.0 ⎰ 53.4	5.9 ⎰ 39.1
e. Don't know	6.4	9.3	19.6

Although substantial portions of the memberships of both parties were in agreement, the "centers of gravity" of the two groups were on opposite sides of the issue presented. These differences in attitude toward public policy appear to be consistent with expectations inferable from the differences in party composition shown in Table 10.

A closer look at some of the vocational groups represented substantially in both parties discloses further contrasts in party composition. Note that in Table 10 the business community appears to have its feet in both parties. To a degree this reflects the sectional distribution of business; southern business finds it advantageous to be Democratic for

reasons of state and local politics.   But other differences in the composition of the business element in the two parties exist.   A bit of evidence
on the subject comes from an analysis of the contributors of gifts of over
$1,000 to the party war chests in 1944.   The information is presented in
Table 11.   Note that the business groups predominantly Democratic
in financial affection differ markedly from those who put their money
on the Republican candidate.   The liquor industry, movie magnates
and amusement impresarios generally, contractors, and merchants were
Democratic, whereas the financiers, manufacturers, utility men, and
mine owners gave more generously to Mr. Dewey's campaign fund.

TABLE 11

**Percentage Division of Total Contributions by Persons of Specified Occupational
Affiliation between Democratic and Republican Campaigns, 1944 [a]**

Group	Democratic	Republican
Brewers, distillers, soft drinks	95.5	4.5
Amusements and the arts	93.8	6.2
Officeholders	88.4	11.6
Contractors, builders, building materials	65.4	34.6
Merchants, wholesale and retail	58.2	41.8
Professions	48.1	51.9
Publishers, radio, advertising	47.7	52.3
Public utilities	36.2	63.8
Real estate	35.7	64.3
Insurance	35.1	64.9
Oil	33.6	66.4
Manufacturers	19.8	80.2
Bankers, brokers, financiers	18.8	81.2
Mining	5.3	94.7

[a] Computed from data presented by Louise Overacker, "Presidential Campaign
Funds, 1944," *American Political Science Review*, 39 (1945), p. 916.

The similarities and differences in party composition account for the
similarities and differences in party policies.   It is, of course, incorrect
to say that American parties have no principles or policies.   They have;
but their principles tend toward similarity.   To see that American
parties stand for certain governmental policies and values, although
essentially the same, it is only necessary to compare their outlook with
that of the Communist party of Russia, the erstwhile Fascist party of
Italy, or any one of the more extreme parties of the right or left of Republican France.   The programs of both American parties change from
time to time, but they both change at nearly the same rate and generally
in the same direction.   Their policies are the policies of a capitalistic
society, modified as recurring internal crises demand.

But how is the similarity of the general views of the two major parties to be explained? It has been indicated that a basic factor in the biparty division has been the necessity for a program and combination powerful enough to capture the Presidency. Although these combinations have been primarily sectional in character, all kinds of persons with all kinds of conflicting and divergent interests have been resident in the winning sectional combinations. The party has had to gain the support of a cross section of the entire population. Instead of dividing society vertically into parties of farmers, laborers, and businessmen, the party system has been so constructed that each party contains farmers, laborers, and businessmen. Parties compete for the support of the same kinds of people; the general objectives of both must, then, have a considerable similarity. Incidentally, this necessity for gaining support among a wide variety of classes also gives the party a degree of independence from the demands of extremist groups. Although the party has to appeal to many groups, it may form a winning combination without yielding to the demand of every small group.

The composition of parties probably also has a significant influence on the kinds of presidential candidates chosen. In candidates, as in platforms, the tendency must be to seek a candidate who antagonizes no important group by his undeviating attachment to some competing group. The candidate must personify the lowest common denominator of agreement among the elements of the party structure. Especially in the selection of new candidates, in contrast with the renomination of a sitting President, this principle seems to govern. An aspirant for a nomination who appears to be somewhere near the center of the divergent factions of his party usually seems to have a better chance than a person identified with any extreme faction of the party.

The inclusion of a cross section of the major interests of the country within each political party accounts for a peculiar function of the American party. It is often said that within the party machinery and through the party processes conflicts that would otherwise be mediated within the government itself are reconciled. In a multiparty situation the combination and compromise necessary to form a majority are made in the parliamentary body. In the United States it is said that these differences have to be adjusted within the party as an antecedent to co-operation in the campaign for the Presidency. There is an element of truth in this view of the party's function, but the degree to which compromise on policy is effectuated within the party machinery through agreement on platforms is often slight. About all that is done in the platform is to hold down the extremist elements in the party whose views might give offense in the campaign. The chief consensus arrived at through the party machinery is agreement on candidates; the battles on issues are fought out later in Congress, and there the play of interest often shatters party unity.

Identification of party differences. Though American parties tend toward similarity, they also have their differences. The difficulty that the majority of us have is in determining just what those differences are when we cast our ballots. In state and local politics, it must be said, that in most places only despair rewards him who tries to ascertain the issues between the parties. In a few states, as perhaps in New York, the voter has something of an alternative in choosing between the two parties. In presidential elections, the issues that divide parties are often more easily identified in retrospect than in prospect at the time of the election.

Party platforms offer a guide of little usefulness to the significant divergencies between the two parties. Even in a national election such as that of 1936, proclaimed at least by Liberty League orators as a great referendum on whether alien institutions and practices were to be substituted for traditional Americanism, the platforms of the two parties manifested a high degree of agreement on fundamental matters. A sample of the platform enunciations in that bitter campaign make the point. The Republicans attacked monopoly as "indefensible and intolerable" and promised "vigorous enforcement" of the laws against monopoly and the "enactment of such additional legislation as is necessary." The Democrats branded monopolies "the creature of Republican rule and privilege" and the "exploiter of the consumer," and pledged themselves "vigorously and fearlessly to enforce the criminal and civil provisions of the existing anti-trust laws" and, if necessary, to "restore" the efficacy of these laws. Regarding labor, the Republican platform makers promised to "protect the right of labor to organize and to bargain collectively through representatives of its own choosing without interference from any source." The Democrats pointed with pride to the fact that they had enacted legislation protecting the right of collective bargaining and declared that they would "continue to protect the worker and . . . guard his rights, both as wage earner and consumer. . . ."

Presidential campaign speeches are a better guide than platforms, but the preparation of speeches in the modern manner by the use of research experts, party conferences, and drafting experts may conceal the candidates' views as thoroughly as a platform conceals the interests underlying the party. The bewildered citizen could listen to the speeches by Messrs. Roosevelt and Dewey in 1944 and conclude that the principal issue was which party could do the same thing better. Indeed, in the nature of American politics, that is invariably one of the major issues. But in campaign oratory both candidates speak of the nobility of the American working man, the sacred values associated with the American farm home, the solid contributions of American business, the unsurpassed virtues of the great middle classes, and pledge themselves to defend and to promote all these things.[28]

The gyrations of Congress are no better guide. Within the party groups in both houses of Congress are to be found reactionaries and radicals. The voting record of the individual Representative or Senator may furnish a very satisfactory guide to whether a citizen wishes to return him to office,[29] but it may give no clue to the general trend of policy to be expected under one party or the other.

About the best index to party differences is an appeal to the record of this century with admixture of judicious guesses about whether the trend is likely to continue. It was pointed out that the Democratic party draws more support from workers than do the Republicans, that the center of gravity of wealth appears to be on the Republican side. The record of party promise and performance contains a parallel divergence. The Democratic party in this century has elected Woodrow Wilson and Franklin D. Roosevelt. Both administrations were characterized by programs of economic reform and an inclination to control the power of business. Yet in neither period of Democratic dominance was business crucified, despite wails to the contrary. Under the leadership of both these Presidents policies calculated to improve the lot of labor gained headway, although it cannot be said that the Democrats had a monopoly of this achievement. Democratic administrations promoted the cause of the farmers, but so did the Republicans. Of the Democratic leaders who did not achieve the Presidency during this period, Bryan belonged to the same tradition as Wilson and Roosevelt, but Parker and Davis would have felt completely at home in the Republican party. In affairs international the Democrats have been less disposed toward isolationism than the Republicans.

[28] The appeal to ambiguity reaches down the ranks to the lesser candidates. Consider the following classic straddle by the Honorable Wilmer C. Carter, candidate for renomination as a Democratic State Senator in Baltimore in June, 1946: "Although a church member, I have liberal views and am without prejudice. I am reasonably sympathetic to both labor and capital, believing both can live the American way by co-operative understanding that must be made possible by application of the Golden Rule, and the principle of live and let live."—Baltimore *Evening Sun,* June 22, 1946.

[29] The voting record is, of course, not conveniently available to most voters. A move to fill the void, however, was taken by the publication by Penguin Books before the election of 1946 of a *Handbook of Politics,* at 25¢, which contained roll calls and other information to enable a voter to find out what kind of a person his Congressman had turned out to be.

Over this period, on the whole, the driving force in the Republican party has been the financial and manufacturing community. Within the Republican party solvent citizens who feel that they can take care of themselves without government intervention, unless it is on a matter like the tariff, have exerted great influence. Hence, the Republican party has been less disposed to advance the cause of labor by governmental action; it has felt that what is good for business is good for the country. Yet Republicans in power ordinarily have not moved away from reforms already adopted. In 1936, for example, they viewed the Social Security Act with some disdain, but in 1944 Mr. Dewey was reproaching the Democrats for not extending its coverage. In this century the Republicans have no great reform for the regulation of business to their credit, yet at times they have proceeded with great vigor against business abuses, as under Theodore Roosevelt and Taft in the prosecution of combinations in restraint of trade. In general, it is probably not incorrect to conclude that the Republican party in this century, judged by the record, has been less inclined than the Democratic to use the powers of government to promote mass welfare.

In so far as we have a "conservative" and "liberal" cleavage, that cleavage is along Republican-Democratic lines. Even this sort of distinction fails in many times and situations. Yet after discounting the statement to allow for campaign exaggerations, a residue of fact remains in Wilson's assertion that "the chief difference between the Democratic and Republican parties is that in the Republican party the reactionaries are in the majority, whereas in the Democratic party they are in the minority." [30] The troubled voter cannot use this as an infallible guide, for in each party sometimes the minority gains the upper hand, and always broad areas of agreement exist between the parties. Furthermore, what a party actually does in office is perhaps dictated more by the necessities of the times than by party doctrines. Hence, it is hazardous to predict what the Democrats would have done had they won in 1920; or the Republicans, had they won in 1916.

Consensus: Curse or blessing? The broad area of agreement among political parties and the coyness with which major party leaders approach contentious issues are basic characteristics of our party system. In consequence, issues are dodged, clean-cut decisions avoided, and the animosities of party conflict are muffled. Party leaders often repress and ignore fundamental issues rather than bring them out into the open and thresh them out in discussion, debate, and polling. Charges, founded and ill-founded, are made with wild abandon, but the issues

[30] Quoted by Josephus Daniels, *The Wilson Era, Years of Peace, 1910–1917* (Chapel Hill: University of North Carolina Press, 1944), p. 11.

have a way of never being joined. Often basic questions are ignored and discussion concentrated on spurious or trivial matters. Thus, in 1932, when it would be supposed that the occasion existed for a thorough debate on the adequacy of our arrangements for managing our economic life, a visitor from Mars might have supposed from the campaign that the great issue before the American people was whether a citizen should be allowed to buy his liquor openly or be required to purchase it from a bootlegger.

Yet let it be said that a judicious avoidance of issues is not without value. It can be contended with great force that temporization on divisive questions gives time for public discussion to proceed, for information to be disseminated, for experience to accumulate, and for the composition of conflict. Time and patience may bring a happy outcome to an apparently insoluble problem; or the burning issue, avoided, may appear tomorrow to have been no issue at all. The problem is when to temporize; delay on the wrong question may only accelerate disaster.

The minimization of conflict inherent in our two-party arrangements results from the necessity under which our politicians labor of seeking common ground for all groups in contrast with leaders in a multiparty system who must stimulate particularism to live. The question may well be raised of how much political conflict we would tolerate. Could the nation continue an elective system, with alternating groups in control, if it were known that a change in party control would bring with it genuinely radical changes in governmental policy? [31] The alternative to our present two-party system may not be two parties between which genuinely sharp differences of policy exist. It may be a multiparty system with the concomitant of governmental instability. [32]

---

[31] Pendleton Herring concludes that in the United States "both parties must cherish the same basic values. They may offer slightly different interpretations of the public interest but they can not advocate fundamental change, for the loyalty of the voter must be to the same general economic system and to the same general political values. We can not have a radical party standing for revolutionary change and a conservative stand-pat party. Such parties may exist only on the plane of discussion. Revolutionary communism can be tolerated by democracy as long as it remains an academic question."—"Political Parties and the Public Interest" in *Essays in Political Science in Honor of W. W. Willoughby* (Baltimore: Johns Hopkins Press, 1937), p. 102.

[32] A recurrent expression by American politicians appears in the following remarks by James A. Farley, in his capacity as New York State Democratic Chairman: "The genius of our representative democracy is the two-party system—one party entrusted with power to carry out the will of the majority; the other, vigilant in criticism but always loyal in opposition, always loyal to the fundamental principles of the Republic. The alternative to the two-party system is a jumble of special-interest groups who, even in coalition are in disagreement, and in crisis are too disunited to act. To thus weaken our political system would be to destroy the very basis of our demo-

With the sharpening of political issues, the increasing importance of the stakes of political struggle, and the spectacle of liquidated democracies abroad since 1930, the traditional rationalizations and justifications of our bipartisan, principle-less politics has undergone some re-examination. The most spirited and facile defense of the traditional arrangement has been made by Pendleton Herring in a brilliant book entitled *The Politics of Democracy*. The essence of his argument is that the American political system has rested in considerable measure on the fact that differences between parties have been slight. Under such circumstances the vanquished in elections have been willing to accept the outcome; the victors have not been inclined to push their advantage to the point of outraging the sensibilities of the losers. Both parties have been carried along in the process of political change by common influences and have thereby adapted themselves to the needs of the nation.

Other observers are less sanguine about the prospects of meeting national necessities through the bumbling delays and compromises characteristic of the past. Some sober people profess to see underlying social tendencies driving us toward a one-party system. The stakes of the game, they believe, are already becoming so great that the time is approaching when internal disputes and differences cannot be tolerated to the extent that they have been in the past. Others place emphasis on the fact that the economic order and the governmental system are becoming so intertwined that continuity in governmental policy and control may become necessary; shifts in political control might come to result disastrously for the economic order. Whatever the prognosis may be, it is certainly correct that the traditional, easy-going technique of the two-party system in coping with public problems will be put to an increasing strain.[33]

4. DEVIATIONS: THIRD PARTIES

Designation of the American party system as a two-party system is not strictly correct, for at every presidential election candidates other than those of the two major parties are on the ballot. Despite the efforts of the major parties to broaden their appeal so as to bring within their ranks a cross section of the entire population, their adaptability has not been great enough to prevent the rise of third parties to advocate policies that neither of the two great parties would embrace. At times

---

cratic government." *Congressional Record* (daily edition), September 24, 1941, p. A4625.

[33] For a thoughtful review of these problems, see Norton E. Long, "Party and the Constitution," *Journal of Politics*, 3 (1941), pp. 198–209.

these third parties have split off from a major party that was unable to find a formula under which party unity could be maintained; at other times the minor party has not been generated by dissension within a major party but has grown up outside.

The relative insignificance of minor parties in recent years makes it pointless to devote extended attention to their activities, yet these parties possess sufficient historical interest to merit brief notice.   On two occasions since 1900 third parties have polled substantial proportions of the total popular vote: Theodore Roosevelt as the Progressive candidate in 1912 and Robert M. La Follette, Sr., as the Farmer-Labor standard bearer in 1924.   At other campaigns the small, continuing third-party vote was cast.   The percentages of the total popular vote going to third-party candidates during the past fifty years has been as follows: 1896, 3.03; 1900, 2.78; 1904, 5.96; 1908, 5.35; 1912, 34.93; 1916, 4.68; 1920, 5.52; 1924, 17.13; 1928, 1.08; 1932, 2.93; 1936, 2.90; 1940, 0.54; 1944, 0.87.   Thus apart from the two instances in which great personalities led minor parties, their vote has been a very small proportion of the total.

Representative minor parties.   A persistent element in the continuing minor party vote is that for Prohibitionist candidates.   This party represents an example of a party founded to promote a principle to which neither of the major parties respond with alacrity.   The party has nominated presidential and vice-presidential candidates at every election since 1872.   The formation of the party itself was preceded by temperance agitation dating from the earliest days of the Republic. Even before the Civil War, temperance leaders considered the advisability of forming a political party devoted to the cause of prohibition. After the Civil War it came to be thought that with the abolition of slavery the time was propitious for bringing forward another great issue.   Some temperance leaders believed that new parties and new alignments should be formed as new issues arose.   They had before them the experience of the Liberty, Free Soil, and Liberal Republican parties; and many of them had been abolitionists and were disposed to use again the technique of forming a new party to bring an issue to national attention.

At a meeting of the Right Worthy Grand Lodge of Good Templars, a temperance society, at Oswego, New York, in 1868, a call was issued for a national convention to form a party.   Later in the year at Chicago the first national convention was held, at which an organization was perfected and a platform adopted.   The Chicago *Times,* commenting on the convention, foresaw only slight hopes for prohibition:

When our Senators and Representatives come reeling to their desks in a state of intoxication and when all the avenues of political life are crowded with debauchees it is idle to hope that prohibitory laws could be enforced.

Undiscouraged by such comment, the Prohibition party held its first nominating convention in 1872 to name candidates for the Presidency and Vice-Presidency. Although the party made prohibition the primary issue, its platform-makers even in the first convention broadened the program and showed remarkable prescience by advocating other policies that were eventually to be adopted. They favored the direct election of Senators, woman suffrage, and civil service reform. At each succeeding convention various other policies, in addition to prohibition, came to be advocated.

The leaders of the party believed that they could gain greater concessions from the major parties as the vote for Prohibition candidates increased. In the campaign of 1884 the tactics of the Prohibition party chairman were "to strike a crushing blow at one wing of the liquor army. He believed if the Republican party could be beaten it would show the strength of prohibition and lead to a later alignment of the prohibition forces against the liquor forces." He concentrated the work of the party in pivotal states. In New York, Blaine, the Republican candidate, lost to Cleveland by 1047 popular votes and thereby lost the Presidency, while the Prohibitionists polled 24,999 votes. Whether the Prohibitionists were responsible for this turn of affairs is debatable; the result is more often attributed to the boomerang effect of the unfortunate reference of one of Blaine's ministerial supporters to the Democratic party as the party of "Rum, Romanism and Rebellion." At any rate, the Prohibitionists found that, as their vote increased, state legislatures were more inclined to submit the question of prohibition to popular vote and to adopt restrictive measures short of complete prohibition.

The Prohibition party serves mainly as a medium for agitation. In this function it came to have a great competitor in the Anti-Saloon League, which, in contrast with the party, nominated no candidates and encouraged its members to support those individuals, regardless of party, committed to the League's policy. The party persisted, however, in its campaigns for office. "There was an irreconcilable difference," said the party's official historian, "a great gulf between the low ideals of satisfaction with the rum-ridden old parties and perpetuation in office of low-grade politicians on the one hand, and on the other the ideals of the Prohibition party which sought a regeneration of poli-

tics and statesmen to match the grandeur of the cause." [34]   Such a spirit
has great vitality.   The party polls no impressive vote.   In 1940 its
candidate received less than 60,000 votes.   But the party has kept the
issue alive and at times, especially in an earlier day, influenced legislatures and other officials.

The Populist party represents another type of third party.   Instead
of persisting as did the Prohibitionist, the Populist movement flared up
and soon died out.   In another connection,[35] the monetary, transportation, and crop conditions in the Northwest that gave rise to the agrarian
unrest of the 'seventies and 'eighties have been recounted.   The largest
and most influential political party emerging from the discontent of
that period was the Populist, or People's, party.   In the campaigns of
1890, independent and "People's" candidates, backed by the Farmers'
Alliance and allied groups, working either through the Democratic
party in the southern states or through independent state and local
parties in the northwestern states, met with success in a considerable
number of instances.   But experience with both these modes of operation pointed toward the necessity for a national party organization to
fight for reforms on a nation-wide basis.

After negotiation and conference among the divergent factions interested in a third party, a party was formed at a convention in Cincinnati
early in 1892.   Later in that year the Populists nominated for the Presidency General James B. Weaver of Iowa, who had had other experience
in minor parties.   He had been the Greenback candidate for the Presidency in 1880.   The party received a total of over a million popular
votes and twenty-two electoral votes.   The party won a handful of
seats in the lower house of Congress, placed its candidates in the governor's chair in three states, and elected hundreds of local officials.   In
the presidential contest the strength of the Populists was greatest in the
western and southern states.   In no state east of the Mississippi and
north of the Ohio did Weaver poll more than 5 per cent of the popular
vote.[36]

Between 1892 and 1896 there was a struggle within the Populist
party over the silver issue.   The faction favoring the free coinage of
silver finally gained control, and in 1896 the Populists supported Wil-

[34] D. L. Colvin, *Prohibition in the United States,* copyright, 1926, Doubleday,
Doran and Company, Inc., p. 392.   See also Roger W. Babson (Prohibition presidential candidate in 1940), *Our Campaign for the Presidency in 1940* (Chicago: National Prohibitionist, 1941).

[35] Chapter 2.

[36] The states of greatest Populist strength in order of the per cent of the popular
vote polled by Weaver were: Nevada, 66.7; Colorado, 57.0; Idaho, 54.6; North Dakota,
48.9; Kansas, 48.4; Wyoming, 46.1; Nebraska, 41.0; South Dakota, 37.5; Alabama,
36.6; Texas, 23.6; Washington, 21.7.

liam Jennings Bryan, the Democratic candidate, who went down before the onslaughts of the Republicans, ably managed by Mark Hanna. The Populists were not so unsuccessful in the state and local campaigns, but their day as an independent party was done. In 1900, 1904, and 1908 a few of the faithful convened to nominate presidential and vice-presidential candidates, who made no substantial showing in the campaigns of those years.

Although Populist candidates failed to win the Presidency, many of their ideas have become law partly because of the persistent agitation by the Populists. One of their fundamental tenets, that the people should control the government, grew out of their seeing, on every hand, corrupt machines, often supported by the railroads, ignoring the public interest. To remedy the situation the Populists demanded the Australian ballot; they protested against the indirect election of United States Senators; they sought to substitute the direct primary for the convention system of nomination; they advocated the extension of the suffrage to women; and they urged the adoption of the initiative, referendum, and recall as means to achieve more popular control of government. These changes in the machinery and procedure of government have long since come about, in part because of the original exertions of the Populists.

The Populists were not concerned alone with the machinery for the expression of the popular will. They agitated for the adoption of new policies. In the field of money and banking the Populists, viewed at the time by all the "best" people as cranks and crackpots, criticized the inelasticity of the currency and argued that the matter could be solved by the issuance of paper money. Later monetary legislation, in particular the Federal Reserve Act, created the basis for an elastic national currency, although by means different from that urged by the Populists. The germ of the idea of the present extensive system of federally sponsored credit agencies for farmers was to be found in the Populist platform, and increased governmental control of the railway system held an important place in Populist principles. Antitrust laws were pushed by the Populists, and the tendency toward more strict governmental control of business continued after the Populist party disappeared from the scene. It is, of course, not to be contended that the Populists were solely responsible for the eventual adoption of all the policies that they advocated, but their party did serve as a channel for the expression of discontent and for the propagation of ideas later taken up by the major parties and put into law.[37]

[37] The chief work on the Populists is John D. Hicks, *The Populist Revolt* (Minneapolis: University of Minnesota Press, 1931). See also S. J. Buck, *The Agrarian Cru-*

The Socialist party represents still another type of minor party. It promotes no political program of indigenous origin as does the Prohibitionist. It grows out of no specific domestic unrest as did the Populist. American socialism, in its many varieties, is a transplanted growth that has failed to take political root in new soil. The great thinkers and philosophers of socialism have been Europeans; their ideas of objectives and of political strategy have been formulated from observation of European conditions. Almost all movements in socialist thought have been reflected in the formation of movements and organizations in the United States. Utopian socialism, guild socialism, Christian socialism, Marxian socialism, and revisionist socialism have had their effects in this country. Yet none of the socialist sects has succeeded in establishing a formidable working political party; perhaps their influence has been greater in the propagation of ideas. Although several socialist groups have nominated candidates for national, state, and local office, the Socialist party, formed in 1901, has polled the largest vote.[38]

The socialist vote for President rose to peaks in 1912, 1920, and 1932. It climbed steadily from only 94,000 in 1904 to 897,011, polled by Eugene V. Debs, in 1912. The distribution of the Socialist vote indicates a curious characteristic of the American socialist movement. The party was designed to be a party of the industrial proletariat, but its greatest electoral strength was in the western agricultural and mining states, areas in which the Populists had earlier made the strongest showing. In 1912 the highest Socialist vote was in Oklahoma, where 16.6 per cent of the voters indicated a Socialist preference; the states with more than 10 per cent of their votes Socialist were Oklahoma, Nevada, Montana, Arizona, Washington, California, and Idaho. Voters of the industrialized states were much less inclined to vote Socialist.[39] In Massachusetts, for example, the Socialist candidates polled only 2.6 per cent of the total vote cast. In 1920 the party candidates polled 919,799 votes; in 1932, 884,781. In neither instance was the vote so high a percentage of the total as in 1912.

The Socialist party has been under the control of right-wing So-

---

sade (New Haven: Yale University Press, 1920); F. E. Haynes, *Third Party Movements Since the Civil War, with Special Reference to Iowa* (Iowa City: State Historical Society of Iowa, 1916); Anna Rochester, *The Populist Movement in the United States* (New York: International Publishers, 1943).

38 Those interested in the extremely complicated story of socialist politics may find the details in such volumes as Nathan Fine, *Labor and Farmer Parties in the United States, 1828–1928* (New York: Rand School, 1928); W. E. Walling, *et al, The Socialism of To-Day* (New York: Holt, 1916); Morris Hillquit, *History of Socialism in the United States* (New York: Funk & Wagnalls, 1910).

39 F. E. Haynes, *Social Politics in the United States* (Boston: Houghton Mifflin, 1924), p. 206.

cialists, who have faith in parliamentary methods and institutions. Gradual achievement of a socialist society through the ballot box and through the instruments of representative government is the hope of the Socialist party. In 1919 the left-wing faction split off and formed the Communist party, which hoped to reconstruct the socialist movement on undefiled Marxist principles. Participation in political campaigns was purely a means for agitation and for education and not an acceptance of the doctrine of gradualism. The socialist society was to be achieved by a dictatorship of the proletariat set up by violent revolution. The revolutionary potentialities of the Communist party in the United States have been vastly overrated, and even the party itself came eventually to lay less emphasis on preparation for the great day when heads will roll. As a compact and disciplined minority, however, it gained influence in other organizations, such as some trades unions, by capturing key posts. Its chief political function, however, eventually came to be that of serving as a butt for the fulminations of frustrated statesmen in search of a scapegoat.[40] The more extreme doctrines of the Communist party have given respectability to the Socialist party and to the moderate preachings of its leader, Norman Thomas, and Communists are now subjected to the repressions and discriminations that were the Socialists' in an earlier day.

Occasionally a third party exists on a state or local basis and in limited areas becomes in fact one of the major parties. The Non-Partisan League in Dakota, the Farmer-Labor party in Minnesota, the Socialist party in Milwaukee are examples of third parties that have gained considerable state and local power, at least for a time. The development of a third party locally is often followed by a coalition of the Democratic and Republican parties within the state on local issues.[41] The maintenance of a third party with its power centered in a small area is attended by no little difficulty. To exert influence in national affairs the party often fuses with one or the other of the major parties and is swallowed up in the process. In any case, whichever party is in power nationally is likely to use its patronage to maintain its own

[40] See G. S. Watkins, "Revolutionary Communism in the United States," *American Political Science Review*, 14 (1920), pp. 14–33; Barrington Moore, Jr., "The Communist Party of the USA," *American Political Science Review*, 39 (1945), pp. 31–41; Irwin Ross, "It's Tough to Be a Communist" and Granville Hicks, "The Spectre That Haunts the World," *Harper's*, June, 1946. The American Communist movement has also been beset by the battles of the Leninites and Trotskyites. Furious and intent little men armed with fountain pens and typewriters assault each other over issues of monumental insignificance. See, for example, J. P. Cannon, *The Struggle for a Proletarian Party* (New York: Pioneer, 1943).

[41] On this phenomenon in Minnesota, see J. R. Starr, "Labor and Farmer Groups and the Three-Party System," *Southwestern Social Science Quarterly*, 17 (1936), pp. 7–19.

local organization in spite of the support it may receive from a third party.

In New York the American Labor party is a state and local party that also reflects a dream of many American labor leaders that some day labor may organize its own party to capture control of the government. It was established in 1936, primarily on a trade-union basis, with the International Ladies Garment Workers Union as its principal financial angel. Because of the election system of New York, the ALP has been able to nominate as its candidate on several occasions the candidate of a major party and establish by the election returns that its votes constituted the balance of power. Thus in 1944 the distribution of the sources of the popular votes for the major candidates for President in New York state was as follows: [42]

Dewey as Republican nominee	47.5
Roosevelt as Democratic nominee	39.4
Roosevelt as American Labor nominee	7.9
Roosevelt as Liberal nominee	5.2
Total Roosevelt percentage	52.5

In the 1938 governor's race the American Labor party also held a pivotal position. The distribution of the vote among the party nominations was as follows:

Dewey as Republican nominee	48.8
Dewey as Independent Progressive nominee	0.5
Total Dewey percentage	49.3
Lehman as Democratic nominee	41.8
Lehman as American Labor nominee	8.9
Total Lehman percentage	50.7

Since the voting strength of the American Labor party centers mainly in New York City, its proportion of the vote in city elections is considerably higher than in state elections. In 1941 its support, added to the Republican vote, gave the mayoralty to LaGuardia. The breakdown of the vote follows:

O'Dwyer as Democratic nominee	47.1%
LaGuardia as Republican nominee	29.8
LaGuardia as American Labor nominee	19.4
LaGuardia as City Fusion nominee	2.8
LaGuardia as United City nominee	0.9
Total LaGuardia percentage	52.9

[42] The percentages are of the total vote for the two major candidates in each instance.

The New York system of nominations makes it possible for a minority party to fuse with a major party without losing its identity and also to prove the dependence of the major candidate upon its support. Yet the American Labor party has been rent by internal dissension turning chiefly around the issue of relations with the Communists. In 1943, after a battle for control of the ALP between Sidney Hillman, leader of its left wing, and David Dubinsky, right-wing leader, the right-wingers withdrew and formed the Liberal party.[43] The possibility of alliance between minor party and a major party in New York rests on the willingness of the major parties to tolerate such coalitions. In New York major-party leaders from time to time have considered repealing the statute permitting dual nominations. Repeal of the act would make third parties much less attractive vehicles of agitation and of campaigning and perhaps compel them to work within one or the other major party.

Role and nature of minor parties. The foregoing discussion treats only a few of the minor parties that have been active on the American scene. These cases, however, furnish sufficient evidence to suggest some general observations about the role and nature of minor parties. When discontent arises with the existing political order and a movement for or against some policy is born, its leaders have several alternative courses of action in striving toward their objective. They may form a pressure group and attempt to bring their influence to bear on both major parties. They may, as did the Anti-Saloon League, command a large enough popular following to hold the balance of power between the major parties and therefore be able to compel the candidates of both parties, at least for lower offices, to yield to their demands. They may choose to work within an existing party and seek to impress their policy upon it by "boring from within." Or they may form a third party and attempt to elect their own nominees for local, state, and national office.

Under what conditions do third parties arise? The question is not easy to answer. The correct analysis probably is that different circumstances govern in each instance. In most important minor-party movements neither of the major parties has been receptive to a point of view that commanded a rather large popular following. The leaders of dissident groups usually had no special desire to form a minor party but did so only when it seemed impossible to convert the dominant elements in one of the major parties to their views. But not all minority parties have resulted from splits of the major parties; some have been

---

[43] See Hugh A. Bone, "Political Parties in New York City," *American Political Science Review*, 40 (1946), pp. 272–282; Daniel Bell, "New York's 'Third Parties,'" *Common Sense*, June, 1945, pp. 14–15.

formed, as was the Socialist party, to propagate an idea or a philosophy that would not even be seriously considered by either major party.

It is easier to state the function of minor parties than to isolate and define the conditions under which party movements arise. "Looked at from the social point of view the chief function of third parties has been to bring new issues before the people: they force new policies upon the older parties, and after accomplishing their work they pass away." [44] An assortment of examples of this role of the third party has been furnished in the foregoing pages. Although the minor party has been a formidable method for bringing an issue to public attention, not all minor parties see their reason for existence disappear because their ideas have been taken over by one of or both the major parties. Even when the minor parties have no perceptible effect on the policy of government, they may serve a useful social function. They operate as a channel for the expression of discontent, which is often dissipated and rendered harmless by the exertions of verbalization and electoral activity. Theodore Roosevelt must have had something of this notion in mind when he said that reformers "will get together in a large hall, will vociferously demand 'reform,' as if it were some concrete substance which could be handed out to them in slices, and will then disband with a feeling of most serene self-satisfaction, and the belief that they have done their entire duty as citizens and members of the community." [45] The "safety-valve" function of the minor party depends on a tolerance, by the majority, of the political deviates who seem to gravitate toward the minor party ranks.[46] Now and then a minor party serves a significant function by publicizing an issue that neither major party has the temerity to raise.

Occasionally third parties have held the balance of power in presidential elections. Hicks says that "in possibly half a dozen instances the third party vote has snatched victory from one major party ticket to give it to the other." [47] Minor-party leaders assume that by building up enough popular support to hold the balance of power they can

[44] Haynes, *Third Party Movements*, p. 3.

[45] Quoted by E. D. Ross, *The Liberal Republican Movement* (New York: Henry Holt, 1919), p. 3.

[46] When that tolerance disappears, extremist parties are likely to be suppressed. Witness the treatment accorded Socialists during World War I. In 1939 and 1940 numerous measures of official discrimination against Communists were adopted. More practically for political action, many states changed their election laws to make it extremely difficult for small parties to place the names of their candidates on the ballot. See Hugh A. Bone, "Small Political Parties Casualties of War?" *National Municipal Review*, 32 (1943), pp. 524-528.

[47] John D. Hicks, "The Third Party Tradition in American Politics," *Mississippi Valley Historical Review*, 20 (1933), p. 26.

gain greater concessions on questions of policy from the leaders of the major parties. Most instances in which it is suggested that a minor party threw an election one way or another are not susceptible of proof. The election of Wilson in 1912, however, offers a clear-cut instance in which the third-party candidacy of Theodore Roosevelt as a Progressive divided Republican strength and gave the Presidency to Wilson. And, in a sense, the Progressives were the true victors, for the Wilsonian program brought the adoption of measures thoroughly in accord with the spirit of the progressive movement.[48]

The distribution of minor-party strength suggests a hypothesis about the conditions that permit and discourage minor-party activity. The strength of these parties has been greatest in those western states without strong and long traditions governing political behavior, with a social system in a state of flux, and with comparatively weak and unstable governing groups. In the South the third-party strength, over the entire period of 1864–1936, was at its weakest. Social stratification, political tradition, and the pressure to conform from the governing groups have been very different in the South than in the West.[49] One kind of condition may facilitate the operations of dissenting groups; the other definitely discourages such movements.

In the study of minor parties it is well to assign importance to the factor of the personality of leaders. Some minor parties have tended to be one-man affairs. For many years the Socialist party was centered around the personality of Eugene V. Debs; in later years the Socialist party has been Norman Thomas and Norman Thomas has been the Socialist party. The elder LaFollette was the central figure of the Farmer-Labor party, while Theodore Roosevelt gave life to the Progressive party. "The Progressive party, in large measure, was the outward expression of the love and admiration, amounting almost to idolatry, that the overwhelming majority of its members felt for Theodore Roosevelt," says Harold L. Ickes, who was a Progressive leader. "They believed that by unfair tactics and crooked machinations he had been denied the Republican nomination in 1912. Personally or politically, with only a relatively few exceptions none of the people who took their political lives in their hands when they left the Republican and Democratic parties 1912 to follow Roosevelt had a thing to gain. Yet

[48] For a careful statistical analysis of the role of minor parties in presidential elections, see C. A. M. Ewing, *Presidential Elections* (Norman: University of Oklahoma Press, 1940), chap. 3.

[49] Louis Bean has also shown that states with strong third-party votes have also been states in which the greatest shift from one major party to the other occurs. See his *Ballot Behavior* (Washington: American Council on Public Affairs, 1940), chap. 6.

they were willing to risk all, if necessary, to sacrifice all, because of their faith in one man." [50]

It should not be concluded that the minor party is either the only or the most effective channel for the popularization and eventual effectuation of a new policy. The range of diversity of views within both major parties is great, and under certain conditions it is feasible for a movement to exert a mighty influence within the party ranks. To work from within on national issues, the faction must at least be strongly entrenched within some area where it can control the state party organization. The LaFollettes, for example, controlled the Republican machine of Wisconsin for many years against the efforts of the dominant elements of the Republican machine nationally to purge them from the party. In 1928, when Senator Robert M. LaFollette, Jr., offered a minority platform to the Republican national convention he "prefaced it by reminding the hostile delegates that of the 35 planks which the left-wing Wisconsin delegation had offered to the Republican Party since 1908, only to be hissed and spurned, 32 had been enacted into law." [51]

Hicks has suggested that perhaps the day of the sectional third party is nearly done. Under the system of nominations by direct primary it is not necessary to organize a minor party to capture office. The leaders of protest movements of all shades and hues may, if their following is strong enough, capture the nominations of either major party for legislative and local offices. Neither party has any means for protecting itself from appropriation by groups that might otherwise form a new party.[52] This suggestion is undoubtedly true, and in this respect the direct primary has facilitated the process of "boring from within" the major parties and made it less necessary for the leaders of movements of dissent to form new parties.

[50] "Who Killed the Progressive Party?" *American Historical Review,* 46 (1941), p. 329.
[51] Roy V. Peel and T. C. Donnelly, *The 1928 Campaign* (New York: R. R. Smith, 1931), p. 25.
[52] Hicks, *Mississippi Valley Historical Review, op. cit.,* pp. 3–28.

Chapter 9

RECENT PARTY HISTORY

ROBERT BENCHLEY, the late humorist, disposed hilariously of the history of American political parties in two essays of four pages each.[1] In his remarks he caricatured the perplexities of the undergraduate trying to learn when the Democrats were Republicans and the Republicans something else, the difference between the Federalists and the Whigs, and when and why the waters were muddied by the Antimasonic party, Know-nothingism, and the Liberal Republican movement.   In this chapter Mr. Benchley's predicament can be sidestepped by limiting the review of party history to the period since 1896.   Since that time the nomenclature of the parties at least has remained uniform, and the campaign of 1896 perhaps marked a turning point at which the party battle began to take its modern form.   The student with historical inclination and interest may be referred to books dedicated to the comprehensive chronological analysis of American parties.[2]

In any case the student may well ask why he need be bothered by a consideration of party history, even if it is confined to the period since 1896.   In truth, political history is usually sterile stuff, a collection of names, dates, titles, and events, beaded on a chronological string.   Yet, by historical analysis of events, one can gain a comprehension of the interrelation and unfolding of streams of action possible by no other type of approach.   By tying together in an historical pattern developments that would be treated separately in other types of analysis a

---

[1] "Political Parties and Their Growth" and "A Short (What There Is of It) History of American Political Problems" in *20,000 Leagues under the Sea or David Copperfield* (New York: Holt, 1928).

[2] The best party history is by W. E. Binkley, *American Political Parties* (New York: Knopf, 1943).   A brief account has been written by C. A. Beard, *The American Party Battle* (New York: Macmillan, 1928).   Other party histories include: W. S. Myers, *History of the Republican Party* (New York: Century, 1928); F. R. Kent, *History of the Democratic Party* (New York: Century, 1928); Francis Curtis, *The Republican Party, 1854–1904* (New York: Putnam's, 1904); E. E. Robinson, *The Evolution of American Parties* (New York: Harcourt, Brace, 1924).

better understanding of American politics as a whole may be obtained.
By an examination of the recent history of parties one can test the
notions advanced in the preceding chapter about the nature of parties,
as well as acquire an elementary knowledge of the facts of our political
life useful in other connections.

1. CONSERVATIVE DOMINANCE TEMPERED BY INSURGENCY, 1896–1912

The Republicans controlled the Presidency from 1896 through 1912,
but theirs was an uncertain hegemony.   The dominant eastern wing of
the Republican party during this period was almost constantly be-
deviled by the party's progressive wing.   Eastern finance and industry,
energetically increasing its power by the formation of combinations
and trusts and its wealth by reaping the fruits of the protective tariff,
aroused the opposition of western agriculture and of middle-class leaders everywhere, who viewed with alarm the rapid rise of plutocratic
powers.   These anxieties fed opposition to the standpat Republican
organization and they also had their effects in arousing progressive
clamor within the Democratic party.

1896: Referendum on silver.   Ostensibly the campaign of 1896 was
fought on the issue of the free coinage of silver, but underlying the
question of bimetalism was a struggle in which disadvantaged groups
sought economic redress against those enjoying the fruits of economic
and political power.   In the preliminaries to this alignment in the
campaign the forces of economic protest gained control of the Democratic organization.   President Grover Cleveland, by his support of the
gold standard, alienated the silver faction of his party, and, by his use
of troops in the Pullman strike of 1894, aroused the animosity of labor.
Silver Democrats, representative of debtor sections anxious to avoid
the burdens of an inelastic currency in the payment of debts and of
silver-mining interests desirous of a ready and easy means of convert-
ing their product into money, laid the groundwork for control of the
Democratic convention of 1896.   The Democratic platform flatly declared for the "free and unlimited coinage of both silver and gold at
the present ratio of sixteen to one. . . ."   In debating this plank William Jennings Bryan stirred the delegates to a frenzy by his speech
containing the famous passage:

We shall answer their demand for the gold standard by saying to them:
"You shall not press down upon the brow of labor this crown of thorns.   You
shall not crucify mankind upon a cross of gold."

By their stand on silver and their nomination of Bryan, the Democrats appropriated the chief issue of the People's party, the political expression of western agrarian discontent, which had polled over a million votes in 1892. As a result, after some debate on the dangers of fusion, the Populists also nominated Bryan.

The Republican party had its own internal disputes over the silver issue, but the eastern wing of the party overwhelmingly defeated the silverites and adopted a sound money plank:

> The Republican party is unreservedly for sound money. . . . We are unalterably opposed to every measure calculated to debase our currency or impair the credit of our country. We are therefore opposed to the free coinage of silver, except by international agreement with the leading commercial nations of the earth.

The Republicans nominated William McKinley, whose record on the money question was not completely orthodox but who personified Republican attachment to the doctrine of protectionism.

The campaign attained a high intensity of feeling, similar perhaps to the tone of the 1936 campaign. The crusading Bryan was pictured as the leader of a rag-tag band of radicals that would upset the foundations of the Republic. Eastern finance and industry were terrified and contributed generously to the Republican campaign ably managed by Mark Hanna. Hanna's record of frank and open dealings with organized labor stood the party in good stead, as did McKinley's own actions earlier in his career in defending striking workingmen against prosecution. The Republican promise of a "full dinner pail" was not lacking in appeal to laborers unemployed as a consequence of the panic of 1893, and they no doubt responded favorably to the argument that the protective tariff assured employment of American workers. In this they were given encouragement by the threats of their employers of the dire consequences that would follow a Democratic victory. The oblique reference by the Democratic platform to the action that should follow a reversal by a reconstituted Supreme Court of a decision holding the income tax unconstitutional spurred the Republicans to greater effort and fed the anxieties of men of substance.[3]

The high turnout at the election reflected the sharp popular interest in the campaign. About 1.9 million more people voted than in 1892; the turnout was almost as high as in 1900 and exceeded that of 1904. The electoral vote was 271 for McKinley and 176 for Bryan. The Democrats carried the states of the Solid South and the western farm-

[3] See Herbert Croly, *Marcus Alonzo Hanna* (New York: Macmillan, 1912).

ing and mining states in which the doctrine of free silver held sway. Thus in the Democratic column were Colorado, Idaho, Kansas, Missouri, Montana, Nebraska, Nevada, South Dakota, Utah, Washington, and Wyoming.

The usual interpretation of the outcome of the election of 1896 is that the manufacturers and financiers of the East succeeded in persuading the workers to help them beat off the threat of the embattled debtors of the West. Superficially this is what happened, but the struggle was not purely sectional. The issue of men against property was fought in every section, and McKinley, the "advance agent of prosperity," annexed nearly everywhere a greater proportion of the increased outpouring of electors than did Bryan. Even in most of the states of the Solid South the Republican percentage of the total vote increased between 1892 and 1896. The Republican percentages of the total vote in these states in 1892 and 1896 were as follows:

	1892	*1896*	*Republican Gain or Loss*
Alabama	3.9	28.6	24.7
Arkansas	32.0	26.7	−5.3
Florida	0.0	24.3	24.3
Georgia	21.8	37.9	16.1
Louisiana	11.6	18.1	6.5
Mississippi	2.7	7.0	4.3
North Carolina	35.7	46.8	11.1
South Carolina	18.9	11.2	−7.7
Tennessee	37.5	46.8	9.3
Texas	19.3	30.3	11.0
Virginia	38.7	45.9	7.2

The silver-mining states responded differently. In these states all classes zealously supported free coinage of silver, and election returns reflected their sentiments. The Republican percentages of the total vote in 1892 and in 1896 were as follows:

	1892	*1896*	*Republican Loss*
Colorado	41.1	14.1	−27.0
Idaho	44.3	21.3	−23.0
Montana	42.5	19.7	−22.8
Nevada	25.0	18.8	−6.2

In the sparsely settled states of the great plains the repayment of debts in a dear currency burdened men most heavily. Presumably here the demand for free coinage of silver would express itself decisively. Yet in these states the local business allies of eastern finance aroused themselves—as manifested by William Allen White's famous editorial, "What's the Matter with Kansas?"—and in the main lost little ground in comparison with 1892. The Republican percentages of the total popular vote in 1892 and 1896 in these states follow:

	1892	1896	Republican Gain or Loss
Kansas	48.4	47.4	—1.0
Nebraska	43.6	46.2	2.6
North Dakota	48.5	56.0	7.5
South Dakota	49.5	49.5	0.0
Wyoming	50.6	47.7	—2.9

These shifts between the two presidential elections were comparatively small. The nature of the political alignment in the election is suggested by comparing with these figures the Republican percentages of the total vote in states in which manufacturing and finance were centered:

	1892	1896	Republican Gain
Illinois	45.7	55.8	10.1
Maryland	43.5	54.6	11.1
Massachusetts	52.8	69.5	16.7
New Jersey	46.1	59.6	13.6
New York	53.5	57.6	4.1
Ohio	47.6	51.8	4.2
Pennsylvania	51.5	61.0	9.5
Rhode Island	50.7	68.3	17.6

1900: Imperialism. The McKinley Administration redeemed its tariff pledge by the Dingley bill of 1897, which tied the manufacturing interests of the nation even more closely to the Republican party. Before the campaign of 1900 the Spanish-American War intervened and furnished the new issue of imperialism. The national fervor induced by war redounded to the advantage of the party in power, which also had the good fortune to have the currency problem eased through no effort of its own. New gold strikes increased the money supply. McKinley had no difficulty in obtaining renomination by the Republican convention; the principal event of the convention, as it later turned out, was the nomination of Theodore Roosevelt for the Vice-Presidency. Boss Platt of New York wanted to be rid of Roosevelt as governor of New York. Western Republicans, restive under control of the party by financial and manufacturing interests, welcomed his nomination.

The Democrats, exhausted from their unsuccessful exertions of 1896, again nominated Bryan, who contended that the campaign was only another episode in the battle of "Democracy against Plutocracy." The contestants were the same; only the issues were new, he argued. He viewed imperialism as merely another manifestation of plutocratic influence. The party platform asserted "that no nation can long endure half republic and half empire." Imperialism "abroad will lead quickly and inevitably to despotism at home." The Democracy declared monopolies to be "indefensible and intolerable." The charge was that "trusts are the legitimate product of Republican policies, that they are fostered by Republican laws, and that they are protected by the Republican administration, in return for campaign subscriptions and political support." The Democrats denounced the Dingley tariff as a "trust breeding measure," and re-affirmed the 1896 declaration in favor of the free coinage of silver. They opposed "government by injunction" and proposed the creation of a Department of Labor.

The Democrats concentrated their campaign on the issues of imperialism and trusts; the Republicans stood on their record and won the popular mandate. The Democratic percentage of the total popular vote fell only slightly, but the electoral vote, 292 to 155, was more favorable to the Republicans than in 1896. Kansas, Nebraska, South Dakota, Utah, and Washington returned to the Republican fold, while Kentucky atoned for its apostasy of 1896 by going for Bryan.

Roosevelt the First. After McKinley's assassination the succession of Theodore Roosevelt to the Presidency threatened the Democratic monopoly of championship of the underdog. The Democrats had pictured themselves as a party of protest against plutocratic domination as represented by the Republican party and, in so doing, had had to settle disputes between their own right and left wings—although those were not the terms of the day. By his policies Roosevelt stole some of the Democratic thunder. At the same time he brought to the surface latent differences within the Republican party, whose right wing had triumphed, in contrast with the situation in the Democratic party. Roosevelt clearly recognized the danger to the Republicans of loss of western and progressive strength from too exclusive control by the eastern wing of the party. He sought to shift Republican policies in the same direction that the Democrats had been moving, only not so far. He was performing the historic function of national party leaders in bringing the two major parties more nearly into parallel courses.

For the duration of the unexpired term of McKinley, Roosevelt accomplished little in the way of positive legislation. The conservative wing of the party, under the leadership of Senator Nelson W. Aldrich, held firm control of Congress, and the President was too wise a politician not to recognize the strength of such formidable opponents.

Instead, he acted in areas in which he did not need congressional collaboration.

In 1901 the railroad titans competing for Chicago-Seattle traffic found competition unprofitable and arrived at peace terms embodied in the formation of the Northern Securities Company. In 1902 Roosevelt's Attorney General instituted antitrust proceedings against the Northern Securities combination and thereby lifted the spirits of western Republicans, who regarded trusts and railroads as the villains grinding down the poor and honest. In the same year the anthracite miners struck, and the operators stood on the God-given rights of property and refused to negotiate. Roosevelt intimated that federal troops might be used to take control of the mines, which would be operated by the government unless the mine owners saw the light and arbitrated the dispute. Up to this time the use of troops in industrial disputes had been reserved for the benefit of employers. Roosevelt's action set off fine displays of profanity in the Union League Clubs, but renewed the Republican loyalties of workers and progressives.

1904: Democrats as reactionaries. Roosevelt's policies confused the Democrats as the campaign of 1904 approached. Members of the radical wing of the party, under Bryan, argued that to retain their position as the party of liberal protest they should take even more advanced positions, while the conservatives of the party wished to move in the other direction. The conservative wing triumphed in the nomination of Judge Alton B. Parker of the New York Court of Appeals. The platform rang with denunciations of the trusts, but candidates are more important than platforms and Parker's nomination squeezed the meaning from the platform. Nor did the eastern wing of the party have its heart in the platform declaration in support of the popular election of Senators.

Roosevelt's gestures to the progressives held their support; to the conservatives his bark seemed louder than his bite; the Republicans rode to an easy victory over Parker. The Democratic percentage of the total popular vote fell to 37.6, the lowest point it was to reach until 1924. Roosevelt, President in his own right, felt himself freer to take a more independent policy line.

After Roosevelt's election in 1904 the rifts within the Republican ranks became wider. The battle was joined in the congressional dispute over railroad regulation; Aldrich led the eastern wing of the party against granting power to the Interstate Commerce Commission to fix rates to go into effect immediately. The western radical wing of the party, supported by shippers, recruited support from the Democrats to bring about the passage of the Hepburn bill. Roosevelt stirred up popular enthusiasm for other measures that the conservative branch of his party viewed with alarm. He placed himself among those Presidents who relied on a widespread popular following to aid in whipping Congress into line with their legislative recommendations. The Pure Food and Drug Act thus became law, as did legislation providing for the inspection of meat-packing houses.

1908: Taft and the progressives. As 1908 approached, the Democrats realized that by abandoning their position as the party of protest in 1904 they had surrendered popular support. A Bryan boom made itself heard long before the 1908 Democratic convention. Roosevelt exerted himself to unite the Republican party on William Howard Taft, an heir to carry on the Roosevelt tradition. In this endeavor he had to conciliate the party's conservative branch, which had begun to regard him as not unlike Bryan and feared a continuation of his policies. He also had to persuade the progressive element of the party that Taft subscribed to the articles of progressive faith. The conservatives, oddly enough, swallowed Taft with bitter protest; the progressives took Roosevelt's word that Taft was one of the anointed.

Taft, victorious over the luckless Bryan by an electoral vote of 321 to 162, soon departed from the Roosevelt policies—and the fat was in the fire. By this time the Republican progressive element had become stronger, and the spirit of revolt within the party flourished. To reconstruct the atmosphere of the times is difficult. The progressive movement was a mixture of economic discontent, of middle-class protest against plutocratic influences, and of moral and religious fervor, as well as of some sectionalism. On every hand established institutions were said to be threatened, and so-called right-thinking men bemoaned the decay of our society, the rise of the proletariat, and the wickedness of demagogues, like Roosevelt, who catered to the masses. The muckrakers uncovered graft and corruption in high places; the new cheap magazines disseminated their writings widely. The direct primary, which was coming into use, gave the people a chance to clip the wings of party bosses. Direct election of senators was urged, and in some western states was becoming a reality although the constitutional forms were preserved. The Senate, the "millionaires' club" and a bulwark of property, was thus threatened. In Wisconsin La Follette preached the doctrine that the people should rule, and conservatives became panicky as the initiative and referendum spread. State after state elected progressive governors, who proceeded to drive through their legislatures tax and regulatory measures unpleasant for corporation executives to contemplate. Courageous men challenged the pillaging of municipalities by combinations of corrupt political organizations and special interests.[4]   City after city elected reform administrations, and municipal ownership of street railways became a favorite topic of discussion among reformers.   Gambling houses were raided and houses of joy closed.   Business enterprise of every kind quaked; the day of judgment had come.[5]

Fate dropped the amiable and obese Taft into this situation.   As he was at heart no crusader, his sympathies lay with the conservative wing of the party.   Desirous of maintaining party unity, he lacked enough political adroitness to manage its divergent factions.   He had in his following Republicans like Aldrich of Rhode Island, high priest of protectionism,[6] and equally genuine Republicans like La Follette of Wisconsin, hero of the progressives.   Their presence as communicants in good standing of the same faith reflected a curious characteristic of the American party system.   People find it convenient to make themselves felt through whatever party is dominant in their locality rather than to move over into the opposite party.   State and local party organizations find it expedient to respond to these great swells of public opinion, even if it puts them in opposition to the national leadership. The alternative would be to remain faithful to the national leadership at the cost of control of state and local governments.   The progressives having taken over many Republican state organizations, Mr. Taft was confronted by rebels duly enrolled in his ranks.

His administration got off to an inauspicious start in a battle over tariff revision.   The 1908 platform had declared "unequivocally for a revision of the tariff by a special session of Congress immediately following the inauguration of the next President. . . ."   Taft called the special session and Aldrich led the high-tariff forces in Congress. Chided about his deviation from party promises, Aldrich responded that the promise was for "revision" not necessarily downwards.   Middlewestern Senators—La Follette of Wisconsin, Dolliver of Iowa, Beveridge of Indiana, Cummins of Iowa, Bristow of Kansas, Clapp of

[4] Thus, in an open letter to the Republican members of the Colorado legislature, Edward P. Costigan and others declared in 1911 that a recent Republican convention of Denver county had been "dominated by public utility agents, attorneys and discredited politicians."   The convention, they asserted, "was the natural flowering of several years of party subservience to political trickery, crimes against the ballot, thefts of franchises, violations of law and bold invasions of public rights."   C. B. Goodykoontz (ed.), *Papers of Edward P. Costigan Relating to the Progressive Movement in Colorado* (Boulder: University of Colorado, 1941), p. 152.

[5] The spirit of the progressive movement can be grasped from *The Autobiography of William Allen White* (New York: Macmillan, 1946).   Keen insights may be obtained from G. E. Mowry, *Theodore Roosevelt and the Progressive Movement* (Madison: University of Wisconsin Press, 1946).   See K. W. Hechler, *Insurgency: Personalities and Politics of the Taft Era* (New York: Columbia University Press, 1940).

[6] See N. W. Stephenson, *Nelson W. Aldrich* (New York: Scribner's, 1930).

Minnesota—opposed the Aldrich leadership in a battle royal, but the
right wing of the party triumphed and passed a bill distinctly to the
advantage of eastern interests. Taft's ineptitude in gaining tariff reductions brought disfavor in the Middle West. Soon Taft's handling
of conservation policies stimulated the true adherents of the Roose-
veltian doctrines to further gnashing of teeth.

In the 1910 congressional primaries Taft ingloriously failed in an
effort to purge the Republican party of progressives, and in the elections
a Democratic majority was returned to the House. The remaining
years of his term were marked by further division within the Republican party and the formation of the battle lines for 1912. His belated
attempts to bring party unity failed; perhaps the issues were beyond
compromise.

2. DEMOCRATIC INTERLUDE AND THE NEW FREEDOM, 1912–1920

When Republicans engage in a family fight, Democrats are sure to
capture the Presidency. The progressive movement within the Republican party reflected a moral and political ferment in the nation
that affected both parties. It led to a split within the Republican
party, to nomination of a progressive by the Democrats, and to a period
of notable legislative action under the leadership of Woodrow Wilson.

Campaign of 1912. The campaign of 1912 stands out as one of the
fabulous chapters of American party history. Roosevelt campaigned
energetically for the Republican nomination, but Taft controlled
enough state organizations to command a majority of the delegates.
Roosevelt was undoubtedly the choice of the mass of the party in so
far as their wishes were expressed in those states employing the primary
method of choosing convention delegates.[7] Taft, however, had early
signed up the delegates of the southern states and was able to control
a convention marked by unprecedented disorder.[8] The progressives,
asserting that they had been robbed,[9] proceeded to bolt the Republican
party and found a new party, called the Progressive party, with Roosevelt as its standard bearer. It was a personal party, a party permeated
with intense moral flavor, a crusade for righteousness or at least a movement rationalized in terms of righteousness. Progressive conclaves were
wont to sing the "Battle Hymn of the Republic," and Roosevelt's speech

[7] Edward P. Costigan reported from Colorado on the campaign for progressive
delegates to the national convention: "The wealth of the state is mostly against us,
but the rank and file are with us." Goodykoontz, *op. cit.*, p. 178.

[8] See chap. 13.

[9] Victor Rosewater, Republican national chairman in 1912, rebuts the charge of
thievery in *Back Stage in 1912* (Philadelphia: Dorrance, 1932).

to the Progressive convention was billed as a "Confession of Faith." With the preliminaries out of the way the doughty champion of the right went forth to smite the wicked.

Roosevelt, with his doctrine of "New Nationalism," lifted political discussion to a new plane of sophistication. He attacked the virtues of weak government and expounded the idea that a government, as strong as it need be, should use its powers to promote the liberties of the weak against the greed and oppression of those in high places. For the traditional antitrust demonology that proposed to cure economic ills by jailing a few rascals he substituted the idea of public control of more or less inevitable industrial combines. This idea was not unacceptable to Progressive men of wealth, who regarded some type of governmental control as in the cards. Roosevelt espoused all the progressive panaceas calculated to make government more responsive to the people: direct primaries, a nation-wide preference primary for candidates for the Presidency, the popular election of Senators, the initiative, referendum, and recall. The Progressives also pledged themselves to use the power of government to accomplish a long list of specific reforms: prohibition of child labor, minimum wages for women, the eight-hour day, regulation of security sales, social insurance, the establishment of a Department of Labor, and others.

The Democrats, still mindful of the electoral catastrophe that followed their conservative turn in 1904, determined to set a progressive tone for their own campaign. But this determination came after no little dispute in their national convention. Bryan, still the outstanding figure of the party, early put the convention in an uproar by proposing the following resolution:

Resolved, That in this crisis in our party's career and in our country's history this convention sends greetings to the people of the United States, and assures them that the party of Jefferson and of Jackson is still the champion of popular government and equality before the law. As proof of our fidelity to the people, we hereby declare ourselves opposed to the nomination of any candidate for President who is representative of or under obligation to J. Pierpont Morgan, Thomas F. Ryan, August Belmont, or any other member of the privilege-hunting and favor-seeking class.

Be It Further Resolved, That we demand the withdrawal from this convention of any delegate or delegates constituting or representing the above-named class.

The conservative wing of the party fumed and frothed, but to have voted down the resolution would have been bad politics indeed. To accept it would make difficult the nomination of a conservative candidate. Mr. Bryan had the conservatives in a corner—his enemies, had

they been equipped with modern vocabularies, would have called him
a crackpot, but the man had a streak of genius. The conservatives,
after Mr. Bryan withdrew the second paragraph of the resolution,
manfully voted for it. And the cartoonists pictured Bryan burning
the progressive brand into the hide of the Democratic party.[10]

Woodrow Wilson won the nomination, after Champ Clark of Missouri had attained a majority but failed to obtain the two thirds then
necessary to nominate under the rules of the Democratic convention.
Wilson, a recent convert to progressivism, had been president of Princeton University and governor of New Jersey. His doctrines belonged
to an older tradition than those of Roosevelt; his "New Freedom"
stemmed from Jefferson. He sought to free men from restraints,
monopolistic or otherwise, which restricted their liberties and prevented the full use of their talents. He regarded Roosevelt's "New
Nationalism" with its powerful state as a threat to liberty. This kind
of doctrine, Roosevelt retorted, was "rural toryism," which would, if
applied, lead to the repeal of all legislation for the protection of the
social and industrial rights of man.

Taft could not compete in the campaign with men of the histrionic
talents of Roosevelt and Wilson. He was a poor third in the running,
polling 3,486,000 votes to 4,118,000 for Roosevelt and 6,296,000 for
Wilson. The Republican split gave Wilson the victory although the
Democratic proportion of the popular vote fell from 43.1 in 1908 to
41.9 in 1912. In the electoral vote the figures were: Wilson, 435;
Roosevelt, 88; Taft, 8. The split within the Republican party was
not sectional, although Roosevelt's popular vote was highest generally
in the Middle West and the Far West. The territorial distribution of
the popular support for Roosevelt is shown in the map in Figure 13.
He won the electoral vote of Michigan, Minnesota, Pennsylvania, South
Dakota, and Washington, and 11 of the 13 electoral votes of California.

Wilson and the Presidency. Wilson brought to the Presidency definite conceptions about the role that a President should play as party
leader in the execution of a party program. He also brought to the
Presidency experience as a college executive that stood him in good
stead in the practice of the art of pacifying and managing his party
followers by the cold-blooded distribution of patronage and pap. For-
tified by these skills and supported by the undoubted spirit of pro-

[10] For Bryan's account of the convention, see W. J. Bryan and M. B. Bryan, *The
Memoirs of William Jennings Bryan* (Philadelphia: United Publishers, 1925), Pt. I,
chap. 10. See also A. S. Link, "The Baltimore Convention of 1912," *American Historical Review*, 50 (1945), pp. 691–713.

gressivism abroad in the land, he succeeded in pushing through Congress a remarkable program of legislation.

Tariff had been debated for over a decade, but the Wilson Administration actually reduced the tariff. The tariff bill included an income tax; the Democrats came to power just as the income tax amendment, proposed in 1909 by a coalition of Democrats and Republican insurgents, had finally been approved by the requisite number of states. The currency problem—reflected in the agitation of the Grangers, the

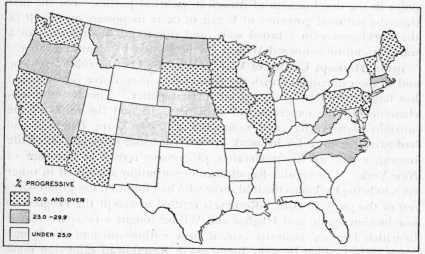

% PROGRESSIVE

30.0 AND OVER

25.0 –29.9

UNDER 25.0

Figure 13. Percentage of Total Popular Vote Polled by Progressive Ticket in Presidential Election of 1912, by States

Greenbackers, the Populists, and the free-silverites of 1896—was dealt with in the establishment of the Federal Reserve System, which provided an elastic supply of money. The solution differed from early panaceas, but the problem dealt with was the same as that which had plagued the country for decades. The Federal Trade Commission was created to attack the problem of restraints on competition in a different manner and in supplementation of the traditional antitrust procedures. The Clayton Act, in addition to its provisions regarding monopolies, contained clauses affecting labor. It exempted labor unions from the antitrust laws and contained other provisions that enabled Samuel Gompers, overoptimistically, to hail it as the "Magna Carta of Labor." Wilson approved an act safeguarding the rights of seamen, a measure that had been pocket-vetoed by Taft in a different form. The Adamson Act embodied an eight-hour day for railroad workers. After reversing his earlier views, Wilson urged the adoption of a statute prohibiting child labor, a law later to be held void.[11]   The Democrats also had something for the farmer: they enacted the Federal Farm Loan Act under which the government subscribed the capital stock to banks especially created to make long-term loans to farmers at low rates of interest.

Professor Binkley suggests that perhaps Wilson's aggressive support of legislation for the benefit of the laboring masses marked a turning point in the development of American political parties.   For the first time the national government began to exert its powers on behalf of the workingman on a broad scale, and this trend was reflected in a warm friendliness toward Wilson by the leaders of organized labor.[12]

1916: "He Kept Us Out of War."   War checked the tide of reform, and in the campaign of 1916 the conservative-progressive issue loomed less large than that of American foreign policy.   The Republicans, chastened by the experience of 1912, went beyond the ranks of the outright conservatives and nominated Charles Evans Hughes, who had gained renown for his work in the Armstrong investigation of life insurance and for his moderately progressive record as governor of New York.   The regular Republican organization attempted in other ways to bring back into the fold those who had followed the Progressives out of the party in 1912.   Roosevelt refused to accept the Progressive nomination again, and Hughes and Wilson fought a two-party battle in which Hughes' austerity evoked little enthusiasm and the Democratic record, aided by some ineptness in Republican campaign management, brought victory.

The Democratic organization in the campaign emphasized the slogan, "He Kept Us Out of War," but the candidate cagily refused to commit himself to a position that might later restrict his freedom of action.   On foreign policy the issue was not clearly drawn; both parties were for American rights and adequate preparedness.   They differed on who should be responsible for executing the policy.   Perhaps, as often happens, the fundamental issue was not presented in clear alternatives to the electorate.

The polling resulted in an electoral vote of 277 to 254, but the Democratic proportion of the total popular vote increased to 49.3 per cent from the 1912 level of 41.9.   Wilson carried the states of the Solid

[11] Paul McKown, *Certain Important Domestic Policies of Woodrow Wilson* (Philadelphia, 1932).

[12] *Op. cit.,* p. 367.

South and the West and broke into Republican territory to capture Ohio and New Hampshire.[13]

Soon war came, and of war little can be said. Domestic politics was not adjourned, but the issues became different. Wilson's handling of foreign affairs aroused the animosity of senatorial Republican leaders, who succeeded in winning their battle against the proposed League of Nations. The senatorial cabal that defeated the League won control of the Republican party and removed from it the last taint of the progressive spirit of 1912. In the campaign of 1918 Wilson appealed to the country to return Democratic Congressmen who would support him in his policies, but the country did not respond. It returned a Republican majority to the House; the period of normalcy had begun.

3. NORMALCY AND ITS AFTERMATH, 1920–1932

In 1920 the pendulum swung to the right. The movement had begun in the congressional elections of 1918 and continued in the presidential election of 1920. The hopeful spirit of the crusading progressives largely disappeared as the temper of the country was modified by the undeviating and wholehearted pursuit of speculative gains.

Harding and Coolidge. In the preliminaries to the Republican convention of 1920 the Republican senatorial leadership held control of the Republican organization. It was clear that the nominee would be a safe and sane man unlikely to challenge the primacy of the elder statesmen of the Senate. The mantle fell on Warren G. Harding, undistinguished in his record as a Senator and unmarked by any characteristic of greatness as an Ohio newspaper editor and publisher.

The Republican platform reflected the views of the dominant interests in the party, but made some genuflection to progressive principles. It promised "to end executive autocracy and restore to the people their constitutional government." On the great issue of the campaign, if it can be said that there was an issue, the party stood for an "international association" to be based upon "international justice." However, presaging the veto system of the United Nations, the party promised international agreements to "meet the full duty of America to civilization and humanity," but "without surrendering the right of the American people to exercise its judgment and its power in favor of justice and peace." In characteristic partisan language, the platform condemned the record of Wilson and praised the actions of the Congress

13 The electoral vote is shown on the map in Figure 6, page 159.

in which a Republican majority had prevailed since the elections of
1918.

Within the Democratic party also the crusading spirit had sagged.
It chose another undistinguished Ohio newspaper editor, James M.
Cox, as its presidential candidate.   Franklin D. Roosevelt, then a young
man of no great consequence who had been Assistant Secretary of the
Navy, accepted the vice-presidential nomination.   The Democratic
party stood on the Wilson record, advocated entrance of the United
States into the League of Nations, condemned the Republican party
generally, and went down to inglorious defeat.   Harding's promise of
"normalcy" voiced the feelings of a nation weary of war and anxious
to achieve a restoration of things as they had been.

Harding swept the nation with an electoral vote of 404 to 127.   The
western states moved back into the Republican column, and Cox carried only eleven southern states.[14]   The Democratic proportion of the
total popular vote dropped to 34.1 per cent; the Democratic percentage
of the popular vote declined in every state although desertions to the
Republicans were at a lower rate in the southern states than elsewhere.

In the administrations of Harding and Coolidge finance and industry
again became dominant.   None of the measures put on the statute
books by the Democrats for the control of business were repealed, but
they were tempered in their application.   Government by injunction
prevailed, and Andrew Mellon, as Secretary of the Treasury, preached
the reduction of taxation of the rich in order that they might invest
their money in employment-producing enterprise.   Most of it, however,
apparently went into stock market speculation.   The Republican administration put through measures for the enlargement of the farm
credit system, but this step was not enough to quiet the farmers.   Even
in Coolidge's first administration the midwestern farmer was on a
rampage, asserting that prosperity did not trickle down to him in adequate degree.   The advocates of farm relief in the form of the McNary-
Haugen bill, the spiritual ancestor of the Agricultural Adjustment Act,
were beginning to make themselves heard.

1924: Mediocrity *vs.* Mediocrity.   The New England rectitude of
Calvin Coolidge and mounting prosperity carried the Republicans
triumphantly through the election of 1924; so weak was the spirit of
protest that the country paid little heed to the Teapot Dome scandals.[15]
The Democratic party, rent by internecine struggle, did little to encourage the public in the belief that it had the capacity to govern.   Its
1924 national convention was a savage bout beautiful to behold.   The

14 The electoral vote is shown on the map in Figure 7, page 160.
15 See M. E. Ravage, *The Story of Teapot Dome* (New York: Republic, 1924).

points of internal weakness in the coalition which is the Democratic party made themselves manifest; when urban Irish Catholics disagree with rural Protestants bitterness is bound to ensue. The New York convention fought over what, if anything, should be said in condemnation of the Ku Klux Klan, but most of all it fought over whether Alfred E. Smith or William G. McAdoo would be the nominee of the party. Behind Smith were arrayed the urban, Catholic, and "liberal"— by now some people were beginning to suspect that prohibition did not come up to forecast—elements of the party. McAdoo had the support of the southern, rural, dry, Protestant elements of the party. A hundred ballots could not break the deadlock and on the one hundred and third ballot the convention compromised on John W. Davis.

The Democracy, in its platform, flayed the Republicans with might and main, but the conservative John W. Davis had neither the beliefs nor the manners requisite for a leader of protest. Such a candidate could give no tone of urgency or sincerity to the platform charge that the Republican party believed "that prosperity must originate with the special interests and seep down through the channels of trade to the less favored industries, to the wage earners and small salaried employes." The resolutions writers proclaimed: "A vote for Coolidge is a vote for chaos." They charged that the Mellon tax plan was "a device to relieve multimillionaires at the expense of other taxpayers"; they denounced the Fordney-McCumber tariff as "class legislation which defrauds the people for the benefit of a few." They announced that the "predatory interests" had "by supplying Republican campaign funds, systematically purchased legislative favors and administrative immunity."

This sort of oratory had little effect on the electorate. Probably the Republican affirmation of "its devotion to orderly government under the guarantees embodied in the constitution" had no more effect. The Republicans pointed to prosperity, to the reduction of taxation, to the wise tariff provisions that had been enacted, to measures for the benefit of agriculture.

The Republican landslide gave Coolidge 382 electoral votes to 136 for Davis. The Democratic proportion of the total popular vote fell to an all-time low of 28.8 per cent. Wise men freely predicted that the day of the Democratic party was done; but not all was well within the Republican party. Its midwestern wing was again restive and some secession occurred in 1924 in support of the Farmer-Labor candidacies of Robert M. La Follette and Burton K. Wheeler, who carried the state of Wisconsin and polled about one out of every eight popular votes in the nation. The Farmer-Labor platform proclaimed the great issue as "the control of government and industry by private monopoly." It pointed to the distress of the American farmer and to the usurpation of legislative powers by the courts. The distribution of the vote for La Follette identified areas of future difficulty for the Republican leadership. The Farmer-Labor candidates polled more than 30 per cent of the popular vote in California, Idaho, Minnesota, Montana, Nevada, North Dakota, South Dakota, Washington, Wisconsin, and Wyoming.

After the election of 1924 the Coolidge Administration yielded no great legislative achievement. The midwestern agrarians of the Republican party became more vocal and succeeded in passing the McNary-Haugen bill, which Coolidge vetoed. The plaints of the farmer were drowned by the unprecedented prosperity of the speculators. Whether Coolidge was wise enough or whether he could have done anything to check the coming crash is problematic. In his revealing study of Coolidge, William Allen White concluded that Coolidge was a perfect democratic expression of the dominant forces of the day.[16] However that may be, Coolidge rode the tide, but apparently sensing what was coming, in 1927 chose not to run in 1928. Mrs. Coolidge, in a family gathering, was reported to have explained: "Poppa says there's a depression coming." [17]

Hoover and the crash. With Coolidge's renunciation of the 1928 nomination, Mr. Herbert Hoover, his Secretary of Commerce, was soon in full cry after the nomination. Tagged by friend as the "Great Engineer" and by enemy as the "Wonder Boy," Hoover easily outdistanced other aspirants for the Republican nomination. Hoover had to convince the Republican organizations that he could win; he did not belong to the inner circle of Republicanism as had Harding and Coolidge. In a sense by the nomination of Hoover, the Republicans yielded somewhat to the discontent within the party, for Hoover had accomplishments to his credit that placed him in a different category from the old-fashioned stand-patter.

Northeastern elements of the party dominated the convention and easily overrode the objections of midwestern farm leaders to the agricultural plank. Midwesterners demanded more positive promises to farmers than the limited policy the easterners were willing to concede. The prohibition issue aroused debate, but the party pledged itself to the vigorous enforcement of the prohibition provision of the Constitution. The old Republican standby, the protective tariff, was acclaimed as the source of all prosperity and as a boon to every section and to every class,

16 *A Puritan in Babylon* (New York: Macmillan, 1938).
17 *Ibid.*, p. 366.

although it was conceded that some revision of existing arrangements might be required in the light of the world situation.

The Democrats again assayed their role as the party of protest, but again demonstrated the incohesiveness of the elements that must make up such a party in comparison with the ties that bind a party whose ranks include the solid industrial and financial interests. The conditions were not ripe for a party of protest to win, but in making their nomination the Democrats conspired with the forces working for their defeat.

They chose Alfred E. Smith of New York as their nominee. A dripping wet, he renounced the party's dry platform plank. A child of the streets of New York, he could not induce the midwestern farmers to believe that the more liberal farm relief plank meant what it said. A Catholic, he could not persuade many Protestants of the party that the Pope would not make of the White House a branch Vatican.

Of the issues, probably prosperity was the most influential outside the South. The Republicans could point with pride to the Coolidge market. They could concede the existence of limited agricultural prosperity, but that was to be taken care of by generous upward revisions of the tariff on agricultural products. In the South Smith's religious affiliation and his wetness were too much for dry, native-white Protestants. Hoover broke into the Solid South, and in that area Smith carried only Alabama, Arkansas, Georgia, Louisiana, Mississippi, and South Carolina. The Republicans won the traditionally Democratic states of Florida, Kentucky, Maryland, North Carolina, Oklahoma, Tennessee, and Texas. The electoral vote was 444 to 87. Had they studied the election returns more closely the Democrats could have found cheer. Their proportion of the total popular presidential vote jumped to 40.8 per cent from the 1924 figure of 28.8. They won the electoral vote of Rhode Island and Massachusetts, an omen of further growth of Democratic support in urban, Catholic, industrial centers. In every state north of the Ohio and east of the Mississippi their proportion of the total popular vote increased over the 1924 level. Although Smith shook the loyalty of the southern wing of the party, he helped lay the groundwork for the future by annexing the wet vote and by regaining a sizeable proportion of the vote of workingmen.[18] The distribution of the Democratic strength by states in 1928 is shown by the map in Figure 14.

Herbert Hoover came to the Presidency with greater ability and

[18] See R. V. Peel and T. C. Donnelly, *The 1928 Campaign* (New York: R. R. Smith, 1931).

greater promise than his immediate predecessors. A man of humanitarian impulses, of great knowledge, of demonstrated administrative capacity, perhaps fate dealt with him worse than he deserved. Crisis after crisis was his lot, and he met them as they came, sometimes skilfully but sometimes ineptly. A recalcitrant Congress did not ease his task. During his entire administration a Democratic-Progressive Republican coalition controlled the Senate at critical moments. This combination sought to go beyond the scope of farm relief that Hoover recommended at the special session called soon after his inauguration.

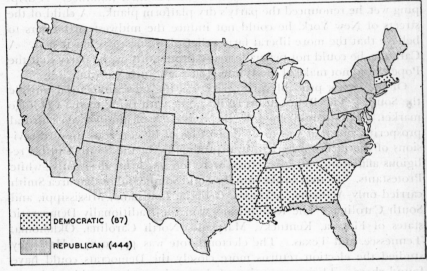

Figure 14. **Electoral Vote by States in Presidential Election of 1928**

It ignored his recommendation for a "limited revision" of the tariff to lift rates on agricultural commodities, and he was unable to prevent the enactment of the Smoot-Hawley tariff, which perhaps worsened conditions. During the last two years of his administration the Democrats, in control of the House of Representatives, did not dedicate themselves to co-operation with him in grappling with the problems of the day.

Perhaps the puzzle of Hoover is to be explained by the fact that he was in a way the first President who took his ideology seriously. The American political tradition had been pragmatic; we dealt with whatever came in whatever way seemed to be appropriate at the moment, using the government as an instrumentality if need be. Hoover, however, adhered to principle, and his principles were those of reliance on private initiative, of abhorrence of governmental action, especially by the national government, and of individual responsibility. All these doctrines happened to coincide with the interests of the predominant sections of the Republican party, but Hoover's sincerity could not be questioned, for he acted consistently with his principles as disaster after disaster overwhelmed him.

In his inaugural address we hear him interpreting the election as a confirmation of the "determination of the American people that regulation of private enterprise and not governmental ownership or operation is the course rightly to be pursued in our relation to business." We see him calling in the officials of the New York Stock Exchange and telling them that, although the exchange was under the jurisdiction of the State of New York, unless it reformed its ways demands for federal control would certainly come. We see him organizing a huge drive to collect private funds to furnish aid to the destitute; if the federal government paid for relief it would result in graft, politics, bureaucracy, corruption. In the face of senatorial demands for appropriations for relief, he contended that we should "maintain the spirit of charity and mutual self-help, through voluntary giving and the responsibility of local government. . . ." [19] Eventually federal action became necessary, but it took the euphemistic form of loans to state and local governments. We see him coping with bank failures. He summons bankers and insists that they subscribe funds to a private association that would loan money to banks under pressure from their depositors. Becoming concerned about the problem of security in old age, he calls in the presidents of life insurance companies and persuades them to give thought to ways and means by which the matter can be handled by private enterprise. Nevertheless, economic conditions grew worse and worse; many steps were taken by the government, but Hoover fought doggedly for individual initiative, private enterprise, local governmental responsibilities. Yet in his administration there were initiated, in a tentative, tardy, and small-scale way, many of the measures that the New Deal later expanded to huge dimensions.

4. THE NEW DEAL AND AFTER

The presidential election of 1932 marked another great turning point in American party history. The disastrous economic fate of the country under Republican leadership—whether the Republicans had anything to do with it—gave the Republican party a blow from which

[19] W. S. Myers and W. H. Newton, *The Hoover Administration, A Documented Narrative* (New York: Scribner's, 1936), p. 63.

it would take time to recover. The same record laid the basis for the formation of a new Democratic party, perhaps not fundamentally different from its former self but incorporating a much larger proportion of the less-favored groups economically than in the past. The discrediting of business leadership paved the way for the broadest governmental intervention in economic affairs that the nation had seen in times of peace and for far-reaching measures of reform.

1932 and the New Deal. The campaign of 1932 presented no great uncertainties for the political forecaster. The Republican delegates who convened at Chicago to renominate Mr. Hoover produced a synthetic enthusiasm in public but were privately appalled at the prospects. The Democrats, sure of victory, vied with one another for the nomination and after a warm dispute among themselves agreed upon Franklin D. Roosevelt as their nominee.

The campaign gave to the public no clear-cut alternatives of policy, except with respect to prohibition. The Democrats were thoroughly wet. But no other issue of a major nature presented itself sharply and dramatically in the campaign. The times called for a great debate on measures to lift the American economy out of the morass, but a stranger might have presumed that all the fighting was about when and whether one could get a glass of legal beer. Mr. Roosevelt expressed some doubt about the Republican theory that by helping employers the lot of the workingman could be improved significantly, but the issue was not made plain to the mass of voters. Mr. Roosevelt's promises and his record with respect to the regulation of public utilities, some of which had been involved in scandalous financial transactions, were much stronger than those of Mr. Hoover. Probably the genius of Roosevelt's strategy was in his appeal to all classes of citizens; he proposed a farm program, a labor program, a banking program, a business program, and stood for the theory of working in concert with all groups rather than relying chiefly on industrial and financial leadership to lift the country out of the depression.

Yet it is doubtful that the rational appeals of either candidate had much to do with the election results. All types and classes of people had suffered deprivations; all of them were anxious for a change. Poor men, rich men, middle-class men, farmers, workers, all moved over into the Democratic ranks in sufficient number to give Roosevelt a resounding victory. All these classes could identify themselves with the "forgotten man," and they could equally feel themselves deserving of a "new deal" without necessarily insisting on exactitude in the definition of what the "new deal" was to be. The Democracy won 57.4 per cent of the total presidential vote in contrast with Smith's poll of 40.8 per cent in 1928. The electoral vote was 472 to 59; Hoover carried only Connecticut, Delaware, Maine, Pennsylvania, and Vermont.[20]

Washington was soon treated to a spectacle the like of which it had never seen, except on the occasion of Jackson's inaugural reception when staid personages reacted with horror at the lack of decorum of the common people who invaded the White House as if they owned it. The Democrats assembled to take control of the government were a motley crew indeed. Southern statesmen of the old school mixed with

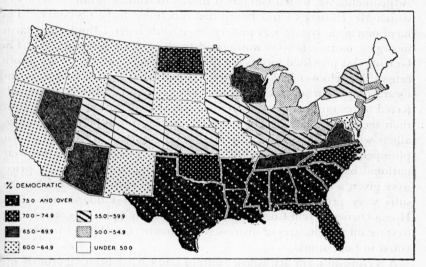

% DEMOCRATIC
75.0 AND OVER
70.0 - 74.9   55.0 - 59.9
65.0 - 69.9   50.0 - 54.9
60.0 - 64.9   UNDER 50.0

Figure 15. Democratic Percentage of Major-Party Popular Vote by States in Presidential Election of 1932

Bull Moosers, with suave and tough labor bosses, with intellectuals, with the Democratic contingent from big business, with bright young men from the Harvard Law School. Ghosts of the past were resurrected as former lieutenants of Bryan and Wilson emerged to take high places, and now and then an old Socialist who had been converted to the Democracy made a place for himself. Presiding over this assemblage, representative of every element of protest and discontent, was a man who, to the surprise of all concerned, turned out to be a genius at the art of political leadership and the first President to be a master of the use of the radio in arousing mass support for his measures.

The country cried for action, and Roosevelt gave it action. After dealing with the immediate problem of restoring the nations' banks to

[20] See Roy V. Peel and T. C. Donnelly, *The 1932 Campaign* (New York: Farrar & Rinehart, 1935).

operation, he proceeded to drive through a not unwilling Congress a
series of measures for recovery and reform without parallel. Yet most
of the measures stemmed from the American stream of reform agitation
Planks in the Democratic platform of 1908 and later years, the Progres
sive platform of 1912, and other long-past campaign promises were re
deemed; in many instances measures inaugurated by Mr. Hoover were
pushed only a step, perhaps a long stride, forward.

The farmers were taken care of by the passage of the Agricultura
Adjustment Act, which embodied means to control production, a step
which Mr. Hoover's Farm Board had concluded to be necessary. The
farm mortgage system was underpinned with federal funds, and farm
mortgage moratoria were authorized to check farm foreclosures. The
Grazing Act provided means for the regulation of the use of the publi
ranges; Mr. Hoover had appointed a commission to look into ways and
means of preventing over-grazing. Banks received aid and were sub
jected to restraints. A major reform was the separation of banks from
their security affiliates. The bank deposit insurance plan became law
albeit without Mr. Roosevelt's support. The Democrats in 1908 had
plumped for a "guarantee fund" to pay off "depositors of any insolven
national bank." The dollar was devalued; thereby commodity price
were given a boost and the burdens of debtors eased. Horrendous re
sults were predicted by spokesmen of the gold-standard cult. The
Home Owners' Loan Corporation was created and given $3,000,000,000
to stave off foreclosures of distressed homeowners, and relief funds were
voted in huge sums.

A reciprocal tariff act, whose concept had earlier been vigorously op
posed by the Republicans, was adopted, and a securities act became
law. Its objectives recalled the Progressive platform of 1912, which
had pointed out that people were "swindled" out of millions every year
by investing in stocks offered by "highly colored prospectuses" and tha
it was the duty of the government "to protect its people from this kind
of piracy." The Tennessee Valley Authority Act settled the long
drawn-out feud between farmers and the power companies over the
utilization of the Muscle Shoals Dam and the development of the water
power resources of the Tennessee Valley. Business leaders met in the
annual session of the Chamber of Commerce and advocated a large
measure of governmental compulsion to aid business in its attempts a
self-regulation. The National Industrial Recovery Act, one of the
less well-advised New Deal measures, became law and was put into
operation with great fanfare by General Hugh Johnson.

All these measures, and others too, left Congress a bit groggy; Con
gressmen who were inclined to balk heard from their constituents, and

in 1934 the Democratic party gained congressional strength in the mid-
term elections, the first time an administration in power had done so
since the Civil War. There was more to come. The Social Security
Act provided for a system of old-age assistance based on a means test;
for a system of old-age insurance on a contributory basis for persons in
industrial employment; for assistance to the blind and to dependent
children; for unemployment insurance; and for enlarged public-health
services. All these measures had behind them a long period of agitation by liberals and progressives. The National Labor Relations Act
undertook to guarantee to labor the right to bargain through representatives of its own choice; the Farmer-Labor platform of 1920 had
pledged such legislation and as early as 1908 the Democrats had made
tentative moves in the same direction. Although most of the New
Deal program had roots in earlier political discussion, the program as
a whole marked a sharp deviation from the policies of the preceding
years, which had been dominated by the notion that the public good
was promoted best by a government that restricted the sphere of its
activities. One scholar concludes that "the New Deal represents the
most zestful and thorough attack yet seen on those Whig principles
which, with relatively minor exception, have dominated public policy
since the days of the Federalists." [21]

1936: Roosevelt, Landon, and the Liberty League. As the campaign of 1936 approached—there was no doubt that the Democrats
would renominate Roosevelt—the Republicans began to give thought
to the strategy of attack. The big-business element in the Republican
party, with returning business activity, began to be dubious about the
New Deal. The Republican party was not an adequate vehicle for the
expression of their indignation; they formed the Liberty League to save
the country and conducted a vigorous campaign of protest reminiscent
of Herbert Hoover's attachment to "ordered liberty." The Republicans nominated Alfred M. Landon, Governor of Kansas, to serve as
martyr in the campaign and promulgated a platform dedicating themselves to "the preservation of . . . political liberty." They invited
men of all parties to join them in defense of American institutions and
pledged themselves to maintain the Constitution and to preserve free
enterprise. They condemned unemployment insurance and old-age
annuities, provided by the Social Security Act, as "unworkable." They
proposed that labor have a right to bargain through representatives
"of its own choosing without interference from any source," a qualification that presumably implied some modification of the National

[21] T. P. Jenkin, *Reactions of Major Groups to Positive Government in the United
States, 1930–1940* (Berkeley: University of California Press, 1945), p. 396.

Labor Relations Act. They pledged themselves to "balance the budget," to maintain a "sound currency," not to devalue the dollar further.

The country failed to be disturbed by Republican forecasts of disaster; Roosevelt was returned by a larger majority than in 1932. He carried every state save Maine and Vermont, with an electoral vote of 523 to 8. By now the public-opinion polls had come into operation, and it was easier to discern the exact kind of coalition that Roosevelt had built up. He had brought together the votes of traditional Democratic territory and the northern urban laboring vote. The population dependent upon public relief overwhelmingly supported him, and the Negroes had been wooed away from their habitual Republicanism. Businessmen in the main remained Republican, but each successively lower-income group voted Democratic in larger proportions.

The problem of holding this diverse coalition together grew more difficult after the President's 1937 proposal for the "rejuvenation" of the Supreme Court.[22] The Supreme Court had long been regarded as the great bulwark of property rights, and to earn that reputation it had over the years invalidated a considerable quantity of state and federal legislation. Supported by conservatives generally, it had often been attacked by labor and protest groups. The Progressives in 1912 had demanded restriction of the power of the courts so that the people might have "the ultimate authority to determine fundamental questions of social welfare and public policy." La Follette's 1924 platform favored an amendment to the constitution to permit Congress to override judicial veto of a statute. The Democrats in 1936 proposed, if necessary, a "clarifying amendment" to the Constitution to permit the enactment of laws necessary "to regulate commerce, protect public health and safety, and safeguard economic security." This declaration had been preceded by Supreme Court decisions invalidating the Agricultural Adjustment Act and the National Industrial Recovery Act. Roosevelt went beyond the platform and proposed to "pack" the court and thereby set off a battle that solidified the conservative interests of the country and opened a little wider the split between his party's conservative and liberal factions. Defeated in his court proposal, Roosevelt won his primary objective. The Court itself soon altered the direction of its decisions, and retirements permitted him to name judges of a more acceptable political philosophy.

In 1938 Roosevelt faced the same problem that confronted Taft in 1912. Taft had within his own party an insurgent wing that deviated

22 See Joseph Alsop and Turner Catledge, *The 168 Days* (Garden City: Doubleday, Doran, 1938).

from the official line of the party; he tried to drive it from the party. In 1938 Roosevelt had a right wing in the Democratic party that rebelled at the Supreme Court proposal and on other issues had a marked kinship with the right wing of the Republican party. He tried to persuade the Democrats in several state primaries to purge the "Old Dealers," but in this he failed in almost every instance.

1940: Third term. A new ingredient came into the political picture in the campaign of 1940. The outbreak of European war and the consequent threat to American safety brought foreign policy to the fore as the chief question before the country but not the chief issue in the campaign. Willkie, the Republican nominee, agreed substantially with Democratic pronouncements on foreign affairs. The foreign-policy issue was thus officially taken out of the campaign although minor Republican orators called the Democrats a "war party" and Democrats questioned the sincerity of the Republicans by pointing to the conspicuous isolationists in their ranks.[23] "Don't Change Horses in the Middle of the Stream" became the Democratic slogan; Republicans attempted to raise the specter of dictatorship, attacked Democratic domestic policies, and appealed to the hallowed two-term tradition, but to no avail. Roosevelt won by 449 to 82 electoral votes. Willkie captured the loyalty of the mass of Republicans but was viewed coolly by the Republican machines as an amateur and a renegade Democrat. He carried only ten states, among them Indiana, Iowa, Kansas, Michigan, Nebraska, North Dakota, and South Dakota. A combination of isolationism and agrarian dissatisfaction with Democratic policies brought these states to him in a Republican trend that had begun in 1936.

Even before the election of 1940, the New Deal was dead as a moving force for additional innovation. It had run its course and lost its momentum, and the approaching war diverted attention from domestic matters. Yet the New Deal had left a thick residue of legislation and had introduced a new sharpness into American political debate. Although the Democratic program merely executed in many instances projects long considered in American politics, the total effect was to present in new form the broad issue of individualism versus collectivism. The New Deal emerged from the tradition of American progressivism, but it operated with a superior political leadership and applied its measures with a more sophisticated administrative technique. Instead of relying on moral castigation and the penalization of a few rascals to promote the public weal, it spent money, set up commissions

[23] See the discussion by C. A. Berdahl, "Political Parties and Elections," *American Political Science Review*, 37 (1943), pp. 68–80.

and agencies, issued orders and rules and regulations, and generally used the powers of government.[24]   All these measures sharpened political conflict and raised broadly the question of the role of government in promoting the interests of its citizens.   The overwhelming support of labor—and most people are workers in one way or another—gave strength to the government, but it also solidified upper-class sentiment in opposition.   Spokesmen for the more prosperous contended that the American way was threatened, that dictatorship was coming, that individual liberties were being bartered for a mess of pottage.   This sort of discussion was not new; Theodore Roosevelt and Woodrow Wilson had been cursed with almost the same abandon as Franklin Roosevelt.   Yet the New Deal strained the capacity of the upper classes to accede to peaceful change, and right-wing predictions of leftist dictatorship were matched by leftist assertions that men of property and wealth had too little belief in democracy to stand idly by and allow the fulfillment of the logic of rule by the will of the masses.

Of the politics of World War II it needs only to be noted that Roosevelt managed to hold together with great skill the amalgam of antithetic elements composing the Democratic party, an essential for the successful prosecution of the war.   The internal strains made themselves more apparent in the events leading to the campaign of 1944.   At the Democratic convention southern state organizations, conservative Democrats elsewhere, and the A.F. of L. succeeded in preventing the nomination of Henry Wallace, strongly backed by the C.I.O., for the Vice-Presidency. But the party closed ranks for the campaign and again defeated the Republican nominee, this time Governor Thomas E. Dewey of New York, by an electoral vote of 432 to 99.   The Democratic proportion of the total popular vote again declined, but between 1940 and 1944 Roosevelt acquired additional support from business and professional groups, reflective perhaps of the Administration's swing toward the right and of the sense of responsibility of these groups in the sphere of foreign affairs.   The farming classes, however, continued their movement toward the Republicans, resentful of Democratic policy toward labor and of Democratic policy calculated to keep food prices down.

With the death of Roosevelt, Truman inherited both the Presidency and the problem of juggling the pieces of the Democratic party.   In maintaining unity among labor, southern conservatives, metropolitan bosses, and urban people generally, it appeared that Mr. Truman faced a task to which he did not bring the skills of group diplomacy with which Mr. Roosevelt had been endowed.   This appearance was con-

[24] See the discussion by Edgar Kemler, *The Deflation of American Ideals, An Ethical Guide for New Dealers* (Washington: American Council of Public Affairs, 1941).

firmed by the mid-term elections of 1946, in which the Republicans won a majority in both House and Senate.

5. ARE THERE POLITICAL CYCLES?

In a two-party system the answer to the question whether there are political cycles must obviously be in the affirmative unless one of the parties is perpetually out of power. If power alternates between two parties, cycles there must be although they may be of uneven length and there may be those who question the applicability of the term cycles. As a conclusion to this discussion of recent party history, it is appropriate to examine some of the evidence pointing to the existence of political cycles and to speculate a bit about their nature and their bearing on interpretations of the character of the party battle.[25]

Evidence of cycles. In one theory of cycles, Arthur M. Schlesinger insists that in the identification of cycles one must by and large ignore parties and Presidents and search for shifts in the nature of governmental policy and parallel changes in the general mood of the nation. Applying this method he finds that politically the nation alternates between eras of conservatism and liberalism or between eras of emphasis on the rights of property and of emphasis on human welfare. In each of these types of periods, he contends, the predominant public sentiment converts parties, Presidents, and Congresses to the mood of the day. Thus he breaks recent United States history into the following periods: 1841–1861, 1861–1869, 1869–1901, 1901–1918, 1918–1931. The first, third, and fifth of these periods he denominates conservative; the others, liberal. He contends, for example, that the period 1901–1918 can be characterized as liberal, for even the Taft Administration had to yield to the temper of the times and enact quite as much progressive legislation as the preceding Roosevelt Administration. This liberal period came to an abrupt end with Republican resurgence in the congressional elections of 1918, which marked roughly the beginning of a period in which the dominant national mood was conservative. By ruling out the two periods in which extraordinary circumstances prevailed from 1861 to 1901, Schlesinger arrives at the conclusion that over the entire period of United States history conservative epochs average about 15 years, liberal ones 16.5 years. On this basis, writing in 1939, he suggested that the liberal period beginning in 1931 would come to an end in 1947 or 1948.[26]

---

[25] These remarks bear solely on national politics. The cycle phenomenon in state and local politics remains to be investigated.

[26] Arthur M. Schlesinger, "Tides of American Politics," *Yale Review*, 29 (1939), pp. 217–230.

Another student of political cycles, Louis Bean, takes another approach to the problem. Instead of setting off one cyclical phase from another by qualitative judgments of the country's mood or the liberal or conservative temper of public policy, he looks at the election returns for the House of Representatives and for President. The Democratic percentage of the House membership as well as the Democratic percentage of the popular vote for President shows ups and downs indicative of cycles of irregular duration, with majorities moving from the Democratic column over to the Republican and back.[27]   A chart illus-

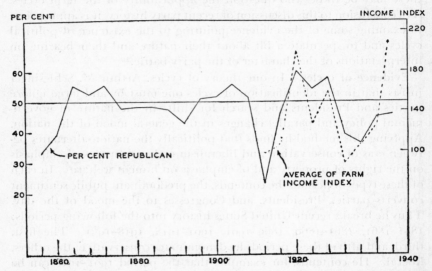

Figure 16. Republican Percentage of Total Presidential Vote, 1856–1944, and Average of Farm Income Index for Each Election Year and the Preceding Two Years, 1912–1944

trative of one part of Mr. Bean's theory is presented in Figure 16. Note in this chart that in recent American history the Republican percentages of the total popular vote for President reached peaks in 1904 and 1920 and troughs in 1892, 1912, and 1936.[28]   These "cycles" are different in duration from those of Schlesinger.   Thus Schlesinger designates the entire period from 1901 to 1918 as a liberal era, but voting cycles do not coincide with this period.   The difference between the two views are not necessarily irreconcilable.   Economic cycles also

[27] Louis H. Bean, "Tides and Patterns in American Politics," *American Political Science Review*, 36 (1942), pp. 637–655.   See also his *Ballot Behavior* (Washington: American Council on Public Affairs, 1940).

[28] The chart presents a slightly different appearance if percentages of major-party, rather than total, presidential vote are used.   See Figure 10 on page 218.

are not simple phenomena in which everything moves at the same direction at the same time; there are all sorts of cycles of varying duration and amplitude included within the great swings of economic activity. A convenient differentiation would be to refer to Schlesinger's concept as "policy cycles" and to Bean's as "party cycles."

Significance of party cycles. If it is assumed that there are party cycles of a fair degree of regularity, that condition has consequences of singular importance for speculation about the nature of political behavior. Of course, it may not be correct to assume that party cycles are a permanent feature of American politics. The behavior of the curve in Figure 16 in the period following the Civil War suggests that one may not be on completely solid ground in supposing that we will continue to have our party ups and downs, with the periods of dominance of each of fairly regular duration. But let it be assumed for the sake of discussion that the behavior of the curve of party strength since 1888 reflects a more or less fixed pattern in American politics.

One immediately searches for causes of these party cycles. Bean finds, in relation to party strength in the House of Representatives, a tendency for a decline in business activity to be followed by a loss of seats by the party in power. An upswing in business activity, however, does not seem to be uniformly followed by a gain of seats by the party in power. But he also concludes that analysis needs to be carried "much farther" to determine the exact relation, if any, between business conditions and political tides.[29] A cursory inspection of the curve in Figure 16 suggests the limitations of the notion that the business cycle parallels the party cycle. Sometimes the party cycle follows the business cycle; sometimes it does not.

In Figure 16 the dotted curve shows the fluctuations in the index of the average per capita income from farming of persons living on farms from 1912 to 1944. For each presidential year the average of the index for the election year and the two preceding years is shown on the theory that political behavior of farmers would be influenced by shifts in income over such a period. Since 1912 the percentage of the total vote polled by Republican candidates has in general increased and declined with shifts in the average per capita farm income. The inference might be that traditionally Republican western farmers veer away from the G.O.P. in times of stress and return as conditions improve. In Figure 16 there appears to be one exception to this generalization: Republican strength declined between 1932 and 1936 despite a rise in the farm income index. In midwestern farming states, the Republican percentage did rise, but it was offset in the national total by Democratic gains in the

[29] *Ballot Behavior,* chap. 8.

industrial states.[30]   It is not suggested that variations in per capita
farm income underlie party cycles; those fluctuations may be one influence but the causes are much more complex.   The parallel is indicated merely to suggest the need for further inquiry into the factors
underlying party cycles.[31]

If party cycles come and go with inexorable regularity, we need to
revise some of our ideas about the nature of electoral choice and the
effects of political campaigning.   Campaigns used to be thought of as
the presentation of alternatives in candidates and in policies to an
electorate that weighed the pros and cons and expressed its choice at
the polls.   The propaganda experts arrived on the scene and began to
recognize nonrational elements in electoral behavior and spoke of the
effects of the personality of candidates, the consequences of the manipulation of significant symbols, and the general technique of the manufacture of opinion.   Yet both these approaches to the interpretation of
political behavior receive a jolt at the hands of the cycle theorists.   If
we have cycles, the general trend apparently cannot be stopped; once
the tide starts running against one party, it will run until it is reversed.
Extravagant and skilled campaigning may serve perhaps only to increase or reduce the amplitude of the cycle.   Parties and candidates are
gathered up and moved along by great tides of sentiment that travel
with irresistible force until they have run their course.   Rational choice
of the electors does not determine the trend; it is governed rather by
factors that are not clearly understood.   At least these are the kinds of
interpretations that might flow from the cycle theory.

Highly unsatisfactory explanations of party cycles come in part from
the fact that our knowledge of who votes how in elections is limited to
findings of opinion polls and other types of analyses made chiefly since
1930.   If we had had the Gallup poll since 1860, for example, we should
know much more exactly the nature of the shifts among voters that
make for party cycles.   It may be that what happens in the cyclical
process is something like this: The Republican party, in the North
claiming the loyalties of most businessmen, bankers, manufacturers,
larger farmers, and the top economic classes generally, succeeds in retaining power when it can gain the support of an adequate number of

---

30 See Figure 26, page 608.
31 W. C. Clark finds that for the country as a whole from 1936 to 1940 Roosevelt's
"popularity" varied with fluctuations in national income.   Events such as the Supreme Court fight affected "popularity," but such happenings merely ruffled the
surface for the broad movements of sentiment seemed to be associated with changes
in national income.   The index of "popularity" was built from responses to Gallup
poll questions.   See his *Economic Aspects of a President's Popularity* (Philadelphia:
University of Pennsylvania, 1943).

workers and middle-class persons. Saenger suggests that middle-class groups and workers have little difficulty in identifying their interests with the upper classes when general prosperity reigns.[32] On the other hand when times are not so good middle-class groups, urban and rural, decline to identify themselves with the economically dominant. The Democratic party, the party historically of economic protest, then benefits from the rift between classes of Republicans.

The evidence seems to support this general description of what has happened in the party cycle since 1932, but the data on party cleavages prior to that time are limited. Information from a study of Pennsylvania indicates that at the Republican peak of 1920 class lines were scarcely drawn at all in politics; workers and middle-class groups in large numbers supported Republicans. By 1936 a marked shift of lower and middle-class support to the Democrats had occurred, and it is known that after 1936 a trend back toward something approximating the 1920 pattern seemed to be under way.[33] Investigation of earlier presidential elections on a broader scale would be required to know whether the true pendulum in American politics consists of those disadvantaged economically or otherwise who swing from party to party and thereby produce cycles in party control of the government.

Another hypothesis with an element of plausibility is that a party in power for a period of years of necessity in the process of governing antagonizes many individuals and groups. One group becomes dissatisfied because it does not get everything it wants. Individual aspirations are blocked in a thousand ways. Over a period of time these discontents cumulate. The party in power may also suffer from the inversion of individual frustrations that flow from no action of its own but which manifest themselves in electoral aggression against the party. Frustrated persons, unable to identify the obstructor of their ambitions, seek a substitute object on which to attach the blame. Contrariwise, the party of opposition attracts to itself the oppressed (and those who believe themselves to be oppressed), dissenters and protestants of all varieties, and benefits from the mental processes of those who blame the party in power for their misfortunes. At some point the cumulation of grievances and the transfer of loyalties goes far enough to result in the replacement of the "ins" by the "outs," and the cycle begins over again. Undoubtedly factors like these are operative, but whether they are adequate in their effects to account for party cycles is another matter.

[32] G. H. Saenger, "Social Status and Political Behavior," *American Journal of Sociology*, 51 (1945), pp. 103–113.

[33] See H. F. Alderfer and R. M. Sigmond, *Presidential Elections by Pennsylvania Counties, 1920–1940* (Pennsylvania State College Studies, No. 10, 1941).

Chapter 10

PARTY ORGANIZATION

A POLITICAL party, like any other well-developed group, possesses machinery of organization. In earlier discussions of associations, such as the American Federation of Labor, the Farm Bureau Federation, and the Chamber of Commerce of the United States, it was noted that these groups have created organizations for the expression of their wishes and for the achievement of the purposes of the group. In like fashion the political party has its machinery of action. The terms "machine" and "machine politician" are usually terms of reproach, but even a municipal reform league must have a machine if it is to be effective. A group cannot act as a whole; it must have its specialized organs of expression and action manned by competent personnel.

In the study of the organs of group government a distinction may be made between policy-forming organs and the administrative or executive machinery of any group. Broadly, the distinction is that between congresses and bureaucracies (or administrative organizations). These concepts serve as tools of analysis of the organs of group government in general, but in the study of the organization of political parties they are not of very great utility. Thus, although parties have their parliaments in the form of conventions—to be dealt with in later chapters—the principle that conventions are controlling organs of parties is largely fiction. In most states, state and local conventions have been stripped of their chief power, the nomination of candidates, and retain only perfunctory duties. The national convention has maintained its importance, but not as an organ for the control of the bureaucracy of the party. This party bureaucracy or organization carries on its affairs without a high degree of control by the mass of party membership. As a result, the party machine or organization is, for all practical purposes, the party. It is the inner core of the party. It is a more or less cohesive group held together by the ambition to gain power. Each party machine benefits from a substantial following of party "members." To gain control of the government, it must annex additional support from among the "independent" voters or from the followers of the other machine.

To present a meaningful picture of the party organization is extremely difficult. The structure and functions of the organization are set forth in statutes and party rules, but this formal organization often differs radically from the actual machinery of the party. In some areas political parties are highly organized; in other areas they are loosely organized and come alive only in the days immediately preceding a primary or a general election. In some places the organization is weak; in others it is strong. In some localities the organization is clean; in others it is most corrupt. In some cities the party machine is virtually the government; in others the official bureaucracy is so strong and competent that the party machine has nothing to do with the day-to-day acts of government. In some localities a strong leader rules the organization with an iron hand; other state and local organizations lack a czar. For these reasons, generalizations are hazardous and whatever is said must be discounted in application to specific local situations.

1, FORMAL PARTY ORGANIZATION

The party organization may be thought of as a more or less cohesive group of persons united to control the party and to seek control of the government. To gain power it must conduct campaigns and win votes. To run campaigns effectively the party workers must be properly "organized," with tasks assigned to each and with lines of control and leadership defined.

The problem of organization arises when a job is to be done that requires the services of more than one man. The total task has to be broken down into parts and each part assigned to those involved in the performance of the entire task. As assurance that each person carries out this assignment in the right way and at the right time, supervisory and directing authority must be centered in some individual. Hence, there are created relationships of authority and responsibility between superior officers and their subordinates. By management, direction, and leadership the entire personnel of the organization may work together effectively in the achievement of group objectives. Organization is thus a condition precedent to the accomplishment of tasks that require the co-operation of many individuals. By organization each man may know his part in the whole, and appropriate sanctions are available to ensure that he does it. But organization involves more than the mechanical assignment of duties and the definition of lines of authority and responsibility. A spirit of devotion to the common cause, common loyalties, and high morale must animate the organization if its personnel is to work together effectively.

The form of a particular organization will be determined by the nature of the task to be accomplished. The division of labor among the individuals in an organization for the manufacture of automobiles differs from the division of labor among the individuals of a department store organization. Yet each organization is adapted to its own ends. Similarly, party organization takes on the form and structure indicated by the nature of the job to be done. The major objective of the party organization is the winning of elections. Hence, the party organization is built around the divisions of the country for electoral purposes. The unit cell of the party organism is the precinct executive, who is immediately concerned with getting out the vote of the precinct to which he is assigned. The precinct executive, committeeman, or captain (the terminology varies from place to place) is the private of the party army. Next up the hierarchy comes the ward committeeman or the district leader in whose jurisdiction a number of precincts are grouped. From the wards or districts, councilmen or legislators are elected. The city or county party committee is built on a combination of wards or districts and is concerned with city- or county-wide matters. The party has a state committee, and at the apex of the pyramid, a national committee.

On paper at least, there is a perfect party hierarchy based on the precinct executive and capped by the national committee, with special organs formed around each important electoral unit—ward, city, county, legislative district, state, and nation. Thus, the form of organization is dictated by the function to be performed—which is, to campaign for candidates elected by the voters of wards, cities, counties, legislative districts, states, and the nation. Yet, as will be shown presently, the party organization in actuality rarely coincides with the party organization on paper.

National committees. The capstone of the formal party hierarchy is the national committee. Both Republican and Democratic national committees consist of one man and one woman (the latter a precipitate of woman suffrage) [1] from each state (plus a number of members from the possessions and dependencies). In form the national committee is elected by the national convention of the party to serve for the succeeding four years, but in practice the national committee members from each state are selected by the delegates to the national convention from that state. Election by the convention is mere formality. In turn, the

[1] On the infiltration of women into the national party organizations, see Marguerite J. Fisher and Betty Whitehead, "Women and National Party Organization," *American Political Science Review*, 38 (1944), pp. 895–903.

state delegations, in nominating the committeemen, are often bound by the action of a direct primary, party convention, or party committee in their respective states.

The national committeemen may or may not be powerful in the politics of their states. Bankers and insurance men, lawyers, railroad and utility men, manufacturers, and publishers are the largest occupational classes on the national committee.[2] Some of these gentlemen are accomplished practitioners of the political art, but often they are overshadowed by other party leaders in their own states. Membership on the national committee may be a recognition by the state organization for financial support or an accolade for an elder statesman of the state organization. On occasion, the national committeeman may be the real chief of the state organization. The women members of the national committee usually play a secondary role.[3]

The duties of national committees include the fixing of the time and place of the national convention and the issuance of the call for the convention. The committees prepare the temporary roll of delegates to the convention, a function that may be of great significance. For example, actions by the Republican national committee in 1912 in placing stalwart delegates on the temporary roll gave control of the organization of the convention and the nomination to Taft. Generally, however, the formal functions of the committees are outweighed by their informal activities and the behind-the-scenes maneuvering that takes place at their periodic meetings.

The meetings of the national committees prior to the conventions bring together party leaders from all over the country and furnish opportunity for consultation, combination, and maneuver concerning the next nominee of the party. If the party is in power and the President is in line for another nomination, the committee may adopt a resolution commending his administration and demanding that he accept a renomination. In January, 1944, for example, the Democratic national committee expressed its confidence in Roosevelt and "earnestly" solicited "him to continue as the great world leader." If the party is out of power, the managers of contenders for the nomination at the next convention will be on hand busily negotiating for support among the

[2] See W. S. Sayre, "Personnel of Republican and Democratic Committees," *American Political Science Review,* 26 (1932), pp. 360–362; Odegard and Helms, *American Politics* (New York: Harper, 1938), pp. 287–289.

[3] On the origin of the national committees, Kleeberg says: "Although the early national conventions, like the first State conventions, usually elected a committee of correspondence, it was not until the Democratic convention of 1848, that a permanent national committee consisting of one member from each State was chosen, with power to call the next national convention."—*The Formation of the Republican Party as a National Political Organization* (New York, 1911), p. 193.

political leaders assembled, but in such situations the national committee itself makes no formal endorsement in advance of the convention. Thus, at the December, 1946, meeting of the Republican national committee the chief subject of informal discussion was the party's nomination for 1948.

Since the conventions meet only once every four years, significant issues of national policy arise between conventions on which an expression of party policy is desirable. In the interim the national committee sometimes constitutes itself into a policy-making body and issues pronouncements of party policy analogous to the planks of a national platform. The Republican National Committee, for example, in its April, 1942, meeting became embroiled in battle between the isolationists, led by Robert A. Taft, and the international collaborationists, led by Wendell Willkie. The Committee adopted a resolution to serve in effect as a platform for the 1942 congressional campaigns and in this resolution attempted to cleanse the party of its pre-Pearl Harbor isolationism by recognizing an "obligation to assist in bringing about of understanding, comity, and co-operation among the nations of the world."

National chairman: General position. The national committee, from its very size, cannot function as the executive head of the party. For that reason the kingpin of the national organization is not the national committee but its chairman, whose chief responsibility is the management of the presidential campaign. At national headquarters he has under his supervision a staff of assistants. During campaigns the national staff mushrooms, and special units are created to care for special phases of the campaign: a woman's division, labor division, foreign language division, business and professional men's division, publicity division, research division, and others, as circumstances dictate. After the campaign is concluded, the electioneering machinery is dismantled and the national chairman is left with a small staff in his domain.

In form, the national committee chooses the national chairman, but in fact he is designated by the presidential nominee of the party. If a vacancy occurs between campaigns, the President, in his capacity as leader of the party in power, fills the vacancy. The national committee of the party out of power elects a new chairman if the post becomes vacant between campaigns. These elections often constitute a test of strength between leaders or factions of the party and sometimes reflect a dispute over policy. In December, 1942, the Republican national committee, following a cat-and-dog fight between the Willkie faction and the "regular" Republicans, elected Harrison Spangler, of Iowa, as national chairman. Spangler, a dark-horse, managed to annex the support of a bloc led by Robert A. Taft, who was successful in defeating the Willkie candidate. In April, 1946, the Republican national committee again elected a chairman, Carroll Reece of Tennessee, in a fracas lost by the internationalist-liberal faction of the party to the stand-patters.

The national chairmanship is what the national chairman makes it, no more and no less. Men like Mark Hanna and James A. Farley invested the office with prestige and power. Farley's position as chief leader of the party workers rested partly on close ties of personal friendship with key figures in state and local organizations over the country. The mass of professional party workers had a deep affection for him. Sentimental ties of loyalty can be and often are powerful sources of cohesion within the organization. Although the national chairman may build up a following that enables him to operate a smooth-running organization, he remains in a sense a hired man subject to the party's real leader, the presidential candidate. Thus, despite John Hamilton's service in nursing the Republican organization through the dark days from 1936 to 1940, when Willkie won the nomination in 1940 Hamilton was, as a matter of course, relegated to a subordinate position to be replaced by Willkie's designee, Representative Joseph Martin of Massachusetts. Similarly, Farley, apparently in disagreement with Roosevelt, resigned to make way for Edward Flynn as Democratic national chairman in 1940. In other words, no national chairman has succeeded in building himself up as national boss stronger than the presidential nominee. This situation is in contrast with the role of superiority to mayors that local party leaders often play. The national chairman is, in effect, a technician, a specialist in campaign management and machine tending, who exercises his power only so long as he enjoys the confidence of the presidential nominee.

National chairmen: Activities between campaigns. During the periods between campaigns the role of the chairman of the victorious party differs materially from that of the chairman of the losers. The chairman of the winners usually becomes Postmaster General, a position that at an earlier time controlled the largest single repository of federal patronage. Especially when there has been a change of party control of the government the national chairman takes on importance. Applicants for patronage jobs usually must "clear" through his office, and their success in obtaining "clearance" depends on how their sponsors stand with the national chairman. The national chairman, in turn, must dispense patronage and favors in a manner that will keep peace and harmony in the organization, for there is always another election in the offing. Furthermore, he has to satisfy, in so far as practicable, those who hold liens on party action by virtue of their campaign contributions.

The life of the national chairman of the party out of power is beset by far fewer worries. Not long since, the national committee and the national headquarters of the minority party were practically nonexistent between campaigns, but the tendency of the past thirty years has been for the committee and its chairman to become more active in the period between presidential campaigns in preparation for future congressional and presidential elections. After the defeat of Smith in 1928, the latter suggested that the minority party carry on a positive educational program rather "than sit by and adopt a policy of inaction with the hope of profiting solely by the mistakes or failures of the opposition." In 1929, with the appointment of Charles Michelson as director of publicity for the Democratic national committee, the minority party took the offensive. The publicity division prepared statements to be released mainly under the name of Democratic Senators and Representatives in criticism of the policies of the majority party. The minority obtained a wide hearing for its attacks on majority policy, irritated Republican leaders, and seldom failed to take advantage of an error by the majority. The constant publicity helped lay the basis for Democratic victory in 1932.[4]

The Republican national committee profited by the Democratic precedent and in 1936 established at its headquarters a research and editorial division. The staff of this division prepared factual material for Republican members of the Senate and House, assisted "in a technical capacity" in the drafting of minority reports of congressional committees, coached Republican Congressmen on legislative subjects, issued propaganda material, prepared memoranda for "insertion in the Congressional Record and subsequent distribution to the electorate under frank," and, in general, served as a research agency for Republican leaders.[5]

In their operations between campaigns national chairmen must steer a careful course to avoid antagonizing factions of the party. Herbert Brownell, Republican national chairman designated by Dewey, found it expedient to resign in 1946. One of the considerations leading to the resignation was the fear in some sections of the party that Mr. Brownell might use the organization to promote the renomination of Mr. Dewey

[4] See T. S. Barclay, "The Publicity Division of the Democratic Party, 1929–30," *American Political Science Review*, 25 (1931), pp. 68–72; Charles Michelson, *The Ghost Talks* (New York: Putnam's, 1944), chap. 2.

[5] C. A. H. Thomson, "Research and the Republican Party," *Public Opinion Quarterly*, 3 (1939), pp. 306–313.

in 1948. At a meeting of the national committee preceding Mr. Brownell's resignation one committeeman had expressed the view that there should be a new chairman "as pure as Caesar's wife, who does not have to determine whether his personal interest and his interest in Tom Dewey are more important than his interest in the Republican party and the United States of America." Nearly always the national chairman has to tread warily among factions interested in competing candidacies, but he must also watch lest he antagonize factions attached to particular principles. Robert Hannegan, Democratic national chairman, for example, in 1946 got caught in the crossfire between the conservative and liberal wings of the Demcratic party. A series of pronouncements by the national chairman and by the editors of propaganda sheets issued by the national committee led to a caucus of southern Democratic House members who wanted Hannegan's scalp but agreed to be satisfied with apologies and retractions.[6]

Senatorial and Congressional committees. Both parties maintain senatorial and congressional committees, whose function is the conduct of campaigns for Senators and Representatives. These committees are not subordinate to but work closely with the national committees. Their origin may be traced to the conflict between President Johnson and the Republican majority of Congress in 1866. The party majority in Congress forced its will on the President and wrested from him the leadership and control of the government. Since the President had been elected as Vice-President on the Republican ticket and was influential with the Republican national committee, the party in Congress formed an independent congressional committee to campaign for the election of Republican Representatives in 1866. Later the Democrats created such a committee, and with the adoption of popular election of Senators the need for senatorial committees arose.[7]

State committees. Next down the party hierarchy comes the state central committee of the party. In most states the composition, method of selection, and duties of the state committees are determined by law, in contrast with the national committee, which is created by and receives its powers from the national convention, an extralegal agency. The members of the state central committees represent various electoral units of the state. In some states each congressional district is represented by one or more members on the state central committee; in other states each county has one or more members; in still others, judicial

---

[6] A thorough study of the role of the national chairman remains to be written. For the story of one national chairman, see James A. Farley's *Behind the Ballots* (New York: Harcourt, Brace, 1938).

[7] See Jesse Macy, *Party Organization and Machinery* (New York: Century, 1904), pp. 31–32.

districts and state legislative districts are the basis of representation. Or there may be a combination of such areas as in Arkansas where the Democratic state committee is composed "of three members from the state at large, one of whom shall be chairman, a woman who shall be vice-chairman, and a secretary; two members from each congressional district, one of whom shall be a woman; and one from each judicial district." [8]

The method of selection of the state committee again varies from state to state.   In some states selection is by direct primary; in others, by state conventions; in others, by county or district conventions. In South Carolina, for example, the committee is composed "of one member from each county, to be elected by the county conventions, and the state Chairman and State Vice-Chairman, who shall be a woman, to be elected by the State convention." [9]   At times county chairmen or committeemen from some other subdivision of the state collectively compose the state committee.[10]

County and city committees.   Toward the base of the party machinery come the county and city committees.   These committees, like the state committee, are built on electoral units.   The county committee may be composed of members selected from townships, precincts, or other subdivisions of the county; the city committee is often composed of ward representatives.   At the base of the party hierarchy are precinct captains or committeemen, sometimes elected by the members of the party in the precinct through the direct primary, sometimes selected by precinct conventions or caucuses, and in some instances appointed by higher party authority.   In addition to these committees, the state organization often includes congressional district committees, legislative district committees, and committees for judicial districts.

Formal and actual organization.   The determination of the structure of the formal party organization is a simple matter.   The rules of the national conventions prescribe the powers and composition of the national committees, and state legislation or party rule does the same for the state organization.   But the organization as it appears on paper has little or no relation to the organization as it actually functions. For aid in campaigning, the national chairman may depend on state leaders, who occupy no position of importance in the state's formal party organization, and he may recognize them in the distribution of

---

[8] *Rules of the Democratic Party in Arkansas, January 15, 1946,* p. 6.

[9] *Rules of the Democratic Party of South Carolina, May 15, 1946,* p. 6.

[10] The most complete recent account of the formal party organization in the states is by E. M. Sait, *American Parties and Elections* (New York: Appleton–Century, 3rd ed., 1942), chap. 15.

patronage. In turn, the state central committee and its chairman may exist largely on paper. The "real" chairman may be someone other than the titular chairman. Within each party factional leaders of state-wide importance may have their county managers and leaders, loyal to them but not necessarily occupying positions in the formal party hierarchy. The machine that a national chairman, a state chairman, or a county chairman forms tends to be hierarchical, with lines of influence and authority binding it into a closely knit unit. Yet the hierarchy in fact often does not coincide in many respects with the formal organization as outlined in the laws and regulations.

2. DISCIPLINE AND DIVISION IN THE PARTY ORGANIZATION

From the foregoing account one gleans a conception of the skeleton of the party organizations, but one must go farther to gain an understanding of how the party organization is wrought into a functioning and cohesive unit. A simple chart of the party hierarchy conveys the impression that the party machinery might be military in character, with its generals, colonels, captains, lieutenants, sergeants, and privates all bound together and closely articulated by commands from above. While the military analogy has its usefulness, it conveys an inaccurate conception, for, although at times and in limited areas the party organizations may be as well disciplined and as responsive to command as an army, there is during most of the time within each party organization a struggle for its control.

This competition for power within the organization is sometimes nothing more than a struggle between individuals seeking the prestige and power that come from dominance within the machine. Conflicting personal ambitions appear to predominate in the internal struggles of state and local parties where place far outweighs policy. One must look more deeply to find the explanation for forces tending toward and against cohesion in the party organizations viewed nationally. The fratricidal conflicts there are not uncolored by competing personalities, but underlying most of the problems in the maintenance of national organizational cohesion and discipline are great issues between liberal and conservative, West and East, labor and agriculture, city and country, and other groups that struggle for ascendancy within our parties.

National party a coalition. From the formal structure of the party organization it might be expected that the national committees and the national chairmen of the major parties would occupy positions, if not of command, at least of potent leadership in the party machinery. But the center of gravity or of power in each party is farther down the hierarchy and is vested in state and city committees, leaders, and bosses. The party, nationally, tends to be a loose alliance of state and city leaders who work together most faithfully during a presidential campaign. The national committee is more a gathering of sovereigns to negotiate and treat with each other than a gathering of subordinates of the national chairman. Its members convene as equals to agree upon a course of action acceptable to the majority; the national chairman resembles more a moderator than a boss.

The nature of the position of the national committee may be illustrated by contrasting its role with that of a state or city committee. On the one hand, although it is by no means the practice in every city, it is not uncommon for the city committee to form an "organization slate" of candidates that the organization will support for party nomination in the direct primaries. On the other hand, the national committee does not agree in advance on an "organization slate" that it will back in the national convention for the party nominations. Much less does it propose an official slate for nominations for the House and Senate by state conventions and primaries. The national party organization gains whatever unity it has by common agreement on candidates and policies in the national convention. The candidate who succeeds in lining up the largest bloc of state machines usually takes the nomination. Now this coalition of state organizations may be given impressive cohesion by the strength and determination of the social interests supporting it. The professional politicians are held together by an ambition for office, but their unity may also be re-enforced by a united and disciplined economic or sectional interest. In some cases, however, the party coalition may possess only the most tenuous unity because of differences of interest among state leaders, differences that in turn parallel conflicting views on questions of public policy on the part of their principal supporters in their states.

Party discipline in presidential campaigns. During the course of a national campaign the lines of authority and leadership from the office of the national chairman down to the state organizations are usually tighter than at other times. The mutual hope for victory induces a degree of discipline. In earlier times, the national organization doled out sums from its war chest to state and local organizations and gained authority over the general conduct of the campaign. Although subventions from the national party to state parties have declined since the Hatch Act limited national committee expenditures to $3,000,000 in any one year, the national leaders are in contact with the sources of funds and can aid a local organization by steering contributions to it. Even in presidential campaigns the national leadership has its trou-

bles in developing such relations that state and local organizations
will respond quickly to national guidance in strategy and tactics. Part
of this problem comes from deliberate withholding of support by state
leaders; part flows from the simple administrative weaknesses of a huge
campaign organization built up in large part of volunteer workers. In
the campaigns of 1932 and 1936 James A. Farley, chairman of the Democratic national committee, undertook to tie the local party committeemen in more closely with the national committee. A complete list of
precinct committeemen was collected at the national headquarters, and
campaign literature was sent directly to each of these workers in small
quantities; this was in contrast with the previous practice of sending
literature in bulk to state committees for redistribution to local workers.
Mr. Farley observed that the

worker in the field who gets ten lithographs of the presidential candidate soon
has them distributed, and he likes to "jack up" headquarters by demanding
more and insisting upon prompt delivery. . . . The county or precinct worker
also seems to feel that he has a new standing in his home community if he gets
his orders directly from the "generals" who are directing the campaign against
the political enemy. It gives him a sense of satisfaction to be let in as part
of the show, and the degree of loyalty awakened by this simple gesture is truly
gratifying. The fellow out in Kokomo, Indiana, who is pulling doorbells night
after night and respectfully asking his neighbors to vote the straight Democratic ticket gets a thrill if he receives a letter on campaigning postmarked
Washington or New York; and we made sure that this pleasure was not denied
him.[11]

So long as the head of the national ticket lends strength to state and
local tickets, state and local organizations can be expected to work in
harmony with the national leaders. Occasionally a state leader sulks
and refuses to fight for the party nominee; David B. Hill, of New York,
for example, after failing to block the nomination of Bryan in 1896, declared himself to be still a Democrat but "very still." When the presidential nominee is a handicap to the party's candidates for state and
local office, the state and local organizations may virtually desert the
national nominee. Professor Salter quotes a letter from a Republican
leader in Philadelphia concerning the 1936 campaign: [12]

The result was such an overwhelming repudiation of the Republican party
in our section that I have never seen the like of it, and hope never to see it
again. In a normal Republican district of 9,000 votes Landon was able to get

[11] James A. Farley, *Behind the Ballots* (New York: Harcourt, Brace, 1938), pp. 159–
160.
[12] J. T. Salter, "Letters from Men in Action," *National Municipal Review,* 26
(1937), p. 422.

only 1,300, a little over 7,700 going to Roosevelt. I might say that as soon as I sensed the sentiment I considered it advisable to go easy in my efforts to push the candidacy of Landon and concentrated on the local ticket. In this I was successful to a degree, having a difference of nearly 500 votes in favor of the local candidates over the head of the ticket. Nevertheless I was not able to carry them because people were still afraid to split their vote on the machine.

The national party authorities have no very effective sanction to prevent the "knifing" of the head of the ticket by state and local machines. Moreover, the national organization is generally lacking in power to purge local organizations of elements that give the party a bad name nationally. Not infrequently a local organization elects a rogue on the strength of the popularity of the party's presidential nominee. From time to time, to be sure, the national leaders of a party may exert some influence in the councils of a state organization, with the result that the party takes on a semblance of national unity. The national leaders of the Democrats in 1928, for example, persuaded Franklin D. Roosevelt to accept the nomination for the governorship of New York in order to strengthen the ticket in that state; and in 1936 the national leadership was influential in bringing about the renomination of Governor Lehman for the same purpose. In 1940 the New York state Republican convention acceded to the request of the presidential candidate, Wendell Willkie, that Bruce Barton receive the New York senatorial nomination. Other like instances occur sporadically, but by and large the reins of the national leadership over state and local machines are loose.

Patronage: A cohesive factor? The party in power nationally has much greater opportunity and much greater resources than the party out of power to construct a truly national party organization. The patronage in the hands of the national leaders is great enough to weld the state machines into a semblance of national unity. In the next chapter we shall observe the actual mechanics of the patronage system, but here we shall look at it as one of the more important forces giving cohesion to the party. The power of patronage, among a great many other things, is reflected in the fact that a President can usually gain a renomination at the end of his first term.[13] The most striking example

[13] One of the famous examples of the exertion of patronage pressure is furnished by the statement of W. Irving Glover, Second Assistant Postmaster General, during the 1932 campaign to a convention of postmasters:

"Get out on the firing line in support of President Hoover. I'll be back in Washington Monday and I'll be glad at that time to take the resignation of any of you postmasters who don't want to do it.

"You are a part of this Administration. When you hear anybody assailing that man Hoover, remember what I said or go read a book and answer them. As long as you do that you are filling the job of postmaster.

"To make the world safe again for democracy, you must stand behind that man

of the use of patronage in attaching state organizations to the national headquarters is to be seen in the behavior of Republican organizations in the southern states during the periods that the party controls the national government. In those states the party has lacked substantial popular support; the control of the party organizations by small cliques of officeholders has, therefore, been quite easy. In turn, the officeholders may be readily controlled by the national headquarters of the party. The situation is, of course, somewhat different when the Republican party is not in power nationally.

But the power of federal patronage is limited. In considerable measure its distribution may be governed by commitments made in the formation of the combination that won the presidential nomination for the successful candidate. State organizations, moreover, demand their share as a matter of right and attempt to reduce the President's discretion in using patronage to strengthen his personal following. Furthermore, in the distribution of patronage, Senators and Representatives have an important voice. Now, these members of Congress are not generally interested in building an organization with power centered in the hands of the national leaders, the President, and the national chairman. Instead, they are concerned with using the patronage to strengthen their own organizations or those state organizations with which they are affiliated. And when patronage appointments are made on the recommendations of Senators and Congressmen, the appointments will be such as to strengthen allegiances to the state and local organization.

These remarks are illustrated by the following letter, dated June 9, 1933, signed by the Democratic Senators and Representatives from Texas, and addressed to the Democratic national chairman: [14]

The Texas delegation in Congress has unanimously agreed upon the following:

The two Senators are to control the following patronage: District and appellate judges, district attorneys, United States marshals, internal revenue collectors, customs officers, postmasters in their respective home cities, all State-wide appointments, and all appointments requiring confirmation of Senate.

The Congressman in each district is to control subject to above, all post-

---

of peerless leadership—of brains, ability, and steadfastness. I ask your faith in God, that our country shall not fail."—Quoted by Peel and Donnelly, *The 1932 Campaign* (New York: Farrar & Rinehart, 1935), pp. 58–59.

On Lincoln's use of the patronage to give unity to his party, see H. J. Carman and R. H. Luthin, *Lincoln and the Patronage* (New York: Columbia University Press, 1943).

[14] *Congressional Record* (daily edition), January 9, 1935, p. 225.

masters in his district, all appointees in his district to be made by Mr. Morgen-
thau, the Reconstruction Finance Corporation, the Census Bureau, the Agricultural Department, the Treasury Department, and other appointments in
his district not Statewide.

Until a successor for the Briggs district has qualified, appointments in that
district, not controlled by Senators, are to be jointly controlled by the present
three Congressmen-at-large.

Until January 1, 1935, the present Representatives of districts shall control
in the counties of their present existing districts, and the redistricting is not
be recognized until January 1, 1935. We ask that this agreement be respected
by all Department and offices.

It can be inferred from the mode of distribution of federal patronage
that even when a party is in power nationally, the perquisites of power
may be used to build up federal organizations loyal to the Senators or
Congressmen or to strengthen the state organizations with which they
are affiliated rather than to construct a truly national organization.
Such power as patronage does give the national leadership was weakened by the passage of the Hatch Act in 1939. This act forbids federal
employees with the exception of the Chief Executive, heads and assistant heads of departments, and certain other policy-forming officials,
to take any active part "in political management or in political campaigns." All persons employed in "any administrative position" are
prohibited from exercising their "official authority for the purpose of
interfering with, or affecting the election or the nomination of any
candidate for the office of President, Vice-President, Presidential elector,
Member of the Senate, or Members of the House of Representatives,
Delegates or Commissioners from the Territories and insular possessions." Prominent among the congressional supporters of the legislation were Republicans supported by organizations built around state
and local governments and Democrats fearful that their own political
careers might be endangered by strong national party leadership built
in part on patronage.

Party leadership in legislative elections. Centripetal influences of
the presidential election force a degree of unity and of discipline in
the party organization over the entire nation during a presidential campaign, but the behavior of the national party machine in campaigning
for Senators and Representatives portrays the weaknesses of the national
party structure. A truly national party would have some influence over
candidacies in the states and congressional districts; a slate of candidates
would be supported for nominations consisting of persons with views in
accord with the national party policies. In fact, state and local leaders

insist that the determination of party candidates for the Senate and House is a local matter. They resent interference by the national leadership and generally defeat such efforts at interference. The retention of a local monopoly of these matters is re-enforced by the rule of local residence for candidates for nomination and for office.[15] The national party leadership, in turn, usually considers itself bound to support for election the local nominees bearing the party label whatever their views on party policy may be.[16] Thus early in 1944 Robert Hannegan, the Democratic national chairman, stated that Democratic Senators and Representatives, even those with violent anti-New Deal records, would be given financial and other support by the national committee in their campaigns for re-election.

National party leaders occasionally attempt to purge the party of the disloyal, but their success is invariably slight. In 1910 President Taft and the conservative wing of the Republican party attempted to drive the progressive element out of the Republican party by defeating its legislative leaders for renomination in the primaries and conventions that year. Under the leadership of President Taft and Senator Aldrich, the spokesmen for industry and finance in the Republican party, the eastern standpat Republicans proposed to raise money and to conduct a campaign against the renomination of western progressive leaders. The Republican Congressional Campaign Committee propagandized the western states against progressives such as Dolliver, Cummins, and Beveridge, and urged the nomination of true Republicans. Eastern money began to flow into these areas to finance the intraparty fight, and Taft withheld patronage from progressive Republicans. Patronage referees from the other wing of the party had the distribution of local jobs. Conservative leaders traveled to the West and opened fire against La Follette. Even in some eastern states the insurgent wing of the party was strong enough to merit the opposition of the official or regular party organization. When the returns were all in the national party leadership had almost completely failed. In state after state con-

---

[15] Contrast the situation in England: "In the matter of candidatures the Central Offices have control. The Labour Party in its constitution requires that before any parliamentary candidate can be regarded as finally adopted for a constituency as a candidate of the Labour Party, his candidature must be sanctioned by the National Executive. This requirement goes farther than that of either of the two other parties but the practice is quite the same in all parties. A Tory who is *persona non grata* is not likely to be nominated against the objection of the Central Office, and in normal times the same has been true of the Liberals."—J. K. Pollock, "British Party Organization," *Political Science Quarterly*, 45 (1930), pp. 164–165.

[16] See C. A. Berdahl, "Party Membership in the United States," *American Political Science Review*, 36 (1942), pp. 16–18.

ventions and primaries resulted in the renomination of progressives, who were as thorns in the flesh of the national party leaders. Taft failed to make the party a simon-pure conservative party.[17]

In 1930 officers of the Republican national committee exerted their best efforts to defeat the late Senator George W. Norris of Nebraska, who had long been a minority figure of note in the Republican party. The surreptitious manner of the national opposition, however, illustrates the great strength of the tradition that the national leadership is expected to keep hands off local nominations. In the preliminary maneuvers the standpat leaders in Nebraska hired an obscure grocery clerk by the name of George W. Norris to file for the senatorial nomination in order to make it virtually impossible to count the votes cast for either Norris. The filing of "Grocer" Norris was thrown out on legal grounds. After the failure of this plan, the primary campaign continued with a well-financed opposition to the genuine Norris. It eventually developed, after a senatorial investigation, that some of the cash for the opposition had come from an official at the headquarters of the Republican national committee. Every means had been taken to conceal the source of the funds; but when the facts finally came out, the national committee officials defended their actions on the ground that they had been trying to defeat a Democrat, for they regarded Norris as no Republican.[18]

Republican national leadership failed in efforts to upset state organizations of a progressive tinge; the Democratic national leadership has also failed to upset its conservative state machines. In the senatorial primaries of 1938 President Roosevelt sought to exert his influence as the party's national leader. Battles in Congress over the President's proposal to revamp the Supreme Court, over the administrative reorganization bill, and over the wages and hours bill had indicated sharp cleavages within the Democratic party. The first primary of the year occurred in Alabama, where J. Thomas Heflin was opposed by Lister Hill, a New Dealer. "The support of all three branches of labor," Professor Shannon concludes, "and the inferential blessing of the President, who allowed Hill to ride on his train across Alabama, together with the aid of Governor Bibb Graves' political organization seemed to have been decisive in Hill's victory." [19]

In Florida the sitting Senator, Claude Pepper, who had supported

---

[17] G. E. Mowry, *Theodore Roosevelt and the Progressive Movement* (Madison: University of Wisconsin Press, 1946), chaps. 4 and 5.

[18] *Fighting Liberal, The Autobiography of George W. Norris* (New York: Macmillan, 1945), chap. 28.

[19] J. B. Shannon, "Presidential Politics in the South: 1938," *Journal of Politics*, 1 (1939), p. 150.

the President on all his major measures, was opposed by Representative Wilcox, an anti-New Dealer, and by former Governor Sholtz who professed friendship for the President. James Roosevelt, son of the President, announced that "we" desired the return of Pepper to the Senate, and the victory of Senator Pepper was followed by a bold declaration by the President:

As President of the United States, I am not asking the voters of the country to vote for Democrats next November as opposed to Republicans or members of any other party. Nor am I, as President, taking part in Democratic primaries.

As the head of the Democratic party, however, charged with the responsibility of carrying out the definitely liberal declaration of principles set forth in the 1936 Democratic platform, I feel that I have every right to speak in those few instances where there may be a clear issue between candidates for a Democratic nomination involving principles or involving a clear misuse of my own name.

Do not misunderstand me. I would certainly not indicate a preference in a state primary because a candidate, otherwise liberal in outlook, had conscientiously differed with me on any single issue. I should be far more concerned about the general attitude of a candidate toward present-day problems and his own inward desire to get practical needs attended to in a practical way. We all know that progress may be blocked by outspoken reactionaries and also by those who say "Yes" to a progressive objective, but who always find some reason to oppose any specific proposal to gain that objective. I call that type of candidate a "Yes, but" fellow.

In Oklahoma the President made an address in which he spoke of "my old friend, Senator Thomas," who was seeking renomination against Governor Marland and Gomer Smith. Senator Thomas won the nomination. In Kentucky, Roosevelt supported for the senatorial nomination Senator Alben W. Barkley, the majority leader in the Senate. Governor Chandler mobilized his state organization in an unsuccessful effort to gain the nomination against Barkley, who "had had twelve years in the Senate and before that twelve years in the House. He had built up a federal machine of employees in the state, for Kentucky has been especially favored by a large number of New Deal appointments." [20]

In Georgia the President supported Lawrence Camp against Senator George. In his Barnesville speech the President said that the Senator "is beyond question a gentleman and a scholar—but so also are other gentlemen for whom I have an affectionate regard but with whom I differ heartily and sincerely on the principles and policies of how the

[20] *Ibid.*, p. 165.

government of the United States should be directed." "To carry out my responsibility as President," said Roosevelt, "it is clear that there should be co-operation between members of my own party and myself. That is one of the essentials of a party form of government." Camp was defeated. In South Carolina the President indicated a preference for Governor Olin Johnston over Senator "Cotton Ed" Smith, who had voted against important administration measures. Senator Smith, supported by his own organization and by that of Senator Byrnes, won the nomination. In Maryland the President backed Representative Davey Lewis against Senator Millard Tydings, who "had shown himself more opposed to the President's program than many of the Republicans." [21] Again the national leader of the party was successfully resisted by an entrenched state leader, who called on all Marylanders to keep the Free State free.

After his survey of presidential intervention in the Democratic primaries, Professor Shannon asks: [22]

> What conclusions may be drawn from this survey of an effort by a party leader to determine the composition of his party? First of all, it is clear that in the South all incumbent senators were renominated and reelected except Senator Berry of Tennessee, who had held office but a short time and was opposed by powerful local and federal organizations. It is evident, therefore, that a potent if not decisive factor in the primaries was the control of the local party organizations. A sitting senator, especially if he has held office for a long number of years, is well nigh invincible and not even a person as powerful and popular as Franklin Roosevelt can unseat him.

When the national party leader went up against a candidate backed by the state organization, the national leader went down to defeat.[23]

In whatever manner one views the national party hierarchy, one is driven to the conclusion that the actual power of control over the party

21 *Ibid.*, p. 290.

22 *Ibid.*, p. 295.

23 In 1918 President Wilson appealed to the country for the election of Democratic Congressmen and failed. His appeal, unlike those of Franklin Roosevelt, was made in the election rather than in the primary campaigns. His statement of October 25, 1918, was: "They [the Congressional elections] occur in the most critical period our country has ever faced, or is likely to face in our time. If you have approved of my leadership, and wish me to continue to be your unembarrassed spokesman at home and abroad, I earnestly beg that you will express yourselves unmistakably to that effect by returning a Democratic majority to both the Senate and the House of Representatives. . . . The leaders of the minority in the present Congress have unquestionably been pro-war, but they have been anti-administration. At almost every turn since we entered the war they have sought to take the choice of policy and the conduct of the war out of my hands and put it under the control of instrumentalities of their own choosing. This is no time either for divided council or for divided leadership."

machinery with its tremendous influence in nominations has rested with state and local leaders. Whether they be conservative Democrats or progressive Republicans they can generally resist the national leadership. There are, of course, many leaders of state organizations who ally with and support the national leaders, but their support is not the result of authoritative direction by the national leaders. In speculation on the nature of the distribution of power between national and state leaders, a theory advanced by Michels is of suggestive value. He contends that centralization of power is the work of the majority of the moment in the party; minorities, on the other hand, demand decentralization in order that they may retain a degree of autonomy in their home areas.[24]

Bases of organizational decentralization. The impotence of the national party executive in the control of the party organization flows in part from our federal form of government. State and local party organizations are built up around the patronage of state and local government; and these organizations, particularly in cities and states dominated by one party, have a continuous life regardless of whether the party is in or out of power nationally. State and local patronage makes the local machine financially independent of the national headquarters and contributes to a spirit of independence. Federalism in our formal governmental machinery includes a national element independent of the states, but in our party organization the independent national element is missing. Party structure is more nearly confederative than federal in nature. The state and local machines, built on state patronage, are allied with or paralleled by machines built around the patronage controlled by Senators and Representatives; and owing to the method of dispensation of this patronage, the resultant machines are quite as independent of central control as are the purely local organizations.

Federalism in government tends toward confederation in the party's government, but deeper forces are also at work. Each party, as has been indicated in another connection, encompasses groups with divergent views and aims. These conflicting interests often find expression through state and local party organizations. It is not clear why it is impossible to drive the progressives from the Republican party and purge the Democratic party of the conservatives. One factor rests in the strong traditionalism in party affiliation in many areas. In these areas to influence state or local government one must be affiliated with the party dominant locally. Control of the state or local government aids in controlling the local activities of the party nationally. No group

[24] Robert Michels, *Political Parties* (New York: Hearst's International Library Co., 1915), pp. 196–197.

is anxious to move over to the opposite party for the sake of its principles on national questions if that will mean loss of state or local government.

Patronage and party cohesion in state and city.   It has been suggested that the centers of power in the party organization are the leaders of state and local organizations.   Even in state and local organizations the widest variety of arrangements prevails.   In the one-party states the party organization is apt to be a congeries of factions, and in some states party organization is practically nonexistent, with something approaching popular government actually prevailing.   All that can be said is that state and city organizations are often more tightly knit than is the national organization.   Sometimes they are in fact virtual dictatorships.[25]   The difference between the discipline in the organization nationally and that within the states and cities is one of degree, but often of substantial degree.   At times a city organization may be under absolute control of a city boss or city chairman; at other times the city boss may be merely a figurehead at the mercy of a coterie of ward leaders.   And there are constant battles for supremacy within the state and city organizations.   These contests do not always result in dominance of one leader or another but more often in a stalemate, different leaders holding dominion over different segments of the party organization.

An important factor in building up lines of command and internal cohesion and discipline within state and city party organizations is patronage.   Leaders of a political organization, the inner core of which is composed largely of persons dependent upon them for a livelihood, have a tremendous power.   A large proportion of the officials of the party organization in many jurisdictions also holds public office, appointive or elective.   Those not in public office may enjoy other perquisites or may be inspired by a hope for public place.   In a study of party committeemen in selected upstate New York cities, Professor Mosher found that 19 per cent of 3,618 committeemen had places on the public pay roll.   In Albany, 35 per cent of the Democratic committeemen were also public officials, and in Syracuse and Auburn the figure was 28.[26]   In Chicago in 1928, 59.2 per cent of the precinct captains had public jobs.[27]   "In the 689 districts in Pittsburgh," it was said in 1926, "all the outstanding district leaders, people that like to

[25] See Charles W. Van Devander, *The Big Bosses* (New York: Howell, Soskin, 1944).
[26] W. E. Mosher, "Party and Government Control at the Grass Roots," *National Municipal Review*, 24 (1935), pp. 15–18.
[27] H. F. Gosnell, *Machine Politics: Chicago Model* (Chicago: University of Chicago Press, 1937), p. 54.

work at the polls and are interested in politics, are on the city or county pay roll." [28]

Lines of control do not, of course, run directly from each individual in the organization to the state or city leader. The organization tends to assume the form of clusters of personal loyalties about nuclear individuals. The latter, in turn, are bound to persons higher up the hierarchy by materialistic ties eventuating in a more or less rigid control of the whole by a few individuals at the apex.[29] The result is an army amazingly responsive to commands, behind which rests a potent pecuniary sanction. This explains in part the strength, unity, and persistence of such groups in the face of movements carried on by unpaid and, hence, usually undisciplined volunteer campaigners.

That the possibility of discharge from office is a potent factor in creating discipline in the party organization is obvious. The threat of discharge is well understood when there is likelihood of the exercise of this sanction, and it requires no verbalization to have its effect. Now and then the threat gets into writing. A few instances will suffice to give the atmosphere.

In a speech to a gathering of city employees, the Pittsburgh *Press* reported the late Mayor Kline as saying: [30]

Let me tell you, ladies and gentlemen, it doesn't require any intelligence to cheat. But the only unfortunate part of it will be that it will take me only to May 19 to find out who did cheat, and if then I found out a man who has cheated—notwithstanding we have civil service in Pittsburgh I would not keep him five minutes after I discovered it.

This is Charlie Kline's fight. And I'm to fight to the bitter end.

I'm going to ask every man on the pay roll to come to our aid and assist us, I never was so deeply interested in any struggle as I am in this struggle.

County Commissioner Armstrong, presented by the chairman as "our honored former mayor," was reported as saying at the same meeting:

Joe Armstrong and E. V. Babcock represent the county and make the appropriations in the county. If you like Kline and like Armstrong and Babcock, you ought to hold up Kline's hands. Now, boys and women, love those that's loving you. . . . I want you to get behind the ticket.

[28] Testimony of Charles C. McGovern, *Hearings before a Special Committee Investigating Expenditures in Senatorial Primary and General Elections*, U.S. Senate, 69th Congress, 1st Session, pursuant to S. Res. 195 (1926), Part 1, p. 109.

[29] For an excellent analysis of the New York organization, see Roy V. Peel, "The Political Machine of New York City," *American Political Science Review*, 27 (1933), pp. 611–618. See also Hugh A. Bone, "Political Parties in New York City," *American Political Science Review*, 40 (1946), pp. 272–282.

[30] *Hearings before a Special Committee Investigating Expenditures in Senatorial Primary and General Elections*, op. cit., pp. 639–642.

Commissioner Babcock added:

Now, we county commissioners are going to take care of those who take care of us. . . . Give us honest and full support, and you may expect our comfort, succor, and aid.

Bernard W. Snow, former chairman of the Cook County, Illinois, Republican central committee, contrasts the effectiveness of paid and voluntary organizations in this way: [31]

The Chairman [Senator Nye]. Mr. Snow, do you not very often get as thorough service from volunteer workers as you do from those who are paid?
Mr. Snow. I think that any precinct committeeman or any ward committeeman will tell you that he has in his organization many people who are volunteers who do give exceptionally good service. But the ward committeeman must have an organization which will respond very quickly to the demands made upon it, and that is the reason why in the securing of registration, in the circulation of pledge cards, there is a legitimate expense.

How the organization is brought to "respond very quickly to the demands made upon it" is shown by the following speech by a Chicago ward leader to the precinct captains in his organization prior to a party primary: [32]

"I don't want applause; what I want first is pledge cards, but, more than that, votes. This is a real fight, and every man must do his share. Look at that chart—some of the precincts show no pledge cards at all. Who is the man from this precinct?"
"That's mine, Mr. ——. I have thirty cards at home and am just waiting to copy them before turning them in."
"You're expecting a raise in salary in your job, aren't you?"
"Yes sir."
"Carry your precinct or you not only won't get it, but you'll lose your job altogether.
"I don't want to scold, but I believe I've been as good to this ward as it has to me. . . . I want to say to you that if any man does not carry his precinct on the thirteenth of April, he'll be fired on the fourteenth. If a man means anything in his precinct, he can carry it. If he doesn't mean anything in his precinct, he has no business in politics and holding a job. The reason that —— is on the ticket for municipal judge in spite of the fact that he is a new man in the ward is that he had the banner precinct. . . . I promise that whoever turns out the biggest vote in his precinct will be on the next county ticket, if I sit on the state committee, and I think I will.

[31] *Hearings before a Select Committee on Senatorial Campaign Expenditures,* U.S. Senate, 71st Congress, 2nd Session, pursuant to S. Res. 215 (1930), Illinois, Part 2 p. 249.
[32] C. H. Wooddy, *The Chicago Primary of 1926* (Chicago: University of Chicago Press, 1926), pp. 7–8.

"What is more, any of you that don't get out the vote and have jobs will lose them, and they'll go to those who do work and have no job. I'm looking at one right now that has no job, and he'll have one that someone else now has unless you get out the vote. Don't think I don't mean this. I've fired the ward committeeman and I've fired the president of this ward club, although he had a $6,000 job."

The upshot of all this is that the persons who control the patronage have a highly organized and well-disciplined army of voters and campaigners ready to go into any campaign and wield a powerful influence. Under ordinary circumstances when the party organization is not rent by internal dissension, it is almost futile to challenge its slate in the party primaries. And if one controls the primary, he has gone a long way toward controlling all. In the election itself the votes of the members of the organization, public employees subservient to it, and their dependents are not inconsequential in many jurisdictions.

Stress on the power of patronage is likely to give an exaggerated notion of discipline in the party organization. The element of patronage does not relieve organization leaders of the necessity of paying heed to the sentiments of their subordinates in the party machinery. In some situations decisions on the distribution of patronage, and other matters as well, actually rest in the lower reaches of the party hierarchy. The location of the power of command and decision apparently tends to rise to the top of the hierarchy as the pressure on the organization or the intensity of the struggle in which it is involved increases. In times of stress autocracy becomes real, and either the organization is perfectly articulated or it is wrecked. When the strain is relieved, the power of decision tends to gravitate downward although nominally and in form control from above persists. The relationship of leader and led involves reciprocal interactions, the balance of power turning this way and that with the demands of the situation.

Moreover, the ambitions of the more lowly within the party organization offer a continuous challenge to the power of those higher up in the machine. The precinct captains, for example,[33]

. . . are rivals for the favor of the ward boss. Each of them hopes to control the ward some day. Each tries to spread out from his own precinct and pick up a personal following in the other precincts of the ward. . . . In due course some one of these precinct leaders wins his way to recognition as the right-hand man of the ward boss, while another, taking umbrage at this, begins to feel himself strong enough to 'buck the ward machine' as it is called. By and by a showdown comes. At primary election there is a pitched battle between

[33] From W. B. Munro, *Personality in Politics* (New York, 1924), pp. 50–51. Quoted by permission of the Macmillan Company, publishers.

the two. The old machine usually wins, and the precinct leader who has matched strength with it goes into the discard. Somebody else takes over the precinct in his place. Occasionally, however, the rebel wins the fight, supplants the boss, and takes the role for himself. Most of the young hopefuls are eliminated in these ward insurrections. It is only the most capable who survive them.

The same kinds of contest occur further up the hierarchy. Speaking of New York City in 1933, for example, Peel reported for Queens borough: [34]

. . . the district leaders have frequently been on the edge of revolt. At the present time, the county leader there is little stronger than his district leaders, and some of the latter are in turn hard pressed by the zone-leaders, regional lieutenants exercising authority over subordinate districts within the assembly districts. District leaders in Manhattan and in Brooklyn have frequently rebelled against the county leaders. Some of these insurrections have been put down by disciplining the district leader (depriving him of his job or his patronage); in other cases, the district leader has been conciliated by the grant of wider powers than formerly enjoyed.

By the struggles within the ranks of the party leadership is renewed and maintained. The common assumption is, and it is probably true, that those individuals most competent in party warfare make their way to the top of the heap. No comprehensive studies have been made either of the progress of the rise of party workers in the party hierarchy or of the effect of the struggle and compromise, the give and take, which seem to be necessary to reach points of prestige and leadership in the party organization. Without the analysis of many parallel political careers one cannot speak with certainty, but the impression is that powerful party leaders do not spring into power. With exceptions, they climb to the top of the ladder by arduous work. The career of the late A. J. Cermak, once mayor of Chicago, is a case in point. He became precinct captain, secretary of the ward organization, and leader of the ward organization. He became a leader of the Bohemian groups, and in 1902 the Democratic organization sent him to the Illinois Legislature. He served four terms and became floor leader. He then went to the

---

[34] Peel, *American Political Science Review, op. cit.*, p. 614. The penalty for internal revolt is further illustrated by the following incident reported by the Baltimore *Evening Sun*, April 6, 1940: "Philip J. Wallace, for years the leader of Mayor Howard W. Jackson's political organization in the Twenty-first ward, was ousted from the post today in retaliation for his support of the Senate candidacy of Howard Bruce. [The Mayor had supported Bruce's opponent.] In his place, the Mayor's forces appointed John J. McMenamen, 28-year-old clerk in the office of Comptroller J. Millard Tawes and a political protege of Julian B. Carrick. The change was announced by the City Register Eugene H. Beer, who is the Mayor's representative in the campaign headquarters of Senator George L. Radcliffe."

Chicago city council, was elected bailiff of the municipal court, and then back to the council. He ran for president of the Cook County board of commissioners and held that post from 1922 to 1931, when he became mayor of Chicago, leader of the Democratic party in the state, and a power in national politics.[35] In seeking to understand what holds a party organization together, what gives it discipline and coherence, one must keep in mind factors such as the friendships and alliances formed through long careers like the one mentioned.

To offset further the impression that loyalty in the party organization is purely a pecuniary matter, it should also be remembered that personal loyalties develop in many other ways. "Persons young and unsophisticated, who knew of his power," it is said of Uncle George Aldridge former party leader in Rochester, "went to him for help. He usually rendered assistance. One young man wanted to study law. He needed a job in Albany to see him through the Albany Law School. Aldridge helped, even advanced money to him for a year. He never had cause to regret it. This man became his staunchest supporter." [36] "In a few cases," Gosnell says in his study of Chicago precinct captains, "precinct captains were bound to their ward committeemen by personal ties of loyalty which grew out of crisis situations. When a ward boss could dramatically come to the rescue of some man who was in trouble with the police, he could count on that man for steady precinct work from that time on." [37] We have the testimony of no less an authority than James A. Farley that "those people who are inclined to imagine that patronage and patronage alone, is the only thing that keeps a political party knit together are off on a tangent that is about as far wrong as anything humanly could be. I am convinced," he says, "that with the help of a few simple ingredients like time, patience, and hard work, I could construct a major political party in the United States without the aid of a single job to hand out to deserving partisans." [38]

In addition to its uses within a party organization, patronage has been used from time to time in municipal politics to maintain a subservient opposition. By the feeding of a little patronage to trustworthy individuals in the minority camp, the enemy may be kept under control and the "good will," that is, the socially inherited voting strength, attached to the symbolism of the opposition party kept out of the hands of persons who might become really dangerous opponents. For

---

[35] Chicago *Tribune*, March 6, 1933.

[36] C. G. Lanni, *Beat 'em or Join 'em* (Rochester N.Y.: Rochester Alliance Press, 1931), p. 17.

[37] *Op. cit., Machine Politics: Chicago Model*, p. 67.

[38] *Op. cit., Behind the Ballots* (New York: Harcourt, Brace, 1938), p. 237.

example, before 1933 the Philadelphia Democratic organization was merely a subsidiary of the Republican machine. As Professor Salter said: "There is only one party organization in Philadelphia; the Democratic end is part of it under another name." [39] Even if bipartisan collusion is limited to municipalities and a few states, it probably has at times a strong influence on the vote in national elections in those areas.

3. PARTY MACHINE AND PARTY MEMBERSHIP

Political reformers often observe that the party membership has only slight control over the party machine, and reformers with a mechanical turn of mind have tried to devise ways and means of making the official structure of the party more responsive to the wishes of the mass of the membership. Students of social institutions will find profitable a comparison of the oligarchical tendencies in various kinds of social groupings. It will be recalled from the earlier analysis of the government of the American Federation of Labor that labor organizations are not always democratically controlled. In probably every sort of group activity there is a tendency for the affairs of the group to be managed by a relatively small minority. The professional leaders and organizers and the paid bureaucracy of almost all groups make it their business to remain in control. They work at it. Certainly there may be a leadership responsive to movements of sentiment in the mass. Another leadership may attempt to ignore or suppress dissent. But the differences are differences of degree. It is not surprising, then, in political parties especially, where the sense of membership on the part of the rank and file is so weak, that the tendency toward oligarchy should make itself manifest. The organization leaders and their subordinate associates control the organization because they make it their business to do so. And they remain in control until ousted by another faction equally intent on devotion to the business of politics.

The power that the party machine possesses arises from the collaboration of a minority—the adherents of the machine—to control the entire party. "The power of any minority," says Mosca, "is irresistible as against each single individual in the majority, who stands alone before the totality of the organized minority. At the same time, the minority is organized for the very reason that it is a minority. A hundred men

[39] J. T. Salter, "Party Organization in Philadelphia: The Ward Committeeman," *American Political Science Review,* 27 (1933), p. 619. See also A. F. Macdonald, "The Democratic Party in Philadelphia," *National Municipal Review,* 14 (1925), pp. 293-299.

acting uniformly in concert, with a common understanding, will triumph over a thousand men who are not in accord and can therefore be dealt with one by one." [40]

The minority that gives the party machine its power consists of the members of the party hierarchy itself plus those persons whose vote can be controlled by the members of the hierarchy. This is the "organization vote." In the mustering and disciplining of this vote, the chief workers are the precinct committeemen, whose labors are led and directed by the higher party officials. The precinct executive "is the actual connecting link between the people and the organization, and he is the only connecting link—the only man in the machine who has any point of direct contact with the voters, who knows anything about them, who has any real influence with them." [41] "These precinct officials are the backbone of any political machine, and upon them rests the responsibility for seeing and winning the voters." [42]

The precinct executive in recruiting the organization vote in his precinct can begin with the vote of himself and his relatives. In New Orleans, according to Reynolds, "every precinct leader had a personal following of at least ten voters made up of his family, relatives and close personal friends." [43] And to this nest egg the votes of those whose support can be recruited through the distribution of election-day perquisites. The precinct executive can usually designate two or three precinct election officials and thereby annex their vote and their following. If he belongs to the majority party, he can usually select the quarters to be rented for the polling place and thereby pick up more support. On primary and election days he has at his disposal funds allocated to him from the city or county campaign chest for election-day expenses. He may have from $25 to $100, depending on the prosperity of the party, to hire watchers, runners, and other persons to get out the vote. With each accession to his pay roll a vote or two or more is added to his little bloc.

The precinct captain, however, works throughout the year and adds to his strength by continuous service to the voters of his precinct. Especially in the poorer neighborhoods he is likely to become a sort of social agency, distributing food to the needy and from time to time paying

[40] *The Ruling Class*, p. 53.

[41] Frank R. Kent, *The Great Game of Politics* (Copyright, 1923, Doubleday, Doran and Company, Inc.), p. 1.

[42] H. F. Gosnell, "The Political Party versus the Political Machine," *The Annals of the American Academy of Political and Social Science*, 169 (1933), pp. 21–28.

[43] G. M. Reynolds, *Machine Politics in New Orleans, 1897–1926* (New York: Columbia University Press, 1936), p. 114.

their rent and furnishing them with coal. W. S. Vare, Philadelphia Republican boss, boasted: [44]

In every precinct of the city there are two representatives of the Organization, elected directly at the Republican primaries and who are known as committeemen. They maintain contacts with the voters and are at their beck and call for 24 hours of each day of the year. In time of stress the poor or other unfortunates always turn to these Organization representatives to assist them. It is they that see that the sick are cared for and that the poor are provided for, and that even in death aid may be rendered. The Philadelphia Organization gives a real social service and one without red tape, and without class, religious, or color distinction.

Beyond services of this kind the precinct executive serves as a buffer between governmental agencies and the voters of his precinct. He steers the alien through the naturalization procedure. He aids in obtaining governmental employment for the people of his precinct and private employment as well. And it is through public and private patronage that he adds substantially to his following. He aids in contacts with public social agencies. He may see the judge and attempt to mix mercy with justice. In all these relationships the precinct captain may from time to time obtain treatment for his friends that amounts to favoritism, but in a substantial proportion of these services he is primarily a guide. Governmental agencies are so numerous and complex that the average citizen is bewildered and does not know to whom to apply for any given service. The precinct executive "knows the ropes" and can be of service even when no question of favoritism is involved. Yet when he can have the traffic ticket "fixed" he can create a great obligation to himself.[45]

By these various means the working precinct executive can build up a substantial bloc of votes in his precinct, a bloc that can be swung to the support of the organization slate in the primaries.[46] And the organization power is probably of greatest importance in the primaries. If the machine can control nominations, it automatically captures in

[44] Quoted by D. H. Kurtzman, *Controlling Votes in Philadelphia* (Philadelphia, 1935), p. 29.

[45] See H. F. Gosnell, *Machine Politics: Chicago Model*, chaps. 3 and 4; Roy V. Peel, *The Political Clubs of New York City* (New York: Putnam's, 1935); Sonya Forthal, "Relief and Friendly Service by Political Precinct Leaders," *Social Service Review*, 7 (1933), pp. 608–618; idem, "The Small Fry and the Party Purse," *American Political Science Review*, 34 (1940), pp. 66–76.

[46] Many are the tales of prodigious feats of precinct leaders in swinging the voters as they wish. Kurtzman, for example, tells of two Philadelphia committeemen who had been pardoned through the efforts of a man who subsequently became a candidate for a judgeship. Out of gratitude to this man they delivered to him 450 of the 460 votes cast in their division. For accounts of other like incidents, see Kurtzman, *op. cit.*, pp. 33–34.

the election the "good will" attached to the party name—that is, the habitual Republican or Democratic vote. Estimates of the size of the vote controlled by precinct executives vary. Frank Kent says: [47]

. . . it is not far wrong to credit the precinct executive in any great city with sixty-five deliverable votes which he can swing in any direction and at any time he wants. Some of them have less than this number, but most of them have a good many more, and sixty-five is not far from the minimum. Multiply that by the number of precincts in any city and it is a pretty accurate estimate of the minimum machine strength when the machine is united, financed, and fighting.

In New Orleans, Reynolds estimated that the Choctaw, or regular organization, precinct leader [48]

. . . had over one hundred votes of which he was absolutely certain before election day. In some of the larger precincts, the number of certain votes might go as high as one hundred and seventy-five. In the average sized precinct of four hundred votes a leader controlled one hundred through his prerogatives and patronage. To carry the precinct such a leader had to have two hundred and one votes. The task then was to manage the campaign so as to get voluntarily one hundred and one more votes out of the three hundred remaining. Compared to the task of the opposition, which ordinarily had no patronage on which to build up advance commitments, this was comparatively easy.

By binding together workers in each precinct, each with his following, the city or county leader may form a compact minority to act in concert within the party. By so acting the disciplined minority composing the party machine may control or have an important voice in the determination of the candidates to be chosen by the party as a whole either through direct primaries or conventions. If the party wins in the election, it will be through the party machine that favors are dispensed. Even if an antimachine man wins the party nomination in the direct primary, the same clique is likely to remain in control of the party hierarchy. And so the snowball-like procedure of machine-building goes on.

How is the party organization to be kept in leash by the party membership? The answer is that it is not. The party machine, like the controlling clique of a reform league or an ecclesiastical body, is self-perpetuating. Usually the party officials are elected, directly or indirectly, by the voters registered as members of the party, but the accredited candidates of the regular organizations enjoy a great advan-

---

[47] From *The Great Game of Politics* (Copyright, 1923, Doubleday, Doran and Company, Inc.), p. 22.
[48] *Machine Politics in New Orleans, 1897–1926*, pp. 115–116.

tage in the contests for these posts. In an analysis of popular control of the party organization in Indiana, F. H. Guild observed that the law governing the party organization was "based upon the assumption that the proper place at which popular control should be applied" was the precincts. Provision was made for the election by each party of precinct committeemen who, in turn, elected the county chairmen. The county executives met in each congressional district and elected members of the state central committee, who selected the state chairman. But, at the point at which popular control was to be applied, the precincts, there was no popular interest. In most instances, Guild found, "the county chairman or other active party workers have to select someone in each precinct who can undertake the work of political organization necessary for party success in the election, and in many instances have to persuade that person to accept the position." In not over 10 per cent of the precincts were there contests for the position of precinct committeeman.[49] He concludes that "popular control of party organization through the primary does not exist in Indiana; has never existed; and, which is more important, has never even been attempted."

In Iowa, according to Horack, the law permits the voter to stick a paster on the ballot containing the names of precinct delegates to the county convention or to write in their names on the ballot. Horack concludes: [50]

> In practice, few voters find themselves able, on the spur of the moment, to write out a list of from ten to twenty names of persons whom they know to be residents of the precinct and members of the party designated. The result is that the party organization or some of its members distribute lists of delegates and candidates for party committeemen printed on gummed paper, in practically every voting precinct. The voter obediently licks this gummed slip of hand-picked delegates and pastes it on the proper place on the ballot, without knowing who they are or for what they stand. . . . Thus the party organization perpetuates itself and may often be altogether out of accord with the mass of the voters.

In Chicago the important functionary in the party hierarchy is the ward committeeman, elected by the voters of each party in each ward. The stability of the party organization is illustrated by the fact that out of a total of five hundred contests for the post of ward committeeman between 1928 and 1936, "only thirteen city committeemen were 'licked.'

[49] F. H. Guild. "The Operation of the Direct Primary in Indiana," *The Annals*, 106 (1925), pp. 172–180.
[50] Frank E. Horack, "The Workings of the Direct Primary in Iowa, 1908–1922," *The Annals*, 106 (1923), pp. 148–157.

Their superiors might change, but the ward bosses clung to their posts in spite of economic and political storms." [51]

The task of the party organization in bringing about the continued re-election of its members to party posts is simplified by the fact that a relatively small proportion of the total registered membership of the party expresses a choice on these posts. In eighteen upstate New York cities, Mosher found that only 36 per cent of the registered voters voted for party committeemen. In eight of the eighteen cities "the percentage voting was 20 per cent or less. In two only 6 or 7 per cent found it worth while to vote for committeemen." [52] In Chicago between one half and two thirds of the registered voters express a choice for ward committeemen.[53] In an analysis of ten rural counties in Illinois, Weaver found that 82.5 per cent of the voters going to the polls voted for precinct committeemen; if the total party enrollment had been used as a basis for computing the percentage, the figure would have been considerably lower. For these counties the conclusion was that popular interest in party committeemen was not appreciably less than popular interest in the selection of the party nominees for public office. But in both instances the less the popular participation the greater is the probability that the wishes of the party organization will prevail.[54]

Some observers profess to see underlying forces operating to weaken the control of the party oligarchies over the affairs of the rank and file. They see the development of public social services that dwarf the charitable activities of the ward boss. Moreover, the public services are coming to be manned by a professionalized personnel that both resents and makes less necessary the activities of the party functionary as an intermediary between the citizen and the government. These trends, it is declared, are breaking down the group loyalties nucleated about each party worker. The gradual centralization of power, from local to state government, from state government to national, is encroaching upon the independence of state and local political machines. In another direction it is becoming more feasible for leaders to appeal effectively to the masses directly through such channels as the radio and the press rather than through the thousands of organization workers. According to the hypothesis, the declining significance of the mass of the party hierarchy eliminates the real check of the party oligarchy

---

[51] Gosnell, *Machine Politics: Chicago Model*, p. 27.

[52] W. E. Mosher, "Party Government and Control at the Grass Roots," *National Municipal Review*, 24 (1935), pp. 15–18.

[53] Gosnell, *Machine Politics: Chicago Model*, p. 34.

[54] Leon Weaver, "Some Soundings in the Party System: Rural Precinct Committeemen," *American Political Science Review*, 34 (1940), pp. 76–84.

upon the leaders at the apex of the party pyramid. These leaders are now coming to draw their power from their direct influence over the masses of the people without the aid of the party machine; and the masses of the people, unlike the party oligarchy, are unable to control those whom they have catapulted to power. In a somewhat larger context Norton Long in 1941 stated some of the consequences of these tendencies: [55]

A characteristic of recent times, however, is the emergence into political consciousness of voting masses, still divided to be sure into groups, but no longer meekly and unquestioningly loyal to their customary group leaders. . . . The political meaning of the masses is to be found in the existence of a political power in the community capable of raising its representatives to power but incapable of controlling them. That there should be masses, rather than groups, available for direct organization behind a novel leadership is a sign of the decay or collapse of existing institutions. That infinite gradation of social authority leading from the smallest social nucleus to the highest command in the state is disrupted. The destruction of intermediate leadership, although by some, especially by liberals, viewed as a genuine emancipation of popular energies, is what Burke saw as the creation of a dangerous social vacuum. . . . In view of Italian, German, and Russian experience, however, it seems at least as likely that a fatal choice, that is, fatal to the chance of further choice, may be made. For the commitment to a leadership not held in check by powerful interests within it which are capable and ready to moderate its action and resist the drive toward dictatorship may result in the destruction of any alternative leaderships to which the mass may turn. . . .

From scattered events and straws in the wind it is difficult to determine the degree to which American party organization is being affected by these tendencies. Certainly the party machines do not possess the potency that used to be attributed to them. Some great local machines have crumbled away. Others have preserved themselves and even prospered, particularly Democratic ones, but only at the cost of surrendering to the national leadership of the party. But machines have always been disintegrating and forming anew. Whether we are undergoing a fundamental change in which the "intermediate leadership" of the party organization is being squeezed out of existence by the closer communion of national leadership and the masses can be determined better in retrospect than in prospect.

4. PARTY MACHINE AND POPULAR LEADERSHIP

The party organization—the inner core of the party—gives the party vitality and continuity, but it also contributes elements of rigidity

[55] "Party and Constitution," *Journal of Politics*, 3 (1941), p. 203.

and inadaptability. The party workers, attached to the organization in many instances by the simple necessity of earning a livelihood, have also an inbred sense of loyalty and regularity. They place a high value on staying with the party through thick and thin and insist that the party rewards go to those who have records of party service and regularity. These factors contribute to institutional longevity. Yet they also weaken the party in the performance of the function of popular leadership.

The professionalization of the party organization tends to produce a party bureaucracy. The party bureaucracy in turn tends to control the party. Bureaucracies are notoriously poor in either sensing or leading public opinion. Yet the party bureaucracy desires to furnish from within its own ranks candidates and leaders, and only infrequently does the party organization produce a great popular leader. In part, the infirmities of the party machine as a cradle for popular leadership can be traced to the kinds of skills required for routine party work. The business of machine-tending has become in considerable measure the art of getting votes quite separated from the consideration of issues of public policy. Thousands of workers trod the sidewalks in their precincts, doing favors, getting acquainted with the folks, reminding them to go to the polls on primary and election day, distributing literature, and doing all the errands and odd jobs that are the lot of a private in the political army. On the whole, this kind of work appeals to those who want political jobs and to those who want to advance their private interests, law practices for example, in the process. The skills necessary to perform these party tasks are not the same as those required for great popular leadership.

Yet the rank and file of the party organization feels deeply that the rewards for party work should go to those who have labored loyally in the vineyard. They usually resist the award of party nominations to those without a record of service in the party ranks. The institutional behavior is quite similar to that in almost any large-scale hierarchy; the inevitable demand of the mass of the hierarchy is that respect be accorded to seniority and that the top jobs be filled by promotion from down the ranks. Yet rarely does any large-scale organization produce within the ranks adequate timber for top leadership. Similarly, the party organization must go outside the ranks of the simon-pure party workers for candidates for top positions.

Only grudgingly does the party organization realize the need for going outside the inner circle for candidates. In times of stress these leaders virtually force themselves on the party organization, which may have little choice in the matter if it is to have a winning candidate.

One can call the roll of great popular leaders, and nearly all of them have had to overcome resistance of the organization of their party.

Although Theodore Roosevelt placed great store on party regularity and solidarity (until he felt that the presidential nomination was stolen from him in 1912), he was not an "organization" man and the party machine accepted him reluctantly. Woodrow Wilson was not cherished by many Democratic machine leaders. Old-line Republican machine tenders could scarcely stomach Wendell Willkie. Party conclaves are much happier when they can nominate men like Calvin Coolidge, John W. Bricker, Harry S. Truman. Similarly in states and cities nominations for the prominent posts of governor and of mayor often mark a battle between a regular party candidate and a popular leader who seems better able to sense the undercurrents of popular sentiment and the needs and ambitions of the people than do men who have fought their way gradually up within the party organization.

These observations point to the extraordinary sterility of the American party as an originator of policy and as a proponent of action. The popular leader with an idea and a program comes along and forces himself upon the party organization, which reluctantly nominates a winner. This state of affairs comes about in part because the party organization—Democratic and Republican—tends toward conservatism. It wants to upset no applecarts and conduct no crusades. Organization conservatism, in turn, flows from the fact that bureaucracies tend always to be attached to the status quo and from the fact that the funds for the maintenance of party organizations come from elements of the community attached to the status quo. Great popular leaders invariably want to upset somebody's applecart and to conduct some sort of crusade. To do so they first have to conquer the structural inertia and conservatism of the party machine.

These remarks may suggest the query, Why do we have such extensive party organization? Why does society support elaborate party machines built up of thousands of party workers doing the daily chores of the organization? Could not politics be conducted without them? In truth, some states and cities do get along very well without elaborate party organization. In such states and cities the party organization is likely to consist of a great variety of amateurs and part-time workers thrown together for the duration of a campaign. And in the campaign greater reliance is placed on publicity by means other than the precinct workers. Yet a strong and continuing party organization lends a much higher degree of stability and certainty to public affairs and is likely to check upsurges of popular sentiment that might make themselves felt through the government. The political organization has, of course, its own reason for existence, but one must add to this the interests of those elements in the community that believe they profit from stability and certainty. In every state and city where strong and well-nurtured party organizations exist they will be found to have as their allies substantial interests in the community, interests that have something to defend. These conservative elements in the community pay premiums to the organization just as they pay insurance premiums. In every social organism, ecclesiastical or political, well-knit hierarchies limit the liberties of the subject.

On the other hand, the party organization exists ultimately by its capacity to win votes, and this necessity from time to time compels it to abandon those interests in the community that regard it as a bulwark against political insecurity. The organization possesses strength in its own right; in the absence of a fairly strong machine other centers of power lack a counterbalance. In communities without well-organized machines for example, the press is apt to wield great power in a quite irresponsible way. The existence of an organization may also temper the animosities of political combat, for the machine may hesitate to antagonize large groups by inflammatory appeals; the organization wants to live and fight another day, whereas a candidate with only a personal following may regard a campaign as only a matter of the moment.[56] Finally, although in many states and cities the parties are overorganized, it must be recognized that they have moved in to perform a function of community leadership long since abdicated by the part-time community leaders characteristic of true self-government.

[56] Contrast mayoralty campaigns in Detroit and Boston in 1945. The Detroit campaign, conducted without the participation of extensive political organization, was marred by the most inflammatory appeals to race and class hatred. In the Boston campaign the Curley machine included prominently in its higher ranks representatives of all racial groups and the tactic was to decry racial discrimination. See J. S. Bruner and S. J. Korchin, "The Boss and the Vote: Case Study in City Politics," *Public Opinion Quarterly*, 10 (1946), pp. 1–23; C. O. Smith and S. B. Sarasohn, "Hate Propaganda in Detroit," *idem*, pp. 24–52.

Chapter 11

PARTY MACHINE AS INTEREST GROUP

IN EARLIER chapters the idea is put forward that organized social interests—business, labor, agriculture, religion, reform—are concerned with the acquisition of political power and influence in order that they may promote public policy or administrative action favorable to their interests or block action deemed unfavorable. Political parties are differentiated from pressure groups; they, unlike pressure groups, nominate candidates who seek formal control of the government. In doing so, parties must in their following campaign appeal to the entire community rather than to a single interest. Yet the inner core of the party—the machine or the party organization—may be considered in one respect to be in the same category as a pressure group. The party machine, like the Chamber of Commerce of the United States, wants to obtain certain types of governmental action and to prevent others on questions of immediate concern to the organization. Like pressure groups, the machine is a compact, well-organized group of individuals with fairly well-defined group objectives. Those objectives may be quite at variance with the interests of the party as a whole.

From one point of view the party machine is one of the chain of interests that coalesce to gain by alliance power to control a community. From another point of view the party machine is one of the many interest groups that the public official must placate, satisfy, or discredit in order to retain community confidence and consent to govern. The party machine seeks many things from government, but the end that concerns the largest proportion of its members is public employment.[1] The machine, in effect, may be considered as a pressure group that

[1] Kurtzman reports that a Philadelphia ward leader remarked to a gathering of Republican committeemen: "Every vote should go to the Organization candidates. The Organization must exist if you want jobs for yourselves and your friends. Every city and county office from the Mayor down should be occupied by Organization men. We must have the county offices so that we may be able to give jobs to the political workers and to our constituents."—*Methods of Controlling Votes in Philadelphia* (Philadelphia, 1935), p. 25.

desires to control the selection of as many public employees as possible and to control the distribution of other favors and perquisites in which members of the party hierarchy have an interest.[2]

The character of the party machine as an interest group was long ago demonstrated by A. Lawrence Lowell. He investigated the voting behavior of the Pennsylvania legislature to ascertain the degree of party cohesion on measures before the legislature in the palmiest days of Republican bossism in that state. On only a few issues did the legislature divide along party lines. The machine meddled "very little with general legislation." But the party leaders rallied and held together the party's representation on measures affecting the electoral machinery or touching the interests of persons from whom the machine drew its revenues.[3] In other words, generally on questions of public policy the organization had no "interest," but in legislation endangering the revenues and perquisites of the party as a party, the members of the organization had a common interest and acted in concert to protect that interest.

The object of this chapter is to describe the principal matters with which the party machine is concerned as an interest group. The chief of these is control or influence over appointments to public places— in which the party organizations have been more and more circumscribed by civil service laws. But the party machine is also interested in other public perquisites as a means of party sustenance.

1. THE PATRONAGE SYSTEM

The patronage system may be viewed in several ways. From one angle it may be considered as the response of government to the demands of an interest group—the party machine—that desires a particular policy in the distribution of public jobs. That policy is phrased by the more moderate party men in some such terms as these: "Other things being equal, a party worker in our party should be appointed

[2] Samuel Seabury concluded from his investigation of Tammany-dominated New York: ". . . in a very large measure the affairs of the City of New York are conducted, not with a view to the benefits which can be conferred upon the residents of our city, but for the profit which the dominant political organization in the City and its satellites can make out of the running of it. The consequence is that widespread inefficiency and sloth are tolerated in politically appointed and protected city employees, and every subterfuge is availed of to furnish excuses for the spending of money, not because the spending thereof is necessary, or even desirable, in the public interest, but because of the opportunities for graft incident thereto." Quoted by New York City Commissioner of Accounts, *Investigating City Government in the La Guardia Administration* (1937), p. 7.

[3] "The Influence of Party Upon Legislation in England and America," American Historical Association, *Annual Report,* 1901, Vol. I, p. 349.

to public appointive office." The more extreme adherent of the spoils doctrine would omit the phrase, "other things being equal," from the statement of policy.

From another direction the patronage system may be considered as a method of financing party activity. The operation of a party organization requires the services of many men and women. The social and friendly functions of the organization go on the year round; during campaigns, when literature must be distributed, electors canvassed, meetings organized, voters brought to the polls, and many other campaign chores done, the work reaches its peak. Although much of this work is performed by unpaid volunteers, their efforts are not adequate. In effect, a considerable part of party expenses is met by the public treasury, and the chief means of diverting public funds to party purposes is through the appointment of party workers to public office.

From still another point of view the patronage system, with the rotation in office it involves, has been considered as a means of filling offices that is peculiarly in keeping with democratic theory. Andrew Jackson was the great proponent of this conception of the patronage system. He argued:

There are, perhaps, few men who can for any great length of time enjoy office and power without being more or less under the influence of feelings unfavorable to the faithful discharge of their public duties. Their integrity may be proof against improper considerations immediately addressed to themselves, but they are apt to acquire a habit of looking with indifference upon the public interests and of tolerating conduct from which an unpracticed man would revolt. Office is considered as a species of property, and government rather as a means of promoting individual interests than as an instrument created solely for the service of the people. Corruption in some and in others a perversion of correct feelings and principles divert government from its legitimate ends, and make it an engine for the support of the few at the expense of the many. The duties of all public officers are, or at least admit of being made, so plain and simple that men of intelligence may readily qualify themselves for their performance; and I cannot but believe that more is lost by the long continuance of men in office than is generally to be gained by their experience. I submit, therefore, to your consideration whether the efficiency of the government would not be promoted, and official industry and integrity better secured, by a general extension of the law which limits appointments to four years.

Because of his expression of this doctrine, Jackson is generally given more credit than he deserves for the introduction of the spoils system. It appears, in fact, that the roots of the patronage system antedate Jackson. "It is admitted now that President Jefferson removed about the same proportion of office-holders as did Jackson, and further that the principles governing his removals were essentially the same as Jackson's," says E. M. Ericksson. He concludes: "If one would be just in his estimate he must admit that the development of the spoils system was a gradual process for which no one man or administration can be blamed." [4]

Pressure on executives for appointments. However the system started, it has been the source of continued pressure on Presidents, department heads, governors, and others in executive positions to make appointments in government agencies as a reward for party service. President Polk, for example, in January, 1847, recorded in his diary that many persons had called on "the contemptible business of seeking office for themselves or their friends." He felt that in making appointments he was unable to rely on the recommendations of Congressmen and others of "high station" who imposed on him and induced him "to make bad appointments." [5]

Succeeding Presidents were subjected to the same sort of demands. In Cleveland's first administration the demands on the President's time by office seekers was so great that he issued a public announcement stating that he would no longer "grant interviews to those seeking public positions or their advocates." In explanation of this policy he stated that a large part of his time during the first eight months of his term had been devoted to the consideration of applications for office. The public welfare, he thought, required that "the time of the President should be differently occupied." [6]

In the present century the pressure on the President for appointments had been reduced by civil service legislation, but it has by no means been eliminated. James A. Farley described the movement of would-be officeholders on Washington following the Democratic victory in 1932: [7]

---

[4] "The Federal Civil Service under President Jackson," *Mississippi Valley Historical Review*, 13 (1927), pp. 517–540.

[5] Allan Nevins (ed.), *Polk, The Diary of a President*, 1845–1849 (New York: Longmans, Green, 1929), pp. 183–184.

[6] Allan Nevins (ed.), *Letters of Grover Cleveland*, 1850–1908 (Boston: Houghton Mifflin, 1933), pp. 88–89.

[7] *Behind the Ballots* (New York: Harcourt, Brace, 1938), pp. 226–227. William Jennings Bryan, when he was Secretary of State, contributed a famous phrase to our political vocabulary in the following letter to the Receiver of Customs in San Domingo: "Now that you have arrived and are acquainting yourself with the situation, can you let me know what positions you have at your disposal, with which to reward deserving Democrats? . . . You have had enough experience in politics to know how valuable workers are when the campaign is on; and how difficult it is to find rewards for all the deserving. . . . Let me know what is requisite, together with the salary, and when appointments are likely to be made." Letter of

I had anticipated quite a rush of deserving patriots who were willing to help F. D. R. carry the burden. But, to be frank, I had never had the slightest conception of what was about to happen. They swarmed in and flocked in by the hundreds and thousands until it seemed as though they must have been arriving by special trainloads. . . . For two or three months I was compelled to hand over the running of the Post Office Department to my worthy assistants. . . .

Congressmen and patronage. In the filling of federal offices not within the competitive civil service, formal authority is vested in the President and in the heads of the administrative departments and agencies. The chief spokesmen for party workers in quest of jobs are Representatives and Senators, and usually there exists some sort of system to apportion the appointments more or less fairly among the faithful. The Postmaster General is traditionally the patronage secretary, but the President usually has also in his immediate entourage a secretary who deals with patronage matters. Early in the Roosevelt administration it was reported that patronage seekers "cleared" through the offices of Democratic national chairman Farley, who was aided in this work by Emil Hurja. According to newspaper accounts, Hurja maintained records showing for each Democratic Senator and Representative the appointments made at their request. When Democratic leaders demanded jobs for their followers, it was a simple matter to determine whether they had already received a disproportionate share of the patronage or whether they were equitably entitled to additional appointments. Hurja's records were also reputed to include election figures so arranged that the justice of claims for patronage on the basis of success in delivering the vote to Roosevelt could be readily determined.[8] Systematic arrangements for the division of the spoils may contribute to party harmony by preventing disaffection based on the feeling that some party leaders are receiving more than their fair share of the patronage.

August 30, 1913; published in the New York *Sun*, January 15, 1915. Quoted by Charles Seymour (ed.), *The Intimate Papers of Colonel House* (Boston: Houghton Mifflin, 1926), Vol. I, p. 178.

[8] Paul Mallon in the Chicago *Daily News*, August 10, 1934. Newspapermen described Hurja's system as if it were novel. It was not actually new. W. D. Foulke has given an account of an investigation of the Census Bureau many years ago in which the patronage records were inspected. In a ledger the names of the employees were classified under the names of the Congressmen charged with the appointments. "In the left-hand column were the numbers of the files containing the recommendations and credentials, then followed the names of the appointees and the grades and salaries. By means of this book the relative rights of members of Congress could be adjusted and it could be seen at a glance whether any particular member had overdrawn his account."—*Fighting the Spoilsmen* (New York: Putnam's 1919), pp. 73–74.

The degree of actual control that a member of Congress exercises over appointments depends to a considerable extent upon his position within the party organization in his state or district. If he is master of his own organization, he is free to make his own decisions upon recommendations to the appointing authority. If he owes his election to a powerful machine, he will perforce accept and forward the recommendations of the organization within his district. Under these conditions the Congressman may be merely a channel for the transmission of the wishes of the party organization. Sometimes, however, members of Congress may be practically ignored by the party leaders, who make their recommendations directly to the officials with the power to appoint.

In those states and districts where the administration has no Congressmen the distribution of patronage is handled by the party organization or by the faction "recognized" by the President, if there happen to be competing factions, as there often are. In making his decisions for appointments the head of the state organization generally advises with the interested county or city organizations. The Republican national committeeman from Georgia told a Senate committee that when, during the 'twenties, a vacancy arose in a post office in his state the Post Office Department would furnish him and the chairman of the state central committee with a list of eligibles and they would make the choice. He said that in reaching a decision he would "inquire of the county organization, the district organization, and in some cases, where it was not convenient to hear from them, sometimes I would ask the Congressmen; . . . and I would ask others sometimes. I would inquire—if it was in some settlement where I did not think it was safe for my folks to have anything to do with it, I would ask some white man that I knew in the settlement."[9]

During the same period the procedure of appointment to federal offices in Texas was systematized by the Republican organization. Persons applying for appointment were furnished a printed form on which they indicated their education, business experience, previous federal service, age, marital status, and other relevant facts. A blank was provided for the endorsement of the Republican county chairman and of the member of the Republican state executive committee of the senatorial district in which the county was located. After these endorsements were made, the form was checked and approved by the state director of organization and then by the national committeeman.[10]

[9] Testimony of Benjamin J. Davis, *Hearings before a Subcommittee of the Committee on Post Offices and Post Roads*, U.S. Senate, 70th Congress, 2nd Session, pursuant to S. Res. 193, Part 1, p. 7.

[10] *Ibid.*, Part 2, p. 311.

State and city patronage procedures. In states the process of distribution of patronage bears a close resemblance to the federal procedure. In Illinois, for instance, after the inauguration of Governor Horner in 1933, the county organizations of the down-state counties prepared recommendations, which were passed upon by John H. Steele and Bruce A. Campbell, both high in the party ranks in that section of the state, before presentation to the governor. Recommendations from Cook County originated with the Chicago ward committeemen and were presented to the party leaders of the county, who in turn made the final set of recommendations to the governor.[11] In states where little integration of the administrative system or of the party organization exists, a series of parallel organizations of a personal character tends to develop around the patronage controlled by each elective state officer.

In cities the tendency is to divide the mass of patronage among the leaders—committeemen, or whatever title they bear—of the larger political divisions of the city. Thus, in Chicago the patronage appears to be largely in the hands of the ward committeemen, the number of jobs under control of each varying with the population of the ward, with the ramifications of the committeeman's power beyond his ward lines, and with the esteem in which he is held by the higher party leaders. A similar practice was inaugurated by Croker when he became chief of the Tammany organization in New York. His predecessors had personally dispensed patronage, but he delegated to the assembly district leaders the control of all appointments within their respective districts. This change, Croker said, made the district leaders "more powerful, and at the same time relieved me of infinite worry and left me free to attend to other business."[12]

Sometimes practically all patronage will be handled personally by a city leader or boss. When patronage is centralized, frequently the leader will delegate the task of dispensing jobs to an immediate subordinate, who becomes in effect a personnel agency for the party. Mayor Thompson's patronage committee in Chicago maintained offices in the Hotel Sherman across the street from the City Hall where the prospective job holder called. "If he was found to be deserving, and the quota from his ward was not already full, he was given a card which was good for a job when presented to the proper department head."[13]

11 "Democrats Get Ready to Shake Big 'Plum' Tree," Chicago *Daily News*, December 19, 1932.
12 W. T. Stead, *Satan's Invisible World Displayed* (New York: R. R. Fenno & Co., 1897), p. 293.
13 J. B. Kingsbury, "The Merit System in Chicago from 1915 to 1923," *Public Personnel Studies*, 4 (1926), pp. 313–314.

In this sort of procedure the appointing officer may reject the name submitted or may be given a choice of two or three individuals nominated by the organization.

From these outlines of the procedure of the distribution of patronage it is plain that the patronage problem is not solved for the party when it wins an election. Procedures have to be established to allocate patronage according either to fairness or to the strength of the factions of the party machine. These procedures are also designed to insure that applicants will be vouched for by the proper functionaries of the party. In general, recommendations for appointments go from the lower reaches of the party hierarchy toward the top, being communicated to the appointing official at the appropriate level of government. The formal appointing authority possesses a widely varying discretion—ranging from complete freedom from his party leaders to complete abdication to them.[14]

Costs of patronage. The stake that the party machines have in the game of politics through their control over patronage appointments has not been estimated in any accurate way, but certainly the annual cost runs into the millions. In 1932 Raymond Moley estimated that "roughly half" of the cost of support of the magistrates' courts of New York City at that time went "either to political work or to utter waste and inefficiency." [15] In May, 1933, the New York Civil Service Reform Association found that the annual pay for positions exempt from civil service requirements in New York City was "only $7,000,000, but about half of this sum" the association estimated to represent "sheer waste of public funds." Most of the exempt positions were "passed around to the district leaders and their henchmen." [16] In 1937 Professor Pollock found that in Michigan the annual turnover of public employees, owing to the patronage system in the main, was 25 per cent. He esti-

[14] Patrick Nash, chairman of the Cook County Democratic Committee, made the following statement after the election of Edward J. Kelly as mayor of Chicago by the city council in 1933: "Before Mr. Kelly was definitely selected he promised that all jobs be filled through the ward committeemen. We all want jobs. But I know that no ward committeeman wants a job at the expense of another ward committeeman or of the taxpayers. For that reason there will be no one chasing Mr. Kelly around. All applications will come through the ward committeemen."

[15] Raymond Moley, *Tribunes of the People* (New Haven: Yale University Press, 1932), p. 263.

[16] Efforts of the La Guardia administration in New York City to wipe out certain unessential county offices were blocked by the party organization. "The county offices contain 834 exempt positions which are used for the most part for rewarding political henchmen. The city pays to this group of 834 exempt employees $2,300,000 a year. Since they are nearly all chosen by the direct orders of county and district political leaders, the city is in effect sustaining the political machine by feeding its officers."—New York City Commissioner of Accounts, *Investigating City Government in the La Guardia Administration* (1937), p. 9.

mated the annual cost of breaking in new employees at around half a
million dollars.[17]

The cost of the patronage system is, of course, not to be measured in
the salaries of inefficient employees alone. The effects of the errors of
the incompetent employee may be extremely costly. For example, a
Chicago building inspector, appointed through party channels, inspected a water tank atop a building. The 40,000-gallon tank later
collapsed and fell through six floors of the building, killing five men
and injuring six others en route. The inspector's testimony before
the coroner's jury follows: [18]

Q. How long have you been a building inspector?
A. Nine months.
Q. What were you before that?
A. I was a malt salesman.
Q. When you were made a building inspector did you know anything about
   the work?
A. No. I didn't know anything about it.
Q. When did you inspect the building and the tank?
A. It was in January.
Q. Did you find anything wrong with the tank?
A. No. It looked all right to me.
Q. Are you in a position to know whether it was all right or not?
A. No. I'm just the same as you or anybody else who might inspect it.
Q. Did you inspect the anchor plates?
A. Well, I looked at them.

It is not to be concluded that all appointees who owe their jobs to the
party organizations are unfitted for the duties of their office. Many persons of ability, industry, and loyalty to the public weal become public
servants through party channels and remain permanently, to serve
whatever party comes to power. They are overshadowed in public
attention by such individuals as the building inspector whose disarm-
ing testimony has been quoted and by such rollicking cases as the
minority registrar of the Baltimore Board of Supervisors of Elections.
A patronage-starved Republican organization in 1941 and 1942 was so
hard pressed for jobs that this $3,000 place was filled by a series of Re-
publican ward executives. One would serve for a month, resign, and
be replaced by another. Republican leaders defended the arrangement
as a means of avoiding the evils of long continuance in office.[19]

[17] J. K. Pollock, "The Cost of the Patronage System," *The Annals of the American
Academy of Political and Social Science,* 189 (1937), pp. 29–34.
[18] Chicago *Tribune,* June 2, 1934.
[19] Baltimore *Sun,* April 13, 1942.

2. POLITICAL NEUTRALIZATION OF THE CIVIL SERVICE

The existence of a large body of civil employees of federal, state, and local governments active in support of the party in power supposedly tips the scales in favor of the party that controls the electioneering activities of these employees. Often the party in power is tempted to improve on this advantage by increasing the number of patronage employees. While the party out of power does not have the advantage of the public treasury to support its workers, it has the activities of workers anxious to obtain office as a result of future electoral victory. And the hungry sometimes work harder than the well fed.

Whichever party wins an electoral victory under the patronage system, the public pays the cost of the system. Hence, there has arisen a persistent effort to remove the public employee from political activity. By political neutralization of the government service technical merit may be established as the basis for the selection of public employees. The forces contending for political power will no longer need to form alliances with machines consisting primarily of public employees; and the control of government may be shifted from party to party without the disruption of the public service attendant upon large-scale turnover in subordinate administrative positions.

The neutralization of the civil service requires that the civil servant serve with equal loyalty whatever party is in power. Permanence of tenure of office is in one respect a condition of neutrality, in another respect a consequence of political neutrality. Political neutrality is an essential condition precedent to permanence of tenure, since no party can be expected to retain in the public employ individuals who have actively campaigned against it. On the other hand, when civil servants refrain from active participation in electoral campaigns, the government of the day may be stronger in its efforts to resist the demands of party workers that a clean sweep be made of the administrative services to provide places for those who have loyally served the party.

Pendleton Act of 1883. The principal type of public policy to neutralize politically the great mass of administrative employees of government has been so-called "civil service" or "merit system" laws. The Pendleton Act of 1883 created the Federal Civil Service Commission and provided for recruitment of persons to fill positions in the "classified services" by competitive examination. By "classified service" was meant the aggregate of positions covered by the legislation; those positions outside the "classified service" remained subject to the patronage system. In the excluded class of positions were such offices as United States marshal, collector of internal revenue, federal district attorney, and (with modifications from time to time) postmasters. Since 1883 the scope of the "classified service" gradually has been increased, with the defenders of the patronage system fighting a slowly losing fight.[20]

A corollary of appointment through competitive examination and tenure during good behavior is neutrality in political campaigns. In practice political neutrality has been difficult to enforce, but the tendency in the long run in the federal service has been to make more stringent the rules against partisan activity by employees in the classified service. The original rule of the Civil Service Commission provided: "No person in the said service shall use his official authority or influence either to coerce the political action of any person or body or to interfere with any election." Apparently this rule did not adequately cover the situation, for President Cleveland in 1886 issued an executive order exhorting federal officeholders to refrain from "obtrusive partisanship." When Theodore Roosevelt was a member of the United States Civil Service Commission, he observed excessive partisanship among federal employees and was moved to write for the 1894 annual report of the commission:

A man in the classified service has an entire right to vote as he pleases, and to express privately his opinions on all political subjects; but he should not take any active part in political management or in political campaigns, for precisely the same reasons that a judge, any army officer, a regular soldier, or a policeman is debarred from taking such an active part. It is no hardship to a man to require this. It leaves him free to vote, think and speak privately as ·he chooses, but it prevents him while in the service of the whole public, from turning his official position to the benefit of one of the parties in which the whole public is divided; and in no other way can this be prevented.

Almost the same language was used in 1907 when the rules under the Civil Service Act were amended to provide: "Persons who by the provisions of these rules are in the competitive classified service, while retaining the right to vote as they please and to express their opinions on all political subjects, shall take no active part in political management or in political campaigns." [21] In the application of the rule against taking "active part in political management or in political campaigns," fine distinctions have to be made between what is and what is not permissible behavior by a civil servant. He may express his views "privately" but not in public places or by the publication of a letter or article in favor of any party or candidate. He may make political con-

---

[20] For an account of the civil service reform movement, see F. M. Stewart *The National Civil Service Reform League* (Austin: University of Texas Press, 1929).

[21] For a full account of the evolution of federal policy, see Wei-kiung Chen, *The Doctrine of Civil Service Neutrality in Party Conflicts in the United States and Great Britain* (Chicago: University of Chicago Libraries, lithoprinted, 1937).

tributions, but only to persons not in the service of the United States and to them only "voluntarily." A fine jurisprudence separates the "voluntary" and the "involuntary" contribution. He may be a member of a political club, but he must not be an officer of the club. He may not be a candidate for elective office. He may attend a political convention as a spectator but not as a member. He must not wear campaign badges or buttons.

Hatch Act. In 1939 Congress, in the Hatch Act, adopted another method of bringing about political neutrality of federal employees. As has been noted, the provisions of the rules and regulations under the Civil Service Act applied only to those persons in the federal classified service. The exclusion of the unclassified employees from the provisions of the regulations left a substantial number of federal employees free to engage in political activities. The Hatch Act declared it

. . . unlawful for any person employed in the executive branch of the Federal Government, or any agency or department thereof, to use his official authority or influence for the purpose of interfering with an election or affecting the result thereof. No officer or employee in the executive branch of the Federal Government, or any agency or department thereof, shall take any active part in political management or in political campaigns. All such persons shall retain the right to vote as they may choose and to express their opinions on all political subjects and candidates.

Certain policy-forming officials, such as the President, the Vice-President, the heads and assistant heads of departments, and other high officials whose business it is to make and defend governmental decisions are, of course, excluded from the prohibition of political activity. But the main effect of the Hatch Act was to extend to most of the employees outside the classified service the rules that have long governed those in the classified service.[22]

Quite apart from legislative enactments, such as the Civil Service Act and the Hatch Act, federal employment of specialized professionals has tended to create a more or less permanent, expert body of civil employees relatively unconcerned with the changing of administrations. The assumption by the government of highly technical functions requiring the services of these professional classes has made it "bad" politics for the party to apply the patronage system to many departments and agencies. Although Congressmen, for example, often bring

---

[22] See H. Eliot Kaplan, "Political Neutrality of the Civil Service," *Public Personnel Review*, 1 (1940), pp. 10–23; L. V. Howard, "Federal Restrictions upon the Political Activity of Government Employees," 35 (1941), *American Political Science Review*, 35 (1941), pp. 470–489; J. R. Starr, "The Hatch Act—An Interpretation," *National Municipal Review*, 30 (1941), pp. 418–425.

pressure on administrative officers to appoint loyal party workers as clerks, stenographers, messengers, or other routine workers, they will keep hands off the professional and expert groups. Such a rule is not universally followed, but the extent of its observance indicates a recognition by political leaders that it is not to their interest to use a certain class of positions to reward party workers.

Limitation on state and local employees. Parallel to the federal enactments has been the trend toward the adoption of the competitive method for recruitment to state and municipal offices, with the accompanying limitations on partisan activity. It is probably correct, however, to say that, on the whole, state and local laws and rules against the participation of civil servants actively in political campaigns have been less effective than have the federal regulations. In some states and municipalities stringent rules of neutrality in politics are consistently ignored. Sixteen states have civil service commissions or like agencies that conduct competitive examinations for the selection of the employees for most of the state departments and agencies. Much less movement toward the substitution of merit for patronage has occurred in the counties. Of the 3,053 counties of the country, 173 are under some form of merit system rule, either by local charter provision or by state statute. A total of 869 cities have adopted the merit system for all or part of their employees.[23]

A large and important group of state and local employees has been brought under merit system provisions by conditions attached to federal grants to states. Many state activities are financed in part by federal grants, and nearly all these grants are accompanied by a degree of federal supervision respecting the personnel employed by the states to do the aided work. Consequently, these conditions have tended to encourage employment on the basis of technical competence rather than party service. Probably the most thorough-going requirements of this kind are those enforced by the Social Security Board concerning state and local employees in charge of public-assistance and employment-security programs. An amendment to the Social Security Act provided that after January 1, 1940, all state agencies in these fields should, as a condition of receiving federal grants, make provision for "the establishment and maintenance of personnel standards on a merit basis."

In 1940 the limitations of the Hatch Act were extended to a substantial proportion of state and local employees. Normally, of course, Congress would have no power over these persons, but since many state activities have come to be financed in part with federal funds, it was

[23] See, for detailed information, Civil Service Assembly, *Civil Service Agencies in the United States* (Pamphlet No. 16, Chicago, 1940).

possible for Congress to extend the prohibitions to state employees by virtue of the power of the purse. The statutory provision reads as follows:

No officer or employee of any State or local agency whose principal employment is in connection with any activity which is financed in whole or in part by loans or grants made by the United States or by any Federal agency shall (1) use his official authority or influence for the purpose of interfering with an election or a nomination for office, or affecting the result thereof. or (2) directly or indirectly coerce, attempt to coerce, command, or advise any other such officer or employee to pay, lend, or contribute any part of his salary or compensation or anything else of value to any party, committee, organization, agency, or person for political purposes. No such officer or employee shall take any active part in political management or in political campaigns. All such persons shall retain the right to vote as they may choose and to express their opinions on all political subjects and candidates. . . .

If the state authorities fail to remove from office a person found by the United States Civil Service Commission to have violated the act, a sum equivalent to two years' compensation of the violator is deducted from grants to the state concerned. The Civil Service Commission has made findings and issued orders in a few such cases to the accompaniment of strident protests about state rights and the constitutional privilege of the individual to participate in politics.

Over a considerable period of time the patronage system has undoubtedly been reduced in scope. That many positions in federal, state, and local services remain to be used for the rewarding and the supporting of party workers is still true. The degree of prevalence of the patronage system, taking the country as a whole, is impossible to estimate. The situation certainly varies sharply from place to place. In some cities almost the entire municipal service consists of persons who gained their positions through party channels and who devote a portion of their time to the work of the party machine. In a few cities, at the other extreme, the number of patronage employees is extremely small. Some states have developed civil services that serve loyally and impartially whatever party is in power and refrain from partisan activity; other states have an almost completely new set of employees, from the lowliest messenger to the department head, when a new party comes into power.

3. DIVERSE PARTY SPOILS

Public jobs are the objective in which the largest number of party workers are interested. At times other perquisites of power are considered to be more or less legitimate spoils, to be distributed among the leaders of the victorious party organization. These prizes—ranging from contracts for public construction to concessions for operating soda stands in the public parks—affect a small number of machine leaders.[24] The past thirty years have seen an effort to deprive the party machine of these perquisites and to substitute factors of public interest in their distribution, as there has been reform in the sphere of public personnel. It would require much space to list and describe the many kinds of spoils that from time to time go to party leaders. Only a few types may be mentioned.

Judicial spoils. In all political organizations lawyers are to be found in prominent positions, and in some localities the lawyers affiliated with the dominant party machine are favored in the appointment by the courts of masters in chancery, receivers, trustees, and other judicial functionaries. The board of managers of the Chicago Bar Association reported in 1934:[25]

Recently, in exercising their discretion in the appointment of masters, certain judges have deferred to the wishes of politicians. The appointment of a master in chancery as one of the political spoils belonging to a successful political party, regardless of the qualifications of the master, is a subversion of the judicial powers of the court. As a result of this system, many masters in chancery have been nominated by politicians and appointed by the courts, who are wholly unfit to perform the functions required of them.

Similar comments would be applicable to such appointments by the courts in many other localities, and the federal district courts have not been completely free from like practices. The large, sometimes exorbitant, fees drawn by receivers and similar officers acting in a fiduciary capacity under the supervision of courts make these appointments especially desirable to the legal lights of the party machine.

Political contracts. Most urban machines are likely to have several construction contractors occupying important posts in the organization; frequently the contractor may not be a district leader or a ward committeeman but a silent and inconspicuous member of the organization. Contracts for public works may flow to the organization contractors often at unreasonable figures. In turn, the contractor may use a part of his profits to aid in financing the campaigns of the party machine.[26]

---

[24] H. F. Gosnell reports, for example, that in Chicago "Of the seven Democratic ward committeemen who were not employed by some governmental agency in 1928, three were in occupations which enabled them to have many dealings with public authorities. One was in the sewer contracting business; the second was in a law firm which had many political ramifications; and the third was in the insurance business." —*Machine Politics: Chicago Model* (Chicago: University of Chicago Press, 1937), p. 40.

[25] Report by the Board of Managers, Chicago Bar Association, February 1, 1934.

[26] "This reputable firm of architects received $778,000 on four contracts awarded

The many jobs available on public works incidentally furnish an opportunity to allocate employment to the adherents of the machine. The purchase of supplies for public departments and agencies may likewise be used for benefit of members of the party organization. If one examines the records of early city machines, flagrant cases of corruption in the award of contracts for buildings and supplies may readily be discovered. During the Tweed days in New York, for example, a board of audit of three members had the power to approve for payment bills rendered to the city. It arranged with persons from whom supplies were purchased, Tweed said, to "advance bills for work purporting to be done for the city; more particularly for the county, and they should receive only fifty per cent of the amount of the bills." [27] Later the ante to the politicians was raised to 55 per cent and finally to 65 per cent. When payment was made, the city auditor would receive back the excess and distribute it among the members of the ring. Under such a regime items, such as note paper at $14 a ream, $1,294,684.13 worth of repairs on $531,594.22 worth of plaster, and $41,190.95 for "brooms, etc." for the county courthouse, were to be found by examination of the records. Such crude practices are rare now; at any rate prima facie felonious bookkeeping is avoided.

Contracts for garbage collection have been often tinged with a partisan odor. Thus, the Commissioners of Baltimore County, Maryland, in 1946 had contracts with 57 persons to collect and remove garbage, ashes, and refuse. Among the holders of contracts were several members of the Democratic executive committee of the county and other persons with party connections. In several instances the compensation was fixed at a level that enabled the contractor to subcontract the actual work.[28]

Modern reform movements and the general improvement in the quality of municipal administration have reduced greatly the grossness of spoils in contracts and purchasing. In many localities the "organization" contractor has a great advantage in obtaining awards, but he is more likely on the whole to do approximately what he is paid for than he was a few decades ago. Although the tendency has been to attempt to award public contracts on the basis of free competition, legislation requiring awards on the basis of competitive bidding can

---

in the Walker administration, and in one case was so bold as to charge a $10,000 contribution to the Democratic organization on its books as an expense item for work on Riker's Island Penitentiary under the bookkeeping title 'Work in progress, job 394 —Riker's Island Penitentiary.' "—New York City Commissioner of Accounts, *Investigating City Government in the La Guardia Administration* (1937), p. 132.

[27] Quoted by M. R. Werner, *Tammany Hall* (Garden City, N.Y.: Doubleday, Doran, 1928), p. 185.

[28] Baltimore *Sun*, March 8, 1946.

readily be evaded. The economic circumstances are often such that free competition is either discouraged or not feasible.   In a thoroughly corrupt municipality the natural limitations on competition in public construction (through the small number of contractors and their own tendency to combine in limitation of competition) may be supplemented by the actions of officials calculated to favor the organization contractor. Those actions may be in the formulation of specifications so as to exclude all save the favored contractor, or they may be in the inspection after the award of the contract.   Inspection may be strict or lax.

Real estate purchases: "Honest graft."   The purchase of real estate for public improvements has furnished opportunity from time to time for members of the upper strata of the party organization to enrich themselves.   This practice, incidentally, contributed one of the classic phrases of the argot of politics, "honest graft."   The late Senator Plunkitt, a godsend to the authors of textbooks, is reported to have said: [29]

There's an honest graft, and I'm an example of how it works. I might sum up the whole thing by sayin': "I seen my opportunities and I took 'em."

Just let me explain by examples. My party's in power in the city, and it's goin' to undertake a lot of public improvements. Well, I'm tipped off, say, that they're going to lay out a new park at a certain place.

I see my opportunity and I take it. I go to that place and I buy up all the land I can in the neighborhood. Then the board of this or that makes its plan public, and there is a rush to get my land, which nobody cared particularly for before.

Ain't it perfectly honest to charge a good price and make a profit on my investment and foresight? Of course it is. Well, that's honest graft.

TABLE 12

Increases in Value of Real Property Immediately Prior to Acquisition by the City of New York [a]

Tract	Total purchase price to prior owner	Cash payment to prior owner	Award paid by city on condemnation	Time between next prior sale and vesting of title in city
1	$25,000	$8,000	$65,800	1 year, 10 months
2	38,350	12,550	51,425	10 months
3	15,350	4,500	36,000	4 months
4	41,000	7,500	51,230	6 months
5	162,250	27,275	229,500	3 months
6	76,250	27,250	118,026	4 months

a Compiled from illustrative cases described by Leonard Wallstein, *Report on Law and Procedure in Condemnation Applicable to Proceedings Brought by the City of New York* (January, 1932).

29 Quoted in W. L. Riordan, *Plunkitt of Tammany Hall* (New York: McClure, Phillips, 1905), pp. 4-5.

A somewhat different light was put on the matter by Leonard Wallstein in an investigation of real estate purchases by the Tammany administration in New York City during the 'twenties. He found that persons with inside information on the land needs of the city acquired land in the names of dummies with "no apparent financial means, but who produce substantial sums of cash from safe deposit boxes or office safes, buy up property and turn quick profits, which are again immediately converted into cash and vanish. Clearly these operations have been merely the dummies or puppets for influential undisclosed principals." The extent of the profits may be gauged by the instances gathered in Table 12 from Mr. Wallstein's data. In very short periods of time tremendous profits were made on a relatively small cash investment.

Surety bonds. A widely prevalent perquisite of power is control over the bonds that public contractors and officials are required to furnish to insure their fidelity. An excellent example that occurred around 1913–1916 in Boston during the first Curley administration may be used for illustrative purposes. The practice continues in a goodly number of jurisdictions. One of the Mayor's political supporters and friends who was engaged in the business of selling butter, cheese, and eggs from a cart found the time propitious to go into the bonding business after the inauguration of Curley. Persons who had contracts with the city were requested by department heads and other city employees to furnish bonds on their contracts by the National Surety Company, which was represented by the Mayor's friend. The business of the National Surety Company grew rapidly after Mr. Curley came into office. In 1913 it had issued bonds making it responsible for only 6.8 per cent of the total liability on bonds affecting the city; in 1915 the figure was 76.0 per cent.

The Mayor's frank testimony on this matter furnishes a revealing insight into this type of situation generally. He stated that contractors were affected by the same "psychology" as were city employees, who also furnished bonds written by the same agency. They wanted to be "in right" with the administration.

Q. How about contractors? A. Why, contractors are affected by the same psychology.

Q. Why should contractors be affected? A. There isn't any reason—no reason except that they labor under an impression that unless they are friendly with the friends of the administration they will be in bad odor at City Hall.

Q. You were paying political debt to Daly, weren't you? A. You might call it that.

Q. Wouldn't you call it that?   A. I might say that would be as good a name as any other.

Q. A political debt for what he had done for you in your election?   A. I wouldn't say it was in that election. . . . It was personal and political.

Q. Did you communicate to any of the contractors that you would like to have them give bonds to the National Surety Company?   A. I don't recall having communicated with any of them.   They are even more keen than the city employees.

Q. You didn't communicate with any contractors that you would like to have them give their bonds to the National Surety Company?   A. I would say I did not.

Q. Would you say positively?   A. I wouldn't say positively.   If there was occasion. I would, but I don't remember I did.

Q. In other words you gave out the impression that it would be very agreeable to the administrator?   A. It wasn't necessary.

Q. But you were willing to if it was necessary?   A. If it was necessary I would, or send for them.

The commission interpreted the testimony as meaning that if contractors were in "good odor" at the City Hall, they would not be unduly interfered with by inspectors on their work.   If they made the error of offering bonds from the wrong agency, they would be harassed by the inspectors.[30]

Interest on deposits of public moneys.   An old source of revenue to party leaders, for personal or party purposes or both, was the interest paid by banks on deposits of public moneys.   The original custom in many states and cities was to consider the interest paid by the depository banks as a legitimate perquisite of the state or city treasurer. Gradually the principle developed that the interest yield belonged to the public treasury, whereupon methods were devised to evade this rule.   The extent of the evasion in one instance may be gauged by the recovery by the State of Illinois of $650,000 from Len Small, former state treasurer and Republican leader.   This sum represented a compromise payment after the state had sued for $802,992 in interest paid on public deposits but not credited to the state.[31]   The yield of interest has declined greatly because of the development of rules governing deposits and changes in banking practices and conditions.   Yet banks

[30] See Boston Finance Commission, *Reports*, XIII, 163-74 (1918).   It could be noted that similar practices in private business are considered perfectly legitimate.   For example, mortgage and finance companies quite generally insist that insurance on properties that they finance be placed with specified companies.

[31] *People* v. *Small*, 319 Ill. 435; Chicago *Tribune*, June 4, 1927.

with party affiliations may be favored in the deposit of funds.[32]   "If you control public funds to the extent of millions," Merriam observes, "and may determine where they shall be deposited and on what terms (within limits) and for how long, you can deal with some bankers; and you will find allies among them.   Not with all but with some, and they may render you powerful assistance." [33]

Underworld concessions.   Many urban machines have from time to time included in their ranks, either as official members of the party hierarchy or as unofficial members of the ruling coterie, persons engaging in lucrative enterprises on the nether side of legality.   Gambling, prostitution, and, at times, the liquor business could be operated only through arrangements with the law-enforcing authorities.   One of the unlovely aspects of American politics has been the frequent connection between the party organization and this informal licensing of illegal businesses.[34]

Decline of glaring corruption.   Other types of perquisites that have been considered the legitimate spoils of party victory could be mentioned, but the foregoing classes are some of the more important.   Since these practices are not carried on in a goldfish bowl, it is impossible to make any satisfactory estimate of their present significance.   Extensive perusal of the literature of political corruption, of the reports of investigating bodies, and of the decisions of the courts leads to the conclusion that the grosser forms of perversion of public trust to party interest have declined in incidence during the past thirty years.   The exposures by the muckrakers following 1900 had a cleansing effect, and the general upward movement of the level of administrative capacity has had a similar result.   The use of these perquisites as reward for party effort has either declined or come to be more effectively concealed than it was several decades ago.

4. THE FUNCTION OF SPOILS

The patronage system and various other types of spoils tend to be treated as an unfortunate manifestation of the innate perversity of man; and many specific instances of peculation, fraud, and nepotism in the public sphere are no different in motive or effect from departures from the code of proper conduct for persons in positions of trust in

---

[32] On the general problem, see M. L. Faust, *The Custody of State Funds* (New York: National Institute of Public Administration, 1925).

[33] From *Chicago, A More Intimate View of Urban Politics* (New York, 1929), p. 51. Quoted by permission of the Macmillan Company, publishers.

[34] For a case study, see Lloyd Wendt and Herman Kogan, *Lords of the Levee* (Indianapolis: Bobbs-Merrill, 1943).

ecclesiastical, commercial, and labor associations. Yet the patronage
system in the large is something more than a collection of unrelated cases
of individual venality. The spoilsman has his own code of ethics,[35]
and the patronage system as a whole may occupy a significant position
in the configuration of political power.

From one standpoint the patronage system and, to a certain extent,
other types of spoils may be considered a means to aid in financing the
elaborate party machinery that seems to be necessary under our form of
government. With our innumerable offices filled by popular election
and our multiplicity of elections, it seems almost indispensable that
many persons devote their time to the work of the party machine.
What men shall devote their time to this work? Only those who have
adequate private means to permit them to dedicate themselves to the
service of their party. That solution would hardly be in keeping with
the spirit of American democracy and the doctrine of equality of opportunity. Carl Russell Fish argued that "the true cause for the introduction of the spoils system was the triumph of democracy." The work of
the party "requires the labor of many men: there must be captains of
hundreds and captains of tens, district chiefs and ward heelers. . . .
It is an essential idea of democracy that these leaders shall be of the
people; they must not be gentlemen of wealth and leisure, but they must
—the mass of them at any rate—belong to the class that makes its own
living. If, then, they are to devote their time to politics, politics must
be made to pay." [36] Fish contended that the spoils system served in the
period of its establishment "a purpose that could probably have been
performed in no other way, and that was fully worth the cost." Without the inducement of public jobs and other perquisites, the formation
of party organizations becomes difficult. Nevertheless, from place to
place effective local machines of a middle-class character have been
constructed without benefit of spoils.

From another point of view the entire spoils system serves to maintain discipline within the party organization. There may be, of course,
internal contention over the distribution of the spoils, but a powerful
and skilful party leader may maintain his authority by the adroit allocation of rewards. The usefulness of jobs for this purpose is obvious,

[35] An interesting example of this code of conduct is furnished by a quotation from
the official organ of the Republican organization in Philadelphia. It was announced
that steps were to be taken "to comb out of city and county offices the social and
fraternal and 'pull' appointees, so that places can be made for the men who pull
doorbells and produce majorities. . . . This is Senator Vare's idea and comes direct.
Men who can't produce are to 'walk the plank.' This will be good news to the men
who deliver."—Kurtzman, *Methods of Controlling Votes in Philadelphia*, p. 43.

[36] *The Civil Service and the Patronage* (New York: Longmans, Green, 1905), p. 156.
Quoted by permission of the President and Fellows of Harvard College.

but other types of spoils may be employed in the same fashion. A rebellious district leader or ward committeeman may discover that his printing contracts or his fire-hose business has been cut off by the higher-ups in the organization. The spoils system as a whole may serve as a method of consolidating into a cohesive and disciplined group the persons constituting the machine. Without the tradition of a responsible governing elite bound together by ties of tradition and class interest, patronage serves to integrate the activities of individuals bound together by no other tie. It aids in the creation of party loyalties and simplifies the problem of party discipline.

The spoils of power are used to gain support of individuals and of groups under regimes in nondemocratic countries. Many commentators find the like use of spoils in the United States for this purpose to be monstrous and unparalleled, but the practice is as old as human government. The governors of all regimes use the perquisites at their disposal to command the support and loyalty of those susceptible to purchase in this fashion. The striking difference about American practice is the moral reprobation that generally accompanies the practice; matters that elsewhere would be accepted as a matter of course are here considered not quite cricket.[37] Nor can the spoils system be considered or understood in isolation. In a thoroughly machine-ridden city the observer, to comprehend the nature and function of the system, must look for the allies of the machine. "The major interests," says Odegard, "are content to leave minor spoils, such as jobs in the public service, to the party agents as long as these agents direct the affairs of state in a manner to promote the interests of the powerful oligarchies which control the economic and social destinies of the community."[38] If one examines a corruptly governed city of about the beginning of the century, he will observe a powerful political machine utilizing to the utmost the spoils opportunities. But allied with the machine probably would be found the telephone, traction, and power interests, which sought franchises and privileged treatment at the hands of the city, un-

---

[37] On the use of patronage to maintain party discipline, the following comment by Professor J. K. Pollock is relevant: "It has often been contended that patronage is a necessary aid to political leadership in this country. But it is interesting to note that many of our greatest governors—Grover Cleveland, Robert Marion La Follette, Judson Harmon, Hiram Johnson and Albert Ritchie, to name a few—men whose political leadership was undoubted and of a high order, were not merely advocates of civil service but were responsible for its establishment in their respective states. In Great Britain political leadership is all the stronger for being relieved of the sordid patronage duties which bog down the average American political leader. Gladstone was grateful that the only job he could fill was that of his own private secretary."—"The Cost of the Patronage System," *The Annals*, 189 (1937), pp. 29–34.
[38] "Political Parties and Group Pressures," *ibid.*, 179 (1935), pp. 69–81.

derworld syndicates controlling gambling and prostitution, industries that existed by governmental toleration, and perhaps other interest groups that required for their profitable existence a favorably disposed city administration. It was by the combination of the party machine, the utilities, and the underworld that control of the city could be gained, and by that control each of the segments of the power combination could obtain what it wanted.

Thus it came about that important interests outside the party machine itself were content to leave unlimited spoils to the party organization in order that their own interests might be advanced. When all the franchises had been awarded, when privileges sought had been legally granted, the important business interests associated with the party machine were apt to become converts to the doctrine of economy and efficiency in government. Consequently, a sharp decline in the scope of the spoils system has occurred in many American jurisdictions. Where the spoils system still exists unchallenged and unashamed, usually the power combination controlling the jurisdiction contains important elements in addition to the party machine itself—elements that seek to gain, through toleration of their machine allies, governmental action or inaction that might not readily be obtainable in any other way.

The widespread prevalence of graft has had a curious effect on American political campaigns. It has given campaigns, mainly in state and local jurisdictions, a strong moral tone in which the principal issue often turns on the "honesty" of the contending candidates. The concentration of popular attention on the relative degree of probity of the contenders for office diverts attention from their position on economic and social issues. By the distraction of attention from issues that involve matters of great import, the sharpness of social cleavages has probably been kept down. Moreover, the moral tone of campaigns reinforces the doctrine that all "honest" men would arrive at the "right," and the same, solution of any public question. It is, of course, untrue that all "honest" men are of the same view. An "honest" labor sympathizer can take one position; an "honest" middle-class leader, another. By wholehearted attention to the relative "honesty" of candidates, however, public discussion and recognition of the very real differences that may occur on questions of public policy between equally "honest" men is minimized.

The interest of the party in patronage and in other perquisites encounter opposition from other social groups. The party hierarchy is in this respect like any pressure group: the unlimited prosecution of group interests may meet a countermovement from people adversely affected. In this process the long-term trend has undoubtedly been to limit more and more the perquisites of the party hierarchy. Merit system protection has been extended to most federal employees and to a substantial proportion of state and local employees. Many kinds of party spoils have been made illegal. Public services have come to be manned to a higher degree by a professionalized personnel animated by a higher professional ethic than prevailed in the past. Yet party machines resist encroachments on their ancient prerogatives, and movement toward weaning them away from their perquisites is slow and halting.

The truth of the matter is that we have found no other way to assure the performance of the functions that the party machine carries on. The party organization makes a democratic government work and charges a price for its services. Sometimes it becomes corrupt and levies a high price. The plunder of Jersey City by the Hague machine, for example, has made it the highest-taxed city in America. Corrupt political machines, like other interest groups, once they gain unchecked power will take, and take, and take until another group resourceful enough and courageous to drive them from power enters the fray. Fortunately, not all political organizations are corrupt. Usually those who protest most loudly against political machines are least disposed to undertake the responsibility of community leadership that work in a party organization entails. Former Governor Edison of New Jersey, for example, reports that his attempts to interest distinguished citizens in service to their state almost uniformly failed.[39] When such citizens abdicate their political duties, where does one turn for political leadership? Citizens who have to punch time clocks can scarcely afford to devote time to public affairs. Until we invent some other system of political financing or new incentives for public service, the government, directly or indirectly, will support party activity in considerable measure.

[39] Charles Edison, "Effective Democracy," *New Republic,* March 20, 1944, pp. 369–371. Men of substance in New Jersey may have hesitated to associate themselves with Governor Edison because of the effective punitive measures within the power of the Hague machine, which was opposed to the governor. See D. D. McKean, *The Boss, The Hague Machine in Action* (Boston: Houghton Mifflin, 1940).

Chapter 12

NOMINATIONS IN THE STATES

THE PRIME function of the political party is the nomination of candidates for public elective office. Indeed, the great achievement of party government has been the development of pacific means, as a substitute for the earlier methods of violence and inheritance, for determining succession to positions of power. It has been indicated in previous chapters that the American political party tends to be weak in the formulation of principles, that on the ground of principle the major parties are more alike than unlike, that new principles, new policies, and new ideas are likely to be first championed by pressure groups or minor parties. Yet the party remains unchallenged in the field of the selection of government personnel. It is an elementary observation that in large constituencies it is necessary to have a winnowing process to sift out a few persons from whom the entire electorate may choose; it is equally elementary that various coalitions will agree in advance on individuals whom they will support both for the party nomination and for election.

Nominating processes in the United States are much more elaborate than in any other democratic regime. In most countries nominations are handled informally by the party organization or by a caucus of party leaders operating entirely as a private group. In the United States nominations are usually made under detailed rules prescribed by public authority. Instead of being a virtually private matter, the nominating process in the United States is publicly controlled and is a part of the electoral procedure.

The reasons for the peculiar emphasis on nominating procedures in the United States are several. A far heavier burden is carried by political parties in the selection of governmental personnel in the United States than elsewhere because of the large number of offices filled by popular election. This fact alone gives the nominating process much greater significance in the United States. Moreover, the existence of vast areas over which a single party holds virtually unchallenged sway in state and local governmental matters elevates nominations to the status of elections and precludes their consideration as private questions to be settled by a few party leaders. Finally, from time to time in many states and localities both party organizations have been dominated by fundamentally similar interests. The achievement of popular control could not be accomplished without popular participation in nominations. When there is genuine competition for power between parties, nominating procedures may be of little public concern, for the electorate has a choice. But when parties are similar in their views, a surge of antagonism against the ruling interests must express itself at the stage of nominations. Hence, the initiation of regulation of nominating methods in the United States has almost invariably been associated with popular protest against oligarchical rule.

The general scheme of this chapter is to trace the evolution of the nominating process, with primary attention to the permutations of procedures within the states. The trend of its development will incidentally throw considerable light on the struggle for democracy in America as well as on the nature of political parties.

1. RISE AND DECLINE OF THE LEGISLATIVE CAUCUS

In reality, the development of nominating methods has consisted in the adaptation, to larger areas and to more complex situations, of the techniques of the caucus that met in Tom Dawes' garret in colonial Boston (see page 209). The informal caucus of local leaders was a means whereby the inner core of the party could agree in advance on candidates to be supported in the formal election. This type of agreement to work in concert seems to be more or less inherent in "group" action; indeed, it is said that "parlor caucuses" were employed even in the selection of the judges of Israel.[1] The caucus as it was known in colonial Boston, however, was best adapted to the selection of candidates for small areas from which the leaders or inner core of the party could readily and conveniently assemble to carry on their work. The nomination of candidates for state-wide and nation-wide offices was a matter that the caucus in its primitive form could not easily handle, such were the hardships and inconveniences of travel at that time.

Post-Revolutionary nominating methods. Various methods were used to nominate candidates for district or state offices after the Revolution. In some instances "the views of the inhabitants of various counties were . . . ascertained by means of a very extensive correspondence;

[1] F. W. Dallinger, *Nominations for Elective Office in the United States* (New York: Longmans, Green, 1897), p. 3.

a number of circulars were despatched, and from the replies received a list was drawn up of the candidates who had received the most votes, and it was returned by the same channel for ratification by the counties. These consultations were led by a few public-spirited men with a taste for election work, who made themselves into a committee of correspondence for the occasion." [2]   In certain states, after the adoption of the Constitution, full-fledged conventions, as they later developed, were used for a time.   In some states candidates for governor were nominated by meetings of local party leaders assembled at the chief city of the state.

Legislative assumption of nominating function.   The difficulties of assembling a convention at a central point in the state permitted the assumption of the function of nomination for state-wide offices by the members of the party in the state legislature.   The legislators had to gather at the state capital anyway to carry out their legislative duties, and they were, of course, men of influence in their respective constituencies.   Obviously here was a group of men that could readily assume the function of the selection of candidates to be offered by the party to the voters of the state.   "This reflection occurred to the public, and in particular to the members of the state legislatures themselves, and they laid hands on the nomination of the candidates to the state offices." [3] The meetings of the members of the party in the legislature to make nominations consisted of a joint session of the members in both houses and came to be known as legislative caucuses.   The decisions of the caucus were formulated as proclamations or addresses by the participants in their capacity as individuals and not in their capacity as legislators.   Ostrogorski finds that the first instance of the use of the legislative caucus was in 1790 in the nomination of candidates for governor and lieutenant governor; by 1800, according to Dallinger, the legislative caucus was the prevailing mode of nomination in the states.   The same method came to be used in making nominations for the Presidency, beginning in 1800.

Rise of the "mixed" caucus.   The reign of "King Caucus" was to be short.   The legislative caucus had hardly become firmly established in the states when modifications began to be made to meet its apparent shortcomings.   The caucus was unrepresentative, in that a legislative district was unrepresented in the party legislative caucus if that district was controlled by the opposite party.   To remedy this defect, the "mixed caucus" came into use from place to place.   In the "mixed cau-

[2] M. Ostrogorski, "The Rise and Fall of the Nominating Caucus, Legislative and Congressional," *American Historical Review,* 5 (1900), pp. 255–256.
  [3] Ostrogorski, *op. cit.*, p. 257.

cus" special delegates sat to speak for the party members in those legislative districts represented in the legislature by the opposite party. In
1817 in New York, for example, a mixed caucus was held, "composed of
the Republican members of the legislature, together with delegates
chosen by the Republican voters in those counties represented in the
legislature by Federalist members." [4]

It was not devotion to the abstract notion of representation for all
that led to the introduction of the "mixed caucus"; it was the practical
fact that the pure legislative caucus might bring one result, the mixed
caucus another. "The real reason for the calling of this mixed convention," in New York in 1817, Dallinger tells us, "was the fact that the
friends of De Witt Clinton, who was the real choice of the people, feared
that on account of the opposition of Van Buren and the Albany Re-
gency, their favorite might be defeated in a Legislative Caucus, especially
as Clinton was especially strong in the Federalist counties." [5]

In other states similar alterations in the composition of the legislative
caucus were made after about 1810. The course of evolution is often
traced in the following way. The legislative caucus was replaced by the
"mixed caucus," which, in turn, gave way to the "mixed convention."
In the mixed convention, legislators were permitted to sit only if a
delegate especially elected by their county or district to serve in the
convention was not present.[6] Finally, the pure convention came to prevail. It is not necessarily to be supposed, of course, that the nominating process uniformly went through all these phases in each of the
states, but it tended to follow this pattern of development.

Jackson and the congressional caucus. The disappearance of the
congressional caucus as the means for making presidential nominations
gave the *coup de grâce* to the legislative caucus in the states. The congressional caucus fell before the onslaughts of Andrew Jackson, the hero
of New Orleans, the idol of the West, the symbol of a rising spirit of
democracy and egalitarianism. As an aspirant for the presidential
nomination in 1824, Jackson could hardly hope to gain the nomination
at the hands of an unsympathetic congressional caucus. His backers
inaugurated a campaign to discredit the caucus itself. Niles, the editor
of an important journal of the day, observed:

"As my soul liveth" I would rather learn that the halls of Congress were
converted into common brothels than that caucuses of the description stated
should be held in them. I would rather that the sovereignty of the States
should be re-transferred to England, than that the people should be bound to

4 Dallinger, *op. cit.*, p. 28.
5 *Ibid.* Quoted by permission of the President and Fellows of Harvard College.
6 Ostrogorski, *op. cit.*, p. 279.

submit to the dictates of such an assemblage. But the people will not succumb
to office-hunters. . . . The great mass of the American people feel that they
are able to judge for themselves; they do not want a master to direct them how
they shall vote.

A meeting of citizens of Jefferson County, Ohio, late in 1823 resolved: [7]

The time has now arrived when the machinations of the *few* to dictate to
the *many,* however indirectly applied, will be met with becoming firmness, by
a people jealous of their rights . . . the only unexceptional source from which
nominations can proceed is the people themselves. To them belongs the right
of choosing; and they alone can with propriety take any previous steps.

The friends of Jackson boycotted the 1824 Republican caucus, which
was attended by only about one fourth of the Republican members of
Congress. William H. Crawford received the caucus nomination.
The results of the election in November, 1824, indicated that the caucus
as an institution had been discredited.[8] The nominations for the election of 1828 were made by "State legislatures, State legislative caucuses,
public meetings, and by irregular conventions of the people." [9] Only
in 1831 did the convention method of nomination take on final form at
the national level.[10]

The decline of the legislative caucus, of course, represented more than
a mere change in the method of nomination. The adoption of the new
form of nomination reflected a far-reaching shift in political power.
The broadening of the suffrage that was occurring at this time, the increasing influence of the West, and the rise toward political influence of
the less affluent classes all combined to wipe out the legislative caucus,
the instrument and symbol of government by an aristocratic elite. The
old system had its mourners. In 1843, for example, a Whig convention
in Illinois offered a nomination to Governor Duncan of that state who
rejected it with these words: [11]

---

[7] Both quotations are from *ibid.,* pp. 272–273.

[8] For the minutes of the 1824 caucus, see C. L. Jones, *Readings on Parties and
Elections in the United States* (New York: Macmillan, 1912), pp. 44–46. The proceedings contain this recitation: "Resolved, That, in making the foregoing recommendation, the members of this meeting have acted in their individual characters, as
citizens; that they have been induced to this measure from a deep and settled conviction of the importance of union among republicans, throughout the United States,
and, as the best means of collecting and concentrating the feelings and wishes of the
people of the union, upon this important subject. The question being put upon
these resolutions, they were unanimously agreed to."

[9] Dallinger, *op. cit.,* p. 20.

[10] See H. F. Ford, *The Rise and Growth of American Politics* (New York: Macmillan, 1898), chap. 16, on the origins of the convention system.

[11] Quoted by C. E. Merriam and L. Overacker, *Primary Elections* (Chicago: University of Chicago Press, 1928), p. 256.

This convention system, if adopted by both parties, will make our government a prize to be sought after by political gamblers. It throws the chains of slavery and degradation around its votaries, prostrates the fine feelings of nature, extinguishes every spark of patriotism, creates jealousies, distrusts, and angry divisions in society, and will ultimately make us an easy prey to some fiend, or despot, at the head of an army or church, whose followers, like themselves, love the spoils of power better than the liberty of their country. . .

In fact, I look upon the convention system as designed by its authors to change the government from the free will of the people into the hands of designing politicians, and which must in a short time drive from public employment every honest man in the country. Is it not so to a great extent already?

2. THE CONVENTION SYSTEM

The convention system that was gradually substituted over the entire country for the legislative caucus as a method of nominating party candidates was essentially an indirect selection of nominees by the entire party membership. For the nomination of candidates for offices filled by a state-wide vote, the state convention came everywhere to be used. In practice the state convention consisted of delegates chosen directly by the party membership in local units, towns, cities, or counties; or it consisted of delegates chosen by county conventions, the delegates to which had been selected by the party membership in smaller local units.

The procedure for setting in motion and conducting the state convention resembled in general that now followed with respect to the national nominating convention. The initial step was the issuance by the state central committee of a call for a convention; the call indicated the time and place for holding the convention and the number of delegates that each city, town, or county was entitled to send to the convention. Each local unit would then select its delegates either to the state convention or to the county convention, which, in turn, would select the delegates to the state convention. The meetings of voters or party members to select their delegates were called variously "precinct conventions," "caucuses," or "primaries." The delegates assembled from the entire state in convention would proceed to nominate the party candidates. Similar procedures and practices prevailed in the nomination of candidates for city, county, and state legislative offices, and for the national House of Representatives. The convention was adapted to whatever territorial unit served as the area for the selection of public officials.[12]

Democratic spirit of convention system. In spirit the convention

[12] For a full description of the convention system, see Dallinger, *op. cit.*, chap. 3.

system marked a sharp break with the tradition represented by the legislative caucus. The convention mechanism constituted a means for transmitting, from local assemblies of the rank and file of party membership, the wishes and impulses of the mass of party membership to a central point, where the selection of nominees was made. The adoption of the convention system thus reflected a profound change in the distribution of political power. The aristocratic leadership working through the legislative caucuses was gradually deposed, and the notion that the "general will" of the mass of party membership should govern in the selection of party nominees became dominant. The convention was a means for the expression of that general will; it was a representative government of the party.

Factional control of conventions. In the previous consideration of the general nature of party and party organization the possibility and, in fact, the tendency for groups to be controlled by small cliques of men working in concert toward a common end were indicated. The convention system was susceptible to control and management in this fashion, and party organizations and factions soon set about to determine the outcome of the representative process within the party. Moreover, coincident with the introduction of the convention certain developments occurred that greatly increased the burden of parties. The broadening of the suffrage through the reduction or elimination of property-holding and tax-paying qualifications increased the number of persons eligible to vote and to participate in party affairs. The convention and the broadening of the suffrage, in a way, were parallel results of a common cause. In addition to the broadening of the suffrage, in the 'thirties and 'forties other elements enlarged the task of the party system. Jacksonian democracy had its repercussions in state constitutions, city charters, and local government law in general; officers formerly appointed were made directly elective by the people; terms of office were shortened. These developments increased the volume of work that the party had to perform.

Urbanism and the convention system. The conditions of party operation came to be seriously altered by the growth of urban communities. The predominantly rural character of the nation at the time of the establishment of the convention system prevented, through the force of community sentiment, abuses that became prevalent as cities grew in size and number. After the Civil War the control of government became an even more valuable prize, and to gain that control men were willing to introduce abuses into the party convention system. The process of concentration of wealth, of gaining control over natural resources, and of gaining monopoly rights or franchises within the rapidly growing cities all required a complacent or friendly government.[13]

Abuses of the convention system. In the workings of the convention certain abuses became widespread. These practices that brought the system into disrepute occurred at either of two points: in the caucus or primary—the initial gathering of voters in precincts or other small units to select their delegates or representatives—and in the convention itself. In the primaries or caucuses there was no assurance in the cities that attendance would be limited to members of the party concerned. In Baltimore, it was said: "The roughs of both parties unite to carry for each other primaries in their class interest, to drive away the respectable element, and when not numerically strong enough, to stuff the ballot box with 'pudding tickets,'—one ticket sometimes enclosing some twenty slips,—which the rascally election judges deliberately open and count for their nominee." [14]

In Boston the Democratic caucuses were "simply meetings to ratify the dictates of the ward committees. In each ward the ward committee, composed of ten or a dozen men, make a 'slate nomination' of those whom they desire to be the party candidates for representatives in the legislature from that ward. These slate nominations are sure to be victorious at the caucus, no matter what the vote may be." [15]

Another practice designed to facilitate machine control of the primary was the so-called "snap" primary or caucus. The organization in control of the party machinery would give only a short notice of the time and place for the meeting of the primary; the controlling faction, ready, informed, and alert, would have the advantage in managing the caucus; minority and opposition elements of the party, taken by surprise, would lose the day.

If the controlling faction within the party did its work well in the caucus, that is, brought about the selection of men in their camp as delegates to the convention, control of the convention itself was assured. This method was not the sole reliance in controlling conventions; abuses and frauds occurred in the conventions as well as in the primaries. The faction in control of the temporary organization of the convention at times unfairly refused to seat duly elected delegates and recognized contesting delegations affiliated with the organization faction. At other times the convention, instead of being a high-minded deliberative body

[13] For a picture of this trend, done in broad strokes, see Matthew Josephson, *The Robber Barons* (New York: Harcourt, Brace, 1934). For a more revealing and more intimate picture, see *Autobiography of William Allen White* (New York: Macmillan, 1946).

[14] Quoted by Dallinger, *op. cit.*, p. 112.

[15] *Ibid.*, p. 117. Quoted by permission of the President and Fellows of Harvard College.

coolly choosing the ablest leaders as candidates, became completely
subject to control by the state or city boss. Conventions, in fact, became a symbol of bossism. Professor Charles E. Merriam records his
experience as a delegate to a nominating convention: [16]

> I recall my last local convention under the old "deliberative" regime. The
> delegates had been chosen on the day before, and as soon as the returns began
> to come in the bosses gathered and began to appraise their strength in terms
> of the new battle. All night long the leaders counting their blocks of dele-
> gates had been sitting in high conclave, dividing the places on the ticket, trad-
> ing back and forth, combining and recombining, bluffing and finessing. There
> were so many commissioners here and so many there, a county office here and
> another there, the patronage value of each carefully calculated in the bargain,
> sub-jobs, arrangements, understandings in regard to a wide variety of per-
> quisites and privileges, all nicely calculated in determining the equitable
> balance. Over all hung the shadow of possible war in the convention, pos-
> sible combination for control between some two or more of the trading powers.
> We assemble at high noon, a restless multitude of delegates; half-past twelve
> comes and nothing happens; one o'clock and we become impatient; but we are
> told that "They" have not arrived. "They" have not finished the slate.
> "They" will soon be here. "They" are coming and finally "They" arrive,
> and the convention solemnly opens. A motion is made here and there. A
> vote is called for and there is a murmur of voices. Many voices, for they must
> all be named by roll-call and the incantation continues. Another and another.
> Who was named then? And finally we hasten out, buying copies of an eve-
> ning extra, and learn the names of the nominees. The ritual is over. And
> this is sometimes called "deliberation."

The tendency toward machine domination of the convention arose
because of several factors. There is, in truth, in almost all kinds of assemblies a tendency for a minority to guide and manage the course of
events. That minority control is especially necessary and particularly
noticeable in *ad hoc* gatherings, which disperse after attending to the
single purpose of their meeting. Furthermore, the magnitude of the
task before the convention—the nomination of a long list of candidates
—stimulated oligarchic tendencies by necessitating many carefully
weighted bargains and a skilful allocation of honors to maintain discipline and unity in the party. Perhaps the factor that contributed most
to oligarchical control of the convention system was the simple fact
that various interests were willing and anxious to spend time and money
to control it. The party organization itself had an obvious interest in
seeking to retain control. Affiliated with the machine were interests
that furnished the sinews of war. In some states it was the railroads

[16] Merriam and Overacker, *op. cit.*, pp. 259–260.

that dominated the machines; [17] in most states the insurance companies had a hand in party policy; in cities the most common cluster of interests was made up of the public utilities, the party machine, and the underworld.

Regulation of conventions. An attempt was made to control the abuses of the convention system by public regulation. Originally the party was a private association; it was no more illegal to commit fraud in the party caucus or primary than it would be to do so in the election of officers of a drinking club. Beginning in California in 1866, regulation of caucuses and conventions by law, at first optional with the party and later compulsory for all parties, was attempted.[18] By the time that regulation became fairly general, the convention system was on the way out. Popular revolt against control by the groups and interests that managed the conventions was directed also against the convention itself, an instrument of domination by the "interests."

Although it has been displaced generally by the direct primary as a method for making nominations, the convention still lives as an institution. It remains on the national level as the method of nominating presidential candidates. In states not using the presidential primary, a state convention generally chooses delegates to the national convention. Connecticut and Rhode Island retain the convention method to nominate candidates for all state offices.[19] The populous, and politically important, states of New York and Indiana use the convention to make nominations for certain offices chosen by state-wide vote.[20] Michigan employs the convention for nominations to lesser offices filled by state-wide vote; in some other states minor parties use the convention; and in some localities it is the prevailing method for making nominations for local office. More generally the convention is retained in direct-primary states as the governing body for the party and as a means for the drafting and adoption of party platforms.

3. DIRECT PRIMARIES

The convention went the way of the legislative caucus and fundamentally for the same reason. "King Caucus" abdicated before the

---

[17] See, for example, W. B. Thorson, "Washington State Nominating Conventions," *Pacific Northwest Quarterly*, 35 (1944), pp. 99–119.

[18] See E. C. Campbell, "Party Nominations in California (1860–1909)," *Southwestern Social Science Quarterly*, 12 (1931), pp. 245–257.

[19] Rhode Island has in recent years considered the adoption of the direct primary. See J. W. Lederle, "Rhode Island Weighs the Direct Primary," *National Municipal Review*, 32 (1943), pp. 258–259.

[20] It would be useful to have studies of the operations of the convention in those states that still use it.

advance of the triumphant Jacksonian democracy, which erected the convention system in its stead as a means whereby the mass of party membership could express its will on party candidacies. Hardly had the convention system been established when it became apparent that the inner core of the party, the party organization, would play an important role in the determination of the choices to be made by the conventions. The advantages enjoyed by those with time and money to devote to politics under the convention system were countered by state regulation of the convention system. But state regulation of the convention system hardly had a trial before the demand arose for the direct primary, the system by which the party membership votes directly on aspirants for party candidacy rather than indirectly through the selection of delegates to conventions.

Movement for direct primary. As early as 1842 the direct primary was employed by the Democratic party in Crawford County, Pennsylvania; other counties in Pennsylvania soon adopted the system. The Crawford *Democrat* in November, 1845, gave the following reply to an inquiry about the Crawford County system: [21]

> Meadville respectfully suggests the adoption of the "Crawford County System" as it is generally known by that name in this state. . . . We consider it the most fair and honorable system that the Democratic party can do battle under. Under its provisions, every member of the party is heard; there can be no intrigue or corruption used. . . . The sovereign voters themselves declare who shall be their candidates, and the cry of bargain and sale, packed conventions, disobeying instructions, &c., will be hushed.

The arguments for the primary advanced in Crawford County in the 1840's were in essence the same as those put forward when the direct primary made its greatest gains, but the widespread adoption of the primary was to await more propitious circumstances.

In the post-Civil War era the party organizations in many states and cities came under the control of plutocratic elements. The elements controlling the state organizations were often the railroads, and in the cities corrupt machines allied with public utilities and other privilege seekers manipulated the convention system to suit their ends. The dominance of the party organizations and the interests affiliated with them was simplified by the fact that in many states, both northern and southern, nomination by the major party was equivalent to election. If the party organization controlled the convention system, it controlled, in effect, the election. The growth of population, particularly in the

---

[21] Quoted by James H. Booser, "Origin of the Direct Primary," *National Municipal Review*, 24 (1935), pp. 222–223.

cities, laid the basis for some of the dissatisfaction with the convention system. "When the population was small, the number of delegates sent to county, district, or state conventions was, relatively to the population, large, and nearly every citizen knew personally the delegate who was to represent him; but when the population increased, the number of delegates became relatively small, their personal relations to most of their constituents were remote, and the delegates came to be what the members of the legislative caucus had been before them, a small ruling class." [22]

New leaders rose to head movements challenging the power of the party machine and of those interests associated with it. The diagnosis of the dissenters was that the "interests" were able to retain their power because of the ease of manipulation of the convention system; therefore, the elimination of the convention system and the substitution of the direct primary were advocated. The Farmers Alliance, the Populists, and, later, the Progressives sought the abolition of the convention system and the establishment of the direct primary. In the cities middle-class reform groups, angered by the abuses of the convention system by the party machine, championed the direct primary.

In South Carolina the direct primary system first achieved fairly complete development. In that state "Pitchfork" Ben Tillman, even before the Farmers Alliance was formed, had "laid his plans for the overturn of the reigning Bourbon dynasty and for the control of the Democratic party by the hitherto inarticulate rural whites." He had "convinced himself" that the misdeeds of the Bourbon rulers of the state "had much to do with the economic distress of the back-country farmers." [23] The triumph of the Tillmanites in South Carolina in 1891 was followed by the replacement of the convention system in the choice of nominees for all public offices, including United States Senators, by the voters at the primaries. Concurrently the primary movement was in motion in Georgia; by 1882 it was widely used in nominating local candidates, and in 1891 the Democratic state committee expressed a desire that it be employed generally in the nomination of local candidates. [24]

Although in various states and localities the direct primary was experimented with in a tentative and cautious way, the system did not come into wide use until the Progressive movement swept the country.

[22] C. B. Spahr, "Method of Nomination to Public Office: An Historical Sketch," *Proceedings*, Chicago Conference for Good City Government, 1904, pp. 323–324.

[23] J. D. Hicks, *Populist Revolt* (Minneapolis: University of Minnesota Press, 1931), pp. 143–144. See also F. B. Simkins, *Pitchfork Ben Tillman* (Baton Rouge: Louisiana State University Press, 1944), p. 124.

[24] L. M. Holland, *The Direct Primary in Georgia* (Urbana, 1945), pp. 5–6.

That movement set off factional strife within the parties, between the progressives and the standpatters, for control of the party machinery and for control of party nominations.

In Wisconsin in 1903 the Progressives, under the leadership of the late Senator La Follette, brought about the passage of the first state-wide direct primary law.[25] Other states, mainly in the West where the Progressive movement was strongest, soon followed. "The years 1907, 1908, and 1909 were banner years for the direct primary movement. In 1907 Iowa, Nebraska, Missouri, North Dakota, South Dakota, and Washington passed such laws; in 1908 Illinois, Kansas, Oklahoma, and Ohio followed; and finally, in 1909, Arizona, Arkansas, California, Idaho, Michigan, Nevada, New Hampshire, and Tennessee were added to the list."[26] By 1917 all the states except Utah, Connecticut, New Mexico, and Rhode Island had adopted the direct primary method of nomination for some or all offices filled by state-wide election. However, in 1921, New York and, in 1929, Indiana returned to the convention system for the nomination of candidates for offices filled by statewide election. In 1927 Utah adopted the direct primary for all nominations. New Mexico followed in 1938 with the enactment of legislation first applied in 1940. Thus, for nominations of party candidates for state and local offices and for United States Senators and Representatives the direct primary is the predominating method.

Organization slates in primaries. The advocates of the direct primary had a simple faith in democracy; they thought that if the people, the rank and file of the party membership, were only given an opportunity to express their will through some such mechanism as the direct primary, candidates would be selected who would be devoted to the interests of the people as a whole. They failed to foresee that within the party some winnowing process would occur to narrow the range of choice in the primary. The inner core of the party, the party organization with its functionaries in precincts, wards, counties, and state, has in many jurisdictions acted in advance of the primary to agree on a slate of candidates to back in the primary. In Cook County (Chicago), Illinois, for example, it is the custom to present to the party membership a slate supported by the party organization for nomination in the primary. The Democratic slate in the 1932 primaries was entitled "Candidates Endorsed by the Democratic County Central Committee and the Democratic State Central Committee." This slate in-

---

[25] See A. F. Lovejoy, *La Follette and the Establishment of the Direct Primary in Wisconsin, 1890–1904* (New Haven: Yale University Press, 1941).

[26] Merriam and Overacker, *op. cit.*, p. 62. This volume contains the most comprehensive account of the direct primary.

cluded forty-three persons supported for nomination for federal, state, and local offices.   At the April, 1934, primaries forty-eight persons were listed as "Regular Republican Candidates, Recommended by the Cook County Republican Central Committee."   At the same primary a list of "Candidates Endorsed by the Regular Democratic Organization of Cook County" was circulated.   In preparation for the Chicago Democratic primary of 1947, Martin Kennelly accepted the organization's support for the mayoralty nomination at a meeting of the city committee of fifty ward committeemen, but the press reported that he had been "picked" earlier by a committee of fourteen Democratic leaders.

In New York City in 1941, to furnish an additional illustration, the five Democratic leaders of the City—Edward J. Flynn of the Bronx, Frank J. Kelly of Brooklyn, Christopher D. Sullivan of Manhattan, James A. Roe of Queens, and William T. Fetherston of Richmond— named a city slate in accordance with the local custom.   After their action Mr. Kelly announced: [27]

At a conference attended by the chairmen of the executive committees of the several Democratic county organizations it was agreed to recommend to the executive and county committees in each county that the Hon. William O'Dwyer, District Attorney of Kings County, be chosen as the Democratic designee for the nomination for Mayor, David H. Knott of Manhattan for Controller and M. Maldwin Fertig of the Bronx for President of the Council. It is expected that the several committees will take the necessary steps to make Judge O'Dwyer, Mr. Knott and Mr. Fertig the regular Democratic designees and that their action will be approved at the ensuing primaries.

Ratification by the county committees was principally a matter of form. The New York County Democratic Committee, more generally known as Tammany Hall, the press reported, "took about a half hour to endorse the city-wide ticket selected by the five county leaders two weeks ago." [28]   Ratification of the party action by the voters at the primary followed.   The Republican organization was unable to reach unanimous agreement on its nominee; two of the five county leaders opposed the nomination of Mayor LaGuardia.   His lead in popular vote in the primary in the three counties in which the Republican county leaders supported him was enough to give him the nomination.   It should not be supposed, however, that the New York practice is universal in direct-primary jurisdictions.   In many areas intraparty differences are not ironed out before the primary, and the action of the voters in the primary is a genuine selection, not a mere ratification.

When one identifies the individuals influential in the determination

[27] *The New York Times,* July 17, 1941.
[28] *Ibid.,* July 30, 1941.

of the make-up of the organization slate, he locates the controlling element in the machine. In some city organizations a single city leader may hold enough power to determine the names to be included on the party slate. Thus, when Vare was the Republican leader in Philadelphia, he dominated in the making of these selections.[29] In another type of situation the organization choice may rest in a small group of city leaders, which arrives at its decisions by a process of trading that is tempered by estimates of the vote-pulling power of those persons prominent enough to be considered for the party slate. The bargaining and compromise within the party organization in connection with the preparation of the slate to be backed by the organization in the direct primary very much resembles the process of trading that went on within the conventions.[30]

In a few instances the role of the party organization in presenting slates has been formalized through the adoption of a pre-primary convention. Always when the party machine presents a slate there must be some sort of informal pre-primary conference or convention of party leaders, but in some instances these conventions are prescribed by law and operate under rules laid down by law. The Colorado law provides for a pre-primary convention at which one ballot is taken, and the name of every person receiving 10 per cent or more of the votes in the convention is placed on the primary ballot. In South Dakota a pre-primary convention system was in operation from 1917 to 1929 under which majority and minority candidates were named for inclusion on the primary ballot. In Massachusetts such a system was adopted in 1932 under which candidates endorsed by the convention were placed on the ballot, but other aspirants for the nomination could be added by petition. The Massachusetts scheme was abandoned in 1937. In 1943 Nebraska adopted a law providing that a pre-primary convention might endorse candidates for nomination by statewide vote in the primary. Utah followed Nebraska in 1947.

Unification of the organization in support of a slate of candidates alone gives the candidates strength in the primary, but the organization's strength is enhanced by the low popular participation in the primary. Participation is likely to be especially low in the voting on minor offices, which may control patronage of concern to the organization. The Democratic primary held in Baltimore in June, 1946, fur-

[29] D. H. Kurtzman, *Methods of Controlling Votes in Philadelphia* (Philadelphia, 1935), p. 15.

[30] The existence of the primary, however, makes it more difficult to maintain discipline over dissentient factions which, if they disagree with the recommendations of the majority of the organization, may appeal to the rank and file of the party in the primary.

nishes an excellent illustration of the power of a small but disciplined organization vote. The strongest city faction, led by Willian Curran, did not carry the primary for its candidates for governor—the nominee incidentally had the support of a lesser factional leader—but it did win the nomination for its candidates for about two thirds of the city's seats in the state legislature and for five of the six court clerkships filled by popular vote. Voting on these lesser offices fell far below the vote for candidates for nomination for governor and for United States Senator, as is pictured in Figure 17, which shows how small a vote it is necessary

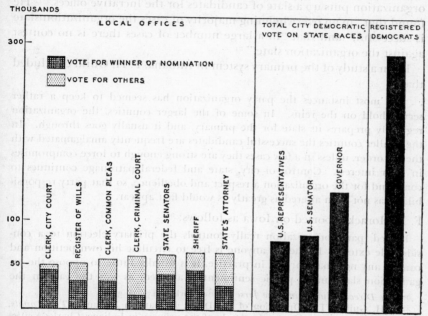

Figure 17. Total Vote Cast in 1946 Baltimore Democratic Primary on State-wide Offices and Local Offices

to mobilize to form a plurality to control the outcome of a direct primary when popular interest is low.

Primaries and organization power. The significant question about the direct primary is whether its use instead of the convention alters the results of the nominating process. Does the primary make it possible for a faction that might be suppressed under the convention procedure to capture the nomination? The evidence on this point is far from complete. One index, however, may be found in the degree of success with which the "organization" candidates win the nomination in the direct primary, if it is assumed that the organization could almost in-

variably control the outcome of conventions. It should be said that
no trustworthy data are available on the extent to which the party
organizations over the country as a whole prepare slates in advance of
the primary. Although information is available only for scattered
localities, that information may be examined to see whether it points to
any general conclusions.

The late R. S. Boots, in a study of the use of the direct primary system
for state and local nominations in New Jersey, published in 1917, concluded that "in almost all of the important primary contests the party
organization puts up a slate of candidates for the lucrative offices." He
found that "in an overwhelming majority of cases the organization slate
is successful," and that "in a large number of cases there is no contest
against the organization slate." [31]

From a study of the primary system in Indiana, F. H. Guild concluded
that [32]

. . . in most instances the party organization has seemed to keep a rather
secure hold on the reins. In some of the larger counties, the organization
regularly prepares its slate for the primary, and it usually goes through. In
the smaller counties the successful candidates are frequently amalgamated with
the old order, unless in a few cases they are strong enough to force compromises
in their interest. Control of city, state and federal patronage continues to
command for the organization a respect and obedience, so that party responsibility has not been altered as greatly as would first appear.

F. E. Horack reported on Iowa as follows: [33]

Indeed, party organization really controls the primary election to a considerable extent. In theory, anyone is free to circulate his own petition and
contest any nomination; but in practice, it is usually futile to oppose the organization slate unless public sentiment is aroused, as was the case in the

[31] *The Direct Primary in New Jersey* (New York, 1917), p. 347.

[32] F. H. Guild, "The Operation of the Direct Primary in Indiana," *The Annals*,
106 (1923), pp. 172–180. In another study of the primary in Indiana, Charles Kettle-
borough assumed that when there was only one candidate for nomination that this
candidate was named by or was acceptable to the organization and ascertained the
number of uncontested primary nominations. "An examination of the primary election returns in Indiana shows that for the years 1916, 1918, and 1920, out of a total
of 1,049 offices for which candidates were to be nominated, there were 623 or 59 per
cent in which no contest developed." The percentages of uncontested nominations
by party were: Democrats, 59; Republicans, 57; Progressives, 89. "The Direct Primary in Indiana," *National Municipal Review*, 10 (1921), pp. 166–170. Professor
K. H. Porter has made a similar analysis of candidacies for nomination for county
offices in Iowa in 1944. In about a third of the counties no office was contested in
either the primary or the election; in over half the counties no nomination was contested in the primary; in many other counties only one or two offices were contested.
"The Deserted Primary in Iowa," *American Political Science Review*, 39 (1945), pp.
732–740.

[33] F. E. Horack, "The Workings of the Direct Primary in Iowa, 1908–1922," *The
Annals*, 106 (1923), pp. 148–157.

senatorial primary of 1922. The failure of the organization to control at all times is one of the chief causes for the demand for the repeal of the law by it.

During the period of use of the direct primary for state-wide nominations in New York, each year of a state election the majority parties held "conferences" or "unofficial conventions." In no instance, said Professor Boots, did an independent candidate defeat "the recipient of a conference endorsement, that is, the regular organization candidate. Can it be that no equally fit candidate has entered the lists against the 'slate,' or is it possible that organization support is so overwhelmingly decisive that successful opposition becomes hopeless?" [34]

In a great many jurisdictions, however, the party organization is moribund and plays no significant role in the primary; and in some instances organization endorsement offers no complete assurance of nomination. The Democratic State Central Committee of California, for example, in 1922 suggested a list of "candidates for all state offices (except governor), for United States Senator, and for members of Congress and the state legislature. These 'suggestions' were not generally accepted. . . . But in a number of districts there were no candidates in the Democratic primaries except those named by the committee. Doubtless there are other cases of the same sort of thing, some perhaps not so open. But those who allege the existence of widespread machine domination of the primaries have yet to prove their case." [35]

Occasionally the party officials, from precinct committeemen to state chairman, selected at the primaries are opposed to a candidate nominated by the same voters at the same primary election; this divergence gives a measure of the significance of the primary as a nominating process. In Indiana, for example, "Mr. Beveridge won the nomination for United States senator in the Republican primary in 1922. But it was unquestionably Senator Watson who secured a dominant control of the party organization through the election of a state chairman and consequent control of the state central committee." [36] In Iowa in one instance the standpat element of the Republican party controlled the state convention that met after the primary at which Brookhart was nominated for the United States Senate. "The convention refused to call upon Mr. Brookhart for a speech, or to indorse his candidacy, demanded the repeal of primary, and inserted a plank against socialists and demagogues." [37] A newspaper organ of the standpat wing of the party

[34] "The Trend of the Direct Primary," *American Political Science Review*, 16 (1922), p. 423.
[35] Victor J. West, "The California Direct Primary," *The Annals*, 106 (1923), p. 122.
[36] Guild, *op. cit.*, p. 179.
[37] Horack, *op. cit.*, p. 149.

spoke of the convention as "the voice of the people speaking through their accredited representatives chosen by the primary to attend the state convention and it adequately and correctly represents the views and wishes of the Republican voters of this state." Certainly the situation indicates the process of refinement of the voice of the people as it passes through the convolutions of the convention system.

The career of "Happy" Chandler of Kentucky throws light on the effects of the primary system. In 1935 it was a foregone conclusion that the next nominee for governor by the Democratic convention would be Thomas S. Rhea, supported by Governor Laffoon, whose administration controlled the Democratic state organization. Chandler, the lieutenant governor, took advantage of the Governor's absence from the state to convene a special session of the legislature to adopt a mandatory primary law. Governor Laffoon rushed back to the state; the legality of the special session was unsuccessfully challenged; and, after various maneuvers, a primary law was adopted providing for a runoff primary to determine the nominee in case no single candidate received a majority. "It would seem," predicted Henry G. Hodges, "that Kentucky's initial try at the double-barreled primary may lead to a defeat of the Democratic organization candidate, a thing which would have been impossible under the Kentucky convention system of nomination." [38] It did lead to a defeat of the organization candidate for the nomination, and gave "Happy" Chandler a boost in his political career.

Primary tempers machine power. Even though the organization slate is nominated in the primary, there is a likelihood that the picking of the slate will have been influenced to some degree by the knowledge that the slate would have to be defended before the entire party membership in the primary rather than before a small hand-picked convention. Professor Merriam says: [39]

The character of the nominations is determined not only by open and successful resistance to organization nominees, but by the possibility and probability of resistance which is anticipated or discounted or thwarted by the character of the nominations made by the organization itself. A wise machine will make many concessions in order to prevent the raising of the standard of revolt by an opposing faction or by unorganized insurgents. Resistance is generally more readily made under the direct primary than under the convention system. There is always a certain protest vote, and a certain disgruntled vote, and there are always groups within the apparently united machines that are

[38] "Kentucky Gets a Primary Law," *National Municipal Review,* 24 (1935), pp. 478–480. See J. B. Shannon, " 'Happy' Chandler: A Kentucky Epic," in J. T. Salter (ed.), *The American Politician* (Chapel Hill: University of North Carolina Press, 1938).

[39] "Recent Tendencies in Primary Election Systems," *National Municipal Review,* 10 (1921), pp. 87–94.

ready to take advantage of any insurgency for the sake of advancing their own ends.

Charles Evans Hughes in 1921 observed that the victory of organization candidates was often declared to be an objection to the primary system. "Why should they not win? If a party organization is clean, vigorous and efficient, if it has the confidence of the party members, as such an organization should have, it will be influential in advising candidacies, and those who are presented as candidates with the approval of such an organization will in all probability be men who ought to be selected." Mr. Hughes regarded the direct primary as a "weapon in the hands of the voters which they can use with effect in case of need. They are no longer helpless. This fact puts party leaders on their best behavior. It is a safeguard to the astute and unselfish leader who is endeavoring to maintain good standards in line with sound public sentiment. It favors a disposition not to create situations which are likely to challenge a test." [40]

It is only easier to challenge the power of the closely knit party leadership by the formation of a competing party faction under the primary system than under the convention system. But the importance of ease of challenging this power is not to be underestimated. As a measure of self-interest, "regular organizations" and the interests associated with them have been behind most efforts to repeal the direct primary and to return to the convention system. Sometimes a good index of the probable effect of a particular procedure is to identify the interests for and against it. During the wave of reaction following the First World War —the era of Harding and normalcy, of Mellon and reduced income taxes in the upper brackets, of Daugherty and injunctions to liquidate labor—a determined effort to repeal direct primary laws was made. The spirit of the movement was expressed in an address in 1924 by the president of the National Association of Manufacturers. He traced the woes of business back to the "unhappy day when the direct primary became a tragic fact." He argued that the direct primary had "caused a pronounced degeneration in the type of men attracted to the public service." Moreover, he added, the direct primary had "diminished the number of those who know the right and have courage to follow its course, regardless of the cost to themselves." The primary and other devices had, he believed, "almost transformed the legislative department of our government into a mere sounding-board to catch and throw back the babble of the voices of the mob." By the continuation of the direct democratic trend represented by the primary he thought that the way

[40] "The Fate of the Direct Primary," *National Municipal Review,* 10 (1921), pp. 23–31.

would "be prepared for the triumphal entry of the Soviet King just waiting outside the gates." [41]   The president of the National Association of Manufacturers apparently thought that the direct primary handicapped the manufacturers in defending their status against the long-run tendency toward more efficacious public regulation of business.   The "cause" of the tendency toward regulation does not go back to the "tragic fact" of the direct primary; rather, social movements in the direction of greater regulation happened to find expression through the primary and probably would have found expression through whatever nominating process existed.

It is apparent that the direct primary system makes more difficult the domination of the nomination process by the political organization. That the party organization has greatest difficulty in winning the nominations for its candidates for the more conspicuous posts, such as governor and United States Senator, also seems obvious.   Furthermore, that the effects of the primary system on the power of the party machine have differed from place to place is a patent conclusion.   Nevertheless to arrive at valid conclusions on the significance of the adoption of the direct primary is difficult in the absence of more first hand studies of its workings in different states and cities.

The variation in the effects of the primary system from state to state suggests that one must look deeper than the nominating process to ascertain the factors responsible for the pattern of political power in a particular state.   The factions battling the old machines had to win under the old convention system before they could bring about the adoption of the direct primary.   This new nominating method was presumably adopted on the theory that the faction that won enough power to institute the primary could retain control of the party more readily under that method than under the convention system.   Consequently, the adoption of the direct primary might be said to be result rather than cause.   The varying power of the party organizations in securing the selection of candidates in the direct primaries suggests further inquiries. In direct primary states like Illinois, Ohio, and Pennsylvania, there are powerful organizations or factions in each party, and often the word of the organization is final.   On the other hand, in the direct primary states of the Far West the veriest political tyro frequently gains the nomination without any organization support; as a matter of fact, "regular organization" slates are not always offered.

Why is there a strong party organization in one instance and not in another?   Obviously the existence or nonexistence of the direct primary has little to do with the situation.   Strong party organizations, with their orderly and effective distribution of favors and penalties, are firmly rooted in the fabric of society. The accepted gradations of rank and status, the habituation to a scale of social priorities, the acknowledgment of the prerogatives of an oligarchical leadership, all depend on factors other than the nominating process.

Primaries in one-party states. Commentators on the direct primary often generalize broadly for the entire country, forgetting that in a great many jurisdictions the primary is really the election. More states are "sure" Democratic or Republican in state elections than in presidential elections. More counties and cities are "sure" for one party or the other than in either state or presidential elections. Probably over one third of the counties are one-party counties locally. For a considerable proportion of the state and local elections the primary must be thought of, not as a means of nomination, but virtually as a means of election. The South is commonly thought to be the principal one-party area, but in local government affairs the one-party system prevails in sizeable areas in other parts of the country.

The extent to which the primary becomes the election is suggested by the material in Table 13 (page 362), which indicates that in the southern states in state-wide elections the primary vote far exceeds that in the general election. The battle is fought out in the primary and only enough voters turn up at the general election to make a formal ratification of the primary choices. A word of caution about the figures is in order. They are for an off-year; the relationship between primary and general election vote is probably different in presidential years. Moreover, the ranking of particular states in the listing gyrates with such factors as the heat of the primary contest, the importance of the nomination being made, and other like factors.

Lest the figures in Table 13 convey the impression that the level of participation in southern primaries equals the level of participation in general elections elsewhere, a few additional figures are in order. In 1944 primary contests occurred in three Mississippi congressional districts. The percentages of the 1940 population of the age of 21 and over and of the 1940 white population 21 and over participating in these primaries were as follows:

	Total	White
1st District	9.6%	15.0%
2nd District	12.6	25.1
4th District	6.6	9.9

With these figures may be compared the rates of participation in the 1944 primaries of three California districts, selected more or less at random. The percentages of the total 1940 population 21 and over voting in the primaries of these districts were: 1st, 33.3; 3rd, 30.5; 9th, 26.7. Although in all these districts one candidate won the nominations of both parties and there was no contest in the general election, the percentages of participation in the general election were: 1st, 42.9; 3rd, 45.4; 9th, 32.8. Of course, much more data would have to be examined to obtain a general valid measure of participation in primaries in one-party states, but these figures are sufficient to rebut broad assertions about high levels of participation in such primaries.

TABLE 13

Total Participation in Primaries as a Percentage of Total Participation in General Elections, 1942 [a]

State	Per cent	State	Per cent
South Carolina	984.0	Washington	62.0
Georgia	487.6	Illinois	59.5
Alabama	403.8	Vermont	57.5
Louisiana	375.5	Pennsylvania	57.2
Texas	340.4	Nevada	53.5
Mississippi	258.6	Kansas	49.7
Florida	241.5	Nebraska	48.8
Arkansas	230.4	Maryland	47.0
Tennessee	173.5	Iowa	44.4
Oklahoma	113.6	Indiana	43.3
Arizona	103.0	Wisconsin	43.2
North Carolina	91.7	Idaho	43.0
North Dakota	76.9	Michigan	41.8
Oregon	75.3	New Hampshire	39.6
Montana	69.5	New Jersey	38.3
New Mexico	68.3	Ohio	37.2
South Dakota	67.2	Colorado	32.4
Wyoming	65.7	Maine	31.1
West Virginia	66.4	Massachusetts	31.1
Minnesota	66.0	Utah	24.9
Missouri	62.9		

[a] The percentages were arrived at by using the total vote for all candidates in all party primaries on the office polling the highest total vote and the total vote on the office polling the highest vote in the general election. The basic figures were from *Statistical Abstract of the United States, 1944–45*, pp. 256–257.

In the one-party states the primaries serve as means for fighting out disputes between factions of the dominant party. Conceivably these factions could amount, for state and local affairs, to something like the two major parties in national affairs. In some instances this condition may be approximated, but more generally the lines of cleavage between these factions are even hazier than those between the parties nationally. The factions are often transient followings of particular leaders based on the force of personality and nothing else. Issues, if they exist, are apt to be well concealed from the voter.[42] The primary, however, permits factions in one-party states to settle their differences without forming two distinct parties and thereby endangering the attachment of the state to one or the other of the parties in national affairs. In the South the primary has served as a means of nullifying national constitutional prohibitions against discrimination in the suffrage on account of color, but in recent years this function has been threatened by Supreme Court decisions.[43]

Runoff primaries. There remain to be mentioned, for the sake of comprehensiveness, certain problems and variations of the direct primary. One problem that framers of direct-primary legislation have had to deal with is the question of nominations by a minority of those participating in the primary. If there are three or more aspirants for the nomination, the vote polled by the leading candidate may fall short of a majority. Should the nomination go to the man with a plurality, or should some device be used to require a majority vote within the party to win the nomination? To prevent plurality nominations and to achieve formal majority decision, some eleven states[44] have at one time or another employed a system of preferential voting in the primary. "Preferential voting is a device whereby a voter in a primary or general election may indicate on his ballot a first and second choice, and, it may be, more choices as to candidates for a particular office with a view to combining or transferring choices when the votes are counted in such a way as to produce at least a nominal majority in favor of a particular candidate."[45] The preferential vote leads to complications in voting and in counting the vote, and for this reason, as well as because of local political circumstances, it has been abandoned in all state primary systems.

An alternative method of preventing nominations by less than a majority of voters participating in the primary is the runoff or second primary. Under this system, if no person obtains a majority at the primary, a second primary is held at which the choice is between the

---

[42] See O. Douglas Weeks, "The Texas Direct Primary System," *Southwestern Social Science Quarterly*, 13 (1932), pp. 95–120; S. D. Myres, Jr., "Politics in the South," *Arnold Foundation Studies in Public Affairs* (1934).

[43] The white primary is treated in chapter 16.

[44] Washington, North Dakota, Idaho, Wisconsin, Florida, Maryland, Minnesota, Alabama, Indiana, Louisiana, Oklahoma.

[45] Weeks, "Summary of the History and Present Status of Preferential Voting in State Direct Primary Systems," *Southwestern Social Science Quarterly*, 18 (1937–1938), pp. 64–67.

two persons who polled the two highest votes at the first primary. Most of the states that have used the runoff primary are one-party southern states in which the winner of the primary almost always wins the election. In a one-party state the possibility of a nomination by a minority is thus a matter of considerably greater importance than in a two-party state. Even in the southern states the adoption of the runoff system has often arisen from local factional disputes rather than from attachments to principle. In such situations an outstanding personality has developed a following great enough to assure a plurality in the primary. His opponents sometimes have brought about the adoption of a runoff device as a means whereby they could unite after the first primary to bring about his defeat. Sometimes when this personality disappears from the scene, the runoff goes out of use.[46]

In principle there can be no objection to plurality nominations; pluralities are adequate for victory in elections. In all probability the existence of a runoff primary encourages a multiplicity of factions within the party. A factional leader may be willing to gamble on winning at least second place in the first primary and run his own candidate, whereas the incentive for combination with other factions would be much greater if a plurality were adequate to nominate. Plurality nominations, like plurality elections, should encourage, although not necessarily assure, a "bi-factionalism" within parties.[47]

Multiplicity of candidacies. The ease with which aspirants for nominations may have their names placed on the primary ballot has at

[46] See, for example, Harry Barth, "Oklahoma Adopts Preferential Voting in the Primary," *National Municipal Review*, 14 (1925), pp. 410–413; L. V. Murphy, "Two Trials of Oklahoma's Run-off Primary," *Southwestern Social Science Quarterly*, 14 (1933), pp. 156–174; Joe Park, "That Elusive Majority," *National Municipal Review*, 29 (1940), pp. 675–678. States that have used the runoff system include Alabama, Arkansas, Florida, Georgia, Kentucky, Louisiana, Mississippi, North Carolina, Oklahoma, South Carolina, Tennessee, Texas, Utah. Most of these states still use it. On the special problem of plurality nominations in New Mexico, see Paul Beckett and Walter L. McNutt, *The Direct Primary in New Mexico* (Albuquerque: Division of Research, Department of Government, University of New Mexico, 1947).

[47] In two states it is possible to win nominations for state-wide offices without a popular plurality. In Maryland and Georgia, usually classified as direct primary states, the nomination is technically made by a convention, but delegates act something after the fashion of presidential electors. The apportionment of delegates in the convention follows that in the state legislature and thus discriminates against the urban communities. One urban primary vote does not equal one rural vote when translated into convention votes. The Georgia unit system in July, 1946, resulted in the nomination of Eugene Talmadge for governor despite the fact that his popular vote was exceeded by that polled by another candidate. A subsequent attack on the constitutionality of the unit system, on the ground of denial of equal protection of the law, was rejected by the Supreme Court. In the Maryland Republican senatorial primary of 1932 a candidate won a majority of the popular vote but lost the nomination because of the unit system.

times resulted in long lists of persons from whom the voter has to choose at the primary. The usual procedure for placing a name on the ballot is by petition signed by a relatively small number of voters. In Michigan, Dorr says, "the circulation of nominating petitions and the ensuing campaigns are viewed by many as a convenient method of advertising business and professional wares, by others as an opportunity for disseminating social, economic, political, and religious doctrines and theories." In that state the general agreement was, he says, that "some system must be devised which would discourage frivolous candidates without imposing undue penalties upon those who were genuinely sincere." The Michigan legislature enacted a law creating alternative methods of getting a name on the ballot for state legislative nominations. The petition method was retained, but a larger number of signatures was required. As an alternative the aspirant might pay a fee of $100, which would be returned if a substantial number of votes was received. A charter amendment in Detroit established the fee method as the exclusive way of placing a name on the primary ballot for city offices, with provision for return of the fee if the aspirant polled half as many votes as the person receiving the nomination. Professor Dorr feels that the excessive number of candidacies for nominations under the primary in Michigan creates a serious problem for the voter,[48] but elsewhere the matter of frivolous candidatures is not viewed so seriously. Although there may be a dozen candidates for the nomination for an office, only two or three attract great attention.

Open and closed primaries. A more important technical aspect of the direct primary is whether it is "closed" or "open." In an open primary a voter may participate in the primary of either party. Participation in a closed primary is limited to the members of the party, and ordinarily a test to determine membership is prescribed either by law or by party rule or by state action supplemented by party rule. The test of party membership is usually in terms of past partisan allegiance, present affiliation, and future intention, or a combination of these. Past allegiance may be determined by the elector's assertion that he supported the party's nominees at a preceding election. Present affiliation consists ordinarily in the elector's assertion that he is a member of the party. Future intention consists in an intention to support nominees of the party in the general election. The Texas primary ballot, for example, contains the following pledge to meet the test of present

[48] H. M. Dorr, "Tightening the Direct Primary," *American Political Science Review*, 30 (1936), pp. 512–522. On the effects of the fee system, see Dorr, "Tightening the Direct Primary in Michigan; First Applications of the Fee System," *ibid.*, 31 (1937), pp. 56–65.

affiliation and future intention: "I am a Democrat and pledge myself to support the nominees of this primary." The difference between the open and closed primary is not always sharp since in many instances the application of the test of party membership is so loose that voters may in practice enter either primary without challenge. In almost half the states, however, party affiliation is determined and recorded at the time of registration; when the primary is held, only those persons registered as members of a party are permitted to participate in its primaries. This method of administration, however, does not prevent changes in party affiliation, but in some instances changes must be made long before the primary and this requirement retards movement from party to party.[49]

Washington in 1935 carried the open primary principle to its logical conclusion by adopting the "blanket" primary, under which a voter can split his vote by voting in different party primaries on different offices. The ballot is arranged in an office bloc form, with the party affiliation of each aspirant for a nomination indicated after his name. The voter may skip back and forth from party to party as he moves down the ballot from office to office.[50]

The open primary is anathema to "regular" party organization men, who contend that it destroys party "responsibility" by making it possible for Democrats to participate in Republican primaries and vice versa. In some instances the voters of one-party may "raid" the primary of the other party and bring about the nomination of a weak or undesirable candidate who will be easier to defeat in the general election. Or voters may be attracted into the party primary in which there is the hottest contest or in which one of the aspirants for the nomination is a popular figure who engenders deep loyalties and hates. The extent to which party "responsibility" is vitiated and the extent to which party principles are diluted by the promiscuous participation of Republicans in Democratic primaries, or vice versa, are matters difficult of determination. Party "responsibility" is often something that persons who yearn for the good old days speak of with nostalgia. It is probable that the lack of a "responsible" party rests chiefly upon such factors as the nature of our governmental structure and the character of our bipartisan system rather than upon the direct primary.

An hypothesis, which may or may not be right, is that in some states

[49] The most comprehensive treatment of the open-closed primary question is by C. A. Berdahl, "Party Membership in the United States," *American Political Science Review,* 36 (1942), pp. 16–50, 241–262. See also Illinois Legislative Council, Research Department, *The Direct Primary Ballot* (Publication No. 25, July, 1940).

[50] See C. O. Johnson, "The Washington Blanket Primary," *Pacific Northwest Quarterly,* January, 1942, pp. 27–39.

with open primaries there is a much greater awareness of issues among the electorate than in many states with well-knit "responsible" party organizations. In some of the western states using the open primary there appears to be a sharper appreciation of the stakes of politics and a keener identification of the real policies of candidates, whatever their party, than in states with stronger traditional party ties. The open primary in such states may not contribute to party responsibility, but it may contribute to a sharper definition and determination of political issues. In other states the open primary, rather than serving this purpose, has been an element in short-term, factional maneuvers for advantage. One faction of the principal party, for example, might gain strength by permitting anybody to participate in the primary. For a satisfactory evaluation of the workings of the open primary additional discerning studies of the primary in a number of states are needed. In one such study, Professor Pollock concludes that in Michigan when party lines are crossed in the primaries, it is not to vote for a weak person to defeat in the elections but "it is almost always to vote for a strong candidate whom they expect to support in the final election." [51]

Cross-filing. Closely related to the question of what voters are to be permitted to participate in the primary is the question of what tests shall be applied to persons who desire to seek a nomination in a primary. In most states a person may seek the nomination in only a single primary and ordinarily he must meet a test of party membership in order to enter the primary race.

In a few states a person may run for the nominations of both parties. This practice is called "cross-filing" or "double-filing" in California, in which state the custom seems most widespread. Maryland permits "cross-filing" only in primaries on judicial offices, the statute being designed as something of an equivalent of a nonpartisan primary. Maine, New York, and Vermont permit "double-filing." In New York nominations for certain state offices are made by conventions that are not limited in their nominees to members of their own parties. Under these arrangements the Democratic and American Labor parties have often nominated the same candidates. For offices for which nominations are made by primary, an act of 1947 limited "double-filing" in New York by requiring that candidates for nomination be enrolled members of a party unless the appropriate party committee or other authority granted an exception to the rule.

California candidates are in the habit of taking advantage of the "double-filing" provisions of the state primary law on a large scale.

[51] James K. Pollock, *The Direct Primary in Michigan, 1909–1935* (Ann Arbor: University of Michigan Press, 1943), p. 60.

Moreover, the voters seem to pay no great heed to party affiliation of a candidate in making their choices, as was demonstrated by Earl Warren's victory in both the Republican and Democratic primaries for the nomination for governor in 1946. In the 1944 primaries nominations were made for 20 senatorial seats and 80 assembly seats. In the election, contests occurred in only 2 senate and 14 assembly districts between candidates of the opposite parties. In the remaining 18 senatorial districts and 66 assembly districts a single person won both party nominations. It should be noted that occasionally a person is disqualified because he loses the nomination of his own party and wins that of the opposition party. Under the California law he can accept the opposition nomination only if he wins his own party primary. The system of cross-filing raises the same issues of principle as the open primary; instead of permitting the voter to migrate freely from party to party the candidate is allowed the privilege of running in both party primaries.[52]

Mandatory and optional primaries. Another distinction among primary forms, which is now primarily of historical significance, is between mandatory and optional primaries. In the early development of party primaries many states adopted laws providing for direct primaries that might be held at the option of the governing authorities of the party. In most instances this optional primary was later displaced by a mandatory primary; that is, the party was compelled to use the direct primary in making its nominations. The optional form continues to exist in Arkansas, Delaware, Georgia, and Virginia.[53] South Carolina has an arrangement different from the usual optional form. The entire matter of nominations is handled by the party authorities, who are unregulated by state law and are free to use whatever nominating method the party desires. This condition came about by a repeal of all state legislation relating to primaries, in an effort to take the white primary beyond the reach of the United States Constitution. The party prescribes its own rules governing the conduct of the primary.[54]

Nonpartisan primaries. Still another variation of the direct primary is the nonpartisan primary. In this type, each party does not have a separate primary, but there is one general primary open to all. The persons polling the first and second highest votes become the candi-

[52] See Robert W. Binkley, Jr., *Double Filing in Primary Elections* (Berkeley: University of California, Bureau of Public Administration, 1945). See the discussion by W. W. Crouch and D. E. McHenry, *California Government* (Berkeley: University of California Press, 1945), pp. 28–30.

[53] *Book of the States*, 1945–46, p. 90.

[54] See *Rules of the Democratic Party of South Carolina*, Adopted by the Democratic State Convention, Holden at Columbia May 15, 1946.

dates at the election. In some jurisdictions, if a person receives a majority of all votes cast at the primary, he is declared elected. The nonpartisan primary is used mainly in municipal, judicial, and various other local elections, although it applies in the selection of state legislators in Nebraska and Minnesota. The chief factor motivating its adoption has been a desire to eliminate national party labels and national party organizations from local elections. The old saying is that there is no Republican or Democratic way to build and maintain a city street. City offices should be filled from the standpoint of local issues rather than national, the argument runs. By the elimination of national party labels in local affairs, the proponents of the nonpartisan primary believe, truly local issues will predominate in local contests.

The workings of the nonpartisan primary depend entirely on the prevailing circumstances in each locality in which it is used, since the primary is only a channel through which prevailing forces will find expression. In some cities with nonpartisan primaries the Republican and Democratic machines are so powerfully organized that they work through the nonpartisan primary unhandicapped by the absence of the party label on the ballot. In other instances municipal groups have been formed to advance candidates committed to certain municipal policies that could be advocated without the embarrassment of attachment to a particular national party label. In some instances the nonpartisan primary has perhaps stimulated realignments on local issues different from alignments in national campaigns. In Seattle, says McKenzie, the "forces which under the old system were concealed in political party organizations, now reveal themselves to public observation. . . . The non-partisan system of election brings into relief many of these forces which were formerly obscured under the partisan system." [55] In Detroit, according to W. P. Lovett, there have been "groups, controversies and alignments, purely local and legitimate, concerning municipal ownership of street cars, preservation or disruption of our clean election system, enforcement of law, honesty as against graft in city governments, preservation of real non-partisanship in elections, economy or extravagance in administration of public schools, and maintenance of an efficient municipal court." [56]

It must be recognized that many advocates of the nonpartisan primary have no understanding of the function of organized groups in politics. Many of them seem to think that by making the primary nonpartisan,

[55] R. D. McKenzie, "Community Forces: A Study of the Non-Partisan Municipal Elections in Seattle," *Social Forces*, 2 (1923–1924), p. 266.

[56] "Detroit Pleased with Non-Partisan Ballot," *National Municipal Review*, 12 (1923), pp. 221–223.

machines and "politics" will be eliminated. But, in truth, an organized group is necessary to win elections, partisan or nonpartisan, and to govern. Such groups will arise regardless of the form of the nominating machinery. Moreover, many advocates of the nonpartisan primary believe that there are really no issues in local politics save those of "honesty" and "ability." And that is a point of view not difficult to understand when it is remembered that the nonpartisan primary is urged mainly by middle-class reformers. There are, however, important issues in urban politics, although they are not always made explicit. It is another question whether people divide in the same way on these local issues as they do in national politics. If they do, the nonpartisan primary is unnecessary. Charles E. Merriam says: "the lines that divide men in national affairs do not run in the same direction in local questions, and the attempt to force them to do so has been a conspicuous failure in this country." [57] Charles A. Beard, on the other hand, concludes: [58]

Viewing the subject from a practical angle we may inquire whether the issues which divide men and women into national politics are issues which have any relation to municipal questions as such. The facile reformer usually answers in the negative. It is true that there seems to be no connection between ship subsidies, tariff, labor legislation, farm loans, and kindred matters and the problems that arise in our great urban centers. Superficially there is none. But I cannot be too emphatic when I say that not a single one of our really serious municipal questions—poverty, high cost of living, overcrowding, unemployment, low standards of life, physical degeneracy—can be solved, can be even approached by municipalities without the cooperation of the state and national government, and the solution of these problems calls for state and national parties. No big vision of this mighty nation as it is to be can exclude from its range an economy which is both urban and rural, one and truly indivisible.

4. NOMINATIONS AND THE NATURE OF POLITICS

A survey of the evolution of nominating methods illuminates the general nature of political behavior and indicates, as well, an important long-run tendency in American politics. It may be observed that, whatever the nature of the nominating process, a relatively small, cohesive group tends to take the lead in organizing support for candidates. Under the system of the legislative caucus the party leaders in the legis-

[57] *Chicago, A More Intimate View of Urban Politics* (New York, 1929), p. 99. Quoted by permission of the Macmillan Company, publishers.
[58] C. A. Beard, "Politics and City Government," *National Municipal Review,* 6 (1917), pp. 201–206.

lative body took the initiative. Under the convention system the party organization, with its precinct, county, city, and state functionaries, constituted the group guiding and managing conventions. Under the direct primary the party organization remained and changed its methods so as to adapt them to the new machinery of nominations. Whatever the form of nominating machinery, its operation has required the collaboration of men working in concert toward common ends. And these men are usually professional politicians, who perform a task that has to be accomplished to operate government. In speculation about the workings of the nominating process, the following comment by H. J. Ford is relevant: [59]

> One continually hears the declaration that the direct primary will take power from the politicians and give it to the people. This is pure nonsense. Politics has been, is and always will be carried on by politicians, just as art is carried on by artists, engineering by engineers, business by businessmen. All that the direct primary, or any other political reform, can do is to affect the character of the politicians by altering the conditions that govern political activity, thus determining its extent and quality. The direct primary may take advantage and opportunity from one set of politicians and confer them upon another set, but politicians there will always be so long as there is politics.

Although the tendency toward leadership and control by the closely knit inner core of the party may prevail, the conditions under which it works may be seriously altered by changes in the nature of the nominating process. The adoption of the convention system marked a revolt against the "autocratic" character of the caucus system. The tendency toward democratization found expression in a new nominating form. Under the convention system there would be, it was thought, a means for the ready expression of the wishes of the mass of party membership. As it developed, the convention system itself was soon labeled with the brand of "bossism." The direct primary was turned to as a means of obtaining a direct expression of choice of the party membership on nominations. Although the machine remained, in the formation of its slate for the primary it apparently has had to be more solicitous of the sentiment of party membership than it was under the convention system. Under this scheme the machine candidates have to run the gantlet of the primary, and this obstacle in the road to election is taken quite seriously by the candidate. But all three methods of nomination have marked further obeisance to the doctrine that the will of the rank and file of party membership should prevail. Yet a change in the system of making nominations does not eliminate the function of the organized minority in leading party opinion; it may, however, make it possible for a different minority to prevail.   "We are always pulling down bosses," Ford observed, "because transient combinations of would-be bosses and reformers may develop strength enough to overthrow a particular boss or a particular machine.   But while bosses and machines come and go, the boss and the machine are always with us." [60]

[60] *Ibid.,* p. 4.

Chapter 13

NATIONAL CONVENTIONS

THE FACT that the founding fathers did not foresee in detail the development of political parties left a gap in the constitutional procedure for
the selection of the President. It early became apparent that the
Electoral College would not operate according to plan. The idea of
electors assembled in each state to deliberate solemnly and judiciously,
without rancor and without issue, over the choice of a President verged
on the utopian. The selection of a President would determine in large
degree in whose interests the government would be run, and even in
the campaign for the adoption of the Constitution sharp cleavages over
public policy developed between two great groups of people. These
groups remained to battle for control of the personnel and policies of
the new government. Hence it became necessary to improvise means
by which the scattered parts of each faction, the Federalists and the
anti-Federalists, could unite on a candidate whom they would support
in the election.

First the causus and then the national convention evolved extra-
legally to meet a need not provided for in the governmental machinery
established by the Constitution. So long as the congressional caucus
included the more important leaders of the party from each state, its
decision on a person on whom their forces would be concentrated for
the Presidency was acceptable to the party. Very early, however, the
Federalists lost control of Congress, and their minority representation
became unrepresentative of the party. Its congressional caucus could
not speak for, nor could it in fact bind, the party as a whole. The
Federalists had to devise other means for agreeing among themselves
on a candidate whom the party would support. In 1808, at a secret
meeting of Federalist leaders in New York, Pinckney and King were
nominated for the Presidency and Vice-Presidency. "This was," says
S. E. Morison, "the original national nominating convention." [1] In

[1] "The First National Nominating Convention, 1808," *American Historical Review*,
17 (1912), pp. 744–763.

1812 Federalist leaders again met in New York to agree on nominations. The sessions "were held privately and there were no reports printed." [2] Eventually the congressional caucus became unrepresentative of the rank and file of the anti-Federalists; and in 1831, under the leadership of Jackson, the first full-fledged national convention was held by a major party.

The early Federalist conventions served the same purpose as those of the present day—the nomination of a candidate—but they were composed of self-appointed leaders, who convened on their own motion. Their character reflected the nature of the Federalist politics of the day. The gentry ruled and they gathered at a central place to agree among and to speak for themselves. In the evolution of the convention a profound change has occurred. In the 1808 and 1812 versions it consisted of men who could make their own decisions and bind the party thereby. In theory it now represents and speaks for the mass of the party membership. It has become a body of delegates who, in form at least, speak for the party in their states. The broadening of the suffrage and the trend toward democratization altered the nature of these national gatherings. Consequently, aspirants for the nomination appeal to the party membership in advance for the support of their delegates or spokesmen in the convention. Thus the process of nomination of a presidential candidate begins, not in the convention, but in campaigns and in maneuvers to sell a potential candidate to the party and to obtain instructed delegates long before the convention meets.[3]

1. PRECONVENTION CAMPAIGNS

The moment a man begins to run for President may be years before his name is put before a national convention. When a person succeeds in hoisting himself above the common run of politicians and attains national political prominence, it rarely requires sustained urging to

[2] T. M. Plaisted, "Origins of National Nominating Committees and Platforms," *Social Studies*, 30 (1939), pp. 199–206; J. S. Murdock, "The First National Nominating Convention," *American Historical Review*, 1 (1896), pp. 680–683.

[3] The student may well supplement this chapter by the examination of accounts of individual conventions, such as the following: H. L. Mencken, *Making a President* (New York: Knopf, 1932); W. A. White, *A Puritan in Babylon, The Story of Calvin Coolidge* (New York: Macmillan, 1938), chaps. 19 and 27; James A. Farley, *Behind the Ballots* (New York: Harcourt, Brace, 1938), chap. 2; Nicholas Murray Butler, *Across the Busy Years* (New York: Scribner's, 1939), Vol. I, chap. 10; R. S. Baker, *Woodrow Wilson, Life and Letters* (Garden City, N.Y.: Doubleday, Doran, 1931), Vol. III, chap. 6; Roy V. Peel and T. C. Donnelly, *The 1928 Campaign* (New York: R. R. Smith, 1931), chap. 2; *idem., The 1932 Campaign* (New York: Farrar & Rinehart, 1935), chap. 4; Josephus Daniels, *The Wilson Era* (Chapel Hill: University of North Carolina Press, 1944), chap. 6.

bring him to consider himself as a presidential possibility. When others also consider him as a possibility, he usually has had a long record of activity in politics. Most presidential prospects are sifted out by the tests of performance in public office, although occasionally generals and others not career politicians win nominations. At some point in his career a man begins to regard himself as a potential occupant of the White House and plans his steps accordingly; the newspapers speak of him as a prospect and the party leaders weigh his vote-getting capacities. Many men make their way into the ranks of the "possibilities," but only two are chosen quadrennially as nominees by the national conventions.[4]

A year or more before the convention the effort is begun to convert a "possibility" into a nominee. The basic objective of the preconvention campaign is to obtain the selection of delegates who will support the aspirant in the convention. To do this, he or his agents must gain the adherence of the leaders of the party's state organizations. The preconvention campaign also involves efforts to create a favorable sentiment toward the aspirant among the rank and file of party members. Success in manipulation of the attitudes of the party membership has much to do with gaining the support of the party's state leaders, who are anxious that the ticket be headed by a man who can win and who can help carry their state and local candidates to victory.

"Availability" of candidates. The presidential bee stings many party figures, but only a few possess the characteristics that make it worth while for them or their friends to campaign strenuously for the nomination. These characteristics are lumped under the term "availability." What is it that makes a man "available" or, better, makes him considered as a possible serious contender for the nomination? One factor is residence. A party leader from a state with a large electoral vote that might be thrown one way or the other in the election is in a much better position to fight for the presidential nomination than one from a state traditionally attached to one party. Since the Civil War, twenty-four of the forty presidential nominees of the major parties have been residents of New York and Ohio.[5] Of the factors contributing to "availability," residence is the only one easily identified. At the present stage of American politics a man must be a Protestant of good "American stock" and name to be "available." He should not be too

---

[4] On preconvention campaigns, see James A. Hagerty, "It's an Obstacle Race to the White House," *New York Times Magazine,* March 26, 1944.

[5] The number of nominees (counting each of the several nominations of the same person) from each state, 1868–1944, has been: New York, 16; Ohio, 8; Nebraska, 3; New Jersey, Illinois, Indiana, California, 2 each; Pennsylvania, West Virginia, Maine, Massachusetts, Kansas, 1 each.

closely affiliated with any particular interest or group nor should he have committed himself on a great and contentious issue before the time is ripe. Yet he must stand for something or a complex of things— a general point of view—in public life.[6]

Luck enters into "availability." To be a serious contender a man must accomplish something spectacular enough to attract the attention of party leaders over the country. Yet he must do this at the right time, that is, when his party is looking for a candidate or when no strong figure is in the saddle of party leadership. Thus, after the defeat of Al Smith in 1928, the Democrats were looking for a winner. When Franklin Roosevelt was re-elected governor of New York in 1930 by a tremendous majority and carried normally Republican territory in up-state New York, he immediately became eligible for the 1932 nomination. After the defeat of Landon in 1936, the Republicans began a quest for a winning candidate. Robert A. Taft, the son of a President, claimed Republican attention in 1939 and 1940 after he had won the Ohio senatorship over Democrat Bulkley and had matched radio oratory with the fluent New Dealer, T. V. Smith. Thomas Dewey's spectacular prosecutions of racketeers in New York, the national center for the manufacture and distribution of news, gave him nation-wide publicity, and his strength in the race for governor of New York against Lehman in 1938 made him a possibility for the 1940 Republican nomination. Although he lost the nomination in 1940, his subsequent election as governor of New York made him an almost certain winner of the 1944 nomination. Similarly Bricker's demonstration of vote-getting capacity in Ohio won the favorable attention of Republican leaders in 1943 and 1944. The chance conjunction of events in the career of an individual with the need of the party for a leader may make a man a presidential possibility.

Organization and strategy of campaigns. Mere possession of the qualities of a candidate does not make of a man a contender; it is necessary to establish an organization to familiarize the country and the local political leaders with a potential candidate's personality and abilities. The manager of the campaign for the nomination publicizes his candidate, keeps in touch with the party leaders in the various states, arranges speeches at appropriate times on major issues, and in general attempts to make it appear that his man is the person who can win for the party. The candidate's backers may spend several hundred thousand dollars in selling him to the party; at times the preconvention

---

[6] The Editors of *Time,* in commenting on the availability of Bricker for 1944, add such features as appearance ("good—but not too good"), personal vigor, and the possession of an attractive wife and children.—*Time,* April 26, 1943, pp. 18–20.

campaign is on a scale that makes it a rehearsal of the presidential campaign itself. Thus, according to press reports, well over a million dollars were raised to finance Harold Stassen's campaign for the 1948 Republican nomination.

It is extremely important that the leaders of state and city party machines be cultivated, since they often can make the decisions of their state delegations. The manager for the candidate early attempts to impress on these men that his candidate would make a strong head of the ticket; the candidate himself usually meets with small groups of these leaders in order that they may look him over. James Farley's travels to line up support for Roosevelt before the 1932 Democratic convention carried him over 30,000 miles.[7]

The leading candidates for the nomination usually make speeches on important current issues at widely separated points in the country for the purpose of letting themselves be seen and heard, of impressing local leaders, and of gaining national attention. In 1940, for example, John W. Cowles and Gardner Cowles, Jr., powerful western Republicans and publishers of newspapers in Des Moines and Minneapolis, heard a speech by Willkie in New York. "They thought my philosophy was right and that I had the power to advocate it, but they didn't know how much discount to give me as a resident of New York City, a public-utility man, and a former Democrat," Willkie said later. Accordingly arrangements were made for Willkie to speak before a group of western Republican leaders in Minneapolis; he made a favorable impression and became a candidate for the nomination.[8]

Dewey's heavy schedule of preconvention speeches in 1940 was deliberately arranged to impress Republican leaders with the popularity of the candidate, to make them believe that with him they could win, and thereby to gain their support in the selection of convention delegates. Many Republican leaders were not inclined to regard the young prosecutor as a man of presidential caliber. In the months before the convention Dewey stumped the country from Massachusetts to California. He spoke in Minneapolis, Philadelphia, Boston, Cheyenne, St. Louis, Milwaukee, and Los Angeles. His speeches and travels in 1939 and 1940 were more extensive than the usual preconvention campaign, but most aspirants who take their prospects seriously generally manage to get around the country to be seen and heard. One speech may be enough to demonstrate that a man cannot capture popular favor, and his boom is deflated early in its career. And if the

[7] Hugh Bradley, "Jim Farley: An Elk on a Tour," *American Mercury*, September, 1932.

[8] Janet Flanner, "Rushville's Renowned Son-in-Law," *New Yorker*, October 12, 1940.

aspirant misjudges the trend of public sentiment, he may ruin his chances by his preconvention pronouncements. In 1940, for example, Dewey's vigorous isolationist stand expressed during the "phony" period of the European war seriously injured him as sentiment for aid to Britain grew.

The difficulty of describing preconvention maneuvers in general terms is well illustrated by Dewey's 1944 strategy, which was quite different from that which he followed in 1940. In 1944 he made few speeches and persistently denied that he was a candidate for the nomination. In accepting the Republican nomination for Governor of New York in 1942 he pledged himself to devote the "next four years to serving the best interests of the people of the State of New York." In January, 1944, at a meeting of the Republican national committee in Chicago, Dewey's political advisers were on hand and in the backstage talk indicated without saying so that he would accept. Meanwhile, the Governor stuck to his knitting in Albany, making a record on questions of state policy and administration. He refused to enter the state presidential primaries where his consent was required to do so, and elsewhere he asked others to refrain from entering slates of delegates on his behalf. In February, however, the *New York Times* reported that the pressure was on local organizations in New York state to select delegates who would support Dewey.[9] In the opinion polls Dewey was demonstrating strength, and he was profiting from the "stop Willkie" movement among the organization leaders who had no great love for Dewey but less for Willkie. Early in April, when a Dewey slate (disavowed by the Governor) led Willkie in the Wisconsin primary and Willkie bowed out of the race, Dewey merely said, "No comment," and continued the pose of indifference. During April and May delegates continued to mount his bandwagon, but he continued to preserve the fiction (not believed by anyone including his managers) that he was not a candidate.[10] In June, as Dewey's managers—Messrs. Sprague, Brownell, and Jaeckle—were leaving New York for the convention, they expressed the view that he would, if nominated, accept. The next day in Chicago they declared, "We're here to draft Dewey for the presidential nomination." But there was yet no direct statement by Mr. Dewey.

[9] "Dewey in the Running While Sticking to Job," *New York Times*, February 6, 1944.

[10] Senator Pepper, Democrat, observed: "The heir-apparent to the Republican throne, that gilded, public-relations-advised candidate, the Governor of New York in his best and most studied pose of the coy maiden who is so diligently sought, the one who says 'no' with lisping lip, but with the dark lashes of her inviting eyes says 'come on.' . . . "—*Washington Post*, February 16, 1944.

TABLE 14

Preferences of Republican Voters for Presidential Nominee, 1943–1944 [a]

Candidate	1943				1944				
	June	Sept.	Oct.	Dec.	Jan.	Feb.	April	May	June
Dewey	37	35	32	36	42	45	55	65	58
Willkie	28	29	28	25	23	21	7		
Bricker	..	8	8	10	8	7	9	9	12
Stassen	7	4	6	6	6	5	7	5	6
MacArthur	15	15	19	15	18	19	20		
	87 [b]	91	93	92	97	97	98	79	76

[a] American Institute of Public Opinion.
[b] The remainder in each case was scattered among other presidential possibilities.

A question of strategy that vexes managers of would-be nominees is whether to enter the presidential primaries that are held by about half the states from March to May to select convention delegates. An early victory in a pivotal state may win the delegation and impress the party in other states with the aspirant's vote-pulling power. On the other hand, a defeat may bring the boom to a premature end. Yet a refusal to enter the primary may be interpreted as timidity and lack of courage, as well as a manifestation of lack of confidence. Since the primary choice is to a large extent governed by the wishes of the state organization, it would be rash to enter a primary unless the candidate has the support of the organization or of an important faction, or felt that he could defeat the state machine. The Dewey leaders in 1940 maintained a poll organization that informed them of the popular sentiment toward their candidate. When their tests indicated a Dewey majority in New Jersey and Maryland, they challenged both Vandenburg and Taft to enter the primaries in those states. Taft and Vandenburg avoided defeat by staying out of these primaries, assuming that it would be better to go into the convention without a record of defeat in the primaries of these two states.

Favorite sons and other bargainers. As the preconvention campaign unfolds, a few serious contenders emerge; and they are faced by the necessity of deciding what to do about "favorite son" candidates. A "favorite son" candidate is an aspirant for the nomination who has the avowed support of the delegation from his own state and usually no other. He is put forward to hold the delegation free for negotiations when the convention meets and on the long chance that the lightning might strike and he would become the nominee.[11] Should the

[11] Governor James of Pennsylvania was in 1940 a typical "favorite son." He modestly announced: "If the delegates find I'm the available man to carry on the fight

leading contenders challenge the favorite sons in their own states? To do so might antagonize men who will control delegates in the convention. One approach is to ask for second-choice support after the favorite son. In 1939 this was the strategy of the McNutt managers, who said, "In no State that has a favorite son are we asking for more than second choice." By such an approach leading candidates hope to keep on good terms with the lesser contenders and perhaps gain their support in the convention.

The candidate who early develops significant strength is sometimes faced by a combination of other candidates who desire to prevent the settlement of the nomination prior to the convention. If a leading contender can be "killed off," the way is left open for a negotiated nomination in the convention, and other contenders will at least have a chance. One technique is not to oppose openly the prominent aspirant in his fights for delegates but to ask for the selection of uninstructed delegates. The state leaders then will also be in a better bargaining position in the convention. In 1932, to illustrate, the Smith forces desired to head off the Roosevelt movement, and Jouett Shouse, a Smith supporter, suggested that "it would be wiser not to instruct delegates to the Democratic convention in favor of any candidate save where such instructions are necessary under the law. The convention should be unfettered by instructions." [12] By this means the Smith faction hoped to stop Roosevelt. The strategy is by no means new. In 1892 those opposing Harrison for the Republican nomination sought the selection of uninstructed delegations with the hope that unpledged delegations could be united around some other candidate at the time of the convention.

Presidents seeking renomination. The preconvention campaign for the nomination of the party in power may or may not differ completely from the general picture that has been described. If the President does not seek a renomination and does not desire to use his position to influence the designation of his successor, the race is "open" to all who wish to attempt to corral delegates. But if the President wants a renomination for a second term, the preconvention campaign is likely to be a prosaic affair of formally lining up the delegates. By custom a President is "entitled" to a second nomination, and he has the advantage of controlling the party machine in obtaining it. Although it is quixotic to challenge his supremacy, some small but noisy dissident faction not infrequently attempts a revolt, proclaiming itself the true

this year, I'd be untrue to myself, my party and my country if I did not accept the responsibility and the duty to carry on the fight this year."
12 Peel and Donnelly, *The 1932 Campaign*, p. 66.

custodian of the party gospel. The President may have great influence, if he chooses, in the designation of the party nominee. Thus, Theodore Roosevelt, much to his regret, passed the Republican mantle to Taft in 1908.

When the President wins the nomination for a third or fourth term —which has not happened very often—the preconvention campaigns do not appear to differ markedly from those in which a nomination for a second term is sought. Nevertheless, the campaigns for the Democratic nomination in 1940 and in 1944 warrant special attention.[13] The 1940 preconvention campaign resolved itself into a struggle primarily between the conservative and liberal factions of the party, with cross-currents of considerations of national policy in times of crisis. Soon after the election of 1936 various aspirants began to try to build themselves up to (and their friends tried to build them to) presidential stature in the public mind, but they were dwarfed by the President. The outbreak of war in September, 1939, gave an entirely different color to the campaign. According to the opinion polls, each time tension in Europe heightened, public sentiment in favor of a third term for Roosevelt increased. In 1939 leaders of the Roosevelt faction of the party began moves to nominate him for another term. In November McAdoo announced his support of Roosevelt for a third term. Secretaries Wallace and Ickes at about the same time issued similar statements. Joseph P. Kennedy, home from his post as ambassador at London, urged the President to run again on the basis that the international crisis overshadowed any "possible objection to a third term." In January, 1940, Mayor Kelly of Chicago claimed that the third-term supporters already had 250 convention delegates pledged for Roosevelt.

Meanwhile the President maintained silence on his intentions, but he did nothing to check the enthusiasm of the promoters of renomination. The conservative wing of the party sought to stop Roosevelt. Vice-President Garner was the "white hope" of the conservative faction for a time; he announced in December, 1939, that he would "accept the nomination for President." Privately he opined that without the President's support no candidacy was better than "a can of stale beer." [14] McNutt had been a candidate for the nomination since 1936, but in December Ickes expressed opposition to him for the liberal faction of the party. The candidacy of James A. Farley was looked on with favor

[13] It is of interest, but perhaps not of cosmic significance, that the Democrats are more disposed than the Republicans to renominate a candidate. Cleveland was the Democratic nominee for President in 1884, 1888, 1892; Bryan, in 1896, 1900, 1908; Roosevelt, in 1932, 1936, 1940, 1944.

[14] Charles Michelson, *The Ghost Talks* (New York: Putnam, 1944), p. 131.

by the right-wing faction. Garner was definitely eliminated as the spearhead of the anti-Roosevelt drive in the early presidential primaries. Roosevelt's name was entered, without his consent, in the Wisconsin primary, and his popular vote far exceeded that of Garner in that state, as well as in Illinois. The conservative faction was unable to produce a candidate commanding impressive popular support. After the early primaries the Roosevelt strength increased by the instruction of delegates by conventions and primaries in state after state. In July the Massachusetts delegates, earlier pledged to Farley, were pledged to assure the renomination of Roosevelt, yet even at that time his intentions had not been announced.[15] Mr. Dewey's 1944 preconvention campaign, in its posed indifference of the candidate, was so much like that of Mr. Roosevelt in 1940 that one may legitimately wonder whether the young governor did not emulate the old master.

The preconvention maneuvers to nominate Roosevelt for a fourth term in 1944 followed a pattern similar to those of 1940. The party had no practicable alternative to the nomination of Roosevelt, and in the conventions and primaries it so decided in state after state as the national convention approached. The middle of a war was no time for a change, the argument went, but the right-wing Democrats made threatening gestures. Considerable press space was given to the formation of the American Democratic National Committee in February, under the leadership of Harry Woodring of Kansas, a former Secretary of War. This self-constituted committee proclaimed itself the true heir of the principles of Jefferson and denounced the "palace guard as trespassers wrongfully in possession of the Democratic Party." The $1,500,000 that the Committee proposed to spend in recapturing the party turned out to be a press agent's dream, and the Committee was never regarded seriously. More portentous rumbling occurred in the South. A "draft Byrd" movement received no encouragement from the Senator, and threats by state leaders and conventions in South Carolina, Mississippi, and Texas to "bolt" turned out to be mainly sound and fury. In truth, the southern leaders, no matter how much they disliked the New Deal, were limited in how far they could go in opposition to Roosevelt.[16] Their antipathies worked themselves out in resolutions advocating "states' rights," "white supremacy," and like old favorites, and in opposition to Wallace as the vice-presidential

[15] For a detailed chronology of events preceding the conventions of 1940, see Roy V. Peel and George Snowden, "From Four Years of Politics the Candidates Emerge," *Public Opinion Quarterly*, 4 (1940), pp. 451–64.

[16] The AIPO poll early in April, 1944, showed the following popular percentages in favor of Roosevelt over all other possibilities both Republican and Democratic: Alabama, 72; Florida, 53; Georgia, 71; Louisiana, 69; Mississippi, 62; South Carolina. 60; Texas, 65.

candidate. Before the convention met it was clear that the nominee would be Roosevelt, who announced "reluctantly" that he would accept.

The candidate may be nominated before the convention meets; the delegates may convene only to ratify an accomplished fact. Even ,if the convention really exercises discretion, it is likely to be limited in its choice to a very few individuals. A true "dark horse" nominee whose selection is a complete surprise is quite rare. Hence, in attempting to comprehend the process of selecting the American chief executive, great weight must be given to the broad range of factors that determine whether a man is considered as a presidential possibility and to the maneuvers in the months preceding the national conventions by aspirants for the nominations. As may be concluded from the meager data presented here, these processes are not easily described in general terms. Each instance is likely to have its own peculiarities, and the most unpredictable developments may occur in the competition to get to the White House.

2. APPORTIONMENT AND SELECTION OF DELEGATES

The delegates whose support the aspirants for the nomination seek are chosen within the states. Hence, the manner of selection of delegates and the method of determining the number of delegates to which each state is entitled are matters of basic importance. During most of the history of the national conventions votes have been apportioned among the states in accordance with their strength in the electoral college. This rule was adopted by the Democratic convention in 1831. Each state was at first entitled to one vote for each of its two Senators and one vote for each member of the House of Representatives from the state. Presently the general practice came to be to allow each state twice this number of votes.[17] Stated in the terms used in the party rules, this means four delegates-at-large from each state (double the number of Senators from the state), two delegates-at-large for each

[17] In the text "delegate" is used synonymously with "vote." In practice the number of delegates may exceed the number of votes to which the state is entitled, in which case each delegate has the appropriate fractional vote. The Democrats especially have been troubled by the designation of delegates far in excess of the number of votes. By this means party faithfuls may be "recognized" and assured of good seats in the convention. The practice, however, makes it difficult to arrange seating and makes headaches for the tally clerks, who may have to record votes in halves, quarters, tenths, sixths, and fifths. In calling the 1940 convention the Democratic national committee "requested" that the number of delegates be limited to the number of votes "as far as possible," but just before the convention met the Sergeant-at-Arms, who arranged seating, feared that if the number of delegates continued to increase "it would take a lot as large as Soldiers Field to hold our next convention." He was having to seat about 1,800 delegates to cast 1,100 votes; one Mississippi district, entitled to two votes, sent 54 delegates to cast them. (It must be kept in mind that a state is entitled also to send an alternate for each delegate, who votes in the absence

Representative elected at large from the states, and two delegates for each Representative in Congress elected by districts. This rule remained in use in unmodified form by the Republicans until their convention of 1916 and by the Democrats through the convention of 1940.

Apportionment: Special problems of the Republicans. The original rule of apportionment presupposed a more or less even spread of party strength over the entire country; as a matter of fact such a distribution did not exist, and solidly Democratic areas had relatively as great strength in Republican conventions as states with heavy Republican majorities. The application of the rule created no serious difficulties in the Democratic party, but its use led to party disaster for the Republicans and a consequent modification of the rule. In the South the Republican vote is usually extremely light; the rule of apportionment gave to these states a relative strength in the national convention much greater than the party vote in these areas warranted. Under these circumstances the Republican organizations in the southern states exist for the distribution of federal patronage—when the party controls the national government—and for the control of delegates in the national convention. The two operations have not been unrelated. The shadow organization in the South has been relatively easy to control through federal patronage when the party is in power nationally. During those campaigns when the party is not in power the managers of aspirants for the nomination may solicit delegates from the "rotten borough" states by questionable means,[18] although it is not clear that the support of these states is always an advantage.

of the delegate. An alternate at the 1940 Democratic convention observed that an "alternate is a guy who when he tries to check in at a hotel the clerk says, 'Sorry, bud, but there's no room, there's a convention in town.' ") The convention attempted to cope with the problem by resolving that in future conventions no "fractional distribution" should be permitted that would give any delegate less than one-half vote. The national committee, at a meeting immediately after the convention, adopted a resolution limiting the number of delegates to the number of votes, save that for each United States Senator four delegates-at-large might be chosen, one-half of whom should be women (see *Proceedings,* 1940, pp. 250, 324, 335, 376). The Republicans allow only one delegate for one vote, and the rule is enforced. Thus, in 1944, when factional contests in the Maryland state convention were happily solved by selecting more delegates to the national convention than the allotted number and giving them fractional votes, the national committee refused to place more than the proper number of delegates on the temporary roll of the convention. The disappointed would-be delegates were mollified by being assigned to such posts as honorary vice-chairman of the convention and membership on the committee to notify the vice-presidential nominee.

[18] The tendency in practice may be inferred from the following statement on the 1912 convention by an "old guard" leader: "A shrewd manipulator could have nominated Roosevelt at that Convention. The Roosevelt group had all the men of wealth,

Although the equity of the system of apportionment had long been questioned, it was not until 1912 that a combination of circumstances occurred to bring about an alteration of the rule. In that year the system of apportionment of delegates, which was partly responsible for Taft's control of the convention, led to a disastrous split in the Republican party, with Taft as the regular nominee and Theodore Roosevelt as the standard bearer of the rebellious Progressive faction. The split in the Republican party gave the election to the Democrats, and the Republican national committee in 1913 took steps to reduce the inequities in the apportionment of delegates by submitting a new plan of apportionment for approval by the state conventions. The rule, approved by the state conventions and first used in 1916, provided that the convention should consist of "four delegates-at-large from each state; two additional delegates-at-large for each Representative-at-large in Congress from any State; one delegate for each Congressional District in each state; and one additional delegate for each Congressional District in each State in which the vote for any Republican elector in the last preceding Presidential election, or for the Republican nominee for Congress in the last preceding Congressional election shall have been not less than 7,500," plus certain delegates from the territories. The change decreased the representation of the Solid South by 76 votes.

The new rule left the weak Republican areas still overrepresented in proportion to their Republican strength. The 1920 convention, "to inspire a greater effort to erect and maintain substantial party organizations in all the states," directed the national committee "within twelve months from the date of the adjournment of this Convention to adopt a just and equitable basis of representation in future National Conventions, which basis shall be set forth in the call for the next Convention and be binding upon the same and all other future conventions until otherwise ordered." The national committee issued a drastic reapportionment rule within the prescribed time, but shortly before the issuance of the call for the 1924 convention it substituted a milder rule. The rule, under which the 1924 convention was selected, made two changes. It awarded a bonus of three delegates to each state "cast-

---

including George Perkins, Bill Flynn, the two Pinchots, and others equally rich and devoted to the Colonel. The Negroes and some white delegates from the South had to have their expenses paid at the Convention, and our fellows ran out of money by Friday night. There was lively scurrying around to try to get funds to sustain them through the next week if we had to remain that long."—J. E. Watson, *As I Knew Them* (Indianapolis: The Bobbs-Merrill Company, copyright, 1926), p. 157. Used by special permission of the publishers.

ing its electoral vote, or a majority thereof, for the Republican nominee for President in the last preceding Presidential election." It raised from 7,500 to 10,000 the number of Republican votes necessary for a congressional district to have two delegates.

The national convention of 1940 changed the system of apportionment to reduce still further the representation in future conventions of those areas with a light Republican popular vote. The rule as amended in 1940 follows:

Delegates at Large

1. Four delegates at large from each state.

2. Two additional delegates at large for each representative at large in Congress from each state.

3. Three delegates at large each for Alaska, District of Columbia and Hawaii, and two additional delegates if the delegate to Congress elected at the last preceding election was the Republican nominee.[19] Two delegates at large each for Puerto Rico and the Philippine Islands.

4. Three additional delegates at large from each state casting its electoral vote, or a majority thereof, for the Republican nominee for President in the last preceding presidential election. If any state fails to cast its electoral vote or a majority thereof for the Republican nominee for President in the last preceding presidential election, and thereafter at the next succeeding election elects a Republican United States Senator, then in that event such state shall be entitled to such additional delegates at large.[20]

District Delegates

1. One district delegate from each congressional district casting one thousand votes or more for any Republican elector in the last preceding presidential election or for the Republican nominee for Congress in the last preceding congressional election.[21]

2. One additional district delegate from each congressional district casting 10,000 votes or more for any Republican elector in the last preceding presidential election or for the Republican nominee for Congress in the last preceding congressional election.

Under the application of the apportionment rules the total number of delegates fluctuates from convention to convention; in 1936, the total number of delegates was 1,003; in 1940, 1,000; in 1944, 1,057.

[19] The bonus of two additional delegates was granted by the 1940 convention.

[20] The last sentence was added in 1940. It gives the state, in effect, an additional chance to earn its bonus of three delegates in the convention.

[21] This section contains the important change made in 1940. Before the adoption of this phraseology each congressional district was entitled to at least one delegate in the convention. Under the new provision the district must have polled at least 1,000 Republican votes to have the right to one delegate. In the 1942 congressional elections in 84 districts in ten southern states less than 1,000 Republican votes were cast.

Apportionment: Democratic practice. The Democratic party has been more fortunate than the Republican party in the matter of apportionment. It has been able to follow the practice of allowing each state a delegation twice the size of its congressional representation without serious controversy because of the lack of a problem such as the Solid South presents to the Republicans. Yet the 1936 Democratic convention, to offset to some degree southern sentiment against the abrogation of the two-thirds rule, adopted a resolution directing the national committee to submit to the next convention "a plan for improving the system by which delegates and alternates to Democratic National Conventions are apportioned." The committee was ordered, in formulating this plan, to "take into account the Democratic strength within each State, District of Columbia, and Territory, etc. . . ." [22] The 1940 convention adopted a rule to grant to states that go Democratic in a presidential election an additional two votes in the next convention. The rule gives only slight additional strength to the states of the Solid South.[23]

Methods of choosing delegates: Conventions and primaries. Once the apportionment of delegates is made among the states, delegates are chosen by two principal methods. In almost two thirds of the states the choice of delegates to represent the state in the national convention is made by state or district conventions. In most other states delegates are selected by the presidential primary, although in a few states they may be chosen by party committees. The call for the 1944 Republican convention indicates the methods employed in the selection of delegates to both party conventions. The national committee directed that delegates should be elected in the following manner:

1. By primary election, in accordance with the laws of the state in which the election occurs, in such states as require by law the election of delegates to national conventions of political parties by district primary. . . .

[22] *Proceedings,* Democratic National Convention, 1936, p. 190. In the 1944 Democratic Convention six votes each were allotted to Alaska, Hawaii, the District of Columbia, the Philippines, Puerto Rico, and the Canal Zone, and the Virgin Islands had two votes.

[23] Since the abrogation of the two-thirds rule for nominations by the Democratic convention in 1936, southern Democrats have agitated for more generous representation in the convention for states and districts going Democratic or casting substantial Democratic votes. Democrats in other parts of the country, however, succeeded in 1940 and 1944 in defeating in the national committee proposals to give the South a larger representation (see the national committee debate printed in *Proceedings,* 1940 Democratic Convention, pp. 341–356). The question of the apportionment of delegates to the Democratic convention is not yet completely settled. The 1944 convention instructed the national committee to "formulate and adopt" a plan for improving the system of apportionment of delegates and resolved that in such a plan the committee should "take into account" the Democratic strength within each state. —See *Proceedings,* 1944 Democratic Convention, p. 62.

2. By congressional district or state conventions, as the case may be, to be called by the congressional or state committees, respectively. . . . In a congressional district where there is no Republican District Committee, the Republican State Committee shall issue the call. . . .[24]

3. By the Republican State Committee or Governing Committee in any State in which the law of such State specifically authorizes the election of delegates in such manner.

4. All Delegates from any State may, however, be chosen from the State at large, in the event that the laws of the state in which the election occurs so provide.[25]

The chief difference in Republican and Democratic procedure in the selection of delegates is that the Republican national convention and committee have generally sought to regulate the conditions under which the delegates are selected, whereas the Democratic national authorities have usually left to state decision the mode of selection of delegates. But this difference is more formal than real. The call for the 1944 Republican convention, for example, set out in some detail the rules under which delegates should be elected. Only "legal and qualified voters" were to participate in caucuses or primaries held for the "purpose of selecting delegates to a county, district or state convention." Delegates to conventions were required to "be apportioned among the counties, parishes and cities of the state or district having regard to the Republican vote therein." Delegates to the national convention were to be "duly qualified voters" and residents of "their respective states." The call for the Democratic convention, on the other hand, merely indicated the number of delegates to which each state was entitled.

The development of state laws regulating the selection of delegates to the national convention has created the possibility of conflict between the regulations of the Republican national convention and the laws of the state. As indicated in the call for the Republican convention just quoted, the party rules have been altered in general to recognize the power of the state to govern the mode of selection of delegates. The Republican rules provide, however, that in any presidential primary state "in which Republican representation upon the board of judges or inspectors of elections for such primary election is denied by

[24] The Republican party has generally preferred that districts be allowed to select their own delegates. If all the delegates from a state are selected by the state convention, the entire delegation may consist of adherents of the presidential aspirant whose managers dominate the state convention, whereas if district conventions select delegates, the state delegation is more likely to be split among several candidates. In earlier calls for Republican conventions the selection of district delegates was permitted by district subdivisions of the state convention.

[25] *Proceedings*, 1944, p. 23.

law, Delegates and Alternates shall be elected" by convention under party rule. The Republican rules further provide that in the selection of delegates "no state law shall be observed which hinders, abridges or denies to any citizen of the United States, eligible under the Constitution of the United States, to the office of President or Vice-President, the right or privilege of being a candidate under such State law for the nomination for President or Vice-President; or which authorizes the election of a number of Delegates or Alternates from any State to the National Convention different from that fixed" in the call by the national committee.[26] Although such prescriptions by national conventions against state laws are not of much current practical effect, the national convention is not bound to seat delegates elected in accordance with state law. It is an extralegal agency and can apply such criteria as it wishes in passing on the credentials of delegates.

Fourteen states use the presidential primary to select delegates to the national convention. Approximately 40 per cent of the delegates are chosen by this means. The adoption of the presidential primary occurred at about the same time and for the same reasons that the direct primary was substituted for the convention method of nomination of candidates for state offices. It will be recalled that conventions were thought to be, and probably were, readily susceptible to manipulation and management by the leaders of the party organizations. Abuses and unfair practices outraged the sensibilities of a substantial minority, which was able to convert itself into a majority and impose the direct-primary method. Similar conditions and circumstances prevailed in conventions for the selection of national convention delegates. It was thought that party leaders could manipulate the convention so as to select delegates committed to the support of presidential aspirants unacceptable to, or at least not desired by, the majority of the members of the party within the state.

Although Wisconsin in 1905 and Pennsylvania in 1906 adopted laws providing for the direct election of delegates—all delegates in Wisconsin and district delegates in Pennsylvania—the birth of the full-blown presidential primary is usually traced to an Oregon law adopted by popular vote in 1910.[27] That law provided for a preference vote by the voters on presidential aspirants, as well as the direct election of all delegates to the convention. Between 1910 and 1916 the presidential primary spread so rapidly among the states that it was freely predicted that within a short period the old-time convention would disappear

---

[26] *Proceedings,* 1936, pp. 13–14.
[27] Louise Overacker, *The Presidential Primary* (New York: Macmillan, 1926). Dr. Overacker's volume is the standard work on the subject.

and that the national convention would become, like the electoral college, a mere mechanism for recording decisions already arrived at by the electorate. The drive for the presidential primary, however, was soon spent, and since the peak in 1916 several states have abandoned it.

Types of presidential primary laws. The wide range of variations in presidential primary laws—partially the result of compromises in their passage because of the opposition of the party organizations [28]—makes it somewhat erroneous to speak of the presidential primary. There is, rather, a variety of presidential primary systems. The only common element among the different types is an intent, accomplished with varying degrees of effectiveness, to allow the party membership to express a choice for the presidential nominee and to select delegates who will seek to bring about the nomination of the popular preference in the national convention.

One type of presidential primary consists simply of the election of the delegates to the convention; this method is used in New York for the district delegates; the delegates-at-large are selected by the state convention. Unless a spirited contest prevails, and the electorate is thereby informed of the preferences of the prospective delegates, the voters have no effective way of expressing a choice for the presidential nomination indirectly through their vote for the delegation candidates. Another method is followed in Maryland, where there is a preference vote in which party members make a choice among presidential aspirants, but the delegates to the national convention are selected by the state conventions. From what has previously been said about the difference in ease of control of conventions and of primaries by party organizations, the likelihood of conflict between popular preference and the preference of delegates chosen by the convention under this system becomes apparent. It is not a matter for surprise, then, that four states have abandoned this combination of convention and preferential vote.

The largest group of primary states combine a preferential vote on presidential candidates with the election of delegates. There are several varieties of this general class of primary system; under all of them confusion may arise because of conflict between popular presidential preference and the preferences of delegates popularly chosen. In one primary of this type there is a presidential preference vote coupled with the election of delegates without knowledge by the voters of the dele-

[28] The opponents of the presidential primary went so far as to contend that the state had no power to regulate the selection of delegates. In New Jersey, for example, the following statement was made in opposition to the law: "New Jersey has no more right to attempt to fix by law the method of selecting delegates to a national convention than it has to attempt to fix the method of selecting delegates to a Knight of Columbus convention or a Knight Templar conclave."—Quoted in *ibid.*, p. 19.

gates' preferences. For example, in North Dakota, which formerly operated under this scheme, the Republican ballot in 1924 had the names of Johnson and Coolidge for President and the names of thirty-nine candidates for the convention delegation of thirteen, without any indication of which delegates were pledged to Johnson or to Coolidge. Under this system in North Dakota in 1932 General Coxey of Ohio and Dr. Joseph I. France of Maryland were entered in the Republican presidential preference race, but no delegates favorable to either were on the ballot. There were two slates of delegates entered, one uninstructed, another favorable to the renomination of Hoover. The voters preferred France over Coxey, "but nine of the eleven delegates favored Hoover, and none of them supported France." [29] North Dakota has since repealed the primary law, and only Nebraska now uses this particular form.[30]

A second variation of the combination of preference vote with election of delegates involves a statement on the ballot whether the candidates for delegate agree to support the popular preference for President, without any indication of their real loyalties. This arrangement prevails in Pennsylvania and was formerly used in West Virginia.[31] A third variety couples the presidential preference vote with the election of delegates, after whose names on the ballot is indicated their preference for President. The assumption is that the voters will cast their votes for the delegates pledged to support their presidential preference, but that does not always occur. In the 1936 Republican primary in Illinois, for example, the state-wide preference vote went for Knox and against Borah, but Borah delegates won in thirteen congressional districts.[32]

In a final group of presidential-primary states the greatest success in obtaining the selection of delegates whose preferences agree with the popular preference has been achieved. In these states—California, Massachusetts, and New Hampshire—there is no separate vote on preference for President. On the ballot, candidates are listed with their preference for President. By voting for the Roosevelt slate, for example, the voter may, in effect, express a preference and at the same time express a choice for delegates pledged to that candidate. In Cali-

---

[29] Overacker in *The American Political Scene* (New York: Harper, rev. ed., 1938), p. 264.

[30] Iowa and Montana at one time had similar systems.

[31] In 1916 and 1920 the Penrose delegates in Pennsylvania "did not hesitate to have printed after their names on the ballot 'Does not promise to support the popular choice of party in . . . . District for President.' "—Overacker, *The Presidential Primary*, p. 69.

[32] Overacker in *The American Political Scene*, pp. 264-265.

fornia, where all delegates are elected at large, it is possible to vote for all the delegates pledged for a particular candidate with one cross mark, the effect of which is to reduce the likelihood of split delegations.[33]

When the Progressive movement was at high tide after the fiasco of the Republican convention of 1912, the prediction was made that the national convention would soon become merely an agency to record the choice of the party arrived at through the presidential primary. The presidential primary, however, has been on the decline since 1916; the choice of the primaries has not been the choice of the convention. Observing the seven presidential contests in the Democratic party since the introduction of the primary, Overacker saw in 1938 only "two cases in which the choice of the convention clearly reflected the choice of the primaries,"[34] and even in those it is not clear that nomination was gained because of victories in the primaries. In 1928 Smith won in the primary states and carried the convention; in 1932 Roosevelt won most of the primaries and gained the nomination. In the Republican party only in 1924, when Coolidge won over Johnson in the more important primary states, did the preferential vote agree with the convention choice. In other instances the nomination has been either a foregone conclusion or the convention went counter to the primary verdict. In 1944 Willkie withdrew from the race for the Republican nomination after an early defeat in the Wisconsin primary. It is doubtful that the presidential primaries have had appreciable influence on the outcome of the nominating process.

The reasons for the failure of the primary to become of greater importance are fairly clear. From the description of the different types of primary laws, it is obvious that many of the laws are defective. They make it difficult for the voters to express their choice unequivocally; it is not without significance that most of the states that have abandoned the system had defective laws. In a sense the presidential primary has never been given a trial; the outcome might have been different had all, or practically all the states adopted the primary. With incomplete coverage, the aspirants for the nomination have been able to ignore or sabotage the system. Not infrequently the leading candidates refuse

[33] The foregoing classification of presidential primaries follows that of Dr. Overacker. The states listed in the discussion have mandatory primary laws. Alabama, Michigan, Florida, and Georgia, however, have optional laws under which presidential primaries may be conducted in the discretion of the state committee of a party. In Georgia the concurrence of the governor is required in such decision. The decision to hold a primary in that state is said to hinge on whether the governor and the party committee happen to be agreed on an aspirant for the Democratic nomination who would probably enjoy an advantage in a primary (see L. W. Holland, *The Direct Primary in Georgia* [Urbana, 1945], pp. 15–16).

[34] *The American Political Scene*, p. 267.

to permit their names to be entered in some or all the state primaries.[35]
Often this refusal is coupled with the fact that the state organization
is running a favorite son; the outside candidate hesitates to antagonize
the organization, which hopes by obtaining the preference vote for a
favorite son to be left free to negotiate in the convention and to throw
its strength where it will do the state organization the most good.[36]
The leaders of state organizations have not generally been enthusiastic
about the primary, and in the conventions they have often paid little
heed to the preferences expressed through it. Interest and participation of the electorate in presidential primaries has on the whole tended
to be less than in primaries for nomination to state offices, although
there have been some notable exceptions to this generalization. Low
popular participation in the primary facilitates, of course, control of
its outcome by the state organization.

Proposals for a nation-wide primary. When the memory of the Republican convention of 1912 was fresh, numerous proposals were made
for the establishment of a nation-wide preference primary, which perhaps would have required a constitutional amendment. President
Wilson, in his first message to Congress, urged a national system in
these words: "I turn now to a subject which I hope can be handled
promptly and without serious controversy of any kind. I mean the
method of selecting nominees for the Presidency of the United States.
I feel confident that I do not misinterpret the wishes or the expectations
of the country when I urge prompt enactment of legislation which will
provide for primary elections throughout the country at which the
voters of the several parties may choose the nominees for the Presidency without the intervention of nominating conventions." Congress
did not act on the recommendation. In 1920 there was renewed interest in the question, and in 1924 the La Follette platform contained a
plank favoring a nation-wide primary. But the proposal has become
a dead issue.

The invention of the straw poll has introduced a sort of nation-wide

---

[35] Although the state laws are not always clear on the matter, the practice is not to
place on the ballot the names of presidential aspirants who object. However, in 1944
delegates pledged to Dewey remained in the Wisconsin race despite a telegram from
Dewey: ". . . I want to make it entirely clear that any use of my name meets my
strongest disapproval." Dewey's "protest" was not addressed to the election authorities.

[36] For example, the California Republicans in their 1944 primary technically
pledged their delegates to Governor Warren. The national committeeman explained
that the state had 50 convention votes and proposed to use them to bargain for a
place in the cabinet, a member of the Supreme Court, and other high positions in the
government, all contingent of course upon the election of the Republican nominee.
The selection of unpledged delegates or the pledging of delegates to nominal candidates is often calculated to lay the basis for such negotiations.

preference primary.   The figures in Table 14 on page 379 show the trend in sentiment among Republicans toward Dewey in the months preceding the 1944 Republican convention.   Whether the polls influence the outcome of the convention or whether the action of the convention is different than it would be in the absence of the polls is a question not readily answered.   It is of some interest in this connection that up to the eve of the 1940 convention Dewey was the poll preference for the nomination, but at the time of the nomination popular opinion had shifted rapidly toward Willkie.   The poll revealing this shift, however, had not been made public at the time of the nomination of Willkie.

3. ORGANIZATION OF THE CONVENTION

On the appointed day [37] the delegates convene to play their parts in our great quadrennial political drama.   The city fathers of the convention city [38] deck out the city in bunting and flags as if a huge county

[37] The Republican convention usually meets in June and is followed two or three weeks later by the Democratic convention.   In 1944 the Republicans met on June 26, 27, and 28, and the Democrats on July 19, 20, and 21.   The timing of the conventions assures a long national campaign in contrast with other great democracies.   In 1944 Frank Walker, Democratic national chairman, proposed that the conventions be held later than usual, possibly in September, to permit a brief wartime campaign.   The Republican national chairman, Harrison E. Spangler, opined that Roosevelt would be the Democratic nominee and that the length of the campaign would not in fact be reduced by the formal device of postponing the conventions.   He refused to discuss the matter unless the Democrats would give assurance that they would not nominate Roosevelt.   This the Democrats refused to give, and efforts to delay the conventions collapsed.

[38] The place of the convention is designated by the national committee.   Esoteric considerations of party advantage are said to have a part in the selection.   It is said, for example, that the Republican convention of 1928 was held in Kansas City on the theory that the farm belt was a potential center of disaffection from Republican leadership and that to hold the convention in that region would help to keep the wheat farmer in the Republican ranks.   It is doubtful that the location of the convention has any effect on the vote cast, but the possibility that it might is certainly urged by the advocates of particular cities.   A representative of Detroit, for example, said to the Democratic National Committee in 1944: "From the political angle, let us be astute; let us use strategy.   Michigan is normally a Republican state.   But in the last ten or twelve years we have had two Democratic governors.   In the last national election we lost the state by relatively few votes.   By taking the National Convention to Detroit, there is an opportunity to bring Michigan back to the Democratic fold."— *Proceedings*, National Convention, 1944, p. 344.   Aspirants for the nomination often attempt to influence the choice of location to avoid cities that would pack the galleries with hostile crowds and to seek the designation of cities where the gallery and newspaper atmosphere would be favorable or at least neutral.   Prime considerations, however, are that the convention city have adequate rail and hotel facilities and that it possess a suitable auditorium for the convention itself.   Beyond these requirements the bonus offered by the local citizenry may be influential.   Thus a consideration in the choice of Philadelphia for the 1948 convention by the Republican national committee in April, 1947, was a certified check for $200,000, although the selection of Philadelphia over Chicago was also regarded as a victory for those favorable to Dewey

fair were in progress. Banners identify the headquarters of the presidential aspirants. Their managers issue optimistic predictions of their first-ballot strength and work frantically behind the scenes to try to approach in fact their predictions. By badges, armbands, and buttons the delegates and visitors proclaim their allegiance. The convention gathers in a great auditorium—such as the Chicago Stadium, the Cleveland Municipal Auditorium, Madison Square Garden in New York—the main floor of which seats the delegates and their alternates, more than two thousand in all; the galleries seat thousands of spectators, both local and visiting, fortunate enough to receive tickets of admission.[39] The heat is usually stifling, the noise deafening, the confusion astonishing to foreign observers. The convention hall is equipped with amplifying apparatus, so that the officials and delegates may be heard. The radio chains have their equipment set up to broadcast the happenings to tens of millions of people listening throughout the nation. In effect, almost the entire nation is in the galleries.

Temporary organization. The convention is opened by the chairman of the national committee, who presides until the temporary officers are elected.[40] The national committee presents to the convention a slate of temporary officers, of which the temporary chairman is, of course, the most important.[41] Generally the nominee of the national committee is approved by the convention, but at times the election of temporary chairman is the occasion for a test of strength of contending factions within the convention. In the Republican convention of 1912, for example, the national committee and the Taft forces suc-

---

rather than Taft for the 1948 presidential nomination. In some recent conventions the leadership has been constrained to hold the convention in session longer than was absolutely necessary in order that local innkeepers and tippling-house proprietors might have a chance to recoup their contributions to bring the convention to their city.

[39] Mary R. Beard has chided me gently for failing to refer in the first edition of this book to the place of women in the national convention (see her *Woman as Force in History* [New York: Macmillan, 1946], pp. 61–62). Let it be noted that at the Republican convention of 1944 there were 96 women delegates and 258 women alternates; and at the Democratic convention of that year there were 152 women delegates and 321 women alternates.

[40] It should be mentioned that each session of the convention is opened with prayer, usually by local clergymen carefully selected to be representative of the leading faiths. Thus at the 1940 Republican convention prayers were offered by a rabbi, a Lutheran, a Christian Scientist, an Archbishop, an African Methodist bishop, a Presbyterian, the Chancellor of an Archdiocese, a Baptist, a Protestant Episcopal bishop, a Methodist, and the Chaplain of the Connecticut State Senate, a divine of undesignated denomination.

[41] The other temporary officers—who are usually made permanent—include the secretary, sergeant-at-arms, parliamentarian, chief tally clerk, chief reading clerk, doorkeeper, and various other assistants and officials necessary for the operation of the convention.

cessfully backed Elihu Root for the temporary chairmanship over the
opposition of the Roosevelt delegates, who supported Governor Mc-
Govern of Wisconsin.   In the same year Bryan opposed Judge Alton B.
Parker, the national committee nominee for the Democratic temporary
chairmanship.   Judge Parker, Bryan said, was backed by Wall Street.
"He asked if such a man should be 'forced on the convention to open a
progressive campaign with a paralyzing speech that will dishearten
every man in it?' " [42]   Parker won through the support of delegates
pledged to Harmon and Underwood, the opposition coming from Wilson delegates.

The chief function of the temporary chairman is to deliver the keynote speech, which is designed to arouse the enthusiasm of the delegates, as well as to set the general tone of the convention.   The keynoter inveighs against the opposition,[43] recites the great achievements
of his own party, and invokes the memory of the great party leaders of
the past.   In 1936 the Republican temporary chairman was Senator
Frederick Steiwer of Oregon, who denounced the New Deal: "For more
than three long years we have had a government without political
morality."   "After three long years of complete control of every branch
of the Federal Government they have failed to provide a permanent
farm program."   He called his hearers to do battle: "To preserve our
country we must get into the American stride again."   He forecast
victory in November: "This wholesome recommendation will be made
in January, by an oath-keeping Republican President."   He invoked
the aid of the Almighty: "To Him let our prayers be offered that an
aroused America, casting out all doubt, will vindicate the faith of the
fathers."   "At the end of the address," the secretary of the convention
solemnly records, "the Temporary chairman received a great ovation,
delegates, alternates and visitors rising, standing on chairs, cheering,
waving hats and flags." [44]

The keynoters in 1944, as befitted the gravity of the times, spoke
more soberly than is usual in times of peace.   Governor R. S. Kerr of
Oklahoma, the Democratic keynoter, declared: "Our aim is complete
and speedy victory.   Our goal is a just and abiding peace.   Our promise to a world at peace is responsibility and co-operation."   He managed, however, to work in some old-fashioned denunciation of the

42 Stanwood, *A History of the Presidency from 1897 to 1916*, p. 256.

43 A sample of the criticism of the opposition is furnished by Senator Barkley's 1932
keynote speech in which he said: "No, my countrymen, there is nothing wrong with
this republic except that it has been mismanaged, exploited and demoralized for more
than a decade by a statesmanship, incapable even now in the midst of its fearful havoc
of understanding the extent of its own mischief."

44 *Proceedings*. 1936, p. 46.

opposition: "To give these modern Bourbons, these Republican leaders, control of the Nation for the next four years would bring about the certain return of 1932." He pointed to the record of a majority of Republican representatives against repeal of arms embargo in 1939, against lend-lease in 1941, against continuation of selective service in August, 1941. He lauded the leadership and statesmanship of Roosevelt. He warned against an untried leader. He feared that the forces of isolationism were striving with "fury and frenzy" to inflict the fate of Woodrow Wilson on Franklin D. Roosevelt. In his peroration he looked forward to victory: "We have overrun the ramparts of special privilege and reaction and planted the banner of Democratic liberalism high on the hill of human progress. Let our opponents—who have grown fat in a prosperity they could not build for themselves—do their worst. Under our great Commander in Chief we will not now retreat. We will not falter in midpassage. We will win."

An early step in the convention is the designation of its four great standing committees: (1) credentials, with the function of examining credentials, hearing delegations contesting for seats, and recommending to the convention; (2) permanent organization, with the function of recommending a set of permanent officers for the convention: (3) rules, with the duty of reporting to the convention a set of rules to govern its procedure, and (4) resolutions, with the task of drafting and presenting a platform to the convention.[45] In practice each state and territorial delegation names a person to sit on each of these committees except that one man and one woman are designated by each delegation for membership on the resolutions committee. The Democrats adopted the innovation of female representation on the resolutions committee in 1940, and the Republicans followed in 1944.

Permanent organization: Rivals maneuver for advantage. The first committee report disposed of by the convention is usually that of the committee on credentials, but, for convenience, the report of the committee on permanent organization may be mentioned first. The item in the report of this committee that may give rise to controversy is its recommendation for the post of permanent chairman. The factions aligned behind each aspirant for the presidential nomination desire the selection of a permanent chairman, if not friendly, at least not hostile to their candidates. A minority report from the committee on permanent organization may furnish the occasion for a test of strength between the opposing candidates for the nomination. In 1932, for example, tl majority of the committee on permanent organization

[45] In 1940 the resolutions committee of the Republican convention was selected and began its labors before the convention itself met.

nominated Jouett Shouse, affiliated with the anti-Roosevelt bloc, for the permanent chairmanship; the Roosevelt forces were able to rally a majority of the convention to support the late Senator Walsh of Montana as permanent chairman.[46]   However, the suspense over who will be permanent chairman is usually not great.   In fact, he may be "chosen" long before he is "elected" by the convention.   In 1944, for example, Harrison E. Spangler, Republican national chairman, announced on April 19 that Joseph W. Martin, of Massachusetts, would be the permanent chairman of the convention to open on June 26. On July 1, Robert E. Hannegan, Democratic national chairman, announced, after consultation with the executive committee of the national committee, that Samuel D. Jackson, of Indiana, would be permanent chairman of the convention meeting on July 19.   The permanent chairman, when he takes over the gavel from the temporary chairman, usually delivers a speech that may be a smaller edition of the keynote speech.[47]

The formal organization of the convention consists of the permanent chairman, the standing committees, and the functionaries necessary for the work of the assembly; but, as with congresses and parliaments, there tends to be also an informal organization of the blocs and factions seeking to steer the deliberations of the convention.   Before the 1932 Democratic convention, for example, the Roosevelt leaders held a caucus at Hyde Park to agree on how to run the convention.   It was decided that Walsh would be permanent chairman, that Arthur Mullen would be the floor manager for the Roosevelt forces, that Senator Hitchcock would be chairman of the committee on resolutions, and that Judge Mack would nominate Roosevelt.   Farley goes on to tell us: [48]

On the night before the convention opened we had another general meeting at headquarters during which we organized our "field" forces for the convention floor itself.   I wanted to make sure that the key men would be recognized immediately by all the Roosevelt delegates.   As each man's name was called, he stepped down front so that all those in attendance had a good look at him.   Those introduced included Floor Leader Arthur Mullen and his assistants.   I also introduced Bill Howes of South Dakota, and a couple of

[46] For an account of this affair, see Charles Michelson, *The Ghost Talks* (New York: Putnam, 1944), pp. 4–8

[47] The exigencies of radio timetables compelled Senator Joseph T. Robinson, 1936 Democratic permanent chairman, to deliver his speech before he had been formally elected as chairman.   The temporary chairman said that "it was expected that the permanent chairman would be elected by this time and deliver an address over the radio. . . ."   Senator Robinson was presented as "the gentleman who is scheduled a little later to be elected as your permanent chairman, but who now speaks in the capacity of a delegate at large from the State of Arkansas."

[48] James A. Farley, *Behind the Ballots* (New York: Harcourt, Brace, 1938), p. 122.

other trusted lieutenants who were to act as emissaries in carrying messages and instructions. Those present were asked to have their delegations go along with whatever these men requested. We were anxious to ensure good teamwork and to avoid the mistakes, which often prove so costly, that come about because of the excitement and confusion on the convention floor.

Similarly, Governor R. E. Baldwin of Connecticut was floor leader of the Willkie forces in the 1940 Republican convention. Mitchell Palmer served as Wilson floor leader in the 1912 Democratic convention.

Frequently the informal organization of the leading candidate plans the management of the convention in great detail. When a convention meets to renominate a sitting President, his leaders generally have the convention proceedings thoroughly in control. In such conventions practically every item of procedure is laid out in advance, even to the allocation of the honors of seconding motions for adjournment and of proposing resolutions of gratitude to the committee on local arrangements. When a stentorian voice echoes through the convention hall, "The chair recognizes delegate Jones from Wisconsin to offer a resolution," the script is merely being followed. To provide for contingencies not foreseen in the planning, remote control may be introduced. Thus, Hoover had a direct line to his managers in the 1932 Republican convention, and Harry Hopkins kept in almost constant telephonic contact with the White House from the 1940 Democratic convention at Chicago.

Credentials: Contested delegations. The national convention is the judge of the qualifications of its own members. In the early history of the convention, examination of delegates' credentials was quite casual. When no formally elected delegation represented a state, chance visitors from the state concerned might be allowed to cast its vote in the convention. With the regularization of convention procedure, a body of precedent developed to govern the determination of the right of delegations to convention membership. Prior to the opening of the convention, the national committee of each party prepares a temporary roll or list of the delegates duly selected to sit in the convention.[49]

[49] The Republican rules provide: "Twenty days before the time set for the meeting of the National Convention, the credentials of each Delegate and Alternate shall be filed with the Secretary of the National Committee for use in making up the temporary roll of the Convention, except in the case of Delegates or Alternates elected at a time or times in accordance with the laws of the State in which the election occurs, rendering impossible filing of credentials within the time above specified. Notices of contests shall be filed in the same manner and within the same limit. Where more than the authorized number of Delegates from any State, Territory, Territorial Possession, or District of Columbia are reported to the Secretary of the National Committee, a contest shall be deemed to exist and the Secretary shall notify the several claimants so reported, and shall submit all such credentials and claims to the whole Committee

In the determination of which names are to be placed on the temporary roll, the national committee must make a preliminary decision on contested elections, if any, and to that end it hears the parties to such contests.[50]   The Republican national committee is required by party rule, however, to place on the temporary roll the names of those delegates certified by appropriate state officials as having been designated in accordance with state law.   The convention itself is not bound by that action.   This rule was adopted following the difficulties in the convention of 1912, when the Taft-dominated national committee excluded from the temporary roll the names of some duly certified pro-Roosevelt delegates.   When the convention of each party meets, the documents and papers used by the national committee in preparing the temporary roll are delivered to the committee on credentials.   It hears the claims of the contesting delegations anew and reports to the convention, which accepts or rejects the recommendations.

The importance of the decision on contests arises from the fact that one delegation claiming to be duly authorized and elected to represent a state may be pledged to one candidate for the presidential nomination; the other delegation, likewise claiming to be duly authorized and elected, may be pledged to another aspirant for the nomination.   In some circumstances the convention, in deciding which delegation to seat, may be deciding which candidate will have enough support to gain the nomination.   Hence the managers for each candidate take a keen interest in the contests and marshal their forces to assure a decision to their advantage, occasionally without much regard to the facts or equities of the contest.

The 1912 Republican convention furnishes the most significant example of the importance of the settlement of contests.   The national committee, in the preparation of the temporary roll, seated delegations pledged to Taft rather than the contesting delegations supporting Theodore Roosevelt.   The committee on credentials and the convention itself followed in general the decisions of the national committee.   The temporarily seated delegations were entitled to vote on all contests save their own; the action of the national committee and of the convention

---

for decision as to which claimants reported shall be placed upon the temporary roll of the Convention: provided, however, that the names of the Delegates and Alternates presenting certificates of election from the canvassing board or officer created or designated by the Law of the State in which the election occurs, to canvass the returns and issue Certificates of Election to Delegates to National Conventions of political parties in a primary election, shall be placed upon the temporary roll of the Convention by the National Committee."—*Proceedings*, 1944, pp. 124–125.

[50] Stenographic transcripts of these proceedings before the Democratic national committee are printed with the proceedings of the national convention.

in seating Taft rather than Roosevelt delegates gave the nomination to Taft.

Democratic conventions have not been without contests for the seating of opposing delegations, but in no instance have the consequences been so serious as the split in the Republican party following the 1912 convention. In 1932, for example, two contests concerning the Louisiana and Minnesota delegations were decided by the convention. The supporters of Franklin Roosevelt for the nomination rallied to seat the delegations from these two states pledged to his candidacy. In both instances the question was, as it generally is in such instances, which authority that named delegates to the convention from the state was entitled to speak for the part within the state. In the 1944 Democratic convention the right of the "regular" Democratic delegates to sit in the convention was contested by delegates chosen by a rump convention in Texas after the "regular" manifested hostility toward Roosevelt. The credentials committee report that was adopted followed an oft-used practice: it recommended that both delegations be seated, each to cast half the number of votes allotted to the state.

4. PLATFORMS

The platform, a statement of the broad program that the party proposes to carry out if its candidates are elected, is presented to the convention by the committee on resolutions.[51] Although this committee holds hearings, at which representatives of various pressure groups present their demands for its consideration, the actual writing of the platform is done by a few party leaders, who may or may not be members of the committee on resolutions. In fact, the business of platform writing begins long before the convention meets. Supporters of particular candidates for the nomination or factional leaders may take the lead in developing platform drafts and in consultation among party leaders about what the platform should contain. Whatever group

[51] It is said that the Democratic convention of 1840 adopted the first full-fledged platform. The resolutions of that convention "involved the three essential factors of a modern platform,—a statement of fundamental party principles, policies to be pursued under the pending circumstances, and pledges that these principles and policies would be carried out."—G. S. P. Kleeberg, *The Formation of the Republican Party as a National Political Organization* (New York, 1911), p. 163. The fundamental idea of the platform antedates even the convention system. The Republican congressional caucus of 1800 passed resolutions stating the principles of Jefferson. The early national conventions often adopted resolutions on questions of policy, although these resolutions were not so comprehensive nor were they in the same form as the present-day platform (see H. J. Ford, *The Rise and Growth of American Politics* [New York: Macmillan, 1898], p. 205).

gains control of the convention and the resolutions committee comes prepared with a platform draft.

Formation of the platform. A sitting President seeking renomination is likely to guide the preparation of the preliminary platform draft. In 1932, although James Garfield was chairman of the Republican resolutions committee, "Secretary of the Treasury Ogden Mills brought the entire platform from Washington, with the exception of the plank on prohibition, which was written in Chicago by men who knew" Hoover's desires.[52] The Democratic platform of 1932 was prepared "chiefly, by A. Mitchell Palmer, former Attorney-General of the United States, after a series of conferences with Roosevelt supporters in Congress and in the various states."[53] The Democratic platform of 1936 was written by Roosevelt and sent to the convention resolutions committee which approved it after the alteration of one sentence, according to Raymond Moley.[54]

Although various leaders may come prepared with proposed drafts of the platform, the work of the resolutions committee is rarely mere formality. It often engages in bitter debate and discussion in the effort to arrive at a wording on which its members may agree.[55] The work of

[52] Peel and Donnelly, *The 1932 Campaign*, p. 86.

[53] *Ibid.*, p. 100.

[54] *After Seven Years*, pp. 346–347.

[55] In preparation for the work of the Republican convention of 1940 an unusual procedure was followed in the creation of a program committee to lay the groundwork for the platform. The program committee was established by the Republican national committee in November, 1937, and Glenn Frank was designated chairman. It consisted of some two hundred Republican leaders, who were divided into regional groups. The program committee was aided by a small research staff working at the national head quarters of the party. Its report, released in February, 1940, was not designed to serve as a platform but to set out facts and, Chairman Frank said, "to discuss, to clarify, and to present the fundamental principles of approach to the various fields of policy." The report was published as *A Program for A Dynamic America*. In addition to this pamphlet the committee and its staff also produced unpublished materials to assist the resolutions committee in its work. See Ronald Bridges, "The Republican Program Committee," *Public Opinion Quarterly*, 3 (1939), pp. 299–306. A different method was used by the Republicans in preparation for the 1944 convention. In September, 1943, the Republican Post-War Advisory Council, a group of Senators, governors, and other Republican bigwigs, met at Mackinac Island and devised a declaration of principles that was notable chiefly for a move away from isolationism in foreign policy. The Council also appointed committees to study current problems and prepare reports and recommendations to aid the resolutions committee of the 1944 national convention. These committees had research assistance and consulted with interest groups in the preparation of their reports. The committee on agriculture, for example, in April, 1944, met in Chicago to hear the views of the principal national farm organizations. Late in 1945 Republican Senators and Representatives drafted a statement of party principles that was regarded by some party leaders outside Congress as too noncommittal on many issues. The National Committee, in December, 1945, endorsed the declaration, but appointed a seven-man committee to collect suggestions for the development of the

the resolutions committee and the parallel discussion among the delegates usually are centered on the one or two questions that are currently foremost in public discussion.   On all matters save a few controversial issues there is likely to be substantial agreement in the platform committee.   The convention leaders exert themselves to bring about harmony within the committee on these controversial matters, so as to avoid an open fight on the floor of the convention.

When these efforts to reconcile differences within the committee fail, the minority submits a separate recommendation to the convention on the bitterly contested items in the platform.   In the 1928 Republican convention, for example, a minority plank on agriculture, proposed by Earl C. Smith, a delegate from Illinois and president of the Illinois Agriculture Society, was supported by fifteen states in the committee on resolutions.   The minority foresaw a defection of midwestern farmers from the Republican party: "We come to you within these four walls pleading with the delegates not to drive the farmers of the Republican States out of their party." [56]   "The farmer furnishes the banquet, but like Lazarus sits at the feet of industry and finance and commerce and picks up the crumbs." [57]   Industry and finance were in the saddle.   The minority plank was rejected, but it was not until 1932 that the midwestern farmers rebelled against commercial and industrial domination of Republican policies.

Other examples of debate on minority platform proposals are furnished by the Democratic convention of 1932.   The majority of the resolutions committee reported a plank advocating "the repeal of the Eighteenth Amendment."   The minority plank, proposed by Cordell Hull, merely advocated submission of the question of repeal to the states.   The minority proposal set off a debate lasting until midnight. Hull and other minority speakers met boos and catcalls from the galleries; Al Smith, Albert Ritchie, and other speakers were greeted with resounding cheers.   The minority proposal was defeated.

The work of both Republican and Democratic resolutions committees in 1940 illustrates the tendency for a single great issue to dominate in platform deliberations.   The Republican committee was vexed by disputes between isolationist and interventionist factions, confounded by the stream of events in Europe, where the Nazis were moving forward daily, and confused by the strategy of the Democratic administration, which had just designated Republicans to head the War and

---

statement to the end that it might represent "the aggregate of the conscience, intelligence and hopes of Republicans in all States."

[56] *Proceedings*, 1928, p. 150.

[57] *Ibid.*, p. 154.

Navy departments. The foreign-policy plank that emerged from days of dispute and deliberation firmly opposed "involving this Nation in foreign war." "Our sympathies," it read, "have been profoundly stirred by invasion of unoffending countries, and by disaster to nations whose ideals most closely resemble our own. We favor the extension to all peoples fighting for liberty, or whose liberty is threatened, of such aid as shall not be in violation of international law or inconsistent with the requirements of our own national defense." In the Democratic convention the interest of the platform committee was similarly centered on the foreign-policy plank. At other conventions the general tendency to concentrate interest on a single great issue is apparent. The Democratic resolutions committee in 1944 was in the position of having to endorse generally the policies of the Democratic administration, but it became involved in a bitter dispute between northern and southern wings of the party over the extent to which the platform should pledge policies against racial discrimination.

The resolutions committee hold hearings at which spokesmen for groups concerned about specific platform planks urge the viewpoints of their organizations. Before the Democratic resolutions committee in 1940 appeared Philip Murray, of the C.I.O., and William Green, of the A.F.L. Walter White, secretary of the National Association for the Advancement of Colored People, demanded a plank promising the repeal of legislation discriminating against the Negro. Joseph Cadden, executive secretary of the American Youth Congress, advocated an extensive program of youth assistance. Clark Eichelberger, secretary of the Committee to Defend America by Aiding the Allies, recommended aid to the British. Dr. Francis E. Townsend sought specific endorsement of the Townsend plan for old-age pensions. Louis J. Taber, of the National Grange, urged schemes to send "American farm surpluses to the starving populations of Europe." Neville Miller, head of the National Association of Broadcasters, asked for greater privileges for broadcasters. A. G. Davis, of the Investment Bankers Association, suggested revision of securities legislation. Representative of the National Woman's Party and the National Women's Trade Union League took conflicting positions on a proposed equal rights amendment to the Constitution. A similar parade of pressure-group representatives passed in review before the Republican resolutions committee. In 1944 a subcommittee of the Democratic resolutions met in Chicago several days before the convention opened to begin hearing representatives of pressure groups.

Nature of the platform. The platform, as finally adopted by a convention, speaks with boldness and forthrightness on issues that are already well settled; it is likely to be ambiguous on contentious questions. Indeed, new and growing issues may not be mentioned at all until a non-party organization or pressure group has conducted so thorough an agitation that the parties cannot ignore the question. The characteristic lack of courageous and bold statement in the platforms calls forth criticism both from those of conservative and those of liberal tendencies alike.[58] But the criticisms of party platforms on grounds of ambiguity on controversial issues overlook the very real political function of the platform. Its vague pronouncements serve as a formula on which the divergent interests and groups within the party may unite for the duration of the campaign; the real settlement of the issue is left until later. To win the campaign it is necessary to unite; to speak forth boldly when majority sentiment is undecided is to invite division. The essential similarity of platforms likewise comes in for criticism; the voter has no choice, it is said. Yet this similarity may be interpreted as an indication of a healthy body politic, or perhaps, more accurately, as an indication that the governing "classes" of our capitalistic democracy are in firm possession of power. In a sense, the continuation of democracy as we know it depends on the absence of extremely abrupt shifts in government policy with each change in party control. With the knowledge that there would be such a swing, it is questionable whether we would have the tolerance, self-restraint, and "democratic discipline" necessary to permit fundamental nonviolent changes.

If the party wins, the platform may be treated in a cavalier fashion. By the naive the platform is considered to be a solemn convenant between party and electorate that the specified policies will be adopted. By the practicing politician, the immediate circumstances are governing; the platform is cited in debate only to taunt the opposition or to defend a course that would have been followed anyway. A characteristic attitude was reflected by Representative Manasco, of Alabama, in December, 1945, in debate on a proposed full-employment bill, when he was reminded of the Democratic platform pledge: "If we had put into law everything that both parties had pledged in their platforms during the last 40 years, the country would have been destroyed many years ago." Nor do the voters regard platforms seriously. Dr. Gallup finds that only a small percentage of the electorate is familiar with the content of either party platform.

It is customary to attribute disregard of platform pledges to the innate perfidy and wickedness of the politician, but, as is usual, the easy explanation does not explain much. A simple fact is that conditions

[58] See, for example, Wendell Willkie, "Cowardice at Chicago," *Collier's*, September 16, 1944.

change between the time the platform is drafted and the time the party takes power. Between June, 1932, when the Democratic platform was adopted, and March, 1933, when Franklin Roosevelt was inaugurated, the banking system of the nation completely collapsed. An extreme example, to be sure, but it is indicative of the significance of the general proposition. Other factors—if not more recondite, perhaps more involved—have greater significance than do changed circumstances in the nullification of platforms. The party platform has a multiple appeal; Senators and Representatives are, in effect, elected, not because of their adherence to a particular party policy or plank, but because they have constructed a strong local organization, or for other reasons. The platform, then, may be the lowest common denominator on which all segments of the party may unite, but in Congress the bloc strongly attached to a particular plank may be definitely in the minority.

Beyond these matters is the practical difficulty of an extralegal, and extraconstitutional body—the national convention—binding its members of Congress and the President—who is nominated after the platform is adopted—to a specific course of action. Carried to its logical conclusion, this process would result in a Congress of automata, at least on those matters on which the platform had spoken. The President and the party in Congress can hardly be reduced to this subordinate role; they became the Government and, for the welfare of the nation as well as for the welfare of their party, must act as the Government and not as the rubber stamp of a party organ. In England, where a much sharper distinction is drawn between the party in Parliament and the party organization outside the government, the parliamentary party has refused to be bound and has demanded that it not be embarrassed by specific and binding instructions—or platforms—adopted by the national organs of the party outside the government.[59] Probably something of the same fundamental tendency—that is, a cleavage between the extragovernmental party organization and the party as government —has operated in this country, although there has been no systematic rationalization of that factor.[60]

Candidates "amend" the platform. The generalities of the platform

[59] On this point, see F. A. Ogg, *English Government and Politics* (New York: Macmillan, 1929), chap. 24. The general proposition was well illustrated by the animadversions of Mr. Harold Laski, chairman of the Labor Party, in 1945. The Laborites in Parliament acted quite differently from the way in which the chairman of the party outside of the government spoke.

[60] Ford observes, however: "The Whigs, a party of political odds and ends, did not formally present a platform either in 1840 or in 1848. The prepossessions in favor of parliamentary control which clung to the Whig party made the laying down of platforms in connection with presidential nominations a disagreeable duty."— *Op. cit.*, p. 205.

are amplified by the presidential candidate in his speeches during the campaign. Occasionally the candidate proceeds to amend the platform before the convention has adjourned. In 1904 the Democratic convention, still suffering from the blight of its espousal of the free coinage of silver in 1896, nominated Parker, a conservative Easterner for the Presidency, and said nothing about coinage in the platform. Parker telegraphed: [61]

I regard the gold standard as firmly and irrevocably established, and shall act accordingly if the action of the convention to-day shall be ratified by the people. As the platform is silent on the subject, my view should be made known to the convention, and if it is proved to be unsatisfactory to the majority, I request you to decline the nomination for me at once, so that another may be nominated before adjournment.

The 1928 Democratic convention pledged "its nominees to an honest effort to enforce the Eighteenth amendment." As the convention was about to adjourn, the following telegram from Al Smith, the nominee, was read:

It is well known that I believe there should be fundamental changes in the present provisions for national prohibition, based, as I stated in my Jackson Day letter, on the fearless application of the principles of Jeffersonian democracy. While I fully appreciate that these changes can only be made by the people themselves, through their elected representative, I feel it to be the duty of the chosen leader of the people to point the way which, in his opinion, leads us to a sane, sensible solution of a condition which, I am convinced, is entirely unsatisfactory to the great mass of our people.

The prohibition plank was, in effect, erased from the platform.

Governor Landon, in 1936, telegraphed the Republican convention before it nominated him expressing his views on several planks of the platform. The platform favored state laws on child labor and on hours, wages, and working conditions of women; Landon favored, if it was found necessary, a constitutional amendment to permit federal action. The platform promised "a sound currency to be preserved at all hazards." Landon interpreted that to mean "a currency expressed in terms of gold and convertible into gold," with certain hedging sentences. The convention pledged the party to "the merit system"; Landon concretized the generality by promising to include within the merit system "every position . . . below the rank of assistant secretaries

[61] Quoted by Stanwood, *A History of the Presidency from 1897 to 1916*, p. 125. The convention telegraphed Parker that since the platform was silent on the subject, "there is nothing in the views expressed by you in the telegram just received which would preclude a man entertaining them from accepting a nomination on said platform."

of major departments." [62]   Every candidate in one way or another finds
it necessary to "interpret" ambiguous platform planks during the course
of his campaign.

5. NOMINATIONS

After the platform has been disposed of, the convention reaches the
main job before it: the making of presidential and vice-presidential
nominations.   Meanwhile, the leaders for each presidential contender,
since the latter, our political etiquette has traditionally dictated, should
remain away from the convention,[63] have been engaged in interminable
conferences, in maintaining the morale and loyalty of the faithful delegations, in trying to induce the wavering enemy to join their ranks,
and in angling for promises of second-ballot support from delegations
pledged to favorite sons and other long-shot candidates.   Each campaign manager has his espionage agents to ascertain the strength of the
opposition, to gain advance knowledge of their strategy, to avoid being
taken by surprise.

Placing the candidates in nomination.   The roll of states is called
in alphabetical order for nominations.   Generally a state near the top
of the list will yield to a state farther down the line that has a serious
contender.   For example, Alabama may yield to New York to permit it
to place its candidates in nomination.   The nominating speeches represent convention oratory at its most extravagant; it must be heard to be
appreciated.   In 1928 Franklin Roosevelt's speech nominating Alfred
Smith concluded with the following climax:

> America needs not only an administrator but a leader—a pathfinder, a
> blazer of the trail to the high road that will avoid the bottomless morass of
> gross materialism that has engulfed so many of the great civilizations of the
> past.   It is the privilege of Democracy not only to offer such a man but to offer
> him as their surest leader to victory.   To stand upon the ramparts and die for
> our principles is heroic.   To sally forth to battle and win for our principles is
> something more than heroic.   We offer one who has the will to win—who not
> only deserves success but commands it.   Victory is his habit—the happy war-
> rior, Alfred E. Smith.

---

62 For the text of Governor Landon's telegram, see *Proceedings,* 1936, pp. 149–151.
63 This custom was broken wholesale at the 1940 Republican convention.   "It has
been a sort of unwritten rule for years past for such aspirants to keep away from the
actual ringside.   Concealing their fierce itching under a pretense of lofty indifference,
and even when that rule has been broken, as at Chicago, in 1920, it has not been
broken by all hands.   But this time each and every one of the boys will be on the
scene, including even the Hon. Herbert Hoover, whose best showing in the straw
polls is two votes, and the Hon. Alf M. Landon, who is himself predicting that he
will not get as many as one vote on any ballot short of the thirteenth."—H. L.
Mencken in the Baltimore *Sun,* June 23, 1940.

In 1928 John McNab nominated Hoover at the Republican convention:

I nominate him for his lofty character as a man and citizen; for his broad and kindly human sympathies; for his wholesome heart that rejoices above all things else that he has been useful to the people of his native land.

And now, engineer, practical scientist, minister of mercy to the hungry and the poor, administrator, executive, statesman, beneficent American, kindly neighbor, wholesome human being, I give you the name of Herbert Hoover.

The custom is, as in the quotations, to describe some mythical character, to extol his virtues, to demonstrate that he can be victorious, and, at last, to reveal, what everybody knew all through the discourse, his name. The name of the candidate is the signal for bedlam to break loose. Supporters of the candidate start processions through the aisles; bands play the campaign song; delegates and spectators yell themselves hoarse; and organized disorder prevails.

These demonstrations are by no means wholly spontaneous; they are merely synthesized in varying degrees. On the day that Hoover was scheduled to be nominated in 1932, delegates to the Republican convention found whistles, horns, other noise-making devices, and bags of confetti in their chairs. When the time came they were equipped for action. The length and exuberance of the demonstration may, of course, vary with the genuineness of the joy of the delegates. In 1936, after the demonstration for Franklin Roosevelt, the convention chairman announced that the seventy-minute demonstration had not only broken the record "of this convention but of all other conventions. It has also," the chairman continued, "broken the instrument on the left of the Chairman designed for registration of applause." The length of the demonstration and the intensity of the applause give a rough index of the strength and popularity of the various candidates, but no votes are changed by the noise. The pageantry and the demonstrations give the delegates something to do while their leaders negotiate behind the scenes.[64]

[64] The following note by the Secretary of the Republican convention describing the demonstration following a speech nominating Taft in 1940 (*Proceedings*, pp. 194–195) conveys something of the atmosphere: "Upon the conclusion of Mr. Patterson's nominating speech the Ohio standard was borne aloft round the hall, followed by other state standards. There were many pictures of Senator Taft, and placards 'Taft the Statesman,' 'Taft Will Win,' and 'Get on with the Winner,' 'We Want Taft,' 'As Ohio Goes so Goes the Nation' and 'Ohio Goes for Taft,' 'No guesswork, just hard work; that's Bob Taft,' 'Bob Taft knows only one way and that is the American way,' 'Out of the Wilderness with Bob Taft,' 'Pick a Man who is big and strong, who knows what is right and won't do wrong, Bob Taft,' 'America is not washed up, Bob Taft,' 'The Best Man for the Biggest Job, Bob Taft,' 'On to Victory with Bob Taft,' 'Come On and Let's Go with Bob Taft.' There were many pictures

Balloting for the candidate. After the nominating speeches have been made, the roll is called again by states for speeches seconding the nominations already made. These speeches are shorter, but on the same order as the nominating speeches. Finally, with the completion of the seconding speeches, the convention is ready to vote, and the roll of states is called. The chairman of each state delegation announces the vote of the state; the announcement may be the occasion for huzzas or for boos. The custom now is simply to announce the vote, but in earlier and more flowery days a short speech was delivered with the vote more often than now. Thus, in 1868, when the name of Montana was called: "The mountains of Montana, from whence flows the waters of the Columbia and the Mississippi, are vocal with the name of Grant, to whom she gives two votes."

If no majority results from the first ballot, other ballots are taken until a decision is reached. As the ballots proceed, state delegations may march out of the hall to caucus to determine what they will do as the political winds shift, or they may go into a huddle on the floor of the convention itself. The announcement of the vote of a state by the chairman of its delegation may from time to time be challenged and the convention chairman orders the delegation "polled," that is, each individual delegate casts his vote. The change of a pivotal state may mark the turn of the tide toward a particular aspirant. In 1932, when Mc-Adoo cast California's vote for Roosevelt on the fourth ballot, the nomination was in fact made and other states rushed to the bandwagon. The nomination is often made on the first ballot; the convention tends in these instances merely to record the accomplished victory of the leading aspirant—the only one who has gathered to his support enough state organizations to command a majority of the convention. Thus in the 1944 Republican convention Dewey's managers were able to negotiate a majority before the balloting; and when the time came to vote, the other aspirants made speeches bowing out of the race.[65] Dewey received all the votes on the first ballot except one cast by a lone delegate from Wisconsin, who held out for MacArthur. The Republicans have had fewer convention struggles than the Democrats. Since the Civil War

of Senator Taft. In the midst of a demonstration Congressman George H. Bender of Cleveland called for 'Three cheers for the winner!' He then called for 'Three cheers for our next President.' The three cheers were given with great enthusiasm, whereupon the marching delegates took up the refrain 'We want Taft,' 'We want Taft,' 'We want Taft.'" Canadian national conventions to choose party leaders are more decorous affairs than our conventions (see J. W. Lederle, "National Party Conventions: Canada Shows the Way," *Southwestern Social Science Quarterly*, 15 [1944], pp. 118–133).

[65] For a detailed account of the 1944 conventions, see Eliot Janeway, "Birth of the Tickets," *Fortune*, 30 (1944), pp. 127–132.

two thirds of the Republican presidential candidates have been nominated on the first ballot. Only half the Democratic candidates during the same period were nominated on the first ballot. The Democrats hold the record with the 103 ballots required to break the deadlock between Smith and McAdoo in 1924. Since the Civil War the highest number of ballots required to nominate in a Republican convention has been 36, in 1880, when Garfield was nominated as a compromise candidate after a deadlock between the supporters of Grant, Blaine, and Sherman.[66]

The better discipline in the Republican organization has various bases. The party has been in power during most of the period and hence has had the cohesion that accrues from the control of patronage. But probably more important has been the fact that the greater divergency of interests within the Democratic party has bred conflict. A factor of some significance also has been the necessity, until 1936, of a two-thirds majority to gain the nomination in Democratic conventions.

When more than one ballot is required to nominate, decisions by state leaders to throw their support to one candidate or another become important. When no candidate has a majority on the first ballot, the way is left open for "negotiated" nominations or nominations determined by conferences between state leaders at the convention. Or, as an alternative, a lesser contender or even a "dark horse" may make such a strong appeal to the delegates and to the public that the leaders of the various delegations are practically compelled to support him.

The 1940 Republican convention is a recent example of a convention that did the unexpected. Dewey came to the convention with the largest bloc of pledged votes, with Taft next. In the few weeks preceding the convention an effective publicity campaign had been carried on in behalf of Willkie, but the number of delegates pledged to him was small. In the face of the probable renomination of Roosevelt by the Democrats, a world crisis, and a split in his own New York delegation, Dewey began to look like a poor bet for the Republican nomination. Even before the convention formally convened, the break to Willkie began when Connecticut announced that its fourteen votes would go to him, and when scattering support from other delegations was pledged to him. During the first days of the convention editorial and popular sentiment turned to Willkie. Kenneth F. Simpson, Republican chairman of New York County, announced that in the twelve days preceding the convention he had received 100,000 telegrams, let-

[66] The figures for the Democratic conventions requiring more than one ballot are: 1868, 22; 1876, 2; 1880, 2; 1884, 2; 1896, 5; 1912, 12; 1920, 44; 1924, 103; 1932, 4. For the Republicans: 1876, 7; 1880, 36; 1884, 4; 1888, 8; 1916, 3; 1920, 10; 1940, 6.

ters, and postal cards urging the nomination of Willkie. This statement was probably an exaggeration, but all the delegates were subjected to like pressures.

Came the balloting. Dewey, according to prediction, led on the first ballot, but all conceded that he had lost before the balloting began. Then came frantic efforts to unite on Taft in order to stop Willkie, but the galleries cried, "We Want Willkie"; and the leaders and managers of state delegations had greater difficulty in keeping their followers in rein. Bitter denunciations of Willkie came from many quarters, and even McNary, later to be the vice-presidential nominee, joined in questioning the advisability of nominating Willkie. On the second, third, fourth, and fifth ballots the Taft strength increased but not so rapidly as that of Willkie, who took the lead on the fourth ballot and was nominated on the sixth. Willkie's nomination has been described by political commentators as an astonishing triumph of the will of the people over that of the professional politician. Perhaps it was in part, but Willkie was not without the support of professionals early in the convention; and, as matters proceeded, others joined his ranks. Yet perhaps the majority of the professionals in the convention would have preferred either Dewey or Taft.

Democratic two-thirds rule. The two-thirds rule and the unit rule are features of the nominating procedure peculiar to Democratic conventions. Until 1936 the Democratic conventions followed the rule that a two-thirds majority of the convention was required to nominate. In the first Democratic convention, that of 1831, the nomination of Jackson for the Presidency was a foregone conclusion, but the two-thirds rule was adopted to govern the decision on the vice-presidential nomination. In the convention of 1835 the committee on rules recommended that "a majority of two-thirds shall be required to elect the candidates for President and Vice-President." The proposed rule was defended as calculated to produce "a more imposing effect." [67] Its adoption perhaps assured this "imposing effect," but the rule also generated difficulties and stimulated attacks based on the majority principle.

Athough the continuance of the rule had been debated from time to time, until 1936 no convention had been able to consider the rule on its merits. The question of its continuance had always been tied up with the fate of particular aspirants for the nomination. Furthermore, the two-thirds rule was supplementary to the unit rule by which the entire vote of a state delegation is cast for the candidate supported by a majority of the delegation. It was argued that the vote of a few large states, actually almost evenly divided but cast as a unit, could give the

[67] Stanwood, *A History of the Presidency from 1788 to 1897*, p. 182.

nomination to a person actually supported by only a minority of the convention. The two-thirds rule made such a result less probable.[68] Moreover, the Solid South, where the greatest consistent Democratic strength has been concentrated, has viewed the two-thirds rule as operating to its advantage, by giving it a veto on candidates unfavorable to the desires of that area.

In 1932 an attack, destined eventually to be successful, was begun against the two-thirds rule by the forces seeking the nomination of Franklin D. Roosevelt. The Roosevelt managers were, prior to the convention, sure of a majority for their candidate, but, lacking enough committed delegates to assure a two-thirds majority, they undertook to change the rules of the game. The committee on rules, by a vote of 30 to 20, decided to propose a resolution to the effect that the two-thirds rule be followed for six ballots. If no nomination were made within that time, the convention would vote on whether to make its decision by a simple majority. It soon became apparent that, if presented, the proposal would be defeated; and the defeat would, of course, have constituted a serious blow to the Roosevelt candidacy. The Roosevelt managers hastily reconvened the rules committee, which rescinded its action and adopted a report recommending that the 1936 convention "consider" the abolition of the two-thirds rule. In 1936 the report of the committee on rules, presented to the convention by Bennett Champ Clark, whose father had lost the nomination in 1912 because of the operation of the two-thirds rule, recommended the abrogation of the rule. With Roosevelt the certain nominee, the adoption of the change was unmixed with the interests of any aspirant for the nomination. Southern Democrats continue to complain that this action reduced their influence in the convention and to seek a reapportionment of delegates in the convention to give them greater strength. Before the 1944 convention Representative Eugene Cox of Georgia agitated for a return to the two-thirds rule. "When the two-thirds rule was abrogated," he asserted, " the South completely lost its power independently to influence party affairs." There was at least a trace of arithmetical nonsense in the Congressman's reasoning. In the 1944 convention the ten states of the Solid South had 21.2 per cent of the delegates. To exercise a veto under the two-thirds rule, these states would have to be united—which is not always the case—and also able to carry with them enough other states to make one third plus one of the convention.

Democratic unit rule. The Democratic unit rule requires that the entire vote of a state delegation shall be cast as the majority of the dele-

[68] Carl Becker, "The Unit Rule in National Nominating Conventions," *American Historical Review,* 5 (1899), p. 62.

gation desires, if the state delegation has been so instructed by the state convention. The national convention, however, recognizes state laws that do not subject delegates chosen within congressional districts to the operation of a unit rule imposed by the state convention.[69] For example, if the Virginia state convention instructs its delegates to the national convention to abide by the unit rule, the convention will recognize the instruction as binding upon it. The unit rule, then, is not imposed on the state delegations by the national convention; the convention merely enforces the instruction of the duly constituted agencies of the party within the states. The Republican national convention, on the other hand, does not recognize as valid a state instruction to its delegation to operate under the unit rule.

During this century, with the increase in the number of states failing to instruct their delegations to act as a unit, the importance of the unit rule in Democratic conventions has considerably diminished. As an indication of the practical degree of departure from the unit rule, it may be noted that on the first ballot for the presidential nomination at Chicago in 1932, the votes of the delegations from Illinois, Indiana, New York, North Dakota, Pennsylvania, Wisconsin, and Alaska were divided among two or more candidates. On the first ballot on the vice-presidential nomination in 1944 the votes of 21 states were divided among two or more candidates. In both of these examples, of course, additional state delegations may not have been bound by the unit rule but merely happened to be unanimous in their choice.

The selection of the presidential nominee marks the beginning of another demonstration. These demonstrations have probably become a bit less riotous as time has passed; at least certain picturesque features, such as the firing of cannon, have been eliminated. The *New York Times* described the nomination of Lincoln in 1860: [70]

Intelligence of the nomination was now conveyed to men on the roof of the building, who immediately made the outside multitude aware of the result. The first roar of the cannons soon mingled itself with the cheers of the people, and at the same moment a man appeared in the hall bringing a large painting of Mr. Lincoln. The scene at this time beggars description—11,000 inside and 20,000 or 30,000 outside were yelling and shouting at once. Two cannon sent forth roar after roar in quick succession. Delegates tore up the

[69] This exception was introduced by the Democratic convention of 1912 at the instance of delegates chosen by presidential primary and pledged to Wilson. The majority of the Ohio delegation, operating under a unit rule, desired to cast the votes of such delegates for Governor Harmon. *Proceedings*, 1912, pp. 59–60; A. S. Link, "The Baltimore Convention of 1912," *American Historical Review*, 50 (1945), pp. 691–713.

[70] May 19, 1860.

sticks and boards bearing the names of the several states and waved them aloft over their heads, and the vast multitude before the platform were waving their hats and handkerchiefs. The whole scene was one of the wildest enthusiasm.

Naming the vice-presidential candidate. Energies and enthusiasm are exhausted by the strain of the nomination of the presidential candidate; the convention, in a state of emotional deflation, then proceeds, often hurriedly and without much relish to finish its business, with the nomination of a candidate for the Vice-Presidency. The factors governing the selection of the running mate for the head of the ticket are numerous, but a few patterns recur. A frequent persuasive consideration is the necessity of "balancing the ticket." In this matter a party faction or a geographical section of the nation other than the one represented by the presidential candidate is recognized.[71] Thus, in 1912 the Democrats nominated Wilson of New Jersey and Marshall of Indiana; the Republicans, Taft of Ohio and Sherman of New York. In 1880, after the nomination of Garfield, "some of the prominent leaders of the Grant movement were sullen and discontented." The vice-presidential nomination was conceded to the Grant faction, and Senator Conklin, the chief leader of that faction, named Chester A. Arthur of New York.[72] In 1928 the Democratic convention selected Senator Robinson of Arkansas as the running mate of Alfred E. Smith. "Robinson was a Southerner, a Protestant, and a Dry, and his selection was dictated by the northern Democracy's desire to divide honors with the South and hold it in line for Al Smith. Thus, as one writer remarked, 'The Democratic donkey with a wet head and wagging a dry tail left Houston.' "[73]

The nomination for the Vice-Presidency occasionally is connected with the nomination for the Presidency. In the 1932 Democratic

[71] L. C. Hatch and E. L. Shoup, *A History of the Vice-Presidency of the United States* (New York: American Historical Society, 1934), p. 415.

[72] Stanwood, *A History of the Presidency from 1788 to 1897*, p. 408.

[73] Peel and Donnelly, *The 1928 Campaign*, p. 34. It is extremely doubtful whether the doctrine that the "balancing of the ticket" swings support to the party has real validity. Consider the nomination of McNary by the Republicans in 1940. In May preceding the convention the American Institute of Public Opinion found that the greatest G.O.P. gains since 1936 were in the midwestern and Great Lakes states. In May Dr. Gallup reported that 16 per cent of the Oregon voters had moved over to the Republican ranks since 1936; in the election, 15 per cent transferred their allegiance. In May Dr. Gallup estimated that 10 per cent of the Iowa voters had since 1936 returned to their traditional Republicanism; in November, 8 per cent did so. McNary's presence on the ticket did not swing enough Oregon support to put that state in the Willkie column, nor did Iowans consider the nomination of Wallace enough of a compliment to dissuade them from their Republican leanings of the spring. Apparently the vice-presidential nominees had little or no influence on the vote in their own states.

convention the California delegation, pledged to Garner, swung the presidential nomination to Roosevelt. The convention next day unanimously placed Garner on the ticket with Roosevelt. In the Republican convention of 1944 a similar sequence of events occurred when Governor Bricker yielded the presidential nomination to Dewey without a fight and subsequently received the second place on the ticket. The vice-presidential nomination thus becomes something of a consolation prize to the unsuccessful presidential aspirant, who allies his forces with the winner. Often the presidential nominee in fact names the vice-presidential nominee. In 1940 there was no real disposition on the part of the delegates to revolt against Willkie's selection of Senator McNary of Oregon as his running mate. The 1940 Democratic convention, however, reluctantly and with loud manifestations of displeasure ratified Roosevelt's designation of Henry Wallace as the vice-presidential nominee.

Ordinarily the choice of a vice-presidential nominee is a relatively peaceful affair, but the battle over this nomination in the 1944 Democratic convention brought out for exhibition all the internal wrangles of the party. Henry Wallace went into the convention with the support of the CIO-PAC, the liberal and New Deal elements of the party, the state machines from several industrial states, and a good representation of states west of the Mississippi. Against Wallace most of the states of the Solid South were aligned, and they had as allies the AFL, right-wing Democrats generally, and a number of northern city machines whose leaders were alarmed by the strength being gained within the party by the CIO-PAC. In the maneuvering immediately preceding and during the convention President Roosevelt played a cagey game, and Robert Hannegan, Democratic national chairman, contrary to the custom of party officials, worked feverishly to line up delegates for Senator Truman of Missouri. The left wing of the party succeeded in vetoing James Byrnes of South Carolina, but it was unable to muster enough support to nominate Wallace. On the first ballot Wallace led Truman, 429½ to 319½. With the substantial strength Truman demonstrated on the first ballot, states that had stayed on the side lines by voting for favorite sons and other unlikely aspirants were encouraged to turn to Truman, who won the nomination on the second ballot. Candidates initially backed by both the conservative and liberal wings of the party had been rejected, and the party was able to maintain a tenuous unity by nominating a person not entirely acceptable to either of its extreme factions.

Notification of the nominees. It has been the custom for the convention to appoint a committee to notify both the presidential and vice-presidential candidates of their nomination. Under the usual pattern a committee of dignitaries makes a journey to the home of the nominee. The chairman of the committee makes an appropriate speech of notification and the candidate responds with a speech of acceptance. The notification ceremony is often an important political ceremony and the speeches are significant campaign documents. Yet the procedure in a day of rapid communication has the quaintness of an anachronism and has frequently been deviated from since 1930. In 1932 Roosevelt flew to Chicago to accept the nomination.[74] In 1940 and 1944 his acceptance speech was delivered by radio to the convention. In 1944 Dewey went to Chicago to deliver his acceptance speech to the convention.

6. ROLE AND FUNCTION OF THE CONVENTION

How is the national convention to be evaluated? A favorite critique of the national convention is that by Ostrogorski, who called the convention a "colossal travesty of popular institutions"; the platform "a collection of hollow, vague phrases." He with approval quoted the saying: "God takes care of drunkards, of little children, and of the United States!" [75] Other observers, both imported and indigenous, remark on the hilarity and unseemly demeanor of delegates gathered together for the solemn business of nominating a candidate for the Presidency of the United States. It is indeed true that the conventions are rarely august assemblages. They partake of the more robust features of American character, but on the whole the level of sobriety is not markedly different from that of most national nonpolitical gatherings of comparable size.

The sensitive soul may be troubled by the lack of dignity, the noise, and the confusion of the national convention; yet the ultimate tests of the convention are whether it works and how well it works. Obviously it works. Without it the presidential system could not be operated; it is difficult to conceive of a practical substitute. Criticisms of the convention system are sometimes based on the contention that the convention is not an accurate reflector of popular wishes regarding the nominee. Lurid pictures of conferences in "smoke-filled" rooms and

---

[74] In the speech Roosevelt said: "The appearance before a National Convention of its nominee for President, to be formally notified of his selection, is unprecedented and unusual, but these are unprecedented and unusual times. I have started out on the tasks that lie ahead by breaking the absurd traditions that the candidate should remain in professed ignorance of what has happened for weeks until he is formally notified of that event many weeks later."

[75] See his complete statement in *Democracy and the Party System in the United States* (New York: Macmillan, 1910), pp. 159–160.

of secret caucuses and of bargaining characterize this type of criticism. Sessions of this kind do go on behind the scenes, but it is probably erroneous to attribute them to a desire to thwart the will of the rank and file of voters. It is a difficult matter to foist off on the voters a candidate whom they positively dislike; for pure self-interest, if for no other reason, the politicians who steer the work of the convention earnestly consider the probable reaction of the voters to potential nominees. If the wrong nomination is made, the election may be lost. In a broad sense the kinds of nominations made by conventions are governed by the conditions of the time and by the estimates by political leaders of the temper of the people.

Scholarly critiques of the convention system are often at bottom criticisms of the presidential system as contrasted with the cabinet system, in which the chief leaders are thrown up by the process of struggle within the party group in the parliament. The general drift of this type of argument is that under the cabinet system potential prime ministers receive long training and testing in national affairs through their experience in parliament and in minor ministerial posts. By a practical demonstration of ability, prime ministers more or less select themselves. Under the presidential system, on the other hand, the presidential nominee may have had no experience in national affairs. The channel for political advancement is different under the presidential system. It is not, the argument runs, a channel that permits practical testing and demonstration of capacity. The test of this kind of criticism of the presidential system (of which the convention is a part) is an estimate of the men who have come up through the selective machinery. It can be contended with considerable force that the convention system has yielded results quite as satisfactory as those of the cabinet system.

From another point of view the national convention is part and parcel of the magic by which men rule. It is a great ceremony in which the forms of the expression of the will of the mass of party membership are followed. It is a miracle play from which the hero emerges triumphant to fight the battles of the party. It is a drama played in terms that the simplest spectator can understand and in which he can hiss the villain and applaud the hero. That the convention may not, in fact, constitute a precision instrument for gauging and expressing the "will" of the rank and file of the party is, in one sense, immaterial. It works; it arrives at acceptable decisions, at least most of the time. The institution of the convention constitutes one of the great contributions of parties to the American system of government. Evolving completely outside the Constitution and laws, it fills a void in our formal governmental system by providing a workable means for designating candidates for the Presidency.

Chapter 14

CAMPAIGN TECHNIQUES

WITH the broadening of the suffrage the battle for control of the government has come to involve a large proportion of the entire people. Consequently the work of political leaders in maintaining the enthusiasm and loyalty of their supporters, in bringing about defections from the ranks of the opposition, and in rallying the wavering and weak of heart has increased correspondingly. At the same time there has come about a fundamental change in the method of "manufacturing consent," as Walter Lippmann has called the process of popular government.

Under a narrowly restricted suffrage the task of reaching the electorate was not so great, and different methods might be used in seeking support. At one time word of mouth, personal influence, and parlor caucuses were of considerable importance as methods of carrying a campaign to the voters. These more intimate relationships, characteristic of campaigns in the period of very limited suffrage, have come to be supplemented and to a large degree superseded by newer techniques of appeal to the great mass of the electorate. The party organization has continued, with workers in almost every precinct who seek to build up person-to-person contacts with the electors; but the radio, the newspaper, and the mass meeting are more and more important as channels for the dissemination of appeals to the electorate. With improved technologies of communication has come increased sophistication in the management of mass opinion. And probably these trends are making a greater change in the nature of political power than has been recognized. Political power has been based on a stable network of the party machine, around each member of which was clustered a little group loyal through thick and thin. For this source of strength there seems to be in the process of substitution a power structure broadly based on mass consent and support. As leaders have available devices and methods for appealing directly to the great mass of people, the representative and opinion-managerial function of the party machine apparently is becoming less important than it once was.

1. CAMPAIGN ORGANIZATION

The conduct of a presidential campaign requires the collaboration of thousands of men and women. Thorough organization is necessary if each person working in the campaign is to do his part in the right way at the right time. Campaign organization consists of two kinds of party machinery. The permanent party organization—that is, the national chairman, the national committee, state and county committees, precinct captains and committeemen, and other party functionaries—comes to life during the campaign and carries a major part of the burden.

Temporary party machinery. The regular party machinery, however, is supplemented by additional party organs, spawned in great numbers during the course of a campaign. The staff of the national committee is enlarged, and new divisions designed especially to handle phases of the campaign are added to national headquarters. In most states similar temporary enlargements of the party headquarters occur. And each party stimulates the creation of temporary nonparty organizations to support its candidate.

The specialized divisions set up at the national headquarters are usually created to handle special aspects of the campaign. A finance unit has the job of raising money. Usually a labor division, headed by a prominent union labor leader, is created for the purpose of handling relationships with labor. In 1940 and 1944, for example, Daniel J. Tobin, a vice-president of the American Federation of Labor and president of the Teamsters Union, was in charge of the labor bureau of the Democratic national committee. The Republican national committee has a naturalized-citizens division. Each party usually has a Negro division, and there is a special unit in charge of women's activities. The national headquarters is always equipped with a publicity division, which prepares leaflets, press releases, and other types of propaganda. Usually a speakers' division recruits speakers and arranges their schedules.[1]

A question that almost invariably arises in the establishment of the temporary campaign machinery is whether to provide for a single national headquarters or to divide the management of the campaign among regional divisions under the general supervision of the national

[1] See T. M. Black, *Democratic Party Publicity in the 1940 Campaign* (New York: Plymouth, 1941), chaps. 2 and 3; John Stanton, "The GHQ's of the Two Political Armies," *New York Times Magazine*, October 8, 1944.

chairman. In 1928 the Republicans established their main campaign headquarters at Chicago, primarily because of its central location. An eastern division was located in New York. In 1932 the Democrats had a single national headquarters in New York against the desires of regional leaders, who thought that James Farley had not had enough experience in national campaigning to exercise complete direction over the campaign. A factor in the decision to centralize was "the avoidance of possible jealousies by not having to select men to head branch headquarters." [2] In 1940 Chairman Flynn of the Democratic national committee established a new precedent by creating four regional campaign headquarters to supplement the work of the national office in New York. The campaign in the northeastern states was handled from New York under the direction of Mr. Flynn. Senator Scott Lucas directed the midwestern division from Chicago; Senator John H. Bankhead, the southern division from Birmingham, Alabama; former Governor Leslie Miller of Wyoming, the far western division from San Francisco; and Representative Sam Rayburn of Texas, the southwestern division from Dallas. Sometimes a factor in the determination of the question of decentralization is the supposed effect of the location of a branch headquarters on the enthusiasm of the party workers in that area and the consequent effect on the popular vote.[3]

Auxiliary nonparty organizations. A uniform feature of campaign organizations is a number of auxiliary or nonparty organizations, agencies that are set up with nonparty names on the theory that by this means the party can mobilize voters beyond reach of regular party organization. In 1936, for example, the Good Neighbor League was established, Farley says, on the suggestion of Louis Howe to reach "a large body of independents and of socially minded people" who disliked "to affiliate with any political party." [4] In 1940 the Republicans relied heavily on the Associated Willkie Clubs, clubs that had been formed to bring about the nomination of Mr. Willkie and continued after the convention to work for his election. The Democrats formed a Committee of Independents for Roosevelt, with Senator George W. Norris serving as honorary chairman and Mayor La Guardia as its active head.

Somewhat similar to nonparty committees are special committees of leading figures from the opposite party, a feature of almost every presi-

[2] Roy V. Peel and T. C. Donnelly, *The 1932 Campaign* (New York: Farrar and Rinehart, 1935), pp. 112–113.

[3] For example, see Grover Cleveland's comments on the desirability of establishing a western headquarters in 1892.—Allan Nevins (ed.), *Letters of Grover Cleveland, 1850–1908* (Boston: Houghton Mifflin, 1933), pp. 294–295.

[4] *Behind the Ballots* (New York: Harcourt, Brace, 1938), pp. 301–302.

dential campaign.   In 1944 the Republicans had the support of "Democrats for Dewey," which supported Mr. Dewey for the Presidency but expressed a preference for Democratic candidates for state and local offices.   The supposition underlying the establishment of these adjuncts to the regular party organization is that an appeal from them may have greater effect in weaning away nominal supporters of the other party.   It hardly needs to be said that the committees of independents, of labor leaders, of farmers, of citizens, of lawyers, of businessmen, and of others that spring up during every campaign work in close collaboration with the regular party organizations.

Role of the national chairman.   In the presidential campaign, general direction of the entire party organization is vested in the national chairman, who is a nominee of and acts for the presidential candidate. His job breaks down into two principal tasks: the direction of the subdivisions of the national committee staff, and the guidance of state organizations of the party.

The general management of the staff of the national committee is of special importance, for it is here that a substantial proportion of the propaganda work is conducted.   Unless the different units into which the work is divided are well managed, one division may issue appeals that embarrass other divisions, and internal jealousy and conflict may detract from effectiveness of the campaign.   Casey cites the national Republican organization of 1936 as an example of poor organization. Instead of creating a unified publicity agency with responsibility for all propaganda, John Hamilton, the Republican national chairman, "divided the propaganda function into too many fields; failed to delimit the scope of activity of each aspiring propaganda service; built propaganda organizations within organizations, and laid the seeds of inefficiency and waste. . . ." [5]

In dealing with the state organizations, the national chairman exercises a role of general guidance and leadership; he attempts to speed up the work of lagging state and local organizations.   Before the passage of the Hatch Act limiting the amounts of money that can be raised by the national committee, he was usually in a position to aid deserving state organizations with subsidies from the national campaign chest.   Now he can guide individual contributors in the financial centers to worthy and needy state committees elsewhere.   He supplies the state organizations with speakers of national reputation and confers with state leaders on questions of strategy.   In some instances the national organization may be at odds with the party leaders in a state; in such a situa-

[5] R. D. Casey, "Republican Propaganda in the 1936 Campaign," *Public Opinion Quarterly,* April, 1937, p. 29.

tion the national chairman may establish and deal with a state campaign organization loyal to the presidential candidate.

Work of local organizations. It is the local organizations that bear the burden of personal solicitation of voters and of "getting out the vote." The traditional view is that the party that has the most efficient and loyal staff of precinct workers, supplemented by large numbers of workers hired for election-day work, enjoys a tremendous advantage in the campaign. The theory is that the able precinct captain who, through his connections with the local machine, has been able to do favors and make friends will have a store of good will to draw on at election time, a following that will stick with him regardless of candidates or issues.

Knowledge of the relative effectiveness of the personal work of precinct workers and canvassers and of propaganda slanted to the masses through the radio, newspapers, and political rallies is slight. Stories are told of the great ability of precinct workers to gain the loyalty of the voters of their bailiwicks and to swing their votes this way or that as occasion demands. In some localities at some times "organization" work undoubtedly is of great importance in terms of votes.[6] It may be suspected, however, that it has become of less significance since 1932 in presidential campaigns. The adoption of governmental policies on a broad front in the public welfare field has made the welfare work of the party organization picayune indeed. Urban Democratic machines in several conspicuous instances allied themselves enthusiastically with New Deal policies and consequently found themselves on the winning side. Yet it is probable that the precinct work of the Democratic machines contributed only slightly to the outcome. There is substance in David Lawrence's theory that in 1936 "the party organizations, state and national, really played for the first time in our history a relatively incidental part in a national election. Even the political machines in the big cities were, in a sense, swallowed up by a bigger and more powerful mechanism of vote-getting than we had ever witnessed."[7]

2. THEORY OF PROPAGANDA

The term "propaganda," because of its various meanings in popular usage, is difficult of employment in exact discussion. It is often used to indicate either an underhand campaign to influence public opinion or

---

[6] See the suggestive consideration of this question by P. F. Lazarsfeld *et al.*, *The People's Choice* (New York: Duell, Sloan and Pearce, 1944), chap. 16. See also Oliver Carlson and Aldrich Blake, *How to Get Into Politics, The Art of Winning Elections* (New York: Duell, Sloan and Pearce, 1946).

[7] *Who Were the Eleven Million?* (New York: Appleton–Century, 1936), p. 34.

the dissemination of falsehoods and misrepresentations. In this analysis, however, its connotation is somewhat different. We shall follow Harold Lasswell, who defines propaganda as "the management of collective attitudes by the manipulation of significant symbols." [8] Under this definition the propagandist becomes one who endeavors to manage collective attitudes, whatever his motive. He may attempt to present the cause of a small minority that pursues selfish gain in such a light that the cause will be acceptable to the public generally. He may be promoting an unselfish project that unquestionably is consonant with prevailing concepts of the general welfare. He may shade the truth, suppress matters of negative propaganda value, and emphasize those of positive propaganda value for his cause. On the other hand, he may be completely veracious. But in any case he is a propagandist. Thus considered, propaganda is "no more moral or immoral than a pump handle." [9]

Symbols: Tools to influence people. What are these "significant symbols" by which collective attitudes are managed? Lasswell says, "these objects which have a standard meaning in a group are called significant symbols. The elevated eyebrow, the clenched fist, the sharp voice, the pungent phrase, have their references established within the web of a particular culture. Such significant symbols are paraphernalia employed in expressing the attitude, and they are also capable of being employed to reaffirm or redefine attitudes. Thus, significant symbols have both an expressive and a propagandist function in public life." [10] Thus the phrase "more business in government" is a verbal symbol designed to manage collective attitudes; its efficacy depends on the cultural predispositions of the persons to whom it is directed. The person using this slogan or symbol presumes that "business" enjoys prestige; that "government" enjoys a less favorable rating in public attitudes; that the propagation of the symbol "more business in government" will evoke the desired reaction or organize collective attitudes around the symbol. Political campaigns become in a degree a battle of competing symbols, and perhaps the winner is the party that can formulate a system of symbols that either better expresses or more effectively manages collective attitudes.

Propaganda evokes nonrational responses. Observe the assumptions of the theory of propaganda. They presuppose a method of in-

---

[8] H. D. Lasswell, "The Theory of Propaganda," *American Political Science Review,* 21 (1927), p. 627.

[9] Lasswell, "The Function of the Propagandist," *International Journal of Ethics,* 38 (1928), pp. 258–263.

[10] Lasswell, *American Political Science Review, op. cit.,* p. 627.

luencing attitudes that is different from the process of deliberation or reasoning. "Deliberation," says Lasswell, "implies the search for the solution of a besetting problem with no desire to prejudice a particular solution in advance. The propagandist is very much concerned about how a specific solution is to be evoked and 'put over.'" Deliberation may enter into the formulation of the program that the propagandist desires to carry into effect, but the process of selling it to the public is not deliberative. And the development of an extensive propaganda system is more or less inherent in universal suffrage since millions of people cannot collectively deliberate, yet under the theory of democracy they have the job of deciding many issues. The propagandist assumes that the decisions will be made for the electorate and will be made acceptable—or the "consent" of the public will be obtained—through the process of propaganda. The decision of the electorate becomes a choice between competing propagandists. And this may turn out to be no decision at all, for the victory may belong to the more skilful symbol manipulator and may be without much concrete influence on the stream of events. Moreover, in many situations the propagandist has no competitor for public favor, and he may carry his cause to success without opposition.

Implicit in the theories of the propagandist are certain assumptions about the psychology of human behavior. Every student is familiar with Pavlov's dog, the unfortunate animal that thought it was going to be fed when the bell rang. A more recent example related by E. B. White, not a professional psychologist, is as follows: [11]

A friend of mine has an electric fence round a piece of his land, and keeps two cows there. I asked him one day how he liked his fence and whether it cost much to operate. "Doesn't cost a damn thing," he replied. "As soon as the battery ran down I unhooked it and never put it back. The strand of fence wire is as dead as a piece of string, but the cows don't go within ten feet of it. They learned their lesson the first few days."

In the terminology of the psychologist, the cows were "conditioned" to respond in a certain way to the stimulus of the wire, which they associated with the shock. In the language of the theory of propaganda the wire was a significant symbol; the collective bovine attitude evoked or expressed by the symbol was the tendency to stay away from the wire. It would perhaps libel the propaganda theorists to attribute to them the view that humans are either canine or bovine, but in their work there is an assumption that, within limits, the collective attitudes of

[11] *Harper's Magazine,* January, 1940, p. 217.

humans may be managed by the manipulation of symbols to which men have been conditioned to respond in a predictable way.

Adapting propaganda appeals to group prejudices. If the propagandist is to be successful in molding the attitudes of the group to which he makes his appeal, he must know intimately the existing attitudes of the group and to what symbols its members have been conditioned to respond. His problem, says Lasswell, is "the presentation of an object in a culture in such a manner that certain cultural attitudes will be organized toward it. The problem of the propagandist is to intensify the attitude favorable to his purpose, to reverse the attitudes hostile to it, and to attract the indifferent, or, at the worst, to prevent them from assuming a hostile bent." [12] Ralph Turner observes that "the cultural fixations of the population are especially important for the development of a successful propaganda; indeed, if a propagandist can identify the opinion he desires to fix with an element of the tradition of the population, he is likely to succeed. Competition for the sanction of tradition is not only a normal element in propaganda but also a usual aspect of politics." [13] Something of the same notions are implicit in Walter Lippmann's concept of "stereotypes." Words evoke certain pictures in our minds; propaganda technique involves the selection and use of words that will create the desired pictures.

The necessity for thorough knowledge of the "cultural fixations" of the people to whom propaganda is directed is apparent enough, but it has been demonstrated experimentally in a small way. Using students as guinea pigs, Menefee found that 64 per cent of the experimental group agreed with the proposition: "We should stand solidly upon the Constitution of the United States because it is the bulwark of our liberty." When the statement was made to read: "We should uphold the past interpretation of the United States Constitution because it guarantees certain privileges as it stands," only 24 per cent were found to agree. With the statement, "I may not agree with what you say, but I will defend with my life your right to say it," 42 per cent agreed. Changed to this: "One should face death rather than allow any person to be denied freedom of expression," the support fell to 16 per cent.[14] In another experiment Menefee found that the symbols "conservatism" and "radicalism" called forth vastly different responses from the experimental group. Statements labelled as typical of conservatism drew

---

12 *American Political Science Review, loc. cit.*

13 Ralph Turner, "Culture, Change and Confusion," *Public Opinion Quarterly* 4 (1940), p. 596.

14 S. C. Menefee, "Stereotyped Phrases and Public Opinion," *American Journal of Sociology*, 43 (1936), pp. 614–622.

a high percentage of agreement; but when the same statements were labelled as typical of radicalism, the degree of agreement among the subjects of the experiment dropped sharply.[15]   In dealing with this group, the propagandist would need to formulate his campaign in terms of conservatism.

The necessity for a close relationship between the symbols of propaganda and the cultural fixations of the group propagandized explains the repeated appeal by politicians to tradition, precedent, and established practice.   Those who seek to introduce innovations are more likely to succeed if they can formulate their program in terms of the accepted values of the group, and make the innovation appear to be no innovation at all or at most an adaptation to approximate more closely the spirit of the old.   But cultural fixations, of course, change; old symbols lose their power.   The politician who fails to keep abreast of these changes may lose his ability to sway the masses and be succeeded by another with a keener sensitivity to the currents of mass attitudes. "Brain trust" may evoke favorable responses at one time; sneers, at a later time.   This would be a short-run change, but there are more fundamental long-run changes.   Dr. Turner has argued, for example, that the movement of people from rural environment to the great cities has created a situation in which vast numbers of persons have been uprooted from their cultural habits.   The cultural fixations are in the course of profound alteration.   Under such circumstances the task of the propagandist becomes greater; he has lost his relatively stable pattern of response as the basis for propaganda planning.[16]

The effect of the same symbol on different groups and types of individuals may be quite different.   To use an extreme example, "commissar" is presumably a term of prestige in Russia; in the United States the assumption of propagandists who referred to Commissar Ickes and Commissar Hopkins was that the term automatically evokes responses of dislike.   But within a single culture, persons of different classes attribute a different content to the same symbol.   The phrase "pump priming" may arouse very different emotions among upper-class taxpayers than among men employed on public works undertaken as pump primers.   On the other hand, a symbol involving generalities may have different meanings to different people and have a unifying rather than a divisive effect.   This explains why so much political propaganda is completely meaningless when subjected to rational analysis.   Mr. Willkie said:

15 Menefee, "The Effect of Stereotyped Words on Political Judgment," *American Sociological Review,* 1 (1936), pp. 614–621.

16 "Culture, Change and Confusion," *op. cit.,* pp. 579–600.

I see an America whose representatives in Washington believe in America. I see a country governed by men in whom our producers—labor, agriculture and business—have confidence. . . . I see an America from which democracy will arise to a new birth; an America which will once more provide this war-torn world with a clear glimpse of the destiny of man.

President Roosevelt said:

We can assert the most glorious, the most encouraging fact in the world today, the fact that democracy is alive; it is alive and going strong. We are telling the world that we are free, and we intend to remain free and at peace. We are free to live and love and laugh. We face the future with confidence and courage. We are American.

Both statements are noble, yet almost meaningless, but they may mean all things to all men, and thus men of divergent views may be brought together. Walter Lippmann has remarked that when political parties declare for Americanism, Justice, or Humanity, "they hope to amalgamate the emotion of conflicting factions which would surely divide, if instead of these symbols, they were invited to discuss a specific program." [17]

One of the propositions of the theory of propaganda is that simple repetition is the most effective means of getting across the "message." One formulation of this doctrine is that of LeBon: [18]

Affirmation pure and simple, kept free from all reasoning and proof, is one of the surest ways of making an idea enter the minds of crowds. The conciser the affirmation is, the more destitute of every appearance of proof, the more weight it carries. . . . Affirmation, however, has no significance unless it is constantly repeated, and so far as possible in the same terms.

On this theory, successful campaigners, like successful advertisers, are repetitive: they din their message into the ears of the people by endless repetition.[19]

Economic determinism *versus* propagandistic manipulation. An apparent conflict may exist between the theory of propaganda and the

---

[17] *Public Opinion* (New York, 1922), p. 206. Quoted by permission of The Macmillan Company, publishers.

[18] Quoted by N. C. Meier, "Motives in Voting: A Study in Public Opinion," *American Journal of Sociology,* 31 (1925), pp. 199–212.

[19] For a guide to the extensive literature on propaganda, see B. L. Smith, H. D. Lasswell, and R. D. Casey, *Propaganda, Communication, and Public Opinion: A Comprehensive Reference Guide* (Princeton: Princeton University Press, 1946). The student will find suggestive ideas about propaganda in general in L. W. Doob, *Propaganda* (New York: Holt, 1935); H. L. Childs, *An Introduction to Public Opinion* (New York: Wiley, 1940); H. D. Lasswell, *Propaganda Technique in the World War* (New York: Knopf, 1927); H. D. Lasswell and Dorothy Blumenstock, *World Revolutionary Propaganda* (New York: Knopf, 1939).

theory that voting behavior may be determined by some external condition, such as economic deprivation. Between extreme formulations of the two doctrines a conflict exists, yet a line of reconciliation may be pointed out. It would be absurd to say that an adroit manipulator of symbols could influence mass behavior in certain ways under certain conditions; in times of piping prosperity the advocate of economic reform may make little headway. But when the time is ripe for economic reform, the group with the keener perception of the expectations of the populace and with the better judgment of the sorts of symbol appeal to make may wield the greater influence. And it can be argued, and probably established, that the skilled propagandist in politics (as in mass advertising) may induce the objects of propaganda to follow, within limits, a course of action contrary to their interests, or to what would be expected *a priori* from the application of a doctrine, such as economic determinism or any similar theory of behavior.

3. ART AND STRATEGY OF CAMPAIGNING

Most practical politicians and most political propagandists have not had the benefit of extensive training in psychology, social psychology, or propaganda techniques. Yet among political campaigners there have developed rules-of-thumb, setting forth what should and what should not be done. Supposedly they are based on experience regarding the response of the electorate to different types of campaign appeals and methods, but the relationship between appeal and response has never been measured conclusively. Hence the commonsense rules of campaigning traditional among practical politicians may be superstition rather than the product of the observation of experience—a body of superstition, incidentally, that is drawn on and elaborated by the writers of Sunday features. Whether the maxims of the practicing politician have any validity, they are relevant as a part of the folklore of the trade.

Picturing the candidate to the public. In campaigns that lay great emphasis on the personality of the candidates rather than on issues of public policy—and such campaigns, if one includes state and local campaigns, are certainly the more frequent—it is extremely important that the candidate and his propagandist present to the electorate the desired impression of the personality of their candidate. Or the candidate may be made to personify the issues. At the hands of the propagandist the candidate becomes a fictional or mythical character. "In our day," says Mosca, "sects and political parties are highly skilled at creating the superman, the legendary hero, the 'man of unquestioned honesty,' who serves, in his turn, to maintain the luster of the gang and brings in wealth and power for the sly ones to use." [20]   Before Charles Michelson became director of publicity for the Democratic national committee he commented on the process of making imaginary characters of the candidates, thus: [21]

The American people will elect as President of the United States in November a nonexistent person—and defeat likewise a mythical identity.

They will vote for and against a picture that has been painted for them by protagonists and antagonists in a myriad of publications, a picture that must be either a caricature or an idealization.

Herbert Hoover, the miracle man, the perfect human machine, destitute of error, with a vision beyond cosmic bounds, who resolves every problem into its mathematical elements; who has on tap all the wisdom of the universe, who plots all his tasks with unerring curves and discharges them by rule and measure; who has not time for mirth or diversions; no thought but of duty before him.

Alfred E. Smith, the ingenuous child of the New York sidewalks, simple beyond belief, but with that simplicity is combined a knowledge beyond that given in books; a demigod to whom all the complexities of government are clear as day; a paragon of wisdom, gentleness and righteousness, whose facile mind fathoms automatically every depth of economics and politics.

Senator Watson of Indiana records that prior to the 1920 convention Penrose of Pennsylvania attempted to persuade him to accept the Republican presidential nomination.   In the course of the discussion Penrose replied, " 'Well, Jim, we'll have votes enough to nominate you, and always after a man is nominated they bring out the royal robe and put it on him, and that covers up all the cracks and nail-holes.'   A wise remark, for it always happens just that way." [22]   After Calvin Coolidge succeeded to the Presidency it was necessary to "humanize" that dour New Englander prior to the presidential campaign of 1924.   Bernay says that [23]

. . . [it] was suggested that an event in which the most human groups would be brought into juxtaposition with the President would have the desired result. Actors and actresses were invited to breakfast with Mr. Coolidge at the White House.   The country felt that a man in the White House who could laugh with Al Jolson and the Dolly sisters was not frigid and unsympathetic.

20 *The Ruling Class* (New York: McGraw-Hill, 1939), p. 194.

21 Quoted by Casey, "Party Campaign Propaganda," *The Annals of the American Academy of Political and Social Science,* 179 (1935), pp. 96–105.

22 James E. Watson, *As I Knew Them* (Indianapolis: Bobbs-Merrill, copyright 1936), p. 208.   Quoted by special permission of the publishers.

23 E. L. Bernays "Manipulating Public Opinion: The Why and the How," *American Journal of Sociology,* 33 (1928), 958–971.

What kind of a picture of the candidate should be implanted in the people's minds? Frank Kent quotes a practicing politician as follows: "It is bad publicity to convey the impression of superiority of any sort— but particularly of intellectual superiority. Be a little dumb. Never be subtle and ironical." [24] This maxim parallels the more sophisticated argument by Professor Salter that the politician, to be successful, must be considered as a prototype of the electorate to which he appeals. He contends: [25]

The citizen in the United States votes for someone like himself or as he imagines himself to be, or as he would like to be. I do not mean solely as the voter might profess to want to be, but as in his secret heart he unerringly wishes to be. Of course, this is not true of everyone in the electorate or of every politician, but the politicians who are elected term after term are likely to be as descriptive of their constituency as the sidewalks are of the streets.

The exact nature of the fictional picture of the candidate that it is necessary to plant in the minds of the people varies, of course, from time to time. In 1932, for example, Franklin Roosevelt thought it desirable to "dramatize himself as a breaker of custom, a daring, resolute champion of action, establishing a bold contrast with the country's picture of Hoover as timid, hesitant, irresolute." [26] Immediately after his nomination, he went by plane to Chicago to accept the nomination before the convention itself rather than await the customary formal notification of the nomination weeks later. By action, then, rather than by words, he created the desired impression in the minds of the electorate.

There is another side to the propagation of myths about candidates, and that is the prevention of the successful dissemination of myths of prestige about the opposition candidate. Of the 1936 campaign, Charles Michelson said, "my department of the Democratic organization began with the theory that the correct strategy was to insure, if possible, that the candidate of the opposition should not be built up to an inspiring figure." [27] The Democratic publicity men concentrated on the inexperience of the Republican candidate. "I believe," Michelson said, "we got across the idea that here was a man who, granted all his good qualities, either had no definite views on the great problems of the time or was willing to adopt any position that he, or his advisers, thought might attract votes." In the 1940 campaign the Republican publicity

[24] From *Political Behavior*, p. 271. Copyright, 1928, by William Morrow and Company, Inc., quoted by permission.
[25] J. T. Salter, "The Pattern of Politics," *Journal of Politics*, 1 (1939), pp. 258–277.
[26] Raymond Moley, *After Seven Years* (New York, 1939), p. 26. Quoted by permission of Harper and Brothers.
[27] "Democratic Strategy Is Told by Michelson," *The New York Times*, November 5, 1936.

staff, besides attempting to get across the idea that Willkie was a businessman who understood production and could make the economic system work, attempted to destroy the popular conception of Roosevelt. This effort was directed mainly toward ridicule of the doctrine that Roosevelt was indispensable, but it may be suspected that the repeated negation of the doctrine of indispensability really helped Roosevelt by suggesting to the voters that, perhaps, after all, he was indispensable. In the 1944 Republican campaign the accent was on youth: Dewey and his entourage were pictured as young, aggressive, forward-looking men; Roosevelt and other Democratic leaders were attacked as tired, old, quarreling men.

The kind of conception the voters gain of the candidates may determine the margin between victory and defeat, so close are many elections. Moreover, a choice between candidates is one most easily made by voters. Hence, great importance is attached to the choice of candidates and the propagation of the desired conception of a candidate. The candidate is not only a personality; he symbolizes a general approach to public questions or a general spirit in public policy. Consider: Bryan, a fearless crusader attacking the strongholds of special privilege; Harding, the easy-going, pleasant embodiment of the yearning for normalcy; Coolidge, the conservative, shrewd, safe, New Englander; Wilson, the militant battler for a new freedom; Franklin Roosevelt, the champion of the forgotten man. Voters in the mass find it easier to decide between personalities than between policies; campaigners build into their candidates a personification of the policies that they think will appeal to a majority. In the process, the actual individuals are often caricatured into abstractions quite unlike themselves, or special aspects of their personalities are highly distorted. Of course, many candidates attain no sharply defined image in the minds of the mass of the voters; they ride along with the ticket. But presidential candidates, gubernatorial candidates, mayoralty candidates, and sometimes senatorial candidates make a distinct impression.

Choosing campaign issues. Perhaps the prime question in campaign strategy is the selection of the points to emphasize in the campaign. What feature of the party's program or candidate is to be chosen as the main selling point? What aspect of the opposition record is to be singled out for repeated attack? The theory is that concentration on the strongest or most popular point will gain the most votes, and likewise that concentration of fire on the most vulnerable phase of the opposition will have the greatest possible effect. On the contrary, a multiplicity of appeals creates confusion and eliminates the cumulative impact that results from ceaseless repetition of one effective appeal.

Campaign managers have not often disclosed the processes of planning campaign strategy; it is probable that not so much cool calculation or cold cunning enters into the process as might be supposed. In 1936 the entire Democratic campaign, according to James Farley, was "based on the proposition that Roosevelt, and Roosevelt alone, was the issue before the voters." [28] In the speeches of party orators and in the literature distributed by the national committee, "the central theme was always the 'gallant leadership' of the Chief Executive." On the negative side of strategy, or the attack phase, in the early stages of the 1936 campaign the Democratic strategy was to "ignore the Republican Party and to concentrate fire on the Liberty League." The Liberty League and its denunciations of the New Deal received great attention in the press of the country early in 1936, but by the time of the national conventions Democratic propaganda had effectively discredited the League and as effectively associated that discredit with the Republican party. "In point of fact," Mr. Farley concludes, "the G.O.P. never did recover from the initial blunder of permitting the Shouse organization to direct the firing during the preliminary skirmishing." [29]

In the 1896 campaign the association of John D. Rockefeller, Cornelius Vanderbilt, C. P. Huntington, J. P. Morgan, and Andrew Carnegie with the Republican party, and of Bryan and his "cross of gold" with the Democratic party, gave color to the belief that the campaign involved a struggle between the rich and the poor. How were the Republicans to meet the situation? McKinley in accepting the nomination declared: "All attempt to array class against class, the classes against the masses, section against section, labor against capital, poor against rich, or interest against interest, is in the highest degree reprehensible." This statement amounted virtually to the defense of a class interest by denying the existence of conflicts, but it was effective.

Public opinion polls now can be used to supplement the politician's intuition in the determination of the strategy of issues. At the beginning of the 1944 campaign, for example, the opinion polls indicated that twice as many people thought the Democrats could bring the war to a successful conclusion at the earliest time as believed the Republicans could do so. Similarly, a majority believed that Roosevelt would be a better man than Dewey to represent the United States at the peace conference. On the other hand, Dewey and Roosevelt ran neck and neck on the question of which man would do the best job of managing domestic affairs, and the people who believed that the Republican party would bring the greatest postwar prosperity were slightly more numer-

[28] *Op. cit.,* p. 314.
[29] *Ibid.,* pp. 294–295.

ous than those who placed their faith in the Democrats on this point. In the actual conduct of the campaign the Democrats and Republicans tended to stress those points in their records and in their promises that had the strongest appeal to the voters.[30]

Defensive strategy: Reply or ignore? One of the problems in the strategy of issues is what the campaigner should do about attacks made by his opposition. Should he answer them or should he ignore them. "There's an old bromide in politics that goes something like this: 'If your opponent calls you a liar, do not deny it—just call him a thief.' " [31] One possibility is to have the attack answered, not by the head of the ticket, but by a lesser political figure. In 1936, Charles Michelson says, "Governor Landon's acceptance speech put us somewhat on the spot. It did not seem fitting that the President should answer it—for he could not take a defensive attitude. We finally decided on an hour's program in which a chain of four Democratic Governors participated, chiming in, each from his own State House." [32] As another alternative the candidate chooses carefully the charge that he will answer; naturally it will be the one that can be answered in the most devastating manner. In the 1940 campaign, for example, Roosevelt chose to answer the charge of a Republican campaigner that the President's only supporters were "paupers, those who earn less than $1,200 a year and aren't worth that, and the Roosevelt family." An extreme charge of this sort made by a minor figure of the opposition can be answered advantageously.

On the other hand, it may be judged preferable to ignore an attack altogether, for if you answer an attack you fight on terrain chosen by the enemy. In the presidential campaign of 1936 the Republicans "took as their targets Chairman Farley and Rex Tugwell" and other Democratic figures. "Farley was not a conscienceless villain; Tugwell was not a Socialist gone mad, and Dubinsky was not a Communist; but," said Michelson, "if the Republicans could get us arguing on such points they had a better chance than if the battle line remained straight. So Farley took it on the chin and we made no replies to the collateral assaults." [33] In the 1932 campaign the Republican campaigners ridiculed and belittled John N. Garner, the vice-presidential candidate. The Democrats paid little heed to the attack, but they assigned to Mr. Garner a very inconspicuous part in the campaign. A consequence of the parrying of campaigners is that often the issues are not joined.

[30] See Hadley Cantril, "The Issues—As Seen by the American People," *Public Opinion Quarterly,* 8 (1944), pp. 331–347.
[31] "The ABC's of Political Campaigning," *The New York Times Magazine,* September 22, 1940.
[32] *The New York Times,* November 15, 1936.
[33] *Ibid.*

One party talks at great length about its strong points and keeps quiet about its weaker points, not even attempting to defend them. The opposition party does the same thing. For example, in 1940 the Republicans spoke frequently and vociferously on the third-term issue; the Democrats scarcely mentioned it. They spoke of the desirability of an experienced administration at a critical phase in foreign affairs. The Republicans did not deny this need; they talked about the dangers of a third term.[34]

Geographical concentration of effort. An elementary principle of campaigning is that efforts should be concentrated where they will do the most good: usually in closely contested and doubtful states. Presidential campaign forays into the Solid South are extremely rare, for the outcome of the voting in those states has, since the Civil War, almost always been known in advance. Elsewhere the greatest outlay of energy and of funds is likely to occur in the areas believed to be close. Thus in the closing days of the 1940 presidential campaign the Democrats sent into Ohio—a state thought to be slipping toward Willkie— the President, Henry Wallace, Mayor La Guardia, Senator Norris, and other Democratic bigwigs. In the same campaign the Democrats-for-Willkie focused a large-scale mail circularization campaign in states that could be converted to Republicanism by a slight shift. Even in speech-making tours there may be a concentration of effort in doubtful areas. In 1944 Dewey made a 6,700-mile swing to the Pacific Coast with only seven scheduled speeches, most of them in supposedly doubtful states. By contrast, Willkie in 1940, talked his heart out at every whistle-stop; he talked himself hoarse and did not conserve his energy for major speeches. The principle of concentration of fire is further illustrated by the selective purchase of radio time. In 1936, for example, the Republicans excluded from their network deals southern stations; dissemination of Republican propaganda in that area would have been an unfruitful expenditure.

Campaign timing. An element in strategy is the timing of campaign efforts. Since campaigns in the United States tend to be stretched over a long period of time, this factor may be of considerable significance. If all resources are thrown into the campaign too early, the campaign may reach its peak prior to election day and exhaust the campaign chest and the party personnel before the moment that the greatest exertion is needed. The campaign should reach its apex just prior to the election. Mark Hanna, for example, planned that his campaign work

---

[34] Lazarsfeld, *The People's Choice* (New York: Duell, Sloan, and Pearce, 1944), pp. 38–39. On strategy of issues in the 1916 presidential campaign, see D. C. Roper, *Fifty Years of Public Life* (Durham: Duke University Press, 1941).

would "be cumulative in its effect, culminating a few days before the
election in an outburst of common conviction and enthusiasm." [35]   The
1944 Dewey campaign presented perplexing problems in timing.   Early
in the campaign the Republican high command chose to concentrate
on the need of the country for a peacetime President rather than a
Commander-in-chief.   At the time, the movement of military events
looked extremely favorable, and under these circumstances the Republicans were emphasizing a point in which they were strong and the
Democrats weak, in popular estimation.   As the campaign progressed,
military reverses made peace seem more remote, and the Republican
appeal appeared to have been erroneously timed.   Military events did
not move in accord with the assumptions underlying the party's campaign strategy.   The timing and strategy of the Republican campaign
was in fundamental error—perhaps unavoidable error—because it appeared that the controlling factor in the campaign was the judgment of
the electorate whether a President was being elected for peace or for
war.[36]

Front porch or swing around the circle.   In a presidential campaign
a recurring question of strategy relates to the extent of the speaking and
traveling schedule of the head of the ticket.   Should the candidate
make an extensive swing around the country and speak at as many
places as practicable or should he make the type of campaign traditionally known as the "front-porch" campaign?   The decision on this
question may depend on the kind of candidate the party has.   In the
1920 Republican campaign the strategy was to keep Harding at home
in Marion, Ohio.   "Keep Warren at home," the Republican leader
Penrose is reported to have said.   "Don't let him make any speeches.
If he goes out on a tour, somebody's sure to ask him questions, and
Warren's just the sort of damn fool that'll try to answer them."   "The
Front Porch campaign," according to Samuel Hopkins Adams, "was
determined upon.   The role assigned to the candidate was that of the
modest, simple, sagacious, home-loving, home-staying statesman.   He
was to be 'just folks.'   To the Mecca of Marion would come the devout,
and the Prophet would edify them with the sound doctrine of orthodox
Republicanism." [37]

In the 1932 Democratic campaign James Farley says that a vexing
question was the determination of whether Franklin Roosevelt should
stay at home and issue statements on the occasion of the visits of party

[35] Herbert Croly, *Marcus Alonzo Hanna* (New York: Macmillan, 1912), p. 322.
[36] See Hadley Cantril, "The Issues behind the Issues," *New York Times Magazine*,
October 22, 1944.
[37] Samuel Hopkins Adams, *Incredible Era* (Boston: Houghton Mifflin, 1939), p. 170.

dignitaries or travel about the country "flinging bold challenges at the Republican foe." The leading Democratic Senators and Representatives, according to Farley, advised that a front-porch technique be used, but Roosevelt decided to follow the alternative method. Farley believed that the speech-making trip to the west coast and back was influential in increasing the Roosevelt vote in the states that he traversed.[38] The swing around the circle was incidentally calculated to rebut opposition insinuations about the state of the candidate's health and physical vitality.

The strategists of the 1928 Hoover campaign had the problem of what to do about the speaking schedule of a candidate whose oratorical abilities were hardly notable. Something of a compromise between the "swing around the circle" and the front-porch technique was adopted. Only Grover Cleveland and Calvin Coolidge, according to Peel and Donnelly, had delivered fewer speeches during a presidential campaign than Hoover made in 1928. And the strategy was to play up the notion that Hoover, a dignified and statesmanlike figure of legendary proportions, could hardly bemean the presidential office by anxious appeals to the mob on the hustings. The suggestion to the electorate was that a man of Hoover's dimensions would hardly stoop to the same sort of tactics as his competitor, the rough diamond of the streets of New York, Al Smith.

Driving a wedge between the opposing candidate and his followers. An old campaigning maxim is that " a candidate should always separate his opponent from the rank and file of the party." Willkie in 1940 strove to draw a line between Roosevelt and the Democrats. The "New Dealers" (not the Democratic administration) had, he argued, departed from the precepts of Democratic heroes and saints. "So if there is any Democratic disciple of Thomas Jefferson in Dubuque he ought to vote for me," Willkie asserted. "Surely any Andrew Jackson Democrat should vote for me and not for my opponent. . . . No Cleveland Democrat should vote against me." He talked to the Democrats as if they had been betrayed by Roosevelt and the "New Dealers." Similar is the direction of intensive criticism against minor figures rather than the chief of the opposite party. Roosevelt attacked the men around Willkie in 1940; Republican orators aimed much of their fire at the "Corcorans and Cohens"; the "brain trusters"; the city bosses Kelly, Flynn, and Hague; "Reds"; and "fellow travelers." But Republican orators did not limit their attack to the minor figures, and it is not improbable that the intense criticism of Roosevelt hurt the Re-

---

[38] *Op. cit.,* pp. 163–165; Charles Michelson, *The Ghost Talks* (New York: Putnam, 1944), pp. 11–12.

publican cause. That would be the deduction if there is any validity in the theory that relentless and untempered criticism may redound to the benefit of its victim.

Ridicule: A double-edged sword.   A subtle art of campaigning is the use of ridicule, sarcasm, scorn.   Not many presidential candidates are masters of the art.   In Roosevelt's speech to the International Teamsters Union in September, 1944, he skilfully poked fun at the opposition.   In this speech the President rose to the defense of his dog Fala. The President's wife, the President's sons, the President could ignore attacks on themselves, but Fala's "Scotch soul was furious."   Listeners laughed raucously before millions of radios: "I think I have a right to object to libelous statements about my dog."   The speech, however, had far-reaching effects.   A rip-roaring declamation, it was calculated to arouse the voters from their apathy.   Perhaps it was also designed to anger the opposition candidate.   The next day Dewey promised "unvarnished candor"; and his next speech, thrown together in haste, did not reflect the same sober consideration as earlier speeches and paved the way for campaign boners, or so the political writers opined.   Invective, sarcasm, satire, ridicule, when used by the head of the ticket, may boomerang, as will outright misrepresentation.   In the 1944 campaign, for example, Dewey used quotations from Roosevelt's earlier statements out of context in a manner to misrepresent Roosevelt's position.   The Democratic reaction was prompt and Democratic speakers condemned the G.O.P. for trying "to lie its way into office," for "wholesale falsehood."   The dirtier side of campaigning at times moves over into slander and raises questions of ethical standards of political behavior.   Campaigns are probably cleaner than they were a century ago.[39]   Nevertheless, in the 1940 campaign many very fine specimens of smear literature were circulated.[40]   Consequently it was felt that legislation was necessary to re-enforce the voters' intolerance of intolerance, and Congress in December, 1944, required that campaign literature in all its forms include the names of the persons responsible for its publication or distribution.[41]

Another of the more shady campaign practices is the surreptitious backing of phony candidates who will draw strength from the opposition.   This practice is not at all infrequent in state and local campaigns, but it is rare in presidential campaigns.   In 1884, for example, the Republican managers largely financed the campaign of the Greenback

[39] See Samuel Hopkins Adams, "Presidential Campaign Slanders," *Life,* October 2, 1944.

[40] Hugh A. Bone, *"Smear" Politics* (Washington: American Council on Public Affairs, 1941).

[41] Public Law 544, 78th Cong., approved December 23, 1944.

candidate on the theory that his campaign would draw strength from Cleveland.[42]

Maintaining the illusion of victory. The major objective of a campaign is to maintain the illusion of victory among the partisans of a candidate. A campaign serves the purpose of keeping up the courage of souls already saved, as much as it does that of winning converts. Hence, the candidate keeps up to the end of the campaign an appearance of confidence that victory is inevitable, and his lieutenants frequently issue reports of surveys indicating that the election is in the bag. Thus, early in September, 1944, Herbert Brownell, the Republican national chairman, announced that an extremely careful analysis of political sentiment had been made and that Messrs. Dewey and Bricker would be elected with "votes to spare." Mr. Brownell was "tremendously encouraged" by the trend that, it was predicted, would also bring control of the House and Senate. Such pronouncements occur in every campaign and are made on behalf of every candidate.

4. CHANNELS OF PROPAGANDA

One phase of propaganda analysis is the study of the media or channels used to reach the groups whose opinions are to be influenced. The development of media of communication in an astonishing manner during the past century, in fact, underlies propaganda in its modern scale and method. Without the technological developments in communication and dissemination of news that have been invented or perfected in relatively recent times, mass propaganda as it is currently practiced would be impossible.

Communications in Jackson's time and now. Professor Eriksson has described the facilities Andrew Jackson had for reaching the electorate. During the campaign of 1828 and until 1830 Jackson's chief means for the circulation of his views was the United States *Telegraph,* a partisan newspaper that built up a large circulation, 40,000 copies weekly. The successor to the *Telegraph,* the Washington *Globe,* reached by 1834 a daily circulation of 12,000.[43] The leading articles of this newspaper were reprinted and commented on by newspapers of local circulation scattered over the country, but only after the Washington newspaper had been conveyed to their offices by the primitive means of transport of the day. In addition to the party press the party campaigners could reach as large a crowd as could be assembled within the range of their

---

[42] Nevins, *Grover Cleveland,* pp. 173–174.

[43] E. M. Eriksson, "President Jackson's Propaganda Agencies," *Pacific Historical Review,* 6 (1937), pp. 47–57.

voices—a range that was determined by lung power and not by electrical amplification.

Since Jackson's time the weapons at the command of the propagandist have multiplied.   The invention of the telegraph permitted the simultaneous publication of the same item in every city of the land.   The parallel improvements in printing technology and newspaper merchandising brought newspapers within the economic reach of practically everyone.   Decreasing illiteracy widened the market for printed matter, and the number of periodicals with a nation-wide circulation increased with the improvements of the means for their distribution.   Naturally, advances in the means of travel made it feasible for the candidate to conduct more extensive campaigns and bring more people within the range of his voice.   The introduction of movies made it possible for the candidate to be seen as well as heard simultaneously by millions of people.   The inauguration of radio broadcasting after 1920 brought the entire nation within earshot of the campaigner.   All these developments in communication markedly changed the nature of propaganda, political and otherwise, and probably profoundly altered the nature of political power, by making it possible for national leaders to reach and influence mass opinion directly without heavy reliance on an intermediate network of party workers.   By the use of the modern channels of propaganda, vast influence may be exerted by a very few men through the use of the new instruments of power.

The press: Reporter and partisan.   Newspapers are a channel for propaganda; they also are usually propagandists.   In their reporting of events and in their advertising columns they furnish a medium through which the party and the candidate may reach the electorate; in their editorial columns and in their reporting of the news they are likely to play the part of a partisan.   It is not necessary to establish the existence of a gigantic conspiracy on the part of newspapers and business interests to color and control the news, as is sometimes alleged to exist; publishing is in itself a big business, and what is astonishing is not that newspapers take on the tone of their proprietors, but that they have so often conducted crusades in the general interest.

Whatever the attitude of the newspapers toward a candidate, the latter cannot afford to be ignored by the press, and in his entourage are usually to be found men whose special job it is to handle relations with the press.   When the presidential candidate goes on tour, ample provision is made for newspaper correspondents to accompany him; and they are furnished with advance copies of speeches and with other facilities to aid them in covering the campaign.   Similarly, in state and local campaigns, efforts are made to expedite and facilitate the work of the press. Apart from the newspaper coverage that comes from press representation at party meetings and speeches, the campaigner uses other channels to get his message into the editorial rooms. In the 1936 Republican campaign, for example, the publicity department made arrangements to furnish its press releases in mat, plate, and proof form to weeklies and small dailies. "At their own request 7,000 weeklies and 280 dailies received W.N.U. plate service; 430 weeklies and 557 dailies got mat service, and proof service was supplied to 25 weeklies and 780 dailies." [44] The total number of press releases distributed during the campaign was estimated at 361,000. The publicity divisions of both parties are diligent in furnishing partisan argumentation to the press, and column after column of small dailies and country weeklies is filled with material supplied from party headquarters in the form of "editorial suggestions."

The candidate must make news. It sometimes appears that the routine of the life of the candidate is geared to newspaper deadlines. Candidates strive to keep in the headlines; every day there must be some sort of news for the press. The theory of the practicing politician is, according to Frank R. Kent, that "it is better to be roasted than ignored." He says that the late Claude A. Swanson of Virginia framed the maxim in this way: "When they stop writing about you in politics, you're dead." [45]

In reporting the news, the newspaper may give the advantage to one or the other candidate by giving its favorite more space, by giving stories of his speeches and activities greater prominence, by colored and misleading headlines, and by various other means that may be observed during any campaign. In a study of attention given in twenty-one newspapers to the candidates during the 1936 presidential campaign, E. O. Stene found that "all except one of the twenty-one dailies gave a majority of their political news space to the candidate who was supported through the editorial pages." This tendency held whether the paper was supporting Roosevelt or Landon. Stene concludes that if it be assumed that impartiality in reporting means approximately equal treatment of both candidates, "few newspapers could claim impartiality" during the 1936 campaign. Stene also examined newspapers in the 1944 campaign and reached a similar conclusion for that campaign. [46] Incidentally, in the campaign of 1944, according to a survey

[44] Casey, *Public Opinion Quarterly, op. cit.*, pp. 27–44.

[45] *Op. cit.*, pp. 252–253.

[46] E. O. Stene, "Newspapers in the Campaign," *Social Science*, 12 (1937), pp. 213–215; *idem.*, "Newspapers in the Presidential Campaign," *Southwestern Social Science Quarterly*, 25 (1945), pp. 258–264. See also Bureau of Applied Social Research, "Front-Page Bias in Newspapers," *Nation*, 159 (1944), p. 348.

by *Editor and Publisher* in September, dailies with 64 per cent of the total circulation supported Dewey, dailies with 14 per cent of the circulation backed Roosevelt, and the remainder, with 22 per cent of all circulation, announced no stand.

The advertising columns of the newspapers are always open to party committees, but usually at a somewhat higher rate than is charged to ordinary commercial advertisers. Among politicians the opinion is that newspaper advertising involves a waste of money; yet when one side advertises, the other feels that it must do so, too. Frank Kent diagnoses the failings of political advertisements in this way: ". . . if they are written by the skilled advertising writer, they lack the political knowledge, background, instinct and feel; and if they are written by the politically minded man, brought up in the political school of politics, they lack the skill of the trained writer of advertisements." [47] Casey says that the advertising and publicity experts of the Republican national committee in 1936 were not "as closely in touch with the political thinking of the lower-income and wage-earning voters as political symbol specialization demanded. This is not to be wondered at, however, since their vocational lives had been spent largely in contact with commercial propaganda enterprises." [48]

What of the influence of newspapers? Do people vote as their favorite editors recommend? The evidence on these questions is extremely limited. It is quite apparent that in a presidential campaign the newspapers cannot always swing the election; this was clearly demonstrated in 1936, 1940, and 1944 when the preponderance of the press of the nation opposed the re-election of Roosevelt. Yet it is probable that some voters were influenced by newspapers. It is also probable that newspaper influence is greatest on questions about which the voter has least information on which to base an opinion of his own. Furthermore, newspapers are doubtless influential in jurisdictions that have the long ballot and must elect many obscure candidates to fill inconspicuous positions and in jurisdictions that vote on many constitutional amendments, charter amendments, and initiated and referred measures. Regarding charter amendments and like questions in Seattle, McKenzie concluded: "Apparently the electorate is more ready to follow the advice of the press on minor and more technical questions, such as the majority of the charter amendments are, than on the more important issues, especially those involving the expenditure of money." [49]

[47] *Op. cit.*, p. 266.
[48] "Republican Propaganda in the 1936 Campaign," *Public Opinion Quarterly*, April, 1937, p. 35.
[49] R. D. McKenzie, "Community Forces: A Study of the Non-Partisan Municipal Elections in Seattle," *Social Forces*, 2 (1923–24), p. 271.

On the other hand, the newspaper is sometimes more a reflector than a leader of public opinion. "Newspaper opinions," says Lundberg, "are perhaps themselves the products of the various forces which make opinion in a community. Of these, the newspaper is undoubtedly one, but its influence as such has perhaps been grossly overestimated or at least the nature of this influence has been misunderstood." [50] Whatever the influence of the newspaper on electoral behavior is, the degree of that influence is extremely difficult to measure. The difficulty of that measurement may be indicated by an examination of articles by Professor Gosnell in which he employed complex statistical techniques to ascertain the influences of the press on voting in Chicago. His conclusion was: "In those sections of the city where their circulation is largest, newspapers are important influences over a period of time in determining the fate of factional leaders in primary elections. In general elections, the papers which have followed a consistent policy regarding a given party faction may influence their readers to split their tickets in favor of or in opposition to that faction." [51] The last sentence refers to the success of two newspapers in persuading their readers to split their Republican tickets and support the Democratic nominee for governor of Illinois in 1932.

Party literature. The production of leaflets, pamphlets, and circulars by the publicity divisions of the national committees during a presidential campaign is stupendous. Charles Michelson says that "100,000,000 pamphlets, fly sheets and other pieces of paper would be a modest estimate" of the literature distributed by the Democratic publicity division in 1936. Estimates of the total number of pieces of literature issued by the research and editorial division of the Republican national committee during the same campaign range from 125 million to 170 million. Including all the divisions of the Republican committee issuing literature during that campaign, Casey hazards the "guess that . . . 400,000,000 pieces of literature flooded the country in the effort to persuade a majority of the electorate to vote for Landon." [52]

Through leaflets and pamphlets the party can deliver its message to people not reached by the newspapers, furnish ammunition to its

[50] George A. Lundberg, "The Newspaper and Public Opinion," *Social Forces* 4 (1926), pp. 709–715.

[51] H. F. Gosnell and M. J. Schmidt, "Factorial Analysis of the Relation of the Press to Voting in Chicago," *Journal of Social Psychology*, 7 (1936), pp. 375–385; "Relation of the Press to Voting in Chicago," *Journalism Quarterly*, June, 1936, pp. 129–147. See also Bernard Berelson, "The Effects of Print upon Public Opinion" in *Print, Radio, and Film in a Democracy*, edited by Douglas Waples (Chicago: University of Chicago Press, 1942); Gerhart Saenger, "The Press and Public Opinion," *New Republic*, 111 (1944), pp. 123–124, 157–159.

[52] Casey, *Public Opinion Quarterly, op. cit.*, April, 1937, pp. 27–44.

friends, and present arguments and material that would not be printed by newspapers or transmitted by the radio stations. A 1940 Democratic leaflet entitled "Life Lines vs. Spite Lines," for example, presented the T.V.A. record and the Commonwealth and Southern record in parallel columns. A Republican leaflet, "A Third Term?" gave in parallel columns pictures and statements of pro- and anti-third termers. Among the former were, according to the leaflet, Earl Browder, "Boss Edward J. Kelly," "Boss Frank Hague," and Harold L. Ickes; the latter, George Washington, Thomas Jefferson, Andrew Jackson, and Woodrow Wilson. Even the most partisan newspaper rarely prints its news in so partisan a fashion as campaign literature may be prepared.

The distribution of literature is costly. If it is mailed, a large outlay for postage and clerical labor is required. If it is entrusted to the party workers for distribution, it may not be distributed, for the party organization is seldom so efficient as it is reputed to be. Louis Howe, late secretary to President Roosevelt, found in a survey of national campaigning that only about 3 to 5 per cent of the literature distributed to state committees by national headquarters ever reached the hands of the voters. In the 1932 Democratic campaign the practice was inaugurated of sending a few pieces of each kind of literature to each of about 140,000 local committeemen instead of depending on the state committees to accept bulk shipments and then distribute it through subordinate party workers. Howe found that the new method of distribution resulted in about 90 per cent of the literature reaching the voters.[53]

Radio. The newest gift of communication technology to the campaigner is the radio. Apparently if the campaign budget has to be reduced, the tendency in national campaigns is to squeeze expenditures for newspaper advertising, organization work, and literature rather than to eliminate items for time on the radio networks.

Exact measurement of the relative advantages and disadvantages of the radio as a channel for propaganda over other media has not been carried very far,[54] but a few comparisons may be noted. Listeners to a radio speech obviously lack the emotional stimulus of the crowd that operates in mass meetings. In an ordinary political meeting there

---

[53] Howe's account of the methods used in 1932 is quoted by Peel and Donnelly, *The 1932 Campaign*, pp. 115–116. The distribution of literature from national headquarters has long presented a problem. In the campaign of 1896 two weeks before the election several carloads of pamphlets had not even been unloaded from the freight cars at Columbus, Ohio. The Republican national committee in that campaign mailed many documents directly to the voters to assure distribution.

[54] See Paul F. Lazarsfeld, *Radio and the Printed Page* (New York: Duell, Sloan and Pearce, 1940); Paul F. Lazarsfeld and Frank N. Stanton, *Radio Research 1941* (New York: Duell, Sloan and Pearce, 1941).

exists not only an interaction between the speaker and each auditor, but, in addition, relationships among the listeners, which may reinforce the admonitions and urgings of the speaker. The individual listener is carried along by crowd compulsion to cheer, to agree; and the emotional experience shared by the individuals in an audience may be very stirring indeed. The radio listener, on the other hand, is usually, at most, one of a handful listening. The social stimulus of the crowd is absent; even when the cheers and cries of the speaker's immediate audience are broadcast, the effect on the radio listener is certainly not so great as if he were in the crowd.[55]

The radio listener receives only those impressions that can be conveyed by the sound of the human voice. The effects of the gestures, the smiles, the bearing of the speaker are lost to him. James Farley was willing to concede that the radio was a "tremendous factor" in the Roosevelt political fortunes, but, he said, "to my way of thinking, there is no substitute for the personal touch and there never will be, unless the Lord starts to make human beings different from the way he makes them now."[56]

Radio presentation has marked advantages over printed propaganda in several ways. A matter of great importance is that the campaigner can control what reaches the voter's mind; whereas, if he relies on newspapers to report his speeches and statements, distortions may occur.

A factor governing radio speeches, as found by Merton E. Carver, is that "the effectiveness of auditory presentation tends to vary inversely with the difficulty of the material presented." In less technical language, the simpler the speech is, the more likely is its content to be implanted in the listeners' minds. This factor, together with the costliness of radio time and the difficulty of holding listener interest for long, has made the finished radio speech a very different article from the long-winded political oration of earlier days. Carver also finds that critical attitudes and discriminatory comprehension tend to be aroused more by reading than by listening. The persuasive affirmations of the seductive radio voice are more likely to be accepted than are the same words in print.[57] The radio handicaps candidates deficient in radio "personality" and radio "voice," and gives a corresponding advantage to the candidate who has mastered the use of this medium.

Political rallies: The personal touch. The political rally and the

[55] For discussion of this point, see Hadley Cantril and G. W. Allport, *The Psychology of Radio* (New York: Harper, 1935), pp. 9–14.

[56] *Op. cit.*, pp. 192–193.

[57] Note the comment of an Illinois farmer: "Sometimes when I listen to Roosevelt I even get to thinking he's right and all the time I know he's wrong." Lazarsfeld and Stanton, *op. cit.*, p. 267.

campaign tour are means by which the candidates may be seen as well
as heard. The voter may size up the candidate from his appearance
and manner; the voter shares in the intoxication of the crowd; the
candidate builds up emotions of affection on the part of his auditors.
Or, it may not always be necessary for the candidate to speak to obtain
an effect. Candidates and potential candidates like to show themselves before the public as often as possible. Roosevelt, for example,
between campaign years made many expeditions across the continent.
Farley says that he always urged the President to make these journeys,
and he quotes a Republican politician on the prospects for the election
in North Dakota in 1936: "Roosevelt has been across North Dakota
three times, and those visits sewed up the State. . . ."[58]

In his tours the presidential candidate travels by special train and
is accompanied by an entourage that includes a research staff, publicity
men, political advisers, office staff, radio technicians, newspapermen, newsreel photographers, newspaper photographers, and others.
Dewey's train in 1944 consisted of thirteen cars. Included was a car
equipped for the operations of the candidate's research staff, a lounge
car for conferences, a car prepared as a workroom for the 60 reporters
on the tour. The baggage car contained darkroom facilities for the
photographers. The train carried sound amplification apparatus for
rear-platform speeches, which were piped into the press car to enable
the reporters to cover the speeches without leaving the train. Such a
traveling hotel and party headquarters is to be contrasted with William
Jennings Bryan's campaign tour in 1896, when the presidential candidate traveled in day coaches, occasionally in Pullmans, and depended
on the newspaper reporters in the towns he visited to cover his speeches.

5. EFFECTS OF CAMPAIGNS

What of the effects of campaigns? Is one type of campaign more
effective than another? Does the use of the radio yield more votes
than reliance on printed literature? Can a campaigner with a particular type of personality sweep the electorate off its feet? What proportion of the voters change their minds as a result of the barrage of
speeches, of literature, and of personal solicitation? Does the debate of
the campaign set off a national deliberative process in which the people
listen to the evidence, weigh it, and form an opinion on how to vote?

Trustworthy data on the effects of campaigns are extremely limited,
and the information that exists relates primarily to national campaigns.

[58] *Op. cit.*, p. 317.

One way to narrow the problem of estimating the effects of campaigns is to examine, first, other factors that perhaps have greater weight in determining the outcome of elections than campaigns themselves. One of these factors is the traditional or consistent vote. It is apparent that a large proportion of the electorate votes for the party in one election that it supported in the preceding election. These diehard partisans are seemingly untouched by the events of the campaign. Around four fifths of the voters may ordinarily be placed in the category of loyal partisans. This matter of the extent of consistent party voting is treated at some length later in Chapter 19.

Another point that aids in getting down to the effects of campaigns is this: Changes in party loyalties and voting intentions occur all during the four-year period of a President's incumbency. The trend of opinion may be such that the changes in voting intentions during the more than three years before the campaign proper begins may exceed the changes occurring during the period of intensive campaigning. The "propaganda of events" or the "propaganda of deeds" may make or lose more votes than all that is said during the course of the campaign. Consider the period from 1928 to 1932. Hoover won in 1928 by an impressive majority, but after the crash of 1929 his popularity rapidly declined and the trend away from the Republican party found expression in the congressional elections of 1930 and in many state and local elections. In all probability the changes from Republican to Democratic occurring before the campaign of 1932 began exceeded those brought about by the hullabaloo of the campaign. Consider also the sharp increase in Democratic strength from 1932 to 1936. The dramatic series of governmental acts from 1933 to 1936 that affected directly millions of people constituted a powerful propaganda of deed, with great influence on the voting in 1936. The campaign was over before it began.

Some evidence is available to support the assertion that long-term trends of sentiment may be more efficacious in altering voting intentions than campaign oratory. In an intensive study of Erie County, Ohio, in the 1940 campaign, a sampling of the electorate indicated that the change in sentiment in the county from November, 1936, to May, 1940, accounted for twice as many votes as did the events of the campaign itself.[59] The use of nation-wide poll findings at intervals between elections also suggests that in the country as a whole the change in sentiment over the long term as a consequence of non-campaign fac-

[59] Paul F. Lazersfeld and Others, *The People's Choice* (New York: Duell, Sloan and Pearce, 1944), p. 102.

tors may exceed the shifts in voting intentions occurring during the campaign itself. The campaign may serve to accelerate or to retard a pre-existing trend.

In the important pioneer study of campaign behavior involving an intensive analysis of Erie County, Ohio, Lazarsfeld suggests that campaigns may have three principal effects: reinforcement, activation, and conversion. The reinforcement effect consists simply in the fact that the events of the campaign reinforce the voting intentions and party loyalties of the die-hard partisans. Speeches, parades, and other campaign festivities keep up the courage of those whose minds are already made up. They furnish the loyal with reasons for their loyalty and maintain the exuberance of their spirits. Party managers have long been aware of this general proposition,[60] but Lazarsfeld's careful analysis furnishes factual support for the supposition. The loyal partisans expose themselves to more political propaganda than others. Moreover, they expose themselves to propaganda favorable to the point of view that they already have. Thus a major function of campaign propaganda is to confirm those already decided in their convictions.

The activation effect of campaigns consists in the arousing of persons indifferent at the outset and inducing them to vote. In considerable measure those whose disinterest is turned into an inclination to vote are persuaded to vote in the manner in which one would have predicted on the basis of their personal characteristics. Thus, in his study of Erie County, Ohio, Lazarsfeld discovered that persons who were prosperous, Protestant, rural dwellers tended toward Republicanism; on the other hand, urban Catholic workers had a predisposition toward Democratic affiliations. On the basis of extensive interviews it appeared that in the majority of instances those undecided at the beginning of the campaign whose views crystallized during the campaign drifted to the party toward which they were predisposed by their characteristics. In reality, the activation effect consists in arousing the lethargic and bringing them out to vote. This campaign effect may, of course, determine the outcome of an election. The 1944 presidential election furnishes a striking example of the effect of bringing out the vote. The apathetic were more disposed toward the Democratic party than toward the Republican. A vigorous campaign to get out the vote brought more Democratic than Republican voters to the polls.

Very few people are converted by a campaign, that is, change their voting intentions between the time of the beginning of the campaign

---

[60] See Turner Catledge, "Is Campaigning Worth While?" *New York Times Magazine,* October 15, 1944.

and the election itself.   The small margin of conversion may, of course, in a close election determine the outcome.   Lazarsfeld produces evidence that indicates that campaign propaganda itself may bring about these conversions.   His findings showed, for example, that persons of Republican predisposition exposed mainly to Democratic propaganda voted Democratic in larger degree than did those who happened to be exposed in large degree to Republican propaganda.

The state of research on the effects of campaigns, let it be repeated, is such that only limited conclusions may be drawn.   Yet the available studies and common observation suggest that campaigns mainly renew the loyalties of the faithful, bring the apathetic out to the polls for the expression of their predispositions, and effect the conversion of a very few electors.

PARTY FINANCE

THAT he who pays the piper calls the tune is often said to be the entire story of party finance in a democracy. But in politics there are different pipers competing for power and pay; there are people with divergent tastes in tunes often paying the same piper. The repertoire of the pipers is limited and there are arias beyond purchase; but no performer likes an empty house, and the piper may choose to be governed by the tastes of his impecunious listeners. Undoubtedly the parable of the payer and the piper correctly describes a recurring tendency, but campaign finance is more complex than the saying would indicate. It is certainly true that some campaign contributions are thinly disguised bribes, that is, payments to persons who have the power to exercise official discretion to the advantage of the contributors. More often, however, although the contributor may hope that he will receive a *quid pro quo,* he has no expectation based on explicit promise. Perhaps even more generally the expectation of reward is not in terms of a specific desired action; it is rather a belief that the general trend of events will be more favorable if one candidate wins rather than another. The contributor pays his money and takes his chances. If his party wins, he feels, right-thinking men like himself will regard his problems sympathetically, and the fact that he has made a campaign contribution will not be held against him. In other instances contributions seem inexplicable in terms of rational self-interest; some contributors are either quite nonrational or very poor judges of how to spend their money.

The financing of campaigns presents a perplexing problem in democracy. A relatively small number of people furnish a large proportion of the money to keep the machinery of the party going. This dependence on the gifts of a few to finance the campaigns of those who are bound to govern for the welfare of the many supposedly gives great advantage to those with money. To deal with such questions, it is necessary to examine the available facts about party finance. Incidentally, such a survey furnishes an insight into many aspects of political activity. The cost of campaigns and the purposes for which money is expended give us a notion of the magnitude of campaign efforts and an impression of the relative importance attached to different methods of campaigning. The sources of campaign funds show to some extent the differences in the composition of the parties and help in the identification of the groups clustered about each party banner. Analysis of efforts to regulate and control campaign funds illuminates one segment of the struggle between interests and groups for political power.[1]

1. WHAT CAMPAIGNS COST

The magnitude of the task of effectuating the democratic doctrine that the people shall choose their rulers may be measured by the expenditure of a total of over 20 million dollars by the major parties in a presidential campaign. The outlays in congressional, state, and local campaigns are, of course, on a smaller scale, but the person who aspires to be a member of Congress, the governor of a state, or the mayor of a large city must either have a goodly sum to finance his campaign or be able to command the support of persons with money to spare. The facts on campaign costs are only approximate. The completeness of our information depends on the scope of laws requiring campaign costs to be reported, on the degree of compliance with these laws, and on the thoroughness with which investigations of campaign expenditures are conducted. Furthermore, almost every political organization has at its disposal volunteer workers and also receives contributions of materials and quarters. The evaluation of these items is seldom attempted; hence, an organization that depends in large measure on volunteer services of campaign workers may appear to be able to carry on a campaign at a much lower cost than is actually the case.

Outlays in presidential election years. In presidential election years party expenditures reach a peak. Prior to the conventions aspirants for the nominations carry on campaigns in quest of favorable delegates. Although information on the costs of these preconvention activities is

[1] The principal source of information about American party finance is provided by the writings of Louise Overacker, to whom all students of politics owe a great debt. See her *Presidential Campaign Funds* (Boston: Boston University Press, 1946); also her *Money in Elections* (New York: Macmillan, 1932) and her articles analyzing the data on each subsequent presidential campaign, published in the *American Political Science Review*. An earlier but still useful, study is J. K. Pollock, *Party Campaign Funds* (New York: Knopf, 1926). On European practices, consult Pollock, *Money and Politics Abroad* (New York: Knopf, 1932). On regulatory measures, see E. R. Sikes, *State and Federal Corrupt-Practices Legislation* (Durham: Duke University Press, 1928).

not reported to any national authority, it is occasionally brought to light by investigations. In 1928, for example, the preconvention campaigns involved an outlay of almost $900,000. The largest sums were spent on behalf of Hoover ($395,000), Smith ($152,000), Lowden ($87,-000), Willis ($66,000), and Reed ($52,000).[2] In the Democratic preconvention campaign of 1912 the Wilson forces spent $208,000; the Harmon forces, $77,000.[3] To be a serious contender for a presidential nomination a person ordinarily has to be able to attract the support of at least a quarter million dollars, but it should not be supposed that a quarter of a million dollars alone can make a person a serious contender for the nomination.

After the conventions have made their nominations and the presidential campaign itself gets under way, expenditures mount. The determination of what is actually spent is attended by no little difficulty. The information on what is actually paid out is incomplete. The allocation of known expenditures to campaigns for particular offices challenges accounting ingenuity. A committee finances campaign work for "the ticket," which includes every party candidate from that for the Presidency to the aspirant for the precinct constableship. How shall the outlays be allocated? It is obviously impossible. From the data available, about all that can be done is to attempt to build up a relatively comparable set of figures on expenditures by specified party and nonparty agencies from campaign to campaign. Table 15 presents such information for the years 1928, 1940, and 1944.

Completeness and reliability of campaign cost data. The figures in Table 15 will bear closer examination. The reliability of the data, which are based on reports of expenditures filed under requirements of law and of statements filed with senatorial investigating committees, varies. Reports filed by the national committees of the major parties probably are fairly reliable. Reports filed by state committees are considerably less so, and reports filed by independent committees are of highly variable reliability. These committees spring up overnight, collect and spend money, and disappear with equal rapidity. Their records are sometimes nonexistent and often highly informal. On occasion these committees have good reason to keep their affairs secret. Thus, in 1944, after some urging, the California Committee of Real Democrats submitted a statement. The Committee, it turned out, had functioned only for two weeks prior to the election, and all radio broad-

[2] Roy V. Peel and T. C. Donnelly, *The 1928 Campaign* (New York: R. R. Smith, 1931), p. 20.

[3] Josephus Daniels, *The Wilson Era* (Chapel Hill: University of North Carolina Press, 1944), p. 83.

casts and newspaper advertising in the name of the committee were financed directly by the Dewey Non-Partisan Finance Committee.[4]

TABLE 15

Expenditures in Democratic and Republican Presidential Campaigns of 1928, 1940, and 1944, by Type of Committee or Agency [a]

(In Thousands of Dollars)

Committee or agency	Democratic			Republican		
	1928	1940	1944	1928	1940	1944
National	$3,157	$2,198	$2,056	$4,065	$2,243	$2,829
State [b]	2,445	2,786	2,033	4,762	10,791	9,260
Independent	1,550	872	3,352	607	3,587	1,106
	7,152	5,856	7,441	9,434	16,621	13,195
Transfers [c]					1,680	
Net Total	7,152	5,856	7,441	9,434	14,141	13,195
2-Party Total				16,586	19,997	20,536

[a] L. Overacker, "Trends in Party Campaign Funds," in *The Future of Government in the United States* (Chicago: University of Chicago Press, 1942), p. 125; and "Presidential Campaign Funds, 1944," *American Political Science Review*, 39 (1945), p. 906.

[b] Republican finance committees as well as all state committees are included in this group.

[c] Transfers between committees deducted to produce net expenditure total.

Apart from the reliability of the available information the data in the table are incomplete. Not all agencies that spend money in a presidential election year are included. It is extremely difficult to obtain data on the finances of the many nonparty committees that enjoy a transient existence during a campaign. To illustrate the problem of constructing a complete picture of campaign finance, it is necessary only to name a few of these committees. In 1936 nonparty organizations supporting Roosevelt included the Good Neighbor League, Labor's Non-Partisan League, and the Roosevelt Agricultural Committee. On the Republican side, a total of $653,000 was spent by the Independent Coalition of American Women, the Liberty League, and the Women's National Republican Club. Among the nonparty organizations supporting the Republican ticket in 1940 were the following: Associated Willkie Clubs of America, National Committee of Democrats for Willkie, People's Committee to Defend Life Insurance and Savings, National Committee to Uphold Constitutional Government, Anti-Third Term Association of New York City, and the Clearing House for National Interest. In 1944 a Senate committee used several pages of fine print to list the independent or nonparty campaign agencies it discovered. On the Democratic side were such

[4] Senate Report No. 101, 79th Cong., 1st sess., p. 9.

organizations as Business Men for Roosevelt, Inc., Committee to Enlighten the Electorate, Independent Voters Committee of the Arts and Sciences for Roosevelt, National Citizens Political Action Committee, and the Samuel Goldwyn Southern California Committee for Roosevelt. Among the groups supporting the Republican candidates were the American Democratic National Committee, Constitutional Democracy Crusaders, Girls Who Save Their Nickels to Elect a Republican President Club of Chicago (expenditures $37.80), Jeffersonian Democrats of California, and the Independent White Democratic League of Thomas County, Georgia.[5]

Sometimes these nonparty committees are publicity shy for good and sufficient reasons. An example is furnished by the New Jersey State Republican League and the Republican Citizens' Committee of Jersey City. These organizations had no connection with the Republican party, but their managers pirated the good will of the Republican name and solicited funds in the campaigns of 1940 and 1942. The funds, a Senate committee found, went mainly to the high-pressure promoters rather than to political activity: "Palpable fraud had been practiced upon a number of the unsuspecting donors."[6]

From the listing of only a few samples of the nonparty organizations that make expenditures in a presidential campaign year, one may gain a notion of the difficulty of getting complete coverage in the reporting of expenditures. In addition, expenditures are made by city, county, and other local party committees, and these outlays have never been adequately estimated on a national basis. The data in Table 15 show the totals as reported by state committees for selected presidential years.[7] Expenditures by city and county committees from local party revenues are an unknown quantity. Available evidence, however, suggests that they spend considerable sums. In 1944, for example, county committees in the state of Pennsylvania reported total expenditures of $857,000.[8]

Cost of state and local campaigns. From what has been said it may

---

[5] *Ibid.*, pp. 134–37.

[6] *Ibid.*, p. 30.

[7] Total expenditures by the regular party committees in selected states in 1944 may be of some interest: California, Democratic, $119,000, Republican, $140,000; Florida, Democratic, $33,000, Republican, $12,000; Illinois, Democratic, $58,000, Republican, $418,000; Massachusetts, Democratic, $25,000; Republican, $544,000; New York, Democratic, $399,000, Republican, $353,000; Ohio, Democratic, $29,000, Republican, $379,000; Texas, Democratic, $35,000, Republican, $42,000. These figures, from the report cited in the preceding note, are of little use in comparisons from party to party or state to state since in many states the main burden of finance was carried by committees other than the state party committee, and in other instances the figures suggest almost indubitably incomplete reporting.

[8] Senate Report No. 101, 79th Cong., 1st sess., pp. 241–242.

be seen that it is difficult enough to build up information both reliable and complete on expenditures in presidential campaigns. The evidence is far less complete when one attempts to answer the question, "What do campaigns cost?" with respect to races for local, state, and other offices. In a presidential year the expenditures for campaigns for many of these offices are intermingled with the general funds to support the entire party ticket, and in that way we obtain some light on these expenditures. Outlays in campaigns in other years, however, are unknown in any comprehensive way. A great deal of information, incomplete though it may be, is available in reports filed in state and local offices, but it has never been systematically collected and analyzed. Occasionally scandalously large expenditures stimulate investigations that bring to light the facts on particular campaigns. For example, about $190,000 was spent on behalf of Truman H. Newberry in his successful primary campaign against Henry Ford for the Republican senatorial nomination in Michigan in 1918.[9] In 1926 Frank L. Smith was nominated for the United States Senate in an Illinois Republican primary that involved the expenditure of slightly more than $1,000,000, about equally divided between Smith and his opponent.[10] In the 1926 Pennsylvania Republican primary a total of $2,265,000 was spent in the fight for the nominations for governor and United States Senator. These spectacular campaigns in which huge sums were spent are offset by many other campaigns in which only nominal outlays are made.

In some states and cities groups concerned about issues voted upon—constitutional amendments, initiated measures, referenda, charter amendments, and the like—spend considerable sums to influence the electorate. Thus, in California a total of $1,207,000 was spent for and against in the referendum campaign on a chain-store tax passed by the 1935 legislature. The California Retail Chain Stores Association and allied groups reported that they had spent $1,142,033 to defeat the tax. The Anti-Monopoly League, representing the nonchain group, spent $65,731 in a vain attempt to retain the statute. In 1936 $170,000 was spent in a referendum contest on a measure designed to tax and regulate the sale of oleomargarine. The opponents of this measure reported expenditures of $115,000, and the dairy and creamery interests spent $55,000 in its unsuccessful support. These are exceptionally large expenditures for campaigns on issues.[11] Less controversial meas-

[9] See Spencer Ervin, *Henry Ford* vs. *Truman H. Newberry* (New York: Richard R. Smith, 1935).

[10] See C. H. Wooddy, *The Case of Frank L. Smith* (Chicago: University of Chicago Press, 1931).

[11] See V. O. Key, Jr. and W. W. Crouch, *The Initiative and the Referendum in California* (Berkeley: University of California Press, 1939), chap. 5.

ures evoke much smaller outlays. Yet these activities are a part of the total campaign finance picture, and the recorded data are quite incomplete.

Significance of size of campaign outlays. The foregoing outline of the areas of ignorance about what campaigns cost brings one back to the question of what can be concluded from the known data. Information on expenditures in presidential campaigns is most complete. It is probably as complete from one party as another and for one election as another. Hence, whether the specific figures are complete does not invalidate certain general observations about expenditures in presidential years. From the figures in Table 15, it is apparent that in recent national campaigns the preponderance of the cash has been on the Republican side. The Democratic party is not without men of money, but affluent individuals more generally find themselves on the Republican side of the fence, a fact reflected in the expenditure figures.[12]

The comparison of total expenditures from year to year means little unless the changing size of the electorate and, hence, of the campaigning job, is taken into account. According to calculations by Dr. Overacker, the total outlays by both national committees amounted to the following number of cents per vote cast in the years indicated: 1912, 19; 1916, 19; 1920, 20; 1924, 15; 1928, 20; 1932, 13; 1936, 32. Figures for later years would not be comparable with those shown. After 1936 the Hatch Act, with its limitation of $3,000,000 for expenditures by any single committee, resulted in a reduction, not of total expenditures, but of the proportion borne by the national committees. Viewed in the light of the per-vote expenditures, the totals take on greater meaning. Observe the relatively slight fluctuation in the per capita series. The figures are fairly uniform except for 1924, a year with no serious

---

[12] Expenditures by the national committees of the major parties for recent campaigns other than those covered by Table 15 show a uniformly higher Republican expenditure. The figures (from Overacker, *Money in Elections*, p. 73) are as follows:

Year	Democratic	Republican
1916	$2,284,590	$2,441,565
1920	1,470,371	5,417,501
1924	1,108,836	4,020,478
1932	2,245,975	2,900,052
1936	5,194,741	8,892,972

If it is assumed that expenditures by party and nonparty organizations are divided among Republican and Democratic campaigns in the same ratio as expenditures by the national committees, Democratic expenditures were exceeded by the Republicans in each presidential campaign from 1916–1944. It should be noted that the abrupt drop in national committee expenditures after 1936 was induced by the Hatch Act limitation of $3,000,000 on expenditures by any single committee. That legislation, to be discussed later in the chapter, forced parties to allocate their expenditures differently among state, national, and other committees in order that no committee would exceed the $3,000,000 limit.

contest, 1932, a depression campaign, and 1936, a year in which the Republicans spent money rather recklessly. Yet the data for 1936, 1940, and 1944 suggest that perhaps the more bitter the contest and the greater the stakes are believed to be, the greater will be the expenditure.

Another way of thinking about the significance of the sums spent on presidential campaigns is to compare these outlays with the costs of advertising products sold on a national market. The conduct of a presidential campaign is a task comparable in magnitude to the advertising of a commercial product. To make known the virtues of cigarettes, laxatives, or cereals to the nation entails enormous expenditures. Eighty-six advertisers, who spent more than one million dollars each in 1944 for magazine, radio, and farm journal advertising, made a total outlay of 265 million dollars. Four large tobacco companies in that year paid out almost 19 million dollars to extol the merits of their cigarettes and other tobacco products. If data on newspaper advertising costs were available, they would undoubtedly show that the cost of tobacco advertising in 1944 exceeded the reported campaign costs of that year. In 1944 two large soap companies spent a total of more than 30 million dollars to bring their soaps and related products to the attention of consumers.[13] It does not follow, of course, that because soapmakers spend 30 million dollars, president-makers should do likewise. Nevertheless, such comparisons furnish some measure of the problem of gaining the nation's attention through publicity channels.

The data on total expenditures for presidential campaigns are so limited that few conclusions of general significance can be drawn from them. No very profound observations can be made about the facts. About all they mean, in the calculus of the average man, is that it takes a lot of money to finance the business of electing the representatives of the people. Even that conclusion may be of profound significance for the working of a democratic system.[14]

2. WHAT THE MONEY GOES FOR

A useful approach toward an understanding of the size of campaign funds is to look at the sorts of purposes for which the money is spent.[15]

[13] *Printers' Ink* publishes annually a compilation of data on outlays by the leading advertisers. The above comments are based on data in the issues of March 2 and 9, 1945.

[14] The same problem exists in Great Britain. Although total campaign expenditures in Britain are less than in the United States, the financial requirements on the candidate are such that the range of choice of persons for Parliament is sharply limited. See J. F. S. Ross, *Parliamentary Representation* (New Haven: Yale University Press, 1944), chaps. 14 and 15.

[15] On this subject, see Pollock, *Party Campaign Funds*, chap. 6; Overacker, *Money in Elections*, chap. 2.

Here again, the data are limited; both the information and the inferences therefrom should be accepted with more than a grain of salt. Before the Hatch Act limitations on total outlays by any single committee encouraged a dispersion of financing among many committees, it was possible to gain a rough notion of the general trend of expenditures for various purposes by analysis of the operations of the national committees.   Since 1936, however, study of expenditures by the national committees reveals very little, for the essential information is scattered in the records of other committees.   To discover, for example, how much the Democrats spent for radio time in 1944 would necessitate the compilation and analysis of data on the outlays of many committees. And that information simply is not available.   Nevertheless, one can indicate in a general way the main purposes for which money is spent. Judgments about the relative weight given in party expenditures to different purposes, however, involve considerable guesswork.

Most campaign expenditures may be grouped in the following categories: (1) general overhead, which includes salaries for headquarters staff (such as stenographers, clerks, research workers), postage, telephone, rentals; (2) field activities, under which item would be included payments to speakers, their transportation, and like activities; (3) publicity—the largest item—including radio costs, payments for direct-mail campaigns, literature, photographs, billboards, newspaper advertising, and the like; (4) grants to subsidiary committees, such as payments by the national committee to aid state committees and to aid special organizations set up for the duration of the campaign; and (5) election-day expenses, including outlays for watchers, runners, election-day workers, and the conveyance of voters to the polls.

Expenditures for overhead and field activities. The breakdown of total expenditures into these general categories, however, can be only a rough estimate.   Dr. Overacker estimates that "from twenty to forty per cent" of the expenditures of national committees and of state committees is devoted to the item of "general overhead."   The pay roll for publicity experts, research workers, stenographers, clerks, and other personnel in the national headquarters is large.   Seemingly inconsequential items, such as telephone, telegraph, and express, amount to huge sums.   In the 1936 campaign, for example, the Democratic national committee paid $206,000 for postage, or 4.6 per cent of all their expenditures; and the Republican disbursement for this purpose was $264,000, or 3.9 per cent.   In 1920, according to Pollock, the Republican outlay for the maintenance and operation of national headquarters was $800,000; in 1924, $450,000.   In the last six months of 1940 the Republican national committee outlays included $361,986 for salaries and

$108,850 for "office expenses including rental, furniture, taxes, supplies." [16]

The category of expenditures for "field activities" covers items for "organization" and "contact work," and hence it is likely to include expenditures shading into bribery—not the bribery of voters but the purchase of the services of individuals thought to be influential enough to "swing" particular groups to the party. It also covers the services and expenses of speakers and expenses of special trains for the candidate and his entourage. Thus, in the second half of 1940 the Republican national committee paid out $259,172 for "Travel, including special train, aviation, and expenses of speakers."

Publicity costs. The largest of the categories is that for publicity in its various forms. The long-term trend in the distribution of campaign expenditures appears to be toward the use of a larger and larger proportion of available funds for publicity. This development has, of course, paralleled the rise of new media for propaganda, such as the radio, and the development of more refined techniques of propaganda. County and city organizations have probably not been so seriously affected as have the national organizations, for in state and local campaigns it is likely that a larger proportion of the money goes for field activities and election-day expenses than the national committee expends for these purposes. Dr. Overacker estimates that 50 per cent of campaign expenditures go for publicity.

The use of the radio for campaigning has introduced a new and expensive type of publicity. In 1936 the Democratic national committee spent $582,327 for radio time, or 12.9 per cent of their total outlay; the Republicans, $757,737, or 11.1 per cent. Or, to put it another way, about one out of every eight dollars spent by the national committees in 1936 went for radio time. In 1932 the Democratic committee expended $551,972, or about 17 per cent of their total expenditures, for radio; the Republicans, $551,972, or more than 20 per cent. In more recent campaigns a larger proportion of the funds of the national committees has gone for radio but not necessarily, of course, a larger proportion of all campaign expenditures. For radio time in 1944, the Democratic national committee paid $925,000; the Republican national committee, $841,600. Other committees may also buy radio time. In 1940 toward the end of the campaign the Democratic national committee found itself in peril of exceeding the 3 million dol-

---

[16] Louise Overacker, "Campaign Finance in the Presidential Election of 1940," *American Political Science Review,* 35 (1941), p. 707. In this article Dr. Overacker includes a statement of the objects of expenditure by the Republican national committee for the period June 29 to December 31, 1940.

lar limit fixed by the Hatch Act. It hurriedly arranged for costs of some of the closing broadcasts to be borne by various state Democratic committees. There is some indication that party managers regard radio as more essential than other types of publicity and that when money is scarce they will reduce other expenditures before they will pare the radio bill.

Newspaper advertising quickly runs into money. A full-page advertisement in a metropolitan daily may cost as much as $3,000. Payments to lesser newspapers are sometimes said to be for editorial support. The foreign-language press especially has gained the reputation of being susceptible to offers of advertising in exchange for editorial support in the campaign. Ordinarily, rates for political advertising substantially exceed commercial rates, a genteel form of extortion against which candidates cannot afford to protest. Billboard rentals require considerable sums. The amount required for national coverage may be gauged from the fact that the Wood managers spent $10,800 in the 1928 preconvention campaign for seventy-four billboards in the single state of Illinois. Extensive use of the mails for circulars and letters is extremely costly. The postal costs alone to send a postal card to 1,000,000 voters would be $10,000; to send a first-class letter to the same number of voters would cost about $30,000. To print, address, and fold the same number of circulars for mailing would cost an additional $16,500. In a national campaign a party may spend around $500,000 for the printing of pamphlets and leaflets. And in local campaigns the preparation and printing of campaign literature may be costly. Lithographs, photographs, and campaign novelties add to publicity costs. In 1940 the Republican national committee spent a total of $48,000 for Willkie buttons.

Subventions to subsidiary committees. The item of subventions to subsidiary and auxiliary committees used to be much more important in the finances of the national committees than it has been since the Hatch Act limitation on expenditures by single committees. National committees in 1940 and 1944 aided state committees and other campaign organs to a limited extent, and nonparty committees collected money and transmitted it to other committees. State committees continue to grant subventions to county committees. Since the passage of the Hatch Act, instead of funneling funds through the national committee to state and nonparty committees, contributors divide their gifts among different committees, a plan which enables the national committees to keep within the letter of the law and also enables contributors to avoid violations of the $5,000 limitation on individual gifts to any single committee. Of historical interest, then, are some examples of earlier subsidies by the national committees and transfers by committees in "sure" states to the national committee. In 1936 the Democratic national committee paid to the Roosevelt Agricultural Committee, for campaign work among farmers, $244,087; to the Young Democratic Clubs of America, $10,750; to the Good Neighbor League, $34,750. It gave $50,000 to the Kansas state committee; $40,000 to the New York state committee. The Republican national committee contributed $15,000 to Kansas; $166,000 to Missouri; $155,000 to Ohio; $255,000 to Pennsylvania. State committees, if the race does not seem to be close in the state or if it is hopeless, may contribute to the national organization for use in more necessitous areas. The Florida Democratic committee in 1936 gave $28,500 to the national committee; Louisiana gave $61,845; Mississippi, $65,000; Texas, $179,000.

Election-day expenses. Election-day expenses are heavy for city and county organizations. The polls must be manned with watchers; runners are needed to bring out the voters; men and women must be stationed near the polling places to distribute literature and sample ballots; automobiles must be on call to transport the lame, the blind, and the lazy to the polls. The precinct captains and their assistants, sometimes on the public pay roll, are assigned election-day duties, but helpers are employed to aid them in their precincts on election day. Lavish expenditures for election-day work at times closely approach bribery. Some observers, notably Frank R. Kent, attribute great significance to the funds available for election-day work in the determination of the outcome of the balloting, for an invariable condition of election-day employment is that the party worker cast his vote right and bring out his family, friends, and relatives for the same purpose. The level of election-day expenditures differs enormously from place to place. In "sure" states and cities where the contest is more or less a formality these disbursements are nonexistent or at a minimum; in closely fought races the outlay is likely to be at a higher level. In some states and cities the custom of heavy election-day spending is more deeply rooted than in others. It is probably correct to surmise that the influence of election-day outlays varies with popular interest and participation in an election. With low public interest, general unconcern about the issues, and low participation, the efficacy of election-day outlays increases. However, election-day money is often inefficiently spent. A considerable percentage may lodge at various levels of the organization as it percolates down toward the election-day workers.[17]

[17] The following example illustrates the possibilities: "Robert Dougal, a candidate for committeeman in the 34th ward on the Igoe ticket in the April primary, was found guilty of campaign-finance cheating by Judge Thomas A. Green in State street

From the available facts it is plain that the conduct of campaigns on the scale to which we have become accustomed requires large sums for perfectly legitimate objects of expenditure. Since the information about how money is spent is so scant, no well-supported conclusions can be drawn about how much ought to be adequate to conduct a campaign. Certainly too much is often spent, and campaigns are often models of waste and inefficiency. The competitive factor induces high outlay. Each party or faction feels that it must attempt to match the expenditures and make the showing of the other, for undoubtedly in many elections and primaries money helps mightily in gaining victory. If one group has plenty of money to hire watchers and to man the polls, its longer purse may be the deciding factor. Yet campaign cost data are so meager that no satisfactory standards for controlling the purposes or amounts of expenditure can be formulated. Moreover, it is doubtful that enough information on the relative efficacy of different objects of expenditure exists to enable campaign managers to budget their outlays except by hunch.

3. WHO GIVES AND WHY

Systematic knowledge of the sources of campaign contributions is limited mainly to the funds of the national committees. That information is not obtained automatically from the official reports filed by the national committees; it is available because those reports have been carefully and painstakingly analyzed by Dr. Overacker, from whose work this section is primarily drawn. Of the sources of state and local campaign funds, our systematic information is extremely limited. The reporting of these contributions is not nearly so complete as it might be, and the reports on file in public offices have not been analyzed and published in usable form.

Economic affiliations of generous contributors. In Table 16 is presented a grouping of the large gifts to the major parties in the campaigns of 1932, 1940, and 1944. In the preparation of the data underlying the table persons giving more than $1,000 were identified as bankers, manufacturers, miners, and so forth, and classified accordingly. Necessarily, such a classification involves an element of judgment in determining to which category a particular individual shall be assigned. In order to clarify study of the table another word of

---

court today and placed on probation. Martin Moloney, 2141 Richmond street, said Dougal received $300 expense money to pay precinct workers, but 'blew in' part of it and paid several of them, including Moloney, in 'rubber checks.' Dougal pleaded he had a wife and seven children and was out of a job. Judge Green gave him six months to make restitution."—Chicago *Daily News*, June 10, 1932.

warning should be interposed. When making comparisons between parties one should understand that 10 per cent in one party column does not in one sense equal 10 per cent in another party column. In 1940 persons associated with mining and the oil industry furnished 5.3 per cent of the total in large gifts to the Democrats and 5.9 per cent of those to the Republicans. This approximate equality of the percentages does not mean that the actual sums were approximately equal; the amount given to the Democrats from this source was $27,500, to the Republicans, $72,000. What is being compared is proportions in totals of different sizes. From these figures it may be concluded that gifts from the oil and mining group, although of different absolute size, were of about equal proportionate importance in the receipts of both parties from large contributions.

TABLE 16

Percentages of Total Contributions from Gifts of $1,000 or More to Democratic and Republican Presidential Campaigns from Persons Identified with Various Economic Pursuits, 1932, 1940, and 1944

Group	1932 [a] Dem.	Rep.	1940 [b] Dem.	Rep.	1944 [c] Dem.	Rep.
Bankers, brokers, manufacturers, oil, mining, utilities, real estate, insurance	45.2	60.6	21.1	57.0	24.3	59.4
Brewers, distillers, soft drinks, contractors, builders, building materials, publishers, radio, advertising, amusements, professions, officeholders, merchants	21.7	11.0	46.8	9.2	46.2	15.6
Others and unidentifiable	33.1	28.4	32.1	33.8	29.5	25.0

[a] Derived from data presented by Louise Overacker, "Campaign Funds in A Depression Year," *American Political Science Review,* 27 (1933), p. 776. The percentages are based on gifts to the national committees.

[b] Derived from data presented by Overacker, "Campaign Finance in the Presidential Election of 1940," *American Political Science Review,* 35 (1941), p. 723. In this table the gifts from organized labor included in the original tabulation were omitted to obtain comparability with the 1932 and 1944 figures. The figures for 1940 are based on contributions to the national committees.

[c] Derived from data presented by Overacker, "Presidential Campaign Funds, 1944," *American Political Science Review,* 39 (1945), p. 916. These figures include gifts of $1,000 or more to the national committees and to certain related organizations as well.

With these explanations, some observations on the data in Table 16 may be offered. Compare first the gifts to the two parties in the campaigns of 1940 and 1944. Note the differing composition of the big givers to the two parties. Banking, finance, manufacturing, utilities furnished a much larger proportion of the substantial gifts to the Republican party than to the Democratic. The figures confirm the common knowledge that in these campaigns heavy industry and finance in the main were generous in their support of Willkie and Dewey. On the other hand, the Democrats had to rely largely on a different type of person for their large gifts. Brewers and distillers rallied around the party that espoused prohibition repeal in 1932. Officeholders, as usual, furnished substantial contributions to the party in power. Many Hollywood stars and producers supported Roosevelt with their pocketbooks as well as their hearts. Professional men, traditionally a more important source of large gifts for the Democrats, performed as usual. Gifts from merchants likewise bulked larger in the Democratic campaign chest than in the Republican. Thus in 1940 and 1944 the composition of the group of generous donors to the Democrats differed sharply from the Republican group.

Another significant fact may be observed from the data in Table 16. Contrast the sources of big gifts to the Democrats in 1932 and in subsequent campaigns. Note the striking decline in the relative importance of gifts from bankers, manufacturers, and other important industrial groups after the campaign of 1932 and the parallel rise in the proportionate significance of the odd assortment of, big givers who furnished most of the large gifts to Democrats in 1940 and 1944. As the full import of the New Deal became apparent after 1933, the few big industrialists and financiers who had been traditionally Democratic began to shift to the Republicans or to withhold support from the Democrats. The intensification of upper-class opposition to the Democratic party manifested itself in the politically inept operations of the Liberty League in the campaign of 1936. In subsequent campaigns the general sharpening of political conflict along class lines manifested itself in the pecuniary loyalty of finance and heavy industry to the Republican party.

Contributions analyzed by size. Another method of analysis of the sources of campaign funds is to compare the extent to which the two parties rely on contributors who are able to make gifts of various sizes. Presumably if one party relies to a greater extent than another on givers of large sums or of small sums, such facts have considerable significance. The available information is presented in Table 17.

The data in Table 17 reveal trends of some significance in the comparative analysis of our major political parties. Observe that in both parties the proportion of total receipts coming from contributions of $5,000 or more declined from 1928 to 1940. The sharp decline in 1940 reflected the effects of the Hatch Act, which prohibited gifts in excess of $5,000, but the trend had set in before this act became effective. In comparing the receipts of the two parties it is significant that the Republicans relied to a greater extent on persons able to give from $100 to $5,000 than did the Democrats. The Democrats, on the other hand, relied more on gifts of less than $100 than did the Republicans. During the period covered by the table both parties were able to increase the proportion of their receipts coming from small givers, but in this endeavor the Democrats were the more successful. In general, the data in the table confirm common knowledge: viz., that the center of gravity of the Democratic party is somewhat farther down the economic scale than that of the Republican party.[18]

TABLE 17

Percentage Distribution by Size of Cash Contributions to the Democratic and Republican National Committees, 1928–1940 [a]

Size	Democratic				Republican			
	1928	1932	1936	1940	1928	1932	1936	1940
$5,000 and over	52.7	43.7	26.0	13.1	45.8	40.1	24.2	3.8
$1,000–$4,999	17.0	14.4	19.4	19.6	22.6	24.8	26.8	38.3
$100–$999	16.3	14.5	18.0	17.3	21.9	23.4	23.9	30.7
Less than $100	12.5	16.0	18.5	23.3	8.2	9.1	13.5	13.4
Impossible to allocate: [b]								
Labor	..	..	5.1	6.2	..	..	..	..
Other	1.5	11.4	13.0	20.5	1.5	2.6	11.6	13.8
Total	100.0	100.0	100.0	100.0	100.0	100.0	100.0	100.0

[a] Source: Louise Overacker, "Trends in Party Campaign Funds," in *The Future of Government in the United States* (Chicago: University of Chicago Press, 1942), p. 128.
[b] "Impossible to allocate" includes group contributions remitted to the national committees in lump sums. Contributions from the United Mine Workers and other trade-union groups are classified as "labor"; gifts from local party committees and clubs as "other."

Both major parties have attempted to increase the number of contributors of small sums; neither party relishes its dependence on large contributions. In the campaign of 1936 the Democratic managers per-

[18] The data on the size of contributions to 1944 campaign funds are not exactly comparable with the information shown in Table 17 (in part because of the omission of information on receipts classified as "labor" and "other" in Table 17). Gifts to the Democratic national committee and the One Thousand Club and to the Republican national committee and the United Republican Finance Committe of Metropolitan New York have been classified by Dr. Overacker (*American Political Science Review,* 39 [1945], p. 908) as follows:

	Democratic	Republican
$1,000 and over	56.7%	51.5%
500 to 999	6.9	12.7
Less than $500	36.4	35.8

suaded a large number of individuals to become "nominators" by giving a minimum of $1.00 to the campaign fund. Over $1,000,000 was raised in this way, but it is impossible to say how many individuals contributed to the fund. The Democratic committee has used the Jackson Day dinners as a means of raising funds. The top charge has been $100 per plate for the Washington dinner; the price per person ranged downwards to $5 in smaller centers. The party committee netted over $300,000 from this source in 1936 and over 300,000 persons participated. In 1937 the yield went to $422,000; in 1938, $415,000; in 1939, $322,000; and in 1940 the dinners brought $422,000 to the party treasury.[19] The New York daily, *PM,* in the campaign of 1944 collaborated with the Democratic national committee in the stimulation of small contributions by printing appeals for funds accompanied by coupons to be used in transmitting small gifts. Such headlines as, "It Cost $37,000 to Air Dewey—Send Your Dollars and Hear FDR," brought enough responses to add considerable sums to the Democratic radio fund.

The Republican national committee in 1936 and the following years experimented with a fund-raising technique modeled after that of community-chest campaigns, described by the head of the finance division of the national committee as "volunteer solicitation under professional direction." The plan involved co-operation between the national committee and state committees to avoid overlapping and competing solicitation. "Organized professionally directed solicitation" was employed in several of the states in the 1936 campaign. "In every case," says the director of the finance division, "it resulted in a huge increase in the number of givers, a substantial growth in the amount raised, and a cost low in proportion to the returns. Supplemented by a mail appeal in the closing weeks of the campaign, it brought a total of more than 650,000 separate givers to the Republican fund."[20] The huge figure probably involved a degree of exaggeration; the national committee itself claimed in its report only 331,037 contributors; and Dr. Overacker, the most thorough student of party funds, concludes that the total number of contributors to both party funds is "veiled in uncertainty." It is certain, however, that the democratization of campaign finance remains to be accomplished. The finances of neither party are dominated by the contributions of the small giver; both still

---

[19] Overacker, "Campaign Finance in the Presidential Election of 1940," *American Political Science Review*, 35 (1941), p. 715.

[20] C. G. Ketchum, "Political Financing, 1937 Model," *Public Opinion Quarterly*, 2 (1938), pp. 135–140. The Hatch Act of 1940, through its limitation on total amounts spent by committees, compelled abandonment of co-operation of national and state committees in fund raising.

rely in large degree on people who can afford to give $100 or more.[21]
The significance of reliance on the wealthy donor may be judged by the
receipts of both national committees in 1936, the last year for which
data are conveniently available in comprehensive form.   In that year
the two national committees received donations totaling $10,224,291;
of this total, $5,069,011 was given by 1,945 contributors of more than
$1,000 each.   At the time there were approximately 73 million persons
in the United States over 21 years of age.   Hence, about 49.5 per cent of
the total receipts of the national committees came from slightly more
than 2/1000 of 1 per cent of the adult population.

Indirect contributions from the public treasury.   Private contributors furnish the bulk of the sinews of political war, but the government itself, in one way or another, finances a not inconsiderable share
of party activity.   One of the more innocent of these methods is the
use of the congressional frank for the distribution of campaign literature by sitting Congressmen.   A Congressman may extend his remarks
in the *Congressional Record;* that is, he may have printed in the *Record*
remarks never delivered orally, obtain copies at cost from the Government Printing Office, and frank them to his constituents without postal
cost.   In some instances the use of the congressional frank on campaign literature is simply a means by which a party committee, by agreement with the Congressman, transfers to the government the postage
cost on huge quantities of campaign literature.   In other instances the
frank is used in a purely individual campaign endeavor by a member
of Congress.   The Honorable Joachim O. Fernandez of Louisiana,
for example, early in 1940 extended his remarks under the heading,
"I Am a Candidate for Re-election."   He had asked leave to extend
his remarks "in answer to thousands of letters" from his "people" as to
his "disposition to run again for Congress."   His extension of remarks
traced his political career and set out his accomplishments.   Among
those accomplishments were "constructive agitation" for the new federal building in New Orleans, sponsorship of a bill for a new lighthouse
supply depot in New Orleans, extensions of mail-carrier service, support of maximum funds for Mississippi flood control, obtaining aid "for
all the needy muskrat farmers" of his district, support of all veterans'
legislation, "which was of a worthy nature," and support of "labor
100 per cent." [22]   Immediately prior to primaries and elections many

---

[21] For an account of the success of the British Labour party in financing its operations from small contributions, see Pollock, *Money and Politics Abroad*, pp. 43–52.
In the Weimar Republic the Social Democratic party perfected a revenue system in
which about a million party members made no less than 25,000,000 individual contributions per year.   For a description of the system, see *ibid.*, pp. 228–235.
[22] *Congressional Record* (daily edition), March 11, 1940.

literary contributions like that of Representative Fernandez appear in the *Record,* are reprinted, and circulated to constituents. The possibilities are further illustrated by a composition in the *Record* in 1942 under the title, "Reasons Why Edwin Arthur Hall Should Be Re-elected to Congress."

The man in office is almost continually running for re-election and enjoys certain perquisites and advantages that might be said to constitute public support of partisan activity. John T. Salter has given as an example the activities of legislators of "Everystate," presumably Wisconsin. "Many legislators," he says, "are able to help their local Isaac Waltons secure supplies of fingerlings for the streams in their districts" from the conservation commission. They may bring about the adoption of resolutions congratulating important individuals and groups of their districts on noteworthy accomplishments. Publications of state departments are distributed to interested constituents by the legislator. Bills are introduced often solely for the consequent publicity in the home district. In a variety of ways the man in office is able to give personal attention to his constituents that the outside opponent is unable to match.[23]

The greatest contribution of the public treasury to party finance is made through the public employment of persons who devote a large part of their time to the work of the party organization. In pre-La Guardia New York, the Civil Service Reform Association reported: [24]

The total annual pay for exempt employes in New York City is only $7,000,-000, but about half of this sum represents sheer waste of public funds. Half of these positions could be safely abolished without loss of service or efficiency in the city government. Most, if not all, of the exempt positions are passed around to the district leaders and their henchmen. . . . With what brazen contempt of the public interest such positions are still filled with untrained, unqualified persons is well illustrated by such recent appointments as that of

[23] J. T. Salter, "Personal Attention in Politics," *American Political Science Review,* 34 (1940), pp. 54–66. An additional illustration is furnished by the following letter published in the *Congressional Record,* June 26, 1930:
"Hon. U. S. Stone,
"Member of Congress, Washington, D.C.
"My dear Mr. Stone: I have your telegram of October 4, 1929, informing me that my pension had been allowed at the rate of $20 per month beginning on July 16, 1929.
"This is mighty fine work, and I thank you for putting this through for me so quickly.
"I was for you in your former race, and I hope to be able to do you some good if you are a candidate again.
                                                                "Your friend, Fred E. Hysell."
[24] Report of the executive committee, Civil Service Reform Association, May 16, 1933.

Charles P. Sheridan, Democratic leader of the 16th Assembly District, a former dockmaster in the Department of Docks, to the position of clerk of the Surrogate's Court, New York County, at $9,000; Thomas J. Culkin, son of the Democratic leader of the 3rd Assembly District, Manhattan, as a deputy commissioner in the Fire Department at $8,000; George J. Ryan, 24-year-old son of the Democratic leader of the 4th Assembly District, Queens, as chief clerk of the district attorney's office in Queens at $4,500.

These were merely typical examples.

No feasible way is known of estimating the contribution of federal, state, and local governments to the maintenance of party organizations through the patronage system. It is expected, of course, that Presidents, governors, Congressmen, and legislators shall defend and advocate policies before the electorate, but the doorbell ringing and electioneering activities of the lower ranking administrative employees are on a different plane. Of the latter employees, some devote a large proportion of their time to precinct work; others may spend only a few days immediately prior to the election. Some are competent and able public employees; others are on the public pay roll only because they have special skills in the management of the electorate. From these facts the difficulties of the computation of the cost of patronage element in party finance become apparent.

Motivation of contributors: Public policy. The foregoing discussion indicates some of the principal sources of campaign funds. The analysis of sources and of the distribution of funds among the major parties suggests the answer to the question, Why do men contribute to party funds? In national campaigns the motivation behind the mass of contributors is usually not mysterious. In elections in which great issues are at stake the cleavage has been fairly plain. The bulk of the money from men of wealth has been on the side of the party that promised least disturbance of the status quo. In the campaigns of 1936, 1940, and 1944 a fairly sharp difference in the sources of campaign contributions of the two parties indicated the objects that the givers hoped to promote by their pecuniary support of the parties. Big business backed the Republicans; labor, officeholders, and an odd assortment of contributors supported the Democrats. Yet in these campaigns not all the money was on one side and not all contributions could be explained in terms of the donor's hope for gain. In any case, the understanding of what is to be had in return for a campaign contribution is often tacit, if it exists at all.[25] The contributor, in so far as the

[25] The nature of the understanding of the contributor and the receiver is indicated by Herbert Croly's statement that in one instance in the campaign of 1896 a check for $10,000 was returned by the Republican national committee to a firm of Wall

evidence goes, gives usually on the theory that the candidate is attached to principles similar to his own rather than on the specific understanding that he is purchasing a particular action. But the evidence is limited. Fund solicitors avoid goldfish bowls. Furthermore, the insidious effect on candidates and party committees of the need for raising money should be kept in mind. In the positions they take and in the questions they avoid, they must find it difficult to avoid being influenced by the fact that some courses of action would certainly cut off the flow of contributions. This sort of reasoning would perhaps be the

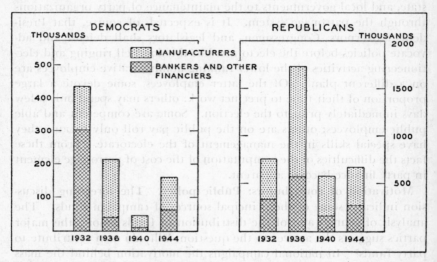

Figure 18. Total Yield of Gifts of Over $1,000 to Democratic and Republican Campaigns from Manufacturers, Bankers, Brokers, and Other Financiers, 1932–1944

most charitable interpretation of the charges made in 1946 against Edwin Pauley, Treasurer of the Democratic National Committee. It was stated that in conference with other Democratic leaders in the campaign of 1944 he had asserted that if suits claiming federal ownership of oil-bearing tidelands were dropped he could raise $300,000 in California for the campaign fund. The party in power is in the special danger that its actions may drive contributors to the other party in the next campaign. Reflect on the significance of the data shown in Figure 18. Note that the New Deal program in the first Roosevelt

Street bankers, which had made the donation with the implied condition that a specific favor would be granted in return. The etiquette was not to purchase particular services but to give on the general understanding that the party would run the country as business desired.—*Marcus Alonzo Hanna* (New York: Macmillan, 1912), p. 326.

Administration was followed by a sharp drop in Democratic contributions from bankers, brokers, and other financiers in 1936. This decline was paralleled by a rapid rise in contributions to the Republicans from these sources.

Occasionally investigations reveal the considerations underlying campaign contributions. In the campaign of 1896, for example, panicky businessmen gave freely in support of McKinley lest Bryan and "free silver" triumph. In subsequent investigations of life insurance companies by the Armstrong committee, John A. McCall, president of the New York Life Insurance Company, testified: [26]

. . . I felt that if Free Silver coinage was going to prevail and Byran was going to be elected President of the United States that we almost might put up our shutters on the New York Life doors. Knowing that and believing it in 1896, I consented to a payment to defeat Free Silver, not to defeat the Democratic party, but to defeat the Free Silver heresy, and thank God that I did it.

The president of the Metropolitan Life testified in a similar vein:

Our directors felt that a contribution to the defeat of that effort was more a matter of morals than it was of policy; they were fearful of the disturbance of values and the impairment of those things which we had which made for security of the policyholders.

Senator Guffey, Democrat of Pennsylvania, in the debate on the extension of the Hatch Act in March, 1940, explained steel contributions to the Republican cause: [27]

In 1884 the first steel man took an active part in national politics. I refer to B. F. Jones, who was chairman of the Blaine and Logan campaign committee. Prior to that time the railroads and the Standard Oil group had controlled the politics of the State. As the steel industry expanded and grew, those connected with it became much more active in politics, and it is common knowledge in Pittsburgh that in 1896 Mr. Frick furnished the sinews of war that secured the Presidential nomination for William McKinley, of Ohio, from the late Speaker Thomas B. Reed, of Maine.

From the time when the steel corporation was formed it was quite apparent that the president of that corporation, the late Charles M. Schwab, took charge of financing the Republican organization in Pennsylvania. He was in my office. . . .

He said, "Senator, I used frequently to come to Washington. I never received a telegram from the late Senator Penrose without dropping everything and coming to Washington. He never asked for less than $250,000 on each visit, and sometimes more. It reached the maximum in one Presidential

[26] Quoted by Overacker, *Money in Elections*, p 181.
[27] *Congressional Record* (daily edition), March 9, 1940, p. 3988.

campaign when I raised the sum of $8,000,000; and, as Max Leslie, the former city leader in Philadelphia, would say, most of that was free money." By "free money" in Pennsylvania, I presume as elsewhere, is meant money that does not have to be accounted for.

. . . Of course, we all know why the steel people have contributed so much in the past. It was entirely due to the high protective tariff. . . .

The interests of campaign contributors may not lie in the field of legislation but in the administration of existing law. In the Illinois Republican senatorial primary of 1926 Samuel Insull, the late utilities magnate, contributed $125,000 to the campaign of Frank L. Smith and at the same time spent some $33,000 on an anti-World Court campaign which presumably redounded to the benefit of Smith. At the time, Smith was the chairman of the Illinois Commerce Commission, with rate-making power over the utilities headed by Insull. Insull told a Senate committee that he spent money in the campaign because ". . . of reasons that I have not told you and do not intend to tell you, because it involves a dead man, and other reasons, because I am very much interested in politics generally." [28] The reference to the dead man, it was rumored, was to Smith's opponent in the race, who had been at an earlier time a bitter rival of Insull in business. Naturally the charge was made that the object of the liberal contribution was to induce favorable treatment by the regulatory commission rather than to satisfy a grudge against an erstwhile competitor.

The kind of appeals made by fund solicitors may be suggested by the following extract from a letter sent to the principal shipbuilders by A. P. Homer, chairman of the marine committee of the finance division of the Democratic national committee, in 1932: [29]

As a result of the events of the last 3 weeks, we believe that if the shipbuilders of the United States are to get a square deal it will be necessary to make a change on November 8. I hope that you are in accord with this idea. If so, we ask that you help us with a contribution in the campaign fund of Governor Roosevelt, who, as you know, is marine-minded and hasn't the opinion that international affairs can be settled with a blueprint navy. Checks should be made to F. C. Walker, treasurer (personal check, of course), and mailed to him in the enclosed envelope. The writer will personally acknowledge your contribution and see that the news of it reaches the Governor's ears.

[28] C. H. Woody, *The Case of Frank L. Smith* (Chicago: University of Chicago Press, 1931), p. 61.
[29] U.S. Senate, Special Committee on Investigation of the Munitions Industry, Preliminary Report, Naval Shipbuilding (74th Cong., 1st sess., S. Rep. No. 944, 1935), p. 272.

In some situations the contributor may be motivated by dislike of the actions of the man in office rather than by a deep attachment to the beneficiary of the contribution. In May, 1946, for example, A. F. Whitney, of the Trainmen's Brotherhood, was in high dudgeon about President Truman's handling of the railroad strike. Whitney announced that his union, with $47,000,000 in assets, was the richest union in the world and intimated that it was prepared to spend a sizable chunk of its resources to defeat Truman in 1948. Whitney stated that his board of directors, as a starter, had authorized him to spend $2,500,000 to defeat members of Congress who had voted for the strike-control legislation proposed by Truman.

Contributions to the organization treasury may be motivated by a desire to retain the favor of those already in power. The author of the following newspaper story probably would have us infer that such was the purpose in the situation described.

One of the most auspicious Christmas charities in the political world this year is that sponsored by the 27th Ward Democratic Club. . . .

The program for the charity comes fresh from the press of M. Ph. Ginzburg, 1214 South Halsted Street. The cover of the bulky document designates it as the souvenir program of an amateur boxing exhibition to be held Dec. 14 at the 132d regiment armory, but the contents are all advertising.

Business men in the district had the "bite" put on them at the rate of $100 a page of advertising in the publication. The follow-up was a bunch of tickets for the event, ranging from 25 to 100 and priced at $1 apiece. There are 111 solid pages in the book, and if everybody paid the same rate, the return on this should be $111,000.

Saloons, of which there are plenty in the district, comprising the near west side, were the chief contributors. This was in the way of natural law, because a saloonkeeper never knows when he is violating the highly complicated liquor laws. All the tavernkeepers know is that violations by those who are not right-minded means license revocation.[30]

[30] *Chicago Daily News,* December 5, 1935. *The Book of the Democratic Convention of 1936* could be said to be of the same character as the program of the boxing exhibition of the 27th Ward Democratic Club in Chicago. *The Book,* containing a variety of information about Democratic leaders and about the national government, contained paid advertisements, in many instances from corporations, and was sold in several editions. The de luxe edition, autographed by the President, was sold at $100 a copy. The sale of advertising and of copies of *The Book,* Dr. Overacker estimates, netted the Democratic national committee at least $250,000 (see *American Political Science Review,* 31 [1937], pp. 479–480). The Hatch Act amendments of 1940 made it unlawful for any person or corporation "to purchase or buy any goods, commodities, advertising, or articles of any kind or description where the proceeds of such a purchase, or any portion thereof, shall directly or indirectly inure to the benefit of or for any candidate for an elective Federal office (including the offices of President of the United States, and Presidential and Vice-Presidential electors) or any political committee or other political organization engaged in furthering, advancing,

Motivation of contributors: The special case of assessments against jobholders. The motivation of one important group of contributors to party funds is obvious. The payment of party assessments on the salaries of officeholders is made under a threat, at least tacit, that discharge may follow a refusal to pay the "income tax" levied by the party in power. There are two sources of assessment income, party nominees for elective offices and persons occupying administrative posts. Party committees customarily assess nominees on the ticket specified sums for the general costs of the campaign and nominees usually spend on their own account additional amounts.[31] In fact, the party organization not infrequently awards nominations to persons because they are able to contribute liberally to the party war chest. However, assessments or "contributions" by the mass of administrative employees probably bulk considerably larger in state and local campaign funds than do contributions from the nominees for elective offices. The ultimate sanction for the enforcement of an assessment is the power to remove from office. An official's livelihood may depend upon whether he "contributes" a portion of his salary. The techniques for stimulating payment vary from brutal extortion upon threat of removal to a mild suggestion by the appropriate persons to the administrative personnel that contributions will be appreciated. The changes in methods of collection have arisen in response to legislation prohibiting assessments: assessments tend to be made to appear as "voluntary contributions."

In the federal service the practice of levying assessments on employees sprang up in the 1830's; by 1842 assessments were rigorously collected in the New York post office and customs house, and the practice became quite general in the federal service by the time of Buchanan's administration. Concurrently the practice arose in state and local governments. The present extent of the practice of assessment is difficult to gauge. At the federal level, the outright assessment of classified civil service employees has apparently become negligible. Employees, however, are solicited with varying degrees of thoroughness. In Kentucky, during the senatorial primaries of 1938, federal employees, for example, were found to have contributed about $24,000 for use in Senator Barkley's campaign.

---

or advocating the nomination or election of any candidate for any such office or the success of any national political party."

[31] Expenditures by candidates, incidentally, are not deductible as an expense of doing business in the computation of federal income taxes. A judge of a court of Luzerne County, Pennsylvania, who was running for re-election for a ten-year term as judge at $12,000 per year, paid an assessment of $8,000 for the general campaign fund and expended $5,017 directly in the campaign. The Supreme Court held these expenditures not deductible, although a strong dissent was registered.—*McDonald* vs. *Commissioner of Internal Revenue*, 65 S. Ct. 96 (1944).

Among state employees assessment seems to be the general rule. One of the widely publicized examples of recent years involved Kentucky. During Governor Chandler's campaign against Senator Barkley in 1938 for the senatorial nomination, collections from state employees who were paid in whole or in part from federal funds alone were "in the neighborhood of $70,000." [32] Another case attracting considerable attention was that of the Two Per Cent Club, sponsored by the Indiana Democratic organization built up by Paul McNutt. The amounts collected were reputedly 2 per cent of the annual salaries; the total yield is unknown, but in 1938 the club donated $110,000 to the Democratic state committee. In cities and counties the practice of assessment seems to continue wherever there is intense organized partisan activity. No complete picture either of the extent or of the thoroughness of the practice in local governments is available,[33] but the custom is so general that its absence rather than its presence is noteworthy. Again, trustworthy figures are not available, but the general opinion among investigators of the problem is that the revenue from assessments bulks much larger in the income of city, county, and state party committees than do contributions from officeholders in the receipts of national committees.

Motives of friendship, admiration of the candidate as a person, and personal ambition frequently enter into campaign contributions. A wealthy man may have a friend running for office; a gift of a few thousand dollars will help the cause and not hurt the donor financially. A wealthy man himself may have an itch for public office and become a candidate himself or back another candidate with the hope of receiving an appointive office. The diplomatic service, with its social prestige, is often attractive to the wealthy contributor. The Newberry campaign for the Republican senatorial nomination in Michigan in 1918 illustrates some of the foregoing statements. The campaign contributions totaled around $190,000, of which $99,900 came from John S. Newberry, the brother of the candidate, Truman S. Newberry. A gift of $25,000 was made by Victor Alfred Barnes, an intimate friend and brother-in-law of Newberry. Henry B. Joy, another brother-in-law and a retired businessman, contributed $25,000, and his wife, $10,000. Lyman D. Smith, an old friend in New York, gave $10,000. Frederick

[32] Senate Report No. 1, 76th Congress, 1st Session (1939), p. 12.

[33] The most thorough survey of any single jurisdiction was made of Philadelphia by M. L. Cooke in 1913. He found that "94 per cent of all city employees paid assessments" and that "these 'contributions' totaled several hundred thousand dollars every year." During Mayor Blankenburg's administration the practice was stopped in the departments under his control, but assessments have been since resumed. See *Report of the Director*, Department of Public Works, Philadelphia, 1914, pp. 28–29.

Brooks, who had been at Yale with Newberry, contributed $2,500. Between $12,000 and $15,000 was contributed by Andrew H. Green, who had served on the same ship with Newberry in the Spanish-American War.[34]

Although it is easy to point out that campaign contributions are frequently made without any expectation of governmental favors, it should also be observed that wealthy campaign donors seem to have few friends among the Socialist, Communist, or liberal candidates. Occasionally men of wealth support liberal candidates and causes. The late Charles R. Crane, for example, contributed to the preconvention campaigns of both Wilson and La Follette in 1912 because he was interested in the election of a liberal candidate by one party or the other. Other instances might be cited, but as a general rule the wealthy contribute to candidates not intensely interested in fundamental changes in the political order—whatever their party affiliations may be.

4. REGULATION OF PARTY FINANCE

In practice, the regulation of party finance is not inspired by abstract and rigid ethical notions. The use of money in politics may give power to one group or another. The moneyed groups may gain influence at the expense of those not so affluent. Laws concerning party finance are usually put through in an effort to curb or weaken the influence that is gained by one group at the expense of another or to prohibit particular methods of using money that give the party with the larger purse an advantage. Thus statutes regulating party finance merely constitute maneuvers in the struggle for political power. At their inception at least they are designed to aid or handicap particular interests in the acquisition of power and influence.

Requirement of publicity. One of the more important types of party-finance regulation is that requiring publicity of the amounts of contributions, the names of contributors, and the nature of expenditures. Under a regime of secret campaign funds the electorate has no means of knowing what financial clique is backing a candidate. Also, secrecy of funds may encourage purchase of governmental favors through campaign contributions. In 1896 Mark Hanna, manager of McKinley's campaign, systematized and perfected a scheme for raising campaign funds from corporations. Corporate contributions were not novel, but the thoroughness with which the Republican national committee assessed corporations more or less according to their ability to pay at-

34 Spencer Ervin, *Henry Ford* vs. *Truman H. Newberry* (New York: Richard R. Smith, 1935), pp. 21–25.

tracted attention. In 1904 Alton Parker, the Democratic candidate, made an issue of the secrecy of campaign funds by the assertion that corporations were furnishing funds to the Republican campaign to purchase the favor of the Republican party. The Democratic campaign treasurer of 1904, Perry Belmont, led a movement to regulate campaign funds. He organized the Publicity Law Organization of the State of New York and later the National Publicity Law Association.[35] The first fruits of the work of Belmont and his allies were not publicity laws but certain laws prohibiting corporate contributions. By 1908, however, the sentiment against secret funds had become so strong that both parties made their financial records public; in 1909 Taft recommended to Congress that an act be passed requiring political committees and candidates for Congress to file with some public officer a statement of their campaign receipts and expenditures. Congress adopted such a law in 1910, which was subsequently amended and extended.

As the federal law now stands, "political committees" are required to file at certain intervals statements with the clerk of the House of Representatives. The term "political committees" includes organizations accepting contributions or making expenditures to influence the election of candidates "in two or more States," or in a single state if the committee is a branch or subsidiary of a national organization. The reports must include the name and address of each person who has contributed more than $100, the total of all contributions, the names and addresses of persons to whom payments of $10 or more have been made, the total expenditures, and certain other information. Somewhat similar reports are required of candidates for Senator and Representative.

In a large proportion of the states somewhat similar legislation exists. Candidates, political committees, and campaign managers are required to file with the secretary of state, the county clerk, or other official a statement of receipts and expenditures. These statements are open to public inspection and usually become the subject of newspaper stories.[36]

Although laws requiring reporting and publicity of the details of party finance have been enacted by the federal government and most of the states, there are many dark corners not reached by the glare of

---

[35] See Perry Belmont, *An American Democrat* (New York: Columbia University Press, 1940), chap. 17.

[36] For an analysis of the state laws, see Overacker, *Money in Elections*, chap. 12. A summary of state corrupt practices laws, prepared by Harry Best of the University of Kentucky, has been published as Senate Document No. 11, 75th Congress, 1st Session. Dr. Best has also prepared a study of the judicial interpretation of these laws, which has been issued as Senate Document No. 203, 76th Congress, 3rd Session. See also a more recent tabulation by S. S. Minault, *Corrupt Practices Legislation in the 48 States* (Chicago: Council of State Governments, 1942, mimeographed).

publicity. In many instances the laws are defective. In some states, for example, the financial reports are filed after the primary or election. Publicity before the election is necessary if knowledge of the sources of a candidate's funds is to be given to the voter at the right time. Some laws have inadequate coverage: in some states they apply only to expenditures by the candidate, and thus campaign committees that collect and spend money are exempt from the reporting requirement. The federal act requires that a candidate for Congress report money received and expended by himself "or by any person with his knowledge or consent." Money spent by a local committee without the "knowledge or consent" of the candidate would not have to be reported by the candidate.

Difficulty has been encountered in defining in the laws precisely who should report; nonparty groups have often been opposed to the extension or interpretation of the legislation so as to cover their activities. In 1928, for example, the Board of Temperance, Prohibition, and Public Morals, according to its general secretary, did all that it was capable of "in bringing about the election of Herbert Hoover as President and Charles Curtis as Vice-President." An official of the board contended that it was not covered by the federal law requiring reports of receipts and expenditures because "criticism of the opinions of a political candidate in regard to a moral concern can not legitimately be called participation in politics." The federal law applies to "political committees." [37] Another example of how groups sometimes try to crawl outside the "political committee" definition is furnished by the activities of the Committee for Constitutional Government in the campaign of 1944. A volume widely distributed by the committee began with these sentences: "This book shows how the New Deal is taking

---

[37] See Overacker, *Money in Elections*, pp. 259–262. Certain constitutional questions concerning the extent of the power of Congress to compel the filing of reports have been answered in the case of *Burroughs* v. *United States*, 290 U.S. 534 (1934). In 1928 the Anti-Smith Democrats, an organization led by Bishop James Cannon, Jr., collected and expended funds in a campaign against Al Smith. In defense against an indictment for violation of the Federal Corrupt-Practices Act through failure to file a report, Cannon and his secretary, Burroughs, contended that Congress had no power to regulate presidential elections, and therefore no authority over the campaign activities of individuals. (The Constitution provides that presidential electors of each state shall be appointed "in such manner as the legislature thereof may direct.") The Supreme Court held that Congress had acted within its power: "To say that Congress is without power to pass appropriate legislation to safeguard such an election from the improper use of money to influence the result is to deny to the nation in a vital particular the power of self-protection. Congress undoubtedly possesses that power, as it possesses every other power essential to preserve the departments and institutions of the general government from impairment or destruction, whether threatened by force or corruption."

America into national socialism. Its bureaucrats are fastening on our economic life permanent controls similar to those Hitler and the Nazi Party have fastened on Germany." Such passages in the committee's literature suggested that perhaps it was opposed to Mr. Roosevelt. Although it spent $250,000 in the first nine months of 1944, it refused to disclose the names of its contributors. The committee averred that it did not support any candidate or party: "We support the Constitution and free enterprise." [38]

Since 1925 the federal law regulating expenditures has not applied to expenditures in primaries, although primaries are generally regulated by state legislation. In 1925 an amendment was adopted removing primaries from the sphere of federal regulation, as a consequence of the Newberry decision of 1921, which involved charges against Truman H. Newberry in connection with his campaign for the Republican senatorial nomination in Michigan. In some quarters the decision in the Newberry case [39] was interpreted to mean that Congress was without power to regulate primary elections, although it was somewhat difficult to say precisely what the court decided, since different members of the court arrived at the same conclusion for different reasons. A 1941 decision, involving the application of a different type of legislation, seems to make clear that Congress could extend its regulation of campaign finance to primaries for the nomination of Senators and Representatives if it cared to do so.[40]

In addition to patent defects in the laws, other factors operate to prevent the attainment of complete publicity. An obvious one is the failure of candidates and committees to file reports. Often incomplete or false reports are filed. Quite complete reports may be unrevealing. Both the Democratic and Republican national committees file reports, but to know their significance requires extensive analysis. Who makes the analysis that becomes available to the public? This comes mainly from newspaper reporters, who sketch through the reports hurriedly to select newsworthy items that may be made into stories by the next deadline. To determine the total gift by any single individual may require the collation of different donations indicated at scattered points throughout a bulky report. Sometimes lengthy itemizations of expenditures and receipts that have not even been totaled are filed. Reports may be extremely complete, but the form in which the facts are presented conceals their significance.

Limitation of source of funds. One of the oldest and most common

[38] Sen. Rep. 101, 79th Cong., 1st sess., p. 10.
[39] *Newberry* v. *United States*, 256 U.S. 232 (1921).
[40] *United States* v. *Classic*, 61 Sup. Ct. 1031 (1941).

limitations on the source of funds is the prohibition against campaign contributions by corporations. Legislation of this sort was a logical consequence of the efficiency with which Mark Hanna levied on the corporations for the support of the Republican campaign in 1896, but there were other factors. The widespread corruption of state and city governments by corporate contributions, as revealed by the "muckrakers" and capitalized on by the progressive and antiplutocratic elements in both parties, gave impetus to the movement to limit corporate contributions. The federal law, as adopted in 1907, makes it unlawful for "any national bank, or any corporation organized by authority of any law of Congress" to contribute "in connection with any election to any political office," or for "any corporation whatever to make a contribution in connection with any election at which presidential and vice presidential electors or a Senator or Representative . . . are to be voted for. . . ." The more inclusive limitation on national banks arose from the fact that the Congress had broad power over corporations chartered by itself. The narrower limitation on other corporations was based on the authority of Congress over the election of presidential electors and over the election of its own members. Another group of corporations, utility holding companies and their subsidiaries, was brought under federal control by the Public Utility Holding Company Act of 1935. These companies are forbidden to contribute to federal, state, or local campaigns.[41]

About three fourths of the states limit corporate contributions. Some states prohibit contributions by any and all corporations. Others forbid contributions by public utility corporations. Still others forbid contributions by other types of corporations: banks and insurance companies are frequently specified. Thus the limitations on corporations vary from state to state, from election to election, and with the type of corporation.[42]

Although these restrictions have been placed on corporate contributions, it would be erroneous to conclude that the political wings of corporations have been clipped. A contribution of $100,000 by the board chairman of a corporation may be made with the same design as a contribution of $100,000 from the treasury of the corporation itself.

---

[41] The practices that the legislation sought to prevent may be glimpsed from the case of the Union Electric Company, which was in 1942 found guilty of violation of the act. During the 'thirties it made contributions to candidates and party committees in Missouri, Illinois, and Iowa. It accumulated a fund of $591,000 for these purposes by obtaining rebates from persons to whom it made payments and by the use of false expense accounts, and thus concealed the political use of its funds. See *Egan* v. *United States*, 137 F. (2d) 369 (1943), certiorari denied, 320 U.S. 788.

[42] See E. R. Sikes, *State and Federal Corrupt-Practices Legislation* (Durham: Duke University Press, 1928), pp. 127–129.

Yet the number of individuals who can give $100,000 from their own funds is considerably smaller than the number of corporations that can do so. Moreover, the prohibition on corporate contributions offers a measure of protection to stockholders who are, in effect, assessed by the corporate management when contributions are made from the resources of the company.

The legislation restricting corporate subsidization of party organizations contains a most significant loophole; the federal law, for example, prohibits contributions in connection with the election of individual officials—in one instance, "any political office," in another, "presidential and vice presidential electors or a Senator or Representative." This prohibition does not apply to expenditures for lobbying before Congress. The public-utility corporations could, for example, spend some $4,000,000 in an effort to prevent the passage by Congress in 1935 of the Public Utility Holding Company Act without violating the Federal Corrupt Practices Act. A corporation may contribute to its trade association, which carries on campaigns of public education in favor of or opposing certain governmental policies of interest to the membership of the association.[43] These campaigns often become in reality efforts to promote particular candidates. A House Committee, reporting on the presidential campaign of 1944, commented on the increasing importance of thinly veiled political propaganda carried on as "education" and as advertising. This "education"

takes the form of promoting in a "nonpartisan manner" social and economic doctrines clearly associated in the public mind with one major political party or the other; and of publications and comment on the records of Members of Congress who will be candidates in the not too distant future. The commercial sponsorship of news broadcasts by commentators with a definite political slant, under the guise of advertising of a product, is a familiar device; and the bulk purchase of literature from pseudo-educational organizations which em-

---

[43] Some discouragement to the expenditure of funds for lobbying and propaganda to influence legislation is furnished by the legal provision that such outlays are not deductible as a business expense in the determination of income-tax liability. For an application of the rule, see *Commissioner of Internal Revenue* v. *Textile Mills Securities Corporation*, 117 F. (2d) 62 (1940). The Federal Power Commission, through its control of the accounting of its licensees, may require that political expenditures be charged to surplus rather than to operating expense, and thus compel the stockholders rather than the customers of the utility to pay the cost of propaganda calculated to enable the utility to persuade the consumer that its overcharges are justified. For an illustration of the operations of the commission, see In the Matter of Northwestern Electric Company *et al, 2 Op. and Dec. of the Fed. Power Comm.* 369 (1941). In the years 1935-40 several companies had spent $790,000 for "definitely political" purposes. A principal object of the outlays was to defeat public ownership proposals; the utilities made extensive use of "front" organizations, such as the Washington State Taxpayers' Association.

ploy the profit from those sales to distribute more political propaganda, is still another device encountered more than once in the course of the committee's investigation.[44]

Congress, by the Smith-Connally Act of 1943, prohibited "contributions" by "labor organizations" in "connection with any election at which Presidential and Vice Presidential electors" or a Senator or Representative are to be voted for. The move for such legislation began after the 1936 campaign, when union contributions constituted an important part of the Democratic fund. The United Mine Workers, the Amalgamated Clothing Workers, the International Ladies' Garment Workers' Union, and other labor organizations gave a total of $770,000 to the Democratic campaign in that year.[45] The agitation to limit union contributions met with a more enthusiastic reception from the Republican party and from antilabor groups than it did from Democratic leaders. Proponents of the limitation pointed to similar legislation in England,[46] and pictured themselves as the champion of the wronged union member whose leaders assessed him against his will for funds for political purposes or who diverted union funds for partisan use. The effort to curb union political financing succeeded, as a part of general restrictive legislation regarding unions passed in the midst of war.

The limitation on trade-union contributions contains loopholes. The statute applies to contributions in connection with an "election" and thus leaves nominations untouched. The C.I.O. Political Action Committee in 1944 received contributions of about $650,000 from trade unions and spent about $475,000 from this fund prior to the nomination of Roosevelt and Truman. The trade-union fund was then "frozen," and expenditures were made from funds received from the solicitation of individual members of the unions. These funds, not being contributions from union treasuries, could be legally used in campaigns for "election" as distinguished from campaigns for "nomination," although, of course, the administrative machinery of the trade unions was used in the solicitation of contributions. About $375,000 was collected in this manner. There was also organized the National Citizens Political Action Committee to collect funds and to campaign beyond the limits

[44] House Rept. No. 2093, 78th Cong., 2d sess. (1945), p. 9.
[45] Louise Overacker, "Labor's Political Contributions," *Political Science Quarterly,* 54 (1939), p. 59.
[46] For the English situation as of that time, see Pollock, *Money and Politics Abroad,* chap. 4. Later, in February, 1946, the Labour Government repealed the act limiting union participation in party finance.

of trade-union membership. This committee spent about $375,000.[47]

Apart from the fact that the law did not apply to contributions made in connection with nominations, the unions asserted that a distinction might be drawn between "contributions" and "expenditures." The law clearly forbade contributions by unions to political committees or candidates, but it said nothing about "expenditures" made directly by unions in connection with elections. A union might, for example, hold meetings, distribute literature, ring door bells, or engage in other activity in support of candidates for election and remain within the letter of the law.[48] By the same reasoning "expenditures" by corporations would not run afoul of federal law, for the statutory language applicable to corporations is identical with that referring to labor organizations. It should also be noted that several states have followed federal precedent and enacted statutes forbidding political contributions by labor unions.[49]

In 1946 and 1947 efforts were in motion to clarify the federal law relating to unions and party finance. The Smith-Connally Act of 1943, with its prohibition against union contributions, expired June 30, 1947. In anticipation of this expiration Senate and House committees proposed to extend the prohibition against contributions by unions and to broaden the legislation to apply to expenditures by unions as well.

Another source of party revenue regulated by legislation is assessments on public employees. Legislation to prohibit assessment, or "macing" as it is called in Pennsylvania, is designed to deprive the party in power of the advantage of access to this source of revenue, as well as to protect the rights of government employees in their wages and salaries. The defenders—and there are defenders—of the practice of assessment con-

---

[47] The reports filed by the CIO-PAC and by the NC-PAC showed receipts and disbursements in 1944 as follows:

	Contributions	Expenditures
Trade-union account	$647,903.26	$478,498.82
Individual contributions account	376,910.77	470,852.32
Subtotal: CIO-PAC	1,024,814.03	949,351.14
National Citizens Political Action Committee	380,306.45	378,424.78
	1,405,120.48	1,327,775.92

[48] See Sen. Rep. No. 101, 79th Cong., 1st sess., pp. 20–24. A.F.L. unions, as well as C.I.O. unions, were advised of this distinction between "contributions" and "expenditures." See Joseph Padway, "Political Contributions," *American Federationist*, March, 1944, pp. 24–25.

[49] The Alabama statute was held unconstitutional because a like prohibition was not applied to employers' associations. *Alabama State Federation of Labor* v. *McAdory*, 18 So. (2d) 810 (1944).

tend that by raising funds in this fashion the party is able to maintain its independence of the corporations, of the wealthy contributors, and of the vested interests. Perhaps occasionally the assertion is true, but more generally the party organization that assesses public employees will be found to be accepting "tainted" money with the other hand.

The Federal Civil Service Act of 1883 forbade the solicitation or receipt by any officer or employee of the United States of any "assessment, subscription, or contribution, for any political purpose whatever" from any officer or employee of the United States and made it unlawful for any person to solicit political contributions from employees in their offices. The legislation has certain patent defects: employees may not be solicited for contributions by another employee of the government, but they may be assessed by outsiders, such as the agents of a party committee who may be able to bring about their discharge. Most subordinate personnel in the federal service are not compelled to contribute to party funds, but occasional instances of assessment come to light. In 1934, for example, the President requested the resignation of a collector of internal revenue in Pennsylvania because of assessments in his office. Similarly, the Detroit collector of internal revenue resigned after charges of assessment had been made against him.[50] In the 1938 congressional campaign, scattered instances of solicitation from federal employees were uncovered, but generally the solicitation was within the letter of the law: it was done, not by a federal official or employee, but by party managers or other private persons.[51]

Less than half the states prohibit assessments against state and municipal employees. Even in those states with anti-assessment laws the legislation itself is in some instances defective; everywhere, whether prohibited or not, the practice of assessment appears to be much more general among state and local employees than in the federal service. At times the collections are made in a most systematic manner. In West Virginia, according to evidence presented in a 1940 congressional debate by Senator Neely, the system was so thorough that a road worker

[50] Chicago *Tribune*, May 23 and June 13, 1934. "One witness," from the Philadelphia office, "said he had always contributed to the party in power, to Republicans before and now to Democrats. Another witness testified the only difference between the system now and in former years was that the Republicans only ask for 3¼ per cent, while the Democrats asked for 5."

[51] After the 1938 campaign Congress, in the Hatch Act, made it unlawful "for any person to solicit or receive" any subscription, assessment, or contribution for "any political purpose whatever from any person known by him to be entitled to or receiving compensation, employment, or other benefit" from federal funds for work relief or relief purposes. This protection of this group of employees from assessment by "any" person is broader than the earlier act, which applies only to solicitation of one employee by another employee.

who received a check for $3.50 had to contribute 2 per cent, or 7 cents, to the party fund.[52]

State legislation prohibiting assessment of state and local employees was supplemented in 1940 by congressional action. An amendment to the Hatch Act prohibits assessments of state and local employees paid wholly or partly from federal grants or loans. This legislation, like that applicable to federal employees, prohibits assessment by one employee of another, but does not reach assessments by nonemployees. The Hatch Act applies, of course, only to part of the state and local employees. In several instances the Civil Service Commission, which administers the act, has invoked its penalties against state officials guilty of collecting political funds from state employees.

Contractors, suppliers, and other persons having financial transactions with the government have been important donors to campaign funds. In corrupt situations contractors may be virtually compelled to contribute to the party treasury. The 1940 amendment to the Hatch Act attempted to prevent contributions from persons dealing with the federal government. The act prohibits contributions by contractors and the solicitation of contractors for contributions "during the period of negotiation for, or performance" of a contract with a federal agency.

Limitation of purpose of expenditures. Expenditures for specified purposes are prohibited primarily by state legislation. The earlier tendency was to select and prohibit certain expenditures believed to be corrupt. The bribery of voters, for example, is everywhere unlawful. In various states expenditures are prohibited for treating, for conveying voters to the polls, for election-day workers. The more recent tendency in legislative control of the purpose of campaign expenditures is to specify by law the objects for which money may legitimately be spent. In a primary in California, for example, a candidate is limited to "lawful" purposes of expenditure that are defined as follows:

1. For the candidate's official filing fee.
2. For the preparing, printing, circulating and verifying of nomination papers.
3. For the candidate's personal traveling expenses.
4. For rent and necessary furnishing of halls or rooms, during such candidacy, for public meetings or for committee headquarters.
5. For payment of speakers and musicians at public meetings and their necessary traveling expenses.
6. For printing and distribution of pamphlets, circulars, newspapers, cards,

[52] *Congressional Record* (daily edition), March 8, 1940, p. 3947. The Senator relates: "The poor man had but 2 cents to his name, and consequently borrowed 5 cents from a friend in order to pay the ransom necessary to obtain his check."

handbills, posters, and announcements relative to candidates or political issues or principles.

7. For his share of the reasonable compensation of challengers at the polls.
8. For making canvasses of voters.
9. For clerk hire.
10. For conveying infirm or disabled voters to and from the polls.
11. For postage, expressage, telegraphing, and telephoning, relative to candidacy.

Well over half the states have legislation enumerating lawful items of expenditure, although these items vary from state to state.

Limitation of amounts spent. Efforts to limit the amount spent in campaigns has been one of the most prevalent types of legislation and at the same time one of the most generally ineffective. Congress has placed a limit on the amount to be spent by "a candidate" for the House or Senate in his election campaign, and thereby has excluded from the limitation expenditures in the primary campaign and those made by persons other than the candidate. The federal limits, unless the law of the state sets a lower maximum, are "the sum of $10,000 if a candidate for Senator, or the sum of $2,500 if a candidate for Representative, Delegate, or Resident Commissioner." However, to meet the greater needs of candidates in the larger states, a sliding maximum has been established, which raises the above limits in some states. This sliding maximum is defined as follows:

An amount equal to the amount obtained by multiplying three cents by the total number of votes cast at the last general election for all candidates for the office which the candidates seeks, but in no event exceeding $25,000 if a candidate for Senator or $5,000 if a candidate for Representative, Delegate, or Resident Commissioner.

The limits fixed in the congressional act are deceptive, for certain types of expenditures may be made over and above the maximum. Not included in the limitation are expenditures for the candidate for "necessary personal, traveling, or subsistence expenses, or for stationery, postage, writing or printing (other than for use on billboards or in newspapers), for distributing letters, circulars, or posters, or for telegraph or telephone service," and certain other expenses. In other words, a candidate might legally spend $50,000 for postage and distributing letters, circulars, or posters so far as the federal law is concerned. The limitations on amount apply only to certain types of expenditures.

In the states legislation to limit the amount of expenditures is common. In Idaho primaries, for example, expenditures by candidates are limited to $5,000 for the office of United States Senator; $2,000 for

Representative in Congress; $2,000 for state offices; $250 for county offices and membership in the state legislature. In some states limitations are specified in terms of percentages of the salary of the office concerned. In Iowa, for example, a candidate may spend in a primary or in a general election not more than 50 per cent of the annual salary of the office sought. In other states variable limitations, depending on the number of voters, are established by law.

By a farcical provision Congress in 1940 halfheartedly attempted to limit the total amount spent in presidential campaigns. The Hatch Act provided: "No political committee shall receive contributions aggregating more than $3,000,000, or make expenditures aggregating more than $3,000,000, during any calendar year." The simple method for avoidance of this limitation is to organize several political committees to collect campaign funds. Early in the 1940 campaign Henry P. Fletcher, general counsel to the Republican national committee, advised that the Republican national committee, the Republican congressional committee, and the Republican senatorial committee could each collect and spend $3,000,000 without violating the act. He suggested, in addition, that state committees, instead of relying on grants from the national committee, collect funds directly from donors. Funds formerly collected by the national committee and distributed to the states would not then come under the $3,000,000 limitation. Fletcher's opinion dealt also with the status of an independent Willkie-McNary committee: "It is our opinion that donations to such a committee would not have to be included in the Republican National Committee's limitation of $3,000,000 if such Willkie-McNary committee is independently organized and does not consist of members of the Republican National Committee." [53]

Mr. Fletcher's opinion undoubtedly interpreted the statute correctly, and both parties have simply divided their expenditures among several committees. The statute does not limit total expenditures; it merely puts the party managers to the trouble of dividing their fund-collecting and spending activities among different agencies. The Republican national committee reported for 1944 receipts of $2,999,999.48, and thereby kept within the letter of the law by a margin of 52 cents. Supporters of both candidates in the campaigns of 1940 and 1944 spent much more than $3,000,000, but the expenditure was nicely divided among different committees to allow each to remain within the legislative limitation. The multiplication of committees makes the enforcement of publicity requirements difficult. In 1945 a Senate committee recommended that the $3,000,000 limitation, which does not

[53] For the text of Fletcher's opinion, see *The New York Times*, August 4, 1940.

limit, be repealed and that greater efforts be made to obtain publicity of campaign finance on the theory that publicity of the facts would do more to cleanse party finance than impotent legislative limitation.[54]

Statutes attempting to limit the amount of expenditures in campaigns have certain defects. In one respect, many laws fix limits so low that it would be possible to conduct only the most feeble of campaigns if expenditures were kept within the permissible limits. The alternatives are either to ignore or to evade the law. Many statutes apply only to expenditures "by candidates"; in many instances outlays made by committees or persons in behalf of a candidate are not covered by the law. A fundamental difficulty in the limitation of campaign expenditures arises from the nature of our electoral system. If in a particular campaign only a single office were to be filled in any one area or district, it might be feasible to control the amount of expenditures. In the American electoral system, however, that condition is exceptional. A party committee may be working for the election of a ticket of twenty or thirty names, from the presidential electors down to the precinct constable. How are general expenditures in support of the entire ticket to be allocated among the different candidates? If one candidate on the ticket operates under a limit, the expenditures may be charged to the candidate having no statutory limitation.

Limitation of size of individual contribution. The fact that individual contributions to campaigns are at times extremely large has been a matter for criticism, and in 1940 Congress in amendments to the Hatch Act sought, in an ineffective fashion, to limit individual contributions to $5,000. But the limitation was not applied to gifts to state or to local committees. The Fletcher opinion quoted above pointed out the obvious loophole: "It is therefore our advice that donors desiring to give more than $5,000 to Republican candidates or committees should give only one gift of $5,000 to the Republican National Committee or the Republican Senatorial Committee or the Republican Congressional Committee. Any amounts above $5,000 that a donor desires to give should be given to State or local committees." [55]

[54] For an expression of a similar view, see J. W. Lederle, "Political Committee Expenditures and the Hatch Act," *Michigan Law Review*, 44 (1945), pp. 294–299.

[55] The division of contributions may be illustrated by the gifts of Lammot Du Pont in 1944. He gave a total of $31,322 to different committees in amounts of less than $5,000, including $2,000 to the Republican national committee, $3,000 to the Delaware Republican state committee, $3,000 to the New York County Republican committee, and $3,000 to the Kings County Republican committee. Marshall Field gave a total of $14,000, similarly divided, including $2,000 to the Democratic Senatorial Campaign committee, $3,000 to the New York State Democratic committee, $4,000 to the Democratic national committee, and $2,000 to the Illinois State Democratic committee

5. PARTY FINANCE AND POLITICAL POWER

Those who are critical of large expenditures by political parties often overlook the hard fact that large sums are necessary to carry on a modern political campaign. Even without the use of money for veiled purchase of votes or support of organization leaders who in turn can deliver votes, enormous sums legitimately may be spent to inform, persuade, and manipulate the electorate. The dissemination of party propaganda in a national campaign or in a large state campaign is a large-scale advertising job and accordingly necessitates large expenditures.

If one admits the necessity of large funds in modern campaigns, the important question for the observer of political behavior remains: What is the effect of the methods of raising and spending funds on the distribution of political power. The broad tendency has certainly been that the greater part of campaign contributions are made with the object of checking any fundamental political change. The essential similarity of the two parties has not prevented the same motive from governing contributions to both parties, but it is significant to note that, when the cleavage between the parties has been sharper, as in 1896 and 1936, the contributions of wealth have tended to be concentrated on the side more attached to the *status quo*. It need not be concluded, however, that all contributions, large or small, are made after a nice calculation of the potential gains or losses. Factors of personal ambition entirely apart from views on public policy may enter into contributions. Nevertheless, the fact that both parties draw most of their income from an infinitesimal proportion of their following certainly gives to the financial supporters a voice in party affairs far disproportionate to their numbers.

It need not be supposed that the power of wealth is the only means of gaining influence in party councils and in the formulation of public policy. The rise of agricultural groups to a position of great power in party activities and in government itself has not been accomplished by means of lavish campaign contributions by agrarians. Labor, similarly, achieved considerable influence long before it became of importance in party finance. Agriculture and labor, through force of numbers, can exert influence; holders of concentrated wealth resort to other means to retain their status in the political and economic order.

The long-run tendency has been repeated efforts, under the leadership of middle-class groups, to curb the power of great wealth. Although the contributors of large sums remain important in campaign finance, their contributions are probably but a tithe of what they would be had not the coffers of the corporations they control been closed for party purposes by legislation. Corporate financing of political activity through pressure groups and lobbying campaigns against particular public policies, however, remains unchecked. The influence of great wealth in party activities is persistent and at times unchallenged; it is kept in check only by the challenge of other groups with power enough to rise from time to time and erect an effective barrier to the progress of wealth.

In any attempt to evaluate the importance of campaign funds in influencing public policy it is well to keep in mind that there are enormous gaps in our knowledge of campaign finance and that most campaigns are conducted with much less publicity of party finance than are presidential elections. In the choice of state legislators, for example, the level of public interest is low and the level of interest of those affected by state legislation is high. In such situations small amounts of money may produce high returns, and from such scraps of evidence as there are one can surmise that campaign donations play a not unimportant role in keeping state legislatures in leash.

Does the side with the most money win in the electoral campaign? Generally, it does. George Lundberg collected data on 156 elections in various parts of the country and found that in fourteen out of fifteen instances "campaign expenditures, as reported, constitute an absolutely reliable index of the outcome of the election." [56] The question arises: Does the side with the larger purse win because of the purse, or does it receive the money because it is in the habit of winning? There is undoubtedly a little of both elements; but there are campaigns in which the most generous expenditures would not have turned the tide. In the 1932, 1936, 1940, and 1944 presidential campaigns the Republican party had the larger war chest; however, it seems doubtful that even a greater disparity in campaign funds would have led to the defeat of the Democratic candidate.[57]

[56] "Campaign Expenditures and Election Results," *Social Forces*, 6 (1928), pp. 452–457.
[57] It has been proposed from time to time that the public treasury bear the cost of campaigns, but the idea has not caught on. Several western states distribute publicity pamphlets to the voters. Arizona, California, Massachusetts, North Dakota, Ohio, Oregon, Utah, and Washington distribute pamphlets containing the text and arguments pro and con on proposed constitutional amendments and initiated and referred measures. Oregon and North Dakota publish candidates' pamphlets that contain information about the candidates supplied by them. Candidates' pamphlets in North Dakota are issued only at primary elections at which a measure is also voted on. The practice varies, but in some states candidates and supporters and opponents pay a fee for space that covers only a part of the cost of publication and distribution. See W. L. Josslin, "Oregon Educates Its Voters," *National Municipal Review*, 32 (1943), pp. 373–379.

Part Three

THE ELECTORATE AND
ELECTORAL METHODS

Chapter 16

THE ELECTORATE

ONCE the practice of deciding public issues by counting heads is instituted, the problem is posed of what heads to count. The settlement of questions by vote probably antedates the idea of voting by the citizen. Decisions by vote in juries, councils, and assemblies is an ancient practice, but popular suffrage gives voting a different meaning. The extension of the privilege of voting to all or part of the adult population for the determination of questions of governmental personnel or policy has been one aspect of the development of democracy and of representative government. The consultation of the electorate through voting introduced a new factor profoundly altering the appearance, if not always the reality, of the relationship of the governor and the governed. Mosca declares that popular suffrage gives a democratic system [1]

. . . greater powers of self-preservation than other systems. That is because its natural adversaries have to make a show of accepting it if they wish to avoid its consequences to a greater or lesser extent. All those who, by wealth, education, intelligence or guile, have an aptitude for leading a community of men, and a chance of doing so—in other words, all the cliques in the ruling classes —have to bow to universal suffrage once it is instituted, and also, if occasion requires, cajole and fool it.

It is not improbable that Mosca overestimated the tenacity of systems based on universal suffrage. Yet even the dictatorial regimes resort to plebiscites, although under such systems the voting is in a different social context and has a different significance than under democratic conditions.

Universal suffrage is now regarded as a commonplace, but it did not emerge full fledged with the birth of democratic governments. Popular governments at first allowed only a small part of the populace to vote. In western democratic societies the privilege of the suffrage has been gradually extended to new groups; each step in its extension has been in response to the demands of a group emerging from political sub-

[1] *The Ruling Class* (New York: McGraw–Hill, 1939), pp. 333–334.

ordination and demanding a voice in the management of public affairs. Whether, by the acquisition of suffrage, these new groups always actually gained power and influence or merely won a symbol of emancipation may be questioned; nevertheless, the step-by-step extension of the suffrage has been resisted by the older holders of the privilege lest their own political power be diminished. Moreover, the extension of the suffrage has brought far-reaching changes in the methods and strategy of politics. In monarchial and aristocratic regimes the gaining of power was a matter of personal intrigue among a small group of people. Success in that endeavor depended upon the possession of qualities and the employment of techniques quite different from those necessary to gain the favor and support of the electorate under a system of universal suffrage.

A broad popular suffrage is, then, a constant that conditions both the methods and the substance of American politics. The development of the suffrage in the United States to its present status is principally a matter of historical interest, but in the story of the rise of popular suffrage may be seen some of the main currents in American politics. The first great suffrage battle involved the breaking down of property-owning and tax-paying qualifications for manhood suffrage. The outcome of this struggle included a weakening of the power of the colonial and early American aristocracies and the rise in power and influence of the common man. The question of Negro suffrage was debated and, in the main, settled against the Negro prior to the Civil War; the Fifteenth Amendment was calculated to extend the suffrage to the Negro, but it was ineffective and the question of Negro suffrage remains. The third great dispute over the suffrage turned on the question of its extension to women.

1. MEN WITHOUT PROPERTY GAIN THE VOTE

Early property qualifications. Until the triumph of Jacksonian Democracy, property-holding and tax-paying qualifications for the exercise of the suffrage were common. The American Revolution had brought no abrupt change in the fundamental nature of the suffrage; changes were made, but they were in the direction of lowering, not eliminating, the property qualification. The nature of suffrage qualifications in the colonial period may be best indicated by a few illustrations. A Virginia act of 1736 provided

That no person or persons whatsoever shall hereafter have a right to vote at any election of members to serve in the general assembly, for any county, who hath not an estate of freehold, or other greater estate, in one hundred acres of land, at least, if no settlement be made upon it; or twenty-five acres with a house and plantation, in his possession, or in the possession of his tenant or tenants, for term of years, in the same county where he gives such vote.

To cover the special situation of holders of real property in urban communities, the act contained the following: [2]

Provided always, that nothing in this act contained shall be construed to hinder any person to vote at such elections, in respect or in right of any houses, lands or tenements, lying and being in any city or town, laid out and established by act of assembly, as such person be a freeholder, in any house or lot, or a house, and part of a lot; but where the interest in any such house and lot, or house and part of a lot, is or shall be divided among several persons, no more than one single voice shall be admitted for one and the same house or lot.

Thus in Virginia the suffrage qualifications were defined, except for the cities and towns, in acreage of real estate. In Georgia, North Carolina, and New Jersey colonial suffrage qualifications were defined in like terms. In New Hampshire, New York, and Rhode Island, however, the real-estate qualifications were in terms of the value of the real estate. The pre-Revolutionary requirement in New York, for example, was ownership of real estate worth forty pounds. In the other colonies the requirement was ownership either of real estate or of personal property. In Pennsylvania a person owning fifty acres or other property worth fifty pounds might become an elector. In Massachusetts ownership of real estate yielding forty shillings annual income or of other property worth forty pounds gave the right to vote. In South Carolina the suffrage came with ownership of property or payment of ten shillings in taxes. During the Revolution eight of the thirteen states altered their suffrage requirements, "and the modifications were not such as to indicate that statesmen had abandoned the principle that only property holders should vote. The only tendency manifest was to reduce the amount." [3]

The effect of the colonial restrictions on the suffrage is problematical. Figures on voting at that time, and even on population, are unreliable. McKinley attempted to estimate the numbers entitled to vote and the numbers actually voting in the colonial period, but the available data justified only the conclusion that the potential voters varied "from one-sixth to one-fiftieth" of the total population and the proportions of actual voters varied over about the same range.[4] The effect of a narrow

[2] A. E. McKinley, *The Suffrage Franchise in the Thirteen English Colonies in America* (Philadelphia: University of Pennsylvania, 1905), pp. 38–39.
[3] K. H. Porter, *A History of Suffrage in the United States* (Chicago: University of Chicago Press, 1918), p. 10.
[4] McKinley, *op. cit.*, pp. 487–488.

suffrage may better be visualized if we consider these figures in relation to our present electorate and suffrage. If a figure of 10 per cent of the population be assumed as the colonial suffrage for purposes of comparison, a like limitation on the suffrage today would have in 1940 disfranchised over 35 million persons who voted in the presidential election.

Elimination of property requirements. The general pattern after the American Revolution was gradually to eliminate the property-owning qualification, to substitute a taxpaying qualification, and eventually to remove the taxpaying requirement for the exercise of the suffrage. South Carolina substituted a taxpaying requirement for the property requirement in 1778; Georgia, in 1789; Delaware, in 1792; Maryland, in 1810; Connecticut, in 1818; Massachusetts, in 1821; New York, in 1821; Rhode Island, in 1842. A few states did not pass through the stage of substitution of taxpaying for property holding. Virginia persisted in the property qualification until 1850 when it was removed; at that time the taxpaying requirement was gradually passing out of use.[5]

The struggle over the property qualifications in Virginia illustrates the kind of cleavage that occurred elsewhere. The demand for the extension of the suffrage came primarily from the more recently settled western sections of the state; it was resisted by the tidewater section. In the state constitutional convention of 1829–1830, the westerners cited Thomas Jefferson in support of a broadened franchise; easterners, such as John Randolph of Roanoke, opposed the change. He refused to be struck down by the authority of Jefferson, a man of "theory and reveries." Randolph said: "Such is the wisdom of our existing form of government that no proposition can be brought forward with a view to making an inroad that can demand a respectable majority. The lust of innovation has been the death of all republics. All men of sense ought to guard and warn their neighbors against it." A property qualification was retained by the convention of 1829–1830, to be eliminated in 1850.[6]

In the states of the West the conflict between frontier and tidewater, between an aristocratic group enjoying the suffrage and a democratic group clamoring for its extension, did not occur as in Virginia. The western states came into the Union with no property or taxpaying requirements or only nominal ones. Porter comments:[7]

---

[5] Porter, *op. cit.*, p. 110.

[6] J. A. C. Chandler, *The History of Suffrage in Virginia* (Baltimore: The Johns Hopkins Press, 1901).

[7] Porter, *op. cit.*, p. 48.

In these frontier states there was an entirely unique situation. All men were on a plane socially, and government was merely a convenience to them, not a semi-sacred institution. That all men should participate in what government there was, was a foregone conclusion. There was no aristocratic element to deal with, no poor-servant and artisan class, there were no scholars, no philosophers, no theologians, just hardy pioneers setting up a frame of government because the population was getting big enough to need it. There was no suffrage problem for them.

These conditions of the frontier regions contrasted sharply with the situation in the older states. In the New York constitutional convention of 1821, for example, a leading opponent of the proposal to abolish property qualifications for voters for the state senate, Chancellor Kent, phrased his opinion in this fashion:

Such a proposition, at the distance of ten years past, would have struck the public mind with astonishment and terror. The apprehended danger from the experiment of universal suffrage, applied to the whole legislative department, is no dream of imagination. It is too mighty an excitement for the moral condition of men to endure. The tendency of universal suffrage is to jeopardize the rights of property and the principles of liberty. There is a constant tendency in human society—and the history of every age proves it—there is a constant tendency in the poor to covet and to share the plunder of the rich; in the debtor to relax or to avoid the obligations of contract; in the indolent and profligate to cast the whole burthen of society upon the industrious and virtuous; and there is a tendency in ambitious and wicked men to inflame those combustible materials. . . . We stand, therefore, on the brink of fate, on the very edge of a precipice. If we let go our present hold on the Senate, we commit our proudest hopes and most precious interests to the waves.

Fear of the propertyless people of the growing cities motivated some opponents of removal of property and tax qualifications in the eastern states. A member of the Pennsylvania constitutional convention of 1837 spoke as follows: [8]

But, Sir, what does the delegate propose? To place the vicious vagrant, the wandering Arabs, the Tartar hordes of our large cities on the level with the virtuous and good man? . . . These Arabs steeped in crime and in vice, to be placed on a level with industrious population is insulting and degrading to

---

[8] Quoted by Porter, *op. cit.,* p. 92. Tom Paine's ridicule of property qualifications was used by a delegate to the Massachusetts convention of 1853: "You require that a man shall have sixty dollars' worth of property, or he shall not vote. Very well, take an illustration. Here is a man today who owns a jackass, and the jackass is worth sixty dollars. Today the man is a voter and he goes to the polls with his jackass and deposits his vote. Tomorrow the jackass dies. The next day the man comes to vote without his jackass and he cannot vote at all. Now tell me, which was the voter, the man or the jackass?"—Quoted by Porter, p. 109.

the community. . . . I hold up my hands against a proceeding which confers on the idle, vicious, degraded vagabond a right at the expense of the poor and industrious portion of this commonwealth.

Property and income qualifications for the exercise of the suffrage largely have been swept away. In some jurisdictions a remnant persists in the limitation of voting on local bond issues to persons paying property taxes. Occasionally the idea is put forward that persons on relief should be disfranchised. In 1940 a Seattle manufacturer gained publicity by proposing the "One-Two Plan," a scheme that would not disfranchise the propertyless but would give two votes to each person who could present a real-estate or income-tax receipt. Movements of this sort recur but rarely gain much strength.

2. THE NEGRO AND THE VOTE

Prior to the Civil War the Negro was disfranchised in practically all the states. In the southern states slaves were, by virtue of being slaves, excluded from the ballot; the only issue was whether the privilege of voting should be extended to the free Negro. In Virginia, although there was no constitutional limitation of the suffrage to white men until 1830, free Negroes did not vote from the Revolution to the Civil War. Even in West Virginia, which seceded from Virginia to remain in the Union, the constitution of 1864 enfranchised whites only. The status of Negroes in the other southern states was similar. In North Carolina, however, free Negroes who met the other qualifications were permitted to vote until the constitutional convention of 1835, which adopted a Negro exclusion rule by a vote of 66 to 61. "This was the end," says Weeks, "of Negro suffrage in North Carolina and in the South until the days of Reconstruction." [9] The status of Negro suffrage was not markedly different in the other states of the Union before the Civil War. Weeks points out that by the time of the Civil War there were only five states in which no color qualification existed for the exercise of the suffrage. These states were Maine, Rhode Island, Massachusetts, New Hampshire, and Vermont; and in practice the free exercise of the suffrage by the Negro was said to be restricted to Maine.

Grant of Negro suffrage. The grant of Negro suffrage was a phase of the power politics of the post-Civil War period. Negro suffrage had no part in the reconstruction schemes of Presidents Lincoln and Johnson, but the so-called radical group in Congress favored suffrage. Stevens, one of the congressional leaders of this group in 1867, said:

[9] S. B. Weeks, "The History of Negro Suffrage in the South," *Political Science Quarterly*, 9 (1894), pp. 671–703.

White union men are in a minority in each of those states. With them the blacks would act in a body, form a majority, control the states and protect themselves. It would insure the ascendency of the Union Party.

Sumner advocated Negro suffrage for similar reasons. Not only would the extension of the suffrage to the Negroes give the Union party control in the southern states, but it would swing the vote in the same direction in certain doubtful northern states. In 1867 Sumner wrote to the editor of the *Independent:* [10]

You wish to have the North "reconstructed," so at least that it shall cease to deny the elective franchise on account of color. But you postpone the day by insisting on the preliminary of a constitutional amendment. I know your vows to the good cause; but ask you to make haste. We cannot wait. . . . This question must be settled forthwith: in other words it must be settled before the presidential election, which is at hand. Our colored fellow-citizens at the South are already electors. They will vote at the presidential election. But why should they vote at the South, and not at the North? The rule of justice is the same for both. Their votes are needed at the North as well as at the South. There are Northern states where their votes can make the good cause safe beyond question. There are other states where their votes will be like the last preponderant weight in the nicely balanced scales. Let our colored fellow-citizens vote in Maryland, and that state, now so severely tried, will be fixed for human rights forever. Let them vote in Pennsylvania, and you will give more than 20,000 votes to the Republican cause. Let them vote in New York, and the scales which hang so doubtful will incline to the Republican cause. It will be the same in Connecticut. . . . Enfranchisement, which is the corollary and complement of emancipation, must be a national act, also proceeding from the national government, and applicable to all the states.

The introduction of Negro suffrage in the former Confederate states was accomplished by the Reconstruction Act of 1867, which declared the governments of the southern states to be provisional until, among other requirements, new constitutions were formulated by "delegates elected by the male citizens of said state, twenty-one years old and upward, of whatever race, color or previous condition." In July, 1868, the Fourteenth Amendment became effective. Section 2 of the Amendment, calculated to stimulate the states to grant the suffrage to the Negro, reads:

Representatives shall be apportioned among the several states according to their respective numbers, counting the whole number of persons in each state, excluding Indians not taxed. But when the right to vote at any election for the choice of electors for President and Vice-President of the United States, Representatives in Congress, the executive and judicial officers of a state, or the

[10] Quoted by Weeks, *op. cit.,* p. 682.

members of the legislature thereof, is denied to any of the male inhabitants of such state, being twenty-one years of age, and citizens of the United States, or in any way abridged, except for participation in rebellion, or other crime, the basis of representation therein shall be reduced in the proportion which the number of such male citizens shall bear to the whole number of male citizens twenty-one years of age in such state.

The exaction of the penalty thus provided is the responsibility of Congress, whose duty it is to apportion the membership of the House of Representatives among the states.[11]   The penalty has never been exacted.

The Fifteenth Amendment, adopted in 1870, deprived the states of their legal power to bar persons from the suffrage on account of color. It reads: "The right of citizens of the United States to vote shall not be denied or abridged by the United States or by any state on account of race, color, or previous conditions of servitude." With the enfranchisement of the Negro, rule of the southern states by a combination of Negroes and carpetbaggers ensued for about eight years.   The results were not considered good by even the most sympathetic observers.   Unprecedented extravagance, corruption, and administrative incompetence prevailed.[12]

White control reestablished.   Federal reconstruction policy wiped out party differences between the whites, formerly divided between the Whig and the Democratic parties.   United by external pressure they determined to use whatever tactics were necessary to regain control. The activities of the Ku Klux Klan were the most striking example of the methods of intimidation used to prevent Negro political activity, although the same object was served by other organizations, such as the Rifle Clubs of South Carolina.   Apart from intimidation and fraud, the return of white supremacy in the South was facilitated by relaxation of federal policy.   The withdrawal of federal troops from the South by President Hayes in 1877, for example, removed a strong prop from the remaining reconstruction governments.

A period of experimentation in the disfranchisement of the Negro followed.   In addition to intimidation, a variety of legal means was used to disfranchise or otherwise reduce his influence.   Gerrymandering legislative districts against the Negro was a favorite device.   Poll-tax requirements were established, as were "elaborate and confusing registration schemes, and devious complications of the balloting proc-

---

[11] See H. E. Flack, *The Adoption of the Fourteenth Amendment* (Baltimore: The Johns Hopkins Press, 1908).   The adoption of the Negro-enfranchisement amendments was not accomplished without serious opposition in the northern states.

[12] Paul Lewinson, *Race, Class, and Party* (New York: Oxford University Press, 1932), p. 48.

ess." [13]   Some states disqualified voters because of conviction for petty larceny, on the theory that these convictions occurred, or could be made to occur, more frequently among the black population.   Control of the electoral machinery, regained by the whites, facilitated election frauds to reduce the effective Negro strength.

Lewinson, the leading student of the subject, holds that the cleavages among the whites as a result of the agrarian movement of the 'eighties and 'nineties, served as a factor in the development of more perfect techniques of disfranchisement.   His argument is that the dominant groups in the post-Civil War white governments were the new business, railroad, and financial classes rather than the old planting aristocracy.   White dominance depended on white unity.   The agrarian movement challenged Bourbon control, and in the struggles between white groups both sides were tempted to recruit Negro support.   In Texas, according to Martin, [14]

. . . while in a great many counties with a large Negro population the People's Party managed to convert one-half or more of the native white vote, it had still to compete with the Democratic Party for the control of the Negroes. In county after county the identical story was told: the white vote divided about equally between the Democratic and the Populist parties and the Negroes held the balance of power.   In such a situation the strategists of the two parties went out on the open market to deal with the Negro voter, and circumstances combined to throw so great advantage on the side of the Democrats that they were able ordinarily to return with the larger vote to show for their efforts.

Under such circumstances there was in the South generally, in Lewinson's opinion, strong reason for white factions to unite in order to deal with the question of Negro suffrage.   Only by disfranchisement could political dispute among the whites follow its natural course, and the expense and fraud associated with Negro suffrage be eliminated. [15]

The problem facing the drafters of new southern constitutions was to circumvent the Fifteenth Amendment legally, disfranchise Negroes, and at the same time leave the way open for all whites to vote.   The Mississippi constitutional convention of 1890 was fertile in the invention of contrivances to serve these purposes, and its handiwork found imita-

[13] Lewinson, *op. cit.*, p. 65.   An example of these devious complications of the balloting process is furnished by the South Carolina Eight Box Law of 1882.   At the polling place as many ballot boxes were provided as there were contests.   A ballot deposited in the wrong box was invalid.   A voter unable to read operated under something of a handicap in casting a valid ballot.

[14] R. C. Martin, *The People's Party in Texas* (Austin: The University of Texas, 1933), p. 96.

[15] Lewinson, *op. cit.*, p. 79.

tion in other states. To vote, the elector was required by the new constitution to pay a $2.00 poll tax and, if requested, to present his tax receipt at the polls. The assumption was that Negroes were neither inclined to pay the tax nor habituated to the preservation of records. A two-year residence requirement was imposed, on the doubtful theory that Negroes were more migratory than whites. The legislative districts were gerrymandered to discriminate against the sections of the state most heavily populated by Negroes. Conviction for bribery, burglary, theft, arson, obtaining money under false pretenses, perjury, forgery, embezzlement, murder, or bigamy was made a disqualification. If the Negro passed all these bars, there remained the literacy test, to become effective in 1892. With it was coupled an "understanding" clause, the crowning achievement of the Mississippi convention. The clause read that after 1892 qualified voters must be able "to read any section of the state constitution; or to be able to understand the same when read to him, or give a reasonable interpretation thereof." [16] Illiteracy was common among both Negroes and whites, but in the administration of the alternative test—the "understanding" clause—discrimination against the Negroes was definitely contemplated.

In the discussion of similar provisions in a Virginia constitutional convention, one speaker explained:

I do not expect (them) to be administered with any degree of friendship by the white man to the suffrage of the black man. I expect the examination with which the black man will be confronted, to be inspired with the same spirit that inspires every man in this convention. . . . I would not expect for the white man a rigid examination. The people of Virginia do not stand impartially between the suffrage of the white man and the suffrage of the black men. . . . We do not come here prompted by an impartial purpose in reference to Negro suffrage.

Another speaker, Carter Glass, replied to the question whether disfranchisement would be accomplished by "fraud and discrimination" under the scheme: [17]

By fraud, no: by discrimination, yes. But it will be discrimination within the letter of the law. . . . Discrimination! Why, that is precisely what we propose; that, exactly, is what this convention was elected for—to discriminate to the very extremity of permissible action under the limitations of the Federal

[16] W. A. Mabry, "Disfranchisement of the Negro in Mississippi," *Journal of Southern History*, 4 (1938), pp. 318–333. The South Carolina constitutional convention of 1895 followed the Mississippi precedent and adopted an "understanding" clause. See F. B. Simkins, *Pitchfork Ben Tillman* (Baton Rouge: Louisiana State University Press, 1944), chap. 20.

[17] Quoted by Lewinson, *op. cit.*, pp. 85–86.

Constitution, with a view to the elimination of every Negro voter who can be gotten rid of, legally, without materially impairing the numerical strength of the white electorate. . . . It is a fine discrimination, indeed, that we have practiced in the fabrication of this plan.

Early tests of constitutionality. The constitutional clauses employed to disfranchise the Negro did not expressly refer to Negroes. Litigants were not lacking to try to persuade the Supreme Court to look beyond form and to examine the substance of the disfranchising clauses in relation to the Fifteenth Amendment. In *Williams* v. *Mississippi*,[18] decided in 1898, the Supreme Court reviewed the indictment of Williams for murder. Williams' case was built on the state law requiring that jurors be electors. The contention was that the practical administration of the Mississippi constitutional suffrage requirements manifested "a scheme on the part of the framers of that Constitution to abridge the suffrage of the colored electors in the State of Mississippi on account of the previous condition of servitude." Furthermore, the coupling of suffrage requirements with the qualifications for jurors constituted a deprivation of the equal protection of the law by the state, a matter prohibited by the Fourteenth Amendment. The Supreme Court agreed that it should go behind the form and examine the substance of the requirements, but in this proceeding the Court found that the constitution and statutes of Mississippi did "not on their face discriminate between the races" and that it had "not been shown that their actual administration was evil, only that evil was possible under them."

In 1903, in the case of *Giles* v. *Harris*,[19] the Supreme Court had before it the question of the constitutionality of the suffrage provisions of the constitution of Alabama that permitted permanent registration as a voter before 1903 of all persons "of good character . . . who understand the duties and obligations of citizenship under a republican form of government," as well as all persons who served in the Revolutionary and certain other wars, together with their descendants. After 1903, suffrage requirements under the Alabama constitution were to be stiffened to include a literacy test, among other things. Giles, a Negro, alleged that the constitutional provisions were part of a conspiracy to disfranchise Negroes because of their race and, therefore, void under the Federal Constitution. The Court, in an opinion by Mr. Justice Holmes, refused to grant an order in equity to compel the election officers of Alabama to place the name of Giles and other Negroes on the voting lists. The Court's decision was justified on two principal bases.

---

[18] 170 U.S. 213 (1898).
[19] 189 U.S. 475.

If the Alabama constitution were held invalid, as Giles asked, how could the court order his registration under a void law? "If, then, we accept the conclusion which it is the chief purpose of the bill to maintain, how can we make the court a party to the unlawful scheme by accepting it and adding another voter to its fraudulent lists?"

Another basis for the Court's decision was the simple fact that it had no instruments at its command to prevent Negro disfranchisement.

In determining whether a court of equity can take jurisdiction, one of the first questions is what it can do to enforce any order that it may make. . . . The bill imports that the great mass of the white population intends to keep the blacks from voting. To meet such an intent something more than ordering the plaintiff's name to be inscribed upon the lists of 1902 will be needed. If the conspiracy and the intent exist, a name on a piece of paper will not defeat them. Unless we are prepared to supervise the voting in that state by officers of the court, it seems to us that all the plaintiff could get from equity would be an empty form.

Holmes concluded the opinion by saying that relief against political discrimination must be given by the people of the state "or by the legislative and political department of the government of the United States."

The "grandfather clause," another method of Negro disfranchisement, encountered constitutional obstacles in *Guinn* v. *United States.*[20] This was usually a temporary means for permanently registering all those persons who could vote, or whose ancestors could vote, prior to the adoption of the Fifteenth Amendment. Those whose ancestors could not vote at that time had to jump some other hurdle, such as a literacy test, to establish their right to vote. In conjunction, these two requirements meant that whites who could show that they or their ancestors could vote prior to the adoption of the Fifteenth Amendment could gain registration regardless of their literacy and that Negroes, who were legally barred from the vote prior to the Fifteenth Amendment, could not establish a voting ancestry and were in large measure barred by the literacy test. The Oklahoma constitutional clause, invalidated in *Guinn* v. *United States,* provided:

No person shall be registered as an elector of this state or be allowed to vote in any election held herein, unless he be able to read and write any section of the Constitution of the state of Oklahoma; but no person who was, on January 1st, 1866, or any time prior thereto, entitled to vote under any form of government, or who at that time resided in some foreign nation, and no lineal descendant of such person, shall be denied the right to register and vote because of his inability to so read and write sections of such constitution. . . .

[20] 238 U.S. 347 (1915).

The state of Oklahoma contended that the Fifteenth Amendment did not grant the franchise to the Negro but merely prohibited denial of the vote on "account of race, color, or previous condition of servitude." Since the grandfather clause, so the argument ran, "does not in terms make any discrimination on account of race, color, or previous condition of servitude, since all, whether Negro or white, who come within its requirements, enjoy the privilege of voting, there is no ground upon which to rest the contention that the provision violates the 15th Amendment." The Court, in its opinion, inquired why the date of January 1, 1866, was set unless the object was to evade the Fifteenth Amendment. The Court said: ". . . we are unable to discover how, unless the prohibitions of the Fifteenth Amendment were considered, the slightest reason was afforded for basing the classification upon a period of time prior to the 15th Amendment. Certainly it cannot be said that there was any peculiar necromancy in the time named which engendered attributes affecting the qualification to vote which would not exist at another and different period unless the Fifteenth Amendment was in view." The invalidation of the grandfather clause was not a victory of importance to the Negroes who sought the vote since the clause was only a temporary means to permit the permanent registration of those meeting the "grandfather" qualifications.

White primaries: Their rise and vicissitudes. The most recently developed device to disfranchise the Negroes in the South is the white primary. Long before the rise of the direct-primary method of nomination in the South, Negroes had been excluded from participation in the affairs of the Democratic party. With the birth of agrarianism in the 'nineties and the subsequent adoption of the direct primary, a means was at hand by which the battles between the whites could be fought out within the Democratic party, from which the Negro could be excluded. As early as 1907 the Negro was said to have been practically eliminated from politics in Georgia by the white primary. Rules of local and state party committees were gradually adopted in other states to exclude Negroes from the primary, and by 1930 eight states had state or local party rules of this kind. Nevertheless, in some communities Negroes were permitted to participate from time to time because of their attachment to local white factions.

A "minor squabble among white politicians in Texas," as Lewinson calls it, resulted in the substitution of state legislation excluding Negroes from the Democratic primaries for the pre-existing party rules. This development brought an important series of decisions by the Supreme Court on the white-primary method of disfranchisement. In Bexar County, in which San Antonio is located, Negroes were permitted to vote in the Democratic primaries despite the state committee's exclusion rule. In a race for the nomination for district attorney both aspirants sought the Negro vote; the defeated contender, having lost the Negro vote, successfully agitated for the passage of an act by the state legislature excluding Negroes from the primaries. The law provided that "in no event shall a Negro be eligible to participate in a Democratic primary election held in the State of Texas."

Subsequently, in 1924, Dr. L. A. Nixon of El Paso, a Negro, attempted to vote in the Democratic primary. After the election officials rejected his request to vote, Nixon sued Herndon, an election judge, for damages. He challenged the act of the legislature under the Fourteenth and Fifteenth amendments of the Federal Constitution. In a laconic opinion the Supreme Court did not consider the validity of the act under the Fifteenth Amendment, which prohibits denial of the right to vote on account of race or color, but held the act void as a denial of the equal protection of the laws guaranteed against state action by the Fourteenth Amendment. The Court found it "hard to imagine a more direct and obvious infringement" of the Fourteenth Amendment, which was passed "with a special intent to protect the blacks from discrimination against them." [21]

To meet the Supreme Court decision the Texas legislature in 1927 repealed the statutory rule barring Negroes from the primary and substituted a clause authorizing "every political party in this State through its State Executive Committee . . . to prescribe the qualifications of its own members." By virtue of this grant of power by the legislature the state executive committee of the Democratic party adopted a resolution "that all white Democrats who are qualified under the constitution and laws of Texas . . . and none other, be allowed to participate in the primary elections." Again Dr. Nixon was denied the ballot by the election judges and again he sued for damages. The defense argument was that the rule under which Nixon was excluded from the primary was an act of the party; that the prohibition of denial of equal protection in the Fourteenth Amendment applies only to action by the state itself; hence, the party rule was not in violation of the equal-protection clause. The Supreme Court refused to say whether the party could exclude Negroes. It observed that the state executive committee possessed no inherent power to exclude Negroes or any other group from the party. "Whatever power of exclusion has been exercised by the members of the committee has come to them, therefore, not as delegates of the party, but as the delegates of the state." And later in the opinion: "The pith of the matter is simply this, that, when

[21] *Nixon* v. *Herndon,* 273 U.S. 536 (1927).

those agencies (the state executive committee) are invested with an authority independent of the will of the association (the party) in whose name they undertake to speak, they become to that extent the organs of the state itself, the repositories of official power." In other words, the Supreme Court was of the opinion that in the first case the state was acting through the legislature; in the present case, the state was acting through the executive committee of the political party. The exclusion of Negroes by a party committee acting under state authority constituted a denial of equal protection by the state.[22]

The rebuff by the Supreme Court stimulated the imagination of Texas Democrats, and in 1932 another rule limiting participation in the direct primary to whites was adopted, not by the legislature, not by the state executive committee of the party, but by the state convention of the party. The question came before the Supreme Court in *Grovey* v. *Townsend*. Was the party's action through its convention the action of a private voluntary association, or was it the action of the instrumentality of a state and as such an infringement of the equal-protection clause? It was necessary to examine the legal nature of political parties in Texas. The Court observed that parties were compelled by the law of Texas to use the direct-primary method of nomination, but that the primary was a party primary. The expenses of it were borne by the members of the party seeking nomination, the ballots were furnished by the party, and the votes were counted and returns made by agencies of the party. Furthermore, the Supreme Court looked to the decisions of the courts of Texas on the nature of parties in that state. The highest state court had held that parties "are voluntary associations for political action, and are not the creatures of the state"; that the party "by its representatives assembled in convention, has the power to determine who shall be eligible for membership and, as such, eligible to participate in the party's primaries." As a private association, therefore, the party might exclude Negroes without violating the equal-protection clause, which applies only to action by the state.[23] Thus, the legality of the white primary under the conditions described was established.

The legal merry-go-round, however, had not taken its last turn. It

[22] *Nixon* v. *Condon*, 286 U.S. 73 (1932).

[23] *Grovey* v. *Townsend*, 295 U.S. 45 (1935). For accounts of the white primary litigation, see R. W. Hainsworth, "The Negro and the Texas Primaries," *Journal of Negro History*, 18 (1933), pp. 426–450; Louise Overacker, "The Negro's Struggle for Participation in Primary Elections," *Journal of Negro History*, 30 (1945), pp. 54–61; C. S. Mangum, Jr., *The Legal Status of the Negro* (Chapel Hill: University of North Carolina Press, 1940), chap. 18. For a case study on the origin of the white primary in a Texas county in 1898, see J. A. R. Moseley, "The Citizens White Primary of Marion County," *Southwestern Historical Quarterly*, 49 (1946), pp. 524–531.

was given another push by the Supreme Court's decision in the *Classic*
case [24] in 1941, which upset the general belief, based on the *Newberry*
case, that the federal government had no power to regulate primaries
held under state authority.   The contention in the *Classic* case was that
the constitutional provision directing that the House of Representatives be "chosen . . . by the people in the several States" (Art. I, sec. 2)
created a right for the voter under the Federal Constitution that might
be protected by federal action.   The Court accepted this reasoning and
upheld indictments of New Orleans election officials charged with fraud
in a primary to nominate a United States representative and, hence,
with violation of a provision of the criminal code making it an offense
to deprive a citizen of any right or privilege under the Constitution.
The Court observed: "Where the state law has made the primary an
integral part of the procedure of choice, or where in fact the primary
effectively controls the choice, the right of the elector to have his ballot
counted at the primary is . . . included in the right protected by"
Article I, section 2, of the Constitution, just as in an election."

The *Classic* case gave new hope to critics of the "white primary," and
another case was brought by a Texas Negro who had been excluded
from a Democratic primary.   In 1944 the Supreme Court, in *Smith* v.
Allwright,[25] overruled *Grovey* v. *Townsend*.   The reasoning was that
the primary in Texas was an integral part of the machinery for choosing officials.   Although the state convention had acted on its own authority in excluding Negroes, in other aspects the primary was regulated by state law and the state provided procedure by which the party
certified its nominees for inclusion on the general election ballot.   By
such action the state endorsed and enforced the discrimination against
Negroes.   Under these circumstances, discrimination by the party had
to be treated as discrimination by the state.   The Court, in distinction
from the earlier decisions, held the action to be prohibited by the Fifteenth Amendment.

Consequences of the Allwright decision.   *Smith* v. *Allwright* over-
turned the legal doctrines on which southern states had based "white
primaries," and southern lawyers began to look for loopholes in the
decision.   The *Classic* case had laid down two tests for determination
whether a primary came under federal control: (1) when it was an
"integral part" of the election machinery by law; (2) when it in fact
"effectively controls the choice."   *Smith* v. *Allwright* turned on the
"integral part" test.   The test of "control of choice" in the *Classic* case

---

[24] *United States* v. *Classic*, 61 Sup. Ct. 1031 (1941).
[25] 321 U.S. 649 (1944).   See R. E. Cushman, "The Texas 'White Primary' Case—
Smith v. *Allwright*," *Cornell Law Quarterly*, 30 (1944–45), pp. 66–76.

was *dictum* and perhaps not good law, the lawyers argued. Perhaps a way to preserve the "white primary" would be to repeal all state laws concerning the conduct of primaries and leave the matter entirely to party rule. Exclusion of Negroes from such a private primary by party authorities could not be regarded as a denial or abridgment of the right to vote on account of race or color by a state in violation of the Fifteenth Amendment.

In 1944 the South Carolina legislature repealed 147 acts relating to the conduct of primaries and left nominations completely uncontrolled by law and subject to management by the party authorities. In 1945 Georgia took a preparatory step in this direction by repealing a provision of its constitution relating to primaries.[26] In 1947 the Georgia legislature followed the South Carolina pattern and repealed all primary legislation, but the repealers were vetoed by Governor M. E. Thompson, who became chief executive after the state supreme court declared the selection of Herman Talmadge as governor by the legislature void. Governor Thompson asserted that elimination of state regulation of the primaries and the substitution of party control would "allow fraud and stolen elections to run rampant in Georgia."

Reaction to the invalidation of the white primary followed in Arkansas a different pattern from that of South Carolina. The Democratic convention of 1944, following the *Allwright* decision, adopted a rule limiting party membership to whites but permitting nonmembers to vote in the primary provided that they met tests of allegiance to the principles of the party. Among the principles was the "preservation of existing laws relating to the segregation of races in schools, public conveyances and other lawfully designated places" and the "legal prohibition of intermarriage of persons of White and African descent." A Negro who was "loyal" to these principles and who met certain other tests including a pledge to support the candidates chosen at the primary in the general election might vote in the primary. In case of challenge the final determination whether a would-be voter met the tests would be made, under the party rules, by the election judges at the polling place.[27]

In 1945 Arkansas took a further step to avoid the consequences of the

---

[26] A Federal District Court had held that the Georgia primaries came within the rule of *Smith* v. *Allwright*. See *King* v. *Chapman*, 62 F. Supp. 639 (1945).

[27] An odd course was followed in the Virginia Democratic State Convention at about the same time. Eight Negro delegates, duly chosen by local mass meetings, had their names stricken from the list of official delegates by the convention's credentials committee. However, they never received "official" notification of the committee action and sat and voted in the convention without question. It was reported that this plan was followed by the convention leaders to prevent discussion of the "race" question.— *New York Times*, July 9, 1944.

Allwright decision when its legislature provided for a "split" primary; that is, it established a primary to be held at a different time from the regular primary, and in this separate primary candidates for the United States Senate and House of Representatives only would be nominated. In such "federal primaries" no citizen was to be denied the right to vote on any ground "prohibited by the Fifteenth Amendment to the Federal Constitution." By this stratagem a Negro might be deprived of the right to participate in primaries for the nomination of candidates for state and local offices but permitted to vote in other primaries within reach of the federal constitutional guarantees. The apparent theory was that this federal right to vote did not include the right to participate in primaries for the nomination of state and local candidates. The statute was similar in method to 1943 acts of Texas and Tennessee authorizing separate voting on federal offices if and when Congress outlawed the poll tax. In 1947, after one trial in 1946, the Arkansas legislature repealed the split primary law. In practice the law had not kept Negroes from voting in the primaries to nominate state and local candidates.

Still another method to offset the effects of the *Allwright* decision was adopted in Alabama in 1946. In November, 1946, its voters approved a constitutional amendment embodying an "understanding" test. Prior to the adoption of the amendment, registration as a voter was conditional on ability to "read or write" any section of the United States Constitution. The amendment made it necessary to be able to read and write and explain the Constitution. Furthermore, the amendment added the requirement that registered voters be persons of "good character" who understand "the duties and obligations of good citizenship under a republican form of government." The amendment also removed the earlier exemption from the literacy test of persons owning 40 acres of land or $300 worth of real estate or personal property. The arbitrary power actually possessed by local registrars in applying requirements such as the foregoing permits discriminatory administration without effective remedy.

A special session of the Mississippi legislature in 1947 considered ways and means of avoiding the consequences of the *Allwright* case. Leaders of a move to follow the South Carolina precedent and leave nominations to the unregulated actions of party authorities were blocked by sober citizens sensitive to criticism from outside the state. Realistic leaders also saw that it was quite unnecessary to repeal primary laws to prevent Negro voting. "The newspapers of this state," the Jackson *Clarion-Ledger* asserted, "do not think much of the plan of a few professional politicians to put the state back under the old corrupt con-

vention system, under the guise of getting the 'nigger' out of politics."
The upshot of the discussion was the adoption of legislation that provided for exclusion from the primaries of persons not in accord with
the "principles" of the party. This act and related legislation governing registration procedures followed the Arkansas precedent.

The effects of the decision outlawing the white primary remain to
be seen. One immediate consequence was the adoption of expedients
to avoid the decision. The effort to maintain the "white primary" by
removing it completely from state regulation sooner or later will present
the federal courts with a neat issue of constitutional law. Another
consequence has been the strengthening of other methods of disfranchisement. Poll taxes, literacy tests, and other requirements contribute
to the maintenance of white supremacy.[28] When one line of defense
is breached, the opponents of Negro suffrage can withdraw to another.

Nevertheless, the *Allwright* decision was followed by a substantial
increase in Negro participation in Democratic primaries. Probably
from 75,000 to 100,000 Negroes voted in each of the states of Georgia
and Texas in the summer of 1946, and elsewhere more modest increases
in Negro participation occurred. Yet everywhere Negro participation
was not only low in comparison with voting among whites but also was
irregularly distributed geographically. It is doubtful that the removal
of white primary rules and other limitations on Negro suffrage would
in itself bring the vote to the Negro. Nonparticipation in primaries
and elections is the consequence of an elaborate system of social subordination that rests on many factors other than formal legislation
and party rule.[29] One of these factors is suggested in the appeal by
Senator Theodore Bilbo in June, 1946, to every "red-blooded Anglo-
Saxon man in Mississippi to resort to any means to keep hundreds of
Negroes from the polls in the July 2 primary." Negro suffrage tends to
become a reality when crevices appear in white solidarity and white
candidates appeal to the Negro vote. In recent years white candidates
in some southern states have felt it advantageous to recruit Negro support. The situation is illustrated by a February, 1947, resolution of the
North Little Rock (Arkansas) Democratic Central Committee: "It has
been brought to the attention of the Democratic Central Committee
that some of the candidates for the Democratic nomination for city
offices have attended Negro rallies, made speeches and solicited Ne-

[28] In Louisiana, in 1940, 702,545 persons were registered as voters, of whom 888
were Negroes.—A. L. Powell, *Government in Louisiana*, p. 35.

[29] It should be noted that in some communities local party machines find it convenient to encourage a limited degree of Negro voting. On this and other points
concerning Negro suffrage, see the monumental work by Gunnar Myrdal, *An American Dilemma* (New York: Harper, 1944), Vol. I, pt. 5.

groes to vote in the Democratic primary election." After denouncing
the practice the Committee resolved that if "any candidate for the
nomination continues such reprehensible action as herein mentioned
he will be requested to withdraw as a candidate in the Democratic
primary election."

3. WOMAN SUFFRAGE

The crusade for woman suffrage in its beginnings was closely related
to the abolition movement. Woman, because of her extensive legal
disabilities under the common law, was compared with the slave. And,
in truth, the legal rights of the married woman were closer to those of
the slave than to those of free white men. The movement for the
removal of legal disabilities of women and for the right of suffrage
gained headway prior to the Civil War and kept under way until the
adoption of the Nineteenth Amendment to the Constitution in 1920.
This long campaign produced an immense quantity of literature from
both the advocates and opponents of suffrage. Eventually the case for
suffrage came to rest on variations of the doctrine of equality and freedom. An early formulation by an advocate of woman suffrage before
the Massachusetts constitutional convention of 1853 was as follows: [30]

I maintain first that the people have a certain natural right, which under
special conditions of society manifests itself in the form of a right to vote. I
maintain secondly that the women of Massachusetts are people existing under
those special conditions of society. I maintain finally, and by necessary consequence, that the women of Massachusetts have a natural right to vote.

Rationalizations of opponents of woman suffrage. The rationalizations of the opponents of woman suffrage were of a much lower order,
and at this late date it is a bit difficult to see how they could have been
uttered with such sobriety and piety. A few extracts from a statement
by Senator Joseph E. Brown of Georgia in 1884 will illustrate the tone
of the argument. He argued that "the Creator intended that the
sphere of the males and females of our race should be different." Man,
he contended, was "qualified for the discharge of those duties that
require strength and ability to combat with the sterner realities and
difficulties of life." Among these duties were military service, road
construction, labor in the fields, and government. The management
of government, he thought, was "a laborious task, for which the male
sex is infinitely better fitted than the female sex." "On the other
hand," the argument continued, "the Creator has assigned to woman
very laborious and responsible duties, *by no means less important* than

[30] Quoted by K. H. Porter, *op. cit.,* p. 141.

those imposed upon the male sex, though entirely different in their character. In the family she is a *queen*. She alone is fitted for the discharge of the sacred trust of wife and the endearing relation of mother." And, the good Senator said, "When the husband returns home weary and worn in the discharge of the difficult and laborious tasks assigned him, he finds in the good wife solace and consolation which is nowhere else afforded." How could the wife, he asked, with all the "heavy duties of citizen, politician and officeholder resting upon her shoulders, . . . attend to the more sacred, delicate, refining trust . . . for which she is peculiarly fitted by nature? Who is to care for and train the children while she is absent in the discharge of these masculine duties?" The Senator could not bear to visualize the burden of public duties thrust upon woman. He felt that the adoption of woman suffrage [31]

. . . would be a great cruelty to a much larger number of the cultivated, refined, delicate and lovely women of this country who seek no such distinction, who would enjoy no such privilege, who would with woman-like delicacy shrink from the discharge of any such obligation, and who would sincerely regret that what they consider the folly of the State had imposed upon them any such unpleasant duties.

The Senator's argument embodied the stock objections to woman suffrage and it amounted to little more than saying, "Woman's place is in the home." But women were everywhere coming out of the home. Women were beginning to enter the professions; they were working in factories, shops, and stores; in the West they were laboring in the fields; they were making their way into colleges and universities; and some of them came to control great wealth. And as these changes progressed, the demand for woman suffrage became louder and more insistent.

What of the opposition of woman suffrage? Although much of it was simply inertia and resistance to change, a part was based on a belief that substantial interests would be endangered by the extension of the franchise to women. One of the official historians of the suffrage movement states that following 1896 the [32]

. . . Republican party was in complete control of the Government at Washington and was largely dominated by the great financial interests of the coun-

---

[31] The argument is quoted in full by Susan B. Anthony and Ida Husted Harper, *The History of Woman Suffrage* (New York: the Author, 1902), Vol. IV, pp. 93–100.

[32] Ida Husted Harper, *The History of Woman Suffrage* (New York: National American Woman Suffrage Association, 1922), Vol. V, p. xviii. The liquor interests estimated accurately the female attitude on the prohibition question. In every country in the world women, in so far as their votes can be separated from those of men, favor restrictions on the liquor traffic in higher degree than do men. See Herbert Tingsten, *Political Behavior* (London: P. S. King & Son, 1937).

try, and this was also practically the situation in the majority of the States. The campaign fund controlled the elections and the largest contributors to this fund were the corporations, which had secured immense power, and the liquor interests, which had become a dominant force in State and national politics, without regard to party. Both of these supreme influences were implacably opposed to suffrage for women; the corporations because it would vastly increase the votes of the working classes, the liquor interests because they were fully aware of the hostility of women to their business and everything connected with it.

When the suffrage leaders succeeded in persuading a state legislature to submit a suffrage amendment to a popular vote, she records,[33]

. . . It met the big campaign fund of the employers of labor and the thoroughly organized forces of the liquor interests, which appealed not only to the many lines of business connected with the traffic but to the people who for personal reasons favored the saloons and their collateral branches of gambling, wine rooms, etc. They were a valuable adjunct to both political parties. The suffragists met these powerful opponents without money and without votes.

For these and other reasons, the Woman's Christian Temperance Union devoted a considerable part of its efforts to the fight for woman suffrage.[34]

Woman suffrage in state and local elections. The earlier victories for woman suffrage were in connection with school elections. Kentucky in 1838 granted school suffrage to widows and unmarried women with property subject to taxation for school purposes; Kansas in 1861 was the first state to give the vote on school questions to all women. Michigan, Utah, Minnesota, Colorado, New Hampshire, and Massachusetts followed by 1880; by 1890 school suffrage had been gained by women in fourteen states and territories. Wyoming was the first state to grant women the privilege of voting in all elections. It did so as a territory in 1869, and when it was admitted to the Union in 1890 its constitution put men and women on the same plane regarding the suffrage. Three other western states soon followed in the steps of Wyoming: Colorado in 1893, and Utah and Idaho in 1896. After 1896 the suffrage movement began to encounter stiffer opposition, and no state was brought into the suffrage fold until the Progressive movement was fully under way. Here again western states were more receptive to the idea of woman suffrage. Equal suffrage was granted by Washington in 1910; California in 1911; Arizona, Kansas, and Oregon in 1912; and Montana and Nevada in 1914.

[33] Harper, *loc. cit.*
[34] See Mary Earhart, *Frances Willard* (Chicago: University of Chicago Press, 1944). Chap. 12.

Militant movement for nation-wide suffrage for women. The progress toward nation-wide suffrage through action by individual states
had been slow, and during the period from 1913 to 1919 a more militant
sort of tactic was adopted by one set of suffrage advocates. Influential
in the change of method was Mrs. O. H. P. Belmont, who had observed
the activities of the English suffragettes. Mrs. Belmont, a sympathetic
commentator writes, "was practically the only leader formerly associated with the conservative forces who had the courage to extricate
herself from the old routine propaganda and adventure into new paths.
She always approached the struggle for liberty in a wholesome revolutionary mood." [35] However, the leader of the fight in the field was
Alice Paul, an able and resourceful woman. The activities of these
and other courageous and persistent women in the leadership of the
militant campaign for the adoption of nation-wide woman suffrage
constitute one of the most instructive chapters in agitation in American
politics.

The militant suffragettes began with rather mild tactics in the 1914
congressional elections. By that time women had been enfranchised
in several western states, and their campaign was concentrated in those
states. The Democratic party, as the majority party, was to be held
responsible for the failure to propose a constitutional amendment
granting woman suffrage. All Democratic candidates for Congress in
the woman suffrage states were opposed regardless of their individual
stand on the suffrage question. Only twenty of forty-three Democratic candidates in the nine suffrage states won. "It was generally
conceded," Miss Stevens says in her excellent primer on agitation, "that
we had contributed to these defeats." [36] Congressmen and other politicians began to accord a more respectful ear to the suffrage advocates;
and when the national conventions of 1916 were held, both parties included planks advocating the grant of woman suffrage by state action.
These were not satisfactory to the militant suffrage leaders, who organized in the election of 1916 a protest vote against the Democratic party.
Undoubtedly the Democratic opposition to national suffrage cost it
many votes in the suffrage states.

When Congress and President Wilson temporized, new tactics were
adopted. Early in 1917 the women began to picket the White House
and won acres of newspaper space over the country. Day after day,
in both good weather and bad, the women carried their banners before
the White House. The routine was varied by the occasional march
of a delegation to present a petition to the President; sometimes the

[35] Doris Stevens, *Jailed for Freedom* (New York: Boni & Liveright, 1920), p. 32.
[36] *Ibid.*, p. 36.

delegations were received, sometimes not. The militant tactics of the Woman's party aroused criticism, and the government played into the hands of the suffragettes by adopting a policy of suppression. After six months of picketing, the demonstrators were arrested for "obstructing traffic." Others took their place; they were arrested; still others took their position on the picket line.

At their trials the women either stood mute or made speeches for liberty and woman suffrage; they refused to pay their fines on the ground that to do so would be an admission of guilt; they insisted on serving their terms in jail: "As long as the government and the representatives of the government prefer to send women to jail on petty and technical charges, we will go to jail. Persecution has always advanced the cause of justice." [37] Thus spoke one of the defendants. To the workhouse went the suffragettes. Martyrdom had the desired effect; a stream of telegrams in protest began to reach the President and Congressmen. Other women went onto the picket line and thence to jail. This tactic generated publicity for the cause and created a housing problem for the District of Columbia penal authorities. And the primitive facilities of the penal institutions were given nation-wide publicity.

A dramatic touch was added to the campaign by the prisoners' claim for the treatment customarily accorded political prisoners. In all civilized nations, the contention was, persons imprisoned for political offenses were accorded different treatment from that given the ordinary criminal. To reinforce their claim for this status, the prisoners went on a hunger strike. This tactic, Miss Stevens says, brought "the Administration face to face with a more acute embarrassment. They had to choose between more stubborn resistance and capitulation." The administration unwisely resorted to forced feeding of the prisoners, not pleasant for the prisoners and productive of horrendous newspaper stories. But women continued to come to Washington from all over the nation and added to the prison population. The trials furnished glorious opportunities for propaganda for the cause. An elderly woman was given a light sentence and the judge urged her to pay the fine rather than go to jail: "Your Honor, I have a nephew fighting for democracy in France. He is offering his life for his country. I should be ashamed if I did not join these brave women in their fight for democracy in America. I should be proud of the honor to die in prison for the liberty of American women."

In January, 1918, the House passed the proposed suffrage amendment, but the necessary two-thirds majority was lacking in the Senate. A

[37] *Ibid.,* p. 102.

great demonstration was arranged by the women before the White House. Additional arrests occurred; as each speaker rose to talk, she was dragged away to the waiting patrol wagons. Another hunger strike ensued and, finally, the prisoners were released. But additional demonstrations occurred; more women were sent to prison; and those released went aboard a "Prison Special" to tour the country and enlist support.

The President was finally won over to the cause of nation-wide woman suffrage. In 1919 the newly elected Republican House passed the proposed amendment, and Wilson turned enough pressure on the Democratic Senators to win a two-thirds majority. By August, 1920, the necessary three fourths of the state legislatures had ratified the amendment, which provided that "the right of citizens of the United States to vote shall not be denied or abridged by the United States or by any State on account of sex."

Militant tactics won the battle, but it need not be concluded that any sort of political agitation may be carried on solely by picketing the White House, going to jail, and indulging in hunger strikes. The women leading the movement had the backing of local associations and societies over the entire country, and the ordinary strategy of propaganda and pressure went on while the more spectacular acts were being committed in Washington. Moreover, many of the leaders of the movement were persons of high social and economic standing. One of the imprisoned women, for example, had a short time earlier been a guest at the White House. They were women who could not be thrown into jail without regard to the political consequences. Also, the ground had been prepared for the militant climax to the campaign by long years of agitation and education.

The movement also illustrates the problem of government in handling a determined agitation. Mrs. Belmont quoted Wilson who had written: "Governments have been very successful in parrying agitation, diverting it, in seeming to yield to it and then cheating it, tiring it out or evading it. But the end, whether it comes soon or late, is quite certain to be the same." Mrs. Belmont drew a parallel: "While the government has endeavored to parry, tire, divert, and cheat us of our goal, the country has risen in protest against this evasive policy of suppression until today the indomitable pickets with their historic legends stand triumphant before the nation." [38]

[38] Quoted, *ibid.*, p. 246. For a useful collection of essays on the suffrage movement, see National American Woman Suffrage Association, *Victory, How Woman Won It, A Centennial Symposium, 1840–1940* (New York: H. W. Wilson Company, 1940).

4. THE REGULATION OF THE SUFFRAGE

The definition of the suffrage remains a function of the states under the American constitutional system, subject to the limitations imposed by the Federal Constitution.[39]   The principal limitations are contained in the Fourteenth, Fifteenth, and Nineteenth Amendments. The equal-protection clause of the Fourteenth Amendment, as has been shown, has been construed to prohibit discrimination by a state along lines of color in the definition of the electorate. The Fifteenth Amendment specifically prohibits denial of the right to vote "by the United States or any state on account of race, color, or previous condition of servitude." The Nineteenth Amendment prohibits denial of the right to vote "on account of sex." Thus there is left to the states, then, a residual power to impose suffrage qualifications not in conflict with the Federal Constitution. The more important qualifications established by state constitution and law may now be examined.[40]

Poll taxes. The poll tax, a head tax as prerequisite for voting, remains in use in seven southern states. Under this type of suffrage requirement an annual tax of from $1.00 to $2.00 must be paid before one becomes eligible to vote. In some states liability for the poll tax is cumulative; that is, a person may not pay the poll tax for the election year only and gain the suffrage; he must either pay the tax annually for several years before the election or pay the delinquent poll taxes prior to the election. Frequently the tax must be paid at a time long prior to the election.

[39] For the election of Senators and Representatives, the Federal Constitution adopts state definitions of suffrage. Members of the House are to be chosen by "the people of the several states, and the electors in each state shall have the qualifications requisite for electors of the most numerous branch of the state legislature."—Art. I, Sec. 2. The same qualifications for voters for candidates for the Senate were embodied in the Seventeenth Amendment, by which Senators became popularly elective. Although, within the limits of the federal Constitution, the states define the qualifications of voters, the elector's right to vote in elections of presidential electors, Senators, and Representatives is derived from the federal Constitution and the federal government may take steps to protect him in the exercise of this right.

[40] The suffrage is not exercised by residents of the District of Columbia, who persistently seek amendment of the Constitution to permit them to vote in presidential and congressional elections. Congress could legally grant to the residents of the district the franchise to elect their local officials, but the district commissioners are appointed by the President; and Congress, in effect, acts as a city council for Washington. The lack of the franchise apparently does not seriously handicap the citizens of the district in their dealings with Congress. The local social and newspaper lobbies aid in bringing substantial appropriations from the national treasury for aid in financing the government of the district—appropriations of a size that expert investigators find difficult to justify.

As has already been indicated, an important motive in adoption of the poll tax in the southern states was the disfranchisement of the Negro, the presupposition being that the whites would pay and that the Negroes would not. In practice, however, the poll tax, together with the incidental requirements, such as payment long in advance of the election, has operated to disfranchise a substantial number of whites as well as blacks. It is charged, although the case is not well established, that the adoption of the poll tax in the southern states was connected with a desire to disfranchise the poorer whites as well as the blacks. The timing of the adoptions in most of the states gives a color of plausibility to this view, for the tax, save in Georgia, went into effect after other methods had made the blacks timid about approaching the polling places. The tax came about the time the Populists, the Farmers Alliance, and other political dissenters were threatening the ruling oligarchies. The dates of adoption were: Florida, 1889; Mississippi and Tennessee, 1890; South Carolina, 1895; Louisiana, 1898; North Carolina, 1900; Alabama and Virginia, 1901; Texas, 1902; and Arkansas, 1892. In Georgia the poll tax had been in existence since before the Civil War.

Dissatisfaction with the "tax on voting" has led to movements for its repeal both by state action and by federal action. North Carolina abandoned it in 1920, Louisiana in 1934, Florida in 1937, and Georgia in 1945. Tennessee repealed the poll tax in 1943, but the action was held by the State Supreme Court in violation of the state constitution.[41]

The matter has been agitated in other states and unsuccessful attacks have been made on the constitutionality of the tax as applied to voting in federal elections.[42] Poll-tax opponents have not been content with seeking state action. They have advocated federal legislation making the poll tax illegal as a requisite for voting in presidential and congressional elections. The movement for repeal became active in 1940 following the political revitalization of depressed groups in the South as a consequence of New Deal policies. Its leadership has been primarily in the hands of organizations opposed to conservative Bourbon control of the Democratic party in the South, such as the Southern Conference for Human Welfare, the American Federation of Labor, the Congress of Industrial Organizations, the National Lawyers Guild, Labor's Non-Partisan League, the National Association for the Ad-

[41] *Biggs* v. *Beeler,* 173 S.W. 2d 144 (1943). The opinion in this case includes some of the most extraordinary logic in the annals of American jurisprudence. On the movement for repeal in Tennessee, see Jennings Perry, *Democracy Begins at Home* (Philadelphia: Lippincott, 1944).

[42] *Breedlove* v. *Suttles,* 302 U.S. 277 (1937); *Pirtle* v. *Brown,* 118 F. 2d 218 (1941).

vancement of Colored People, and the Workers Alliance. The contention is that the poll tax operates to disfranchise the lower economic classes, both colored and white.

The attainment of positions of great power in Congress by reactionary Senators and Representatives chosen through the influence of the "courthouse crowds" in states and districts with low electoral participation spurs the advocates of national action. It is argued: "If some sections send Representatives to the national Congress who feel no responsibility toward the submerged third, because this third may neither reward nor punish them at the next election, it will naturally become very difficult to put through the Congress Federal legislation for the benefit of these groups." Further, before Congress "can put on the statute books and retain there legislation protecting the rights of labor, the small business man, the farmer, the different racial groups, the unemployed, our young people, and our aged, the poll tax must be done away with in those States where it now exists. The politician who need not take these groups into account on election day need pay no attention to their cries of distress during a session of the Congress." [43]

Senators and Representatives from poll-tax states, as beneficiaries of the system, have rebutted these arguments. Although unable to check legislation in the House, they have invoked the right of filibuster to prevent Senate action.[44] Advocates have been handicapped by doubts about the constitutionality of federal legislative action, and proposals for constitutional amendment to outlaw poll taxes have been put forward as an alternative approach.[45]

The poll tax probably is blamed unduly, yet it constitutes one element in the political sickness of the South. The tax undoubtedly contributes to the low popular participation in southern primaries and elections. Figure 19 shows the trend in total participation in presidential elections in Tennessee, a poll-tax state, and Kentucky, a nontax state, from 1872 to 1940. Note that over the entire period more than 50 per cent of the potential electorate in Kentucky has voted, while

---

[43] Quotations are from a speech by the late Representative Lee E. Geyer, *Congressional Record* (daily edition), March 19, 1940, pp. 1794–1795. See also Frank P. Graham, *et al*, *The Poll Tax* (Washington: American Council on Public Affairs, 1940).

[44] When the House passed an anti-poll tax bill in 1945, only 7.8 per cent of the Democrats from the poll-tax states supported it. Of the Democrats from other states, 80.8 per cent favored the bill as did 93.4 per cent of all Republicans.

[45] On the constitutional issues, see L. B. Boudin, "State Poll Taxes and the Federal Constitution," *Virginia Law Review*, 28 (1941), pp. 1–25; R. A. Hogenson, "Anti-Poll Tax Legislation and the Federal Constitution," *George Washington Law Review*, 11 (1942–43), pp. 73–79.

in Tennessee participation rapidly moved below that level after the introduction of the poll tax.[46]

The elimination of the poll tax in Florida, Louisiana, and North Carolina was followed by substantial increases in popular participation. The significance of the level of participation comes from the fact that generally the lower the participation the simpler becomes machine and oligarchical control. Exclusion of disadvantaged classes from the franchise introduces a definite bias into the attitudes of elective officials.

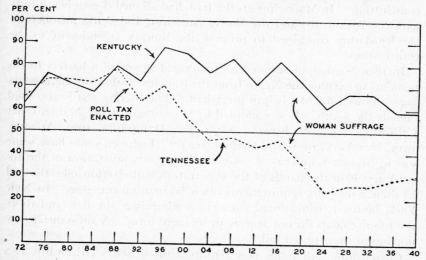

Figure 19. Percentage Participation of Population of Voting Age in Presidential Elections in Tennessee (a Poll-tax State) and Kentucky (a Nonpoll-tax State), 1872–1940

It should not be supposed, however, that complete repeal of the tax would work an immediate revolution in southern politics. Classes long habituated to nonparticipation in political life would require time to become assimilated into political life. Nor is it to be presumed that repeal of the poll tax would immediately bring Negro suffrage. The poll tax is only one element in an extremely complex set of factors conditioning the peculiar structure of political power in the South.[47]

[46] The chart is modeled after one presented by Perry, *op. cit.*, p. 215. However, computations were made independently for this chart, and the results differed slightly from those cited by Perry.

[47] On the poll tax, see Virginius Dabney, "Poll Tax Stirs Revolt," *National Municipal Review*, 31 (1942), pp. 485–491; Stetson Kennedy, "3.2 Democracy in the South," *Survey Graphic*, 33 (1944), pp. 239–241; D. S. Strong, "The Poll Tax: The Case of Texas," *American Political Science Review*, 38 (1944), pp. 693–709; W. M. Brewer, "The Poll Tax and Poll Taxers," *Journal of Negro History*, 29 (1944), pp. 260–299;

Literacy tests. Following the gradual erasure of property qualifications for voting, the advocates of a narrow suffrage hit upon the literacy test as a means for the restriction of the size of the electorate. Connecticut and Massachusetts in 1855 and 1857 were the first states to adopt a literacy test. In both states the older groups were challenged in their hegemony by the wave of incoming immigration. In Connecticut the Know-Nothing representatives in the legislature brought about the submission of the literacy amendment to the state constitution. In Massachusetts the Irish had aligned themselves solidly with the Democrats, and the Native American and Whig members of the legislature combined to propose the literacy amendment to the constitution.

In 1890 Mississippi adopted a literacy test as one of a battery of expedients to exclude the Negro from the franchise; other southern states soon followed the Mississippi precedent. The literacy test is also used outside the South. It was adopted by Wyoming in 1889; Maine, 1892; California, 1894; Washington, 1896; New Hampshire, 1902; Arizona, 1913; New York, 1921; and Oregon, 1924.[48] Eighteen states have some sort of literacy requirement. Generally the administration of the literacy test is in the hands of the registration and election officials, and in their hands the requirements often become meaningless. In New York, however, educational authorities administer the test, and there the requirements do not appear to be mere form. A substantial proportion of those tested fail.[49]

Citizenship. All states now require United States citizenship as a prerequisite to the exercise of the suffrage. "For the first time in over a hundred years, a national election was held in 1928 in which no alien in any state had the right to cast a vote for a candidate for any office—nation, state or local."[50] During the nineteenth century at least twenty-two states and territories gave to aliens the right to vote, pro-

---

Perry, *op. cit.;* Eleanor Bontecou, *The Poll Tax* (Washington: American Association of University Women, 1942); Hearings on S. 1280, Subcommittee of Senate Judiciary Committee, 77th Cong. 2d sess. (1942).

[48] A. W. Bromage, "Literacy and the Electorate," *American Political Science Review,* 24 (1930), pp. 946–962. For a convenient tabulation of the literacy requirements, see H. I. Branse, "Educational Qualifications for Voting," *Monthly Review,* Immigration and Naturalization Service, 2 (1945), pp. 102–103.

[49] Professor Crawford reports that the percentages of those taking the test who failed have been: 1923, 21.4 per cent; 1924, 16.1 per cent; 1925, 17.8 per cent; 1926, 19.6 per cent; 1927, 20.66 per cent; 1928, 10.09 per cent; 1929, 10.84 per cent.—"Operation of the Literacy Test for Voters in New York," *American Political Science Review,* 25 (1931), pp. 342–345. In the year ending June 30, 1942, 57,295 persons applied for literacy certificates; 4,288 failed to pass the test.

[50] L. E. Aylsworth, "The Passing of Alien Suffrage," *American Political Science Review,* 25 (1931), pp. 114–116.

vided, of course, that they met other requirements, such as that of residence. Often it was required that aliens exercising the suffrage should have taken the first steps in the naturalization procedure. About 1875 a trend toward the elimination of alien suffrage began. By 1900 only eleven states continued to grant the right; by 1925 the privilege remained only in Arkansas. By a judicial decision in that state in 1926 a constitutional amendment, voted on in 1920, but theretofore held inoperative, was declared effective and thereby wiped out the last voting privilege of aliens.

Other qualifications and disqualifications. The constitution and laws of each state usually require certain other qualifications for the exercise of the suffrage; or they define the suffrage negatively by declaring persons disqualified under certain specific conditions. All states, except Georgia, require that a person be twenty-one years of age to exercise the suffrage. In 1943 Georgia, under the leadership of Governor Ellis Arnall, amended its constitution to lower the voting age to eighteen. The campaign slogan was, "Fight at 18, Vote at 18." Opponents of the measure derided it as a scheme contrived by long-haired northern professors and Communists. Former Governor Talmadge had chivalrous concern for young women whom ward heelers would have a legal right to approach, "without an introduction," to seek their votes. Thirty other legislatures in 1943 had before them proposals to reduce the voting age.[51] The Democratic party in South Carolina in 1946 adopted the eighteen-year eligibility rule for participation in its primaries. In addition to the age requirement, every state requires a minimum period of residence in the state as a voting qualification; most states also have a supplemental requirement of a minimum period of residence in the county and voting district. In Alabama, for example, a person must have resided two years in the state, one year in the county, and three months in the voting district. Michigan, Oregon, Idaho, Indiana, and certain other states require only six months residence in the state. Mississippi requires two years residence in the state and one year in the voting district, but reduces the latter period to six months for ministers of the gospel.

The list of disqualifying factors varies from state to state. Most states exclude the insane, idiots, and incompetents from the suffrage. In a few states "immoral" persons are not entitled to vote; in some states inmates of prisons and of other public institutions are excluded from the suffrage. A similar end is achieved in other states that deny

---

[51] Ellis Arnall, "Admitting Youth to Citizenship." *State Government,* 16 (1943), pp. 203–204; F. L. Burdette, "Lowering the Voting Age in Georgia," *South Atlantic Quarterly,* 44 (1945), pp. 300–307.

the suffrage to persons convicted of certain crimes. The crimes that disqualify for voting in most states are felonies and election bribery. In some states disqualification follows conviction for treason, bigamy, defalcation, perjury, larceny, forgery, arson, embezzlement, and other acts. In South Carolina, for example, an imposing list of felonies and misdemeanors operates to wipe out the right to vote. It includes burglary, obtaining money or goods under false pretenses, robbery, adultery, wife beating, housebreaking, receiving stolen goods, breach of trust with fraudulent intent, fornication, sodomy, incest, assault with intent to ravish, miscegenation, and crimes against the election laws.[52]

5. SUFFRAGE AND POLITICAL POWER

The broadening of the suffrage over the centuries has been associated with a radical change in the nature and distribution of political power. The discussion and decision of matters of state formerly rested with a comparatively small proportion of the population, an aristocracy, oligarchy, or ruling class. Leadership and, perhaps, it might be said the power of decision continue to be vested in a comparatively small proportion of the population. Yet the conditions of exercise of power have radically changed. The wishes and probable actions of a vast number of people at the polls must be taken into consideration in the exercise of public power. Suffrage is the basis for the welfare state.

Yet there is an odd feature about the expansion of the suffrage that needs some reflection by those seeking to comprehend the nature of political power. Disfranchised groups have gained the right to vote without being able to exert the power of the suffrage. If political power rested on the vote alone, groups enjoying that right could merely have refused to share it with others. But the disfranchised have had power enough to demand and to obtain the vote. On the other hand, a group such as the Negroes, who received the legal right to vote through the gift of others, has not been powerful enough to make the legal right effective in the southern states.

Obviously it is difficult to conclude that the suffrage is the sole cause either of the streams of legislation enacted for the benefit of formerly disfranchised classes or of the power enjoyed by these groups. Movements for the broadening of the suffrage have ordinarily gone hand-in-hand with movements for substantive legislation. Before 1850 agitators

[52] A table showing voting qualifications in all the states appears in *Book of the States, 1945–46* (Chicago: Council of State Governments, 1945), p. 88. On the special problem of Indian suffrage, see N. D. Houghton, " 'Wards of the United States'— Arizona Applications, A Study of the Legal Status of Indians" (University of Arizona Bulletin, Social Science Bulletin No. 14, 1945).

for legislation for the benefit of the working man often also fought for the repeal of property and taxpaying qualifications on voting. The woman suffragists were not interested in the suffrage alone. They were also concerned with the removal of the legal disabilities of women and with such matters as the regulation of the liquor traffic and the promotion of general civic decency. Once a group has gained the suffrage it is in a more powerful position to promote and to protect its cause, but it first must gain, without the ballot, enough power to win the vote.

The effects of the various extensions of the suffrage in the United States have not been adequately analyzed. The early extensions of the suffrage reflected, of course, the profound effects of the democratic revolution. The extension of the vote to Negroes has had limited effects in the South. Yet in those southern communities in which Negroes vote, even in small numbers, they are less discriminated against than in communities where they do not exercise the franchise. It is reported, for example, that in Memphis, where Negroes are a cog in the Crump machine, fewer Negroes are killed by the police than in other southern cities. The vote also brings with it better municipal facilities, such as playgrounds, schools, and streets for Negro neighborhoods.[53] Nobody has tackled the problem of measuring the consequences of woman suffrage. The material question is how women differ from men in their voting behavior. The difference is apparently not great, although participation by women declines with economic status more rapidly than among men. This suggests that perhaps woman suffrage will operate as a disadvantage to labor until the level of female participation in voting becomes comparable with men all the way along the economic scale.

[53] Myrdal, *op. cit.*, Vol. I, chap. 22.

Chapter 17

REGISTRATION, ELECTIONS, BALLOTS

ONCE it is determined that persons possessing specified qualifications shall be entitled to participate in elections, it is necessary to establish machinery and procedures to effectuate that general policy. Although the machinery of elections may be said to be a matter of administrative detail, it is a singularly important administrative detail. All might readily agree that the implementation of the principle of elections requires only simple procedures to permit the qualified electors to express their choice with the greatest convenience and to assure an honest count of the ballots. Yet the field of election procedures contains numerous examples of bitterly disputed issues of form, contested because different factions believed one procedure to favor or to handicap them in the outcome of the voting. The party organization, for example, may desire to include in the election laws procedures making it difficult to become a registered voter, on the assumption that organization voters will be guided through the administrative maze, whereas independent voters will be intimidated by it and hence fail to register.

A review of the administration of election laws furnishes opportunity to note some of the techniques of attaining political power by fraud. Fraud and trickery do not occur solely in democratic regimes, but the practice of voting furnishes an occasion for fraud and trickery peculiar to democracy. It is strange that in the United States, where the principle of popular rule is so universally acclaimed, so little has been done 'to assure a faithful reflection of popular wishes in the election results. The leading authority on elections observed in 1929: "It is highly significant that little progress has been made in the technique of elections in this country. Probably no other phase of public administration is so badly managed. Our elections have been marked by irregularities, slipshod work, antiquated procedure, obsolete records, inaccuracies, and many varieties of downright fraud." [1] Despite improvements

[1] J. P. Harris, *Registration of Voters in the United States* (Washington: Brookings 1929), p. 3.

made in many jurisdictions since 1929, the conclusion would not have to be changed materially today.

1. REGISTRATION SYSTEMS

The function of a registration system is the preparation of a list of names of persons who meet the suffrage requirements of the jurisdiction. On election day the officials in charge of voting permit those persons to vote whose right to do so has been established through the registration procedure. Preferably the registration system should include procedures whereby those persons applying for ballots at the polls may establish that they are the same persons whose names are listed by the registration.

The development of registration systems furnishes an illuminating illustration of the factors underlying administrative procedures and what is often called red tape. Originally in small rural communities individuals presenting themselves at the polls were nearly always well known to the election officials, to the watchers at the polls, and to their neighbors. The officials at the polls knew of their own knowledge whether the person requesting a ballot met the suffrage requirements: whether he had lived in the county and the precinct the prescribed length of time; whether he met the citizenship requirement; whether he was of the necessary age. The formality of establishing the possession of the suffrage qualifications was simple enough to be cared for on election day, if indeed, any attention was given to the matter at all. With the development of urban society and the substitution of secondary or impersonal relationships for the primary group relationships of the rural community, more formal procedures became necessary to identify those entitled to vote.

In urban communities this impersonality of relationships greatly facilitates certain types of election-day frauds, such as the colonization of voters, personation, and the use of gangs of repeaters in different polling places scattered over the city. It is not to be inferred that voting frauds have been, or are, limited to urban communities; conditions in urban communities merely facilitate types of frauds such as those mentioned which involve voting by legally unqualified persons. Consequently, with the broadening of the franchise and the growth of cities, a trend toward the adoption of registration laws, particularly in the post-Civil War period, became apparent. Formalized procedures came into use under which individuals might establish in advance of the election those facts, such as residence, age, citizenship, and other matters, necessary to qualify them to vote. The inclusion of a name on the resulting list of registrants constitutes evidence on election day that the person named is entitled to participate in the election. Thus, administrative formalities arise to replace the common knowledge, and the group discipline arising therefrom, of the smaller community. The influence of these factors is evident in many registration laws that apply only to the larger communities or have more rigorous requirements for the larger cities of the state.[2]

Registration systems of a variety of types are used in the states to prepare the voting lists. Registration may be permanent or periodic; that is, an elector may be enrolled on the lists permanently or there may be a complete reregistration at intervals. Registration may be personal or nonpersonal; that is, for registration, personal application by the elector may be required or the authorities may prepare a list from their own knowledge or from sources of information at their disposal. Registration may be compulsory or noncompulsory; that is, either a person's name must be on the list to qualify him to vote, or he may be permitted on election day to establish by appropriate evidence that he possesses the voting qualifications if his name is not on the list.[3]

Periodic and permanent registration. The chief controversy over registration in the United States in recent years has turned on the issue of periodic versus permanent registration. The older form of periodic registration is being gradually displaced by permanent registration in one form or another. In 1939, according to Professor Weeks, thirty-six states used some form of permanent registration either on a state-wide basis or in designated cities or counties. Under periodic registration completely new lists of voters are prepared annually, biennially, or quadrennially. The customary procedure provides for the decentralized preparation of the lists by registration boards sitting usually at the polling place in each precinct. During specified days the registration boards sit and receive the requests of individuals for the inclusion of their names on the lists. Such is the more general practice under systems of periodic registration, but not all such systems fit into this

---

[2] Urban political leaders at times attribute the greater stringency of laws applying to cities to a rural desire to reduce the urban vote. If city voters are required to go to the polls once to register and again to vote and rural people do not have to make a special trip to the polls to register, the contention is that it is much more difficult to obtain a high popular participation in voting in the cities.

[3] The standard treatise on registration is J. P. Harris, *op. cit.* Statutory changes since 1929 have been collated and analyzed by O. Douglas Weeks, "Permanent Registration of Voters in the United States," *Temple University Law Quarterly,* 14 (1939), pp. 1–15. For a digest of state constitutional and statutory provisions, see J. B. Johnson and I. J. Lewis, *Registration for Voting in the United States* (Chicago: Council of State Governments, August, 1946). A table showing the prevailing registration systems in each state appears in *Book of the States, 1945–46,* p. 89.

pattern. Louisiana, for example, requires a quadrennial registration of all voters, but the voter may register at any time at a central place in each parish rather than only on certain days at the polling places.[4]

Underlying the system of periodic registration is the assumption that it will produce clean lists. Those who have died since the last registration, those who have moved from the precinct, and others disqualified in other ways will not be included on the new lists. This *a priori* assumption appears to be unsupported by experience. Certain cities notorious for registration and election frauds employ periodic registration; the decentralized and more or less irresponsible conduct of the registration in the polling places throughout the city facilitates the padding of the lists. Bipartisan arrangements between registration officials may result in the falsification of the lists; every name of a nonexistent person on the registration lists permits personation under that name on election day. Even if the registration officials are honest, the conditions of urban society are such that in many precincts registration officials have no more personal knowledge of the residence and identity of those applying for registration than the election officials have of those applying for ballots on election day.

As an indication of the degree of fradulent registration possible under a system of periodic registration, experience in Chicago may be cited. A citizens' committee in 1934 sent return postal cards to about 501,000 voters. The return on the cards indicated that in 970 precincts 20.2 per cent of the names on the lists were either fraudulent or were those of persons who had moved and lost the right to vote in the precinct in which they were listed. The entire experiment furnished the basis for an estimate, by the sampling method, that 5.4 per cent of the total registration was fraudulent or of persons not eligible to vote from the addresses given.[5]

Permanent registration involves a single appearance by the applicant for registration before the registration officials. His name remains on the register until he changes his residence or becomes otherwise disqualified. The absence of periodic reregistration requires the substitution of other means to purge the rolls of disqualified persons. In the newer permanent systems a continuous revision of the lists occurs. A central staff in the city or county is charged with the duty of removing from the records the names of disqualified persons. Various sources of information are used. The death certificates filed with the vital

---

[4] See Alden L. Powell, *Registration of Voters in Louisiana* (Baton Rouge: Louisiana State University, Bureau of Government Research, 1940); also his *Government in Louisiana* (Baton Rouge, 1944), chap. 4.

[5] *Chicago Daily News*, April 7, 1934.

statistics unit of the health department may be examined to obtain
the names of electors who have died. Court records may be examined at intervals to obtain the names of persons adjudged insane or
convicted of crimes that disqualify them from voting. The records
of telephone, gas, and power companies may be examined to check on
removals, and from such information in some jurisdictions the voter's
card is shifted routinely in the central office to the records of the precinct
of his new residence. Transfer and moving companies sometimes make
their records available. In areas where transiency is high or fraudulent
registration is suspected, a house-to-house canvass may be conducted to
check the accuracy of the lists. In a few cities a thorough canvass of the
entire city is made by the police department. In some jurisdictions
registrations are canceled because of failure to vote in a specified number of elections. The central staff in charge of the revision of the registration records is usually also vested with the responsibility of accepting the applications of new electors for registration. Except for a short
interval prior to elections the acceptance of new registrations is continuous rather than restricted to a few days during the year as under the
periodic system.

On the issue of fraudulent registration (and hence potential fradulent
voting) neither system is foolproof. The evidence certainly indicates
that the system of periodic registration does not ensure accurate lists
and that the system of permanent registration creates an administrative
situation in which it is possible to bring about less fraud in registration
if there is a will to do so. The decentralized preparation of the rolls
by temporary employees (generally recruited because of their loyalty
to the party organization) characteristic of periodic registration results
in administrative machinery impossible of supervision by the city or
county registration authorities. Precinct registration officials are usually not disinterested individuals; their ward organization is often
eager to have as many imaginary names as possible on the lists in order
to lay the basis for fraudulent voting in the election itself. With a
small permanent staff in charge of the continuous revision of the permanent lists it is more nearly possible through supervision to avoid
these influences. Furthermore, it is possible in a central office to have
access to and to use more trustworthy evidence pertaining to residence,
removal, or loss of voting privilege than is accessible to the precinct
officials. It does not follow, to be sure, that the list under permanent
registration will be freer of the names of persons unqualified to vote.
Yet if the political and administrative will is present, it is more feasible
to maintain clean lists under permanent registration than under the

periodic system. If that will is absent, fraud and error may be quite as prevalent under permanent registration as under other systems. In Philadelphia, for example, the percentage of error under permanent registration seems to have been quite as high as under periodic registration elsewhere.[6]

From the standpoint of cost, permanent registration appears, on the basis of available evidence, to be preferable to periodic registration. Once a system of permanent registration is installed, the principal items of cost are for the support of a small central staff to accept new registrations and to revise the records and for special canvasses. In periodic registration, on the other hand, personnel to accept registrations in every precinct from the entire electorate is necessary, and an entirely new set of records must be purchased at each registration.[7] The tendency is that jurisdictions with permanent registration make use of more modern record keeping and filing systems than is customary under periodic registration.[8] In Table 18 the average annual cost per registered voter under different registration systems is indicated.

TABLE 18

Average Annual Cost of Registration in Cities with Periodic and Permanent Registration [a]

Type of system	Average annual cost per registered voter (in cents)
Periodic:	
Annual (six cities)	72.2
Biennial (two cities)	60.7
Quadrennial (four cities)	55.3
Permanent (six cities)	29.8

[a] Harris, *Registration of Voters in the United States*, p. 105.

[6] See J. P. Horlacher, "The Administration of Permanent Registration in Philadelphia," *American Political Science Review*, 37 (1943), pp. 829–837.

[7] It is not a matter for astonishment that in California, and probably other states also, the printers' lobby actively opposed the adoption of permanent registration. See J. P. Harris, "The Progress of Permanent Registration," *American Political Science Review*, 24 (1930), pp. 963–966.

[8] Recently in Miami, Florida, the punch card was adapted for permanent registration records. The relevant data about the applicant for registration are typed on the face of a punch card that is signed by the elector. "Before each election the cards are mechanically sorted by precincts into alphabetical order. A machine then prints directly from these cards a list of the qualified voters in each precinct. The lists are posted prior to each election so that the electors may see if they are qualified to vote and to check the validity of addresses given by persons living or claiming to live in the precinct." The cards are locked in trays before being sent to the precinct election officials for use on election day. After the cards are returned, the

Personal and nonpersonal registration. Registration may be personal or nonpersonal. The systems that have been described under which the elector must make personal application to have his name placed on the registration list are personal systems. Under a nonpersonal system the lists are prepared by official agencies from information at their disposal. In the United States the nonpersonal scheme generally involves an annual revision by the precinct registration board, which meets to revise the list of the prior year and to add names of new electors in the precinct. The list is usually then posted for the information of the electors of the precinct, and a second meeting of the board is held to permit the appearance of those persons whose names have been omitted and to hear challenges against names incorrectly included in the list. In the United States this form of registration is limited in the main to rural or semirural states or to the rural parts of states, since in only the smaller communities do the precinct registration officials possess the necessary knowledge of the neighborhood to maintain the lists.[9]

In European countries greater reliance on nonpersonal registration prevails. In Great Britain the town clerks send out canvassers periodically to check the lists against the persons actually living in the area in order to add new names and to strike off the names of those no longer eligible to vote. On the Continent the existence of elaborate, continual censuses of the population makes it possible to keep the registration records up to date without the necessity of personal application for registration by the electors.[10]

Compulsory and noncompulsory registration. The classification of registration systems into compulsory and noncompulsory categories is determined by whether there is a compulsory requirement that a person's name be on the list before he is permitted to vote. Under the noncompulsory system it is possible for a voter to be "sworn in" at the polls; that is, he makes an appropriate affidavit that he meets the suffrage requirements and is supported in this statement by witnesses. The noncompulsory system exists primarily as a concession to those groups that originally opposed any registration. The possibility of "swearing in" voters creates a loophole for fraud; the provision is generally used to the greatest extent in those precincts where fraudulent voting is most

cards of those individuals who voted are punched to indicate that fact. This system makes it possible to eliminate mechanically the cards of those persons whose names are removed from the rolls for failure to vote at least once every four years in keeping with the local requirements.—*Public Management,* February, 1941, pp. 52–53.

[9] See Harris, *op. cit.,* pp. 101–102.

[10] H. F. Gosnell, *Why Europe Votes* (Chicago: University of Chicago Press, 1930), p. 185.

probable. To round out the discussion, it should be noted that two states have no formal systems of registration. In Texas and Arkansas poll books are prepared from the lists of those who have paid poll taxes or established their eligibility to vote under provisions of law exempting them from payment of the poll tax. These arrangements constitute, in effect, periodic systems of registration.

The effects of different registration systems on the fortunes of the various contenders for power have not been carefully examined. Party organizations in power have almost uniformly opposed the introduction of permanent registration, which has been advocated by such organizations as the National Municipal League and the League of Women Voters.[11] Party opposition cannot be attributed to refined measurement of the probable effect on the vote of a particular registration system; it has been due, in the main, to the fact that permanent registration eliminates the not inconsiderable petty patronage available through the employment of registration officials in each precinct under the periodic system. It is clear, of course, that any administrative obstacle to voting reduces the total participation; Professor Harris estimates that the number of registered voters is about 15 per cent higher in cities with permanent registration than in cities with annual registration. It is also fairly clear that these obstacles to voting operate in different ways in different socio-economic classes. It is not improbable that the introduction of a well-administered system of permanent registration into a northern city would increase slightly the Democratic percentage of the total presidential vote, under the type of conditions prevailing from 1932 to 1944. In elections in which no perceptible cleavage along socio-economic class lines occurs, the increase in voting probable with the simplifications of administrative requirements might have no effect on the division of voters.

2. ELECTIONS

In the United States, state and local governments conduct elections, even for federal elective officials. And within the states, elections, although governed by state legislation, are generally administered by local governmental agencies, with little or no supervision by state agencies.[12] In the consideration of election administration, therefore, at-

---

11 *A Model Registration System,* prepared by a committee of the National Municipal League, has furnished a model for use in legislation in many states. This report was published as a supplement to the *National Municipal Review,* vol. 13 (1927).

12 The only comprehensive treatment of election is by J. P. Harris, *Election Administration in the United States* (Washington: Brookings, 1934).

tention must be concentrated on counties, cities, or on whatever unit of local government is responsible for the conduct of balloting.[18]

Election organization. The task of conducting an election involves the preparation of ballots; the designation of polling places; the making of arrangements for quarters for the polls; the selection, instruction, and supervision of precinct officials to conduct the election; the preparation and distribution to the polling places of booths, ballots, voting machines, and supplies necessary for election day; the identification of voters as they come to the polls; the presentation of ballots to the voters; and the counting of the ballots after the voting. The conduct of elections is, then, a large but relatively simple administrative task.

Generally a special board of elections commissioners performs this job in the more populous cities and counties. In other places the county board may be the chief local election authority; or the city clerk or the county clerk may be the responsible agency. It is the duty of the central county or city election authority to select precinct officials, to procure and distribute election equipment and supplies to the precinct polling places, to make arrangements for polling places, and to supervise, generally ineffectively, the work of the precinct election officials. The control of the city or county election machinery is a prize eagerly sought by the party organizations, for the control permits the organization to distribute considerable petty patronage and may be used on occasion to prevent embarrassing inquiries into the honesty of the conduct of elections.

The city or county is divided into precincts of varying size but they usually include a few hundred voters. The polling place in each precinct is manned on election day by a group of precinct officials. Their titles, which vary from jurisdiction to jurisdiction, may be "judge of elections," "election inspector," or "clerk." The precinct election officials determine whether persons presenting themselves at the polling place are entitled to vote, give such persons ballots or access to the vot-

---

[18] Federal power is exerted in elections through the Corrupt Practices Act and the Hatch Act. Occasionally fraud in elections of federal officials is obliquely reached through prosecution under a section of the Federal Criminal Code punishing conspiracy to deprive persons of rights guaranteed by the Constitution. The Criminal Law Council of the American Bar Association has proposed the adoption of a "Federal Elections Act" specifically making federal crimes of certain acts by officers of elections in which presidential electors, Senators, and Representatives are chosen or nominated. The acts punishable would include fraudulent acts in the conduct of elections. The proposed act would also reach coercion, intimidation, bribery, personation, and other like acts committed by any person. From 1870 to 1894 somewhat broader federal legislation relating to elections was in effect. For the text of the Criminal Law Council proposal, see *Congressional Record* (daily edition), June 1, 1943, pp. A2900–A2903.

ing machine, count the ballots, and report the results of the precinct
voting to the central election authority.

In form, the precinct officials are appointed by the central election
commission or agency; but in most jurisdictions, they are, in fact, named
by the party organizations. The law usually prescribes that the precinct officials shall be divided between the two major parties; in practice,
the precinct captain of each party has the privilege of naming the election officials to which his party is entitled in his precinct. These
election-day jobs are a part of the patronage at the disposal of the precinct captain, and they are used by him to maintain the loyalty of his
followers in the precinct. It hardly needs to be observed that the
method of appointing precinct officials paves the way for fraud, results
in the selection of many election officials who do not possess rudimentary clerical skill, and brings generally inefficient conduct of an election.
Party control of election machinery is probably most significant in
direct primaries. In primaries the incentive toward fraud is probably
at its peak, and the internal organization of precinct election boards
furnishes no check against it.[14]

In the conduct of the work at the polling place, the first step is the
identification of the person who applies for a ballot. In small communities often no formal procedure of identification is followed because the election officials are personally acquainted with the voter.
Comparison of the voter's signature with his earlier signature in his application for registration furnishes a means of identification in those
jurisdictions with this type of registration practice. Some registration
systems include in the records a description of the voter: height, color
of eyes, color of hair, and the like. Such descriptions are, of course,
practically worthless as a means of identification. Generally, also, the
party watchers may challenge the right of a person to vote; and, if a
challenge is made, various sorts of evidence may be offered to establish
the identity of the would-be voter.

As votes are cast, a list is prepared of those who have voted. The
watchers of the parties also check off on their lists the names of those
who have voted; as the day wears on, they dispatch runners to bring in
the laggards. An incidental but important feature of the voting in

---

[14] In New York City the Board of Elections is required to administer a qualifying
examination to election officials nominated by the party organization. The test, *The
New York Times* observed, "is divested of all nervous strain and everybody concerned
emerges with a glow of righteous satisfaction." This happy state of affairs was
brought about by "printing the questions on one side of the examination sheet and
the corresponding answers on the reverse side. In order to avoid any confusion whatever a notation in bold face type on each page directs attention to the answers." *The
New York Times*, December 12, 1940.

machine-controlled precincts is the general provision for assistance to the voter in making his ballot. Persons incapable of marking the ballot may usually request assistance in this task; the reasons justifying a request for assistance vary from state to state, but they include illiteracy (in those states without a literacy test), blindness, and other physical infirmities. Under this provision the secrecy of the ballot may be destroyed and bargains between party workers and voters may be carried out.

An aspect of election administration of some importance is the practice of making provision for those persons to vote who are unable to appear at the polling place on election day. Absentee-voting laws originated during the Civil War to permit voting by persons serving in the military forces, but the extension of the absentee-voting privilege to civilians occurred principally after 1900. By 1942 all states except Kentucky, Mississippi, New Mexico, Pennsylvania, Maryland, and New Jersey had adopted absentee-voting legislation for the benefit of civilians.[15] In 1936, according to an estimate by Paul G. Steinbicker, about 2 per cent of the votes cast in the presidential election were absentee votes.[16]

Civilian absent voting. State laws on the subject of absent voting by civilians are characterized by almost infinite variation. One point of difference regards the geographical limits on absentee voting. In only two states may a civilian absent from the United States cast an absentee ballot. In a few instances the voter must be outside the territorial limits of the state before he may exercise the absentee-voting privilege. Some states are more generous than others respecting the cause of absence that may justify the casting of an absentee ballot. In Delaware, for example, the elector must be absent "because of the inherent nature of his or her work or business, such as commercial travellers, railroad employees, pilots and sailors. . . ." Other states merely specify absence from the election precinct. Another point of difference concerns the elections to which absentee voting provisions apply. New Hampshire, for example, permits absentee voting only in presidential elections; Tennessee, in "any election for any purpose whatsoever." The Tennessee practice is the more common rule.

---

[15] The Delaware Statute, however, was held void in 1939. See *State* v. *Lyons*, 5 Atl. 2d 495. Two recent summaries of state legislation are available: *Voting in the United States* (Chicago: Council of State Governments, Mimeographed, 1940); Office of War Information, *State Absentee Voting and Registration Laws* (1942).

[16] "Absentee Voting in the United States," *American Political Science Review*, 32 (1938), pp. 898–907. The discussion that follows is based largely on Professor Steinbicker's excellent analysis of absentee-voting legislation. See also J. P. Harris, *Election Administration in the United States*, chap. 8; J. K. Pollock, *Absentee Voting and Registration* (Washington: American Council on Public Affairs, 1940).

Generally in the casting of an absentee ballot, the elector applies to the appropriate election officials. Usually the statutes prescribe a time preceding the election within which this application must be filed. When the ballot is returned to the election officials, it must be accompanied by a properly attested affidavit showing compliance with the requirements of the legislation. These requirements vary but include such matters as a certificate by a notary public or other officer that the person entitled to the ballot actually marked it—a precaution against abuse of the absentee-voting privilege.

Soldier voting. Absent voting by military personnel raised a new set of problems in World War II. The war created a special demand for absent-voting procedures for the military, and the global dispersion of service personnel generated difficult problems in the administration of absent voting. An act adopted by Congress in September, 1942, came into effect too late to permit substantial participation by troops in the election of that year.[17] Less than 30,000 ballots were cast in the election of 1942 under the procedure provided by this act.[18]

The provision of adequate arrangements for soldiers voting in 1944 came to be the subject of bitter dispute. The legal issue was the degree to which the federal government could, through its war powers, take action in an area ordinarily thought to be reserved to the states by establishing a system for soldier voting, which, incidentally, would nullify state registration and poll-tax requirements for military personnel. The main partisan issue arose from the expectation that the soldier vote would be more heavily Democratic than the civilian vote— an expectation that turned out to be well-founded—but southern Democrats feared that a simple federal ballot procedure would permit Negroes to vote. An administrative issue involved the relative ease of administering a uniform federal ballot procedure and a system based on different state laws.

The states' rights bloc won the congressional battle, and President Roosevelt permitted the act to go into effect in March, 1944, without his signature. Two modes of voting were provided by the statute. In the first system the federal government undertook to do no more than to facilitate the transmission of applications for absent ballots and the return of marked ballots to state election officials, who acted under state legislation governing absent voting by military personnel. The alternative was to vote by the "Federal War Ballot" for candidates for President, Vice President, Senator, and Representative. The federal government undertook to prepare blank ballots and to furnish them to

---

[17] 56 Stat. 753.
[18] "The Soldier Vote in 1942," *Elections: 1942*, No. 3, August, 1943.

military and other personnel eligible to vote in those states that recognized the validity of the federal ballot. The acceptance of this ballot form depended on state acquiescence rather than on the exertion of federal power urged by those desiring a simple and uniform method of assuring the ballot to servicemen. In fact, of the 2,691,000 effective ballots cast in the 1944 presidential election, only 84,000 were on the federal form.[19]   Only 20 states agreed to accept these ballots, but the extensive agitation of the subject led to the adoption of more workable state absent voting laws for military personnel. On the whole, a surprisingly large military vote was cast in the presidential election of 1944. It accounted for 5.6 per cent of the total popular vote, ranging from 10 per cent in Georgia to 2 per cent in Alabama.[20]

Practices in absent voting have not been extensively investigated. It is often charged that absent-voting procedures are particularly susceptible of fraudulent manipulation. The bases for such charges are suggested by North Carolina experience. In that state absent voting is permitted in the general election but not in the primary. The local gossip is to the effect that the Democratic legislature made this arrangement to give a little leeway to Democrats, who control the election machinery, in the state's western counties in which the outcome of the battle between Republicans and Democrats is close. In the election of governor in 1944 the absent vote (military and civilian) constituted 6.7 per cent of the state total and in 25 of the 100 counties the absent vote exceeded the plurality of the winning candidate. The absent vote was highest in the western counties; it exceeded 15 per cent of the total vote in seven counties. In one county 25.7 per cent of the total ballots were absentee. Generally the percentage of absentee ballots increased with the closeness of the contest from county to county. One hypothesis would be that fraud had occurred; another, that simply when the contest is close greater efforts are made to get out the vote.

Ballot counting. Here we return to an account of normal election procedure after digression into the problem of absent voting. At the proper time (in some jurisdictions before the closing of the polls) the counting of the ballots begins. The procedure for counting is often prescribed in minute detail by statute. The most detailed statutory provisions require one election official to read from each ballot the

[19] The clause of the statute providing for a federal short ballot was repealed in April, 1946.

[20] See B. A. Martin, "The Service Vote in the Elections of 1944," *American Political Science Review,* 39 (1945), pp. 720–732; "Army and Navy Voting in 1944," *Elections: 1944,* No. 3, April, 1945: United States War Ballot Commission, *Report* (Sen. Doc. No. 6, 79th Cong., 1st sess., January, 1945); Council of State Governments, *Soldier-Sailor Voting, A Digest of State and Federal Laws* (December, 1943).

choices expressed, while two other election officials (one from each party) watch. The choices are supposed to be tallied independently by two clerks, and their counts are supposed to check with each other at the conclusion of the process. In practice these statutory provisions tend to be ignored for the simple reason that to follow them slavishly would make the count almost interminable. The laws, for example, often prescribe that the vote on each ballot on all offices shall be recorded at one time. In practice, often the count is made on a single office at a time. The law usually requires that the tally sheet shall actually be made as the count proceeds, but in practice the count is often made and then the official tally sheets are filled in. Otherwise, the clerks run into difficulty in making their tallies match. Apart from outright fraud, error is likely to creep into the count. The long ballot, the weariness of election officials, and often their indifferent clerical capacities lay the basis for considerable honest error in counting.

To improve counting, some students of election administration have advocated a central count by a special staff. Under this system the ballot boxes are sealed at the close of the polls and transmitted to a central place and counted there by a staff of fresh clerks rather than by precinct officials weary from the work of election day. The advocates of the central count contend that the concentration of the work at one point permits effective supervision of the counting and thus may prevent fraud as well as error. The central count is the prevailing method in England, but it has been used only slightly in the United States. In Indiana, after charges of election irregularities in 1938, the legislature adopted an act requiring a central count within counties. In the primary count in Marion (Indianapolis) County in 1940, the ballot boxes were transported to an auditorium, where the work was conducted under the scrutiny of spectators in the balcony. Three hundred clerks (half Democratic, half Republican) were employed to do the work. J. K. Eads reports that "wide discrepancies in the ability and attitude among the workers were observed almost from the beginning. Some tabulators, as is customary in groups chosen in this manner, were barely literate; others were troubled by weak eyes or deafness." Naturally the failings of the counting personnel were not attributable to the central count and probably were no more prevalent than under the decentralized count. The chief criticism of the central count was that it was slower than the decentralized count had been.[21] Yet no defeated

[21] J. K. Eads, "Indiana Experiments with Central Ballot Count," *National Municipal Review*, 29 (1940), pp. 545–548. On the central count in Kentucky, see J. B. Shannon in Shannon and others, *A Decade of Change in Kentucky Government and Politics* (Lexington: Bureau of Government Research, University of Kentucky, 1943), pp. 11–12.

candidates demanded recounts, as had occurred after the primary of 1938, the irregularities of which led to the enactment of the central-count legislation. Earlier the central count had been used in San Francisco, but it was abandoned partly because of the greater time required in comparison with the precinct count.

After the completion of the count, the precinct election officials prepare a certificate indicating the number of votes received by each candidate and the number of votes cast for and against each proposition on the ballot. This certificate, together with the ballot box, is sent to the central election authority—election commissioners, city council, county clerk, or whatever agency is vested with authority—and the results are "canvassed"; that is, the returns from all the precincts are added together, and the outcome of the election is pronounced. For state offices the county and city results are certified to some state authority—usually the secretary of state—who canvasses or totals the results from all the counties of the state. The process of canvassing is, of course, a simple exercise in arithmetic; and the results have been known, usually long before the official canvass, through tabulations made unofficially by newspapers, party officers, and others.

Election contests. Provision is generally made to permit a contest of the result of an election as declared by the official canvassing authorities. The contest is sometimes heard by the election officials, sometimes by the courts, and, in the case of legislators, usually by the legislative body, which is generally the sole judge of the qualifications of its members. The ease with which a recount may be brought about varies from jurisdiction to jurisdiction. In some instances a recount may be had as a matter of right; in others, proof must first be made of misconduct or errors by election officials. In some states recounts are discouraged by the requirement that the petitioner for a recount finance the work. "An easy, certain, inexpensive, and prompt recount procedure is essential to a sound administration of elections," the leading authority on elections concludes. "It constitutes a valuable protective feature against election frauds and errors. The precinct election officers should always feel that a recount is not unlikely. This will serve to make them more careful of the accuracy of their work." [22]

The settlement of contests over elections to legislative bodies by the legislative bodies themselves, rather than by the courts, is a feature of electoral procedure that has often been criticized. It is said that the majority of Congress or of a state legislature will tend to favor the contestee who is affiliated with the majority party, without regard to the evidence concerning fraud and error in the conduct of the election.

[22] Harris, *Election Administration in the United States*, p. 313.

Enough partisanship has occurred in the determination of these cases to give a color of truth to the criticism, but a recent study by Vincent Barnett indicates that, regarding Congress at least, partisanship in the settlement of contests is the exception rather than the rule. He has found that, of the past sixty contested elections decided by Congress, in thirty-eight instances the decision was awarded to persons affiliated with the minority party. When the majority makes a finding for the minority party contestee in almost two thirds of the cases, it must follow that partisanship in the settlement of contests is certainly not the general rule.[23]

Election costs. The costs of election administration have received much attention in recent years. Studies uniformly disclose that their cost in most jurisdictions is entirely too high. Harris estimates that for the country as a whole the cost is about a dollar per vote cast. Probably the most important source of waste lies in the employment of too many workers to serve at the polls on election day. In Grand Island Township, Michigan, for example, Professor Pollock reports that in 1932 the township had eleven registered voters but for each election six precincts election officers were employed at $3.00 each per day. Other practices that result in an unnecessarily high cost are the renting of quarters for polls when public buildings could be used and the absence of effective competition in the awarding of contracts for the printing of ballots. Professor Harris has accumulated figures for the more important cities on the total cost of registration and elections per vote cast. The figures range from 37 cents per vote in Salt Lake City to $2.13 in Columbus, Ohio. A series of fairly simple reforms would sharply reduce the unit costs of voting, but such reforms are extremely difficult of effectuation because the spoils of the election machinery are controlled by the party machines, which resist with all their resources proposals to reduce their perquisites.[24]

Fraud. The American election system has gained an unenviable reputation for fraudulent practices. Philadelphia, Chicago, Kansas City, and New York have had long, striking records of fraud in elections, but fraudulent acts have been by no means concentrated in large urban communities. On the other hand, it would probably be an error to conclude that the publicized examples of fraud are typical of election

[23] Vincent M. Barnett, Jr., "Contested Congressional Elections in Recent Years," *Political Science Quarterly,* 54 (1939), pp. 187–215.

[24] On costs of elections, see Harris, *Election Administration in the United States,* chap. 10; J. K. Pollock, *County Election Costs in Michigan* (University of Michigan, Bureau of Government, New Series Bulletin No. 2, April, 1935); R. C. Atkinson, "Party Control and Election Costs in Ohio," *National Municipal Review,* 21 (1932), pp. 595–597.

procedure everywhere. The degree of fraud varies from place to place and in individual communities from time to time. Moreover, outright fraud is to be differentiated from machine control. The two things often go together, but machines often build so loyal a following that fraud in the election itself is unnecessary. Yet enough fraud occurs from time to time to depress seriously community morale and to weaken faith in the democratic process. This psychological effect of fraud may be more significant than stolen votes in the power of a corrupt machine; opposition is likely to weaken and falter if there is a feeling that the elections are stolen regardless of how the vote actually goes.

Fraud and error in registration lay the basis for electoral fraud. When the lists of voters contain false names or the names of persons who have moved away, the party organization may readily find persons to vote those names, provided that the precinct election officials are willing to connive in such an arrangement. How do such names get on the registration lists? The lists may be padded with imaginary names by the registration officials in keeping with a definite plan to pad the lists and later to vote the names at the election. Superfluous names may be on the list merely because of failure to purge the lists of names of persons who have died, removed from the precinct, or otherwise lost their eligibility to vote. When the names of persons who die are left on the lists, the basis is laid, as the argot runs, for "voting the cemetery."

Lists with superfluous names are a condition precedent to a simple and easy type of fraud. On election day fictitious names on the registration lists may be voted in various ways. Sometimes the machine employs repeaters or floaters to go from precinct to precinct to vote under false names already on the listing in each precinct. To organize and manage a squad of repeaters is expensive,[25] and the task of voting the

---

[25] The following case report illustrates the nature of this type of fraud: "Two days after the election we look up from our desks to see what is wanted by a tall slender boy who comes in and can hardly believe that it is really Frank who stands before us, smiling with self-consciousness, but with a happiness and satisfaction in his eyes that we have not seen there for over a year. Homeless, jobless, penniless, he has walked the streets for over two years, picking up jobs occasionally, getting thinner and thinner, his clothes completely worn out, and his feet, the last time he came in, literally on the ground. He had grown more and more careless of his appearance, which was not his fault, as he could not get the few things he had wished and rarely had a place to take a bath. Today he stands before us in a light fedora, spring top coat, colorful shirt and tie, new trousers, socks to match and new shoes. In astonishment, I said, 'What in the world has happened?' and he replied, 'I voted on election day.'

"Strolling along on South State Street the night before election, he was approached and asked if he wanted to work the next day. Who wouldn't want to work in his place? He was told to be at State and Harrison the next morning at 4 o'clock, and there, in the early dawn, he and several hundred others were taken out to the respective wards and precincts of the city to help elect our officials. It wasn't as profit-

names on the registers may be left to the precinct election officials, aided by the precinct party workers. A Philadelphia precinct election official testified, for example: [26]

> We didn't record a man as voting unless he actually voted, or unless we knew he could be depended on. For example, I was sure my mother wouldn't come to the polls, so it was quite safe to cast her ballot for her. The people who live next door to us are the right sort, but they're lazy and like to stay at home. So I told them I would cast their votes for them. But we played the game fair.

When a person attempts to vote under the name of some other person, the practice is called personation.[27] When there is no attempt at deception but a wholesale voting of names on the registers by the election officials, the practice is known as "ballot-box stuffing." This practice is cheaper and easier than the organization of repeaters and personators.[28] Cruder practitioners of fraud make no effort to give an appearance of legality to their work and duly record as having voted persons whose names do not appear on the registration lists.[29]

able as usual, for we are in a state of depression, and instead of $10 a day he was to get a dollar for each time he voted and three square meals at a restaurant on the northwest side. 'All they wanted to eat,' he said, 'and, gee, we did eat!'

"It was very simple. He was given cards to remind him whose name he was to vote under at the different precincts. At the first polling place the man behind him said that he knew the man whose name he was using, but one of his gangster employers, armed, as all of them were, stepped up to our friend's challenger, who took back what he said. . . ."—Jessie F. Binford, Executive Director, Juvenile Protective Association, Chicago *Tribune*, April 21, 1932.

[26] A. F. Macdonald, "Philadelphia's Political Machine in Action," *National Municipal Review*, 15 (1926), pp. 28–35.

[27] There is the story of a repeater who had the effrontery to attempt to vote the name of the Episcopal Bishop of Albany, William Crosswell Doane. The precinct official is said to have thought that this was going too far and said: "G'wan! You ain't Bishop Doane." The repeater answered with heat: "The hell I ain't, you —— —— ——!"—T. L. Stoddard, *Master of Manhattan* (New York: Longmans, Green, 1931), p. 45.

[28] The following quotation from a report of the Citizens' Association of Chicago relating to an election of 1927 illustrates the technique in its grosser form: "When there were not voters in the polling place, Sherry would walk to the back door and holler 'all right.' Then men would come from the rear room and from the second floor with bunches of ballots that they had marked, and Sherry would open the ballot box and the men would drop the ballots in the box. At intervals during the day Sherry and O'Malley (an official who has never been apprehended) would take about ten ballots at a time and go into a polling booth and mark them and put them in the ballot box. About 100 ballots were marked in this way. These, with 100 ballots that were marked before the polls opened and put in the ballot box, and a package of 100 ballots that Sherry took to the rear room and upstairs, made a total of about 300 ballots that were marked for persons who did not enter the polling place to vote, and a like number of names were written in the poll books." Quoted by Harris, *Election Administration in the United States*, pp. 351–352.

[29] The charges against the defendants in a Chicago case were that "in 31 instances

Another point at which fraud may occur is during the counting of the ballots. Occasionally the count is a farce; the vote is determined arbitrarily or by agreement among the election officials and the attendant party workers. This type of fraud is most likely to occur at primaries, when the only persons with an interest may be the machine workers for each party organization, and at general elections in precincts where the minority party is either powerless or a subsidiary of the majority party. A Philadelphia election official, to illustrate, testified that the report of the outcome was made long before all the ballots had been counted. "We always do that," he said. "If we actually counted the ballots our job wouldn't be finished until the next morning. At any rate, the division leader is at the polling place all day, and he knows how almost every person will vote. By checking them off as they deposit their ballots he can tell exactly how the election is going." [30] At times the fraudulent count is accompanied by intimidation of election workers who want to count the ballots accurately. But intimidation is seldom necessary. The party worker in the precinct will have brought about the appointment of pliant precinct officials. [31]

---

they allowed persons using the same names to vote twice; that they permitted 26 persons to vote who were not registered, and they let 24 persons whose names had been stricken from the poll books cast ballots." Chicago *Daily News*, August 10, 1934.

[30] Quoted by Macdonald, *op. cit.*, p. 33.

[31] The following testimony of a Chicago precinct election official is relevant: "Robertson and Nathanson, two of the judges, called the ballots and I worked on the tally sheets. They started to call the ballots and I started to take them down. There was much noise from the watchers and cheers for Joyce. I took it for granted right at the start that Joyce had to be elected. Some of the watchers kept saying: 'Put down some more votes for Joyce.' I was keeping proper tally.

"Jim De Lorenzo was sitting on the table sideways, with one foot on the floor, and as the counting of the ballots continued he appeared to be dissatisfied with the number of votes that Joyce was getting legally. It made him sore evidently, for pretty soon he jumped off the table and called out, with some oath, 'Give us a break.'

"It sounded like a threat and I took it to be a threat. The judges stopped counting for an instant and they looked at De Lorenzo. I couldn't see his face but I could see the faces of the judges and it seemed there was some kind of an understanding. When the count was resumed De Lorenzo stayed right there and compelled me to put down more votes for Joyce on the tally sheet than he was entitled to.

"As soon as they finished with the vote for State Senator there was a recess and the judges went into the rear of the room. I never saw the ballots after that. After a few minutes I asked one of the watchers why the count on other offices was not proceeding. He replied: 'We are not going to count those ballots. We will be here until six o'clock in the morning if we do. We proportion the votes off. In fact, we weigh them.'

"Then the number of votes to be credited to each candidate was given to me either orally or written on slips of paper by two or three of the watchers, but mostly by De Lorenzo, who was leading the bunch. I made entries on the tally sheets according to their instructions."—Quoted by Citizens' Association of Chicago, *Bulletin*, No. 86, May 9, 1931.

Moreover, during the count ballots may be altered or removed and substitutions made. Alterations may have several objects. A long ballot may be marked for only a few offices. The counting official may take up the burden where the elector stopped and finish the laborious exercise of the suffrage.[32] The purpose of alteration may be to change the vote completely. In a Chicago precinct, investigators for the Citizens' Association reported, for example, that "after the polls closed many 'straight' Republican ballots were converted into 'straight' Democratic ballots by the simple expedient of erasing the cross in the Republican party circle and putting a cross in the Democratic party circle."[33] Alteration of the ballot may have as its object the spoiling of a ballot, so that it will be thrown out. A cross may be altered, for example, to make it appear to be an identifying mark, invalidating the ballot.[34] Or a mark may be placed in a second party circle with the same effect.

Sometimes fraud or trickery occurs in the certificate of the results. The ballots may be accurately counted and recorded on the tally sheets, but the certificate reporting the results of the precinct is doctored. An old trick is the transposition of figures. The candidate receives, for example, forty-nine votes; in certifying this item it may be written as ninety-four. Or, perhaps the report is prepared without even this sort of attempt to camouflage fraud as error.

The prevention of fraud is difficult, for efforts at prosecution and exposure are usually fought with all the resources at the command of the local political organization. The methods they use in resistance of investigation range from the destruction of records to subornation. Detection of fraud, however, is simple because the people who commit fraud are generally astonishingly stupid. Some operators are intelligent enough, but most of them leave trails readily followed. Sometimes, for example, a simple comparison of the number of votes cast with the number of voters registered in the precinct shows an excess of ballots over registered voters. Precinct reports that show most of the candidates receiving round numbers of votes are an indication of ex-

[32] Indicative of such practices is the following: "Some of these 1,035 votes were marked with crosses plainly different from those before other candidate's names [on the same ballot]. In some instances an 'X' was marked before DeGrazio's name, while other candidates were voted for with crosses made by horizontal and perpendicular lines. In many instances just the opposite was found."—Chicago *Daily News*, June 27, 1934.

[33] Quoted by Harris, *Election Administration in the United States*, p. 352.

[34] There is a recondite jurisprudence defining precisely what constitutes a valid cross mark. See Spencer Albright, "Legislation on Marking Ballots," *Southwestern Social Science Quarterly*, 21 (1940), pp. 221–226; E. C. Evans, *A History of the Australian Ballot System in the United States* (Chicago: University of Chicago Press, 1917), p. 66.

tremely informal counting because the totals do not turn out that way when the votes are actually counted. Likewise, precinct reports that show a series of zeros for the candidates of one party will bear inquiry because that state of affairs seldom actually occurs; and reports that show a uniformity of votes for each of many candidates on a long ballot are patently fraudulent because voters seldom mark all the offices. Inspection of the ballots themselves can easily reveal fraud. Handwriting experts can readily identify crosses inserted after the ballot has been cast by the bona fide voter; they can as easily identify a series of ballots marked and stuffed by a single person because of the characteristics of the crosses. Nevertheless, presumptive evidence of the foregoing nature is not adequate to obtain convictions; it is necessary to follow up the statistical indicators, find the eyewitnesses, and compel them to testify.

No data are available on the extent of fraudulent voting, except respecting situations in which recounts have occurred or in which investigations have been made.[35] Such instances, however, are likely to represent fraud at its extreme because recounts and investigations are made usually only when there is some reason to suspect fraud. An example of a high degree of fraud was revealed by a field investigation of the 1926 Chicago primary. It was found that in certain precincts over 40 per cent of the votes cast were fraudulent. Classified as fraudulent were instances of persons recorded as voting when those persons made affidavits that they had not voted; persons registered from nonexistent addresses recorded as voting; persons who had moved away from the precinct before the primary; and other *prima facie* cases of fraud. The details are presented in Table 19.

TABLE 19

Fraudulent Voting in Selected Chicago Precincts, April, 1926 [a]

Ward	Votes cast	Fraudulent votes	Percentage fraudulent
10 precincts in 20th Ward	6139	2630	42.8
7 " " 27th "	4141	1705	42.1
6 " " 42nd "	2645	1255	47.4

a Derived from data presented by Harris, *Registration of Voters in the United States*, p. 356.

In another analysis of a sample of Chicago precincts a measure of the degree of fraud and error is available. In this study of the vote on

---

35 There are, of course, many instances of unproved allegations of fraud. Some Democrats, for example, firmly believed that Bryan was fraudulently counted out in the election of 1896. See Josephus Daniels, *Editor in Politics* (Chapel Hill: University of North Carolina Press, 1941), p. 199.

referendum measures, the investigation was limited to a recount of the ballots and did not involve questioning of the voters to determine whether they had actually voted. Hence the figures in Table 20 fur-

TABLE 20

Variation in Tallies of Favorable Votes on Propositions in Fifty-Six Sample Precincts in Chicago Election of November, 1926 [a]

	Volstead modifica- tion	I. & M. Canal issue	Constitu- tional amendment	Road bonds	Jail bonds	Day- light saving
Official count ...	72.3%	73.3%	54.7%	59.0%	61.0%	65.3%
Recount	71.7	74.7	50.8	50.5	51.9	61.3
Difference	.6	1.4	3.9	8.5	9.1	4.0

[a] D. M. Maynard, "Fraud and Error in Chicago Referendum Returns," *National Municipal Review*, 19 (1930), pp. 164–167.

nish a measure only of fraud and error in the counting and in the recording of the vote. The precincts recounted were said to constitute a fairly representative sample of all the precincts of the city; therefore the results probably give an indication of the degree of fraud and error in the entire city at this election.

The prevention of electoral fraud is not a matter of obtaining the right kind of election laws. A perfect body of law regulating registration and elections will not prevent fraud; nevertheless such legislation greatly simplifies the task of officials determined to preserve the honesty of elections. Systematic and recurring electoral corruption is not usually an isolated phenomenon; it is generally only one aspect of corrupt rule. To deal satisfactorily with this type of electoral corruption requires a broad attack on community pathology rather than a piecemeal reform movement directed only toward electoral fraud.

3. BALLOTS

Secrecy of the vote. Although secrecy of the ballot has become commonplace, the general use of secret methods of voting is a relatively recent development in American politics. In the colonial period and in the early history of the United States the more prevalent form of voting was the oral, or *viva voce,* method. Under this arrangement each voter would appear before the election officials and announce orally the candidate whom he desired to support. Oral voting gradually gave way to a system of voting by ballots, which by no means assured secrecy of voting. Instead of there being used a single ballot containing the names of all candidates for all offices, the parties or candidates furnished separate ballots. According to Evans: [36]

The ticket of each party was separate, and, as a general rule, could be distinguished, even when folded, from all other tickets as far as it could be seen. Frequently the party tickets were of a different color. In a municipal election in Massachusetts the Republicans used a red ticket and the opposition a black one; and in the same state in 1878 the Republican ticket had a flaming pink border which threw out branches toward the center of the back, and had a Republican indorsement in letters half an inch high. In another election in Massachusetts the Republicans used a colored ballot, while the Democratic ticket was white with an eagle so heavily printed as to show through the ballot. In one election in Orangeburg County, South Carolina, the Republican ticket was of medium-weight paper, with the back resembling a playing-card, and according to statements made, could be recognized across the street. The Democrats had a tissue-paper ticket of a pale-blue color. There were two sizes of this tissue-paper ticket so that the smaller could be folded in the larger one, and an outsider could not tell that there was more than one ticket being voted.

Serious concern over the consequences of the absence of secrecy in voting began to be manifested soon after the Civil War when intimidation and bribery of voters became rife. It will be recalled that the groups benefiting from the earlier restricted suffrage clung desperately to their privileged status and, as they were compelled to yield to the demands for a broader suffrage, predicted dire results for those of property and substance from the enfranchisement of the masses. After the Civil War the full effects of the broadened suffrage began to be felt, and concerted attempts came to be made to neutralize these effects by bribery and intimidation. The lack of secrecy of voting facilitated bribery, since a person was not inclined to purchase a commodity of whose delivery he was not assured. Similarly, the lack of secrecy of the vote enabled those in a position to intimidate to apply their sanctions. Without secrecy of the ballot, employers might control the votes of their workmen; landlords, the votes of their tenants; creditors, the votes of their debtors. The degree to which intimidation existed cannot, of course, be known, but the nature of intimidation may be seen in the report of a Senate committee investigating elections in Massachusetts in the 1870's.[37]

---

[36] Evans, *op. cit.*, pp. 6–7. Fraud with the tissue-paper ticket mentioned in the quotation was simple and in some states the statutes provided for discarding, by random selection, the number of ballots in excess of the number of persons who had voted.

[37] Senate Report No. 497, 46th Congress, 1st Session (1880). It hardly needs to be observed that secrecy of the ballot does not completely prevent intimidation. Attempts to intimidate continue to occur, but with the secret ballot penalization of those who decline to be intimidated is more difficult.

The Boston Elastic Fabric Company employed a large number of hands, most of whom were Democrats, but under the orders of their employer, Mr. McBirney, they were nearly all required to vote the Republican ticket in November, 1878. The foreman of the factory stood at the polls in Chelsea all day on election day between the door and the ballot-box, and required the men employed under him to vote the Republican ticket. Another of the employees was directed to tell them that this was their employer's wish and they must govern themselves accordingly. This was done and the men very generally obeyed the orders given. One testified that he did not and was soon driven out of that employment.

Many states, to ensure secrecy, enacted regulatory legislation to govern the private printing of ballots, but these measures were uniformly ineffective, and the group desiring a truly secret vote turned toward the Australian ballot. This ballot, so named because of the place of its origin, was printed by public authority. It contained the names of the candidates of all parties and was coupled with methods of election administration designed to ensure secrecy of voting. The agitation for the new type of ballot originated in large measure from labor and other minority groups that believed their political strength to be diminished by the intimidation and bribery prevailing under the existing system of balloting. In a volume published in 1889 John H. Wigmore indicated the prime movers in the propaganda in the various states for the Australian ballot. His catalog of these leaders inferentially constitutes an impressive statement of the way bribery and intimidation were thought to affect the outcome of elections. Among the organizations interested in ballot reform in New York were the Reform Club, the City Reform Club, and the Labor party. In Wisconsin the "Labor press . . . earnestly supported the movement." In Indiana the "Democrats, as the defeated party in the national election, and the especial (though by no means the guiltless) sufferers from the corrupt methods employed, naturally took the lead." In Missouri the Civil Service Reform Association and the Single Tax League were active. In Nebraska the bill was drafted by a committee representing the Typographical Union, the Central Labor Union, and the Knights of Labor. Elsewhere the pattern was, in general, similar: early agitation was led by people outside the governing cliques; eventually the reform gained broader support.[38]

The United States trailed other Anglo-Saxon countries in adopting this needed reform. The British Parliament adopted the secret ballot in 1872; South Australia, in 1858. In England its acceptance had been hindered by the powerful influence of John Stuart Mill. Although his

[38] John H. Wigmore, *The Australian Ballot System* (Boston: Boston Book Company, 2nd ed., 1889).

ideas on the subject do not seem to have had much influence in this country, his arguments are worthy of brief review. Mill argued that in the exercise of the suffrage a person was performing a public function and in arriving at a decision he should consider the general interest; his decision and his vote, like the vote of a member of Parliament, should be a public matter. The duty "should be performed under the eye and criticism of the public; every one of whom has not only an interest in its performance, but a good title to consider himself wronged if it is performed otherwise than honestly and carefully." Mill believed that "people will give dishonest or mean votes from lucre, from malice, from pique, from personal rivalry, even from the interests or prejudices of class or sect, more readily in secret than in public. And cases exist —they may come to be more frequent—in which almost the only restraint upon a majority of knaves consists in their involuntary respect for the opinion of an honest minority." Mill conceded that conditions of intimidation might justify a secret ballot: "When the voters are slaves, anything may be tolerated which enables them to throw off the yoke." Although he contended that his argument applied to conditions of universal suffrage as well as to conditions of restricted suffrage, his propositions would appear to have more applicability to the second situation.[39] His conception of the electorate as exercising a function of trust for the entire people has tended to disappear with the broadening of the suffrage. A vote has come to be expected to be governed by a class interest; the general interest is to be promoted by a balancing and synthesis of class and group interests.[40]

In the United States the first Australian-ballot law was enacted by the Kentucky Legislature in 1880. This measure applied only to municipal elections in Louisville, since the state constitution explicitly required *viva voce* voting at elections of state officers. By 1900 a large proportion of the states had adopted the Australian ballot. By 1942, 45 states used this type of ballot; Georgia and Delaware employed a modification of the Australian form, and South Carolina remained the only state untouched by the movement for the Australian ballot.[41]

Intimidation and bribery remain but probably not to the degree that existed before the introduction of the Australian ballot. The secrecy

[39] See J. S. Mill, *Representative Government*, chap. 10, "The Mode of Voting."

[40] It is of interest to note that in England the fears of the Conservative opponents of the secret ballot were not justified by the electoral results after the adoption of secrecy. The groups that feared they would lose power by secrecy actually increased their power, but not, of course, because of secrecy of the ballot. See J. H. Park, "England's Controversy over the Secret Ballot," *Political Science Quarterly*, 46 (1931), pp. 51–86.

[41] Spencer Albright, *Ballot Analysis and Ballot Changes since 1930* (Chicago: Council of State Governments, mimeographed, 1940), p. 1.

of the ballot may be destroyed, as we have seen, by statutory provisions to permit "assistance" to illiterate, blind, or otherwise incapacitated voters. Another device sometimes used to destroy the secrecy of the vote and to facilitate purchase is the "endless chain" or "Tasmanian dodge." Under this scheme it is necessary to take from the polling place an official ballot; the purchaser marks the ballot as he desires it to be voted, delivers it to an elector who enters the polling place and procures a ballot. In the booth the voter substitutes the marked ballot for the fresh one, inserts the marked ballot in the ballot box, and delivers the fresh ballot to the party worker. This ballot is marked, given to another voter who repeats the process; the chain goes on unbroken. To check this practice, a substantial number of states employ a system of numbered ballots. When a voter receives a ballot, the number is recorded opposite his name; before he is permitted to deposit the ballot he must show the numbered stub (the ballot is folded so as show the number) to the election officials who tear it off. In some instances a venal voter may mark his ballot so as to identify it to the election officials and those watching the count; in this way the purchaser may assure himself that he has received delivery. Identification of an individual ballot in this way is illegal; ballots signed plainly fall within the proscription, but other types of symbols designed to identify are more difficult to deal with.

It should be observed that the ballot laws constituted an entering wedge for the detailed regulation of party activity. When it was decided that public authorities should print ballots containing the names of the candidates of all parties, it was necessary legally to define "party" and to define by law the procedure that the party should follow in making nominations; otherwise, the agency in charge of the preparation of ballots might be faced with the problem of deciding which of several party lists should be printed, without having any legal criterion for decision. It was necessary to require that nominations be made far enough in advance of an election to give time to prepare the ballot.[42]

42 The regulation of party action inherent in the Australian ballot law was given as a reason by Governor Hill of New York for his veto of an act passed by the legislature of that state in 1889:

"I am unalterably opposed to any system of elections which will prevent the people from putting candidates in nomination at any time and voting for them by a printed ballot up to the very last minute before the closing of the polls on election day. This is an inherent right under our free institutions, which the people will never knowingly surrender. . . .

"The right of suffrage and the existence of elections are both made absolutely dependent upon previous nominations. If no such nominations should be made, all the people of the state would be disfranchised. It is not enough to say that such event is not likely to happen. A bill which makes the right to vote depend upon irresponsible voluntary bodies, thereby making disfranchisement of all the people

In some instances public control of the ballot is used to exclude minor parties from the ballot or to make it difficult for them to meet the requirements to place their candidates on the ballot. A party is sometimes defined in terms of the number of votes cast for its candidates at the preceding election. In Ohio, for example, "when any political party fails to cast 10 per cent of the total vote cast at an election for the office of governor it shall cease to be a political party within the meaning of this act." By raising the percentage required to keep party candidates on the official ballot, legislatures sometimes discriminate against minor parties. Usually, however, provision is made to permit a new party to place its candidates on the ballot by petition. In Oklahoma, for example, any "political party presenting a petition of 5,000 names of voters . . . shall have the names of its candidates for state and local offices placed on a ballot." The fixing of the number of signatures at a high figure frustrates the desire of minor parties to have the names of their candidates on the ballot.[43]

Ballot forms. No uniform pattern is followed by the different states in the design of ballots. Three principal types of ballot forms have been developed, although there are additional minor variations. They are the office-block ballot, in which all candidates for each office are grouped together; the party-column ballot, in which all the candidates of each party for all offices are grouped together in columns; and the office-block ballot with supplementary provision for straight-ticket voting.

The party-column ballot, used in thirty states, is sometimes called the Indiana-type ballot because the Indiana law of 1889 has served as a model for other states in the adoption of this form of ballot. The Indiana law of that year required that all nominees of any party should be

. . . placed under the title and device of such party or petitioners as designated by them in their certificate or petition; or if none be designated, under some suitable title and device. . . . The arrangement of the ballot shall, in general, conform as nearly as possible to the plan hereinafter given, and the device named and list of candidates of the Democratic party shall be placed in the first column on the left-hand side of said ballot; of the Republican party in the second column; of the Prohibition party in the third column, and of

---

possible, is equally unconstitutional whether such event be probable or not. This result proceeds not from special defects in this particular bill, but is inherent in the very theory of an exclusive official ballot upon which the bill is framed."—Quoted by Evans, *op. cit.*, p. 24.

[43] See W. E. Hannan, *Provisions of the Laws of the Various States with Respect to the Formation of a New Political Party* (Chicago: Council of State Governments, mimeographed, 1938).

any other party in such order as the Board of Election Commissioners shall decide.[44]

In most states using the party-column ballot it is possible to vote a straight party ticket—that is, vote for all the candidates of a single party for all offices—by making a single cross in the circle at the head of the column containing the party candidates.[45] Voting a straight ticket is far easier than voting a split ticket because splitting support among the candidates of the parties requires the recording of a choice for each office. Professional party workers generally favor the use of the party-column ballot on the theory that it discourages independent voting and makes easier the amassing of a large vote for the party nominees for the inconspicuous offices as well as for the more important offices. No careful analysis has been made of the effect of the "straight-ticket" voting provision; indeed, it would probably be difficult to isolate that factor.

In contrast with the party-column ballot is the office-block, or as it is sometimes called by virtue of its origin, the Massachusetts ballot.[46] Names of all candidates, by whatever party nominated, for each office are grouped together on the office-block ballot. The supposition is that the voter will be compelled to consider separately the candidates for each office, in contrast with the straight-ticket voting of the party-column ballot. Pennsylvania employs a variation of the office-block ballot; the candidates of all parties are grouped by offices sought, but provision is made for straight-ticket voting by a single mark.[47]

[44] Quoted by Evans, *op. cit.*, p. 36.

[45] Albright lists and classifies the party-column states as follows (1) states that make provision for straight-ticket voting and print a party emblem at the head of the column: Alabama, Delaware, Indiana, Kentucky, Louisiana, Michigan, Missouri, New Hampshire, New Mexico, Ohio, Oklahoma, Rhode Island, Utah, West Virginia; (2) states that make provision for straight-ticket voting but do not print the party emblem at the head of the column: Arizona, Connecticut, Georgia, Idaho, Illinois, Iowa, Maine, North Carolina, South Dakota, Texas, Vermont, Washington, Wisconsin; (3) states that make no provision for straight-ticket voting: New Jersey, North Dakota, Wyoming.—*The American Ballot*, pp. 50–51. A table giving detailed data about ballot forms appears in *Book of the States*, 1945–46, p. 87.

[46] For a collection of facsimiles of a variety of ballots, see C. O. Smith, *A Book of Ballots* (Detroit: Bureau of Governmental Research, 1938).

[47] Another classification of ballots is partisan and nonpartisan. The partisan ballot includes either party symbols or other identification of the party affiliation of the candidates. The nonpartisan ballot is used primarily in local and judicial elections. Party machines are usually strongly opposed to the nonpartisan ballot; their supposition is that the party emblem or party name attracts voters while the absence of party identification from the ballot makes easier victories by independents. For a discussion of the workings of the nonpartisan ballot, see J. T. Salter, *The Non-Partisan Ballot in Certain Pennsylvania Cities* (Philadelphia, 1928). See also M. C. Moos, "Judicial Elections and Partisan Endorsement of Judicial Candidates in Minnesota," *American Political Science Review*, 35 (1941), pp. 69–75.

Long *versus* short ballot. Whether the ballot is in form a party-column or an office-block ballot, it is usually a long ballot containing a large number of names and perhaps constitutional amendments and other propositions on which the voters are asked to express an opinion. In 1932 the "average party-column ballot consisted of 565 square inches of paper, on which were printed over 102 names and three propositions." In the office-block states the ballot averaged 349 square inches and contained the names of 77 candidates and four propositions.[48] In the off year of 1934 the average ballot had an area of 398 square inches, and the average voter was asked to express 22 choices.[49] The number of expressions of opinion demanded of the American voter under the long ballot constitutes a greater burden than is borne by any other voter in the world. The ballot is so long, in fact, that the voter abdicates and refuses to perform a substantial part of his duty. The tendency is that the vote cast becomes lighter as the office is lower down the ballot.

The variation in votes cast for different offices furnishes to some degree a measure of the effect of the long ballot. In the absence of provision for voting a straight party ticket, the voter will express a choice on the candidates for those offices of greater importance and will neglect to mark the ballot in many other cases. At the November, 1934, election California voters were asked to vote on eight state officers, a United States Senator, a Representative in Congress, and to express a preference on twenty-three constitutional amendments and initiated measures. In addition, in some counties local offices and local issues of policy were included on the ballot. To cast a complete ballot, the voter had to make a choice on at least thirty-three matters. Of the 2,360,916 voters who came to the polls, nearly all (98.6 per cent) expressed a choice for one or the other of the candidates for governor. Only 81.2 per cent, however, put a cross alongside the name of a candidate for the state assembly. Stated in absolute figures, over 440,000 of the voters expressed no preference for candidates for the lower house of the state legislature. The lowest vote recorded was on a proposed constitutional amendment to permit cities and other political subdivisions to adopt agreements for the joint exercise of power and for the joint performance of functions —not a proposal to arouse the most intense passions of the elector. On this measure only 54.5 per cent of those coming to the polls aligned themselves one way or the other; over 1,000,000 voters failed to put a cross in the "yes" or "no" box on this proposition. The complete tabulation is given in Table 21.

[48] Albright, "How Does Your Ballot Grow–" (Bulletin, American Legislators' Association, May 10, 1933).

[49] Albright, "General Election Ballots in 1934," *Southwestern Social Science Quarterly*, 16 (1936), pp. 85–95.

TABLE 21

Total Vote Cast for Candidates for Certain Offices and for and against State-wide Propositions at California Election of November 6, 1934

Office or issue	Total vote cast on each office or issue	Percentage of total coming to polls who expressed choice on each office or issue
Total vote cast	2,360,916	100.0
Governor	2,329,449	98.6
Lieutenant governor	2,249,694	95.2
Secretary of state	2,112,481	89.4
Controller	2,042,854	86.5
Treasurer	2,122,136	89.8
Attorney general	2,063,534	87.4
United States Senator	2,058,940	87.2
State Board of Equalization [a]	2,056,926	87.1
State assemblymen [a]	1,918,213	81.2
U.S. Representatives [a]	2,029,510	85.9
Proposition No. 2, initiative measure on liquor	1,976,618	83.7
Proposition No. 22, constitutional amendment authorizing agreements between political subdivisions [b] ..	1,288,230	54.5

[a] These figures constitute the total of all votes cast for all candidates in all districts of the state.

[b] The two propositions are the ones on which the highest and lowest of the votes on the twenty-three propositions were recorded.

The California figures cited show the variations in the extent to which the ballot is marked for federal and state officers in a general election. A wider range of variation in participation also exists between state offices and obscure local offices. Figure 20 shows the average total participation in both party primaries in Michigan in the years 1922–1934 for various state and local offices. In interpreting the figures on which this chart is based Professor Pollock suggests that participation declines as the voter works his way down the ballot, a tendency that he calls "voter fatigue." The arrangement of the data in the chart in the order in which the offices occur on the ballot suggests the extent to which participation varies with the ranking of the office on the ballot.[50]

The long ballot makes it impossible for the electorate to be informed on the merits of all candidates. The more inconspicuous the office, the fewer the people who know anything about the candidates. The

[50] The data for the chart are from J. K. Pollock, *The Direct Primary in Michigan, 1909–1935* (Ann Arbor: University of Michigan Press, 1943, p. 33. See also his "New Thoughts on the Short Ballot," *National Municipal Review,* 29 (1940), pp. 18–20.

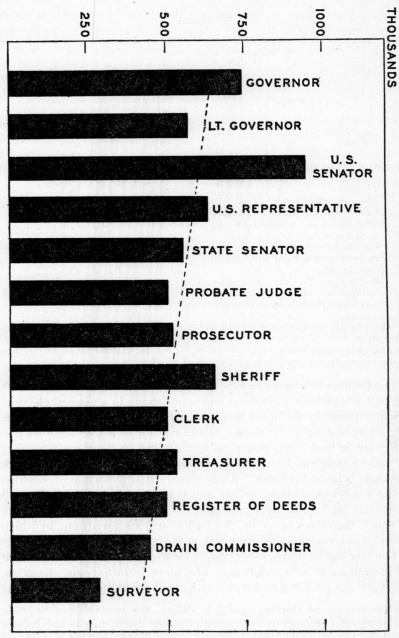

Figure 20. Total Average Participation on Thirteen Offices in Both Party
Primaries in Michigan, 1922–1934

result is that the party organization has an easier task in putting into those offices men allied with it. On the other hand, the head of the ticket is in a glare of publicity, and the machine vote is not so likely to determine the outcome of the election for that position. It must be remembered that the long ballot usually prevails in the direct primaries, as well as in the election, and that voter participation is generally much lower in primaries than in elections. A relatively small vote under machine leadership can exert great influence in the selection of the nominees for inconspicuous offices because the total vote cast in the primaries for these offices is usually light indeed. The long ballot and the structure of government that it reflects can be given considerable credit for the perpetuation of machine control of state and local offices.

Reform groups concerned with local governments place great emphasis on the reduction of the number of offices to be filled by popular election. Their prescription of the short ballot rests on the assumption that if the task of the voter is simplified, he will make more informed choices at the polling place. Furthermore, they believe that, with the short ballot, no longer could minor machine politicos gain lodgment in inconspicuous offices under the concealment of the bed-sheet ballot. The suppositions of the short-ballot advocates are undoubtedly correct under certain conditions, but the adoption of the short ballot does not always throw the machine from power. It may only compel the machine to mend its ways.

The short-ballot movement has been confined mainly to state and local governments, since it has been the structure of those governments that contributed chiefly to the length of the ballot. A minor aspect of the movement to reduce the acreage of the ballot paper has concerned the election of the President. The custom has been to place on the ballot the names of all the presidential electors pledged to each presidential candidate. The presidential electors have had, of course, for over a century no function save that of a rubber stamp, yet their names have been placed on the ballot in conformity with the legal theory that people vote, not for the presidential and vice-presidential candidates, but for electors who in turn select the President and Vice-President. Shortening the ballot presented the legal problem of determining how to remove the electors' names from it and at the same time provide for the popular selection of electors.[51] Nebraska, in 1917, enacted a law that removed the electors' names from the ballot and directed the gov-

---

[51] The Constitution, Art. II, Sec. 2, provides: "Each state shall appoint, in such manner as the Legislature thereof may direct, a number of electors equal to the whole number of Senators and Representatives to which the State may be entitled. . . ."

ernor to appoint as electors the persons "selected in the preceding dele-gates' state convention by the political party whose candidates for Presi-dent and Vice-President received the highest number of votes." Iowa, in 1919, adopted legislation to remove the electors' names from the ballot and at the same time adopted the legal fiction that a ballot marked, let us say, for the Democratic presidential candidate was really a vote for the Democratic electors from the state.[52] The Iowa tech-nique of meeting the legal problem is the method generally used. Spencer Albright points out that the presidential short ballot really received its impetus from the use of the voting machine, which, because of its limitations, required a vote for all the presidential electors of a party at one stroke of the lever. Legislation to permit the use of the machine without a listing of the electors was adopted in Iowa in 1900; other states have since followed. In the 1940 election states with a total electoral vote of 296 used the presidential short ballot.[53] Since most states permit a vote for all the electors for a presidential candidate by marking a single cross, the presidential short ballot does not reduce the burden of the electorate materially but it does, of course, reduce the sheer size of the ballot.

Voting machines. Since 1892, when the city of Lockport, New York, made the first use of voting machines, the voting machine has been gradually taking the place of the paper ballot.[54] In 1898 Rochester, New York, adopted the machine as the sole method of voting, and several other New York cities followed during the next year. Thirty-four states have at one time or another authorized the use of voting machines, but some state laws have been held void while others have been repealed. In slightly more than half the states laws are in effect permitting the use of machines in all or some localities of the state. Most of these laws, however, merely authorize the local governments, which usually administer elections, to install voting machines. Hence, the degree of their use varies greatly among the states with permissive legislation. The Automatic Voting Machine Corporation estimates that machines are used in 3,500 cities and towns in 21 states, and that in the 1944 presidential election 14 million, or about 29 per cent, of the total votes were cast by machine.[55]

[52] L. E. Alysworth, "The Presidential Short Ballot," *American Political Science Review*, 24 (1930), pp. 966–970.

[53] Albright, *The American Ballot*, chap. 5.

[54] On voting machines, see T. D. Zukerman, "The Case for Mechanical Balloting," *National Municipal Review*, 14 (1925), pp. 226–233; J. P. Harris, *Election Adminis-tration in the United States*, chap. 7; Albright, *The American Ballot*, chap. 4.

[55] According to Albright, the following states have never enacted a voting machine law: Delaware, Idaho, Mississippi, Missouri, Nevada, New Mexico, North Carolina North Dakota, South Carolina, South Dakota, Vermont, West Virginia, and Wyoming

In essence, the voting machine is a mechanical device for recording and counting automatically the choices registered by the voter. The machine is provided with a face equipped with levers corresponding to each candidate or proposition to be voted upon. On the face of the machine, adjacent to each lever, is a printed paper indicating the candidate for whom a vote will be recorded if that particular lever is pulled down. See Figure 21. In operating the machine, the voter

Figure 21. Face of Voting Machine
(Automatic Voting Machine Corporation)

pulls a lever to close the curtain to conceal himself. This movement clears the machine for operation, for unless the curtain is closed the machine cannot be operated. The voter then pulls the levers to indicate his choices. Machines are manufactured with a single lever to pull to vote a straight ticket, corresponding to the party-column ballot. If the law of the state concerned prescribes the office-block ballot, the machine is designed to require the movement of a lever for each office. After lowering the levers to indicate his choices, the voter pulls the lever to open the curtain, which movement also actuates the counters to record his choices. At the close of the polls a panel on the back of the machine covering the counting devices is removed, and the election officials read off, record, and report the total vote for each candidate.

The advocates (and manufacturers) of the voting machine are voluble in its praise. The machine prevents certain types of fraud and error in the conduct of elections. The "Tasmanian dodge," for example, cannot be worked on a voting machine. The fraudulent spoiling of ballots by election officials during the count is ruled out by the voting machine. Fraud and error in the count are impossible. The danger of fraud in reporting the precinct results is minimized, since it is a simple matter to compare the machine with the report of the vote by the precinct election officials. The machine makes the results available quickly after the closing of the polls, because it is not necessary to count ballots. The machine speeds up the voting process itself. Secrecy in voting is ensured since the possibility of placing identifying marks on individual ballots is removed.

A point strongly emphasized by the machine manufacturers is the claim that the cost of conduct of elections is reduced by the substitution of the machine for the paper ballot. The Automatic Voting Machine Corporation concludes that it is generally possible to amortize the cost of machines over a period of from ten to twelve years through savings over paper ballots. When the machine is used, the number of precincts may be reduced, with a consequent reduced cost of hiring election officials and renting polling places. The machine does not require so many election officials for each precinct as the older system; nor is it necessary to pay the election officials so much, since they do not have to spend long hours counting the ballots. Although a few ballots have to be printed to serve absentee voters, the major part of the cost of ballots is eliminated, as well as the expense of acquiring, transporting, and installing polling booths. On the other hand, the machines must be stored and transported to and from polling places at election time, and the expense of setting up the machines for use is higher than the cost of installing voting booths. Most writers express the view that voting machines reduce election costs, but frequently their computations do not take into account a capital charge on the investment in the machines and do not include an allowance for depreciation and obsolescence. Joseph P. Harris made a detailed analysis of election costs in New York City and concluded that, if the overhead costs for the machines were included, the use of machines increases costs "rather substantially." Of course, the same increase in cost would not occur in all jurisdictions under all conditions; and, even if it did, it might be concluded that the assurance against fraud and of an accurate count, and other features of the machine would be worth the additional cost.

Chapter 18

STRAW POLLS

In a polity founded on the proposition that the general will should prevail, the determination of the wishes of the people is of fundamental
significance. Elections are classic means for sounding public opinion.
Yet it is not always easy to know what an election decides other than
which candidate shall fill the office. Election results may reflect dissatisfaction with the conduct of the government by the party in power.
They may express discontent arising from conditions over which the
government has no control. Or they may reflect general agreement
with the prevailing orientation of public policy. Sometimes the outcome of an election may furnish a mandate for future governmental
policy, but often no clear-cut understanding exists of what the results
of an election mean in terms of public attitudes regarding specific public policies. In fact, occasionally a majority of people will favor a
candidate and at the same time be opposed to some of his policies.

Politicians have long attempted to ascertain popular attitudes on
issues arising between elections. They have sought to determine public attitudes, not always from deep attachment to the doctrine that
public attitudes should govern public policy, but to facilitate political
survival. The practitioner of politics makes a career of estimating
what the electorate will and will not tolerate, what it likes and dislikes.
His success in judging these matters influences his chances of election
and re-election. Although some practical politicians have a remarkable sensitivity to public attitudes, they often arrive at their estimates of
the state of public sentiment by intuitive means.

The Congressman, state legislator, mayor, or other public official is
likely to pay close attention to his mailbag, but he has no assurance that
the people who feel impelled to write letters of complaint, letters urging
action, or (occasionally) letters of commendation are representative of
his constituency. He must know how to discount a flow of mail that
results from an organized letter-writing campaign. He must recognize
mail that comes from an influential section of his constituency. The

politician has the newspapers as a guide of sorts to the status of the public mind, but the views of newspaper editors may be in complete disagreement with the predominant views of the electorate. The practical politician must by a process of divination determine the weight to be given to the emanations from the editorial sanctum. He has the reports and judgments of the leaders of the party organization on which he relies for support. In addition to these sources of information, most politicians manage to move around among their constituents, keep their ears to the ground, and obtain firsthand impressions of electoral sentiment. By these and other methods the practicing politician has always attempted to estimate the state of public attitudes toward specific public questions. It is not implied that he deems it necessary to follow that estimate, but generally he feels it wise to know the status of public attitudes.

Since the middle 'thirties the time-honored opinion-testing techniques of the politician have been supplemented by the scientific sampling of public attitudes through the public-opinion poll. For many decades prior to this time party organizations conducted polls during campaigns to ascertain the sentiment toward their candidates, but these polls were without the benefit of skilled statistical direction. Newspapers likewise had their early "straw polls," but they, too, were usually defective in technique.[1]

Modern polls, such as those of the American Institute of Public Opinion, *Fortune,* and various newspapers, achieve far greater accuracy than their predecessors. The methods of these newer public-opinion polls have been derived in the main from the experience of market analysts; in fact, the more prominent figures in public-opinion polling either have had experience in market analysis or are also currently engaged in that business. Market analysis methods were devised to enable industrial concerns to measure consumer preferences. If a particular product does not sell, what is wrong? If it does sell, why? Why does it sell in one place and not another? Why do automobile users purchase one car rather than another in the same price range? What features of an automobile do the users like? What features do they dislike? What is the potential market for a new commodity or gadget? What channels of advertising reach the widest audience? Answers to such questions are worth dollars and cents to businessmen, and advertising men developed means for getting the answers.

[1] For a survey of earlier newspaper polls and party-organization polls, see C. E. Robinson, *Straw Votes* (New York: Columbia University Press, 1932). For an elementary survey of polling methods and problems, see George Gallup, *A Guide to Public Opinion Polls* (Princeton: Princeton University Press, 1944).

Specialists in advertising, like politicians, attempt both to mold and to take into consideration public attitudes. To serve their clients effectively they have to know as exactly as possible the attitudes of customers, potential customers, and past customers. If it can be ascertained, for example, what flavor the majority of the people prefer in dentifrices, a new brand can be designed to meet those tastes. To obtain the answer to such a question, it is obviously impossible to query all potential buyers of the tooth paste. The market analysts have devised instead a technique of sampling public attitudes; that is, a small number of persons selected to constitute a representative cross section of the potential market will be questioned. If the sample of persons interviewed is actually representative, the findings will be the same as though all potential buyers had been queried. Thus, a feasible and relatively inexpensive method of ascertaining public attitudes has been devised.

The poll on candidates arouses more popular interest than the poll on issues, but the latter is probably of greater significance. Polls taken during a campaign estimate the sentiment toward candidates—a bit of information that would become available when the votes are counted anyway. The continual sampling of public opinion on issues between elections, however, furnishes fairly reliable knowledge about public attitudes on particular questions. In the past, this information was never available except on the small number of issues on which popular referenda were held by state and local governments.

1. POLL TECHNIQUES

Modern public-opinion polls are based on the principle of sampling; that is, the ascertainment of the opinions of a small representative group from the electorate as a means of estimating the opinion of the entire electorate. Obviously the validity of the results of a poll depends almost entirely on the degree to which the voters interviewed are a reliable sample. In purchasing a bushel of apples, the buyer will not inspect each apple. He will sample the bushel. If he is wise, he will not judge the entire bushel by the large and perfect specimens on top: he will dig down a few layers to see whether the top layer is a representative sample. He may then judge the quality of the bushel by inspecting a few of each sort of apples in the basket. If the bushel consists of one-third large and fine specimens and two-thirds small apples and the buyer looks at a sample of one large and two small, he will have a correct idea of the entire bushel. He has inspected, as the statisticians would say, a "reliable" sample of the "universe" under examination. If the universe is homogeneous, sampling is quite simple. If, for example, all the apples are of the same quality, inspection of a few selected at random will furnish an accurate idea of the quality of the entire bushel. But if the universe is heterogeneous, sampling becomes more difficult. Under these conditions the sample must be made up of specimens from each class in the same proportion as they exist in the entire universe under examination.

Principles of sampling. The principles of sampling may be illustrated by the ill-fated *Literary Digest* poll. The *Literary Digest,* it will be recalled, was a periodical that ceased publication shortly after its erroneous prophecy of the outcome of the 1936 presidential election. The *Digest* had earlier gained renown from the accuracy of its polls, but in 1936 conditions were such that the fundamental defects in its polling technique led to a forecast of victory for Alfred M. Landon, the Republican candidate. The *Digest* in 1936 mailed straw ballots to about 10 million persons. Of these ballots about 2,376,000 were returned and tabulated, of which 1,293,669 were marked for Landon; 972,897 for Roosevelt; 83,610 for Lemke. On the basis of this poll, Landon was expected to receive 57 per cent of the major-party vote; actually, he received 37.5 per cent. The forecast was that Roosevelt would receive 43 per cent of the major-party vote; he not only received 62.5 per cent but carried every state save Maine and Vermont. The poll placed about 19.5 per cent of the major-party votes on the wrong side.

How was it possible to collect such a large number of ballots that diverged so markedly from the division of the electorate as a whole? The *Digest* poll inspected only the apples on the top of the basket. The sample contained too large a proportion of the economically well-to-do. The *Digest* mailing lists were made up from telephone directories and lists of automobile owners. Persons who were sufficiently well off to own automobiles or to have telephones were more inclined to support Landon than were the others in the population. By polling the "tel-auto" list, the *Digest* introduced a bias into its sample that invalidated the results. The *Digest* poll showed about how the "tel-auto" list was going to divide in the election, but it failed to account for the possibility that other people would divide differently. Earlier *Digest* polls had correctly predicted the winner with smaller percentage errors than in 1936; at earlier elections economic status had not been so important a factor in voting behavior.

How can a reliable sample, a miniature electorate, be built up for the purpose of testing accurately the status of public sentiment? The American Institute of Public Opinion questions a sample of from 3,000 to 60,000 persons in its polls; the variations depend on the degree of accuracy desired. If, say 50,000 persons are interviewed, it is necessary that the 50,000 mirror the electorate as a whole. The reliability of the sample may be tested by its comparison with the electorate as a whole. If the voting population as a whole is 50 per cent male and 50 per cent female, the sample should be equally divided between the sexes. Moreover, cities of different sizes must be properly represented in the sample. "If 10.3 per cent of our people lived in cities from 25,000 to 100,000, then we must take 10.3 per cent of our sample from cities of that size." [2] The sample also should be divided, for example, among age groups, rural and urban population, geographic areas, and income levels in the same proportions as these groups are found in the electorate as a whole. On some types of questions, national origin and religion may be important in cleavages of opinion, and the sample must be constructed to take into account these factors.[3]

In general, the sample must be tested against all the important characteristics of the electorate that are associated with the way people vote on candidates or feel about the issue under consideration. It can readily be seen that the ascertainment of the reliability of a sample presents no mean technical problem. It must first be determined what characteristics of the electorate are significant in so far as political attitudes are concerned. Then, as a test of the reliability of the sample, it is necessary to know the characteristics of the electorate as a whole. The census furnishes some information about the characteristics of the population against which the sample may be checked. A few studies of the distribution of income have been made, and these serve as guides against which to compare the distribution of the sample among the different income levels.[4] Despite the difficulties of defining a representative sample, poll experts have made remarkable progress in devising feasible means to test opinion by querying an extremely small number of persons. Illustrative of the possibilities is a special experiment by the Office of Public Opinion Research in 1942, in which a sample of 200 persons was used to forecast the vote in the election of the governor of New York. The OPOR small-sample prediction was 58 per cent for Dewey; he received 53 per cent of 4,100,000 votes. The

---

[2] Elmo Roper, "Sampling Public Opinion," *Journal of the American Statistical Association,* 35 (1940), pp. 325–334. An excellent account of poll methods is contained in the War Department publication *EM 4 GI Roundtable: Are Opinion Polls Useful* (Washington, 1946).

[3] On the problems of sampling, see S. S. Wilks, "Representative Sampling and Poll Reliability," *Public Opinion Quarterly* 4 (1940), pp. 261–269.

[4] On the special techniques of the *Fortune* survey in obtaining a representative sample of economic classes, see Roper, "Classifying Respondents by Economic Status," *Public Opinion Quarterly,* 4 (1940), pp. 270–272.

American Institute of Public Opinion, using a sample of only 2,800, predicted the outcome precisely.[5]

An incidental feature of voting behavior that makes sampling in connection with campaigns especially difficult is the fact that the characteristics of the group that actually votes may differ from those of the population eligible to vote. Women usually do not vote in the same degree as men; generally not so large a proportion of Negroes vote as do whites; participation is less among the young than among the old; the poor do not go to the polls in so high proportions as the more prosperous. When poll takers estimate the division of the voters at the polls, allowance must be made in the sample for the probable variations in participation in voting among different groups of the population. Otherwise, the poll might reflect more accurately than the election returns the attitude of the electorate as a whole and yet fail to predict the winner. Low turnout introduces error into polling only when the nonvoters differ markedly from the participating electors. The small popular vote in the 1942 congressional elections for example, benefited the Republicans and was in part responsible for an overestimate by the AIPO of the number of House seats that would be won by the Democrats.[6]

Problems in poll administration. The definition of the characteristics of the sample to be interviewed presents statistical difficulties, but more perplexing problems must be solved to make sure that such a sample is actually interviewed. When interviewers scattered over the entire nation are allowed to select the specific individuals whom they are to interview, the composite result may not constitute a reliable sample of the entire electorate. Poll experts wrack their brains to devise methods to guide their interviewers in the choice of interviewees. Some poll managers go so far as to designate the exact addresses at which the interviewer shall call. Moreover, it has been found that those not at home at the time of the first call differ in opinion from those more easily accessible. When interviewers enjoy some discretion in the choice of interviewees, as is usually the case, the possibility of the introduction of bias through the normal inclination of man to follow the easy course is apparent. It is especially difficult to make sure that lower economic classes are adequately represented in the sample. The interviewer may "cheat"; it may be simpler to fill in his interview reports without the wearisome task of plodding the streets to find persons who

[5] Hadley Cantril, *Gauging Public Opinion* (Princeton: Princeton University Press, 1944), chap. xii.
[6] C. E. Robinson, "Pre-Election Polls in the 1942 Elections," *Public Opinion Quarterly,* 7 (1943), 139–44.

meet the requirements of the assigned quota. Most "cheating," however, can be fairly readily spotted by the odd statistical characteristics of reports filed by such interviewers.

In addition to problems in the administration of the polls, error may creep in because of the influences generated in the interviewer-interviewee relationship. Commercial polling organizations usually employ white-collar persons as interviewers; in working-class areas the responses obtained by such interviewers on certain types of questions differ from those obtained by working-class interviewers. Similarly, on some types of issues a white interviewer receives one sort of answer and a Negro another in a Negro neighborhood. Polling organizations are well aware of these problems and are applying their ingenuity to their solution, but these observations point to the warning that polls require the most expert and honest management and that the evaluation of poll findings likewise calls for the sure touch of a skilled hand.[7]

Accuracy of polls on candidates. Election results test the accuracy of polls on candidates, a test that is lacking for polls on issues. It may be presumed, however, that issue polls are equally accurate when made by the same methods employed in candidate polls. Among those who have national polling organizations, Elmo Roper, whose work is usually published in *Fortune*, has achieved greatest accuracy in predicting the national popular vote in presidential elections. In 1944 he came within 0.17 of 1 per cent of the actual Democratic vote. The Crossley and Gallup polls were somewhat less accurate. Dr. Gallup's American Institute of Public Opinion, which syndicates its poll findings to newspapers, attempts a state-by-state prediction in the presidential election. This type of prediction, presenting greater technical difficulty than a national prediction, is subject to a much wider margin of error. Because of difficulties in sampling low-income voters, the AIPO has fairly consistently underestimated the Democratic percentage of the presidential vote, but some of its error in 1944 has been attributed to an underestimate of the total turnout, a factor that reduced the estimated Democratic percentage. In his 1944 reports Dr. Gallup's interpretations of his statistical findings also aroused some criticism because his editorial estimates of the Republican trend were borne out neither by

[7] On these problems, see Hadley Cantril, *Gauging Public Opinion* (Princeton: Princeton University Press, 1944); Daniel Katz, "Do Interviewers Bias Poll Results?" *Public Opinion Quarterly*, 6 (1942), pp. 248–268; H. F. Gosnell and Sebastian de Grazia, "A Critique of Polling Methods," *Public Opinion Quarterly* 6 (1942), 378–390; E. R. Hilgard and S. L. Payne, "Those Not at Home: Riddle for Pollsters," *Public Opinion Quarterly*, 8 (1944), pp. 254–261; M. H. Hansen and P. M. Hauser, "Area Sampling—Some Principles of Sample Design," *Public Opinion Quarterly*, 9 (1946), pp. 431–445; National Opinion Research Center, *Interviewing for NORC* (Denver: NORC, 1945).

his own figures nor by the election figures.   Nevertheless, he has built up a creditable record of performance.

During the 1944 campaign two research organizations conducted experimental polls, the results of which were not published.   The Princeton Office of Public Opinion Research, using a sample of only 2,000, produced the forecast second best to that of Roper.   The National Opinion Research Center of the University of Denver, which used a sample of about the same size, made an estimate of the division of the national popular vote slightly more accurate than that by Gallup.[8]   The relevant figures appear in Table 22.   In addition to the well-known opinion-testing organizations, wild-cat polling outfits spring up during campaigns to produce polls for propaganda purposes.   Their findings are usually highly unreliable.   On the other hand, certain newspapers over the country have built up polling staffs that produce estimates of high quality on local elections and issues.   The moral is that persons relying on polls need to know something of the record of the different polling organizations.

TABLE 22

Forecasts of Democratic Percentage of Major-Party Vote in 1944 Presidential Election by Chief Polling Organizations [a]

Polling organization	Prediction	
	Total vote	Civilian vote
Roper Poll	53.6	
Princeton Office of Public Opinion Research	53.3	
Crossley Poll	52.2	
National Opinion Research Center		51.7
Gallup Poll		51.5
Actual	53.77	??

[a] Daniel Katz, "The Polls and the 1944 Election," *Public Opinion Quarterly*, 8 (1944–45), p. 469.

Special problems of polls on issues.   The management and interpretation of polls on issues are beset by special problems.   As in election polls the problem of sampling must be solved and allowance made for the possible introduction of bias by the interviewer-interviewee rela-

[8] Daniel Katz, "The Polls and the 1944 Elections," *Public Opinion Quarterly*, 8 (1944–45), pp. 468–487; E. G. Benson and Others, "Polling Lessons from the 1944 Election," *Public Opinion Quarterly*, 9 (1945–46), pp. 467–484; P. F. Lazersfeld, "Post Mortem," *The Nation*, 159 (1944), p. 613.   On polls in earlier elections, see Daniel Katz, "The Public Opinion Polls and the 1940 Election," *Public Opinion Quarterly* 5 (1941), pp. 52–78; H. F. Gosnell, "How Accurate Were the Polls?" *Public Opinion Quarterly*, January, 1937.

tionship. Beyond such matters common to both types of poll, the formulation of the question may influence the response in a poll on an issue. Questions may be so phrased as to elicit a particular answer. Inflammatory or neutral words may be used to express about the same idea but bring different responses to the question. Paul Studenski has demonstrated graphically how the form of the question may affect the result. He was skeptical of the results of a poll conducted for a national employers association on the question, among others, "Should every worker be forced to join a union?" The association had reported with considerable pleasure that the predominant opinion was heavily in the negative. Studenski used the association's question and a rephrasing of the same question in an experimental poll of 150 New York University students. In response to the question, "Should every worker be forced to join a union?" the replies were distributed as follows:

	% of Vote
Yes	9.3
No	88.9
Don't know	1.8

The reply could have been interpreted as a resounding negation of unionism of the form assumed in the question. A reformulation of the question, however, produced results as follows:

Is it proper for a union to require all wage earners in an industrial enterprise to join the union—	% in favor of each proposition
Under any circumstances?	7.4
When the union controls a minority of the employees?	2.6
When the union controls a majority of the employees?	37.6
Or is it improper under any circumstances?	45.0
Don't know	7.4

The rephrasing of the question demonstrated a much different distribution of opinion to exist than had been found under the original question.[9]

Another example further illustrates the influence of the wording of questions. The following question was asked: "So far as you, personally, are concerned, do you think President Roosevelt has gone too far in his policies of helping Britain, or not far enough?" Another

[9] Paul Studenski, "How Polls Can Mislead," *Harper's Magazine*, December, 1939. See the striking differences in replies to "unloaded" questions, questions with a pro-union bias, and questions with an anti-union bias in a survey of opinion about strikes in defense industries, *Fortune*, June, 1941. Arthur Kornhauser concludes: "In the choice of topics, in the wording of questions, and in the reporting of results, unionism fails to receive balanced and impartial treatment."—"Are Public Opinion Polls Fair to Organized Labor?" *Public Opinion Quarterly*, 10 (1946–47), pp. 484–500.

question was asked with identical phraseology except that "the United States" was substituted for "President Roosevelt." The replies to the two questions differed as follows:

	Roosevelt version	United States version
Too far	20	15
About right	57	46
Not far enough	17	32
No opinion	6	7

The different words of the question both showed, in the pre-World War II period, general approval of the government's policy, but the substitution of "United States" for "President Roosevelt" produced a finding indicating greater popular support for a more drastic policy.[10]

Poll managers interested in eliminating bias in the phraseology of questions have devised a method of pretesting to eliminate this source of error. By asking the same question, phrased in different ways, to small groups, they can ascertain in advance the effect of the wording of the question, if any. Pretesting of the question also eliminates other errors in formulation of the question, such as unintelligibility. A question, for example, that included the phrase "reciprocal trade treaties" was asked by the American Institute of Public Opinion, and it was found that only one person in ten understood the basic principle of the treaties. Hence, questions on the attitude of the public toward the treaties would have to be taken with a grain of salt. Dr. Gallup believes that his institute, through experience and trial and error, "is building up a neutral vocabulary—a public-opinion glossary—within the comprehension of the mass of people." [11] It is only from such a vocabulary that words may be drawn to phrase questions that do not contain the seeds of their own answers.

Poll experts attempt to build a neutral vocabulary, but they realize that they must also deal with other problems in the formulation and interpretation of questions. Some questions simply evoke untruthful replies. Respondents hesitate to admit views or conduct condemned by community opinion. Thus, when absenteeism in industrial plants was being sharply criticized during World War II, replies to questions on absenteeism did not coincide with plant attendance records. The failure to include the consequences of a particular view in a question may influence the validity of the replies. For example, in 1942 the

[10] Donald Rugg and Hadley Cantril, "The Wording of Questions in Public Opinion Polls," *Journal of Abnormal and Social Psychology,* 37 (1942), pp. 469-495.

[11] George Gallup and Saul Rae, *The Pulse of Democracy* (New York: Simon and Schuster, 1940), p. 106.

Psychological Corporation asked: "Do you think that the government should do something to keep prices from going up?" This was followed immediately by the question: "Do you think the government should do something to keep wages and salaries from going up?" To the first question, the replies were 85 per cent yes and 5 per cent no. To the second question, however, the replies were 27 per cent yes and 53 per cent no. What was "public opinion"? Obviously the findings of polls on issues must be warily interpreted. Yet the study being given to polling methods and to the interpretation of poll findings holds promise of developing much more refined methods for analyzing and interpreting public opinion.[12]

2. THE POLLS AND GOVERNANCE

Regardless of the success of the opinion experts in estimating accurately public attitudes is the query, "What is the value of these estimates?" If it be conceded that *Fortune* and the American Institute of Public Opinion have been fairly successful in devising a method for ascertaining the changing state of public opinion, just what is the significance of this new technique in politics and government? The answers to these questions can only be speculative; the speculations can best be presented with reference to the conduct of campaigns, the determination of legislative questions, and the management of administrative agencies.

Polls and campaign management. Presumably the knowledge of the status of public attitudes that comes from the polls should lead to more intelligent management of campaigns; but, since the data from the published polls are available to the campaign managers of both parties, probably the net effect would not be to give advantage to one party or the other. If the polls have any effect at all on campaigning, they would logically be expected to affect both major parties in about

[12] On the problems mentioned in these paragraphs, see Hadley Cantril, *Gauging Public Opinion* (Princeton: Princeton University Press, 1944), Parts 1 and 4; Hadley Cantril, "Experiments in the Wording of Questions," *Public Opinion Quarterly*, 4 (1940), pp. 330–333; H. C. Link and A. D. Freiberg, "The Problem of Validity vs. Reliability in Public Opinion Polls," *Public Opinion Quarterly*, 6 (1942), pp. 87–98; P. F. Lazarsfeld, "The Controversy over Detailed Interviews—An Offer for Negotiation," *Public Opinion Quarterly*, 8 (1944), pp. 38–60; Herbert Hyman, "Do They Tell the Truth?" *Public Opinion Quarterly*, 8 (1944–45), pp. 557–559; G. M. Connelly, "Now Let's Look at the Real Problem: Validity," *Public Opinion Quarterly*, 9 (1945), pp. 51–60; Hadley Cantril, "Do Different Polls Get the Same Results," *Public Opinion Quarterly*, 9 (1945), pp. 61–69; A. B. Blankenship, "The Influence of the Question Form Upon the Response in a Public Opinion Poll," *Psychological Record*, 3 (1939–40), pp. 349–422; Bureau of Applied Social Research, "Bias in the Phrasing of Questions," *The Nation*, 159 (1944), p. 294.

the same way. If the results of a poll, for example, led both parties to espouse bolder policies on a particular issue, the significance might be great, but there is no persuasive way of determining what would have happened in the absence of polls regarding the standing of the candidates and attitudes toward the campaign issues.

An obvious utility of poll data in campaign management is demonstrated in the strategy of presidential aspirants regarding the presidential preference primaries held prior to the national conventions. During the 1940 campaign it was said that the campaign strategy of three aspirants—Dewey, Taft, and Vandenburg, all of whom were eventually unsuccessful at the convention—was governed to a considerable extent by polls. The Dewey organization is said to have maintained its own polling organization to test sentiment as a basis for deciding whether to enter the primaries. When opinion was found to be favorable to Dewey, his headquarters would issue challenges to Taft and Vandenburg to enter the primary of the state in question. Taft, in turn, stayed out of some state primaries, on the plea that his duties as a Senator required his presence in Washington, but his decisions were said to be partially because he did not want to enter the convention with a record of defeat by Dewey in the primaries in the states concerned. In a sense, the polls constitute a national presidential preference primary.

In the management of presidential campaigns the poll results have obvious utility in promoting efficient campaigning by pointing to the states in which the contests are close and to the states in which the results are certain one way or the other. Party resources may be concentrated where the polls indicate the greatest need, and campaign funds saved where "sure" areas are found. Whether the polls furnish more accurate guidance than the private polls of party leaders, which have been made for many years, cannot be determined with certainty. Party managers have always known, of course, that great exertion was neither needed nor worth while in some states, but it is doubtful whether their judgments on the trend of sentiment in the closer states have been as accurate as the polls. Claude Robinson has accumulated estimates made in 1928 by party leaders, and their average error was considerably higher than that of the American Institute of Public Opinion. In that year the Democratic leaders, through self-hypnosis or, as Robinson calls it, an "elation complex," greatly overestimated Al Smith's strength. The estimates Robinson collected were, of course, not those released for public consumption but those prepared for private use in the guidance of the campaign.[13]

13 Robinson, *op. cit.*, Chap. 1.

Polls might be used to guide campaign managers in the selection of appeals and symbols. It is doubtful whether poll research has been carried far enough to determine the effect of particular appeals on the electorate, yet it is possible to determine by the polls viewpoints that are generally unpopular and perhaps should be avoided during a campaign. More aid to the campaigner is probably available from the poll results that indicate the distribution of the strength of competing parties among different economic groups, different age groups, and other subgroups of the electorate. By the observation of this breakdown and of trends within subgroups of the electorate, the politician is able to make a better judgment of the sorts of groups to which he must appeal to retain or to gain strength. The use of polls in the Machiavellian business of devising strategy to get into office is in its infancy. It is difficult to show that the availability of tests of public opinion has had far-reaching effects on campaigning; yet such tests have had some practical use, and their potential influence on campaign appeals and on strategy, as their findings come to be better understood, is undoubtedly great.

The question remains whether the straw poll introduces an element in the campaigning situation that is itself a factor in influencing voters' attitudes. The theory held in some quarters is that the poll results, by indicating the probable winner, produces a "band-wagon" effect. Thus Representative Pierce of Oregon, in a truly self-deprecating fashion, declared in 1940: "I have found in my long political career that the strongest argument I can make in my behalf, that my friends can make in my behalf, is 'He's going to win. You might as well get on the bandwagon.' It takes the starch out of the opponent; it puts backbone into the friends of the one who can create that sentiment." [14] Is there anything to this theory? There is little trustworthy evidence in support of the Representative's theory that the polls accentuate whatever band-wagon effect there might be in their absence. Dr. Gallup has cited several instances in which it appeared that the polls had no band-wagon effect. The Columbus (Ohio) *Dispatch,* for example, has been conducting polls with a reputation for accuracy for about thirty years. In 1932 the first *Dispatch* poll indicated that Roosevelt would receive 65 per cent of the vote of Ohio. Immediately preceding the election the second *Dispatch* poll showed a Roosevelt strength of 51 per cent, about what he received in the election. The band wagon lost rather than gained voters.[15]

[14] *Congressional Record* (daily edition), February 29, 1940, p. 3301.
[15] American Institute of Public Opinion, *The New Science of Public Opinion Measurement,* p. 13.

Dr. Gallup cites the surveys by his American Institute in 1938 during the contest between Barkley and Chandler for the Kentucky Democratic senatorial nomination.   The strength of the candidates as shown by the series of tests was as follows:

	Barkley	Chandler
April 10	67%	33%
May 15	65	35
July 8	64	36
July 24	61	39
August 5	59	41
Election result	57	43

Had there actually been a band-wagon effect from the poll, it would have been supposed that Barkley would have continued to gain from the time of the publication of the first poll.   In fact, however, Chandler's vigorous campaigning turned the tide in the other direction.[16] The forecast of a victory for Landon in the 1936 *Digest* poll had no perceptible band-wagon effect.   Of course, the conclusion that the poll has no such effect rests on two assumptions: (1) that the poll accurately measured the trend of sentiment during the campaign; (2) that the trend would not have been different in the absence of the poll.   If there is anything to the band-wagon theory, perhaps, in the instance cited, the trend away from Barkley would have been greater in the absence of the poll.[17]   A check on the validity of these assumptions, however, is furnished by one American Institute poll in which the interviewees were asked, "Do you happen to know which Republican candidate is leading today in the polls on presidential candidates?" at the time of a preconvention poll on presidential preferences.   The Institute classified the respondents into those who knew and those who did not know the standing of the candidates in the polls.   The vote among those ignorant of poll results "was virtually the same as among those who knew poll results."[18]   About the only conclusion that can be drawn is that although the band wagon undoubtedly carries many voters along with it, the effect of the polls in strengthening the band wagon appears to be slight.

[16] Gallup and Rae, *op. cit.*, p. 250.

[17] More study is required to test adequately the band-wagon theory. Winston Allard, on the basis of experiments with student groups, concludes that in his tests the impression of universality produced by polls constituted a potent influence on group opinion. See "A Test of Propaganda Values in Public Opinion Surveys," *Social Forces*, 20 (1941), pp. 206–213.

[18] Gallup and Rae, "Is There a Bandwagon Vote?" *Public Opinion Quarterly*, 4 (1940), pp. 244–249. See also S. W. Cook and A. C. Welch, "Methods of Measuring Practical Effect of Polls of Public Opinion," *Journal of Applied Psychology*, 24 (1940), pp. 441–454.

Polls and legislation. In the determination of legislative issues and other questions of public policy, the use and potential use of the poll presents a subject for interesting speculation. The more enthusiastic observers of the polls see in them a device for the implementation of the theory of pure democracy; the governor need no longer be much more than a rubber stamp for *vox populi* as evidenced by the poll. The representative, harassed by the raucous demands of lobbyists and letter writers, need only consult the oracle to determine the status of public opinion. At the other extreme, there are those who are skeptical of the wisdom of following public opinion, even if it be granted that the polls measure that opinion with accuracy. They question the capacity of the people to form desirable decisions on broad public issues.

The power of minorities in legislation is a serious problem. They obtain legislation granting unconscionable privileges. They block legislation that might injure them somewhat but promote the welfare of the majority of citizens. Critics of democracy are wont to theorize about the tyranny of majorities. In fact, a more important problem of democracy is how to overcome the tyranny of minorities. It is the organized minorities that maintain lobbyists; that importune representatives to support or to oppose action; that organize campaigns to bring pressure on representatives; and that intimidate representatives with threats of reprisal at election time. The majorities do not indulge in these activities, and the legislative battle is likely to go to the minority through default.

The poll furnishes potentially a means for the deflation of the extreme claims of pressure groups and for the testing of their extravagant claims of public sentiment in support of their demands. Dr. Gallup has referred to his polls on old-age pensions as one instance of the use of the poll to reveal the true extent of public support of an extreme proposal. In 1935 Congress rejected Dr. Townsend's fantastic scheme for pensions of $200 a month to each person over 60 years of age, but the Townsendites did not give up. They organized clubs all over the country to carry the fight into congressional elections. They boasted that by 1936 they would have "their own President in the White House and full control over Congress." Dr. Gallup's poll demonstrated that the country was overwhelmingly in favor of a system of old-age pensions, but only 3.8 per cent of the people would favor the amount of $200 per month. Even in the Pacific Coast states, the birthplace of Townsendism, only 16 per cent voted for $200 a month. Subsequently a congressional investigation did much to discredit the Townsend movement, its demands were revised downward, and the movement as a whole lost strength. At the peak of its strength, however, Townsendism occupied the headlines, filled the editorials, and gave the appearance of being a much more powerful movement than it actually was.[19]

The effect of poll findings on the course of legislation is impossible to estimate, yet it is plain that they give strength to those legislators desirous of combating extreme demands of pressure groups. They remove doubt about the degree of strength behind movements, and that strength is rarely so great as the leaders of a movement assert. On the other hand, the polls leave unanswered questions that need to be known by a legislator who is interested in calculating a course of action that will contribute to his political survival. In the first place, the present polls give no measure of sentiment in the legislator's own district, and that is apt to be the matter of most concern to him. Beyond this, the real meaning of poll results for public policy is often unclear. For example, the poll furnishes no idea of the probable persistence of an attitude. On a question of no great importance, about which people do not feel deeply, an ear-filling clamor may arise at the moment, but the concern will abate shortly; by election time all will be forgotten and forgiven. The poll may show an overwhelming sentiment one way or the other, but it gives no indication whether it is a sentiment that will persist.

Quite closely related is the question of the intensity of public feeling about a particular issue. To a legislator it is important to know whether the opinion in support of a measure is apathetic or active. Are the centers of diffusion of a particular viewpoint in strategic power positions? Can they affect his status if he does not heed their wishes? In March, 1936, for example, 88 per cent of the people, according to the American Institute of Public Opinion, believed that government positions should be given to those with the highest marks on civil service examinations. Yet a poll of this sort carried little immediate weight in terms of influencing congressional action. It was an opinion perhaps on the order of the answer to the question, "Are you against sin?" The difference between views of the public expressed through a poll and policies actually put into effect represents roughly the practicing politicians' judgment of the difference between public sentiment and the actual distribution of power and influence.

The opinion experts have recognized these weaknesses of their find-

---

[19] An additional example of the difference between supposed and actual status of public opinion is furnished by a *Fortune* poll on the question: "Do you think there should or should not be a government agency with the power to force settlement of differences between employers and labor?" The percentages of various groups favoring such an agency were as follows: proprietors, 76.0; executives, 73.8; white-collar workers, 70.2; factory labor, 68.3; miscellaneous labor, 68.8. The similarity of the views of supposedly antagonistic groups was impressive. *Fortune*, June, 1941.

ings and have experimented with polls to ascertain more precisely the intensity of feeling of different groups of people about public issues. They recognize that a requirement of a "yes" or "no" answer forces into two classes people who may view a matter from a third or a fourth point of view. The *Fortune* survey has experimented in a measurement of the intensity of feelings with queries such as the following asked during September, 1940:

With which one of these statements concerning a third term do you come *closest* to agreeing?

The idea that a President should not hold office for three terms is a silly and outworn tradition 13.2%

While it may not generally be a good idea for a President to serve three terms, there should be no rule preventing it at a time of national crisis 51.8

Never under any conditions should a President hold office for three terms 29.9

Don't know 5.1

Presumably a more enlightening notion of the status of public opinion may be obtained through questions, such as the foregoing, that give opportunity for a graduation of public attitudes than from inquiries demanding a simple "yes" or "no" answer.

The question remains what weight the legislator should give to public attitudes in the position he takes on issues. From the standpoint merely of relationship between his vote on particular measures and his chances for political survival, the legislator obtains only slight guidance from the polls. On some issues he may ignore the predominant sentiment, since that sentiment is not likely to persist until the time that he is up for re-election; or that sentiment may be relatively apathetic. Moreover, on the general question of the relationship between a legislator's vote and his chances of re-election, our knowledge is sketchy. He probably cannot long ignore completely the desire of powerful groups in his district, but the poll does not help him very much in deciding which powerful group to ignore and which to follow.

Apart from the consideration of the relationship between the public attitude as shown by the poll, his vote, and the chances for his re-election, the legislator may wonder whether the mass of opinion is the "right" opinion on a particular issue. Antidemocratic theorists rant about the incompetence of the mass, its volatility, its inconsistency, its intolerance, and the folly of the man who would pay heed to mass opinion. Some alarmed commentators see in the poll a threat to representative government. Colonel O. R. McGuire declares that the polls "are positively harmful to the continuation of our present system of government with its checks and balances for the protection of the rights, liberty and property, of all the people, including minority groups." He says that the polls "undercut and discourage the influence of able and conscientious public men and tend to elevate demagogues to power who will go to the greatest extremes in taking from those who have and giving to those who have not." [20]   There is no evidence in support of such statements; mass movements made headway before the introduction of the polls; demagogues gained power both before and after the introduction of polls; and there is no indication that legislators are intimidated by the findings of the polls.[21]   Regarding the supposed desire of the masses to soak the rich, the available evidence seems to show that the inclination is often greatly overestimated.[22]

A slightly different slant has been given by Edward L. Bernays to the foregoing general criticism of the polls.   He recognizes the utility of intelligent and honest interpretation of polls, but he fears that the polls are a danger to democratic leadership.   The polls, he asserts, may inhibit independent thought by leaders and may smother progressive minority ideas.   Leaders have a responsibility to lead, the argument runs.   When leaders are intimidated by polls, they do not perform the function of informing and educating the people.   "We are no longer led by men," he asserts.   "We are led around by the polls." [23]

[20] O. R. McGuire, "The U.S. Constitution and Ten Shekels of Silver," *Public Opinion Quarterly*, 4 (1940), pp. 232–235.

[21] George F. Lewis, Jr., Conducted a questionnaire survey of members of the House and Senate on the influence of the polls and received 117 returns.   To the question "Do the results of public-opinion polls aid you in deciding upon the desires of your constituents?"   9 per cent of the respondents replied "yes" and 30 per cent said "in part."   Mr. Lewis says that the "negative answers of the remaining 61 per cent cannot be accepted as necessarily establishing the fact that they are not subject to an influence which they might be reluctant to admit, even if they were aware of it." Another question was, "Do you think public opinion polls aid other men in public life in deciding their policies about or stands on various subjects or issues?"   To this query, 23 per cent of the Congressmen answered "yes"; 55 per cent said "in part"; 24 per cent replied "no"; and 16 per cent did not know.—"The Congressmen Look at the Polls," *Public Opinion Quarterly*, 4 (1940), pp. 229–231.   See also J. C. Ranney, "Do the Polls Serve Democracy," *Public Opinion Quarterly*, 10 (1946), pp. 349–360.

[22] An AIPO poll of August, 1941, sought to measure general opinion on income-tax rates.   The findings were that mass opinion favored higher rates on the lower-income brackets and lower rates on the higher-income brackets than had been proposed in the tax bill then pending in Congress.   Dr. Gallup interpreted the results to mean that "nothing could be farther from the truth" than the theory "that if the masses had their way in the matter of taxation they would simply gouge the rich indiscriminately."   Release of August 9, 1941.

[23] Edward L. Bernays, "Attitude Polls—Servants or Masters?" *Public Opinion Quarterly*, 9 (1945), pp. 264–268b.   See the replies by poll experts, "The Discussion Goes On," *Public Opinion Quarterly*, 9 (1944–45), pp. 403–410.

The trouble with this kind of criticism is that there is no evidence in support of it. It may be surmised that forces much more potent than poll figures printed on a piece of paper have throttled progressive leaders both before and after the introduction of polls. Nor does the evidence seem to show that legislators place great reliance on polls as a guide to public opinion. A group of Congressmen ranked personal mail, visits to the public, newspapers, and visits from the public as more useful than polls as ways of finding out the public opinion.[24] Obviously more analysis is needed of the relation between polls and governmental action. Probably on many issues it could be shown that public opinion moves more rapidly than governmental action.

In the matter of the influence of poll findings on public policy the real issue is whether the judgment of the mass of the people is any better or worse than that of their elected representatives. The working theory of American politics has been one of faith in the judgment of the mass of the people. Theodore Roosevelt expressed that view in the following sentence: "I believe that the majority of the plain people of the United States will, day in and day out, make fewer mistakes in governing themselves than any smaller class or body of men will make in trying to govern them." Roosevelt's statement was made before there was any mechanism for ascertaining what the mass of people thought about public questions, but the polls are regarded by Dr. Gallup as confirming the Roosevelt pronouncement. It is Dr. Gallup's belief that "the views of the electorate are quite as intelligent as those of their elected representatives." [25] Gallup and Rae conclude: [26]

> The serious observer of public opinion on scores of issues cannot fail to come away with a feeling of intense admiration for the honesty and common sense with which an enormous number of ordinary people in all walks of life and at all levels of the economic scale have continued to meet their responsibilities as citizens. He will be profoundly impressed with the grasp of broad principles which voters of all types possess, and with their capacity to adjust themselves to the ever-changing movement of events.

Elmo Roper, who conducts the *Fortune* surveys, comes to a similar conclusion. Six "years of sampling public opinion," he says, "has given me a profound respect for the wisdom of the American people as a whole and with it a firm conviction that if we keep the power in the hands of the people and further develop techniques for making them

[24] Martin Kriegsberg, "What Congressmen and Administrators Think of the Polls," *Public Opinion Quarterly*, 9 (1945), pp. 333–337.
[25] "Putting Public Opinion to Work," *Scribner's*, November, 1936.
[26] Gallup and Rae, *The Pulse of Democracy*, p. 287.

vocal, we need never have fear that this country will ever face the situation now being faced in certain countries of Europe." [27]

In a consideration of opinion polls, however, it must be kept in mind that only on certain types of issues is the judgment of the public of value. On whether a division of the Treasury should use International or Burroughs business machines, there would be no informed public opinion. On the validity of a test used by the Civil Service Commission, it would not be worth while to conduct a poll. On the relative cost and durability of different types of paving, the answer may be derived by cost accounting and controlled observation. In other words, on a great many questions there is an answer that can be provided by experts. But on many broad questions of public policy, however, there are no "experts." Some people are inclined to believe that all public questions could better be settled by "experts" with their scientific methods and standards, but broad issues of public policy are not susceptible of determination in this manner. For example, a system of unemployment insurance is urged. There are experts in the details of such systems, but on the question whether we want to install such a system the judgment of the "public" may be quite as good as that of the "experts." There is no unquestionably "right" opinion on many issues; the correct decision, from the standpoint of the politician in a democracy, is the decision that provokes the least dissatisfaction and arouses the maximum approbation. The poll is a means for exploring the public mind to ascertain that dissatisfaction and approbation, but the polls have not revolutionized the work of the legislator.

Polls and administrative management. In the management of administrative departments, knowledge of the attitude of the segment of the public with which the agency deals is a matter of basic importance. Administrators have always attempted in various ways to ascertain the views of the public, but the methods used have not been entirely satisfactory. An analysis of complaints, received through correspondence and otherwise, is often made routinely to identify weak spots in administration and to aid in the introduction of corrective measures. Most administrative agencies hold formal or informal hearings to obtain opinion and information before they issue rules and regulations. The representatives of organized groups invariably make the opinions of their constituents, as they estimate them, felt in the administrative

[27] "Sampling Public Opinion," *Journal of the American Statistical Association*, 35 (1940), pp. 325–334. The student can conveniently compare his own judgment on these matters with that of Dr. Gallup and Mr. Roper by examining the extensive reports of poll findings in Jerome Bruner, *Mandate from the People* (New York: Duell, Sloan and Pearce, 1944) and W. A. Lydgate, *What America Thinks* (New York: Thomas Y. Crowell, 1944).

offices. Yet with all these sources of information, the administrator needs additional knowledge about the attitudes of the segments of the public with which he deals.

Although the commercial polls include reports of some value to administrators, the needs of administration have to be met mainly by special polls conducted directly by the government or by private organizations under contract with the government. Reliance on polls by the administrator does not ordinarily raise the same issues of principle as are generated by consideration of polls in relation to legislatures. The administrator can employ a poll to aid him in the execution of policy already fixed by Congress or other duly constituted authority. Such use does not involve one in such questions as whether the polls are undermining representative government. For example, during World War II the War Production Board made considerable use of the poll technique to aid it in determining what goods were most needed for civilian use, in order that scarce materials could be best allocated to meet the most urgent needs. The Department of Agriculture, since the mid-thirties, has carried on opinion studies in connection with its farm programs. In 1941, to illustrate, it proposed to increase the production of dairy products. A survey revealed that few farmers even knew of the price-support program that had been inaugurated and not many were aware of why increased production was necessary. Farmers were hesitant to increase production because of price uncertainty. The findings brought alterations in the promotional program of the Department, so that its efforts might better bring the desired results. The discovery by an opinion survey that 63 per cent of the people of a city were unaware of the existence of the city planning commission pointed to obvious weaknesses in the program. The War Department, during World War II, found polling techniques useful in sounding attitudes of Army personnel concerning existing and proposed policies. These and other uses of polls in administration constitute systematic means by which the management of government activity can discover weaknesses in method and approach and be guided in the contrivance of remedial measures necessary to achieve public purposes more effectively.[28]

[28] Henry A. Wallace and J. L. McCamy, "Straw Polls and Public Administration," *Public Opinion Quarterly*, 4 (1940), pp. 221–223: Rensis Likert, "Democracy in Agriculture—"Why and How?" *1940 Yearbook of Agriculture*, pp. 994–1002; H. E. Skott, "Attitude Research in the Department of Agriculture," *Public Opinion Quarterly*, 7 (1943), pp. 280–292; D. B. Truman, "Public Opinion Research as a Tool of Public Administration," *Public Administration Review*, 5 (1945), pp. 62–72; J. L. Woodward, "Making Government Opinion Research Bear upon Operations," *American Sociological Review*, 9 (1944), pp. 670–677; Princeton Bureau of Urban Research, *Urban*

3. GOVERNMENT REGULATION OF POLLS

Some people have become considerably and probably unduly exercised over the polls and have agitated for governmental regulation of one type or another. Some politicians, particularly when the polls are going against their candidacy, become extremely critical of them. Some observers see in the polls a plebiscital method that threatens to eat away the foundations of representative government and substitute a dreaded direct democracy. Others predict that the polls will hamper social adjustment by giving a voice to mass conservatism.

Congressman Pierce of Oregon fathered a number of legislative proposals directed at the straw polls. In March, 1933, he introduced a bill to forbid the use of the mails by poll takers; at that time mail ballots rather than personal interview was the prevailing poll method. The Postmaster General frowned on a bill that would cut heavily into the postal revenues; the bill was not reported out of committee. Later Mr. Pierce introduced another resolution to provide for an investigation of poll methods by a joint congressional committee. Mr. Pierce's objections to polls were twofold. He felt that the polls influenced the course of elections by introducing a band-wagon effect. He feared that the polls might be used to give an erroneous estimate of public opinion, "if money is used at the right time and right place," and thereby influence the electorate through the band-wagon effect. The band-wagon theory of elections seems to possess no validity, but the Congressman's second point regarding the use of money is of greater importance. In suggesting an investigation of the polls, he expressed the desire that Congressmen who cite polls as authority on what the public wishes should know more about how polls are taken, how they should be interpreted, and what weight should be given to them. Certainly if poll results are to be a factor in determining the attitudes of public officials, these officials should assure themselves that the polls have been conducted in a disinterested way by persons competent to do the work. For polls on candidates, there is a check in the election results, but for polls on issues the principal check is the integrity and ability of the poll conductor. An additional check is available in the comparison of the results of different poll organizations on identical or similar questions, but that control is not always available.

The managers of the chief poll services have agreed that some sort of public control or audit is needed. Dr. Gallup says: [29]

Planning and Public Opinion (Princeton, 1942); Stephen Taylor, "The Study of Public Opinion, An Aid to Administrative Action," *Public Administration,* 21 (1943), pp. 109–119.

[29] Gallup and Rae, *The Pulse of Democracy,* p. 279.

For the protection of those earnestly engaged in polling public opinion, as well as for the general public which uses the surveys as an index of trends and probabilities, it will be necessary to establish some form of public audit to check the various phases of polling procedure. The public is entitled to know all the facts about the polls of public opinion. The people should be informed of the nature of the sponsorship of various polls, and should know where the money for the polls comes from. They are entitled to know the methods used, the number of people in the sample, the method of collecting the ballots, and the margins of error within which the published figures are to be interpreted.

Elmo Roper goes a step further and suggests that the government establish its own polling organization to determine what the electorate wants. Such an agency of government, he says, would have to be managed by persons with "the same high ideals and sense of detached objectivity which are supposed to and in the minds of many do characterize the Supreme Court." He would not, however, desire the government to monopolize the sampling of public opinion; privately owned polls would remain as a check on the publicly conducted sampling.[30] Perhaps persons of these ideals and objectivity could be found. Yet no envy could attach to their task of reporting, for example, the findings of a poll that indicated the people to be at variance with either the expressed policy of the President or of a majority of Congress. But Mr. Roper believes that it would be to the self-interest of politicians to learn as accurately as possible what their constituents want.

The threat of regulation and of investigation constitutes a spur to poll-takers, and competition among various polling organizations in the development of techniques serves to stimulate their efforts. They must strive for accuracy to survive, and an occasional congressional investigation to open their methods to general inspection perhaps serves as a healthy stimulus.[31] Suggestions for more intensive governmental regulation, however, have made no headway.

[30] "Sampling Public Opinion," *Journal of the American Statistical Association,* 35 (1940), pp. 325–334.

[31] Following his overestimate of the Republican vote in the 1944 presidential election, Dr. Gallup was hailed before a House committee and a group of experts also made a report on his methods for the benefit of the committee. See House Committee to Investigate Campaign Expenditures, 78th Cong., 2d sess., *Hearings on H. Res. 551,* Part 12, December 28, 1944 (Washington, 1945).

Chapter 19

ELECTORAL BEHAVIOR

A STRIKING characteristic of the study of politics in the United States is the relatively small amount of effort devoted to the careful analysis of voting behavior. In our society the authority of government is, according to the prevailing doctrines, derived from the popular will as expressed through voting. It might be supposed, therefore, that, merely better to equip those seeking to sway the multitude, there would be ceaseless observation of the electorate to determine who votes, how they vote, why they vote as they do, and what the results mean. The professional politician holds himself out as an "expert" on these matters, but he is not accustomed to presenting and verifying his hypotheses in the fashion of an observer working in the scientific tradition. The results of the elections are ample verification or disproof of the assumptions on which the political practitioner bases his campaigns. In the past few years, however, a few political scientists, sociologists, and social psychologists have attempted to analyze with precision the behavior of man, the political animal. In this chapter some of the studies of the leading students will be summarized for the purpose of indicating their substantive findings, as well as to illustrate various methods of ascertaining with some exactness the nature of mass political behavior.

1. ELECTORAL PARTICIPATION

A high value has been placed on the privilege of voting. The suffrage has been fought for by means varying from force to the tactics of the militant suffragettes. Those within the privileged circle of voters resisted as best they could the demands of the landless, the poor, Negroes, and women for the vote on the supposition that to broaden suffrage would bring with it a reallocation of political power. As the suffrage was broadened, it was supposed that those enjoying a monopoly of political power and influence would have to share their position and perquisites with the upstart groups clamoring for the ballot. Undoubtedly power is not so closely held as it was when the suffrage was narrower, and one factor related to the diffusion of influence has been the broadening of the suffrage. The inauguration of universal suffrage, however, has not been accompanied by its universal exercise. A substantial proportion of the eligible voting population habitually refrains from going to the polls. The effect of this voluntary disfranchisement may be the same as a formal deprivation of the privilege of voting. It is important to know what classes disfranchise themselves and thereby minimize their influence in affairs governmental.

Degree of participation. The computation of the degree of popular participation in elections in the United States presents a difficult problem in arithmetic because no reliable figures are available on the number of persons entitled to vote at particular elections. The voting lists ordinarily include only the names of those who have gone to the trouble to register; they are not a census of all those who meet the tests for the exercise of the suffrage. Hence, to calculate the degree of participation, one has to begin by estimating from the census figures the number of persons in the total population who meet the qualifications of age, literacy, residence, and so forth. Most variations among estimates of the degree of participation spring from differences in the base from which the voting percentages are calculated.[1]

The general trend of participation in presidential elections from 1920 to 1944 may be gauged from Figure 22. The graph shows the total vote in relationship to the total number of citizens 21 years of age or over; hence, it slightly overestimates the participation of eligible voters who are fewer in number than citizens 21 or over. Yet it shows the trend. In 1920 and 1924 less than 50 per cent of citizens 21 and over voted; participation rose to more than 60 per cent in 1940. Study of the graph suggests explanations for variations in participation. The bitterness and closeness of a contest bear on participation. The outcome of the listless campaign of 1920 was a foregone conclusion and no great electoral enthusiasm was aroused. A similar condition prevailed

---

[1] C. H. Titus gives the following estimate of participation in presidential elections: 1880, 78.4; 1884, 76.7; 1888, 78.7; 1892, 76.4; 1896, 79.2; 1900, 73.5; 1904, 65.8; 1908, 66.3; 1912, 60.0; 1916, 63.7; 1920, 49.3; 1924, 49.1; 1928, 57.4; 1932, 57.8.—*Voting Behavior in the United States* (Berkeley: University of California Press, 1935). While his figures picture the trend correctly, they underestimate the participation in each election, since the computations involved no corrections for adults disqualified because of lack of residence, inability to pass literacy tests, insanity, criminality. After allowance for these factors, Harold Gosnell arrives at the conclusion that the following percentages of eligible votes were cast in presidential elections: 1892, 86.2; 1896, 89.5; 1900, 84.6; 1904, 75.3; 1908, 74.8; 1912, 64.7; 1916, 69.6; 1920, 56.9; 1924, 56.6; 1928, 67.5.—*Why Europe Votes* (Chicago: University of Chicago Press, 1930), p. 196.

in 1924, but the hotly fought election of 1928 brought a larger proportion of the voters to the polls. The campaigns of 1936 and 1940 stimulated voter interest to an even higher pitch. The total turnout in 1944 fell by about 1.8 millions from 1940, but the 1944 turnout was extraordinarily high in the light of the numbers in the armed services or made ineligible for voting by inability to fulfill residence requirements in war-manufacturing centers. A factor that may have had some bearing on the upward trend during the period 1920–1940 was the gradual habituation of women to voting. The rate of participation fell sharply

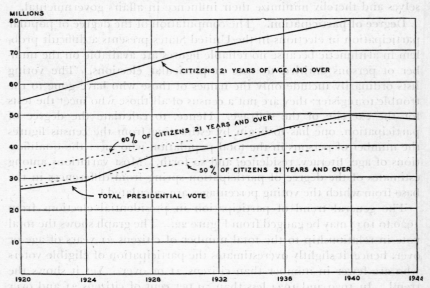

Figure 22. Total Popular Participation in Presidential Elections, 1920–1944, Related to Number of Citizens 21 Years of Age and Over

in 1920 with the enfranchisement of women. It is generally supposed that with the passage of time women in greater numbers have acquired the habit of voting, but there are no conclusive data on this point.

The graph showing the trend in electoral participation in presidential elections for the nation as a whole does not, of course, reveal geographical differences in interest in voting. These variations are indicated in the map in Figure 23, which shows by states the percentage of citizens 21 years of age and over participating in the 1940 presidential election. Examination of the map will bring out the broad range of variation in participation among the states. Lowest popular interest in the presidential election is in the states of the Deep South. In these sure Democratic states there is virtually no presidential campaign. On the other hand, the states with highest participation tend to be doubtful states in which both parties exert themselves to get out the vote.

Participation is usually at its peak in the presidential election. The proportion of the electorate going to the polls is lower in state elections, even lower in state primaries, and often yet lower in city elections.[2] These variations are probably most marked when presidential, state, and local elections are held at different times; even when officials for governments at all levels are chosen at the same election many voters mark their ballots for a presidential candidate but not for candidates for state and local offices.

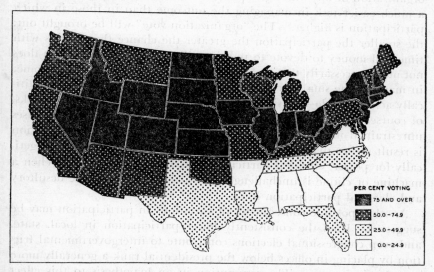

PER CENT VOTING
75 AND OVER
50.0 - 74.9
25.0 - 49.9
0.0 - 24.9

Figure 23. **Participation in Presidential Election of 1940, by States, in Percentages of Citizens 21 and Over**

In a study of voting in Ann Arbor, Michigan, Professor Pollock has shown that, on the average, 25.9 per cent of the potential electorate, that is, those with the legal qualifications to vote, went to the polls. "In other words," he says, "out of the 23,000 people of Ann Arbor, about 3,800 voters run the city and make its political decisions. To put it another way, less than 17 per cent of the residents of the city control its affairs." [3] It must be remembered that these figures are averages; this

[2] A conspicuous exception to this general remark is the Solid South in which the peak vote is cast in the Democratic primaries. For maps showing variations among states in participation in presidential elections, see F. L. Burdette, *Political Parties: An American Way* (New York: Public Affairs Committee, 1945), p. 27.

[3] J. K. Pollock, *Voting Behavior: A Case Study* (Ann Arbor: University of Michigan Press, 1939), p. 6.

average is brought up by the inclusion of votes in presidential elections. Participation in the presidential election was over twice as great as in the state primaries and spring elections, almost twice as great as in the fall state elections, about three times as great as in city elections, and almost five times as great as in city primaries. Although these figures reflect the voting behavior of only one small city, further investigation would probably reveal a similar pattern elsewhere.[4]

What of the effects of differing degrees of participation? In elections and primaries in which there is a relatively small turnout, the party organization or any other group of individuals working in concert has a much easier task in managing the outcome than in those in which participation is higher. The "organization vote" will be brought out; the smaller the participation the greater the chance that groups with time and money to devote to politics will win. This conclusion does not mean necessarily that a corrupt machine will control the outcome; in many of the smaller communities the machine—that is, the politically active people—consists of the leading citizenry. These remarks, of course, do not lead to the conclusion that low participation causes unrestrained machine rule. In a measure at least, low participation is result rather than cause. When different groups compete energetically for power, electoral participation is likely to be high. When a machine or clique is unchallenged, campaigns are apt to be desultory and electoral participation low.

Another possible consequence of variations in participation may be suggested. Does the consistently lower participation in local, state, and even congressional elections contribute to intergovernmental friction by placing in offices below the presidential rank a generally more conservative group? The assumption in an hypothesis to this effect would be that groups desiring to maintain the *status quo* can more easily win in local elections because of lower participation; whereas mass sentiment finds a more unrestrained expression in the election of the President. The answers to these questions are by no means clear, but the hypothesis is worthy of further investigation.

If in national elections 30 or 35 per cent, and in local elections as much as 80 per cent, of the potential electorate disfranchises itself, it is

---

[4] A more complete knowledge of electoral behavior would exist if scholars in widely scattered places would undertake studies on the order of Professor Pollock's excellent monograph. Two subsequent monographs by Professor Pollock, which cover a broader area, confirm the differentials in participation in presidential, state, and local elections. See his *Michigan Politics in Transition* (Ann Arbor: University of Michigan Press, 1942) and *The Direct Primary in Michigan* (Ann Arbor: University of Michigan Press, 1943).

important to know which groups have resigned their political function, which groups have gained whatever power and influence come from the ballot.

Sex variations in participation. Women are less inclined than men to go to the polls. Studies in Sweden, Denmark, Norway, Germany, Australia, New Zealand, and elsewhere reveal this differential with startling uniformity.[5] Data on participation by men and women are less readily available in the United States than elsewhere, but the evidence points to the same differential here. The percentage of popular participation in presidential elections dropped sharply with the introduction of woman suffrage.

Intensive studies of voting in various localities confirm the existence of sex differentials in voting in the United States. A study in 1925 of 4,390 electors in Delaware, Ohio, by Professor Arneson showed that 72.9 per cent of the men and only 57.1 per cent of the women voted.[6] In Austin, Texas, Professor Martin found that, as shown by the 1933 municipal election, men registered as voters in greater degree than women and that of the registered voters, a greater percentage of men voted than of women: of the male registered voters, 58.1 per cent voted; of the female, 44.7 per cent.[7] Similar tendencies were observed by Professor Pollock in Ann Arbor. Over an eight-year period 33.5 per cent of the male registered voters went to the polls; 25.3 per cent of the women. In the presidential elections of 1924 and 1928 a slightly larger percentage of female, than of male, registered voters went to the trouble to cast a ballot;[8] but in all other elections covered by his survey men participated to a higher degree than did women.[9] In Tuscaloosa, Alabama, according to Professor Smith, women constitute about 52 per cent of the population but only about 30 per cent of the registered voters.[10] Connelly and Field suggest, on the basis of opinion poll evi-

[5] Herbert Tingsten, *Political Behavior* (London: P. S. King & Sons, 1937), chap. 1.

[6] B. A. Arneson, "Non-Voting in a Typical Ohio Community," *American Political Science Review*, 19 (1925), pp. 816–825.

[7] R. C. Martin, "The Municipal Electorate: A Case Study," *Southwestern Social Science Quarterly*, 14 (1933), pp. 193–237.

[8] The same was true of women in Lansing, Michigan, in the presidential election of 1928. However, in both Lansing and Ann Arbor a smaller proportion of women than men registered as voters. In Detroit, according to Dr. D. S. Hecock: "Although there were nearly as many women as there were men in the city (and 46% of the population over 21 were women), only 37.9% of the registered voters were women." —Detroit Bureau of Governmental Research, *Detroit Voters and Recent Elections*, Report No. 150, June 1, 1938, p. 3.

[9] Pollock, *Voting Behavior: A Case Study*, pp. 19–24.

[10] C. W. Smith, Jr., *The Electorate in an Alabama Community* (Bureau of Public Administration, University of Alabama, 1942).

dence, that in recent presidential elections about 75 in every 100 men voted, whereas only 61 in every 100 women did so.[11]   It has been suggested that the differential between men and women will gradually disappear, or at least narrow, as women become more accustomed to the exercise of the suffrage.

Age and voting.   Age is another factor that influences participation in elections.   Investigations of voting behavior in relation to age in various countries reveal a remarkable similarity in this respect from country to country.   The proportion of persons voting increases with age until it reaches a peak, usually in the 50 to 60 age group, after which it declines.[12]   Comprehensive data on age differentials in voting in the United States are not available, although straw-poll findings suggest that 76 per cent of those over 40 years of age voted in recent presidential elections but only 59 per cent of those between 21 and 39 did so.[13]   Studies in local situations produce results coinciding with these general conclusions.   In Ann Arbor the peak of voting interest among registered voters was reached in the age group of 51 to 60.   In that range 42.3 per cent of the registered voters went to the polls; in the range 21 to 30, only 22.0 per cent.   Thus electoral participation of persons in their fifties was about twice as high as of those in their twenties.   In Delaware, Ohio, the peak of voting interest was shown to be manifested by persons in the sixties.   Similar findings were reached in the Austin study.   Persons in the age groups over 60 tend to go to the polls less because of illness, incapacity, and related reasons, but a different sort of explanation has to be sought for the low participation of young persons.

Economic status and voting.   Although measures of economic and social status are often crude, in so far as the evidence goes voting participation declines at each stage down the socio-economic ladder.[14] On the basis of polls conducted by the National Opinion Research Center, it has been concluded that in the 1940 presidential election 85 per cent of the upper fourth on the economic scale voted, 69 per cent of the middle half went to the polls, and only 54 per cent of the lowest fourth cast ballots.[15]   Studies made by other methods in scattered localities are in general in accord with these findings.   In both Delaware, Ohio, and Austin, Texas, the occupational group with the highest record of participation was the public-employee group.   It probably would be

---

[11] G. M. Connelly and H. H. Field, "The Non-Voter—Who He Is, What He Thinks," *Public Opinion Quarterly,* 8 (1944), pp. 175–187.

[12] Tingsten, *op. cit.,* chap. 2.

[13] Connelly and Field, *op. cit.,* p. 180.

[14] See Tingsten, *op. cit.,* chap. 3.

[15] Connelly and Field, *op. cit.,* p. 178

found almost everywhere that public employees, by more consistent participation, exert an influence in public affairs disproportionate to their number in the total population. The Austin and Delaware studies are not entirely comparable, but in both places the professional groups ranked high in voting interest. Similarly in Ann Arbor the University of Michigan faculty had a much higher voting record than that of all voters. In Lansing, Michigan, business and professional men manifested a higher electoral enthusiasm than did all men.[16]

Rent paid is an index of economic status often used in social investigations. In a study of voting in Chicago Professor Gosnell concluded that "the better the quarters that a citizen lives in the more apt he is to vote in presidential elections."[17] In Austin, Texas, 53.4 per cent of the registered voters in the wealthier wards voted; in the poorer wards, only 50.5 per cent. Much wider differentials in electoral participation existed between taxpayers and nontaxpayers in Austin. In the Delaware, Ohio, study a much higher proportion of those dwelling in "very good" neighborhoods voted than of those in the "poor" neighborhoods. A study of a sample of the electorate of Lansing Michigan, indicates that in that community women who had telephones and who subscribed to the community chest had more interest in voting than women as a class. In a study of voting in Detroit from 1930 to 1938 Edward H. Litchfield found that participation in elections varied directly with economic status. The group with the highest income had the highest participation, the group with the least income the lowest, with the middle-income groups falling between the two extremes.[18]

National origin and participation. National origin has some connection with voting. Straw-poll data show that persons with both parents native born (even excluding Negroes) have a lower record of participation than do persons with one or both parents born abroad. When the inquiry is narrowed to the voting habits of foreign-born persons, local inquiries show a more complex picture. Professor Pollock found in Ann Arbor that the interest of the foreign-born population in voting was slightly greater than that of the native white group. In Detroit from 1930 to 1938, according to Litchfield's findings, the foreign-born whites had on the average a slightly lower record of

---

[16] Wayne Dennis, "Traits Associated with Registration and Voting," *Journal of Abnormal and Social Psychology*, 27 (1932), pp. 270–278. For evidence of similar tendencies in Battle Creek, see J. K. Pollock, *Permanent Registration of Voters in Michigan* (University of Michigan, Bureau of Government, New Series Bulletin No. 7, 1937).

[17] *Getting Out the Vote* (Chicago: University of Chicago Press, 1927), pp. 90–91.

[18] *Voting Behavior in a Metropolitan Area* (Bureau of Government, University of Michigan), p. 15.

participation in elections than the native whites. Yet "in the non-presidential elections the foreign-born groups participated to a greater extent than did most of the native white groups, though in their own defense the latter groups may point out that in presidential elections the positions were reversed." [19] Moreover, there were important variations in electoral participation among different foreign-born groups, and within the foreign-born groups differences in participation existed among income subgroups. Over the entire period the middle-class Polish electoral interest was only a little less than that of the wealthy native whites, the group with the highest record of participation. On the other hand, the poor Italian group participated to a considerably lesser degree than did the native white group as a whole. Professor Litchfield's findings indicate that broad comparisons of participation of native whites and foreign-born whites are likely to have little significance; in order to ascertain the real nature of participation, it is necessary to go further and determine the participation of subgroups.

Negro voting. Participation by Negroes is less than by whites, even in northern states. The proportion of Negroes who went to the polls in Ann Arbor, Professor Pollock finds, was only about two-thirds as great as the proportion of native whites. In Delaware, Ohio, voting participation of the Negroes was less than that of the whites. Similar, but not unexpected, findings came from the study of Austin, Texas. In Tennessee participation in elections varied from county to county with the percentage of Negro population. Haywood County with 62.1 per cent Negro population had a voting participation of 13 per cent, whereas Bledsoe County with 4.6 per cent Negro population had an electoral participation of 68 per cent.[20] The virtual disfranchisement of the Negro in the southern states accounts for these variations, but less electoral enthusiasm also prevails among Negroes in the northern areas than among the whites.[21]

Effects of education. Participation in elections tends to increase with amount of formal education, although it appears to be more closely associated with economic status. In Table 23 data based on polls by the National Opinion Research Center indicate that within each major economic grouping, voting in the 1940 presidential election increased with education. It may be observed from the table, however, that

[19] *Ibid.*, p. 25.

[20] Paul K. Walp, "Factors Influencing Voting in Tennessee," *University of Tennessee News Letter*, December, 1939.

[21] Dr. Litchfield has suggested that in northern communities Negro participation in elections is gradually approaching that of the community averages. See "A Case Study of Negro Political Behavior in Detroit," *Public Opinion Quarterly*, 5 (1941), pp. 267–274.

economic status outweighed education.   Persons who had gone only to grade school but who were in the upper fourth economically outvoted persons who had gone to college but who managed to stay in the lower fourth economically.

TABLE 23

Participation of Sample of 12,500 Voters in 1940 Presidential Election in Relation to Economic Status and Amount of Formal Education [a]

Persons who went to	Upper fourth	Middle half	Lower fourth	Entire group
College	87%	76%	70%	82%
High School	83	68	54	68
Grade School	83	67	64	63
Entire Group	85	69	54+	..

[a] G. M. Connelly and H. H. Field, "The Non-Voter—Who He Is, What He Thinks," *Public Opinion Quarterly*, 8 (1944), pp. 178–179; and figures furnished and used by permission of National Opinion Research Center.

Reasons for nonvoting.   Another approach to the question of voting has been made by Professors Merriam and Gosnell in their study, *Non-Voting*.   About 6,000 citizens of Chicago were asked why they had failed to vote, and the answers were classified and tabulated.   According to this analysis many nonvoters were deterred by factors beyond their control.   Approximately 12 per cent, or one in eight, of the nonvoters specified illness as their reason for not voting; 11.1 per cent, absence; 5.2 per cent, insufficient legal residence.   Various other explanations classified under the headings of "disbelief in voting" and "inertia" accounted for the majority of the nonvoters.   One factor, "general indifference," accounted for 25.4 per cent of the nonvoters.[22]

Significance of variations in participation.   The general conclusions from the studies of electoral participation can be quickly summarized. The percentage of participation increases group by group up the economic scale.   A larger proportion of men than of women vote.   Participation increases with age up to about 60.   The greater the amount of formal education he has the more probable it is that a person will vote, if other factors are held constant.   Of what significance are these findings?   They have to be related to differences in how these groups vote to disclose their importance.   In presidential elections from 1932

[22] The interviewees did not, of course, answer "I did not vote because of general indifference."   The study gives samples of what they did say.   One young lady "was of the opinion that young girls should have other things to think about besides voting and government."   A young musician "said that he had one of his temperamental spells at election time and neglected to vote."   A Polish woman did not vote "Because she washed that day."

to 1944, the Democratic percentage increased from group to group down the economic scale. Younger persons tended to be Democratic to a higher degree than older persons. The degree of Democratic affiliation increases as the amount of formal education declines. From these facts it follows that other factors being equal, an increase in participation brings an increase in the Democratic percentage of the total vote in presidential elections. Thus, in 1944 Democratic leaders and associated organizations, such as the CIO-PAC and the A.F.L., exerted themselves to get out the vote, and the larger turnout in 1944 undoubtedly contributed to the margin of Democratic victory.[23] Similarly, the explanation for Democratic losses in the 1942 congressional election can be attributed in part to the low popular interest in that election. The effect of the level of participation on state and local elections has not been extensively investigated, but it may be that the relatively disproportionate influence of middle- and upper-class groups in state and local governments is connected with their more assiduous devotion to their electoral duties. It may also be suspected that newspaper editors and civic leaders who organize campaigns to get out the vote are not always aware of the probable effects of a substantial increase in participation.

Dr. Francis G. Wilson has advanced the hypothesis that the curve of participation in voting constitutes a sort of fever chart for the body politic. He says:[24]

In a society in which only fifty per cent of the electorate participates it is clear that politics does satisfy in a way the desires of the mass of individuals in the state. As the percentage of participation rises above, let us say, ninety per cent it is apparent that the tensions of political struggle are stretching to the breaking point the will toward the constitutional.

That is, the will to accept the outcome of elections and the operations of normal governmental procedures may be weakening in a prelude to revolution. "Government by the few voters," he continues, "who make an appearance on election day may be corrupt, it may be the very foundation of the continuance of the old party oligarchy, but at least it is certain that political waste is less than the mass of the people will stand." Otherwise they would not manifest such indifference to elections. There are bits of empirical evidence in support of Wilson's

[23] A special problem of the Democrats was to bring to the polls wage-earning women and wives of wage-earning men among whom the rate of voting abstention is high. See Bernard Berelson and Paul F. Lazarsfeld, "Women: A Major Problem for the PAC," *Public Opinion Quarterly*, 9 (1945), pp. 79–82.

[24] "The Inactive Electorate and Social Revolution," *Southwestern Social Science Quarterly*. Vol. 16, No. 4 (1936), pp. 73–84.

theory. Nonvoters appear to be less dissatisfied with the way political offices are handled than are voters. Nonvoters are more attached to the constitutional *status quo* than are voters. They are less disposed to look with favor on criticism of our form of government than are voters. More of them have no opinion on public issues than is the case with voters.[25] Such opinion-poll data can be supplemented by common-sense observation of variations in participation in presidential elections. Election with highest participation appear to have been conducted at times of higher social tension and more bitter political conflict than in the case of elections with lower rates of participation.

Dr. Wilson's hypothesis is plausible and may account in part for variation in rates of participation. A considerable part of nonvoting, however, may be explained without resort to such recondite theories. Our electoral procedures rather than our relatively less momentous political issues account in some measure for our low popular participation in comparison with other countries. Poll taxes, residence requirements, frequency of elections, complexity of the ballot, and the burdensome character of registration requirements reduce the percentage of participation in American elections.

2. CONSISTENCY OF PARTY AFFILIATION

It is not enough to know who votes. It is also necessary to know how they vote and why they vote the way they do. In an earlier chapter emphasis was placed on the importance, for those who wish to gain power, of control of the party organization and of the nominating process. Control of these matters gives the exclusive right to use the trademark of the party; the party name is a symbol or a trademark with a good-will value, to borrow a concept from economics, capitalized in terms of votes rather than of dollars. The group with the exclusive right to use the party label is certain to receive the habitual party vote, just as Procter and Gamble is certain to receive the business of those conditioned to respond favorably to the trade name "Ivory Soap." It is not to be inferred that the consistent party voter necessarily acts against his own interests. The South has been consistently Democratic, for example, since the Civil War—a large, habitual, unthinking vote, it may be said. Yet the Republican party, led by manufacturing and industrial interests, had little to offer to the agricultural South. When the South, however, thought that it had something at stake in 1928, several of its states deserted the Democratic party.[26] Yet probably

[25] Connelly and Gordon, *op. cit.,* pp. 181–185.
[26] Evidence tending to show that the breaking away from habitual party affiliations is associated with changes in the interests of the individual (rather than personal

habitual attachment to party names causes changes in party allegiance
to lag behind changes in the interests of the voter.[27]   Once established,
party allegiance and loyalty seem to have a remarkable persistence.
Party attitudes seem to be transmitted from father to son, not bio-
logically, to be sure; community, family, and environmental influences
play a part in the fixing of partisan attitudes.

The degree to which the family is an agency for the transmission of
party attitudes has not been extensively studied.   A few professors have
taken advantage of the availability of guinea-pig material in the persons of their students and obtained precise figures for small groups.   At
Dartmouth College in 1928 a study of 375 students showed that 79 per
cent of the entire group voted as their fathers voted.[28]   At DePauw
University the fathers of 77.4 per cent of the students questioned favored
the Republican party in 1932; 67.5 per cent of the students favored
Hoover.   Of the fathers, 21.3 per cent favored the Democratic party;
of the students, 29.7 per cent were for Roosevelt.   Similar variations
existed in the 1936 presidential campaign.[29]   Whether the inheritance
of partisan attitudes is as prevalent in families less favored economically
than those of college students, one cannot say.[30]   The notion of inheritance of partisan attitudes through family influences, of course,
oversimplifies the process of acquisition of party affiliations by young
persons.   The young are subject to the same types of community influences as are their parents and, in most instances, they probably look
forward to a status in society similar to that of their parents.   Identity

appeal of the candidate, the "band-wagon" tendency, or a desire to protest) is
furnished by a sampling study made by S. P. Hayes, Jr.   He found that bolting to
the Democrats between 1928 and 1932 was generally associated with "liberal" attitudes; bolting to the Republicans, with "conservative" attitudes.   "Political attitudes and Party Regularity," *Journal of Social Psychology,* 10 (1939), pp. 503–552.

[27] In a study of 168 persons in Centre County, Pennsylvania, 55.5 per cent of the
persons interviewed agreed with "radical" statements, but 52 per cent of the group
responded most favorably to the Republican party name.   This group when faced
with specific issues favored the introduction of socialistic measures, but was attached
to the Republican party banner.—G. W. Hartman, "The Contradiction between the
Feeling Tone of Political Party Names and Public Response to Their Platforms,"
Journal of Social Psychology, 7 (1936), pp. 336–355.

[28] G. W. Allport, "The Composition of Political Attitudes," *American Journal of
Sociology,* 35 (1929), pp. 220–238.

[29] P. J. Fay and W. C. Middleton, "Certain Factors Related to Liberal and Conservative Attitudes of College Students: II. Father's Political Preference; Presidential
Candidates Favored in 1932 and 1936 Elections," *Journal of Social Psychology,* 11
(1940), pp. 107–119.

[30] A gauge of the degree of inheritance of voting tendencies is furnished by the
estimate of the division of "first" voters in 1940.   Sixty-one per cent of the persons
in that year who had been too young to vote in 1936 cast their ballots for Roosevelt.
The Democratic percentage of "first voters" was thus somewhat higher than of all
voters, 54.7.

of outlook and interest probably have quite as much significance in the "inheritance" of party affiliations as does parental example.

Degree of consistent party voting. The ideal way to estimate the persistence of party preference would be to analyze the political life histories of an adequate sample of individual voters. However, no researcher has had the hardihood to undertake such an inquiry. A simpler method of getting an answer has to be used. By observing the shift of voters from party to party from election to election, one can draw inferences about the proportion of voters whose party loyalty remains constant. Ogburn and Jaffe have applied this rather unsatisfactory method to presidential elections.[31] They compute the percentage of the total vote cast for the Democratic party for each election since 1876. The difference in the percentages polled by the party in any two elections is a measure of the gross shift. For example, in 1928, 41 per cent of the total vote cast was Democratic; in 1932, 57 per cent. The difference between 41 and 57 (that is, 16) is a measure of the net percentage of the electorate that shifted from the Republican to the Democratic ranks between 1928 and 1932. By the application of this method the figures in Table 24 are obtained.

TABLE 24

Estimated Net Shifts from Party to Party between Presidential Elections, 1876–1944

Period	Percentage shift
1876–1880	3
1880–1884	1
1884–1888	0
1888–1892	3
1892–1896	0
1896–1900	0
1900–1904	8
1904–1908	5
1908–1912	1
1912–1916	7
1916–1920	15
1920–1924	5
1924–1928	12
1928–1932	16
1932–1936	4
1936–1940	8
1940–1944	1.3

Inferences from these figures obviously overestimate party consistency in voting. Note that the percentage shift from 1892 to 1896 was zero,

[31] W. F. Ogburn and A. J. Jaffe, "Independent Voting in Presidential Elections," *American Journal of Sociology*, 42 (1936), pp. 186–201.

but shifting went on in both directions in different states to a sufficient degree to alter the outcome of the election. Nevertheless, the figures do suggest a high degree of persistence of party preference from election to election. A different kind of estimate is available from public-opinion polls. The American Institute of Public Opinion made the following estimates of the sources of the popular votes polled by Roosevelt and Willkie in 1940:

	Roosevelt	*Willkie*
1936 Roosevelt voters	19,400,000	4,700,000
1936 Landon voters	900,000	13,300,000
3rd-party supporters in 1936	300,000	400,000
First voters (too young in 1936)	3,000,000	1,900,000
Didn't vote in 1936	3,500,000	1,900,000
	27,100,000	22,200,000

Analysis of these data reveals the shortcomings of the method used by Ogburn and Jaffe. According to the Gallup estimates, 16 per cent of those voting in both elections shifted between 1936 and 1940. Conversely about 84 per cent maintained party regularity. Comparable figures under the Ogburn and Jaffe method would be 8 and 92, respectively.

Neither of the approaches to the problem of measuring party consistency reaches geographical variations in party loyalty nor does either touch the problem of consistency over long periods. A suggestion of the significance of both these factors may be inferred from the graph in Figure 24 showing the Democratic percentages of the total presidential vote in all states in 1920 and 1940. Note that over this period of two decades the net transfer of the electorate from the Republican to the Democratic party differed considerably from state to state. Furthermore, over a long period, such as that covered by the data in the chart, the shift of party strength is greater than that which occurs ordinarily during a four-year period. Thus, the net shift for the entire country during the 1920–1940 period reached about 21 per cent, although it cannot be said to what extent this represented actual transfer of party allegiance and to what extent it represented accession to the Democrats from the ranks of new voters and nonvoters.[32]

[32] The question of the shift of voters from party to party over long periods of time requires further investigation. A plausible hypothesis is that actual transfers of party allegiance by individuals over the long run bulk less large in changes in relative party strength attributable to habitual voting attachments than do differentials in the acquisition of party allegiance among young voters and others beginning to vote. In recent years young voters and other first voters have been predominantly

Several studies have been made to determine the consistency of political affiliation of different geographical areas. If a state or county habitually goes Republican or Democratic, the inference is that the individual voters within the area have a high degree of party loyalty. By this method Ralph and Mildred Fletcher have identified the geographic areas of greatest party consistency and those of the most mercurial political temperament. They tabulated party votes by counties from 1896 through 1932 and ascertained the number of opportunities for a county to change its party allegiance. A county that went Democratic at one presidential election, for example, had an opportunity to change to

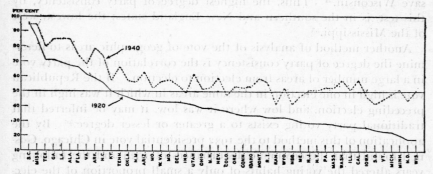

Figure 24. Democratic Percentage of Major-Party Vote in Presidential Elections of 1920 and 1940, by States

Republican at the next presidential election. The tabulation of the data showed 26,151 opportunities for change. In only 29.2 per cent of the instances was there a change in political faith, whereas in 70.8 per cent the county retained its standing at the prior presidential election. The method is, to be sure, a crude measure of party consistency, since there could be considerable shifting of voters from one party to another without changing the political complexion of a county. Dur-

Democratic. In 1946 the American Institute of Public Opinion asked persons 15–18 years of age: "Which political party do you think is the best in the country?" Other age groups were asked: "If a presidential election were being held today, which party would you vote for—the Democratic or Republican?" The replies are (AIPO release of Jan. 24, 1946) as follows:

	Dem.	Rep.
15–18 years of age	65%	35%
21–29 years of age	62	38
30–49 years of age	55	45
50 and over	49	51

It may be that a like analysis in, say, 1900 would have shown a predominance of Republicans among young persons. On the other hand, it may be that persons tend to become more conservative and, hence, more Republican as they become older.

ing the period 1896–1932, 591 counties voted consistently for one party.

By the same method a percentage of consistency was computed for each state. The states with the highest consistency were Louisiana, Mississippi, Rhode Island, South Carolina, and West Virginia, in which the counties remained consistent in more than 90 per cent of the opportunities for political change. In the range of consistency from 80 to 90 per cent were other southern and New England states.[33] At the lowest point in consistency (under 50 per cent) were the western states of Idaho, Montana, Nevada, and Washington. All the states with less than 60 per cent county voting consistency were west of the Mississippi River save Wisconsin.[34] Thus, the highest degree of party consistency, by this test, is in the southern and New England states; the lowest, west of the Mississippi.[35]

Another method of analysis of the vote of geographic areas to determine the degree of party consistency is the correlation of the party vote in a large number of areas from election to election. If the Republican vote is high in one election in the same areas in which it was high in the preceding election, and low where it was low, it may be inferred that traditional party voting exists to a greater or lesser degree.[36] By the application of this method to the 1932 presidential vote in Chicago, Gosnell found that the economic disturbances of 1929 and the following years altered the voting habits of only a small proportion of the electorate.[37] In a study of the 1934 congressional election he concluded that party tradition was the most significant influence in the voting. "The main characteristics of party lines in Chicago, a typical American

---

[33] Alabama, Arkansas, Connecticut, Florida, Georgia, Kentucky, New York, Vermont, Virginia.

[34] The states with between 50 and 60 per cent consistency by this method were California, Colorado, Kansas, Minnesota, Nebraska, Oklahoma, Oregon, South Dakota, Utah, Wisconsin.

[35] Ralph and Mildred Fletcher, "Consistency in Party Voting from 1896 to 1932," *Social Forces*, 15 (1936), pp. 281–285. Hasbrouck found that during the period 1914–1926 there were 148 congressional districts that consistently elected Republican Representatives; 122 regularly returned Democratic Representatives. Thus 270, or 62.1 per cent, of the total membership of the House were elected by districts customarily voting for the same party.—*Party Government in the House of Representatives* (New York: Macmillan, 1927), p. 172.

[36] Without statistical manipulation of the data, similar findings may be made simply by comparing maps showing the party vote for a series of elections. Kinneman and Shipley have applied this method to Bloomington, Illinois; maps showing the presidential vote by precincts in elections from 1928 to 1944 reveal a remarkable consistency of party affiliation within each precinct. See "The Ecology of Pluralities in Presidential Elections," *American Sociological Review*, 10 (1945), pp. 382–89.

[37] H. F. Gosnell, and N. N. Gill, "An Analysis of the 1932 Presidential Vote in Chicago," *American Political Science Review* 29 (1935), p. 984.

metropolitan community, were set long before the depression and the New Deal." [38]

Significance of traditional vote. What conclusions are to be drawn about consistency of party preference? All students are agreed that persistence of party preference is high, but how high is another question. It is probably not far wrong to estimate that from 75 to 85 per cent of persons voting in two consecutive presidential elections support the same party both times.[39] It is commonly said that the strength of the traditional vote has declined since 1900. Certainly the margin of party victory has increased since that time, but since the margin of victory shows only the net rather than the gross shift, it furnishes no valid basis for a conclusion on the long-term trend in party consistency. However, it is extremely likely that partisans have become more fickle since 1900. How much more so, we do not know. Clearly, consistency of party affiliation varies in different parts of the country, with the greatest variation in political preference occurring in states west of the Mississippi.[40]

Such conclusions may be drawn about the facts, but what is the significance of the facts? The large proportion of traditional voters in the electorate may have great influence on public policy. This mass conditioning of the electorate may furnish a brake on rapid change. Under the radical and reactionary surface eddies flow deeper slow-moving currents. To change the figure, consistency of party affiliation represents a powerful mass inertia. Campaigners may declaim that the opposition is leading, or will lead, the country to perdition, but most people remain unmoved. For these reasons those who believe that party consistency is on the decline, look forward with fear to the disastrous consequences in speedy change that may flow from greater electoral fluidity. Disastrous for whom is usually not made explicit. In political innovation there is, indeed, some evidence that American states with high electoral fluidity tend to lead.[41]

Who are the independents? Studies of persistence of party prefer-

[38] H. F. Gosnell and M. J. Schmidt, "Factorial and Correlational Analysis of the 1934 Vote in Chicago," *Journal of the American Statistical Association,* 31 (1936). p. 518.

[39] For discussion of the opinion-poll data, see Hadley Cantril, "Why We Vote the Way We Do," *New York Times Magazine,* Sept. 24, 1944.

[40] Louis Bean, however, shows that differences in state party flexibility have declined since 1896. Or, conversely, the degree of party consistency from state to state has become more nearly the same over the country.—*Ballot Behavior* (Washington: American Council on Public Affairs, 1940), chap. 6.

[41] See T. A. Bailey, "The West and Radical Legislation, 1890–1930," *American Journal of Sociology,* 38 (1933), pp. 603–612.

ence suggest that by identification of the politically fickle, those who transfer their partisan affections from election to election, one could determine who decides elections. Perhaps the "independent" voter often settles elections, but in some instances persons who did not vote at the preceding election are the deciding bloc. Note the Gallup analysis of the 1940 presidential vote quoted on page 598. The majority of the "independents" moved over to the Republican column, but enough 1936 nonvoters supported the Democrats in 1940 to keep them in power. This election, of course, may have been atypical.

One approach to the identification of the "independent" voter is through opinion polls. Dr. Gallup's organization has several times asked the question: "In politics as of today, do you consider yourself a Republican, Democrat, Socialist or Independent?" Usually about 20 per cent of the respondents regard themselves as "independents." If the polled samples have been representative, this would mean that between 9 and 10 million voters place themselves in the "independent" category. The extent to which these persons actually vote independently is another question. It is a matter of some satisfaction—and sometimes self-protection—to regard oneself as an independent,[42] and yet vote quite consistently for one party or the other. Nevertheless, it is fairly certain that persons who declare themselves to be "independents" cross party lines in greater proportions than do diehard partisans. If this is true, the following data on independents in various occupational groups, as revealed by a January, 1940, poll, have special significance:

Professional men	25%	Unskilled workers	16%
Businessmen	22	White-Collar workers	22
Skilled workers	19	Farmers	12
Semiskilled workers	18	Farmers outside the South	14

A plausible conclusion to draw from these data is that the independents do not constitute a narrow group with common class interests that might be promoted by using its pivotal position in the electorate. An appeal for the independent vote almost has to be an appeal to the entire electorate, for the independent vote consists of people of all classes and interests. The independent vote is sometimes thought of as a middle-class vote; but, if these figures mean anything, they refute the popular notion. Confirmation for the proposition that shifting voters are in fact distributed among all social classes is found in the data presented in Figure 25. This chart was built from Gallup poll estimates of the

[42] As a southern gentleman once said to the writer: "My boy, I wear no man's collar. I've always been an independent in politics, but I've never found it necessary to scratch the Democratic ticket."

Republican-Democratic division of broad occupational classes. Thus, in 1936, 49 per cent of the professional group supported Roosevelt; in 1940, 38 per cent. The difference between these figures, 11, represents the degree of net shift within the group. (Undoubtedly shifting occurred in both directions and a gross figure would be higher.) Note from the data in the chart that from 1936 to 1940 the allegiances of all groups shifted toward the Republicans but at somewhat different rates.

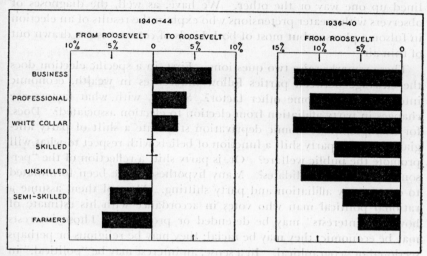

Figure 25. Net Shift from Party to Party, 1936 to 1940 and 1940 to 1944, by Broad Occupational Groups in Percentage Points

From 1940 to 1944 the pattern of transfer was more complex. Some groups moved in one direction, others in another. Conditions of war and the rightward shift of Democratic policy were associated with a move by upper classes to the Democrats, although other classes continued the transfer toward the Republicans that began after 1936.

Obviously the data are scanty on who the independent voters are, but it is clear that in presidential elections voters who cross party lines come from all social and economic classes. The "independent" vote does not make up a narrowly defined class with homogeneous interests that may be promoted because the group holds the balance of power.

3. CHARACTERISTICS ASSOCIATED WITH VOTING

Although it is clear that a substantial proportion of the electorate habitually responds to the leaders of one or the other of the major parties, it is obvious that there is a degree of shifting from one party to another. Moreover, the question remains of how the voters divide, either through response to tradition or to the special appeals and questions of a particular campaign. The reliable data on why voters throw their support one way or the other are limited. We have, of course, the sagacious comments of the editors and columnists, published the day after the election, asserting with force that the Negroes voted this way or that, that the workers turned the trick, that the Catholics were lined up one way or the other. We have, as well, the diagnoses of observers with greater pretensions who explain the results of an election in fulsome phrases; but most of both kinds of comments are drawn out of thin air.

These remarks raise two questions. First, in a specific election does the cleavage between parties follow differences in wealth, economic interest, race, or some other factor? Second, with what factors are changes in party affiliation from election to election associated? Does, for example, an economic deprivation stimulate a shift of party allegiance? Or is party shift a function of beliefs with respect to what will promote the public welfare? Or, is party shift a reflection of the "personality" of the candidates? Many hypotheses have been formulated to cover party affiliation and party shifting. Most of them assume a rational political man who votes in accordance with his estimate of how his "interests" may be defended or promoted. Those interests may be economic; they may be racial; they may be religious or perhaps sectional or geographical. In a sense, an interest may be "political," in that the voter may be concerned about whether a particular course of action will promote the general welfare. Or he may be disposed to vote against the "ins" when dissatisfied, whatever the origin of his ills may be. All these propositions rest upon assumptions about how people behave. An assumption may sound perfectly plausible and be perfectly untrue. Is there evidence to support these hypotheses about how people vote?

The secrecy of the ballot means, of course, that we can have no analysis of the vote at any particular election with nicely totaled columns showing the division of the poor between Republican and Democratic, or the attachment of racial or religious groups to one or the other of the parties. The relationship between characteristics of the voters and party affiliation has to be ascertained by indirect means or by sampling studies. Some scholars have used the statistical method of correlation to ascertain the relationship between characteristics of the voters and their voting behavior. It is known, for example, what percentage of the population of each county consists of Negroes and what percentage of each county vote is Democratic. Is there a tendency for the Democratic vote to rise or to fall with the increase or decline of Negro population? This relationship can be computed and expressed as a coefficient of correlation. The coefficient ranges from o.o to 1.o. If a coefficient of o.o is obtained, it is assumed that there is no relationship between the two factors concerned. As it approaches 1.o, the conclusion arises that as Negro population increases, to use our hypothetical example, the Democratic vote increases. Similarly, the coefficient may range from o.o to −1.o, indicative of a negative relationship. A few of the studies using the method of correlation may be summarized.[43]

The theory perhaps most widely accepted in explanation of political behavior is that of economic motivation. It is simple enough to see this motivation in the activities of pressure groups in promoting and obstructing measures that affect their interests. The plane, however, on which lobbyists and pressure groups operate is a relatively sophisticated one. Is the same awareness of economic interest present among the rank and file of the electorate? Do individual voters act in accordance with their economic interests and do their political attitudes change as their economic fortunes are altered?

Economic status and voting behavior. Most analyses of voting behavior show that there is a measurable relationship between economic status and voting behavior, but other factors also enter into the motivation of voters. In a study of voting behavior in North Dakota, George Lundberg classified the counties of the state into radical and conservative on the basis of their attitude to the candidates of the Non-Partisan League in the elections from 1916 to 1922. "The most striking fact in the comparison of the radical and the conservative counties . . . ," Lundberg concluded, "is the uniformly inferior economic circumstances and prosperity in the radical counties." The radical counties had a smaller per capita value of farm property, a lesser value of land per acre, and a lower per capita value of farm crops. The economic differences were not the only differences between the radical and conservative counties. The radical counties had a much larger proportion of recent migrants, principally of Russian and Scandinavian origin. The prevalence of these migrants, he concluded,[44]

. . . with a highly developed cultural background along the lines of cooperative community enterprises was undoubtedly an important factor in causing the program of state ownership of certain utilities, which was the cen-

[43] Students unversed in statistics should examine the discussion of the technique of correlation in an elementary statistics text.

[44] G. A. Lundberg, "The Demographic and Economic Basis of Political Radicalism and Conservatism," *American Journal of Sociology*, 32 (1927), pp. 719–732.

tral issue during the period considered, to seem less radical, or entirely normal, to this type of population. This same stock (in the conservative counties) reared in American traditions found a larger gap to bridge between their customary way of thinking and the proposed program of the League.

The question arises whether the relatively poorer economic status or the attitudes associated with recency of migration was the more important factor in the more radical voting of the radical counties. Or to put it in another way, would a relatively lower economic status alone have made these counties vote more radically?

Dr. J. A. Neprash made a study, by the method of correlation, of the seven primary and general elections in Iowa from 1920 to 1926 at which Smith Brookhart was a candidate. The former Senator was an insurgent Republican, who made a strong appeal to the farm vote. By the analysis of the vote "a definite tendency was found for sentiment both for and against Brookhart to become concentrated in regions which differed from each other primarily with respect to economic conditions." Moreover, the sentiment toward Brookhart seemed to change with changes in the economic prospects of agriculture. When the prices of livestock and grain were the lowest, the vote for Brookhart rose in the livestock and grain areas. Neprash arrived at the conclusion that "enough voters were swayed by economic considerations to determine the outcome of each election." He observed that "though to a great extent the attitudes expressed in these elections were traditional or otherwise determined, still, the attitudes of a sufficient number of 'marginal voters' were economically determined to materially affect the result." [45] Thus the conclusion of the study of Iowa political behavior was that changes in economic status correspondingly altered political attitudes,[46] not of all but of some of those persons affected by the changes.

The effect of depression and prosperity or changes in economic status has been analyzed by Clark Tibbitts on a larger scale than in Neprash's study of Iowa. He took for analysis congressional elections from 1878 to 1888 and from 1904 to 1911. The elections selected were chosen because of their proximity to upward and downward movements in the business cycle, and the analysis was restricted to nine northeastern

---

[45] J. A. Neprash, *The Brookhart Campaign in Iowa, 1920–1926* (New York: Columbia University Press, 1932), pp. 120–121.

[46] In another study of voting behavior of farmers, John D. Barnhart has found that agrarian unrest in Nebraska in the Populist days was apparently accentuated by drouths. "To suggest," he says, "that the farmer held the politician responsible for the shortage of rainfall would be an unwarranted exaggeration of the thoughtlessness of the voters. But it is quite another matter to suggest that the drouth in Nebraska made a bad set of agricultural conditions worse and that the politicians were held responsible for some of the conditions."—Rainfall and the Populist Party in Nebraska," *American Political Science Review,* 19 (1925), pp. 527–540.

industrial states.   The popular vote of the party in power was found
to have risen with improvements in business conditions; to have declined when the reverse situation obtained.   "When elections occur
during or just following periods of expansion, other things being equal,
the party in power may expect a vote of confidence; while on the other
hand, when an election occurs in a depression period, the majority party
must expect to be shorn of its popularity and even in some cases turned
out of office."   The analysis showed, however, that the vote in many of
the congressional districts studied did not reflect changes in business
conditions.   In from one third to one half of the congressional districts,
voting behavior did not follow the course of business conditions.[47]
How is that substantial degree of lack of responsiveness to changing economic conditions to be explained?   Probably a considerable part of it
is attributable to the traditional party vote.

A simpler and cruder way of ascertaining the relationship between
changes in economic status and political behavior is illustrated by the
graph in Figure 26 showing the relation between per-capita income
from farming of persons living on farms [48] and the Republican percentage of the total presidential vote in Iowa and Nebraska from 1912
to 1944.   Note that as per-capita income increases, the Republican
percentage usually rises.   As per-capita income declines, the proportion
of Democratic and third party vote tends to rise.   The interpretation
of the relationship shown in the chart, however, is not easy.   The relationship obviously does not mean that the party in power is invariably
rewarded with votes when conditions improve.   Note the trend from
1912 to 1916, from 1916 to 1920, and from 1936 to 1940.   The relation
comes closer to meaning that when economic conditions deteriorate,
the party in power loses votes, as from 1920 to 1924 and from 1928 to
1932.   Perhaps an interpretation that better explains the entire trend
is that economic adversity pulls the voters of these states away from
their traditional Republicanism to either the Democratic party or a
third party.   This explanation covers the ups and downs in the Republican percentage, except in 1944 when, despite increasing prosperity,

[47] Clark Tibbitts, "Majority Votes and the Business Cycle," *American Journal of
Sociology*, 3 (1931), pp. 596–606.   Ralph and Mildred Fletcher have approached the
problem by relating turnover in the membership of the House of Representatives to
business conditions.   They concluded that there "is a tendency for the peaks of the
turnover to be associated with periods of depression and that a similar relationship
exists between the lower rates of turnover and periods of prosperity.   This relationship is very slight . . ."—"Labor Turnover of the United States Congress," *Social
Forces*, 7 (1928), pp. 192–193.

[48] The figures are from *Agricultural Statistics*, 1942, p. 663.   Although the income
figures are national, presumably farm incomes in Nebraska and Iowa fluctuated with
the national averages.

there was no change in Iowa and only a one-point Republican gain in Nebraska. For an explanation of this exception one has to go beyond economic variations.

It should also be pointed out that a crude method, like the chart, fails to identify many elements and influences that can be brought to light by the use of more complex statistical methods. The chart, for example, shows only the gross shift away from the Democrats in Iowa

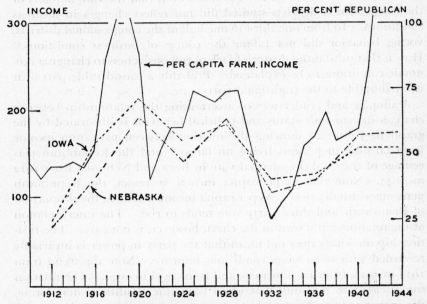

Figure 26. Changes in Republican Percentage of Total Presidential Vote in Nebraska and Iowa in Relation to Fluctuations in Per-capita Farm Income, 1912–1944

between 1932 and 1936. By the use of more refined methods Gosnell was able to arrive at the finding that "the greatest shifts away from Roosevelt between the two elections were in the counties where the voters were in number predominantly dry, native white, and farmers who had suffered considerable corn losses" through drought. "Roosevelt held his ground or gained in 1936 in those counties where there were large percentages of wet, foreign-born, city dwellers, and farmers who suffered only small losses in corn production." [49]

[49] H. F. Gosnell and Norman Pearson, "The Study of Voting Behavior by Correlational Techniques," *American Sociological Review*, 4 (1939), pp. 809–815. Dr. Gosnell has brought this article and other materials into a book which illustrates the uses of statistical technique in the investigation of political behavior. See *Grass Roots Politics* (Washington: American Council on Public Affairs, 1942).

To nail down the general ideas suggested by the cited studies, a few other related pieces of research can be summarized. By use of correlational techniques Ogburn and Hill ascertained for selected areas the relationship between income and Roosevelt support in 1932. In 131 Chicago precincts it was found that "precincts with an average rent of $30 a month gave 73 per cent of their votes on the average to Roosevelt. But, for precincts with $60 rents the average vote for Roosevelt was a good deal lower, 59 per cent. . . . It was not until the voters on the average were paying $80 a month rent, that Hoover received a majority of the votes." The 1932 vote was correlated with rentals and rental values in thirty-nine Illinois cities with between 10,000 and 100,000 population. "The conclusion of the study among the smaller cities of Illinois is that those with the cheaper dwellings gave Roosevelt the larger vote and those with the more expensive homes returned more votes for Hoover." In the urban sections studied, rent paid was used as an index of economic status. A different index of economic status was devised for the rural areas of seventy counties studied by estimating per-capita income through dividing the value of crops and livestock products by the farm population over twenty-one years of age. Comparison with the votes showed that "the counties with lower economic status gave higher percentages of their votes for Roosevelt." [50]

The analysis summarized deals with the relationship of economic status to voting behavior only at one election. The question naturally arises from what groups did the Democrats recruit enough supporters to change the results between 1928 and 1932. After an elaborate statistical analysis of voting behavior in 1932 in parts of Chicago inhabited mainly by whites, Gosnell concluded that the Roosevelt vote varied from place to place in the city according to the traditional Democratic vote. He says that "Democratic party tradition was most important in explaining the variations of the Roosevelt vote in Chicago." This conclusion can be reconciled with the Ogburn and Hill findings by the supposition that a division of income classes something on the order of that which they observed in 1932 must have existed in 1928. But what groups shifted from Republican to Democratic between 1928 and 1932? Gosnell found that the shift was common to all economic classes. All income levels "relieved some of their tensions" associated with depres-

[50] W. F. Ogburn and Estelle Hill, "Income Classes and the Roosevelt Vote in 1932," *Political Science Quarterly*, 50 (1935), pp. 186–193. The Ogburn and Hill study was limited to a small area, and they warn that the conclusion might "not have been true for the Southern states, or indeed, for communities other than those studied." See also W. F. Ogburn and L. C. Coombs, "The Economic Factor in the Roosevelt Elections," *American Political Science Review*, 34 (1940), pp. 719–727.

sion losses and discontent "by voting against the party in power." [51]

Multiplicity of influences impinging on voters. The studies summarized to this point were made by analyzing the election results in relation to the known characteristics of the electorate. They constituted attempts chiefly to test the relation between voting attitudes and economic status or changes in economic status. It is evident that economic influences do not account entirely for voting tendencies. Other factors have a significant influence. Their nature is suggested by a study of Erie County, Ohio, during the campaign of 1940 by Paul F. Lazarsfeld and associates.[52] Instead of correlating election results with economic and social characteristics of the population, their technique of investigation was to interview 1,200 voters, a much larger sample than would be questioned in a county in an ordinary opinion poll. Some of the 1,200 were interviewed at intervals during the campaign to determine the effects of the campaign on voting behavior. The findings were that the factors most closely associated with party preference were social-economic status, religion, residence. A person with low social-economic status, Catholic religion, and a city residence was likely to be a Democrat; a prosperous Protestant farmer was likely to vote Republican.

Thus, many factors motivate voting. If, say, all people were alike except for age and voting behavior, it would be relatively simple to determine the relationship, if any, between the two variables of voting and age. But almost always more than two variables exist. If a given precinct consisting predominantly of wet, Catholic, foreign-born, traditionally Democratic voters gives an overwhelming majority to a Democratic candidate, how can one determine which of these factors is the more important? The statisticians have a way of doing so; this is not the place to explain how, but the existence of the method is worth noting. By holding "constant" all save one of several factors, the varying weights of each factor may be estimated. Ogburn and Talbot examined the vote for Alfred E. Smith in 1928 in 173 counties selected at random from the states of Massachusetts, New York, Ohio, Illinois, Wisconsin, Colorado, Montana, and California. The computations were presented to show the effect of a 10 per cent increase in each of various factors on the Smith vote. Thus, an increase of 10 per cent in the wet voters, all other factors remaining constant, would probably have increased the Democratic vote by 4.1 per cent. The five factors and their estimated importance are as follows:

[51] H. F. Gosnell and N. N. Gill, "An Analysis of the 1932 Presidential Vote in Chicago," *American Political Science Review*, 29 (1935), pp. 967–984.
[52] *The People's Choice* (New York: Duell, Sloan and Pearce, 1944).

Factor which is increased 10 per cent	Corresponding percentage increase in Democratic vote
Foreign born	0.5
Urban population	0.8 (decrease)
Democratic voters	1.8
Catholics	2.8
Wet voters	4.1

Of the factors analyzed, then, wetness was most closely related to support of the Democratic candidate, Al Smith.[53] It needs to be observed that the sample analyzed by Ogburn and Talbot included none of the southern territory that went Republican in 1928; it, therefore, throws no light on the relative importance of Smith's Catholicism and wetness in moving southern Democrats into the Hoover camp.[54]

General conclusions on voter motivation. All the foregoing studies reported attempts to determine what characteristics of voters were associated with voting behavior. Can any defensible general conclusions be drawn from these isolated analyses about voter motivation?

Traditional partisans appear to furnish the core of the vote for both parties in presidential elections. This fact is not necessarily in conflict with the theory of economic motivation of voting behavior; one has to determine with what factors traditional or habitual party affiliation is associated. In so far as the evidence goes, traditional Democrats are, on the average, considerably less prosperous than habitual Republicans. However, the student should be warned that the data on this point does not go back much beyond 1932, but presumably the cleavages since that time were projections of earlier tendencies. Furthermore, other quite obvious elements enter into the traditional vote. Southern Democrats are a different breed from those of the North. To explain a sizeable part of traditional voting, one must include in his analysis some accounting for the influences of the Civil War, which have doubtless projected themselves down through time to the present.

Departures from traditional voting—shifts from party to party from election to election—seem also to be associated in fairly high degree with economic interest. Other things being equal, it is probable that those groups most seriously injured by economic trends will shift in larger proportions to the opposite party. Yet it is not always clear

[53] W. F. Ogburn and N. S. Talbot, "A Measurement of the Factors in the Presidential Election of 1928," *Social Forces*, 8 (1929), pp. 175–183.

[54] For a broader analysis of religion and the 1928 election, see L. H. Bean, *op. cit.*, chap. 9. For a study of the correlation between Catholic population and affirmative votes on constitutional amendments supported by the Roman Catholic Church in New York State, see Madge M. McKinney, "Constitutional Amendment in New York State," *Public Opinion Quarterly*, 3 (1939), pp. 635–636.

that groups benefiting from governmental policies will at the next election reward the administration with an increased proportion of their votes. In an analysis of shifts toward Roosevelt in Pennsylvania between 1932 and 1936 Harold Gosnell found "the existence of a tendency for the counties which had enjoyed the greatest degree of economic improvement to shift markedly toward Roosevelt." [55]   It is evident, nevertheless, that habitual and traditional party loyalties offer great resistance to appeals to transfer party allegiance because of altered economic status for either better or worse.[56]   Under some circumstances, it seems likely that governmental policies that improve the lot of people may simply hasten them in their tendency to return to their traditional attachment to the opposite party.

It is apparent that economic motivation alone is a theory inadequate to cover the facts of voting behavior. All the studies cited have to bring other factors into the picture to account for voting behavior.[57] Sampling studies by the polls are confirmatory. In the elections of 1936, 1940, and 1944, more businessmen were Republican than Democratic, more workers were Democratic than Republican, yet there were substantial numbers of Democratic businessmen and likewise substantial numbers of Republican workers. A different situation would have prevailed had the economic theory of voting behavior covered the whole situation.

A way of isolating these noneconomic influences is to observe the shifts between elections by different economic classes. Thus between 1928 and 1932 all classes moved to some extent over into the Democratic column. These parallel movements suggest that all classes were influenced by common factors. These factors, of course, could be called economic, but the pattern of movement certainly rebuts the idea of class solidarity. Perhaps what happened was that persons of all classes

[55] H. F. Gosnell and W. G. Colman, "Political Trends in Industrial America: Pennsylvania an Example," *Public Opinion Quarterly*, 4 (1940), pp. 473–486.

[56] See the suggestive analysis by H. F. Gosnell and N. M. Pearson, "Relation of Economic and Social Conditions to Voting Behavior in Iowa, 1924–1936," *Journal of Social Psychology*, 13 (1941), pp. 15–35.

[57] The following comment by Mosca is relevant: "The person who wrote that the human being lets himself be guided by self-interest alone stated a general maxim that is almost entirely devoid of practical value, since it can tell us nothing save at the cost of exceedingly minute analysis and distinctions. Anyone who thinks that interest has to be something that can be expressed materially in terms of money and measured in pounds and pence is a person of too little heart and too little head to understand the people about him. Interest is suited in each individual to the individual's own tastes, and each individual interprets his interest in his own individual way. For many people, to satisfy their pride, their sense of personal dignity, their vanities great and small, to humor their personal caprices and rancors, is worth far more than pleasures that are purely material."—*The Ruling Class* (New York: McGraw-Hill, 1939), p. 114.

expressed their resentments of all sorts by voting against Hoover. Observe also the trends from 1936 to 1940, shown in Figure 25 on page 603. All classes moved over to the Republican ranks to some extent. If economic motivation had been the sole factor of influence, it would be expected that at least the workers would have maintained their Democratic loyalties.[58] However, all classes responded in the same way, if not to a single influence, to influences with like effects on their partisan preferences. From 1944 to 1947, according to polls on presidential preferences, the same tendency prevailed. Businessmen, farmers, white collar workers, and manual workers all became slightly more Republican in their inclinations.

The nature of one type of noneconomic influence on electoral attitudes is illustrated by shifts in American partisan attitudes in relation to events in Europe in 1940. During that year the popularity of Roosevelt rose and fell with European crises, according to the reports of the American Institute of Public Opinion. In a poll released on October 22, 53 per cent of the respondents said that they would have favored Willkie had there been no European war. Actually about 55 per cent favored Roosevelt. These figures might be interpreted to mean that almost 4,000,000 voters supported Roosevelt on the basis of their belief that his leadership was preferable in the war situation, although at the same time these voters believed that the election of Roosevelt might be detrimental to some interest or desire of their own. It is probable that many votes were cast on grounds of national defense in a direction contrary to that in which the voter believed his economic interests lay.

Cleavages in state and local elections. Our information about cleavages among the characteristics of voters in state and local elections and primaries is extremely limited, and probably the general ideas discussed above have little validity in application to many such elections and primaries. Dangerfield and Flynn, for example, conclude from the analysis of the primary election in Oklahoma that "personality and speaking ability were more important than economic issues."[59] This

---

[58] Litchfield concludes from his study of Detroit: "From the comparison of the movements of the political behavior curves in all the different economic, race, and ethnic groups one very important conclusion emerged: the behavior curve movements in all groups occur in such a uniform manner that it is clear that the basic influences which cause those movements operate upon and are effective in all the different groups. In the city as a whole, although economic groups are probably more solidified than are ethnic and race groups, none of the groups is so solidified but that the basic character of its political behavior is determined by influences that are city-wide. There is an appreciable element in each group which makes common cause with other unrelated elements in other groups."—*Voting Behavior in a Metropolitan Area* (Ann Arbor: University of Michigan Press, 1941), p. 68.

[59] R. H. Dangerfield and R. H. Flynn, "Voter Motivation in the 1936 Oklahoma

judgment was reached by a process of elimination. The correlation of votes actually cast with available economic indices that might have some conceivable relationship with voting behavior revealed no positive relationship. Additional inquiries of a like character might disclose that in many state and local elections factors such as the personality of the candidate, his speaking ability, his capacity to "make friends," and other like characteristics govern the decision of the electorate and that economic issues are not presented and dramatized in a fashion to divide the electorate along economic lines. Studies by Gosnell of primaries and elections in Louisiana and California suggest the complexity of motivation in state and local elections. In one Louisiana primary it was impossible, as in the Oklahoma study, to relate the vote for Huey Long to any available index of social or economic status. Kaleidoscopic shifts in electoral support of the Long organization from election to election suggested an electoral behavior quite different from the relatively stable pattern of behavior in presidential voting.[60] But about all that can be concluded about voting in state and local elections is that scholars have a wonderful opportunity to narrow our area of ignorance.

4. WHAT DO ELECTION RESULTS MEAN?

The studies of electoral behavior that have been summarized in this chapter have been made mostly during the past ten or fifteen years. They have made available much more precise knowledge of how different types of individuals cast their ballots than existed before. Yet, after an examination of the explorations into the nature of mass electoral behavior, one still wants to ask the question, "What of it all?"

The government of a democracy is supposed to be guided by the "will of the people." Does the detailed analysis of the vote furnish a better guide to what the people will in terms of substantive policy than intuitive judgment? The study of electoral behavior certainly furnishes a better estimate of what classes of voters are responsible for a particular electoral outcome than was formerly available. If an administration holds the support of one group and loses that of another, it has a rough

---

Democratic Primary," *Southwestern Social Science Quarterly,* 17 (1936), pp. 97–105. In a study of the vote for assembly candidates in New Jersey over the period 1877–1924 Stuart A. Rice came to the conclusion that although, there were cycles of voting behavior, these cycles would appear to be attributable "to some factor or factors of changing attitude which are not closely related to changes in business prosperity." *Quantitative Methods in Politics* (New York: Knopf, 1928), p. 292. Compare with this the relationship between economic fluctuations and voting in presidential elections.

[60] Gosnell, *Grass Roots Politics,* chap. 8.

gauge of the acceptability of its policies to different groups of the population. Yet it has, as the result of a victory, no mandate for a particular policy. On the other hand, an administration will know to what general classes of people its policies must be directed if it hopes to hold together the electoral combination that brought it to power. Moreover, the opposition party will know where it must gain recruits if it is to be successful in returning to power.

From these comments it must be supposed that increased knowledge of the nature of electoral behavior would sharpen group conflicts and make more difficult the arrival at a working compromise on questions of public policy. Yet it is conceivable that fuller knowledge of the voting behavior of different classes of the population might serve to minimize class and group friction. From one viewpoint, the discontent and dissatisfaction of particular classes of the population may be identified and dealt with earlier when there is precise knowledge of how those classes cast their ballots. From another viewpoint, the exact analysis of voting behavior seems to indicate that different groups with different interests do not permit those interests to govern their voting behavior so completely as might be supposed. To judge from the exhortations of lobbyists speaking for groups of farmers, laborers, and other groups, one might conclude that it was extremely dangerous for a public official to ignore the demands of pressure groups. Yet analysis reveals that the farmers do not vote as a bloc; nor do the wage earners; nor did even W.P.A. workers act as a unit. These facts have extremely important implications for legislators and administrators. They mean that legislators and administrators, if they have the courage, need not be bludgeoned by the representatives of many special-interest groups. The threat of retribution on election day is often an empty threat. Governments may, if they take heed of the findings of these studies, be left freer to work out programs that reflect more nearly the general interests.

Then what does an election decide? Does it determine the course of governmental policy? Does it give the victor a mandate to carry out a detailed agenda of policies? About all that the election decides conclusively is who shall fill the office in question. "A vote," concludes Lippmann, "is a promise of support. It is a way of saying: I am lined up with these men, on this side. I enlist with them. I will follow. . . . The force I can exert is placed here, not there."[61] We "must adopt the theory," he says, "that, by their occasional mobilization as a majority, people support or oppose the individuals who actually gov-

[61] *The Phantom Public* (New York: Harcourt, Brace, 1925), pp. 56–57.

ern. We must say that the popular will does not direct continuously
but that it intervenes occasionally." [62]

These occasional interventions of the electorate into the direction of
government are in a sense the characteristic that differentiates democracy from other forms of government. "A presidential election," says
Munro, "is merely our modern and highly refined substitute for the
ancient revolution; a mobilization of opposing forces, a battle of the ins
against the outs; with leaders and strategy and campaign chests and all
the other paraphernalia of civil war, but without bodily violence to the
warriors. This refinement of the struggle for political control, this
transition from bullets to ballots, is perhaps the greatest contribution
of modern times to the progress of civilization." [63]

[62] *Ibid.*, p. 62.
[63] *The Invisible Government* (New York: Macmillan, 1928), p. 17.

Part Four

NONPARTY PROCESSES

Chapter 20

THE ROLE OF FORCE

FREQUENTLY textbooks on American politics do not mention the oldest political technique, force. Consequently, it is probably essential that the use of violence be oriented in a concept of politics in order that its political aspects readily may be perceived. It will be recalled that politics has been viewed as a struggle for ascendancy or for power; that those who seek power do so in order to gain certain ends, power either for its own sake or for material or moral values; that the process of politics involves the reconciliation or settlement, at least provisionally, of conflicts of interest between different groups in society; that those seeking power and influence employ certain methods or techniques. The most conspicuous of these methods, in American society, have been the seeking of control of the government through the electoral process by coalitions of interest called political parties; the manipulation of public attitudes, sympathies, and prejudices by propaganda; and the compromise of conflict through representative bodies and through administrative agencies.[1]

Force and violence may be used for political ends, to maintain a stalemate, or to exterminate an opponent. In political conflict the use of violence is almost always an underlying potentiality; if the stakes are not deemed fundamental, if deeply cherished values are not at issue, if the cultural pattern or the customary habits of behavior discourage resort to force, the adjustments arrived at through pacific means may be acceptable to the contenders for power; yet the conditions under which only pacific means are used are transient and may easily be upset.[2] Furthermore, nonviolent methods for settlement of politi-

[1] For suggestive brief treatments of the subject matter of this chapter, see C. E. Merriam, *Prologue to Politics* (Chicago: University of Chicago Press, 1939); James Marshall, *Swords and Symbols* (New York: Oxford University Press, 1939).

[2] See Francis G. Wilson, "Political Suppression in the Modern State," *Journal of Politics*, 1 (1939), pp. 237–257. Consider the following sentences from Wilson's article: "Under what circumstances does the state resort to suppression? A period of repression for any group is a time of strong emotional drives or deep feelings of

cal conflict sometimes work because of the threat of violence in the background. The concentration of scholarly interest on the pacific means of politics has coincided with, and perhaps reflected, a liberal and democratic ideology that frowns on the use of force. The diversion of scientific attention from violence by the barrier of cultural values decrying force has obstructed systematic analysis and description of the role of violence in our political order.

Without pretensions toward precision, a few words are necessary in definition of force and violence.[3] The bayonet, the bullet, the billy, the blackjack are common instruments of force, means of coercion either by actual physical violence or the threat of physical injury. Nor should more subtle instruments of torture or the instruments of the penal law—the gallows, the dungeon, the electric chair—be omitted. The exertion of force may be in the name of the state, through the duly constituted civil or military authorities, or it may be under private auspices acting illegally, since the state claims a monopoly of force. Violence may be resorted to in international political conflict and intranational disputes as well.   Obvious to all, war remains the primary technique for the settlement of serious international friction; yet, not so obvious, in intergroup adjustments in domestic politics not infrequently the exertion of force or the threat of violence occurs.   Violence may be systematically applied to suppress dissent or resolve conflict, or it may occur in isolated, sporadic instances, as in assassination and dynamiting. The ends of violence, the values sought, are almost as diverse as the objectives pursued by other political techniques. The end of an exercise of force may be to preserve the national unit from external aggression, to preserve national security.   In matters internal, the object may be to preserve the distribution of property and income; to prevent rebellion; to suppress dissentient racial or religious minorities; or simply, in the administration of the criminal law, to act for the community to compel adherence to legal principles expressing the consensus of the community as a whole.   That consensus, or law, may, to be sure, reflect class or group interests.

1. THE TACIT ASSUMPTION OF VIOLENCE

In almost all political disputes there is an underlying possibility that one or the other faction seeking ascendancy may resort to the use

resentment and affection. The tolerant days are those of indifference." Again: "Yet democracy continues to be, in no small measure, because a social situation exists in which repression is not needed."

[3] For a more extended definition, see W. Y. Elliott, "Force, Political," *Encyclopedia of the Social Sciences*.

of violence, and this threat of disruption of the peace conditions the operation of representative and deliberative procedures. Although the actual employment of violence in our liberal and democratic society is frequent enough, the saber more often exerts its influence without being drawn. Regimes are always prepared to defend their status, their values and interests, with force if the need arises; and those groups that deem themselves insufferably suppressed may likewise cease to be satisfied with debate and discussion and may resort to arms.[4] Tenuous is the line between conditions under which the arbitration of differences by discussion will bring acceptable results and the conditions under which violence will flare up. A fundamental, although not often recognized, task of democratic government is the adaptation of its policies and the distribution of its favors and honors so as to alleviate conditions that might give rise to insurrection and disorder by group or section. But the task of maintaining that pacific equilibrium is facilitated by the knowledge that insurrection will be met with suppression.

The resort to violence is not difficult to understand; it is the maintenance of peaceful methods of solving political disputes that is sometimes puzzling. What kinds of questions are likely to give rise to violent dispute? What conditions favor settlement of issues without resort to force? Walter Lippman has dealt with such questions by the assertion that in stable and mature societies the differences between opposing factions are not great. If that were not true, he argues that the "outs" would be always considering rebellion and the "ins" would usually adopt policies entirely unacceptable to the "outs." In fact, elections are not followed by such abrupt and wide shifts of policy; the working assumption is that the winners will not push their advantage so far. The basis of that assumption and practice is the fundamental likeness in the views and interests of the "ins" and "outs."[5] John Dickinson has reached similar conclusions:[6]

For representative government, no less than for direct democracy, there must be a willingness on the part of conflicting interests to live together on peaceful terms and to make at least such mutual concessions as are needful for that purpose. Where this is not the case—where the cleavage between particular interests is so deep that they stubbornly refuse all concessions—no form of popular government, whether direct or representative, is possible.

[4] A cardinal doctrine in the American political faith is the right of revolution, a justification of the use of violence to overthrow the government under intolerable conditions. The doctrine is most eloquently formulated in the Declaration of Independence.

[5] *The Phantom Public* (New York: Harcourt, Brace, 1925), p. 127.

[6] John Dickinson, "Democratic Realities and Democratic Dogma," *American Political Science Review*, 24 (1930), pp. 283–309.

Such a condition is ordinarily a mark of the political immaturity of the people among whom it exists.

Whether these speculations really throw any light on the nature of the conditions productive of violence is doubtful. Their substance is that men fight when there are "profound" differences or when something "fundamental" is at stake. That amounts to saying that men resort to force over those things about which they feel like resorting to force—not a very illuminating observation. It is clear, however, that the content of the category of issues soluble only by the sword constantly changes. Issues that at one time create intermittent, bloody internal dissension may at another time be ignored or settled by means no more bloody than the ceremonial bellicosity of parliamentary debate. The things that people feel like fighting about are not always the same. That conclusion points to the great importance of the attitudes of a culture toward violence. A society habituated and attached to debate ʾnd discussion may be able to settle through these means matters that in a different culture or a different time would provoke armed revolt or relentless repression. Yet the veneer of restraint and tolerance is thin; and a constant responsibility of the political therapeutist is the anticipation, prevention, and amelioration of differences based on deep cleavages of sentiment. The task of the political therapeutist is, in the large, the maintenance of faith in representative government. The continued acceptance of the adjustments and decisions between conflicting interests by democratic processes rests in large measure on a general faith in the ultimate improvement of status by peaceful means.

Although settlement of political differences by parliamentary means is the predominant method in the American culture, resort to violence is often in the background as an ultimate possibility. It is difficult to make vivid that possibility except by indication of instances in which violence has actually come to the surface. A recurrent characteristic of American politics is the appearance of cleavages along sectional lines. Generally these disputes are ironed out to the satisfaction of the competing interests, but at times force has been the final arbiter. The Civil War was preceded by a long conflict in polemics that eventuated in a sanguinary conflict. Any other attempt at secession would probably likewise be met with force. Yet to contend that national unity is maintained by force alone is not tenable, for it has more substantial foundations. Nevertheless sectional differences irreconcilable by normal means would have to be resolved by force. And decisions arrived at through parliamentary methods will, if necessary, be carried out by force. Thus violence may break out at two points in the political process: as a means of settlement in substitution for deliberative processes, as a means of compelling acceptance of the result of the deliberative process.[7]

The military establishment thus has its internal potentialities as well as its more obvious external uses. It is prepared to maintain by force, if necessary, the dominant values of a culture in internal conflict.[8] Yet one of the striking developments in liberal, democratic cultures has been the subordination of the military class *per se* to other controlling groups. Political dominance in our time has not been achieved by those most skilled in the management of military operations; the United States has had military leaders as Presidents, Washington and Grant to name two, but it could not be said that these men achieved leadership through military skill in the same sense that a medieval prince fought his way to ascendancy.[9] The replacement of the military class at the apex of the political pyramid by leaders with other skills has not occurred because the warriors were beaten at their own game; the governing classes of a civilization must be recruited from those able to meet the peculiar requirements of a given time and place.

The potentiality of the exercise of violence is not limited to its use by government and by those interests associated with government in the suppression of dissident and dissatisfied groups. Submerged groups may attempt to use force to gain their ends. Sidney Hook has gone so far as to declare that "practically all" successful movements of social revolt have at one time or another in the course of their development used violence. The corollary of this finding is that movements of social revolt will not gain power unless they do use violence. The exception might be a movement directed against a ruling group that for some

[7] An earlier example of a sectional difference in which force was brought into play was the "Whisky Rebellion" of 1794. Farmers in western Pennsylvania beyond the Allegheny Mountains lacked a readily accessible market for their grain which was converted into whiskey, a product more easily transported and sold. Stout resistance to the collection of federal excise taxes brought federal armed forces to quell the insurrection. See B. M. Rich, *The Presidents and Civil Disorder* (Washington: Brookings, 1941), chap. 1.

[8] Friedrich says: "The political scientist must likewise conclude that the military establishment is a necessary concomitant of all government, that it transcends territorial objectives and ultimately is rooted in the general objective of security. Group dissensions within are as threatening as external conflicts. The people of the United States, whose most dangerous war has undoubtedly been the Civil War, should be the last to overlook the lessons which this political rule can teach."—*Constitutional Government and Democracy* (Boston: Little, Brown, 1941), p. 70.

[9] Machiavelli's maxim by inference describes a type of earlier situation: "A prince ought to have no other aim or thought, nor select anything else for his study, than war and its rules and discipline; for this is the sole art that belongs to him who rules, and it is of such force that it not only upholds those who are born princes, but it often enables men to rise from a private station to that rank. And, on the contrary, it is seen that when princes have thought more of ease than of arms they have lost their states."—*The Prince*, chap. 14.

reason or another finds itself unable or unwilling to defend itself. Hook goes further and holds the opinion that so-called "peaceful" reform in which the actual use of violence does not occur succeeds because of an implicit threat of violence. A recurring and telling argument for reform is that it may prevent revolution.[10]

Those who challenge the dominant cluster of interests by force or threat of force are, however, likely to be met by force, applied either by government through judicial or military channels or applied by private militia. Drastic laws, for example, have been enacted in about twenty states for the punishment of "criminal syndicalism." In most states in which these laws were passed there was a background of activity by the I.W.W. or other radical groups that advocated, and from time to time used, violence. One observer notes: [11]

In practically every state where a criminal syndicalism bill was passed, there is evidence of a bill having been sought by those interests and industries which were having trouble with the I.W.W., feared trouble with them, or were apprehensive concerning the effect of the I.W.W. and radical doctrines on the more conservative unions in a period of labor unrest. These interests were found in various forms, as unorganized groups of business men or individual employers in the industries affected, as groups organized in state or city-wide employers' associations, and as corporations or groups of corporations controlling the dominant industry and having a firm hold on the political life of the state.

Although American repression of radical minorities has been, in the main, the result of visions of spooks under the bed, it needs to be pointed out that democratic societies labor under a special handicap in preserving the political regime of debate, discussion, and elections against minorities committed to the use of violence. Commitment to democratic procedures denies resort to violence; effective democracy implies practically universal acceptance of the results of democratic procedures. Speaking of the dead democracies abroad, Loewenstein says: [12]

Democracy and democratic tolerance have been used for their own destruction. Under cover of fundamental rights and the rule of law, the antidemocratic machine could be built up and set in motion legally. Calculating adroitly that democracy could not, without self-abnegation, deny to any body of public opinion the full use of the free institutions of speech, press, assembly,

10 Sidney Hook, "Violence," *Encyclopedia of the Social Sciences.*
11 E. Foster Dowell, *A History of Criminal Syndicalism Legislation in the United States* (Baltimore: Johns Hopkins Press, 1939), pp. 51-52.
12 Karl Loewenstein, "Militant Democracy and Fundamental Rights," *American Political Science Review,* 31 (1937), pp. 417-432, 638-658.

and parliamentary participation, fascist exponents systematically discredit the democratic order and make it unworkable by paralyzing its functions until chaos reigns.

The private army finishes the work when chaos is complete. The difficult problem of a democracy is to sterilize the violent and at the same time leave an avenue of adequate width open for the play, counterplay, and balancing of pressures through debate and discussion.

Consideration of the use and of the possibility of the use of violence on grand issues involving differences between great sections or broad classes should not be allowed to overshadow reliance on force on many lesser matters in the American political scene. The activities of many of the more potent local party machines have been tinged by violence, notably in the management of elections. A lengthy roster could be compiled of killings, assaults, and acts of intimidation committed on election day against those who opposed the dominant organization. Even those who simply demanded an honest count have often been treated quite as roughly as opposition workers. Of course, in some communities the dominant party machine does not limit its use of violence to election day; at other times those disposed to oppose the machine may find that their life expectancy increases with removal from the locality. The most publicized cases of election-day violence occur in poorer urban neighborhoods, but violence is not absent in rural elections.[13]

2. THE STATUS OF LABOR AND VIOLENCE

On two great issues in American domestic politics pacific procedures have been freely supplemented by violence. The parliamentary techniques of discussion, compromise, and acceptance of the outcome of the representative process have not sufficed to resolve conflicts of interest between employer and employee and between white and black. Vivid impressions of the tone of violence in American employer-employee relations are produced by recollection of such episodes as the Haymarket riot (1886), the Homestead riot (1892), the Pullman strike (1894), the dynamiting of the Los Angeles *Times* (1910), the Lawrence strike (1912), the Ludlow massacre (1914), the steel strike of 1919, the murders at Gastonia (1929), and the sit-down strikes of 1937.[14]

[13] As befits the subject the literature is extensive, but for samples see D. D. McKean, *The Boss* (Boston: Houghton Mifflin, 1940); Charles Van Devander, *The Big Bosses* (New York: Howell, Soskin, 1944); C. H. Wooddy, *The Chicago Primary of 1926* (Chicago: University of Chicago Press, 1926).

[14] See Louis Adamic, *Dynamite, The Story of Class Violence in America* (New York: Viking, 1931); Samuel Yellen, *American Labor Struggles* (New York: Harcourt, Brace, 1936); Rich, *op. cit.*

What does the exertion of force in industrial disputes have to do with politics, it may be asked. It all depends on what one means by politics, but a comprehension of the political significance of these examples of violence requires that they be viewed in a larger context than the incidents surrounding individual acts of violence. No particular "political" importance may be attached to the event of a company guard shooting a single striker or a striker blackjacking a strikebreaker. Consider, however, the results of thousands of such individual incidents in the maintenance or disturbance of the power structure of a society. What was the effect of forcible repression of union activity in plant after plant, in state after state, for year after year? Innumerable acts of violence, sometimes brought about or at least stimulated by joint action of employers, undoubtedly had the effect for many years of discouraging collective action by employees, of maintaining a disunited labor movement, of keeping labor weak. Massacres make martyrs, to be sure, but they also make men meek. The total effect of employer violence has been to retard employee organization and consequently to retard the development of a working-class consciousness. A relatively weak labor movement is unable to seek its ends effectively in the political sphere, more narrowly defined, that is, through influencing political parties and through the application of pressure against legislative bodies and other official agencies. The function of violence in the maintenance of the power of the employing classes seems so patent as to require no elaboration. By the same token, when labor groups manage to utilize the technique of violence successfully, they thereby gain potency in the affairs of society as a whole.

In the long dispute between employer and employee, reliance on violence, by both parties to the dispute, has apparently arisen from the fact that matters have been at stake which both disputants have regarded as fundamental and which could not really be compromised. The right to organize and the right of collective bargaining are not subject to compromise; the employers either will or will not "recognize" the union; employees either do or do not enjoy the privilege of freely organizing and bargaining collectively. There is no halfway ground. There is, of course, no halfway ground on many issues, but the issues between employer and employee have been regarded by both as involving rights not to be lightly surrendered. The state of mind of employer and employee has been such as to lead each to believe that it could not yield to the other without irretrievable loss. Senator Kenyon, in a statement resulting from an inquiry into a strike in West Virginia shortly after World War I, described a typical situation: [15]

[15] Senate Report No. 457, 67th Congress, 2nd Session (1922), p. 4.

The issue is plain and perfectly apparent. The operators in this particular section of West Virginia under consideration openly announce, and did before the committee, that they will not employ men belonging to the unions, for, as they say, they believe they will become agitators; and further, that they have the right, and will exercise it if they desire, to discharge a man if he belongs to the union, and in making these claims they believe themselves to be within their constitutional rights.

On the other hand, the United Mine Workers are determined to unionize these fields which are practically the only large and important coal fields in the United States not unionized.

Here we have the situation of two determined bodies trying to enforce what they believe are rights, which rights are diametrically opposed to one another, and we have the situation of an irresistible force meeting an immovable body. In such case there can be nothing but trouble.

The facts about the "trouble" that has occurred in such cases are fairly well known. The strike often involves the direct use of violence. Indeed, it could be said that even the "peaceful" strike is an act of violence. In turn employers have used all manner of violence against their employees. A distinction might be made between public and private violence in industrial disputes. Sometimes the antagonists in an industrial dispute involving violence exert private violence; that is, the parties to the dispute do not act under the color of public authority. In other circumstances the exertion of public authority by police, National Guardsmen, deputy sheriffs, and, occasionally, federal troops is involved. The distinction is not of much import, however, since private violence has often been thinly cloaked with the veil of legality. Company police have often been deputized as public officials and have acted under public authority, but have remained under private direction. In other instances, employer domination of the public authorities concerned has made the public nature of these officials pure fiction.

Some of the most violent industrial disputes have involved the efforts of employers to maintain their position against the right of labor to organize so as to bargain collectively. The dispute has been not so much an economic dispute as a struggle for power: the employers defend their historic position while the employees, driven perhaps by the profound psychological insecurities of the worker in the modern industrial system, seek the right to gain strength through union. In "labor troubles" the unequal distribution of the hazards of the industrial system may be more important than the unequal distribution of rewards. A classic statement of the position of employers on the issues is by John Kirby, Jr., presented by him as president of the National Association of Manufacturers to a Senate committee in 1913: [16]

[16] Senate Report No. 6, 76th Congress, 1st session (1939), p. 28.

The record of organized labor leaves no room for argument as to what the attitude, not only of employers and associations of employers, but of every patriotic individual and newspaper of this land of ours, should be toward it. It pronounces in no uncertain terms that when an employer bows to its demand for recognition he becomes a party to an un-American, illegal, and infamous conspiracy, and adds his strength to a cause which he knows is gradually undermining our industries, intimidating capital, restricting our export markets, fostering the personal interests of the leaders and agitators who preach the doctrine of unrest and hatred of the employer, for the purpose of perpetuating their jobs, and not for love of their fellow workers.

Later public statements by employer leaders were more temperate. In fact, the principle of collective bargaining was often accepted but hedged about with conditions that would prevent true collective bargaining.   Robert P. Lamont, representing the American Iron and Steel Institute, opposed the enactment of Section 7(a) of the National Industrial Recovery Act in the following terms: [17]

The industry stands positively for the open shop; it is unalterably opposed to the closed shop.   For many years it has been and now is prepared to deal directly with its employees collectively on all matters relating to their employment.   It is opposed to conducting negotiations concerning such matters otherwise than with its own employees; it is unwilling to conduct them with outside organizations of labor or with individuals not its employees.   The industry accordingly objects to the inclusion in this pending bill of any provisions which will be in conflict with this position of the industry, or of any language which implies that such is the intent of the legislation.

Industrial warfare became so commonplace that specialized concerns arose to furnish to employers, on a commercial basis, corps of experienced strikebreakers.   Men furnished as strikebreakers by detective agencies and similar organizations were generally not equipped to man the plants; their principal skill was in stamping out labor organizations. Strikebreaking services existed even before 1900, but they became more numerous after that time.   The nature of the service furnished by these companies is illustrated by a circular distributed in 1913 by the Waddell-Mahon Corporation: [18]

As an evidence of our ability as strike breakers, we invite your attention to the labor difficulties now ensuing along the copper range of the Upper Peninsula of Michigan between the Calumet & Hecla Copper Co., the Commonwealth Copper Co., the Quincy Copper Co., *et al.*, and the Western Federation of Miners.   In amount of capital and number of men involved this strike is the most important of the present year.   We point with pardonable pride to

[17] *Ibid.*, p. 78.
[18] Senate Document No. 381, 63rd Congress, 2nd Session (1914).

the fact that this corporation has been selected by Sheriff James A. Cruse, of Houghton County—the storm center of the strike—to aid him in maintaining the integrity of the law. We are now engaged in "policing" the 1,019 square miles of territory contained in Houghton County. We are safeguarding the property of the mine owners against intrusion and violence. We are also protecting the lives and the homes of the 80,098 men, women, and children of Houghton County against overt acts. The Western Federation of Miners is doomed to inevitable disaster and defeat in the Upper Peninsula of Michigan. We make this prediction at this time, and if you will follow the story of the strike as it appears in the daily newspapers, and particularly in the Boston News Bureau, the well-known financial organ, which has a special correspondent on the ground, you will see that our prediction will be fulfilled daily. We are sure of defeating the Western Federation of Miners in this operation because we have met and defeated them before. Last year, when the agitators of this union sought to paralyze the copper industry of Nevada and Utah, we were retained by the Utah Copper Co. and the Nevada Consolidated Co., and broke the great strikes at Bingham Canyon, Utah, and at Ely and McGill, Nevada. We ask you to watch the progress of the present strike, because we know it will be a triumph for law and order, a triumph for the mine owners, and will furnish still another evidence of the success we have always met with in breaking strikes. We ask you to judge us by results.

The number of agencies providing services such as those advertised by the Waddell-Mahon Corporation in 1913 became much larger in the 'twenties and 'thirties. A Senate subcommittee concluded in 1939 that [19]

. . . there exists today a considerable group of persons and firms holding themselves out to supply outsiders in industrial disputes. The news of an impending strike not only finds the larger and well-established detective agencies equipped for strike service, but evokes a response from numbers of fly-by-night strikebreaking agencies, and veteran strikebreakers, all promising to supply strikebreakers or guards. The files show that this latter class of individuals and firms varies from year to year, changing firm names and office addresses. These are the professional "finks" striving to set up in business for themselves.

---

[19] Senate Report No. 6, 76th Congress, 1st Session (1939), p. 29. A droll consequence of the professionalization of strikebreaking was that strikebreakers gained an interest in extending the strike to lengthen their employment and in intensifying disorder to justify the employment of additional strikebreakers or strikeguards. The process of intensifying the strike was called "heating up the job." "In order to do this," one strikebreaker testified, "the men that are hired or already working, or the men that want to get on, either get a delegation of four or five men or they get some of their friends, and the best thing they do is slug a picket or two, which will bring a bunch more out on the line for a while, or go in and throw a rock through a business representative's window, or something like that. During the National Screw they broke out the windows in the Union headquarters there. The fellows would take turn about breaking them out. Of course, that kept the strike going."—*Ibid.*, p. 98.

In some localities employers did not patronize the commercial agencies but obtained strikebreakers from the employers' association which, in this respect, performed the function of a consumers' cooperative.

Alongside the strikebreaking agencies were corporations that sold munitions for use in the suppression of strikes. The inventories of the private arsenals of the Republic Steel Corporation and the Youngstown Sheet and Tube Company, which cooperated in the "Little Steel" strike in 1937, indicate the magnitude of the munitions business as well as the effectiveness with which industry armed itself. These two corporations had on hand 1,881 firearms, 313 gas guns, 153,930 rounds of ball cartridge ammunition, 10,234 rounds of shot cartridge ammunition, and 10,064 rounds of gas ammunition. During the period January 15, 1933, to June 26, 1937, the Republic Steel Corporation "with 52,775 employees, purchased more than 10 times as many gas guns, and more than 26 times as many gas shells and gas projectiles, as the police department of the city of Chicago, with a population of 3,376,438 persons." [20] Employee organizations never had access to the same sources of supplies as employers, and they were usually less well armed. A degree of control over the private use of machine guns and sawed-off shotguns exists under the National Firearms Act of 1934, which placed a prohibitive tax on the sale of these devices to persons other than public agencies. The act, however, has been evaded by means of sales to industrial concerns indirectly through local police officials,[21] and no effective public control of other types of weapons used in industrial disputes exists.[22]

In terms of public policy, the conflict between employer and employee has been one in which the employer has defended the legal *status quo;* the employees of the newer and larger industrial units have sought a redefinition of public policy. The process of accommodating formal public policy so as to bring about workable legal principles governing the relationships of employer and employee lagged. Consequently, in the conflict between employer and employee, the employer was able to picture himself as the defender of the legal order, and the duly accredited functionaries of the legal order tended to be allied with the

20 *Ibid.,* Part 3, pp. 45, 57.
21 *Ibid.,* Part 3, p. 182.
22 As early as 1916 control over industrial munitions was proposed. The Commission on Industrial Relations recommended "the enactment by Congress of a statute prohibiting the shipment in interstate commerce of cannon, gatling guns, and other guns of similar character, which are not capable of personal use, when consigned to anyone except military agencies of the State or Federal governments."— Senate Document No. 415, 64th Congress, 1st Session (1916), Vol. 1, pp. 99. The National Firearms Act was designed primarily to prevent the sale of submachine guns to gangsters.

employer. The employee, on the other hand, was at a strategic disadvantage, since his activities were directed, if not against the legal order, at least toward a reformulation of public policy.

The depth of feeling that characterizes the friction between employer and employee is illustrated by the extreme difficulty of developing and applying new juridical principles to govern their relationships. In a few industries a period of strikes and of strikebreaking was followed by the development of a *modus vivendi,* or an acceptance of the principle of collective bargaining, under which specific problems were dealt with as they arose. In such circumstances, in effect a new "law" or policy was "adopted" by common consent and was obeyed by all parties concerned, although it did not have behind it the power of coercion of the state. In another type of situation, of which the railroad industry was the only specific case, the principle of collective bargaining was enforced fairly early in a particular industry by public authority, an authority generally accepted by all parties concerned. However, the adoption of a like public policy to govern relationships between employer and employee more generally (that is, within federal jurisdiction) under the National Labor Relations Act has not been followed by a complete substitution of pacific for violent means of settlement of disputes. The formal legal order has not reflected a consensus, and the exertion of violence on perhaps a slightly diminished scale has continued.

The National Labor Relations Act provides that "Employees shall have the right of self-organization, to form, join, or assist labor organizations, to bargain collectively through representatives of their own choosing, and to engage in concerted activities, for the purpose of collective bargaining or other mutual aid or protection." The act provides penalties for interference by employers with the exercise of these rights by employees. Public policy is thus, fairly definite, but the reordering of relationships envisaged by the framers of the act has come about only partially, and violence continues to be applied in industrial disputes. The National Labor Relations Board reported in 1938, for example: [23]

In some cases the employer, for the purpose of disorganizing and defeating union activity, has sought to instigate or cause the commission of acts of violence against union organizers and leaders and union members. In one case an overseer of the company offered to buy an employee a gallon of whiskey if he would "stamp hell out of" an active union employee. In another case, a forelady supplemented her attempt to dissuade employees from accepting union pamphlets by the following suggestion having reference to the organ-

[23] National Labor Relations Board, *Annual Report,* 1938, pp. 54–55.

izer who distributed the literature: "What do you say, girls, we give her a
beating?" Marked conduct of this sort was revealed in *Matter of Clover
Fork Coal Company*. The company and the Harlan County Coal Operators'
Association, an employer organization of which the company was a prominent
member, conducted a literal reign of terror against unionization. Union organizers were ordered out of the county at the point of guns; one organizer's
hotel room was flooded with tear gas; another organizer, a minister, was shot
at. The general superintendent of the mine told employees: "If one of my
men will pick up a stick and whip hell out of one of them organizers, I will
. . . see he don't put in a day in jail and I will pay the fine." On another
occasion he proposed that the men throw the union organizers into the river.

In some strike cases, the employer not only sought to incite or did incite
violence against union organizers and members, but in connection
therewith sought to create a situation of general disorder in order to de-
moralize the striking employees and to justify appeals to "law and order."
In *Matter of Remington Rand, Inc.*, large numbers of professional strikebreakers and operatives, known as "missionaries," "nobles," and "undercover"
men, were hired by the company for such purposes. They jostled pickets and
terrorized striking employees. In *Matter of Sunshine Mining Company,*
supervisors fostered the formation of two strikebreaking organizations, the
"Vigilantes" and the "Committee of 356." Through them the company
sought to enlist the intervention in the strike of local law enforcement agencies
and the governor of the State. A mass demonstration was arranged by these
organizations against the strikers, and handbills were distributed stating:
"Vigilantes are ready to take care of any radical organizers . . . ropes are
ready." Confronted by this situation the pickets disbanded before the demonstration was held. There then followed a victory celebration, with the
company furnishing beer tickets, good in any saloon. Violence occurred; in
one instance, a supervisor led a crowd of about 400 men who attempted to
lynch one of the strikers.

On the other side of the picture, strikes and the violence that accompanies them have undoubtedly been an important technique for gaining influence by the employee groups. The use of strikes and violence
by employees has had a peculiar relationship to public policy. "The
two great peaks in the history of industrial disputes in America," John I.
Griffin concludes, "were marked by noteworthy interest in the labor
movement on the part of the government, an interest motivated in the
one case by military necessity and in the other by political expediency." [24] He refers to World War I and the New Deal period. The
conclusion might be that employee groups have been most free to promote their interests by strikes only when the government was favorable
to them. And, in a sense, industrial disputes constitute a kind of civil
warfare permitted by government. The formal governmental machine,

[24] J. I. Griffin, *Strikes* (New York: Columbia University Press, 1939), p. 204.

unable to find a formula to bridge a social cleavage, permits the solution of the conflict by private violence. The side favored by the government tends to have the upper hand. Unrestricted repression of workers is likely to occur with either the tacit consent or open collaboration of the government; labor groups are likely to promote their cause more vigorously when a government is in power that looks with favor on labor.

Labor unions have not hesitated to use violence in industrial disputes. In periods of industrial friction they have met violence with violence, but the resources of unions in such conflicts have not usually matched those of their adversaries. At times when government frowns on the use of violence by employers and does not lend its own forces to the repression of labor unions, employee groups can exert great power without resort to violence against the employer, unless one considers a "peaceful" strike to be an act of violence. By virtue of their numerical superiority, workers do not need to rely on outright acts of violence against employers under such circumstances. However, even in periods when employers are in effect "disarmed" by the government, unions often turn to violence in their relations with nonmember workers. Peaceful picketing is often supplemented by intimidation of potential strikebreakers and the power of union leaders over their followers not infrequently rests at least in part on violence or the threat of violence.

Although the contention has been in tnese pages that, broadly considered, all violence in industrial disputes has a political function, it should be pointed out that a special type of strike is characterized by students of labor problems as a "political strike." Hiller says: "Strikes not only affect the relations between employer and employees, but also disturb the equilibrium between social classes. Such changes arise in part as slow accompaniments of historic movement, and in part as instant results of conflict. Strikes that abruptly change the legal position of the social group involved, or that are intended to do so, are political, in the specific sense of the term." [25] Examples of political strikes are furnished by the series of strikes in Belgium to gain the franchise: in 1891, 1893, and 1913 strikes were called for the specific purpose of compelling suffrage reform.

The general strike, in theory, is a technique of revolution. The theorists of the syndicalist movement considered the general strike as a means whereby the working classes could paralyze a society and wrest control of the government from the dominant classes. Yet the more profound syndicalist thinkers have regarded the idea of the general strike as a social myth. Other revolutionary labor leaders have also

[25] E. T. Hiller, *The Strike* (Chicago: University of Chicago Press, 1928), p. 233.

viewed and used the strike, not primarily as a means for gaining immediate economic advantage, but as a device for creating disorder and
for harrying the capitalist classes as a preliminary for revolution. The
syndicalist movement has been represented in the United States chiefly
by the I.W.W.[26] Communist-dominated unions regard the strike and
the accompanying violence as merely an incident in class warfare—a
different view from that of the conservative unions, which consider the
strike primarily as a means for promoting and protecting labor interests
within the framework of capitalist society.

3. ACCOMMODATION IN RACIAL CONFLICT

One of the most enduring cleavages that divide men and provoke
friction occurs along lines of race.   The contrivance of systems of peaceful relationships between racial groups is so formidable a task that the
instances in which a *modus vivendi* unaccompanied by violence or
repression has evolved are exceptional.   The cleavage between racial
groups is made deep and difficult to bridge by the high visibility of the
insignia of group affiliation; it is either "we" or "they."   Facile identification of the individual's group credentials draws sharp the line between "us" and "them" and solidifies each group internally.   Racial
distinction, of course, involves more than biological differentiation.   It
often includes a wide variety of cultural differences.   Moreover, cultural conflicts are often aggravated by the addition of economic competition along racial lines.   As more and more lines of cleavage coincide, the intensity of friction increases.   A common interest shared by
segments of the membership of both races often mitigates group friction, but the gulf of racial difference often prevents this crisscrossing—
witness the relations of white and black workers in the trade-union
movement.

Violence appears in race relations in a number of forms.   In some
circumstances repression of and discrimination against minority groups
are the accepted public policy; under such circumstances the dominant
group has at its command all the machinery of the state to maintain its

26 Paul F. Brissenden, *The I.W.W.* (New York: Columbia University Press, 1919).
See also the valuable, brief comment by W. H. Crook, "The Revolutionary Logic
of the General Strike," *American Political Science Review*, 28 (1934), pp. 655–663.
Dr. Crook concludes that ". . . in these days a successful general strike in Western
civilization is likely to occur only where the labor forces have faced the full revolutionary logic of that weapon, and where the ruling class or the government has at
the same time remained so blind to progress and so unjust to the masses of the people that anything, even revolution, is preferable.   Even at that, success in the use
of the weapon demands that the cause be so clear that most of the citizens outside the
ranks of labor, and the majority of the military and naval forces, express strong
sympathy with strikers."

status of superordination. In other circumstances the articles of the law may proclaim equality among all individuals regardless of race, but in fact the machinery of government may be used to discriminate against the subordinate group with varying degrees of exercise of legal violence. In other situations interracial friction may be accompanied by the exertion of private violence.

In the United States, friction has flared up from time to time between nativist groups and successive waves of immigrants, but the most persistent social conflict has been between black and white. Prior to the abolition of slavery the laws of the slave states prescribed a special subordinate status for Negroes. Since abolition, the Federal Constitution has prohibited denial of equal protection of the law. In fact, however, the dominant race has controlled the machinery of government, and discrimination in governance has been the practice. Moreover, private violence, the most spectacular form of which is lynching, has played a role of considerable importance in the definition of the relative status of the groups concerned.

The records of the Tuskegee Institute indicate that from 1882-1938 there were 4,687 lynchings, of which 3,398 involved Negroes, and 1,289, whites. The lynching of whites has tended to decrease in relative importance; since 1910 the ratio of Negro to white lynchings has been about nine to one. The number of lynchings alone does not furnish a complete picture of the extent of the will to lynch; in 1938, for example, there were 6 lynchings, but there were 42 instances in which officers of the law prevented lynchings.[27] Apart from the lynching of individuals, large-scale race wars have occurred from time to time in certain cities. In the catalog of violence in race relations there must, of course, be included the activities of the Ku Klux Klan in the restoration of the interracial balance of power that had been upset by the Civil War and Reconstruction.

An interpretation of the function of lynchings in interracial relations similar to that of violence in industrial relations could be made. The individual lynching has an effect far beyond the immediate neighborhood in which it occurs. It serves as a vicarious reassertion of white supremacy for many who do not participate in the event itself; to all Negroes it serves as a reminder of the actual status they enjoy. The lynching dramatizes the relationship between the races and serves to supplement other devices for governing race relations.

[27] See J. W. Johnson, "The Negro and Racial Conflict," in Francis J. Brown and Joseph S. Roucek, *Our Racial and National Minorities* (New York; Prentice-Hall, 1937); Gunnar Myrdal, *An American Dilemma* (New York: Harper, 1944), chap. 27.

4. VIOLENCE AND ITS SOCIAL CONTEXT

To isolate violence for analysis as a technique of politics wrests it from its social setting and perhaps exaggerates the significance of force alone. Exclusive reliance on brute force in political conflict does occur, but in our culture force has usually been only one of a battery of techniques to gain an end or to maintain a status. And probably, to be effective over the long run, force must be supplemented by other methods.[28] Machiavelli perhaps had something of this sort in mind when he wrote: [29]

> You must know there are two ways of contesting, the one by the law, the other by force; the first method is proper to men, the second to beasts; but because the first is frequently not sufficient, it is necessary to have recourse to the second. . . . A prince, therefore, being compelled knowingly to adopt the beast, ought to choose the fox and the lion; because the lion cannot defend himself against snares and the fox cannot defend himself against wolves. Therefore, it is necessary to be a fox to discover the snares and a lion to terrify the wolves. Those who rely simply on the lion do not understand what they are about.

The axiom that "those who rely simply on the lion do not understand what they are about" has repeatedly been a maxim to guide practical conduct. Instead of the fox, propaganda is now the most frequent companion of the lion. The object of the propaganda may be to justify the use of violence or to supplement violence. In industrial disputes neither employer nor employee relies on force or the threat of force alone. A refined technique, publicized under the title of the "Mohawk Valley Formula," was developed in 1936 by Remington Rand, Inc. The "Mohawk Valley Formula" is not radically different from general practice. It was outlined by the National Labor Relations Board as follows: [30]

> First: When a strike is threatened, label the union leaders as "agitators" to discredit them with the public and their own followers. In the plant, conduct a forced balloting under the direction of foremen in an attempt to ascer-

---

[28] John Dickinson argues that political authority does not rest solely on a basis of force. "It rests on obedience, whether produced by reverence, habit, rational conviction, or the fear of compulsory sanctions. That it cannot be said to rest ultimately on force appears from the fact that the use of force against recalcitrant individuals will not be effective unless acquiesced in, and if need be supported by, the preponderance of the impartial elements in the community not directly concerned with the controversy. Only in extremely rare instance can such acquiescence and support be procured by terrorization of the whole community." "Social Order and Political Authority," *American Political Science Review*, 23 (1929), p. 627.

[29] *The Prince*, chap. 18.

[30] 2 N.L.R.B. 664–666.

tain the strength of the union and to make possible misrepresentation of the strikers as a small minority imposing their will upon the majority. At the same time, disseminate propaganda, by means of press releases, advertisements, and the activities of "missionaries," such propaganda falsely stating the issues involved in the strike so that the strikers appear to be making arbitrary demands, and the real issues, such as the employer's refusal to bargain collectively, are obscured. Concurrently with these moves, by exerting economic pressure through threats to move the plant, align the influential members of community into a cohesive group opposed to the strike. Include in this group, usually designated a "Citizens Committee," representatives of the bankers, real estate owners, and business men, i. e., those most sensitive to any threat of removal of the plant because of its effect upon property values and purchasing power flowing from payrolls.

Second: When the strike is called raise high the banner of "law and order," thereby causing the community to mass legal and police weapons against a wholly imagined violence and to forget that those of its members who are employees have equal rights with the other members of the community.

Third: Call a "mass meeting" of the citizens to coordinate public sentiment against the strike and to strengthen the power of the Citizens Committee, which organization, thus supported, will both aid the employer in exerting pressure upon the local authorities and itself sponsor vigilante activities.

Fourth: Bring about the formation of a large armed police force to intimidate the strikers and to exert a psychological effect upon the citizens. This force is built up by utilizing local police, State Police if the Governor cooperates, vigilantes, and special deputies, the deputies being chosen if possible from other neighborhoods, so that there will be no personal relationships to induce sympathy for the strikers. Coach the deputies and vigilantes on the law of unlawful assembly, inciting to riot, disorderly conduct, etc., so that unhampered by any thought that the strikers may also possess some rights, they will be ready and anxious to use their newly acquired authority to the limit.

Fifth: And perhaps most important, heighten the demoralizing effect of the above measures—all designed to convince the strikers that their cause is hopeless—by a "back to work" movement, operated by a puppet association of so-called "loyal employees" secretly organized by the employer. Have this association wage a publicity campaign in its own name and coordinate such campaign with the work of the "Missionaries" circulating among the strikers and visiting their homes. This "back to work" movement has these results: It causes the public to believe that the strikers are in the minority and that most of the employees desire to return to work, thereby winning sympathy for the employer and an endorsement of his activities to such an extent that the public is willing to pay the huge costs, direct and indirect, resulting from the heavy forces of police. This "back to work" movement also enables the employer, when the plant is later opened, to operate it with strikebreakers if necessary and to continue to refuse to bargain collectively with the strikers. In addition, the "back to work" movement permits the employer to keep a constant check on the strength of the union through the number of applications received from employees ready to break ranks and return to work, such number being kept secret from the public and the other employees, so that the doubts and fears created by such secrecy will in turn induce still others to make applications.

Sixth: When a sufficient number of applications are on hand, fix a date for an opening of the plant through the device of having such opening requested by the "back to work" association. Together with the Citizens Committee, prepare for such opening by making provision for a peak army of police, by roping off the areas surrounding the plant, by securing arms and ammunition, etc. The purpose of the "opening" of the plant is threefold: To see if enough employees are ready to return to work; to induce still others to return as a result of the demoralizing effect produced by the opening of the plant and the return of some of their number; and lastly, even if the manoeuvre fails to induce a sufficient number of persons to return, to persuade the public through pictures and news releases that the opening was nevertheless successful.

Seventh: Stage the "opening," theatrically throwing open the gates at the propitious moment and having the employees march into the plant grounds in a massed group protected by squads of armed police, so as to give to the opening a dramatic and exaggerated quality and thus heighten its demoralizing effect. Along with the "opening" provide a spectacle—speeches, flag raising, and praises for the employees, citizens, and local authorities, so that, their vanity touched, they will feel responsible for the continued success of the scheme and will increase their efforts to induce additional employees to return to work.

Eighth: Capitalize on the demoralization of the strikers by continuing the show of police force and the pressure of the Citizens Committee, both to insure that those employees who have returned will continue at work and to force the remaining strikers to capitulate. If necessary, turn the locality into a warlike camp through the declaration of a state of emergency tantamount to martial law and barricade it from the outside world so that nothing may interfere with the successful conclusion of the "formula," thereby driving home to the union leaders the futility of further efforts to hold their ranks intact.

Ninth: Close the publicity barrage, which day by day during the entire period has increased the demoralization worked by all these measures, on the theme that the plant is in full operation and that the strikers were merely a minority attempting to interfere with the "right to work," thus inducing the public to place a moral stamp of approval upon the above measures. With this, the campaign is over—the employer has broken the strike.

The significance of propaganda in industrial disputes is indicated by the fact that strikebreaking agencies came to include propaganda as well as guards in the services for sale to employers. The nature of the propaganda work is shown by a letter of an agency soliciting business from the Republic Steel Corporation in 1934: [31]

In the first place to insure a prompt and early return of your employees, they should be confused, dissension should be spread among them, and they should be influenced, encouraged and urged to go back to their jobs by your own trained agitators and propagandists. Those timid, hesitant, loyal employees, mostly of the better element, also your most desirable and key men in the plant, will only need urging, encouragement and a touch on the elbow to convince them it will be to their best advantage to go back to their jobs.

We have a whole kit of expressions and remarks accumulated by us in the last twenty years that have proven themselves in the handling of industrial disturbances time and again. Facts that the agitators for good reasons have failed to mention to your employees. Facts that are so powerful and put over with such telling effect to each striker by our propagandists that you will note a change at once in their friendly attitude towards you and other officials. . . .

For this purpose we are prepared to supply high pressure salesmen-propagandists possessing natural leadership qualifications, men of intelligence, courage and great persuasive powers, who go right into the homes of the strikers, whose return is desired by you, to carry your side of the story and counteract the evil influence of the strike agitators and the radical element.

Every propagandist used on an operation, before calling on any of the strikers, has connected with a local or nearby merchant to sell specialty products which is a perfect camouflage and does not arouse any suspicion, being apparently just a salesman calling on them. The propaganda being spread to them is considered unbiased as of course we are not known to be connected with your organization. . . .

In industrial disputes the propaganda campaigns of employees are oriented somewhat differently from those of employers. The employer seeks by propaganda to depress the morale of the strikers and to gain the support of community sentiment.[32] Employee propaganda is rarely directed toward the employer. Labor leaders in their propaganda have two objects: to maintain the morale and unity of the strikers; and to gain, if not the support, at least the neutrality of the public generally. Seasoned labor leaders are well aware that a community sentiment favorable to the employer furnishes a framework of attitudes tolerant of violent suppression of labor groups. Generally, however, the facilities and resources of employee groups for propagandizing the gen-

---

[31] Senate Report No. 6, 76th Congress, 1st Session, *Strikebreaking Services* (1939), pp. 38–39.

[32] Employer propaganda directed toward the community as a whole is often managed by citizens' committees or other dummy organizations. See L. G. Silverberg, "Citizens' Committees: Their Role in Industrial Conflict," *Public Opinion Quarterly,* (1941), pp. 17–37.

eral public are quite limited. In some circumstances employee groups succeed in arousing the sympathy and support of the general public; if public sentiment is strong enough, the employees may gain the important point of governmental neutrality in the strike.[33]

Conservative labor leaders usually operate on the assumption that unprovoked acts of violence by strikers may alienate public sympathy. (The contention might well be made that any strike is by nature an act of violence, but strikes may be accompanied by different degrees of actual physical force.)   An important task in strike management is, then, the maintenance of discipline among the strikers. Employers are equally well aware that acts of personal violence by strikers may have the effect of discrediting labor, and employer efforts to provoke violence by workers are not uncommon.   Worker violence will furnish justification for repressive measures.   In an Ohio strike, for example, a company spy worked himself into the inner circles of the union and "tried to get some of the strikers to set off a charge of dynamite in the plant, and suggested that the pickets prevent the United States mail from going into the plant." [34]   In other instances strikebreakers are imported, not to resume plant operation, but to provoke violence by the strikers, to pave the way for the forcible repression of the strike.

Similarly, in interracial relations the individual acts of violence must be viewed as only one of many methods of determining the relative status of the two groups.   Violence tends to be used in what might be called marginal cases.   Customary rules to govern status and relations grow up and tend to govern most situations.   An elaborate system of customs and etiquette of race relations, for example, has grown up in the southern states, and generally these rules are obeyed.[35]   Rationalizations of the prevailing status are preached by both whites and blacks. Apparently, where social stratification is most firmly established and accepted, the incidence of violence is lowest.[36]

Statistically, per ten thousand population, Negroes are safer from mob deaths in the old Black Belt, where more than half the population is Negro, than anywhere else in the South. . . . In the Black Belt race relations revolve about the plantation system, under which Negro tenants and wage hands are practically indispensable. Here the variant economic and cultural levels of the mass of whites and the mass of Negroes are well defined, and far removed.

33 For a discussion of employee tactics in relationship to the public, see E T. Hiller, *op. cit.*, chap. 15.

34 Senate Report No. 6, 76th Congress, 1st Session (1939), p. 46.

35 See the acute analysis by John Dollard, *Caste and Class in a Southern Town* (New Haven: Yale University Press, 1937).

36 Southern Commission on the Study of Lynching, *Lynchings and What They Mean* (Atlanta, 1931), p. 12.

On the other hand, the highest incidence of lynchings is in counties where less than one fourth of the population is Negro. "Here, in the open country, the proportion of Negro farmers who own land is greater than in the Black Belt counties and the proportion of whites who own land is less. This fact makes for a sense of competition." [37] The decline in lynching over a long period suggests that perhaps the customary rules defining the status and relationships of the races have become more firmly established and more generally accepted; thus the necessity for violence to maintain the prevailing relationships declines.

The general arguments have been that violence is likely to be associated with and supplemented by other political techniques, and that it is only under some, not all, conditions that force may effectively be used. Data exemplifying these propositions have concerned relatively minor incidents of domestic politics; but similar interpretations apply to revolutions, domestic upheavals on a much larger scale. A theory has been urged that revolutions are but the skilful application of force at vital points of social power by small groups of conspirators.[38] That idea is "a pure fiction so far as an appreciation of what happens in a real revolution is concerned." [39] Studies of revolutions by Crane Brinton and others suggest that the actual exertion of force is likely to come after a regime has all but collapsed for other causes, and that the dramatic stormings of Bastilles are comparatively insignificant in the total process of revolution.[40]

[37] *Ibid.*

[38] Curzio Malaparte, *Coup d'État, The Technique of Revolution* (New York: Dutton, 1932).

[39] G. S. Pettee, *The Process of Revolution* (New York: Harper, 1938), pp. 5–6.

[40] Crane Brinton, *The Anatomy of Revolution* (New York: Norton, 1938), Louis Gottschalk, "Causes of Revolution." *American Journal of Sociology*, 50 (1944), pp. 1–8.

Chapter 21

EDUCATION AS POLITICS

VIEWED superficially, education is unconnected with politics. Such a conclusion flows from the narrow conceptions of both education and politics customarily propagated. If the analysis of politics is confined to the machinations of the moment of political parties and pressure groups, perhaps politics has only a slight connection with education. If the range of analysis, however, is extended to cover the broad outlines of the political order—or perhaps the "structure of society"—the current maneuvers of politicians become of less significance. The political order, viewed in the perspective of time, has a continuity and a permanence that go unobserved when attention is concentrated on the transient tempest of the day. The material with which politicians must work is rarely notable for its malleability.

The political order is fundamentally an expression or reflection of the beliefs, attitudes, customs, habits, prejudices, hates, and likes of the people. An understanding of the political order requires an understanding of the human beings concerned. How did they acquire the beliefs, attitudes, customs, likes, and dislikes—or the culture—that condition their behavior? The answer is, education, if one defines education broadly enough. Almost from birth the individual is influenced or conditioned by a battery of educational forces. The family, the church, the school, the poets, the novelists, the newspapers, the movies, the radio, political parties, trade unions, and other agencies are all likely to have had a hand in the education of the individual. By all these and other means the beliefs, habits, and values of a society are impressed upon its members. The process of education tends to transmit the beliefs and customs of the group concerned. It molds the beliefs of the members of the society, and those beliefs furnish a framework that profoundly conditions the operation of governments.

1. POLITICAL ORDER AS HUMAN ATTITUDE

To indicate more clearly the political function of education, we must revert to the general theory of politics used as a basis for analysis in this

642

volume. In popular usage, politics generally connotes political parties, political campaigns, the art and practice of intrigue, or other like matters. "But the truth is," as Walter Lippmann said over a quarter of a century ago, "that we overestimate the importance of nominations, campaigns, and office-holding; . . . we tend to identify statecraft with that official government which is merely one of its instruments. Vastly overadvertised, we have mistaken an inflated fragment for the real political life of the country." [1] Beneath the surface manifestations of political life is a more enduring and more fundamental political system.

By politics may be meant the study of the relationships of the governors and of the governed in the broadest sense. By political system may be meant the pattern or form that these relationships take at a given time. Defined in these terms, politics encompasses considerably more than the formal machinery of government. A description of Congress, of the composition of its two houses, of legislative procedure, of the composition, powers, and functioning of the judiciary, of the position of the President, of the mode of making nominations, and the manner of conducting political campaigns give an entirely inadequate answer to the question, "Who rules America?" The abstraction of political institutions and procedures from their social context, as is often done in the analysis of American government, does not promote an understanding of the process of goverance. Nor would a statement of the form and function of the British Parliament furnish any notion of the important role of the British "governing class" in the political system of Great Britain.

Some political theorists describe the relationships of the governors and the governed almost exclusively in terms of political power. The political system in any society, in their terminology, may be envisaged as an equilibrium between the various groups and interests contending for power within the state. The aim of political activity, then, is power. The fruits of power are deference, prestige, income, and safety. The members of the ruling elite enjoy the deference of the masses. The flow of income is allocated among various groups by the political system; the least powerful generally receive the least material rewards. The equilibrium, or balance of power forming a particular political system, may be stable or highly unstable. A thoroughgoing revolution may almost completely change the composition of the ruling groups, and usually the political equilibrium is constantly being adjusted to make allowances for growing strength in one sector of society, for new weaknesses in another. The ruling groups may recruit the more able of the

---

[1] *Preface to Politics* (New York, 1913), p. 46. Quoted by permission of the Macmillan Company, publishers.

submerged classes and thereby forestall serious alterations in the political order. Thus, in a broad view of the political system, it might be concluded that the shifts of control between the Republican and Democratic parties in the national government, in a state, or in a city by no means constitute far-reaching transfers of power in our political system. Such changes merely constitute minor adjustments within the larger capitalistic political order. They are surface ripples that conceal the underlying, stable elements of the political order.

If the emphasis on the element of power in politics is distasteful in a democratic culture, the political system may be conceived as a complex system of loyalties. The phrase "system of loyalties" is used deliberately. A state does not consist of citizens sharing identical loyalties toward identical objects. There may be loyalty to the nation, to the region, to the national heroes, to the capitalistic system, to particular institutions, to the constitution, to abstract national symbols, ideals, and aspirations. The pattern of orientation of loyalties is complicated by the multiple loyalties of individuals. And these may come to be competing or conflicting loyalties. Loyalty to the church, for example, at times weakens, at other times reinforces, the political system as a whole. The makers and the preservers of a political system have the function of weaving these divergent loyalties into a cohesive whole. When in that task there is failure, the political order is likely to be disrupted and to fall.

If analysis in terms of power or loyalty does not seem to cover the situation adequately, political systems could be described in terms of individual attitudes. A political system could be said to exist in the attitudes, and the consequent overt behavior, of its citizens toward a series of matters, such as the distribution of property and income, the nation, other nations, the legal system, the political institutions, the holders of power, the duty of obedience. A political order could be said to derive its fundamental form from the attitudes of its citizens; conversely, a change in the political order either may be caused by, or of necessity may be followed by, a marked change in the attitudes of its citizens. If one contemplates the degree of stability of attitudes toward matters fundamental, he gains a notion of the relative insignificance of political parties in the American political order as a whole.

If one tends to be of a philosophic bent of mind, a description of the political order as a system of values might be more satisfactory. A given political system could be considered as a hierarchy of values— that is to say, a culture of a society attaches value to certain practices, institutions, customs. In the process it frowns upon, or in a sense attaches negative values to, conflicting elements of other ways of life. A scale of values results, ranging from those most sacred to the negative values of darkest hue.

Whatever terminology is employed, however, the essence of the matter is the same. In any political order there are those dominant in terms of power, there are predominant loyalties, there are sets of attitudes that prevail, or there are closely guarded values. It all amounts to saying that in any political order there are those who manage the system because they have the power, because they command the loyalties of the masses, because the generality possesses a system of attitudes favorable to their control, or because they have been able to ensconce themselves as the guardians of the values of the order. In the final analysis the political order reflects the attitudes and beliefs of the human beings making up the society. For a time a tyrannical elite may control, but it soon attempts to convert forced acquiescence into cheerful consent. Moreover, the ideology of a people possesses great staying powers. The long dominance of the ideology of capitalism in the American popular mind illustrates the point. Parties operate within the confines of the prevailing ideology. When one understands the nature of fundamental beliefs and their effect on political behavior, the basis is laid for comprehending the political function of education.

2. POLITICAL FUNCTION OF EDUCATION

One of the first principles of political behavior is that those who benefit from political systems strive to perpetuate them. Abdication occurs infrequently and, then, usually under duress. Those possessing power seek to retain it; the prevailing loyalties are sheltered against competition of possibly more alluring faiths; the dominant values are cherished and protected. The defenses of a political system operate against both external aggression and internal subversion. The process of defense and accommodation of a particular order within its international environment is readily perceptible; but its internal defense and self-perpetuation are not always so apparent, since the observer, as a participant in the system, does not have a psychological base of detachment from which to watch the process. Moreover, although armies, navies, and diplomacy—instruments for external defense and adjustment— are physically and dramatically visible, many of the methods and devices operating to preserve the internal structure of a political system work more subtly or perhaps without conscious direction. The significance of the family, for example, in the perpetuation of political systems remains impressive. The disappearance of formalized hereditary ruling classes did not eliminate hereditary transmission of economic, social,

and political status.[2]   Yet it is not to be supposed that prospective
fathers as a general rule coldly reason that they belong to, let us say,
the bourgeois class, that they desire to perpetuate their class and the
system of which it is a part, and that they therefore decide to become
fathers in order that their class with its power and perquisites may be
perpetuated.   Children tend to grow into adults like their elders, not
because of conspiracy or design, but because there is no one else for them
to imitate.

Role of education in the maintenance of political systems.   One of
the great mechanisms for the maintenance of any political order is its
educational system.   At times the school system is employed to this end
as deliberately and consciously as the military in a war of defense; in
other situations, particularly in well-established political orders, the
school system performs this function without reasoned intent something
after the fashion of our unthinking hypothetical prospective father.
H. D. Lasswell says: [3]

A well-established ideology perpetuates itself with little planned propaganda
by those whom it benefits most.   When thought is taken about ways and
means of sowing conviction, conviction has already languished, the basic outlook of society has decayed, or a new, triumphant outlook has not yet gripped
the automatic loyalties of old and young.   Happy indeed is that nation that
has no thought of itself; or happy at least are the few who procure the principal
benefits of universal acquiescence.   Systems of life which confer special benefits on the other fellow need no plots or conspiracies when the masses are
moved by faith and the elites are inspired by self-confidence.

In other words, when college deans and school superintendents convene, make speeches to one another about the duty of the schools to

[2] The family is an important instrumentality in the projection of a given structure
of politics through time.   In hereditary aristocracies the various classes occupied a
given status and the transmission of political status by inheritance was formalized.
Formalized hereditary aristocracies are largely a thing of the past, but there remains
a tendency for sociopolitical status to be passed on to the younger members of the
family.   In another connection reference has been made to the fact that a marked
tendency exists for the party affiliations and attitudes of children to be similar to
those of their fathers.   Family environment is certainly not the sole conditioning
factor in this process, but the accident of birth into a family of a particular status
subjects the individual to all the forces that play on the family.   Beyond the formation of partisan attitudes, narrowly considered, the younger member of the family
enjoys all the opportunities and limitations of the family status; he has a chance to
obtain and retain a status in society equivalent to that of the family.   "Apart from
brief periods of violent revolution," says Mosca in a generalization based primarily
on observation of European experience, "personal qualities are always less important,
as regards attaining the highest positions in life, than birth or family.   In any type
of society, whether ostensibly democratic or otherwise, being born to a high station is
one of the best claims a person can have to staying there."—*The Ruling Class* (New
York: McGraw-Hill, 1939), p. 123.

[3] *Politics* (New York: Whittlesey House, 1936), pp. 29–30.

teach "citizenship," and issue manifestoes urging all lesser educators to indoctrinate the cherished values of the social system, internal weakness and doubt have probably already gained a foothold. In the absence of doubt, these things take care of themselves more or less automatically.

"The schools," it has been said, "are the organized transmitters of group tradition and of group wisdom. . . ." [4] "Fundamentally and comprehensively considered, education is a process of inducting the young and immature into the life and culture of the group. . . ." [5] Through education there are transmitted to the succeeding generation the traditions, loyalties, values, mythology, mores, attitudes, and folklore as well as the skills of the group. An entire way of life is inculcated. If one views the educational process broadly, the protracted discussion among students of education about the pros and cons of indoctrination becomes patently absurd. Indoctrination is inevitable. Education weaves the moving pattern of the present into the future.

In the selection of the values and attitudes to be inculcated, any school system chooses those that are cherished by the dominant elements in the political order. That this occurs is partially because the educational system cannot extract itself from its matrix within the general social order, and partially because it functions as an agent of or is subject to the control of the governing elite of the political order. The truth of this statement is susceptible of verification by simple observation on every hand, but if documentation is desired one may cite Counts' study of the social composition of boards of education: [6]

The outstanding conclusion to be drawn from this study of the occupations of the members of boards of education is that the control of education and the formulation of educational policy are intrusted very largely to representatives of the more favored classes. To this statement exceptions may be made for isolated city boards here and there and for the boards in the smaller districts and rural communities. The important boards are dominated either by those who control the economic resources of the country or by those who are associated rather intimately with the economically powerful classes. In other words, the ordinary board is composed, for the most part, of merchants, lawyers, bankers, manufacturers, physicians, and persons in responsible executive positions.

These conclusions are not especially startling; what would have been astonishing, knowing what we do about the way our world runs, would

[4] C. E. Merriam, *The Making of Citizens* (Chicago: University of Chicago Press, 1931), p. 89.

[5] G. S. Counts, *The Prospects of American Democracy* (New York: John Day, 1938), p. 296.

[6] *Social Composition of Boards of Education* (Chicago: University of Chicago, 1927), p. 74.

have been a contrary finding. What is perhaps significant is that the "more favored classes" control the schools directly rather than by delegating control to more or less professional, that is, specialized, politicians.

A pertinent inquiry may be, from what source comes this program to be inculcated by our schools? The practicing pedagogue may deny consciousness of systematized compulsion on matters curricular. The student of comparative education will look in vain for an analogy in the United States to the elaborate reorganization of the curriculum and personnel of Italian schools by Mussolini to the end that fascist patriotism might be taught. Nor will he find institutional parallels to the central Ministry of Education of France with its broad authority exercised, ineffectively as it turned out, to strengthen *la belle* France. He perhaps will see here nothing on the order of the educational system in Russia where the Communists "have seized upon the schools as one of the most effective agencies for the purpose of building up a new generation impregnated with Communist doctrines and ideals," where "revolutionary history, struggles, victories, heroes, achievements are developed from the earliest years of the school curriculum to the last, often with great skill and always with great enthusiasm." [7]

The integration of the activities of our loosely organized school system, with its forty-eight state school organizations, is accomplished in large measure through the impact of generally accepted goals, mores, and social values. We do not require an authoritatively or positively promulgated program of education; everyone understands in a general kind of way what sort of things are to be taught. It is primarily when the schools diverge from this poorly defined groove and clash with the dominant groups in the political system that it feels the pressure to conform. Control of the school system is exerted at the periphery of subject matter the great mass of which occasions no disagreement. This would probably tend to be true in any well-established regime.

Inculcation of nationalism. The inculcation of nationalism, which for present purposes may be defined as loyalty to this nation as opposed to others, illustrates these general propositions. That the school system inculcates such attitudes is a commonplace. Indeed, the rise of universal free education has paralleled the development of nationalism, and education has proved a strong prop for intense nationalism. The state schools, says Professor Hayes, "have been the basic and most reliable agencies of nationalist propaganda among the masses." [8]

American school children learn from their textbooks that "America

[7] Merriam, *op. cit.,* p. 93.
[8] C. J. H. Hayes, *Essays on Nationalism* (New York: Macmillan, 1928), p. 86.

stands for one folk equal before God and man in their rights and privileges"; that "ours is a government not of force or fear but of ideals"; that we are "the greatest democratic nation in the world"; that the melting pot has formed "one of the finest systems of population which has ever appeared"; that "the American invents as the Greeks chiseled, as the Venetian painted, as the modern Italian sings"; that the United States "has done more for world advancement than any other nation"; that "our representative system is the oldest in the world, and no country has more safety, more freedom, more opportunities for its people." [9]

Although we usually think of historians as the principal embalmers of our folklore, writers on other subjects also have a nationalistic tinge. As Professor Hayes states it in somewhat picturesque but generally correct terms: [10]

Elementary readers are packed with nationalist poems, with ultrapatriotic legends, and with tales of the mythical and always exemplary deeds of ancestral demigods. Geography is usually centered in the providential economic and territorial primacy of one's own country, and from its study the pupils gather that their nation is, or should be, the most favoured of all God's creation, and that it has, or should have, "natural boundaries," great "natural resources," and vast wealth. From their study of civics, the same pupils are led to believe that their country is the freest, the most liberty-loving, the most progressive, the best governed, and the happiest on earth.

Perpetuation of the structure of power. When one turns from the sphere of nationalism to the internal structure of political power of the nation, it can readily be seen that the schools perform a similar function in the perpetuation of the internal distribution of power. The textbooks, reinforced by classroom teaching, sanctify the existing formal governmental order, which in turn serves as a prop to the general economic order. A set of rigid stereotypes that color thinking and condition reactions for a lifetime is inculated. One text says: [11]

Our country has developed into a true Representative Democracy. That is, our people select their own officials, and have all an equal vote in changing them when necessary. These representatives are pledged to direct our Government for the equal benefit of us all. There is the same law for all, the same permissions and the same restraints. That is the nearest approach to the ideal of equality that man has yet been able to attain.

[9] The quotations are from Bessie L. Pierce, *Civic Attitudes in American School Textbooks* (Chicago: The University of Chicago Press, 1930), pp. 106–125.
[10] *Op. cit.*, p. 88.
[11] From Pierce, *op. cit.*, chap. 11; see W. Y. Elliott, "The Constitution as the American Social Myth," in Conyers Read (ed.), *The Constitution Reconsidered* (New York: Columbia University Press, 1938).

The Constitution is said to be "the most marvelous written political instrument that has ever been made." The general result of the educational process is that the system of separation of powers, the principle of division of powers between state and federal governments, and the position of the Supreme Court are canonized. The prospective citizen is equipped with a ready system of verbal formulae with which to exercise his sovereign functions as a voter.

Apart from notions relating to the formal structure of government, the values of a bourgeois, capitalistic society are inculcated. On these questions there appear to be no extensive studies of the kinds of attitudes transmitted; nevertheless it would probably be correct to say that the notion of the right of private property, the virtues of individual initiative, the certainty of progress, the social wisdom of business and financial leaders are thoroughly instilled by the educational process. These attitudes are quite as important as notions about the formal governmental machinery in the preservation of the existing political order broadly considered.[12]

What is not taught in the schools is perhaps as important as what is taught, in the maintenance of the prevailing attitudes and pattern of politics. In our political order, as perhaps in any political order, the continuation of the existing regime depends in part on the exercise of power in such a way that the masses either are not conscious of the nature of the regime, or are so habituated to the modes of the exercise of power that they are not fully aware of the effects of the order. School pupils learn little of the benefits accruing to the holders of power, of the nature of the distribution income and other perquisites, of the utilization of government by privileged groups. Nor do they learn much of the effects of our political systems on the submerged groups. The result of the press of power is not a major element in the curriculum.

Nature of control of the school system. It has been noted that we do not have a unified educational machine with a duly constituted central organ for the determination of the values to be inculcated through our schools, but that corrective pressure comes to be applied at the margin when the schools deviate from the generally accepted folklore. The detailed story of the nature and application of these pressures has been collected and recorded by Bessie Louise Pierce in her volumes, *Public Opinion and the Teaching of History* and *Citizen's Organizations and the Civic Training of Youth*. The Daughters of the American Revolution insist that "the colleges and schools faithfully present facts of history and government in the United States and inculcate both reverence

---

[12] For a suggestive analysis of the American public mind, see Gunnar Myrdal, *An American Dilemma* (New York: Harper, 1944), vol. i, ch. 1.

for truth and a proper understanding and appreciation of the high destiny for which the Republic was founded." The Veterans of Foreign Wars have as one of their objectives the education of "posterity in the principles of true Americanism through publications and work in public schools and institutions," and to this end the organization has brought pressure on schools and textbook writers. The peace organizations bring their strength, such as it is, to bear, and, like the American Legion, have prepared a book for use in the schools, but the object of the peace leagues is to "help children learn how to live happily in an interdependent world." The activities of the public utilities in seeking a proper presentation in textbooks and schoolrooms of the role of utilities was not so long ago exposed by the Federal Trade Commission. The National Association of Manufacturers occasionally manifests an interest in "subversive" materials in textbooks and, as with other groups, attempts to classify as "un-American" views diverging from its own. On the other side the American Federation of Labor has been vigilant in its surveys of textbooks to assure itself that textbooks "give the labor movement and the problem of industry adequate and just consideration." Throughout the history of American public education the clerics, both Protestant and Roman Catholic, have sought to influence the content of instruction. Almost every group and interest analyzed in the first few chapters of this book exert themselves in one way or another to influence the course and tenor of public instruction, just as they apply pressure to influence the decisions of legislative bodies and administrative agencies.

The nature of pressures on school systems is vividly recounted in Howard K. Beale's *Are American Teachers Free?* He records his findings in over eight hundred pages and emerges with the conclusion, which probably was not unanticipated, that American teachers are hemmed in on all sides. He analyzes with care freedom in the discussion of war problems, peace and internationalism, patriotism, politics, economic and social questions, history, religion, and science. He describes the pressures on text writers and examines the special conditions found in private schools and in Negro schools. He classifies extrascholastic pressures on the teacher and intrascholastic pressures. Without doing violence to his bulky work, it might be compressed into the statement that teachers generally must teach those points of view that find favor in their community.[13] Or, at any rate, they must not teach viewpoints that clash violently with the values held dear by the domi-

---

[13] For a case study of the social pressures of the school system in one community, see R. S. and H. M. Lynd, *Middletown in Transition* (New York: Harcourt, Brace, 1937), chap. 6.

nant classes within the community. What is taught, therefore, varies somewhat from locality to locality, and the pattern of control differs from place to place. In a one-industry town the identity of the controllers of the schools may be quite definite; in a city with varied interests the teacher may be puzzled to ascertain his master in the interplay of conflicting interests.[14]

The discussion thus far has dealt in general with the rather shadowy but none the less effective control over the educational system by the dominant elements of society. In numerous respects this control has been formalized in legislation, and there is a large body of law prescribing the curriculum or phases of it. A special type of this control consists in the legislative insistence that prescribed ceremonies and rituals be performed in the schools, an example of early inculcation of habitual obeisance to institutional symbols common to a variety of organizations.

It is not necessary to prove a conspiracy among the controlling groups of society aimed at guiding the educational system in order to establish the function of the schools in the perpetuation or attempted perpetuation of the main outlines of the prevailing order. The function played by the school system is not necessarily the result of plotting by designing and wicked men. The teacher and the school are a part of the existing political order, and they are immersed in the prevailing beliefs of the society. And they cannot rise above (or very far above) the web of their environment. It is more or less inherent in the nature of social behavior for the educational system to be bound by the prevailing mores.

Thus the educational system is a great instrument of governance, a political device probably more effective than police and prisons, which functions by and large as a means for aiding the dominant elements in any political order to maintain their power. That the hypothesis is generally correct is more or less self-evident and probably would be conceded on all sides. There is nothing startling about the line of argument. A confirmation of the hypothesis, as well as a tribute to the effectiveness of the schools as political tools, is the promptness with which revolutionary groups on attaining power proceed to cleanse the schools of the taint of the old order and to install their own special brand of truth.

It may be concluded that the educational system is in the main a conservative influence in that it tends to conserve or preserve established values. But the heritage transmitted is by no means entirely "conservative." In some respects it may be quite radical. The inculcation of the doctrines of majority rule, of equality, of freedom of

[14] See also H. K. Beale, *A History of Freedom of Teaching in American Schools* (New York: Scribner's, 1941).

speech, of consent of the governed may under some circumstances be a mockery, but a modicum of hope and faith may be instilled under such conditions. The impact may be what is denominated in certain circles as "subversive." In fact, often the pressures on the schools by special interests may be regarded as reactionary (not conservative) attempts to bring by retrogression an identification of special interests with the American tradition. The Constitution, for example, says nothing about the right of one group to exploit another, but interests of all hues try to make certain that the schools do not suggest that their perquisites diverge from the glorious American tradition.

Effects of universal education. A consideration of the political function of education is inadequate, however, if it stops with the conclusion that schools (and other means of education) are powerful instruments for the maintenance of a political system. Universal education results in other political effects of profound significance. They may be suggested by a few comparative remarks on educational systems and by some observations on the genesis of public education in America.

The introduction of universal education may alter significantly the conditions of the exercise of political power. Tyrants and oligarchs, both princely and priestly, almost always seek to keep the masses in ignorance. In fact, the initiation of free, universal education has tended to be associated with popular revolutionary movements and has generally been resisted by the holders of power. Widespread illiteracy simplifies the task of ruling and exploiting groups. When literacy and related skills are a closely held monopoly of a few, a substantial proportion of the population may be virtually inert politically. The reasons are simple. A vast number of people is beyond ready access by systems of communication available to any challenger of the existing order. Authoritarian pronouncements—through the church and state bureaucracy—cannot be readily subjected to competition in the market of ideas. Something of the significance of these observations may be suggested by contemplation of the political differences between, for example, the United States and any Latin-American republic with a high degree of illiteracy.

Widespread literacy, however, does not in itself produce democracy. The examples of Japan and Germany need only be cited. Yet universal literacy alters the requirements for the maintenance of oppression. Tyrannical regimes must establish censorship, maintain "thought control" police, give energetic and constant attention to the suppression of subversive propaganda, and protect themselves in a thousand ways against the dissemination of hostile ideas. A revolutionist with a clandestine printing press (or a mimeograph) may undermine the regime. On the other hand, the existence of general literacy gives a regime new positive instruments of power. Literacy may compel the use of new negative restraints to protect a regime, but the ruling groups also may monopolize the channels of communication to inculcate deference and to generate support. Propaganda ministries are the obverse of censorships. From a comparative analysis of different regimes, which can only be suggested here, it would probably be concluded that universal education and general literacy do not in themselves change the nature of the distribution of political power. It is not the fact of universal education that is of fundamental significance; it is the ideology or the political values that are propagated through the educational apparatus. Inculcation of the doctrine of the master race may produce quite different results from the inculcation of the traditions of American democracy, which include at least a modicum of wholesome disrespect for all holders of authority. Literacy, in association with freedom of speech and press and in association with doctrines of rationalism, of the perfectibility of man, of human progress, produces effects entirely unlike those of universal education and literacy in a different ideological context. However, within a regime like the United States there is evidence that different degrees of education result in sharp differences of political behavior. The less formal education a person has the greater is the probability that he will not participate in political life and the greater is the probability that he will have no views on public issues.[15]

Comparison of the role of education in different societies with variations in educational practice may be supplemented with a few remarks on the evolution of the American educational system. Speculations about education soon after the foundation of the Republic were colored by concern for the creation of a system of education fitted to the peculiar requirements of American institutions and not copied after those of the old world, which were designed to serve monarchical regimes. Republican institutions demanded a general illumination of the public mind, and great faith arose that the salvation of the Republic lay in general education. The doctrine found expression in the famed clause of the Ordinance of 1787: "Religion, morality, and knowledge being necessary to good government and the happiness of mankind, schools and the means of education shall be encouraged." Nationalism was strong in its influence on educational thought, but egalitarianism—

---

[15] A useful analysis could be made of the findings of public-opinion polls relating political attitudes to degree of formal education. It would be difficult, of course, to separate the factor of education from other closely related variables such as economic status but it seems apparent that the degree of schooling itself has significant effects on political behavior.

which was, after all, one element of the new national ideology—was also manifest. In 1791, Robert Coram, in his *Plan for the general establishment of Schools throughout the United States,* exclaimed: "It is a shame, a scandal to civilized society, that part only of the citizens should be sent to colleges and universities to learn to cheat the rest of their liberties." [16] Comments in like vein were to be found in the writings of other agitators for enlarged educational facilities.

Political theorists of the formative years of the nation thus were by no means unaware of the political function of education. They created an ideological basis for universal education, but the development of free public education on a large scale did not come until the nineteenth century. As the movement for the expansion of educational facilities took shape, the issues posed revealed something of the current estimates of the political significance of education. A class cleavage arose, based in part on the opposition of the well-to-do to the assumption of the costs of general education through taxation, but also on the fear of some spokesmen of the more favored classes that their prerogatives would be endangered by a generous extension of educational opportunity to others. Residues of this early array of forces on educational questions remain in many parts of the country in which a principal part of the support for adequate public education comes from labor and affiliated groups while chambers of commerce, taxpayers' associations, and like groups do battle to restrict the scope of public educational activity.[17]

The idea of equality of opportunity in education plays an important role in the American political system. In a rigidly structured society, such as that found in many countries of the world, vertical social mobility is apt to be slight; the sons and daughters of each social group "inherit" a status. The offspring of favored classes enjoy special opportunity, including education, and are apt to constitute most of the favored classes of the next generation. On the other hand, the sons and daughters of the less-favored classes, even though they may be potential geniuses, are likely to remain in the status to which they were born. The philosophy of American education cuts through rigid class lines and proclaims that each person shall have a right and an educational opportunity to attain whatever status his abilities warrant. This sort of educational doctrine is, of course, part and parcel of democratic theory. Thomas Jefferson, hence, was not out of character as a demo-

[16] Quoted by A. O. Hansen, *Liberalism and American Education in the Eighteenth Century* (New York: Macmillan, 1926), p. 71.
[17] See Paul Monroe, *Founding of the American Public School System* (New York: Macmillan, 1940), vol. I; Merle Curti, *The Social Ideas of American Educators* (New York: Scribner's, 1935); Alice Felt Tyler, *Freedom's Ferment* (Minneapolis: University of Minnesota Press, 1944), ch. 10.

cratic theorist when he proposed an educational system that would skim off at various educational levels those persons of genius and provide further training at public·expense. "The object," he said, "is to bring into action that mass of talents which lies buried in poverty in every country, for want of the means of development, and thus give activity to a mass of mind, which, in proportion to our population, shall be the double or treble of what it is in most countries." [18]

Educational systems and the recruitment of governing classes. It may well be asked what all this has to do with the nature of our political system. When class lines are so rigid that men of talent are excluded from the most influential groups, the power of the dominant group is likely to be challenged. A discriminating recruitment of the able into the governing groups is a sign of political health. Aristotle long ago observed that certain governments continued firm and stable as a result of the wise conduct of the magistrates toward those who have no part in the management of public affairs, whose merits they recognize by "introducing those who are of most consequence amongst them into office." Such practices sterilize potential revolutionists. But a more significant and more pervasive political function of the American doctrine of education may be suggested. Utopian ideas have an extraordinary hold on the human mind; a significant clue to the nature of a society is furnished by its utopias. Peoples seem to have to invent heavens for themselves, and their utopian expectations constitute a significant element in the faiths and beliefs that furnish the dynamic forces in a society. If the worker, the janitor, the tenant farmer can achieve very little in this generation, perhaps his son, through education, can in the next. The cult of education undoubtedly has contributed to social morale and created a mass faith in the ultimate rightness of things.

Whether the educational system actually promotes interclass mobility is quite another matter. It is the belief that the system works which has politico-social significance. Such studies as have been made in the United States indicate a fairly high degree of inheritance of occupational and economic status, yet not inconsiderable degrees of vertical mobility are shown to exist. Thus Taussig and Joslyn find that business and professional groups contribute disproportionately to their successors of the next generation although there is substantial infiltration by the sons of members of outside groups.[19] The part played by the

---

[18] Quoted in *The Jeffersonian Cyclopedia*, J. P. Foley, ed. (New York: Funk and Wagnalls, 1900), p. 275.

[19] *American Business Leaders* (New York: Macmillan, 1932). See also P. E. Davidson and H. D. Anderson, *Occupational Mobility in an American Community* (Stanford: Stanford University Press, 1937).

educational system in promoting social mobility is obvious, but few analyses precisely in point are available.[20]

The American educational system has, it may be well to note, never achieved equality of opportunity for all persons regardless of social origin. Yet it has operated with the goal of equality and has probably more nearly reached the goal than other national systems.[21] Opportunity for education is less among the poor than among the wealthy, less among Negroes than whites, lower in the South than in the West, less in the country than in the city. Yet over the long run variations in opportunity have been reduced. Regional differences in educational opportunity are indicated in part by the data in Table 25, which shows the per cent of the population of selected age groups in three great regions attending school in 1940.

TABLE 25

Per cent of Population of Selected Age Groups Attending School, 1940 [a]

Region	7 to 13 years old	14 and 15 years old	16 to 20 years old	21 to 24 years old
North	97.3	93.9	43.9	5.3
South	91.1	82.9	35.1	3.9
West	97.0	94.7	51.3	7.6

[a] Census of 1940.

3. SCHOOLS AND POLITICAL EVOLUTION

The foregoing analysis of the nature of politics and of the role of the educational system in the political order lays a basis for a discussion of the various proposals that it is the responsibility and duty of the schools to remake the social order. It is essential that two basic points already advanced be kept in mind: first, that in the political order there is a ruling group or groups, more or less clearly defined; second, that the educational system, in addition to transmitting skills, tends to aid in the maintenance of the pattern of political power.

Although he is by no means alone, the most vocal advocate of the proposition that the school system should transform the social order is George S. Counts. In numerous books, pamphlets, and articles he has pictured a political order toward which the schools should build. In

[20] See the study of eight Harvard classes by J. B. Knox, "Occupation and Education in a Democracy," *Social Forces*, 20 (1941), pp. 109–115.

[21] Compare the educational practices of England. For significant discussion of the interrelationships between class, educational system, and political power, see H. J. Laski, "The Personnel of the English Cabinet, 1901–1924," *American Political Science Review*, 22 (1928), pp. 12 ff.

one of his recent volumes he has outlined the kind of political system that he thinks should be the objective of the school system. He says: [22]

Conceivably, a closely integrated economy might be managed in the interests of the great masses of the population. Under such an arrangement no class or group would be regarded as a means for the elevation of another, no artistocracy of either birth or property would be allowed, no great concentration of wealth or income in private hands would be permitted, no grinding poverty or degrading slums, placing their indelible stamp on the generations, would be tolerated. On the contrary, the moral equality of all men, as proclaimed in the Declaration of Independence, would be recognized as a controlling ideal and would be accepted as a guiding principle in the reconstruction of social life and institutions. The productive energies of the nation would be devoted first to laying the foundation of material security for all. Thereafter they would be dedicated to raising the cultural level and enriching the lives of the people, to making the entire country a pleasant and beautiful place in which to live. The natural endowment and the resources of technology would be administered in the name of society as a whole. . . . An economy, not only of security, but of abundance lies within the realm of the possible. The American people merely lack the will, the knowledge, and the discipline necessary to achieve it.

With the characteristics of Professor Counts' blueprint one need have no quarrel. The analysis would be the same for any scheme of values different from those prevailing, proposed to be systematically propagated through the schools. The reconstruction of a political order in general means a reallocation of power and pelf, or those things enjoyed in greater degree by the "more favored" or dominant elements of that order. It is proposed that the schools set out to "build a new social order." The proposition is patently fantastic. The educational system is hardly in a position to do battle with the beneficiaries and defenders of the prevailing order; it must, in the nature of politics, be subordinate.

Professor Counts and others have seen the difficulties. "A major task which confronts us," he said in 1927, "is that of devising some means of so controlling the school that it may not become the subservient tool of some powerful interest or group in the community." [23] Later he advanced the notion that the schools, like legislatures, have a representative function. "Whatever may be their legal position," he argues, "they represent the masses of the American people and are therefore under obligation to protect the interests of those masses." [24] If the masses are dominant in the American political order, the schools repre-

22 *Social Foundations of Education* (New York: Scribner's, 1934), pp. 540–541.
23 *The Social Composition of Boards of Education*, p. 91
24 *Social Foundations of Education*, p. 541.

sent them; if the masses are not dominant, the schools cannot represent them no matter what the ethical obligation may be.

George A. Coe has attempted to solve the dilemma.[25] He recognizes that in the modern national state the dominant classes and interests of the state generally bring under their sway all the important institutions. He pleads for a sort of autonomy for the school system. This sovereign agency within the sovereign state would be vested with authority to determine what values and notions would be transmitted through the school system. The observed tendencies of political behavior contradict the validity of the proposal. No political order, unless it is already in the process of disintegration, will tolerate, nor can it afford to tolerate, movements or competing institutions that threaten its existence. It cannot be denied, of course, that our school systems enjoy a certain amount of autonomy, but it is a limited autonomy. The schools can stay in the pantry as long as they do not get into the jam.

About the only sort of regime in which the schools could exercise the power that Mr. Coe suggests would be what could be called a "pedocracy." By that word is meant a state ruled by schoolmen; a theocracy in which the priests would be replaced by pedagogs. Under such a scheme the teachers and others constituting the educational system would become the dominant element in the political order and would be in a position to remake society as they pleased. Now Professor Counts has this to say on ruling classes: [26]

> In shaping educational policy, the peculiar limitations of any dominant social class should be noted. Whether that class is a priesthood, a holy order, a military aristocracy, the bourgeoisie, or the proletariat matters not. They all suffer from the same affliction. A dominant class is a privileged class, a class that is favored by the existing social arrangements. It therefore tends to be conservative, to exaggerate the merits of the prevailing order, and to fear any agitation favoring fundamental changes in the social structure. It represents the past rather than the future; its creative period lies in a preceding age; its genius has already found expression.

Although it may be pleasant to some people to contemplate being governed by a soviet of school superintendents, one will have to admit that such a ruling group would probably suffer from the same afflictions that beset other dominant classes. They would cling to their power and perquisites as desperately as the besieged capitalists or the ruling oligarchy of the American Federation of Labor.

The line of argument may be recapitulated. The first proposition advanced is that in the political system there exists a set of dominant in-

[25] *Educating for Citizenship* (New York: Scribner's, 1932).
[26] *Social Composition of Boards of Education*, pp. 91–92.

terests. It is, to be sure, difficult to define this group sharply in the
United States, but there is a much higher degree of continuity in the
governing interests than would be deduced from concentration of attention on the democratic mechanism of elections and parties. Second,
it is contended that political systems generally seek to perpetuate themselves. That proposition is self-evident; it is extremely rare that the
dominant element in any society knowingly commits political suicide.
(They more often absent-mindedly commit political suicide through
stupidity.) Third, it is stated that the school system performs a political function in the transmission of the prevailing values and attitudes in
the political order. Fourth, it is contended that unless the schools
should themselves become the dominant element in a political system,
they must serve more or less as agents of the dominant classes in society.
Fifth, in the United States it might be argued that the leaders of educational systems occupy a seat at the table of political power, but they by
no means dominate. Finally, it follows that the notion that the schools
can remake the political order has no basis. Political power may be
redistributed gradually or rapidly, but these changes occur by and large
through the action of forces outside the schools. The educational system, like almost any great institution, must generally tend to be a conservative influence in that it conserves present values. The inertia of
the educational organization will probably always tend to keep it somewhat behind, rather than ahead of, the times.

Part Five

THE PARTY AND THE GOVERNMENT

Chapter 22

PARTY LEADERSHIP
IN LEGISLATION

ELECTIONS are dramatic episodes in the struggle for power. In campaigns the party machinery functions at full blast. The high visibility of party activity in campaigns and elections often leads to inadequate emphasis on party activity in the period between elections. Yet it is in the conduct of government after the election that the party in power executes its policies and makes a record to its advantage or disadvantage in the next campaign. The test of a party is in its management of the government. In campaigns party leaders must build a coalition with adequate strength to win the election; the coalition is cemented together by expectations, hopes, and fears. In the conduct of government the party must solve even more difficult problems of political combination. It is not merely seeking power by promises; it has the power. The issues it faces are immediate and urgent; the end-product of the entire political process is in the action and inaction of government.

A distinction, thus, can be made between the functions of parties in campaigns and in the conduct of government, or, if a party happens to be in the minority, in the criticism of the conduct of government by the majority. In a sense, the two functions are performed by two different institutions. The party has its organization outside the government to nominate candidates and to campaign for their election. On the other hand, the party members occupying legislative and executive posts have responsibility for conduct of the government. The party group within the representative body has its own organization and its own identity quite independent of the party outside the government. Thus, the majority leader in the Senate holds his position by virtue of the favor of his colleagues and is an officer of an institution separate from and not subordinate to the party organization headed by the national chairman of the party. In nations with parliamentary governments a clear line is drawn between the parliamentary party and the party outside the government. In fact, on occasion the vote-gathering organization even has a name different from that of the parliamentary group.

In the United States, however, the notion of a dual personality of party is not so commonly recognized, perhaps because complete responsibility for conduct of the government is not held by the majority of a single representative chamber. Nevertheless, the distinction between party as a parliamentary group and party as a campaigning organization serves to give emphasis to the importance of adequate attention to the two separate functions of the political party.

In the performance of the function of nomination of candidates and of campaigning for their election political parties have no serious rivals, but in the conduct of government, especially in legislation, pressure groups are not content to leave the institution and management of affairs to the political party. These private groups try to influence the party program; if they fail in this, they may attempt to wrest leadership from the party and to control the representative body through the formation of a bipartisan coalition. Nevertheless, party machinery and party spirit constitute the principal influences toward a coherent legislative program and the main source of leadership in the process of legislation.

1. GOVERNMENTAL STRUCTURE AND PARTY RESPONSIBILITY

Party performance in the conduct of government is conditioned by the nature of governmental institutions. At times it has been the fashion to say that the structure of government is a matter of indifference: whatever its character may be, the dominant social forces will express themselves through the mechanism. Perhaps such reasoning is perfectly valid if one is concerned with broad social movements sweeping through long periods of history. But in the day-to-day conduct of government the nature of governmental mechanisms is of great significance. Structure and procedure not only influence what can be accomplished and the way it is accomplished but they sometimes determine the outcome of issues. The interaction between party forces and governmental mechanisms, of course, operates in both directions. In the long run party forces also influence the form and nature of institutions, but these influences usually produce gradual change. More clearly perceptible is the fact that, in the everyday business of governing, the institutional tools that party.leaders work with modify, divert, and distort as well as reflect the dominant political forces of the moment.

The problems of the formulation and execution of a party program under the presidential form of government are thrown into bold relief by a comparison of that system with the British system of responsible cabinet government. Under the latter scheme undisputed and undivided party leadership is vested in the cabinet, a body formed of leaders of the majority party in the House of Commons. The cabinet members steer the course of legislation in the House of Commons and individually they head the administrative departments of government. Thus there is unified in the hands of the cabinet both legislative leadership and executive power. The cabinet governs and is, appropriately, referred to as the Government.

The cabinet governs, but it governs subject to the approval of the House of Commons and ultimately of the nation. Approval of the House of Commons, however, comes to mean the support of the majority party within the House, from which the members of the cabinet are generally recruited. Although the cabinet, in its power to dissolve Parliament and call an election, has a potent weapon with which to discipline its followers, the maintenance of party unity depends fundamentally on the enunciation by the cabinet of a party program that will satisfy the party in the House. The members of the Commons tend to reflect, in turn, the attitudes and opinions of their constituents. If party unity cannot be maintained, the cabinet may lose its majority in the House.

In constitutional theory the cabinet may be overthrown, but in practice the only way it could be overthrown would be by a split in the majority party. Such action would bring in its train a general election; members of the majority do not take lightly the responsibility of precipitating an election and of compelling themselves to incur the expense of a campaign. Yet the party leadership does not rely solely on the threat of dissolution to maintain the unity of its following. Cabinet measures that arouse intense criticism may be seriously modified to quell discontent in the party ranks and in the country. The cabinet may even withdraw a measure that threatens party unity if its withdrawal can be accomplished without losing face or prestige. In some situations a minister may be "thrown to the wolves" to satisfy the party or the public. In extreme instances the majority party may change party leadership and, hence, the cabinet, to retain the confidence of the House and of the country, as when, in 1940, Churchill replaced Chamberlain as prime minister.

The machinery of cabinet government thus facilitates the formation and execution of party policy. Party leadership and governmental leadership are in the same hands. Governmental leadership is centered in one place rather than dispersed among institutional entities that induce loyalties in conflict with party unity and hinder consultation and compromise in the formation of governmental policy. The cabinet itself is recruited from among the legislators, and its members are those who have proved themselves in the Commons and have gained the support of their fellows. Consequently it is probable that most shades of opinion within the party will be represented in the government, and will, in turn, be reflected in the measures the government proposes. Moreover, in the give and take between Commons and cabinet a reasonable degree of agreement may be maintained. Nor is the party program subject to veto by an independent judiciary with power to invalidate legislation on constitutional grounds.

Party discipline in the House of Commons flows in part from the nature of party operations in nominations and elections. A high degree of centralization prevails within the party on candidacies. A local Conservative or Labor association nominates persons approved by the national leadership and at times persons suggested by the party's central office. The mandate of the member of Commons is in a sense not to represent his constituency but to collaborate with and to support the leadership of his party in the conduct of the government. The institutional context of the election of Commoners thus imposes upon them a different type of moral obligation than rests upon the American legislator.

It does not necessarily follow that a cabinet system would be workable in the United States; its main features are outlined to serve as a contrast to obtain a better understanding of the effects of the structure of American government on the formation and execution of party policy. The structure of American government impedes the formation of a party policy that would reconcile the differences within the party in control of the government. In the absence of such a policy, party unity is likely to be disrupted. The effect of our governmental structure is to make effective leadership difficult. The obvious feature of structure, both national and state, that handicaps party government is the separation of powers. The President, as leader of his party, occupies a position of leadership in the definition of party policy. But there is no assurance that his program will meet with the approval of all factions of his party in the House and Senate. The machinery of government does not provide a means to be used in the normal course of action for the representation of all factions of the party in the formulation of the presidential program. The mere fact of legal independence of executive and legislature creates institutional jealousies and misunderstandings. In addition, the Supreme Court may exercise from time to time a veto over important party policies.

The calendar of elections contributes to the disharmony of party conduct of the government. The President is elected for a term of four years, whereas Representatives serve for a two-year period. The congressional elections at the middle of a President's term may establish conclusively that the President has lost the confidence of the country, but there is no way to be rid of him until his four-year term has run its course. Even if the country is satisfied with the general program of the President, his party, for some odd reason, almost invariably loses strength in the House at the midterm elections. His party may become a minority in the House or so weak that it lacks an adequate working majority. The tendency of the Administration to lose strength in midterm elections is shown in Figure 27.

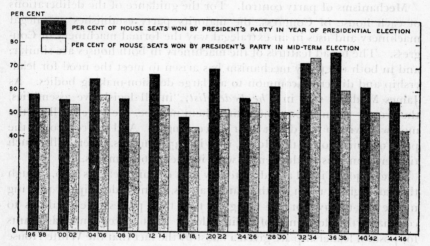

PER CENT

■ PER CENT OF HOUSE SEATS WON BY PRESIDENT'S PARTY IN YEAR OF PRESIDENTIAL ELECTION

□ PER CENT OF HOUSE SEATS WON BY PRESIDENT'S PARTY IN MID-TERM ELECTION

Figure 27. Percentage of House Seats Won by President's Party in Presidential Election Years and in Midterm Elections, 1896–1946

The Senate is renewed by thirds every two years, and the tenor of the Senate may be at variance with either the House or the President without necessarily reflecting the views of the country at the time. And, on occasion, the Supreme Court, with life tenure, appears to speak for a different generation than either the House or the Senate. Thus the pattern of elections may accentuate conflict between the organs of government. But, for the government to function, the obstructions of governmental mechanism must be overcome, and it is the party that casts a web, at times weak, at times strong, over the dispersed organs of government and gives them a semblance of unity.

2. PARTY GOVERNMENT IN CONGRESS

The majority party manages legislative proceedings. In the American Congress the task of the majority in the performance of this duty is attended by much greater difficulty than the cabinet faces in leading the House of Commons. The majority party in the United States must express its will through a more complex machinery of legislative organization. The mechanisms themselves handicap leadership, but to function a majority must be in substantial agreement on the measures it wishes to grind through the legislative mill. In this, American parties are almost always beset by dissent within their own ranks, and it is often difficult to maintain a cohesive majority to control legislation and thereby to fulfill party responsibilities.

Mechanisms of party control. For the guidance of the deliberations of each house of Congress, the majority party establishes extralegal machinery and uses in an extralegal way the formal machinery of Congress. The broad features of the machinery in both houses are similar, and in both the party mechanism has arisen to meet the need for leadership and direction common to all large decision-making bodies. As James Madison said in *The Federalist,* "in all legislative assemblies, the greater the number composing them may be, the fewer will be the men who will in fact direct their proceedings." And the control of the party organization in the House, with its 435 members, is generally much tighter than it is in the Senate with its mere 96 members.

The majority is led and directed by a set of party leaders who, though they are agreed upon by the party caucus, gain leadership by proving in the day-to-day work of Congress that they possess the qualities to command the deference of their fellows. Not infrequently aspirants for posts of leadership are given a boost by the fact that the White House looks with favor upon their ambitions. In the House, the speaker, the rules committee, the chairmen of the important standing committees, the majority floor leader, and the party whip constitute the inner clique that guides the course of action. Both the majority and minority parties in the House have a "steering committee," but these are "an informal and little-used device." They "seldom meet and never steer." [1] Each party also has a committee on committees with the function of nominating the majority and minority members of each of the legislative committees.

Leadership of the House majority is thus dispersed. Before a drastic revision of House rules in 1910–1911, the Speaker of the House, as an agent of the majority, dominated the work of the House as thoroughly as any prime minister ever controlled the House of Commons. In addition to the powers of a presiding officer in the granting of recognition and in the decision of points of order, he appointed committees and sat

[1] Joint Committee on the Organization of Congress, *Report* (S. Rep. 1011, 79th Cong., 2d sess., 1946), p. 12.

as a member of the powerful Rules Committee. Speaker Cannon, a standpat Republican, did not exercise his power in a manner to hold the confidence of all factions of his party. The progressive wing joined with Democrats to divide and disperse the speaker's authority. Stripped of the prerogative of appointment and of membership on the Rules Committee, the speaker remains with his diminished powers a leader and agent of the majority. Designated in form by the House, he is in fact chosen by the majority caucus. The majority floor leader usually ascends to the speakership when vacancies occur. The speaker acts as a party agent in guiding the conduct of House business, but as Hasbrouck has observed, the rules of the House "have so developed as a vehicle for the program of the majority that the Speaker need only apply them, to serve, on the whole, the ends of his own party. There is seldom need for him to discriminate as a moderator in order to promote his aims as a political leader." [2] Yet when he has discretion he does not hesitate to use it to the advantage of the majority, and he collaborates with his juniors in the inner circle of the majority in planning and conducting majority strategy.

The majority floor leader is not, like the speaker, an official of the House; his position is extralegal, but he plays a role in the direction of the work of the House second only in importance to that of the speaker. The floor leader is elected by the party caucus, and his duties are so onerous that he serves on no legislative committee. He functions as a sort of field commander who leads and guides the majority in the legislative battle. He keeps in close touch with the chairmen of legislative committees and, in consultation with other important party figures, guides the course of party action in the House.[3] Subject to his responsibility to his party followers, he arranges the general schedule of work of the House; and in this he is in frequent consultation with the minority leader to assure, in so far as practicable, a mutually acceptable schedule of debate. The formal instrumentality for control of the procedure of the House is the Rules Committee, also dominated by the majority. This committee facilitates the work of House management by proposing special rules determining when bills are to be considered, which bills shall be considered, how long they shall be debated, and the degree to which they shall be subject to amendment.

Another agent of the party leadership is the party whip, a party functionary appointed for each party by its floor leader. The party whip

---

[2] P. D. Hasbrouck, *Party Government in the House of Representatives* (New York, 1923), p. 85. Quoted by permission of the Macmillan Company, publishers.

[3] For a discussion of the floor leader, see F. M. Riddick, *Congressional Procedure* (Boston: Chapman and Grimes, 1941), chap. 4.

serves as something of a top sergeant for the leadership. It is his duty
to keep in close touch with the members. He communicates the wishes
of the party leaders to the rank and file and attempts by persuasion to
keep the members in line with the party program. He scours Washington to bring absent members to the House when their attendance is
imperative. He canvasses the membership to determine their attitudes
on pending questions that seem to endanger party unity. In all this
work the whip of each party is aided by assistants of his appointment,
who are assigned to deal with the members from particular regions.

The relationship between the President and the House leaders is
usually close. Not infrequently the President exerts his influence to
obtain the selection of House leaders disposed to agree with him on
broad lines of policy.[4] It is the House leaders who fight the legislative
battles of the administration on the floor of the House and defend the
work of the administrative departments against their critics. Not only
do the House leaders mobilize their majority to enact legislation; they
use the weapons at their disposal to prevent consideration of undesired
legislation.

A special feature of the House organization (and of the Senate also)
that conditions party leadership and responsibility is the role assigned
to committees. They enjoy great powers over legislation through their
capacity to report or not to report bills and through their prerogatives
in the amendment and rewriting of measures. The committees "form
miniature legislatures with a high degree of autonomy." [5] When committee chairmen (who are, of course, members of the majority in the
House) work in harmony with the House leadership, they may exercise
their powers to accomplish the party program. But the process of
selection of the committee does not insure harmonious relationships.
The majority (through a committee on committees selected by the
caucus) controls assignments of members to each committee, but once
assigned to a committee a member moves gradually upward by seniority
until he becomes chairman (or the ranking minority member). The
chairman, therefore, does not necessarily see eye to eye with either the
Administration or the House leaders.

The complex internal organization of the House often obstructs the

4 Prior to the election of John W. McCormack of Massachusetts as Democratic
leader of the House in September, 1940, the following comment appeared in the
press: "Since the Presidential blessing was reported to have been given to Representative John W. McCormack of Massachusetts, chairman of the House Democratic caucus,
his opponents sought votes to throw the election into the secret stage to permit
members who might wish not to offend the President to vote as they chose."—The
New York *Times,* September 18, 1940.

5 Hasbrouck, *op. cit.,* p. 42.

will of the "majority" of the majority party. Successful management of the House requires that the Speaker, the majority floor leader, the Rules Committee, and the chairmen of the standing committees work in concert. The great authority of committee chairmen, coupled with the fact that their selection results from the fortuitous incidence of political and biological longevity, creates a situation in which a single person or small groups of persons can block the majority program. The Rules Committee, for example, during the later years of the Roosevelt Administration and in the Truman Administration was often at odds with the House leadership and with the President. It obstructed legislation desired by the majority party and facilitated legislation desired by right-wing Democrats and Republicans. Included in its membership were E. E. Cox, of Georgia, Howard W. Smith, of Virginia, and Roger C. Slaughter, of Missouri, widely regarded by their fellow Democrats as Republicans flying false colors. The Rules Committee got so far out of hand in June, 1944, that the speaker and other Democratic leaders spoke against one of its recommendations and induced the House to overrule the Committee, a very rare occurrence. The Rules Committee exercises to some degree the autocracy that used to be attributed to Speakers Reed and Cannon, but it does not always exert its powers in accord with the will of the majority.[6]

Chairmen of standing committees have succeeded in grasping for themselves no small share of the power of the House as a whole. In this they enjoy prerogatives that few great legislative assemblies permit their committees to arrogate unto themselves. Their exercise of the power may not be in accord with the general program of the majority because of their personal predilections. Perhaps more significant in the long run is the tendency of committees as institutions to become special pleaders for particular interests. This tendency, quite apart from the political idiosyncrasies of committee chairmen, militates against the work of the leadership in the execution of a general program of legislation. The formulation of a program in the public weal requires as its first essential power to batter down the more outrageous

[6] An indication of the sentiment toward the Rules Committee is furnished by a statement of Representative Estes Kefauver, who sought a rule to bring a resolution sponsored by himself to a vote: "There is a resolution pending, House Resolution 327, before the Rules Committee, and although I have made request dozens of times of the chairman of the Rules Committee for a hearing, and other Members have expressed great interest in the resolution, and have also asked permission to testify, the Chairman of the Rules Committee has the matter locked up tight, and we cannot even get a hearing before that distinguished committee. The will of the House, in my opinion, is being thwarted by the refusal of the Rules Committee to act. We cannot even get a chance to present our case."—*Congressional Record* (daily edition), June 16, 1944, p. 6159.

demands of narrow interests. The strategic and tactical advantages enjoyed by committee chairmen handicap efforts in that direction.

Superficially the organization of the Senate for the conduct of business resembles that of the House, but in practice the weapons of party control and leadership in the Senate are weaker than in the House. The Vice-President, as presiding officer of the Senate, is more likely to be merely tolerated than looked to as a party leader. The majority and minority usually have floor leaders in the same manner as in the House, but the Senate organization has flexibility. For example, following the death of Minority Leader Charles L. McNary in 1944, the Republicans placed their leadership in a triumvirate of Wallace White, Robert Taft, and Arthur Vandenburg. White had the nominal floor leadership, but some of McNary's duties were assigned to Taft and Vandenburg. The Senate majority leader, like his counterpart in the House, leads the battles of the Administration (if the Administration has a majority of the Senate). Occasionally he asserts the senatorial prerogative of independence. In 1944, for example, Alben Barkley resigned as majority leader in protest against Roosevelt's tax bill veto message. His Democratic colleagues re-elected him unanimously, and he returned to the task of fighting the Administration battle as faithfully and as ably as before. As a consequence of the House rules, discussion is usually brief and proceedings more effectively under the control of the House leaders than in the Senate. In the upper chamber the practice of practically unlimited debate gives to party members hesitant to accept majority leadership ample opportunity to air their views, to mobilize public opinion to their side, to defeat by delay, or perhaps to compel concessions. Senators, moreover, with six-year tenure, do not have to look so often to their party leadership for support in elections.

Formation of party policy. The organization apparatus within the houses of Congress for the effectuation of party policy creaks and groans, but perhaps more important is the fact that the majority in neither house possesses methods for agreeing upon a party policy that takes into account the views of different factions within the party. The party caucus or conference, a private meeting of the legislators affiliated with the party, is supposed to function as an agency for the settlement of intra-party differences. The caucus serves as a means for agreement on party candidates for speaker and other positions in the House, but it meets infrequently to consider the stand the party group will take on questions of legislation. The rules of the Democratic House caucus provide:

In deciding upon action in the House involving party policy or principle, a two-thirds vote of those present and voting at a Caucus meeting shall bind all members of the caucus; Provided, The said two-thirds vote is a majority of the full Democratic membership of the House; And Provided Further, That no member shall be bound upon questions involving a construction of the Constitution of the United States or upon which he made contrary pledges to his constituents prior to his election or received contrary instructions by resolution or platform from his nominating authority.

Although the Republican House conference has no rule similar to that of the Democratic caucus, its decisions are usually accepted as binding upon its members.

The question may be raised why the caucus does not function effectively as a means by which the majority can agree, in advance of action in the House or Senate, on a position to be taken by all its members. Majority leaders usually convene a caucus only as a last resort; they consider the caucus as a place to express confidence in their leadership rather than as an organ for ironing out intraparty differences. In turn, dissident members, who can force the calling of a caucus by petition, regard the caucus as a meeting in which they can embarrass the leadership. Furthermore, the most significant leaders in party formation for the party—the President and his principal executive officers—are outside the caucus. Policy tends to flow from administration, and extensive use of the caucus to determine policy of the House or Senate majority would result in decisions made without adequate information and perhaps would also weaken presidential leadership. A solidified majority view in the House or Senate might confront the Executive with a crystallized view in conflict with the President's views on party strategy at the moment. Apart from such considerations, the day just does not have enough hours for members of Congress to participate extensively in caucus work to debate out policy within the party and at the same time carry on the business of Congress.

In American political mores a strong tradition opposes the idea that a party legislator should be bound by the dictates of the majority of his fellow partisans. Party discipline runs counter to a strain of political romanticism and, perhaps, idealism. After his defeat in the Montana primary in 1946, Senator Burton K. Wheeler stated that his refusal to go along "blindly" with the Democratic Administration had probably contributed to his defeat. "I could not sacrifice my principles for party expediency. I felt it was my duty to vote and fight for my honest convictions." The late Senator William E. Borah for decades was a thorn in the side of the Republican leadership. A constituent chided him for opposing the Republican Administration: "What would you have a Senator do?" he replied. "Sincerely represent his views, however inadequate they may be, or act as an intellectual prostitute for some party

organization?" [7]   It is one of the glories of the American system of legislation that it has enough play in it to allow room for courageous and
righteous men to rise above their party.   One of the drawbacks is that
by the same token the machinery gives considerable license to the scoundrel.   Nevertheless, within Congress the party succeeds most of the
time in subordinating individual wills to the group will sufficiently to
conduct the public business.

The Joint Committee on the Organization of Congress in its 1946
report considered the question of mechanisms by which the party groups
in the houses of Congress could formulate party policy.   The Joint
Committee proposed the creation of "policy committees" by both parties
in both houses of Congress.   It was proposed that these committees
formulate the legislative policies of the two parties and that their decisions be made public.   The Joint Committee proposed no means of
party discipline; each member would be "free to vote as he saw fit, but
the record of his action would be available to the public as a means of
holding both the party and the individual accountable." [8]   These policy committees would have had "$30,000 per year each for the main-
tenance of a high-grade secretariat to assist in study, analysis, and research on problems involved in policy determination."

The House struck from the congressional reorganization bill the
provision for policy committees.   It was reported that the Speaker
and other Democratic leaders feared that such a committee would
encroach upon their traditional sphere of authority.   The Senate, however, on the initiative of Senator La Follette, adopted the policy committee proposal for itself.   An amendment to an appropriation bill
provided funds "for the maintenance of a staff for a majority policy
committee and a minority policy committee in the Senate, consisting of
seven members each, for the formulation of overall legislative policy
of the respective parties, the members of such staffs to assist in study,
analysis, and research on problems involved in policy determina-
tions. . . ."   The practical result of this legislative provision was the
transformation of the party steering committees of each party in the
Senate into "policy committees."   Although each Senate policy committee was given $15,000 annually to employ a staff, it was doubtful that
this change would alter profoundly the nature of the old steering committees.

When the majority of Congress is in opposition to the party controlling the Presidency, special factors condition the formulation of party
policy in the houses of Congress.   Under such circumstances, as follow-

[7] C. O. Johnson, *Borah of Idaho* (New York: Longmans, Green, 1936), p. 466.
[8] *Report*, as cited, pp. 12–14.

ing the elections of 1946, which returned a Republican majority to the House and Senate, the congressional majority operates with a view to the winning of the Presidency by its party at the next election and, naturally, without the benefit of leadership by an executive of its own partisan affiliations. In the session of Congress beginning in January, 1947, the Republican House and Senate majorities set to work to develop party policies that would gain more consistent party support than is ordinarily the case. In this endeavor they were aided by the higher degree of discipline that usually prevails among Republicans than among Democrats. The Republican leaders convoked party conferences for the discussion of party programs more frequently than had been the custom of the predecessor Democratic majority, but frequent conferences did not come about until the newer Republican members had fretted a bit. In March, 1947, Senator Raymond E. Baldwin, of Connecticut, complained in a public statement that the Senate Republican leaders were leading without consultation with their fellow Republicans. He urged that the leadership get together with the Republican members of the Senate and discuss the party program, to the end that the greatest degree of party unanimity possible might be achieved. More frequent party conferences damped out some of the complaints of this sort, but the somewhat higher degree of party cohesion among Republicans than Democrats rested fundamentally upon the greater homogeneity of interest of the Republican party rather than on the mechanisms for consultation among party members in Congress.

Roots of party disunity. One has to look beyond the mechanisms of Congress to find the causes of weak party discipline in the House and Senate. In earlier chapters the diversity of composition of the major parties was noted; both parties are coalitions of conflicting interests. It is the task of party leadership to compromise these differences, to whip together a majority on urgent questions, and sometimes to delay action in order that time and discussion may bring the elements of the party closer together on divisive questions. To illustrate the element of disunity within the legislative groups of the parties, a few congressional roll calls occurring during 1945 and 1946 are shown in Table 26. The votes on these questions are chiefly of value in suggesting the wide differences of opinion within the Democratic ranks, but it is to be noted that on these votes Republicans as the party of opposition were not unanimous either.

When the administration has a majority in Congress and when the administration program is satisfactory or acceptable to all factions of the majority party, the leaders can bring about the enactment of desired

measures and block undesired ones.   Yet party discipline is constantly
challenged and often disrupted.   A great challenge to party unity is
the pressure group which, through lobbying and through its supposed
power of reprisal at the polls, presses for support from Congressmen of
both parties.   Since these groups usually speak for specific interests in
society, their demands are often indefensible from the point of view of
the general interest.   The administration and the legislative leadership
must, if it values its political life, know when to check and when to
yield to the urging of the special interests.   Sometimes, however, a
pressure group becomes more powerful than the ties of party loyalty,
and a bipartisan combination takes over leadership on a particular
measure.

TABLE 26

Divisions within Parties on Selected Congressional Roll Calls

Measure	Yeas	Nays	Democrats				Republicans			
			Yeas	*% Yea*	*Nays*	*% Nay*	*Yeas*	*% Yea*	*Nays*	*% Nay*
SENATE										
9–19–45: To return USES to states in 90 days	56	23	21	48	23	52	34	100	0	0
11–2–45: To exempt Army Engineers from Reorganization Bill	36	18	15	54	13	46	21	84	4	16
2–4–46: To close debate on FEPC bill	48	36	22	44	28	56	25	76	8	24
3–1–46: To restrict REA loans to building generating plants	21	52	8	20	32	80	13	41	19	59
3–29–46: To revise farm parity rule	43	31	24	53	21	47	19	68	9	32
HOUSE										
9–11–45: To give equal party membership on Pearl Harbor Committee	136	168	0	0	168	100	135	100	0	0
12–11–45: Repeal War Labor Disputes Act and limit unions	182	200	96	45	117	55	86	52	81	48
2–7–46: Final vote on Case labor bill	258	155	109	48	120	52	149	82	33	18
2–21–46: To prohibit racial bias in school lunch program	259	109	105	52	99	48	152	94	10	6
3–19–46: To create agricultural credit agency	239	80	87	53	78	47	152	99	1	1

It is necessary to look behind the machinations of pressure societies to discover the basic threats to party unity in the House and Senate. The support of each party tends to come from most classes of society and from most sections of the country. The midwestern Republican speaking for a corn- and hog-raising constituency sometimes finds it galling to work in harness with his party brother from a wealthy suburb of New York City. The Democratic spokesman for a prosperous southern farming area may have points of difference with his fellow Democrat from a northern, urban, industrial constituency. The conservative Democrats are constantly at odds with their New Deal brethren. Progressive Republicans often have more in common with New Deal Democrats than with the reactionary variety of Republican. The differences within the party tend to be as great as or even greater than differences between parties. It is on the differences within parties and on the likenesses between parties that pressure politicians play, to break party unity within the House and Senate.

During periods when control of the majority is threatened by the formation of bipartisan blocs, the basic nature of the major clashes within each party is thrown into sharp relief. In the 1920's the Republican party was torn by dispute between the members from the progressive and agrarian West and the more conservative northeastern faction. The restlessness of the western members was but a continuation of an almost unbroken record of insurgency. The conservative faction of the party had tried in 1906 to "haze" the elder La Follette by "emptying the Senate chamber" when he spoke. His comment was that if the railroad question were not "rightly settled, seats now temporarily vacant may be permanently vacated by those who have the right to occupy them at this time." [9] In 1909 and 1910 western insurgency flared up in both houses against the leadership of the regular party organization.[10] After World War I western insurgents bolted the party to support La Follette and Wheeler for the Presidency and Vice-Presidency in 1924—a much graver breach of party etiquette than failure to follow the party leadership on legislative questions. The Republican Senate conference (or caucus) adopted a resolution to exclude the "disloyal" Senators (La Follette, Ladd, Brookhart, and Frazier) from the conference and not to name them "to fill any Republican vacancies on Senate committees." [11] Within two years, however, the conference relented.

[9] Haynes, *Social Politics in the United States* (Boston: Houghton Mifflin, 1924), pp. 170–171.

[10] E. E. Robinson, "Recent Manifestations of Sectionalism," *American Journal of Sociology*, 19 (1914), pp. 446–467.

[11] Haynes, *The Senate of United States*, Vol. I, p. 478.

Party splits along New Deal-Bourbon or Progressive-Conservative lines reflect deep-seated cleavages of sentiment in the country. Without involving such issues of principle, party discipline occasionally breaks down in the process of voting appropriations. The executive program of expenditures may be modified by logrolling in which enough individual Senators and Representatives combine to amend the appropriation bills for the benefit of their respective constituencies. In this fashion, after the departments concerned with the expenditure of funds, the Bureau of the Budget, and the President have decided that certain items of expenditure are less urgent than others or perhaps entirely unnecessary, combinations may be formed in Congress to add these items to the appropriation bill. "Party discipline in Congress," says Herring, "cannot control members bent on feathering their nests at home, since their political lives depend on local support." [12]

Function of the opposition. The majority party has the responsibility to organize and to lead the houses of Congress. The minority performs a different kind of function. It is sometimes compared with the opposition in a parliamentary system, but it differs in several significant respects. The minority in Congress is not in training to take over the government, although its leaders may, with the victory of their party, take over the posts of leadership in the House and Senate. The great minority leaders may, in fact, be outside Congress. Hence, the actions and pronouncements of the minority congressional leaders are not necessarily to be construed as authoritative enunciation of party policy. The minority in Congress often speaks for an extreme wing of the party. The minority members in most instances come from sure Republican or Democratic districts. When the party tries to win the Presidency it has to water down the views of legislators from its safe territory and attract the support of persons not so deeply dyed with party loyalty. The pronouncements of the presidential candidate and the party platform are likely to differ markedly from the statements of minority leaders in Congress.

The function of the opposition is not so much to challenge the great principles of the majority and to offer an alternative program as it is to obstruct, to harass, to embarrass the majority and the Administration. Its function is to oppose majority proposals whether they be good or bad.[13] The management of a minority is something like the leader-

---

[12] Herring, "First Session of the Seventy-fourth Congress, January 3, 1935, to August 25, 1935," *American Political Science Review*, 29 (1935), p. 997.

[13] Thus, a minority member of an appropriations committee, after raking the spokesman for an administrative agency over the coals, said to him privately: "You are doing your job well, but I am sure that you understand it is my job to make you look sick."

ship of guerilla warfare, a hit-and-run tactic quickly adaptable to a changing situation. In their sniping, the minority may be assisted by a brain trust attached to the party's national committee. During the Hoover Administration, for example, the staff of the Democratic national committee ground out speeches for Democratic Senators and Representatives to use in a campaign to smear Hoover. In the Roosevelt and Truman Administrations the Republican minority leaders had similar assistance in their efforts to discredit the Democrats.

In his Lincoln Day address in 1942 Wendell Willkie proposed a different sort of role for the minority. He asserted that traditionally the role of the minority has been "one of negation—of all out opposition. What the party in power stands for, the party out of power is against." Whatever the situation, the minority attitude, he contended, had been that "those in power are notoriously incompetent and grievously wrong." He thought that this practice, even in ordinary times, was poor politics, for the majority fixed not only its own position but that of the minority as well. He argued for the development of a positive Republican program and for a different sort of minority strategy. Mr. Willkie's plea had little effect. Republicans in Congress were not disposed to follow his leadership. The minority, as well as the majority, has its troubles in maintaining unity. The majority has whatever solidarity is induced by the patronage, prestige, and leadership of the President. The minority lacks this cohesive influence and is not disposed to pay much heed to its own defeated presidential candidates.

In some respects the role of the minority is not so hopeless as is that of the minority in a parliamentary system. With a disciplined majority and minority, all the minority can hope for is a complete turnover at the election. In the American Congress the weak ties of the majority encourage the minority to wean away followers from the majority party and to determine the outcome of legislative issues. And it is not uncommon for the real "majority" to be composed of a substantial part of the minority plus a sector of the nominal majority. Conversely, the majority party leader often carries the day, not by holding his own party together, but by rallying the support of a bloc that cuts across party lines. Thus the genuinely effective "opposition" often consists, not of members of the minority, but of recalcitrant members of the majority who hold a balance of power within the House or Senate.

Nonpartisanship in legislation. From the nature of party in the legislative body and from the nature of legislation, a large part of the work of Congress comes to be transacted on nonpartisan or bipartisan lines. Of the 1,005 bills and resolutions adopted by the Senate during the first session of the Seventy-ninth Congress in 1945, 939 involved

little or no debate. Only 66 bills could be classified as controversial.
In the House at the same session of Congress, debate occurred on only
120 of 1,184 bills and resolutions passed.[14] The figures are similar for
other Congresses.

The tendency for only a small proportion of congressional actions to
be controverted is not new. Many years ago A. Lawrence Lowell attempted to measure the degree of party influence upon legislation in
Congress. He devised a technique for measuring party influence by
defining a "party vote" as one in which more than nine-tenths of the
party members are "on the same side of the question; a nonparty vote
as one in which one-tenth or more of the members are found on each
side—that is, a vote where at least one-tenth of the voting members of
the party split off from the rest." [15] He ascertained the "proportion
of public bills enacted on which there was a party vote at some stage
of their passage through the House of Representatives." For the
Thirty-eighth Congress, elected in 1862, there was a party vote on 18
out of 232 bills, or 7.76 per cent. In the Fiftieth Congress, elected in
1886, "where the President and the House belonged to one party and
the Senate to the other, party legislation was obviously difficult to carry
through, and only 1 public bill, out of 154 enacted, had a party vote
in the House." In the Fifty-fifth Congress, elected in 1896, "the House
cast party votes on 14 out of 195 public bills enacted, or 7.18 per cent." [16]
It should be noted that Dr. Lowell included in his computations only
public bills; party lines are seldom influential in the consideration of
the large number of private bills.[17]

Stuart A. Rice, in a later study, devised another method to measure
the degree of party cohesion. His index of cohesion ranges from 0.0
to 100.0. At the lowest point the party members in Congress are equally
divided, 50 per cent on each side of the question. At 100.0 the party
members act completely in concert. He applied this method to the
Senate in the Sixty-eighth Congress, elected in 1922, with the object of
ascertaining the difference, if any, between the internal cohesion of the
Democrats, the Republicans, a "radical" bloc of thirteen Senators consisting of both Democrats and Republicans, and a larger bloc of twenty-
two "progressive" Senators which included the "radical" group. The

[14] F. M. Riddick, "The First Session of the Seventy-ninth Congress," *American
Political Science Review,* 40 (1946), p. 259.

[15] "The Influence of Party upon Legislation in England and America," American
Historical Association, *Annual Report,* 1901, Vol. 1, pp. 321–542 at p. 323.

[16] *Ibid.,* p. 341.

[17] In one session of the New York legislature 1,296 roll calls were taken and all but
255 were unanimous. "Out of an estimated total of 175,000 votes cast, only 7,595,
or four and three tenths per cent, were cast in the negative."—Stuart A. Rice, *Quantitative Methods in Politics* (New York: Knopf, 1928), pp. 211–212.

average index of cohesion on forty-seven important roll calls, for each
of the groups, was as follows:

Democrats .... 63.1   "Radical" group 71.0
Republicans .... 66.3   "Progressive" group 67.2

These figures give a precise measurement of party discipline. The bipartisan blocs of "radicals" and "progressives" voted together with
slightly more consistency than did the party groupings.[18]

The chaos that results in the legislative process when party leaders,
both inside and outside Congress, lose control of their followers in
Congress has long been a point for criticism by students of our governmental system. The administration not infrequently retains the confidence of the country but loses the confidence of Congress; and after the
patronage has been distributed, presidential leadership may become
impotent. To strengthen party unity and party discipline there have
been proposals, such as that made by Professor Elliott, that the President be given the power to dissolve and compel once during his term
the re-election of a House elected for a four-year term. The House, so
the theory runs, would then be sobered by the knowledge that failure
to unite on a party program would make its members liable to the risk
of their political lives in a campaign for re-election. Moreover, by
the removal of the necessity for the use of patronage in the leadership of
Congress, the way would be opened for the development of a stronger
and more competent permanent civil service.[19]

Yet the looseness of party discipline and the tendencies toward insurgency spring, in part, from the failings of the party leadership.
Since each party consists of representatives scattered along almost the
entire political spectrum, an important shade of opinion may consider
itself outraged or ignored in the administration program. By what
means may progressive Republicans or conservative Democrats make
themselves felt except through the formation of a coalition with kindred
spirits on the other side of the legislative chamber? Since the necessities of the presidential system force into the same party many incon-
gruous elements for the purposes of the presidential campaign, how
are the true interests of all sections of society to be expressed except
through congressional maneuvers? On the other hand, the requirements of modern legislation and administration are such that it seems
to be more and more necessary that all phases of public policy be articulated and co-ordinated. How is this end to be accomplished except

[18] *Ibid.*, pp. 208–217.
[19] See W. Y. Elliott, *The Need for Constitutional Reform* (New York: Whittlesey
House, 1935).

by effective party discipline and more workable machinery for the reconciliation of intraparty differences? [20]

3. PRESIDENTIAL LEADERSHIP

The only common point about which leadership and direction of the party may be established for the conduct of the government is the Presidency. Most important legislative proposals emerge from the problems and the experience of the administrative departments, and with them Congressmen have only remote contact. The sense of reality and of contact with the substance of governance that is an accompaniment of responsibility for administration seldom reaches Congress.[21] The legislator is pressed by a different set of problems, but his position is not conductive to the origination of workable innovations in public policy. Apart from the fact that the legislator's experience in the conduct of the departments of the government is only vicarious, there are other factors, to be mentioned shortly, that make Congress an infertile center for leadership in policy formulation.

It is the President who determines the major issues on which Congress acts; and it is the President who attempts, with or without success, to bring the party members in the House and Senate to the support of his policy. As Professor Ford pointed out: [22]

It is the rule of our politics that no vexed question is settled except by executive policy. Whatever may be the feeling of Congress towards the President, it cannot avoid an issue which he insists upon making. And this holds good of presidents who lose their party leadership as with those who retain it. Tyler, Johnson, and Cleveland, although repudiated by the parties which elected them, furnished the issues upon which party action turned.

The President poses the issues; his party in Congress may or may not accept his views. This is not to deny that in some areas legislative

20 On Congress generally, see Roland Young, *This Is Congress* (New York: Knopf, 1943); F. M. Riddick, *Congressional Procedure* (Boston: Chapman and Grimes, 1941); P. D. Hasbrouck, *Party Government in the House of Representatives* (New York: Macmillan, 1927); Lindsay Rogers, *The American Senate* (New York: Knopf, 1926); G. H. Haynes, *The Senate of the United States* (Boston: Houghton Mifflin, 1938); F. L. Burdette, *Filibustering in the Senate* (Princeton: Princeton University Press, 1940); George B. Galloway, *Congress at the Crossroads* (New York: Thomas Y. Crowell Company, 1946). The hearings and report of the Joint Committee on the Organization of Congress contain valuable information.

21 "Besides, an assembly never personally experiences the inconveniences of its bad measures until they have reached the dimensions of national evils. Ministers and administrators see them approaching, and have to bear all the annoyance and trouble of attempting to ward them off."—John Stuart Mill, *Representative Government*, chap. 5.

22 H. J. Ford, *The Rise and Growth of American Politics* (New York: Macmillan, 1898), pp. 283–284.

proposals develop within Congress over long periods of time. The President pulls them out of the ruck of mere discussion and elevates them to the stature of party issues.[23]

The fundamental basis of conflict between the President and Congress rests on the almost inevitable differences in his point of view and that of the individual Congressman. On the President is focused all sorts of pressure from the entire country; on the individual Congressman is concentrated only the pressures of the interests in his own state or district. In another set of terms, the tendency is that the President considers the welfare of the entire country; the Congressman, the welfare of his state or district. In practical political terms, the President must consider policies and proposals in the light of their probable effect on the strength of the party as a whole. The President's fellow-partisan in Congress is apt to formulate his position in the light of its probable effect on his political career in his own state or district.[24]

The President and the Congressman, thus, may be and often are subjected to conflicting tugs and pressures. The challenge to party unity comes from the divergent interests of the heterogeneous groups that make up the party. Party discipline and party loyalty are not enough to bind the President and his congressional majority together at all times. The question that often faces a Congressman is whether his party is stronger than the American Legion, or the American Farm Bureau Federation, or the American Federation of Labor. And he may decide that his own career is safer if he follows the leader of a bipartisan bloc rather than the leader of his own party.

Apart from the institutional handicaps to presidential leadership, different Presidents have varying capacities of leadership and varying conceptions of the role of the presidential office. Wilson, with his idea that the President should play the role of a prime minister, offered forceful party direction. Harding had an opposite conception of the role of the presidential office; in fact, a handful of Senators had been extremely active in bringing about his nomination because they hoped

[23] See the able discussion by L. H. Chamberlain, "The President, Congress and Legislation," *Political Science Quarterly*, 61 (1946), pp. 42–60.

[24] The following incident, related by a former Secretary of the Treasury, is illustrative: "I was asked to meet a large delegation from the South. I agreed to do so. About forty appeared. Before the meeting, several Senators came in another door and told me in substance that they knew I could not do what the delegation was going to urge, but that they had to appear to be sympathetic, and that they hoped that I understood their situation. I felt like telling them that I did, and that I clearly recognized that they were taking an unfair position, that, if they agreed with me, it was their duty to tell their constituents the truth."—David F. Houston, *Eight Years with Wilson's Cabinet* (copyright, 1926, by Doubleday, Doran and Company, Inc.), Vol. II, pp. 103–104.

to take away from the White House the initiative in legislation. Franklin Roosevelt, on the other hand, exerted a leadership in legislation hardly matched by any other President. Since the Presidency is the only point from which general direction of policy may issue, when the President is incapable or disinclined to play the role, the party in power tends to follow a policy of drift and inaction, with interest groups struggling and trading for mastery in matters of legislation. When the President abdicates his legislative leadership, there is no place for the mantle to fall.[25]

No matter what party is in power or what President is in office, there tends to be a deep anti-presidential sentiment in Congress, even among the members of the President's own party. Legislators encourage the notion that the assertion of presidential leadership somehow violates our constitutional commandments and is a governmental sin to be committed, if at all, surreptitiously. The dignity of Congress is redressed by an occasional setback to the President. At times he may be reversed and rebuked for apparently no reason save an assertion of congressional power. But congressional enunciation of the rights and privileges of the legislative branch of the government may be a mere cloak for allegiance to substantive policies in conflict with those of the President. "It is traditional that those who, yielding to other pressures, fail to ratify presidential proposals should disguise their opposition as an endeavor to maintain the integrity and independence of the legislative branch of the government." [26]

Presidential leadership is apt to manifest itself in ways that threaten party unity in Congress. Special interest groups, more or less clearly in opposition to the general welfare, may attempt to drive measures through Congress. The belief that such pressure groups may control enough votes to swing a state or district one way or another may weigh heavily in the mind of the individual Congressman. The President may attempt to block these special group pressures or to divide and placate by proposing a more moderate measure. He may offer, as Roosevelt did, a social security bill instead of a Townsend scheme. Or he may throw his support toward measures with a broad popular appeal that happen to clash with the narrower and more parochial interests that bring their influence to bear upon the individual Senator and Representative. Ford commented many years ago: [27]

25 See Norman J. Small, *Some Presidential Interpretations of the Presidency* (Baltimore: Johns Hopkins Press, 1932), especially chap. 5, "Legislative Leadership."

26 Altman, "First Session of the Seventy-fifth Congress, January 5, 1937, to August 21, 1937," *American Political Science Review*, 31 (1937), p. 1083.

27 *Op. cit.*, pp. 356–357.

The situation is such that the extension of executive authority is still the only practical method of advancing popular rule. This disposition of American politics to exalt executive authority causes some critics of our institutions to infer that democracy tends towards personal rule. Appearances seem to corroborate this theory; but all that it really amounts to is that at the present stage of our political development American democracy, confronted by the old embarrassments of feudalism, compounded from new ingredients, instinctively resorts to the historic agency for the extrication of public authority from the control of particular interests—the plenitude of executive power.

If we look at the problem from another angle, presidential leadership may be hazardous for the party in power. An ill-considered or unwise presidential proposal may injure the prestige of the President and thereby injure the party as a whole. Not infrequently the President's leaders in Congress can and do take advantage of the lack of clear-cut presidential responsibility to assume the blame for a White House proposal that has turned sour. The combination in a single person of the symbolic headship of the nation and the working political leadership, one that should never err and another that must, offers great practical difficulties.

It is not to be concluded that the legislative proposals of the President are always "right," the position of Congress always "wrong." Of necessity, though, legislative leadership must vest in the President or be non-existent. The fact that the presidential program tends to be formulated without the participation of, and often without consultation with, the party leaders in Congress often accounts for the fact that the unity of the President's majority in Congress is either broken or threatened. Party factions that have had no voice in the formulation of the program may consider that their interests have been either slighted or neglected and refuse to accept party discipline.[28] Nor is it to be supposed that formal association of congressional leaders with the President in the formulation of party policy would alter the situation. Formal linking of the executive and the legislature would not alter the attitudes of individual Congressmen conditioned by the local factors that govern their political survival.

Certain weapons are at the disposal of the President who desires to play an important part in legislation. He has the vast patronage under his control—appointments and specific expenditures—with which Congressmen may be kept in hand. An able and popular President may be able to direct upon Congress a public opinion that clearly favors the

[28] Undoubtedly in some instances congressional criticism and obstruction reflect congressional pique because of the failure of the President and his advisers to consult with party leaders in Congress.

presidential policies.   At the first session of Congress after his inauguration, for example, one observer comments that Franklin Roosevelt [29]

. . . displayed remarkable skill in manipulating the attention of Congress and
of the public.   His messages to Congress were strategically timed and positive and specific in character.   Disagreement with his proposals was interpreted by the general public as obstructionism. . . . His radio talks to the
nation served the double purpose of reassuring the people and breaking down
resistance in Congress.   Legislators were made only too well aware of the
temper of their constituents.

The truth of the matter is that the government of the United States
is not organized for effective party government.   At times of crisis strong
Presidents may rally effectively their party in Congress and drive
through a comprehensive party program.   When the tension eases, however, the party fails to provide machinery for the elaboration and execution of a program that reflects the general interest.   Then special interests and pressure groups take leadership and wreck party discipline,
playing for particular advantage, perhaps without consideration for
the general welfare.   And this fact tends to explain why different administrations are so much alike.   Each President has to contend with
the same class, group, and sectional interests.   Every President has with
him the Association of American Railroads, the American Bankers Association, the Chamber of Commerce of the United States, the American
Legion, the American Federation of Labor, the American Farm Bureau
Federation, and the National Association of Manufacturers.   Each
President has the job of working out a party program to meet or reconcile the demands and needs of these groups.   Moreover, in both parties
all these groups are powerful and their differences are at the root of the
divisions of sentiment and the difficulties of discipline within each
party.   The presidential system sometimes succeeds and sometimes
fails in maintaining a party discipline that recognizes special demands
but does not yield too far to them.   When it fails, a leaderless Congress
may yield to sectional or other demands in a fashion clearly contrary to
the public interest.[30]

[29] "First Session of the Seventy-third Congress, March 9, 1933, to June 16, 1933,"
American Political Science Review, 28 (1934), p. 67.
[30] The principal works on the Presidency are: E. S. Corwin, *The President* (New
York: New York University Press, 1940); E. Pendleton Herring, *Presidential Leader-
ship* (New York: Farrar and Rinehart, 1940); Harold Laski, *The American Presidency*
(New York: Harper, 1940); H. E. Black, *The Relation of the Executive Power to
Legislation* (Princeton: Princeton University Press, 1919).

4. GERRYMANDER: DISTORTION OF POPULAR WILL

A constant that conditions the operations of American legislative bodies is the gerrymander. Narrowly defined, the term gerrymander refers to the deliberate formation of legislative districts in such a way as to gain partisan advantage in the composition of the representative body.[31] By drawing district boundaries in the right manner, one can make one Republican grow where two flourished before. Or the boundaries may be drawn so as to produce one Republican and one Democrat where two Democrats were regularly elected before. These ingenious exercises in political geography are not so significant for the workings of legislative bodies as is systematic discrimination against urban areas in the apportionment of legislative representation. Such discrimination prevails in most state legislatures and in Congress. It sometimes comes about through deliberate policy. At other times it results from the so-called "silent gerrymander," i. e., rapid urban growth in population is accompanied by no revision of legislative districts, with the consequence that the rural population comes to be overrepresented.

State legislatures and the gerrymander. Overrepresentation of rural areas in state legislatures is accomplished by a variety of means. The simple gerrymander involving discriminatory drawing of district lines is, of course, usually the work of the legislature, but the more significant discriminations against urban populations usually have other bases. In the constitutions of some states, territory rather than population is explicitly recognized as the basis for representation in one or both houses of the legislature. According to the constitution of Vermont: "In order that the freemen of the State may enjoy the benefit of election as equally as may be, each inhabited town in this State may, forever hereafter, hold elections therein and choose each one Representative to represent them in the House of Representatives. . . ." In 1938 the town of West Haven cast 78 votes; the town of Poultney, 1,010. Although equal representation of geographical units without regard to population reaches its highest development in New England, the system is not restricted to that section of the country. In New Jersey each county is entitled to elect one senator, and a majority of the senate may be made up of the senators from counties including 15.3 per cent of the population. Essex County has a population of 833,513 and elects one senator; Sussex, a population of 27,830, and one senator.[32] In various states the

---

[31] For the origin of the term and history of gerrymandering to 1840, see E. C. Griffith, *The Rise and Development of the Gerrymander* (Chicago: Scott, Foresman, 1907).

[32] See D. D. McKean, *Pressures on the Legislature of New Jersey* (New York: Columbia University Press, 1938), pp. 38–39.

tendency has been to rationalize the equal representation of towns or counties in one house of the state legislature on the basis of analogy with the national Congress.

A slightly different technique is used in a number of states to discriminate against the urban areas in the representative system. In these states the constitution contains a declaration that representatives shall be allocated among the counties of the state in accordance with population. This declaration is followed by a proviso that each county shall be entitled to elect at least one representative. In North Carolina, to illustrate, the lower house consists of 120 members to be apportioned according to population, except that each county shall have at least one representative. In the distribution of seats the more populous counties do not receive a number of representatives proportionate to their percentage of the population of the entire state.

In some states a constitutional clause is designed specifically to limit the representation of the metropolis of the state. In Maryland the city of Baltimore, with about one half the population of the state, is limited to six of twenty-nine senators. In Pennsylvania no city or county is permitted to elect more than one sixth of the senators, a provision originally designed to limit the influence of Philadelphia. These methods do not exhaust the list of constitutional devices employed to limit the representation of urban areas; nevertheless, they indicate some of the means most frequently used for that purpose.[33]

In many instances simple failure to reapportion representation in the legislature brings glaring inequalities in representation. The state constitutions generally direct the legislature to enact a law reapportioning legislative seats after each census. The representatives from the areas with declining population have often refused to carry out the constitutional mandate to reapportion; the longer the delay, the greater the disparity between population and representation, since the general tendency has been for a larger and larger proportion of the total popula-

---

[33] For a summary of the constitutional clauses governing apportionment of representation, see New York State Constitutional Committee. *Problems Relating to Legislative Organization and Powers* (Albany, 1938), pp. 224–248. The literature on state legislative apportionment is extensive. See the items cited in the first edition of this book, pp. 553–562, and the following more recent studies: Hallie Farmer, *The Legislative Process in Alabama: Legislative Apportionment* (University, Ala.: University of Alabama Bureau of Public Administration, 1944); D. H. MacNeil, "Big Cities and States Rights," *Survey Graphic*, 33 (1944), pp. 405–407; *idem*, "Urban Representation in State Legislatures," *State Government*, 18 (1945), pp. 59–61; D. O. Walter, "Reapportionment of State Legislative Districts," *Illinois Law Review*, 37 (1942), pp. 20–42; Detroit Bureau of Governmental Research Report No. 170, "Representative Districts," January, 1946; L. C. Dorweiler, Jr., "Minnesota Farmers Rule Cities," *National Municipal Review*, 35 (1946), pp. 115–120.

tion to be concentrated in urban areas. In 1946 Minnesota was operating under the apportionment of 1913.

However discrimination in representation is accomplished, the result is substantial diminution of the strength of cities in the legislative process. In 1938 Dr. David O. Walter concluded that the ninety-six metropolitan districts, as defined by the Census Bureau, had "on an average only three-fourths of their proper representation in each house of the legislature." [34] In 1945 D. H. MacNeil found that roughly the same condition continued to prevail. [35] The consequences of maldistribution of representation in the states with large metropolitan centers—the perennial battle between New York City and upstate New York, the stalemate between Baltimore and the "counties," the struggle between Chicago and downstate Illinois—are well known, but in the states without a dominant metropolis, discrimination against the cities as a class also prevail. In Texas 41.0 per cent of the population is urban, but only 19.4 per cent of the senators come from urban districts. In South Carolina 21.3 per cent of the population is urban, but a mere 4.1 per cent of the senators represent urban districts.

The outcome of the apportionment of representation in many state legislatures is that the representatives of the rural minority control the legislature or exert an influence far greater than their proportionate number in the population as a whole. Partly because of the underrepresentation of the cities and partially because of the nature of the single-district system itself, the governmental difficulties inherent in the system of separation of powers are intensified. Since the governor is elected by the state at large, he may be of one party while, through the gerrymander, the legislature is controlled by the opposite party. Short of this situation, party division in the legislature may far from accurately reflect the division of sentiment in the state. This distortion of mass sentiment by the representative system is by no means a new phenomenon. Even before the enormous growth of cities of the past forty years the urban areas had much less influence in the election of members of the state legislature than in the selection of the governor.

If there were no differences of interest between country and city, perhaps the cities would have no serious grievance because of their underrepresentation. Vital cleavages of interest do exist, although there is no satisfactory analysis of the precise nature of these conflicts. In earlier years there were sharp differences of attitude over the liquor

---

[34] "Reapportionment and Urban Representation," *The Annals of the American Academy of Political and Social Science* 195 (1938), pp. 11–20.

[35] D. H. MacNeil, "Urban Representation in State Legislature," *State Government,* 18 (1945), pp. 59–61.

question, and the "wets" asserted that unenforceable and undesired rules were placed on urban communities by legislatures under rural domination. In the depression years the complaint was frequently made, and with justice, that state legislatures did not view with either understanding or sympathy the problems of relief in the metropolitan communities; and it is not improbable that the inflexibility of attitude of the state legislatures has hastened the growth of direct relationships between the cities and the federal government. A perennial point of issue between urban and rural blocs is the question of state taxation; the rural segments of the legislature often attempt to shift as far as possible the incidence of state taxation to the urban areas, although the degree to which they succeed remains unmeasured. In some states the urban-rural cleavage is also a division between native white stock and the foreign born.

It must not be concluded that the rural areas are alone in clinging to their power in the representative body in the face of a declining population. Within many cities the wards of declining population are grossly overrepresented in the city council. Nor should it be concluded that the peoples of the city are unanimously agreed that the cities should have a voice in the legislature proportionate to their population in the state. Certain sections of city population are more closely allied in general political viewpoint with the country than with their fellow city-dwellers. Urban business interests of a conservative character are often found in political alliance with organizations of farmers. Such a coalition may, and frequently does, operate to defeat legislation in the interests of the urban masses. Thus, Alfred E. Smith, in the New York Constitutional Convention charged, with adequate cause, that the upstate Republicans, overrepresented in the legislature, had "opposed every progressive piece of legislation proposed in this State in the last generation." [36]

The effects of this discrimination against the cities is not limited to legislation, since the legislative districts are commonly used as a basis for organization for other purposes. The party organizations are usually built on the legislative districts, and the antiurban gerrymander gives the rural leaders a disproportionate strength in party councils. State constitutional conventions, infrequently held to be sure, are usually elected from the legislative districts, and as the question of reapportionment is often one of the most important issues before the convention, the base of representation in the convention really decides the issue before it is raised. Since the legislature enacts legislation creating districts for the election of representatives in Congress, the

[36] New York State Constitutional Convention, 1938, *Revised Record*, IV, 2881–2884.

composition of the legislature tends to bring a similar antiurban bias in the distribution of congressional representation. In addition, there is some evidence to indicate that the existence of rural rotten boroughs influences campaign tactics and finance. A state-wide interest that desires legislators favorable to it may concentrate its campaign expenditures in the rural districts with small numbers of voters. Scattered data seem to indicate that vote-buying in the rural rotten boroughs is sometimes stimulated by the fact that a small number of votes in such districts exerts a greater proportionate influence in the legislature.[37]

To bring about a fairer distribution of representatives between urban and rural areas, a number of devices have been tried. In a few states the duty of redistributing the seats is vested in a reapportionment commission rather than in the legislature. In some of these states the reapportionment commission may be compelled to act by judicial process, a remedy not available when the function is vested solely in the legislature.[38] In some states the use of the initiative to reapportion is possible if the legislature fails to act. This reapportionment by initiative has been carried out in Washington, as well as in California; but it is significant that in California even through the initiative it was possible to bring about representation according to population in only one house of the legislature.

Congress and the gerrymander. In the House of Representatives the effects of the gerrymander are felt much as they are in state legislatures.[39] The number of members of the House to which each state is entitled is determined by Congress, but the boundaries of the districts

[37] Generally there is no discrimination against the urban communities in the voting for governor, United States Senators, and other officers elected by the entire state, but in a few instances a "county-unit" system has been devised to give rural votes disproportionate weight in the choice of these officials. In Georgia nomination to candidacies for state-wide offices is made by a county-unit system in which each county has twice as many "unit" votes as it has in the lower house of the state legislature. Since the legislature is gerrymandered, the rural counties have a strength disproportionate to their population in making nominations. In 1932 Quitman County, which polled 26 popular votes, had two unit votes in the state-wide Democratic primary; Fulton county at the same primary polled 22,117 popular votes but had only six unit votes. In other words, 26 popular votes in Quitman County had as great strength as 7,372 (or one third of 22,117) in Fulton. See C. B. Gosnell, "The Gerrymander System in Georgia," *Social Forces*, 11 (1933), pp. 570–573. It was under this unit rule that Eugene Talmadge won the nomination for governor in the Democratic primary of 1946 although he lacked a plurality of the popular vote.

[38] The Missouri Constitution of 1945 contains a new twist in sanctions to compel reapportionment. If a commission appointed for the purpose after each census does not redistrict the state within a specified time, the state senators are automatically elected at large at the next election. See V. D. Brannon, "Missouri's Apportionment Key," *National Municipal Review*, 35 (1946), pp. 177–182.

[39] For a thorough survey of the problem, see L. F. Schmeckebier, *Congressional Apportionment* (Washington: Brookings, 1941).

from which they are elected within the states are set by action of the state legislature. Following the census of 1920 Congress failed to reapportion its membership among the states. The population shifts since 1910 had been such that some states would have lost members and others would have gained. Representatives from those states that would have lost opposed a shift that would reduce the representation of their states and deprive some of them of their places in Congress. Consequently the distribution made in 1911 remained in effect until after 1930. Legislation enacted in 1929 provided for an automatic redistribution of seats among the states following each decennial census. The legislation of 1929, as amended in 1940, provides that following each census the President shall transmit to Congress a statement showing the population of each state "and the number of Representatives to which each State would be entitled under an apportionment of the then existing number of Representatives" made according to each of three methods. The law further provides that if Congress [40]

. . . has not, within sixty calendar days after such statement is transmitted, enacted a law apportioning Representatives among the several States, then each state shall be entitled, in the next Congress and in each Congress thereafter until the taking effect of a reapportionment under this Act or subsequent statute, to the number of Representatives shown in the statement based upon the method used in the last preceding apportionment.

After the apportionment of the total House membership among the states has been made, it is the responsibility of the state legislatures to enact laws establishing congressional districts. The legislatures may delay redistricting, may gerrymander for the benefit of the dominant party in the legislature, or discriminate against the urban areas in the distribution of seats.[41] In fact, all these practices occur. In Tennessee, for example, a study covering the period from 1796 to 1941 produced the conclusion that the "party in control in the state legislature has been constantly and uniformly over-represented in the Tennessee delegation in Congress." [42] In Illinois, to illustrate again, the congres-

---

[40] Public No. 481, 76th Congress, approved April 25, 1940.

[41] The degree of underrepresentation in the House of some areas and of overrepresentation of others may be inferred from the varying population of congressional districts in 1940. If each Representative had spoken for the same number of people, his district would have had a population of 302,687. In fact, 95 districts had a population of less than 250,000; 84 had a population of more than 350,000. These tabulations are based on the population of congressional districts before the reapportionments made in some states in 1941. The figures were derived from Census Bureau, Press Release, Series P-3, No. 9, February 5, 1941.

[42] H. N. Williams, "Congressional Apportionment in Tennessee, 1796–1941," *Journal of Politics*, 4 (1942), pp. 507–521.

sional districts laid out in 1901 on the basis of the 1900 census were still in use in 1946.

The general effect of the practices of state legislature in congressional apportionment in the North is an underrepresentation of the urban areas and a consequent diminution of Democratic strength in the House. In the South the effect is to increase the number of rural Democrats. Although no exhaustive study of the effects of the apportionment system has been made, it is fairly plain that it loads the dice against metropolitan interests, particularly labor. It contributes toward the great influence of agriculture in the House and aids those interests, such as business, that from time to time ally themselves with rural spokesmen.[43]

The Senate, of course, is not designed to represent the states in proportion to population. Nevada with its population of 110,247 is entitled to two Senators; New York, with its population of 13,479,142, likewise elects two Senators. If influence through representation could be demonstrated to be determined by percentages (which it cannot), one Nevadan would have 122 times the influence of one New Yorker in the United States Senate. In practice the equal representation of the states in the Senate operates to overrepresent the predominantly rural states and to underrepresent the predominantly urban states. The detailed figures are presented in Table 27.

The important consideration about representation in the Senate, as in other legislative bodies, is the effect of the system of representation on the decisions reached. Would a system of representation based on population alter or modify these decisions? Would the outcome be any different? The evidence indicates that on some questions a minority of the population, through its Senators, is able to defeat or to carry proposals that under a system of representation according to population would have been decided to the contrary. Such evidence is available in the late Carroll H. Wooddy's analysis of the votes in the Senate of the Sixty-fifth Congress, which extended from March 4, 1917 to March 4, 1919. This sitting of the Senate was controlled by a Democratic majority consisting of Senators from states with less than a majority of the population. It could be assumed that, to the degree to which questions were decided on party lines, Senators speaking for less than a

[43] Occasionally the question is raised whether something other than total population should be used as the basis for apportionment of House representation. Southern spokesmen, for example, suggest that aliens should not be counted, which would reduce the representation of northeastern states. Northeastern spokesmen reply with the proposal that the illiterate should not be counted, which would reduce representation of southern states. For an analysis of the effects of the use of such special populations in apportionment, see M. B. Ullman, "Apportionment of Representatives in Congress on the Basis of Special Population," *Journal of American Statistical Association*, 40 (1945), pp. 484–492.

majority of the population would decide the issue. Party discipline is far from perfect, but the likelihood of Senators who represent a minority of the people deciding issues would be greater under such circumstances than when the majority of Senators act for a majority of the population.   Actually it was found that nearly one eighth of all votes on which there was a roll call could be considered "unrepresentative." More than one third of the close votes were carried by a senatorial majority representing a minority of the population.[44] To evaluate fully the effect of the unrepresentative character of the Senate, one would have to analyze additional sessions of the Senate.

TABLE 27

Senate Representation and Urbanism [a]

Degree of Urbanism	1900		1940	
	Percentage of Population	Percentage of Senate	Percentage of Population	Percentage of Senate
States under 25 per cent urban.	32.9	42.2	56.6	10.5
States 25 to 50 per cent urban.	31.9	37.7	33.7	47.9
States 50 to 75 per cent urban.	30.9	15.5	43.4	33.3
States over 75 per cent urban.	4.3	4.4	17.3	8.3

[a] G. H. Haynes, *The Senate of the United States,* Vol. II, p. 1011.

Proportional representation. For the purpose of overcoming the defects of the single-member district, preventing such abuses as the gerrymander, and making representative bodies more representative systems of proportional representation have been devised, advocated, and in some jurisdictions adopted. The essential difference between the single-member district system of representation and proportional representation is this: The majority of the voters in the single-member district select the representative; under proportional representation multimember districts are used and each important group of voters tends to be represented according to its numerical strength. In a three-member district consisting of 66 per cent Republicans and 33 per cent Democrats the Republicans would elect two representatives and the Democrats one, whereas if the same area were divided into three districts, the Republicans might carry all three, depending on how the district lines were drawn.

[44] C. H. Wooddy, "Is the Senate Unrepresentative?" *Political Science Quarterly,* 41 (1926), pp. 219–239.

Many types of proportional representation, bewildering in their mathematical complexities, have been devised, but all of them have the same fundamental objective, namely, the representation of all important shades of opinion in the legislative body. One type of P.R. is the list system. As it was used in the election of the Reichstag of pre-Hitlerian Germany, the governing principle was that each party was entitled to one representative in the Reichstag for each 60,000 votes it polled. The number of members of the Reichstag thus was not fixed but fluctuated with the vote polled at each election. The country was divided into thirty-five districts. The party organizations named a list for each district, and a voter cast his ballot, say, for the Social Democratic list. If the Social Democratic ticket polled 150,000 votes, the first two persons on the district list would be declared elected. But there would be an unused surplus of 30,000 votes. So that this surplus might be used, it was combined through various steps with the Social Democratic surpluses from other districts to make additional quotas of 60,000 and to elect persons from other lists compiled by the party. The outcome was that representation in the Reichstag was divided among the parties in almost precisely the same mathematical proportions as the popular vote.

An incidental outcome of the operation of the list system was the enhancement of the power of the party organization. The party machine prepared the lists of candidates, and it could almost assure the election or defeat of a candidate by its determination of the order in which the names appeared on the list. The first name on the list was usually certain of election. The machine thus virtually appointed the party representatives in the Reichstag and therefore enjoyed great disciplinary powers. Another effect was the tendency for the number of parties to increase, since the system of representation was designed to make its possible for any small fraction of the population to unite and obtain representation.

The form of P.R. that has appealed especially to American proportionalists is the Hare system, which was devised by Thomas Hare, an Englishman, and set forth in a volume published in 1859. The system was brought to the attention of a larger audience when John Stuart Mill advocated its use in his *Representative Government*. Under the Hare system three or more representatives are selected from the same district, but the distinctive feature of the system is the transferable vote. In casting his ballot under the Hare system, the voter indicates first, second, third, fourth choices, and so on, depending on the number of names on the ballot. When all the ballots are in, the total number of valid ballots is determined and a "quota" is ascertained. The formula for obtaining the quota is to divide the total number of ballots by one more than the number of places to be filled and add one to the resulting quotient.

The formula sounds incomprehensible, but it is all quite simple. In fact, when a single person is to be elected from a single district a "quota" is established. If a total of 12,000 votes is cast for two candidates in a single-member district, the winner must receive at least 6,001 votes. Applying the above formula, one is added to the number of places to be filled; the sum is two. Dividing 12,000 by two, the quotient is 6,000. Add one and the quota of 6,001 is arrived at. To be elected the candidate must receive at least 6,001 votes; and not more than one candidate may receive the quota.

In a multimembered district under the Hare system the quota is ascertained in the same way. Assume that 12,000 votes are cast in a district that is entitled to five representatives. Dividing 12,000 by five plus one, the quotient is 2,000. Add one and the quota of 2,001 is found. In the counting of the votes, the ballots are arranged according to the first choices expressed. If a candidate receives over 2,001 first choices he is declared elected. If he receives, say, 2,500 votes, he has an excess; what is to be done with the 499 surplus votes? At this point the transferable feature of the vote comes into play. From the candidate's 2,500 first-choice ballots, 499 would be selected, usually at random, and transferred to the second-choice candidates indicated on those ballots. After the surplus votes have been distributed, the lowest candidate is eliminated and his ballots are distributed among the candidates for whom a second choice has been indicated by the voter. By the process of "transferring" ballots almost all the votes are made to count in the election of a candidate. By the elaborate counting procedure, the details of which have been glossed over in this discussion,[45] every group of voters in the district that can muster enough strength to poll first choices and transferred choices equivalent to the quota elects a representative.

The Hare system has appealed especially to municipal reformers. Apart from the potent appeal of the precise mathematical relationship of voting to representation, the municipal reformers have seen in P.R. a means of assurance that they could elect at least a minority of the city council. With a few strong reform leaders in the city council, so the argument goes, effective opposition could be exerted against the city machine, and the grosser forms of abuse that sometimes occur could be prevented. This argument has prevailed in various American cities, and the following cities either now operate under P.R. or have done so

[45] For the details of the Hare system and other types of P.R. as well, see C. G. Hoag and G. H. Hallett, Jr., *Proportional Representation* (New York: Macmillan, 1926).

at one time or another: New York, Ashtabula, Cleveland, Cincinnati, Boulder, Hamilton, Kalamazoo, Sacramento, and West Hartford. It is often pointed out that the great defect in mechanical and procedural reforms in city government is that the reform group has to gain control under the old system before the new procedures and forms can be adopted. That is, of course, not a vital weakness in their position, since their supposition is that the governmental form may remain after they lose power and enable them to fight a rear-guard action. Nevertheless, it is difficult to isolate the effects of P.R. in those cities that have used it. To be sure, cities such as Cincinnati have gained a reputation for having "good" city government, but how much of that result is attributable to P.R. and how much is attributable to the thorough organization and capable leadership of the Charter Committee in the politics of the city?

The adoption of P.R. for the election of state legislatures and Congress has never been seriously considered except by the small group of advocates of P.R. In political science literature, however, the firm devotees of P.R. were largely unopposed until recently. Fundamentally the argument of the anti-P.R. thinkers against proportional representation is an argument against the multiparty system. The contention is made, on the basis of European experience, that P.R. encourages divisive forces. Under P.R., the forecast is, there would be elected to Congress representatives of farmers, businessmen, Catholics, Protestants, veterans, laborers, single taxers, anti-vivisectionists, and any group, no matter how absurd its belief, so long as it could muster enough votes to meet the P.R. quota. The effect would be, it is said, to emphasize in campaigns and in the thinking of the voters their differences of interest and belief. The conflict between groups of people would become sharper; the difficulties of mustering and leading a majority in Congress would become greater. The single-member district, on the other hand, compels campaigners to make an appeal to as many types of people as possible; they must seek out and appeal to the common interests of the electorate. The necessity of obtaining a majority of the votes to win, as has been shown in an earlier chapter,[46] results in parties of similar views. When power oscillates between parties of similar beliefs, the change from party to party is not too much to be tolerated by the losers.[47]

The dire results predicted for P.R. do not seem to have occurred in

[46] See Chapter 8.

[47] The leading critic of P.R. is Professor F. A. Hermens. See his *Democracy or Anarchy: A Study of Proportional Representation* (Notre Dame, Indiana: *The Review of Politics*, 1941). For his views on P.R. in American cities, see "P.R. and Municipal Reform," *Review of Politics*, 5 (1943), pp. 82–102.

the American cities in which it has been used. It should be pointed out, however, that the great organized interest groups that would be expected to be active under P.R. are more concerned with what the national government does than with the activities of city governments. Hence their lobbying efforts are directed mainly toward the national government. The theory of the critics of P.R. is that the lobbyists would become members of Congress under P.R. Even with the lobbyists on the outside it is extremely difficult to prevent the triumph of special interests at the expense of the general welfare; under P.R. the general interest could hardly govern the behavior of the representative, since he would be elected directly by, and therefore compelled to speak for, a special interest.

5. THE NATURE OF PARTY GOVERNMENT

The workings of party government in the United States do not provide that a party with a definite program gains office with power and machinery for the effectuation of that program. A presidential election may really decide very little in terms of public policy. It decides who is to be in office for the ensuing four years; but the real issues remain to be settled in the friction, the give and take, and the pulling and hauling between the President, the House, and the Senate. It is commonly said—probably with a degree of truth—that the party system, when it operates properly, overcomes the handicaps to governance imposed by the separation of powers and furnishes a common leadership and a bond of loyalty by which the President and Congress may work together. Yet the President and the members of his own party in Congress are rarely in complete agreement on the general program to be followed, and the issues have to be settled by between-elections politics.

Absence of a definite and purposeful party program is sometimes attributed to the system of separation of powers. That system undoubtedly contributes to the confusion of whatever government is in power, but indecision and divided counsels must be traced farther back to the composition of the parties themselves. Each party contains groups of divergent interests with conflicting stakes in the game of politics. They may unite for the duration of an electoral campaign, but internal party differences are bound to reappear when it takes control of the government. And compact, well-organized pressure groups enter into the picture to dispute party leadership and, at times, to threaten Congressmen of both parties with defeat in their districts if they do not desert party leadership and follow a course of action advocated by the group.

The great burden of party leadership is to outmaneuver and overpower particularistic groups usually well represented in the party itself. The promotion of the general welfare does not require suppression of group demands, but it does require control of these demands. The synthesis of a program in the general interest by the party in power is hindered by the division within the party itself, as well as by the fortuitous lodgement at different points in the machinery of government of persons of both parties who can unduly protect and promote the rights of special and local interests.

The absence of clear-cut and congruous party power and responsibility for the conduct of government has led to the propagation of numerous schemes for the reform of the major outlines of governmental organization. At one extreme are those who would attempt to import bodily the system of government by a cabinet responsible to Congress, but this suggestion is met with the hard fact that the Senate, under our federal system, has great vitality, a factor incompatible with responsible cabinet government. An old, old idea is that the members of the President's cabinet should have seats and a right to speak in Congress and thereby bring about a narrowing of the broad gulf between the legislative and the administrative departments. A proposal of some merit is that the House and the Senate be elected for four-year terms at the time of the presidential election. The underlying supposition is that the longer term for members of the House might make them less susceptible to the blandishments and threats of special interests (of both the right and the left) and that the recurring concurrent campaign by the President and members of Congress would perhaps contribute to a tendency on the part of the electorate to view the work of the party as a whole. Another method, already mentioned, that is suggested in some quarters is that the President be given power to dissolve the House and order a reelection to ascertain whether he or Congress has the confidence of the country on a disputed issue. The grave defect of this proposal is that if the country expresses confidence in the House there is no ready and easy means to arrange an immediate succession to the Presidency of a person with the confidence of the country.

It is questionable whether the intraparty conflicts, the rise of bipartisan blocs in Congress, friction between the President and Congress, and the lack of inner consistency in party programs are avoidable. A looseness of party policy, weakness of party discipline, and illogical process of trading between interest groups may contribute to the solution of the sectional and group conflicts that flow up to the national government for reconciliation. The party tie is flexible enough to permit subgroups to meet their own local or regional necessities, yet strong enough to bind in genuinely critical situations of national import. We have, beneath our two-party facade, something of the adaptability of the French multiparty system in that majorities of a new composition can be formed and reformed as new issues arise. However, if the trend in governmental responsibility for the guidance of the national economy continues and with it the necessity for a consistent and interrelated set of governmental policies increases, the need for an overhauling of governmental machinery and party customs to produce that kind of public policy may become serious. Moreover, a nation can afford the luxury of the debate, division, and delay fostered by our governmental mechanism only in a bland international environment. External danger may compel a tightening up of the play in the governmental machinery.

Chapter 23

ADMINISTRATION AS POLITICS

THE victorious political party has responsibility for the formulation of
a legislative program and for the leadership and guidance of legislative
operations. It has a similar responsibility for the direction of the work
of the administrative departments of the government. It executes its
law-making duties by organizing the legislative bodies and devising
methods for holding together and leading the majority as best it can.
On the administrative side it is enabled to carry out its program by
virtue of the fact that the President has the authority to designate the
secretaries and assistant secretaries and like officials in charge of the
administrative departments and agencies of government. They, in
turn, have, within limits, the authority to designate their principal assistants. A relatively small number of persons, politically loyal to the
chief executive and to the party in power and presumably attached to
its program, has the function of controlling and guiding the huge
machinery of government in fulfillment of the party's responsibility to
the electorate.

The control and guidance of administration is in some respects a more
vexing and more difficult matter than the fulfillment of party responsibility in the field of legislation. In some respects the party leaders in
the legislative body come to their tasks better equipped than do the partisans at the head of departments. The legislators have ordinarily had
experience in the House or Senate on the minority side, whereas cabinet
members usually approach their tasks quite innocent of any experience
in federal administration. Furthermore, the President and the department heads do not enjoy undisputed sway in the management of the administration. Their fellow partisans in Congress usually like to take a
hand in the matter and consider that they have a responsibility for the
conduct of administration. The administration, like the majority in
Congress, contains within itself centrifugal forces that strain the capacity of the President, in his role as chief administrator, to prevent special

and partial interests from dominating particular administrative agencies, at least on particular questions.

At one time the belief was that the party in power had to appoint a large proportion of the staff of administrative agencies in order to fulfill its responsibility for the conduct of government.   When the party reserved these posts for appointment, the spoils doctrine was perhaps more influential than the necessities of party responsibility, but it was argued that to satisfy the people with their government the party had to be able to control the appointment of the postmaster in every village, hamlet, and crossroads.   The doctrine of a civil service recruited competitively on the basis of technical merit for more or less permanent tenure has made great inroads against the spoils theory at all levels of government.   Even yet, however, in some cities the conduct of the government is in large measure in the hands of party functionaries who may or may not hold public office.   If one wants a street repaired, garbage service improved, or other public service, he applies to the ward headquarters of the majority party rather than to the appropriate public office.   In the federal government a comparatively small number of persons of admitted partisan attachment have the duty of steering the administrative apparatus.   With a change of party control that involves a sharp deviation in policy, it may be necessary to make personal adjustments over a considerably broader area than the heads of departments and their immediate assistants to assure that the bureaucracy is responsive to party policy.

1. ADMINISTRATION AND PUBLIC POLICY: MOTIVES AND OBJECTIVES

Party control of the administration is of special importance because the administrative departments and agencies are a major source of ideas for new policy and a powerful influence for the adoption of new policy. Moreover, in the exercise of their discretion they make decisions that in their essence are legislative.   Commonly the administrative departments are thought of as mere agents to carry out policies decided upon by representative bodies through the play and interplay of demands by the public, or parts of the public, organized into pressure groups and political parties.   But the execution of legislative policy is not their only duty, though it is their major function; they also have a part in the process that leads to the formulation of public policy.[1]   In this process

---

[1] Georg Jellinek remarked: "The bureaucracy and the army are not state institutions only; they are social groups, too, which independent of their progenitor, react back on his shape and life."—Quoted by Arnold Brecht, "Bureaucratic Sabotage," *The Annals of the American Academy of Political and Social Science,* 189 (1937), p. 56.

the importance of vast aggregations of civil servants organized into well-knit hierarchies and animated by common aims and spirit is often underestimated or even ignored. For the segment of society that they serve, government departments and agencies at times act as spokesmen or representatives before legislative bodies and the public. Through the prosecution of research that reveals public needs and points toward public action, administrative agencies often initiate movements leading to new public policy. In the politics of appropriations almost every administrative bureau or department seeks to maintain or enlarge the scope of its operations; moreover, associations of employees of governmental units attempt to bring about the passage of legislation improving the conditions of their employment. In one respect administrative agencies are like the associations we have called pressure groups: they operate continually, in Republican and Democratic administrations alike, to advance their interests; indeed, often the closest working relationships are maintained between a pressure organization and the governmental agencies in which it is interested. Pressure groups and administrative departments are elements in the pattern of politics that may be jarred and realigned by the results of an election but are rarely completely thrown from power.

The development of administrative agencies employing large numbers of individuals animated by a devotion to a common cause has introduced formidable new forces into the policy-making process. As with private interest groups, the operation of the administrative agency is continuous; the administrative organization exerts its strength through transient department heads and Presidents, no matter what party is in power. With close relationships between its headquarters personnel in Washington and Congress it is able to make its wishes known to Congress either through the department head or through unofficial channels. Often with a personnel distributed over the nation, it is sometimes able to stir up pressure from home to bear on Congress. With almost a monopoly of information in its sphere of interest, the administrative organization is able to release or withold data in such a fashion as to influence the course of legislative action.

What are the motives and objectives of administrative agencies in their efforts to guide legislative action? As regards private pressure groups, motive and objective are usually perceptible to all who will see. Some bloc desires to advance what it conceives to be its own interest. The motivation of the lobbying of the administrative agency is in some respects the same as that of the private group, but it often possesses characteristics unlike those of the private lobbyist.

Narrow interests of administrative agencies in legislation. The ad-

ministrative agency has its selfish interests to promote. Every bureau
is anxious to obtain appropriations to carry out its program on an
adequate scale, and few bureau chiefs believe that last year's appropriation was enough. An organization's prestige is measured in part by the
size of its appropriations and the number of its employees. Larger appropriations may make possible needed salary increases. Apart from
motives of these sorts the personnel of an agency in seeking larger appropriations is often animated by a faith in the worth of the work that
is being done and by a belief that the public interest will be advanced
by the appropriation of the amount requested. In fact, this belief almost always prevails; persons employed by the government, like those
employed elsewhere, are apt to have enthusiasm about what they are
doing.

The administrative agency usually exerts its strength to defend itself
and the program it is carrying out from attack in legislative bodies.
Administrators tend to have a vested interest in the law they enforce;
and when its enemies attack, the agency is quick to line up its legislative
friends in defense. A special type of legislative proposal that arouses
intense interest of administrators is a reorganization bill. Comprehensive schemes to reorganize the administration through legislation
have invariably been defeated in Congress primarily through the pressure exerted by the bureaucracy. Only with the greatest of difficulty
did Franklin D. Roosevelt obtain the passage of a reorganization measure delegating to the President the power to shift administrative agencies from one department to another; yet certain agencies succeeded in
bringing about the adoption of amendments excepting them from the
operation of the act. The Army Corps of Engineers, for example,
which has been one of the most persistent opponents of administrative
reorganization, has succeeded in maintaining the *status quo* with respect to itself. Fights on questions of administrative reorganization are
sometimes battles between two federal agencies for jurisdiction over a
particular matter, such as the dispute between the Department of Agriculture and the Department of the Interior over the Forest Service.
The Forest Service, with its far-flung field service closely knit into the
life of the communities served, has gained strong public support and
has successfully resisted efforts to transfer it to the Department of Interior.

Representative role of administrative agencies. A theory of the
role of administrative agencies widely held by pressure groups is that
the administrative agency has a duty to act in furtherance of the interests of the group it serves. This is something of a doctrine of bureaucratic representation: that the Department of Labor should speak

for and represent the interests of labor in making recommendations for new legislation; that the Department of Agriculture should promote vigorously the interests of the farmer; and so on. A characteristic statement of this notion is one made in 1943 by the National Cooperative Milk Producers' Federation: [2]

> Eleven months from now the people will go to the polls. They will decide many important issues. One of the greatest issues which farmers will help decide will be on the question of who controls the Department of Agriculture. We believe that the organized farmers of America will demand of both political parties that they will provide a reconstituted Department of Agriculture to serve agriculture. Other departments of Government serve the groups for which they are named. The Department of Agriculture today is not being permitted to function for the farmers. We call for definite pledges on this great and fundamental issue.

A statement by Maury Maverick, chairman of the Smaller War Plants Corporation before a Senate committee in 1944 further illustrates the proposition: [3]

> . . . The small manufacturers and the small businessmen of this country are in trouble. Under law enacted by Congress the small plant is in actual fact represented by the Smaller War Plants Corporation. It is my honor to serve as the Chairman of this Corporation.
> Therefore I appear before you as their representative. In preparing this statement we have made extensive studies, and have had many interviews. Thus, what I present is not merely a collection of my own personal views.

With agency after agency attached to the interests of particular groups in society and under pressure to promote those partial interests,[4] the President as the leader of the administration has no little difficulty in bringing about the operation of the government in accord with a party program dedicated to the general welfare. The prevailing practice is that the administrative agencies represent the interests they serve.[5] Many of the great administrative agencies owe their existence to those groups that they serve. As new groups or classes rise to power

---

[2] National Cooperative Milk Producers' Federation, *A Dairy Policy for 1944*, p. 7.

[3] *Statement of Maury Maverick, Vice Chairman, War Production Board, and Chairman Smaller War Plants Corporation before War Contracts Subcommittee, April 20, 1944.*

[4] Consider the following statement by the late Senator Bankhead in 1941: "As you know, there are in the Department of Agriculture, a department which should be representing the farmers to help them get a fair deal and obtain justice, some theorists who assert they are representing the consumers and not the farmers. Everyone of them should be eliminated from the Department of Agriculture." *Congressional Record*, Vol. 87, pt. 4, p. 4020.

[5] See Charles Wiltse, "The Representative Function of Bureaucracy," *American Political Science Review*, 35 (1941), pp. 510–516.

and influence they are recognized through the establishment of governmental departments. The creation of the Department of Agriculture was the first recognition of an economic class in the administrative structure; later the departments of Commerce and of Labor were established; and finally, as the lower-income groups made themselves felt, the services grouped in the Federal Security Agency were inaugurated.

The degree to which an administrative agency becomes an attorney for its constituency varies with circumstances. The Veterans' Administration is rarely in a position to oppose the interests of the veterans. On the other hand, when an agency is subjected to pressure from conflicting interests, it may enjoy a greater freedom in formulating and advocating its own recommendations. The Department of Labor, for example, cannot satisfy both the C.I.O. and the A.F.L. Nor can the Department of Agriculture satisfy, at the same time, the beet-sugar growers, the beet-sugar refiners, the Louisiana cane-sugar growers, and the seaboard cane-sugar refiners. When different interests play on an administrative agency, the agency may seek to work out a program of legislative recommendations appeasing divergent interests in so far as practicable, or it may work out its own program completely.[6]

Administration in quest of the public interest. Occasionally an administrative agency, in its legislative program, ceases to be representative of a particular segment of society and seeks to promote the public interest. Lest this statement be misunderstood, it ought to be made plain what is meant by the "public interest" in this discussion. The Corps of Engineers of the Army, to illustrate, works in co-operation with and under pressure from those interests concerned with river and harbor improvements. Their recommendations are likely to be made without what the railroad and highway groups believe to be ample consideration of the interests of railroad and highway transport. Presumably the "public interest" lies in a "proper" or "economic" relationship and co-ordination of the different forms of transport. In the nature of things it could hardly be expected that the recommendations of the Corps of Engineers would reflect highway and railroad interests, more closely associated with other agencies of government. The legislative recommendations of the Federal Home Loan Bank Board, serving the

[6] Gaus and Wolcott comment that "those who assume that an adequate account of government is given when the term 'pressure group' has been uttered . . . look upon the Departments of Agriculture, Commerce and Labor as so many attorneys for their constituent vocational clients. . . . We point out, however, that agriculture, commerce, and labor are terms each of which covers a multitude of different types of interests that are rarely in total agreement on any save the most general and administratively meaningless abstract slogans."—*Public Administration and the U.S. Department of Agriculture* (Chicago: Public Administration Service, 1940), pp. 282–283.

savings and loan associations, have generally been in conflict with those of the Federal Housing Administration, which works in the main through the commercial banks. Presumably the "public interest" lies somewhere between the two extremes. These examples make clear the reasons that the recommendations of administrative agencies to Congress are often in conflict; their legislative programs frequently appear to be nothing more than projections of the desires of their respective constituencies. Nevertheless, administrative departments, in spite of the pressures brought to bear on them, strive toward the promotion of the public interest.[7]

The goal of the administrative departments is expressed in the inscription on the South Building of the Department of Agriculture: "Dedicated to the Service of Agriculture for the Public Welfare." The achievement of the spirit of such a goal in detail necessitates consideration of the problems of each segment of society in relation to the problem of government as a whole. Within the administrative service of the government there is a much greater tendency to seek to promote the public welfare as a whole than will be found in the ranks of the leaders of private groups. At its best, the thinking and planning of the civil servant approaches the intelligent and informed exercise of a trusteeship of the public welfare. At its worst the lobbying efforts of the administrative departments constitute the shortsighted promotion of the narrow and selfish interests of the agency or its constituency.

In some spheres administrative officials possess something approaching a sovereignty of competence. Since a large proportion of legislation consists of modifications of old policy, those in charge of the administration of law are in possession of the information and experience basic to the formulation of changes. The Bureau of Internal Revenue, for example, in the application of tax laws discovers loopholes facilitating evasion and suggests to Congress methods of remedying the situation. A crusading Food and Drug Administration urges changes in the law in order to broaden the coverage to protect the public and to make effective enforcement more feasible. Scientists of the Department of Agriculture discover means to control a crop pest and recommend suitable measures of control. The Children's Bureau calls attention to the

---

[7] Gaus and Wolcott say of the Department of Agriculture: "Broadly conceived, the Department's major task is to canalize the drive and energy of the pressure groups in agriculture so that they will be less harmful to our economy generally and will contribute to the best use of our natural resources, to the most satisfactory rural life, and to the most economic supply of agricultural products most useful to the consumer. Thus, the Department is not merely an inert and passive transmitter of contending and conflicting pressures but is an active agency in defining objectives and in making adjustments within the scope of legislative policy."—*Ibid.*, p. 379.

high infant mortality rate and agitates for a program to bring about a reduction. In every sphere of governmental activity the influence of the expert knowledge and of the long experience of the administrative official makes itself felt in new legislation.

Institutional inertias in public policy. In the consideration of the role of administration in the formulation and promotion of public policies it is useful to keep in mind a distinction between the politically responsible and politically appointed department or agency head and the department or agency as an institution. The department head may or may not have the confidence of the legislative body; he may have great influence on legislation; he may have no influence. These matters depend to a considerable degree upon the individual qualities of the person who happens to be the chief of the agency. As a consequence they vary from time to time.

Some department heads impress their personality and views on the agency they direct, but it is generally possible to speak of the department as an institution quite separate and distinct from the personality of its chief. "The department" over a long period builds up a tradition, a policy, and, one could almost say, a "personality" of its own. A point of view or general philosophy comes to permeate the organization; and, if new recruits do not have the departmental attitude, they are apt to acquire it in the course of time. These departmental traditions are quite difficult to bring to life on paper, but they are of enormous importance in the determination of the direction in which the department will exert its influence in the legislative process. Moreover, the departmental policy and tradition tend to harden into a form that resists alteration. The institutional pattern of ideas comes to be set in a certain fashion and it tends to stay that way.[8] In consequence, chief executives and legislative bodies often have to seek advice on public policy from outside the existing administrative services.

Intergovernmental administrative lobbying. A special type of administrative lobbying, arising from the form of our governmental contrivances, needs to be mentioned. Associations of state and local officials affiliated with state and local agencies benefiting from federal

---

[8] Public lands, including forested lands, were at one time in the custody of the General Land Office of the Department of the Interior. After considerable political pyrotechnics forests were assigned to the Department of Agriculture for protection and management. "The national forest idea ran counter to the whole tradition of the Interior Department," says Gifford Pinchot who was chief of the Bureau of Forestry of the Department of Agriculture at the time of the administration of Theodore Roosevelt. "Bred into its marrow, bone and fiber, was the idea of disposing of the public lands to private owners."—"How the National Forests Were Won," *American Forests and Forest Life,* October, 1930.

grants-in-aid have become active and powerful lobbying agencies. The American Association of State Highway Officials and the American Vocational Association, for example, have succeeded in pushing through Congress bills upsetting presidential budget estimates. The Association of Land-Grant Colleges and Universities and the Conference of State and Territorial Health Officers are other powerful and influential associations that appear before Congress in quest of appropriations and legislation. These organizations owe their power to the fact that their membership consists of officials in every state usually in a position to bring effective pressure to bear upon their Representatives and Senators in Congress. At the level of local government the United States Conference of Mayors, consisting of mayors of cities of over 50,000 population, has been concerned with federal legislation of interest to the larger municipalities.

In turn, federal administrative agencies are an important lobbying group before state legislatures. The Federal Housing Administration has successfully sought the passage of state legislation amendatory of banking laws to permit state-chartered banks to operate under its mortgage-insurance system. The Farm Credit Administration has been concerned with state laws governing farm mortgages. The Federal Home Loan Bank Board has presented its views to state legislatures on subjects relating to building and loan associations. The Public Works Administration, during the period of its activities, was instrumental in bringing about the passage of over 300 state legislative acts affecting its relationships with political subdivisions of states. The Soil Conservation Service has fostered the adoption of state soil conservation district laws. The Rural Electrification Administration has fought legislative battles for farmers' electrical cooperatives. The Bureau of Narcotics has promoted the adoption of its Uniform Narcotic Law.[9]

This general pattern of administrative pressure prevails also in the states with respect to their legislative bodies. State administrative departments are one of the most important sources of legislative proposals and of pressure on the legislatures.[10] Moreover, associations of local officials have their legislative counsel to present their views and requests to legislative committees and to lobby for and against proposals affecting

[9] See Ruth Weintraub, *Government Corporations and State Law* (New York: Columbia University Press, 1939); Key, "State Legislation Facilitative of Federal Action," *The Annals of the American Academy of Political and Social Science*, 207 (1940), pp. 7–13.

[10] For the situation in a typical state, see McKean, *Pressures on the Legislature of New Jersey*, chap. 5, "Pressures on the Legislature from Other Branches of the State Government." See also Elisabeth McK. Scott and Belle Zeller, "State Agencies and Lawmaking," *Public Administration Review*, 2 (1942), pp. 205–220.

their membership. In many states the state league of municipalities is active in the halls of the state capitol during legislative sessions. Often there is an association of county supervisors or other like officials to present the views of the counties.

Illustrative of the activities of associations of local officials, the New York Conference of Mayors and Other Municipal Officials expressed opinions on 155 bills introduced into the New York Legislature in 1940. "The Conference approved sixty-one, of which twenty-five became law, and disapproved ninety-four of which only four were enacted. Of the twenty-seven recommendations in the conference's legislative program, eight became law." [11] David Kurtzman reports the following groups of local officials active before the Pennsylvania Legislature: Association of Directors of the Poor and Charities and Corrections; Coroners' Association; Probation Officers' Association; Sheriffs' Association; State Association of County Commissioners; State Magistrates' Association.[12]

2. ADMINISTRATION AND PUBLIC POLICY: METHODS

The method employed by administrative agencies to influence the course of public policy are in a considerable measure peculiar to our presidential form of government with its separation of powers. In a cabinet government, such as that of Great Britain, the heads of administrative departments have direct access to the representative, lawmaking body and are its leaders. Their recommendations on new lines of public policy and on alterations in existing legislation are likely, in the great majority of instances, to be adopted as a matter of course.[13] In the United States, and in each of our states, however, executive officers are independent of the legislative body, and between legislatures and executives there is almost inevitably and invariably friction. Yet Congress or the state legislature has the final word on legislation, and, to present effectively the views and desires of administrative agencies, special methods and procedures have been developed. These techniques, although different in degree, are not fundamentally unlike those employed by private pressure and lobbying associations to present their case to lawmaking bodies.

Public-relations activities. In the analysis of the influence of administrative agencies on public policy, a differentiation may be made be-

11 Belle Zeller, "Lawmaker—Legislator or Lobbyist?" *National Municipal Review,* 29 (1940), pp. 523–532.

12 "Influence of Organizations of Local Government Officials," *Annals,* 195 (1938), pp. 103–109.

13 Consult Charles Aiken, "The British Bureaucracy and the Origins of Parliamentary Policy," *American Political Science Review,* 33 (1939), pp. 26–46, 219–233.

tween their public-relations activities designed to mold public opinion and their activities respecting specific bills pending in the legislative body. Almost every governmental agency attempts to reach the public —through newspapers, the radio, and other media—but only a small proportion of the publicity issued by administrative agencies is concerned with the promotion of proposed courses of public policy. The objectives of the bulk of governmental publicity are the performance of a function, such as the dissemination of information on improved farming methods by the Department of Agriculture, or the furnishing of information to the public on the course of public affairs, such as the news releases issued by the Department of State.

Administrative agencies are concerned with the creation of a reservoir of good will among the general public that can be drawn on when specific legislative proposals are under consideration by the legislative body. A "good" press and a "good" name are of great value in convincing Congress of the necessity for an increased appropriation or for other legislation requested by the agency. Sometimes the public-relations strategy is to dramatize the agency through publicizing its chief. The Federal Bureau of Investigation furnishes an excellent example of this technique. Its chief, J. Edgar Hoover, has diligently cultivated public favor with after-dinner speeches, dramatic news releases, and books and articles extolling the fearless work of the "G-Men." So effective has been his continuing campaign that when Mr. Hoover makes a request of Congress newspaper editors all over the land editorialize in support of his position.

The armed services, in peacetime at least, do not build up a single personality but seek to create a public opinion favorable to the service as an institution. The special facilities extended, for example, by the army and navy to motion picture companies for the filming of pictures presenting the services in a favorable light, to the accompaniment of a certain amount of romance, undoubtedly aid in creating favorable attitudes.[14] Other agencies seek to propagate an idea. The motion pictures *The River* and *The Plow That Broke the Plains*, prepared by the Resettlement Administration, were powerful and dramatic presentations of the effects of abuse of the soil.

Often the appeal is not to the "general" public, as in the examples cited, but to special groups of the population with a particular interest in the work of the agency. This preoccupation with what the public believes about the administrative agency is not entirely a matter of manipulating the attitudes of the public. The public often in turn in-

[14] See James R. Mock and Cedric Lawson, "Public Relations of the U.S. Army," *Public Opinion Quarterly*, 5 (1941), pp. 275–282.

fluences the work of the administration. Practices that evoke criticism
may be modified; or, if the criticism is poorly founded, increased efforts
are made to present the facts, so as to offset criticism.

None of the examples of public-relations activities cited involve an
appeal for public support for any particular policy advocated by the
agency; rather, they are calculated to establish a favorable general attitude toward the personalities, services, and ideas concerned. If this
type of generalized publicity is effective, an underlying sentiment is
formed or crystallized that is likely to help when specific legislation is
under consideration in Congress. A different type of publicity—a sort
of administrative guerilla warfare—flows from the informal and almost
surreptitious relations of administrators, often at subordinate levels,
with columnists and other journalists. Information is often fed to
these persons who report it on "high authority" or as from "informed
sources." By this means Congress may be needled, the President
nudged, a fire lighted under a superior, and, on occasion, officials in another department may be stirred to action or to anger.

Administrative origination of legislation. Since a large proportion
of the legislative output grows both from the need, demonstrated by
administrative experience, for modifying existing legislation and from
the need, demonstrated by administrative research and inquiry, for
adopting entirely new policies, administrative agencies play an extremely important role in the process of lawmaking as a whole. They
originate legislative proposals; they attempt, at times, to defeat legislative proposals originating from other sources; and, at other times, they
seek to bring about alterations in proposals pending in the legislative
body. The organization of the various departments of the federal government for carrying on this work varies. All agencies have facilities
for watching the course of legislation, in order to keep informed on
proposals that might affect their work. For the preparation of legislative proposals there exists in the office of the General Counsel of the
Treasury Department, for example, a legislative division that drafts all
proposals for legislation from the different units of the department for
presentation to Congress. Most of the other departments of the federal
government do not possess special units for handling this work, but
generally, the legislative proposals from the bureau of the department
pass over the desk of the head of the department for approval.[15]

Most legislation is of a routine character and arouses no controversy.
It seeks to accomplish objectives that, by common consent, are wise and

[15] E. E. Witte in President's Committee on Administrative Management, *Report
with Special Studies*, pp. 361–378; *idem*, "Administrative Agencies and Statute Lawmaking," *Public Administration Review*, (1942), pp. 116–125.

necessary for the conduct of public business. In support of such bills, representatives of the administrative agencies appear before the committees of Congress and present information indicative of the circumstances that appear to make the changes desirable. The departmental officials then have to do little more than watch the bill to see that it is not neglected in the many steps of the legislative process.

Bills, however, that propose a major change in public policy are likely to affect adversely some private interests and hence to create a conflict in Congress that calls for a more vigorous presentation of the administrative department's case. Under these circumstances the department may call on its allies among the pressure groups for assistance in dealing with Congress. When the objectives of the Department of Agriculture, for example, are coincidental with those of the American Farm Bureau Federation, the lobbyists of the Federation will appear, present testimony, buttonhole members of Congress, and perhaps focus upon Congressmen pressure from their constituencies. Or perhaps the Farmers' Union is with the department and the Federation against it; under these circumstances the department may plan its legislative strategy in collaboration with officials of the Farmers' Union. Connections exist between nearly every administrative unit and outside private associations, and these relationships are of great importance in the promotion of legislation. There is a deep-seated congressional jealousy of "bureaucrats," and the bureaucracy is restricted in the methods that it may use in dealing with Congress. If it seeks to stir up popular pressure on Congress in support of particular legislation, it is likely to arouse criticism and resentment in Congress; but its allied private pressure groups may turn the pressure on Congress.

It is chiefly in political disputes involving questions of high policy that the administration attempts to crystallize and focus a supporting public sentiment on Congress. And the important figures in these affairs are not petty bureaucrats but the principal leaders of the administration. On these great questions the President or cabinet members may appeal to the country for support in defeating congressional opposition.

The requests of administrative agencies for legislation often conflict and thereby create confusion. In earlier days bureau chiefs might approach Congress directly to obtain legislative action; now legislative requests generally flow through the department head. In recent years a further clearance has been established within the administration: most departmental requests for legislation are routed through the Bureau of the Budget, which acts for the President to reduce interdepartmental conflicts and to insure that the legislative requests of individual departments are in harmony with the policies and objectives of the administration as a whole.[16]   In the field of appropriations, greater progress has been made in curbing the independent activities of each governmental agency than with respect to general legislation.   Requests for appropriations are submitted to the Bureau of the Budget, as the agent for the President, and the final requests for appropriations are made to Congress by the President.   The chiefs of individual services are not free to advocate appropriations larger than those requested for them by the President.   The establishment of the executive budget thus, with considerable success, restricts administrative lobbying to the limits set in the budget by the Chief Executive.   From time to time, however, the interest groups allied with particular governmental functions lobby increases of the presidential estimates through Congress; or the initiative in increasing presidential estimates comes from within Congress itself.

3. LIMITATIONS ON ADMINISTRATORS

By various means Congress has sought, on the whole ineffectually, to limit the activities of administrative agencies designed to influence public opinion and legislative action.   These legislative acts have been motivated in part by congressional jealousy of the growing power and influence of the bureaucracy; in part by adherence to the theory that administrative agencies should have no place in the initiation of legislation; in part by congressional resentment of the actions of particular administrative agencies in specific situations.

Prohibition of employment of "publicity experts."   The first limitation applicable to all administrative agencies was enacted in 1913.   It grew out of the announcement of a civil service examination to select a "publicity expert" for the Office of Public Roads.   The duties of this position, it was announced, would "consist of the preparation of news matter relating to the work of the Office of Public Roads and securing the publication of such items in various periodicals and newspapers, particularly in country newspapers."   It was desired to obtain the services of a man "whose affiliations with newspaper publishers and writers is extensive enough to insure the publication of items prepared by him."   The phraseology of the examination announcement could not have been better calculated to arouse animosity in Congress.   Congressman Gillett observed: "The different departments of the administration certainly are not very modest in finding men and means to put before

---

[16] See Carl R. Sapp, "Executive Assistance in the Legislative Process," *Public Administration Review*, 6 (1946), pp. 10–19.

the country in the press the duties and purposes of their administration."
And Congressman Fitzgerald agreed "that there was no place in the
Government Service for an employee whose sole duty was to extol and
to advertise the activities of any particular service of the Government."
The outcome was the following legal provision: "No money appropriated by this or any other act shall be used for the compensation of any
publicity expert unless specifically appropriated for that purpose." [17]

Congress has made no specific appropriation for the employment of
publicity experts. Consequently, there has resulted, says McCamy,
"the evasive hiring of publicity experts under such titles as 'Director of
Information,' 'Chief, Division of Information and Education,' 'Chief
Educational Officer,' 'Editor-in-Chief,' 'Assistant to the Director' or 'Assistant to the Administrator,' 'Supervisor of Information Research,' 'Assistant to the Chairman,' or 'Director of Publication.' " [18] It should be
said, however, that many laws authorize administrative agencies to carry
on educational work or to inform the public, and the expenditure of
funds for publicity work can be justified under these authorizations.
The principal effect of the legislation of 1913 has been to outlaw the
title "publicity expert."

Prohibition of expenditures to influence Congress. In 1919 Congress
enacted the following legislation: [19]

No part of the money appropriated by any act shall, in the absence of express authorization by Congress, be used directly or indirectly to pay for any
personal service, advertisement, telegram, telephone, letter, printed or written
matter, or other device, intended or designed to influence in any manner a
member of Congress, to favor or oppose, by vote or otherwise, any legislation
or appropriation by Congress. . . .

Indicative of the practices toward which the legislation was directed is
the statement in congressional debate that this clause would "prohibit
a practice that has been indulged in so often, without regard to what administration is in power—the practice of a bureau chief or the head of
a department writing letters throughout the country, for this organization, for this man, for that company to write his Congressman, to wire

---

[17] 38 Stat. L. 212. In 1909 Congress had placed the following limitation on the
Forest Service: "That hereafter no part of any funds appropriated for the Forest
Service shall be paid or used for the purpose of paying for, in whole or in part, the
preparation or publication of any newspaper or magazine article, but this shall not
prevent the giving out to all persons without discrimination, including newspapers
and magazine writers and publishers, of any facts or official information of value to
the public."

[18] J. L. McCamy, *Government Publicity* (Chicago: University of Chicago Press,
1939), p. 7.

[19] 41 Stat. L. 68.

his Congressman, in behalf of this or that legislation." [20]   The law does permit executive employees to communicate with members of Congress at the request of Congressmen or through "the proper official channels" respecting legislation or appropriations.

Further statutory limitations on publicity by governmental agencies were imposed by Congress in 1939.   By an act effective July 1 of that year, Congress prohibited administrative agencies from sending through the mail free of postage, books, documents, pamphlets, and like materials unless a request had been received.   This limitation was adopted as the result of the objections of some Congressmen to the practice of New Deal agencies of transmitting large volumes of publicity matter through the mails.

Enforcement of prohibitions by criticism and publicity.   In practice the principal sanction for the enforcement of the foregoing limitations on administrative agencies is the possibility of adverse criticism in Congress, to which the executive officers of the government are extremely sensitive.   The absence of a body of case law interpreting the statutes as applied to different kinds of situations makes it difficult to say precisely what is prohibited.   Every administrative agency aspires and hopes to influence the course of legislation.   The law does not prevent recommendations on new legislation through proper channels—the President and the heads of departments.   The chief effect of the regulatory legislation seems to be to discourage administrative agencies in openly organizing support throughout the country for or against specific bills.

The kinds and tenor of congressional criticism of administrative activity in relation to public policy may be illustrated by a few examples. In 1940 Congressman Smith of Ohio assailed Nathan Straus, administrator of the United States Housing Authority, and members of his staff for "gumshoeing about the Capitol and offices of Congressmen lobbying for the passage of the housing bill. . . ."   He described the activities of Mr. Straus and his staff as "perfidious action" and announced that "every bureaucrat should be put in jail for lobbying to put his schemes through Congress." [21]   Again in 1940 Congressman Smith of Virginia, bitter critic of the National Labor Relations Board and leader of a congressional bloc united to weaken the Labor Relations Act, charged that the officials of the board had used public funds to line up labor organizations and their sympathizers to use their influence on congressional committees against changing the law or reducing the appropriation of the board.   He asserted that the available data indi-

[20] *Congressional Record*, Vol. 58, Part 1 (1919), p. 403.
[21] *Congressional Record*, April 30, 1940, p. 8060.

cated a violation of the law and demanded that the responsible officials be prosecuted.[22]

Similarly in 1945 Senator Robert A. Taft made an extended criticism of the Treasury Department for its "information" activities in support of the Bretton Woods agreements. The Senator showed that the Department had circulated hundreds of thousands of pamphlets and that its staff had spoken at many meetings and to many organizations in support of the agreements. He contended that such action violated the statute of 1919 and that it also subverted the normal constitutional processes by enabling the administration to organize and direct public pressure upon Congress. Such practices raise genuinely important constitutional issues, but congressional attitudes seem to be grounded more on attitudes toward the particular issue than toward the principle involved. A legislator seems more likely to become critical if he opposes a particular measure that is being aided by administrative propaganda than if he favors it. Thus, in 1946 when President Truman instructed the admirals to refrain from lobbying against the establishment of a Department of National Defense—an instruction perfectly in harmony with the statute of 1919 and general constitutional principles —the congressional opponents of service consolidation objected vociferously that the experts were being muzzled and other high crimes and misdemeanors committed.

Administrative agencies are also subjected to criticism from private sources for their efforts, alleged or real, to influence congressional action. In the battle in 1933 over the revision of the Pure Food and Drug Act, for example, Daniel A. Lundy, an advertising man connected with the Home Drug Company of Minneapolis, manufacturers of "Prescription No 69," a self-administered cure for gallstones, directed a letter to each member of Congress denouncing Walter Campbell, chief of the Food and Drug Administration. He demanded that Campbell be "dismissed and prosecuted for his alleged gross violations and abuse of authority, in spending government money without permission of the Congress for radio, Paramount News Reels, diversion of his employees' time for selfish purposes and other means to influence passage of the unconstitutional Tugwell-Copeland-Sirovich Food & Drug bills." [23] In 1940 Congressman Disney of Oklahoma, by insertion in the *Record,* disseminated a speech before the Independent Petroleum Association of America, attacking Interior Department radio dramas on oil conservation. The

---

[22] *The New York Times,* March 19, 1940.
[23] Ruth deForest Lamb, *American Chamber of Horrors* (New York: Farrar & Rinehart, 1936), p. 297.

speaker observed a "hysteria and dramatic emotionalism" in these broadcasts and feared that they might lead to "a bloodless revolution, with the transfer of authority over our industrial life from free enterprise to government dictatorship" and cited the gag law.[24]

Outbursts such as those cited have a common origin. They come from critics, inside and outside Congress, of the policies fostered by the administrative agency concerned. Attacks on administrative action, whether based on fact or not, are usually part of a campaign against a particular piece of legislation. Phrased in extravagant language, they are usually designed to attract newspaper publicity calculated to discredit the administrative agency by branding it as a lawbreaker. These attacks serve to keep administrative agencies within legal bounds, but, within the sphere of legality, there is large scope for administrative lobbying. The President and other policy-forming officials have a responsibility to recommend to Congress courses of action; Congressmen, in turn, rely on administrative officials and employees for advice and assistance. The administration remains one of the most important influences on the course of legislative action.

Legal limitations of the sort discussed are likely to be ineffective in stemming the tide of administrative publicity calculated to influence public opinion and the course of legislative action. In some respects, as Harold Stoke has pointed out,[25] the growth of administrative publicity reflects a profound change in the nature of our governmental arrangements. To executive agencies has shifted in considerable measure the initiation of legislative policy. A corollary of this change is the development of administrative propaganda and education to aid in the crystallization of public sentiment concerning new policies. In another respect administrative agencies have themselves become lawmakers through congressional delegation of authority. To make administrative rules and regulations publicly acceptable, propaganda or education has to be carried on as a substitute for the discussion and debate that earlier served in a more exclusive degree to manufacture public consent to governmental action. Yet there remains a serious problem in the definition of the sphere of permissible official propaganda that is in keeping with the theory of representative government.[26]

[24] *Congressional Record*, March 1, 1940, p. 3465.

[25] "Executive Leadership and the Growth of Propaganda," *American Political Science Review*, 35 (1941), pp. 490–500.

[26] There is no denying, says Arthur Macmahon, "that the public-relations activities of governmental agencies may be dangerous for democratic society. Especially when large resources are involved, an agency should not be more interested in perpetuating itself than in enlightening public opinion. The eagerness to win public support may pass beyond the boundary of cultivating consent into demanding obedience. The formula of public relations for modern administration is elusive. The kind of

4. INDEPENDENT COMMISSIONS AND THE PARTY PROGRAM

The party in power has the responsibility and the means for control-ling the ordinary government departments and agencies. Its designees head these agencies, and departmental policy is expected to be in ac-cord with the administration program. The independent commis-sions, however, have broad policy-making power and are beyond the ready and effective control of the government of the day. The inde-pendence of these agencies is justified on the ground that in their quasi-judicial activities the commissions must impartially determine private rights in relationship to law. By that independence, however, the com-missions come to determine political or policy questions with only a tenuous political responsibility. An administration may come into power pledged to adopt altered policies in important spheres, but it may find itself blocked by the fact that the regulatory commissions are con-trolled by men appointed by prior Presidents of a different persuasion on policy.

The situation may be illustrated by a report by David F. Houston, then Secretary of Agriculture, covering a cabinet meeting early in Woodrow Wilson's first administration: [27]

The matter of railway rates was considered at some length. It was agreed that the situation ought to be met squarely and promptly. One of the mem-bers (Lane) said that some of the rates on certain goods were too low. They had been made in the interest of owners of industries along the line: Those he said should certainly be raised, but those on all competing roads would have to be raised also. . . .

It was agreed that the matter was one for the Interstate Commerce Commis-sion and that it should either raise or reclassify rates or insist on greater efficiency in management. It was agreed that no pressure of any sort could be brought to bear on the Commission. The impropriety of approaching it or its members was recognized.

Here the President and the cabinet, with political responsibility for the conduct of government, agreed that the situation "ought to be met squarely and promptly." But it was also agreed that the matter was one for the Interstate Commerce Commission, and that it was improper to approach the commission.

advocacy that prejudices responsible government must be avoided. Yet administra-tors must be left adequately equipped to fulfill their responsibilities. Careful and continuous scrutiny by legislatures and citizens is the best guarantee that the limits of desirable administrative informational activity will be observed."—*The Administra-tion of Federal Work Relief* (Chicago: Public Administration Service, 1941), p. 292.

[27] From *Eight Years with Wilson's Cabinet* (copyright, 1926, Doubleday, Doran and Company, Inc.), Vol. I, pp. 86–87.

When President Coolidge in 1925 appointed William E. Humphrey to the Federal Trade Commission, that body came to be dominated by a Republican majority, and its policy in the enforcement of the prohibition of "unfair methods of competition" in interstate commerce was drastically softened.   Yet for the previous five years the commission had not been in accord with the policy of the Republican administrations. The shift in the commission's attitude with the appointment of Humphrey is indicated by a speech that he made: [28]

> Under the old policy of litigation it [the Commission] became an instrument of oppression and disturbance and injury instead of a help to business.   It harassed and annoyed business instead of assisting it.   Business soon regarded the commission with distrust and fear and suspicion—as an enemy.   There was no cooperation between the commission and business.   Business wanted the commission abolished and the commission regarded business as generally dishonest.

It is a bit difficult to see how a commission that sincerely attempted to prevent "unfair methods of competition" could be "a help to business," except to those businesses injured by unfair competition; at any rate, the commission prior to the Humphrey appointment had apparently been out of harmony with broad Republican policies.   When Franklin D. Roosevelt came into office, his conception of the role of the Federal Trade Commission was more nearly in accord with the ideas of the Wilsonian period and he requested the resignation of Humphrey in the following terms: "I do not feel that your mind and my mind go along together on either the policies or the administering of the Federal Trade Commission, and, frankly, I think it best for the people of this country that I should have a full confidence."   Humphrey resisted the removal order, and the Supreme Court decided that Congress could limit the power of the President to remove members of the commissions exerting quasi-judicial powers.   The consequence of the decision, of course, was to make more difficult the harmonization of the policies of the independent regulatory commissions with the broad objectives of the party in power.

Harding and Coolidge had their troubles with the Tariff Commission, a body with only power to advise on tariff rates.   In 1923 Harding wrote to Culbertson of the Tariff Commission:

> I only venture to say at this time that I think it is altogether desirable to hold up a declaration of broad policy until I can sit down and go over the

[28] Quoted by Herring, *Public Administration and the Public Interest* (New York: McGraw-Hill, 1936), p. 125.   See this volume for a thorough analysis of the position of the independent regulatory commissions.

entire situation with the commission. As I understand it, the commission is the agency of the President in dealing with the tariff problem, and my intimate association and final responsibility in all matters lead me to believe that it is highly essential for a thorough understanding before embarking on any definitely defined course.

When the question of reappointment of one member of the commission arose, Coolidge offered the appointment on condition that an undated letter of resignation be signed by the appointee. Refusal to accede to the condition resulted in failure to receive reappointment. Although the Tariff Commission occupies a position different from that of the ordinary regulatory commissions, these incidents illustrate the difficulties of bringing about a congruity of power and responsibility in the areas carved out for the independent commissions.

What has happened in the creation of the independent commissions is that Congress, unable itself to deal with specific problems, has handed over to the independent commissions a power to arbitrate differences between divergent social and economic interests. The standards to guide the commissions have been extremely vague guideposts, such as "fair," "just," "reasonable," "the public interest," and "the public convenience and necessity." In settling these differences the commissions have adopted a procedure of impartiality, with many of the features and appearances of the judicial process; but in reality the commissions are declaring policy as Congress does when it decides like issues. But mixed with these lawmaking functions is the duty of deciding the rights of individuals. This duty tends to be more or less purely judicial in nature.

The assumption of an independent and impartial attitude by the commissions and their tendency to isolate themselves from the planning and contriving of the administration leaders in the efforts of the latter to meet new situations limit the usefulness of the commissions in an important way. Impartiality and the judicial viewpoint—no matter how essential they are in settling individual cases under established law— are likely to be incompatible with the exercise of leadership in the formation of new policies, in the anticipation of problems, and in the preparation of policies to meet problems as they arise. The Interstate Commerce Commission apparently had something of this sort of thing in mind when it reported: [29]

There is need for readjustments between and within the different branches of the transportation industry, for the consideration of present tendencies and their probable results, for the avoidance of uneconomic and wasteful practices,

[29] Interstate Commerce Commission, 52d *Annual Report* (1938), pp. 24–25.

and in general for the determination, creation, and protection of the conditions most favorable to the development of a transportation system which will best serve the public interest.   There is a field here both for continuing study and research and for active, aggressive, and consistent leadership on the part of the Government which has never been occupied.   The real problem is to fill that void in the best possible way.

With one important governmental agency dealing with certain aspects of the transportation problem, however, it is virtually impossible to create another to assume the function of research and aggressive leadership.   At any rate, the sphere of the independent commission often tends to be outside the main stream of thinking and contriving relative to national economic policy.

The problem of working out the proper relationship of the independent regulatory commissions to the government as a whole remains unsolved.   It seems obvious that a more suitable *modus operandi* will have to be devised, but how it will be done is unclear.   Herring states the dilemma.[30]

> The President has certainly no right to intervene on behalf of any private party who may come before a commission, but this does not mean that he has no concern with its general interpretation of the law.   Can some way be found for admitting his influence upon policy without causing interference with the commission's judicial activities?   How can the chief executive, for example, be given a means of exerting his influence in national transportation problems without disrupting the work of the Interstate Commerce Commission?

Friction will exist until the question is worked out.   And, it may be suggested, the urgency of the need for a satisfactory solution increases as the breadth of government regulation grows.   Since the various aspects of the economic system dealt with by different independent commissions and ordinary government departments are interrelated, a co-ordinated government policy becomes more and more essential.   It is the responsibility of the party in control of the government to devise and execute such a program, but an administration is limited in that responsibility by the independence of the regulatory commissions in their present form.

5. THE PLACE OF BUREAUCRACY IN A DEMOCRACY

The administrative services are not purely inert mechanisms through which the will of the legislature is transmuted into action.   These services themselves are an important force in the state and play an important

---

[30] *Public Administration and the Public Interest* (New York: McGraw-Hill, 1936), p. 224.

part in the determination of what is to be done in the name of the state. Yet their importance is not so great as might be inferred from the more extravagant diatribes against the bureaucracy and its assumption of power.

The trend of events, however, suggests inquiries into the shape of things to come for administrative services and parliamentary institutions. The growing volume and complexity of public functions have reduced to a fiction the theory of separation of powers and the parallel doctrine of the separability of politics and administration. Representatives bodies, the institutional embodiment of democratic ideology, have by the compelling force of the trend of events lost both power and prestige. Their role in the initiation of public policy has been diminished by losses to pressure groups and administrative agencies; their authority to decide many issues has, of necessity, been delegated to the administrative services. They have been driven toward, but not entirely to, a role of futile and uninformed criticism, at its worst motivated either by partisan or picayune considerations.

The administrative services have, in terms of the distribution of both formal governmental power and informal political influence, been the chief heirs of the declining representative bodies. What are the dangers and problems of the growing importance of the administrative services in a culture in which traditionally the theory at least has been that political issues should be decided by popularly elected representatives? Charles E. Merriam points out that as we emerge from the era of corruption, incompetence, and ignorance in administration,[31]

. . . the new possibilities are those of arrogance and indifference to the public, lack of sympathy approaching harshness, and cruelty, devotion to inflexibility and routine, grumbling at theory and change; procrastination, quibbling and delay; or the opposite of too great and rash speed without adequate preparation of the public for the change.

Above all there is the ever impending danger of the desire for personal self-perpetuation and expansion of power, bureaucratic parochialism of the pettiest type; the sabotage of the ends of office by placing the machinery or the person above the function he is there to serve; or the effort of the administrator to take over the role of the policy maker, by various devices, direct or otherwise.

Although tendencies in these directions are discernible, there are offsetting factors. In the initiation and formation of public policy the power of group and class drives, as has been shown, is fundamental. Yet private groups find it difficult, even when the best of intentions are granted, to exert their strength for the general welfare. The legislative

---

[31] "Public Administration and Political Theory," *Journal of Social Philosophy*, 5 (1940), pp. 305–306.

programs of administrative agencies, however, tend to incorporate the objectives of private groups and to temper and to modify them in the public interest. Indeed, in many situations of policy parturition it seems that the bureaucracy is the only participant animated by a devotion to the common welfare. In this connection Gaus and Wolcott inquire: [32]

> At what point in the evolution of policies in the life of the community shall the process take place of transforming a specialist point of view and program, through compromise and adjustment, into a more balanced public program? Much of this process must take place in the administrative agencies through the selection of personnel, their continued in-service training, the content and discipline of their professions, researches, and responsibilities, the attrition of interbureau and interdepartmental contact and association, and the scrutiny of their work by the over-all administrative staff and auxiliary agencies and by Congress. If there is the proper attention to these matters, the viewpoint of the civil service will differ from the surrogacy that one expects from the officials of a pressure group.

A possible line of development, then, would be the direction and harnessing of the power, knowledge, and skills of the administrative services so that they might constitute a powerful force in the initiation of public policies calculated to promote the commonweal. The development of an administrative corps of this character depends in large measure on the further development of techniques of organization and supervision whereby the political heads of administrative services may better overcome the parochialism of the permanent staffs and liberate their talents. This problem of the overhead organization of governmental departments and of the government as a whole is of prime importance in determining the direction in which the powers of the bureaucracy will be exerted. Such responsible officials in collaboration with Congress have the task of orienting public policy, but in the absence of effective techniques for organizing and directing the administration their efforts are likely to be either obstructed or ineffectively carried out by the administrative services. Recent years have seen much attention given to the organization of administration and to administrative planning. This tendency reflects partially a desire to create, within the administrative structure, machinery and procedures for more certain and expeditious determination of the issues in the application of existing policy and the initiation of new policy that otherwise might receive a narrow treatment at the hands of individual uncoordinated and poorly directed administrative services.

The danger of the rise of a bureaucracy aggressively grasping for un-

[32] *Op. cit.,* p. 283.

warranted power is much less than the danger of drifting into a condition in which the bureaucracy is a purely negative force. A seasoned bureaucracy, without heroic measures to the contrary, tends to become attached to the time-honored ways of doing things, hostile toward innovation, lacking in initiative, and timid. These qualities are admirable at the right time and place, but the next few decades in the United States will hardly be the time and place for pleasant habituation to the customary.

This is not to argue for a bureaucracy that will usurp the functions of Congress and the President; the contention is, rather, that present conditions demand a bureaucracy that will minimize the magnitude of the tasks of Congress and the President. How may that be done? The pressure on Congress may be reduced by the development of procedures within the administration for the settlement of matters unworthy of the attention of Congress, by the eradication of parochialism within administrative agencies and the consequent submission of legislative recommendations that are more likely to meet the desires of Congress, and by the development of internal controls that would reduce the task of congressional surveillance of the administration. The task of presidential direction of the administration increases in difficulty with the growth of the number of administrative agencies; the impression of the President's policy on particularistic administrative agencies becomes an almost impossible job (yet that is the President's responsibility and duty). To make the functions of Congress and the President actual as well as nominal, it is essential to have a bureaucracy dedicated to seeking out the general welfare, yet mindful of the final authority of Congress and the President in defining how the general welfare shall be promoted.

The problem of bureaucracy is in a sense not a problem of bureaucracy at all. It is rather a question of recruiting into party service an adequate supply of men competent to manage and control the bureaucracy from their posts as the transient but responsible heads of departments and agencies. Publicists have been greatly exercised about making the civil service attractive enough to draw able men to it as a career. Of no less importance is the attraction of even abler men to the service of parties to direct and carry responsibility for the direction of the career staffs. It is through such persons who owe their posts to the victorious party that popular control over government is maintained.

APPENDIX

APPENDIX

MAJOR PARTY PLATFORMS

DEMOCRATIC PLATFORM, 1944 [1]

I

The Democratic Party stands on its record in peace and in war.

To speed victory, establish and maintain peace, guarantee full employment and provide prosperity—this is its platform.

We do not here detail scores of planks. We cite action.

II

Beginning March 1933, the Democratic Administration took a series of actions which saved our system of free enterprise.

It brought that system out of collapse and thereafter eliminated abuses which had imperiled it.

It used the powers of government to provide employment in industry and to save agriculture.

It wrote a new Magna Carta for labor.

It provided social security, including old-age pensions, unemployment insurance, security for crippled and dependent children and the blind. It established employment offices. It provided Federal bank-deposit insurance, flood prevention, soil conservation, and prevented abuses in the security markets. It saved farms and homes from foreclosure and secured profitable prices for farm products.

It adopted an effective program of reclamation, hydroelectric power, and mineral development.

It found the road to prosperity through production and employment.

We pledge the continuance and improvement of these programs.

III

Before war came, the Democratic administration awakened the Nation in time to the dangers that threatened its very existence.

It succeeded in building, in time, the best trained and equipped army in the world, the most powerful navy in the world, the greatest air force in the world, and the largest merchant marine in the world.

It gained for our country, and it saved for our country, powerful allies.

When war came, it succeeded in working out with those Allies an effective grand strategy against the enemy.

It set that strategy in motion, and the tide of battle was turned.

[1] Adopted at Democratic National Convention held in Chicago, July 19–21, 1944.

It held the line against wartime inflation.

It insured a fair share-and-share alike distribution of food and other essentials.

It is leading our country to certain victory.

The primary and imperative duty of the United States is to wage the war with every resource available to final triumph over our enemies, and we pledge that we will continue to fight side by side with the United Nations until this supreme objective shall have been attained and thereafter to secure a just and lasting peace.

IV

That the world may not again be drenched in blood by international outlaws and criminals, we pledge:

To join with the other United Nations in the establishment of an international organization based on the principle of the sovereign equality of all peace-loving states, open to membership by all such states, large and small, for the prevention of aggression and the maintenance of international peace and security.

To make all necessary and effective agreements and arrangements through which the nations would maintain adequate forces to meet the needs of preventing war and of making impossible the preparation for war and which would have such forces available for joint action when necessary.

Such organization must be endowed with power to employ armed forces when necessary to prevent aggression and preserve peace.

We favor the maintenance of an international court of justice of which the United States shall be a member and the employment of diplomacy, conciliation, arbitration, and other like methods where appropriate in the settlement of international disputes.

World peace is of transcendent importance. Our gallant sons are dying on land, on sea, and in the air. They do not die as Republicans. They do not die as Democrats. They die as Americans. We pledge that their blood shall not have been shed in vain. America has the opportunity to lead the world in this great service to mankind. The United States must meet the challenge. Under divine providence, she must move forward to her destiny.

V

We pledge our support to the Atlantic Charter and the "four freedoms" and the application of the principles enunciated therein to the United Nations and other peace-loving nations, large and small.

We shall uphold the good-neighbor policy and extend the trade policies initiated by the present administration.

We favor the opening of Palestine to unrestricted Jewish immigration and colonization, and such a policy as to result in the establishement there of a free and democratic Jewish commonwealth.

We favor legislation assuring equal pay for equal work regardless of sex.

We recommend to Congress the submission of a constitutional amendment on equal rights for women.

We favor Federal aid to education administered by the States without interference by the Federal Government.

We favor Federal legislation to assure stability of products, employment, distribution, and prices in the bituminous-coal industry to create a proper balance between consumer, producer, and mine worker.

We endorse the President's statement recognizing the importance of the use of water in arid-land States for domestic and irrigation purposes.

We favor nondiscriminatory transportation charges and declare for the early correction of inequalities in such charges.

We favor enactment of legislation granting the fullest measure of self-government for Alaska, Hawaii, and Puerto Rico, and eventual statehood for Alaska and Hawaii.

We favor the extension of the right of suffrage to the people of the District of Columbia.

VI

We offer these post-war programs:

A continuation of our policy of full benefits for ex-service men and women with special consideration for the disabled. We make it our first duty to assure employment and economic security to all who have served in the defense of our country.

Price guaranties and crop insurance to farmers with all practical steps:

To keep agriculture on a parity with industry and labor.

To foster the success of the small independent farmer.

To aid the home ownership of family sized farms.

To extend rural electrification and develop broader domestic and foreign markets for agricultural products.

Adequate compensation for workers during demobilization.

The enactment of such additional humanitarian, labor, social, and farm legislation as time and experience may require, including the amendment or repeal of any law enacted in recent years which has failed to accomplish its purpose.

Promotion of the success of small business.

Earliest possible release of wartime controls.

Adaptation of tax laws to an expanding peacetime economy, with simplified structure and wartime taxes reduced or repealed as soon as possible.

Encouragement of risk capital, new enterprise, development of natural resources in the West and other parts of the country, and the immediate reopening of the gold and silver mines of the West as soon as manpower is available.

We reassert our faith in competitive private enterprise free from control by monopolies, cartels, or any arbitrary private or public authority.

VII

We assert that mankind believes in the "four freedoms."

We believe that the country which has the greatest measure of social justice is capable of the greatest achievements.

We believe that racial and religious minorities have the right to live, develop, and vote equally with all citizens and share the rights that are guaranteed by our Constitution. Congress should exert its full constitutional powers to protect those rights.

We believe that without loss of sovereignty, world development, and lasting peace are within humanity's grasp. They will come with the greater enjoyment of those freedoms by the peoples of the world, and with the freer flow among them of ideas and goods.

We believe in the world right of all men to write, send, and publish news at uniform communication rates and without interference by governmental or private monopoly, and that right should be protected by treaty.

To these beliefs the Democratic Party subscribes.

These principles the Democratic Party pledges itself in solemn sincerity to maintain.

Finally this convention sends its affectionate greetings to our beloved and matchless leader and President, Franklin Delano Roosevelt.

He stands before the Nation and the world the champion of human liberty and dignity. He has rescued our people from the ravages of economic disaster. His rare foresight and magnificent courage have saved our Nation from the assault of international brigands and dictators. Fulfilling the ardent hope of his life, he has already laid the foundation of enduring peace for a troubled world and the well-being for our Nation. All mankind is his debtor. His life and service have been a great blessing to humanity.

That God may keep him strong in body and in spirit to carry on his yet unfinished work is our hope and prayer.

REPUBLICAN PLATFORM, 1944 [1]

The tragedy of the war is upon our country as we meet to consider the problems of government and our people. We take this opportunity to render homage and enduring gratitude to those brave members of our armed forces who have already made the supreme sacrifice, and to those who stand ready to make the same sacrifice that the American course of life may be secure.

Mindful of this solemn hour and humbly conscious of our heavy responsibilities, the Republican Party in convention assembled presents herewith its principles and makes these covenants with the people of our Nation.

THE WAR AND THE PEACE

We pledge prosecution of the war to total victory against our enemies in full cooperation with the United Nations and all-out support of our Armies and the maintenance of our Navy under the competent and trained direction of our General Staff and Office of Naval Operations without civilian interference and with every civilian resource. At the earliest possible time after the cessation of hostilities we will bring home all members of our armed forces

[1] Adopted at Republican Convention held in Chicago, June 26–28, 1944.

who do not have unexpired enlistments and who do not volunteer for further overseas duty.

We declare our relentless aim to win the war against all our enemies: (1) For our own American security and welfare; (2) to make and keep the Axis powers impotent to renew tyranny and attack; (3) for the attainment of peace and freedom based on justice and security.

We shall seek to achieve such aims through organized international co-operation and not by joining a world state.

We favor responsible participation by the United States in post-war co-operative organization among sovereign nations to prevent military aggression and to attain permanent peace with organized justice in a free world.

Such organization should develop effective cooperative means to direct peace forces to prevent or repel military aggression. Pending this, we pledge continuing collaboration with the United Nations to assure these ultimate objectives.

We believe, however, that peace and security do not depend upon the sanction of force alone, but should prevail by virtue of reciprocal interest and spiritual values recognized in these security agreements. The treaties of peace should be just; the nations which are the victims of aggression should be restored to sovereignty and self-government; and the organized cooperation of the nations should concern itself with basic causes of world disorder. It should promote a world opinion to influence the nations to right conduct, develop international law and maintain an international tribunal to deal with justiciable disputes.

We shall seek, in our relations with other nations, conditions calculated to promote world-wide economic stability, not only for the sake of the world, but also to the end that our own people may enjoy a high level of employment in an increasingly prosperous world.

We shall keep the American people informed concerning all agreements with foreign nations. In all of these undertakings we favor the widest consultation of the gallant men and women in our armed forces who have a special right to speak with authority in behalf of the security and liberty for which they fight. We shall sustain the Constitution of the United States in the attainment of our international aims; and pursuant to the Constitution of the United States any treaty or agreement to attain such aims made on behalf of the United States with any other nation or any association of nations, shall be made only by and with the advice and consent of the Senate of the United States provided two-thirds of the Senators present concur.

We shall at all times protect the essential interest and resources of the United States.

WESTERN HEMISPHERE RELATIONS

We shall develop Pan-American solidarity. The citizens of our neighboring nations in the Western Hemisphere are, like ourselves, Americans. Co-operation with them shall be achieved through mutual agreement and without interference in the internal affairs of any nation. Our policy should be a genuine good-neighbor policy commanding their respect, and not one based on the reckless squandering of American funds by overlapping agencies.

POST-WAR PREPAREDNESS

We favor the maintenance of post-war military forces and establishments of ample strength for the successful defense and the safety of the United States, its possessions, and outposts, for the maintenance of the Monroe Doctrine, and for meeting any military commitments determined by Congress. We favor the peacetime maintenance and strengthening of the National Guards under State control with Federal training and equipment as now provided in the National Defense Act.

DOMESTIC POLICY

We shall devote ourselves to re-establishing liberty at home.

We shall adopt a program to put men to work in peace industry as promptly as possible and with special attention to those who have made sacrifice by serving in the armed forces. We shall take Government out of competition with private industry and terminate rationing, price-fixing, and all other emergency powers. We shall promote the fullest stable employment through private enterprise.

The measures we propose shall avoid federalization of Government activities, to the end that our States, schools, and cities shall be free; shall avoid delegation of legislative and judicial power to administrative agencies, to the end that the people's representatives in Congress shall be independent and in full control of legislative policy; and shall avoid, subject to war necessities, detailed regulation of farmers, workers, businessmen, and consumers, to the end that the individual shall be free. The remedies we propose shall be based on intelligent co-operation between the Federal Government, the States, and local government, and the initiative of civic groups—not on the panacea of Federal cash.

Four years more of New Deal policy would centralize all power in the President, and would daily subject every act of every citizen to regulation by his henchmen; and this country could remain a republic only in name. No problem exists which cannot be solved by American methods. We have no need of either the communistic or the fascist technique.

SECURITY

Our goal is to prevent hardship and poverty in America. That goal is attainable by reason of the productive ability of free American labor, industry, and agriculture, if supplemented by a system of social security on sound principles.

We pledge our support of the following:

1. Extension of the existing old-age insurance and unemployment insurance systems to all employees not already covered.

2. The return of the public employment-office system to the States at the earliest possible time, financed as before Pearl Harbor.

3. A careful study of Federal-State programs for maternal and child health, dependent children, and assistance to the blind, with a view to strengthening these programs.

4. The continuation of these and other programs relating to health, and the stimulation by Federal aid of State plans to make medical and hospital service available to those in need without disturbing doctor-patient relationships or socializing medicine.

5. The stimulation of State and local plans to provide decent low-cost housing properly financed by the Federal Housing Administration, or otherwise, when such housing cannot be supplied or financed by private sources.

LABOR

The Republican Party is the historical champion of free labor. Under Republican administrations American manufacturing developed, and American workers attained the most progressive standards of living of any workers in the world. Now the Nation owes those workers a debt of gratitude for their magnificent productive effort in support of the war.

Regardless of the professed friendship of the New Deal for the workingman, the fact remains that under the New Deal American economic life is being destroyed.

The New Deal has usurped selfish and partisan control over the functions of Government agencies where labor relationships are concerned. The continued perversion of the Wagner Act by the New Deal menaces the purposes of the law and threatens to destroy collective bargaining completely and permanently.

The long series of Executive orders and bureaucratic decrees reveal a deliberate purpose to substitute for contractual agreements of employers and employees the political edicts of a New Deal bureaucracy. Labor would thus remain organized only for the convenience of the New Deal in enforcing its orders and inflicting its whims upon labor and industry.

We condemn the conversion of administrative boards, ostensibly set up to settle industrial disputes, into instruments for putting into effect the financial and economic theories of the New Deal.

We condemn the freezing of wage rates at arbitrary levels and the binding of men to their jobs as destructive to the advancement of a free people. We condemn the repeal by Executive order of the laws secured by the Republican Party to abolish "contract labor" and peonage. We condemn the gradual but effective creation of a labor front as but one of the New Deal's steps toward a totalitarian state.

We pledge an end to political trickery in the administration of labor laws and the handling of labor disputes; and equal benefits on the basis of equality to all labor in the administration of labor controls and laws, regardless of political affiliation.

The Department of Labor has been emasculated by the New Deal. Labor bureaus, agencies, and committees are scattered far and wide, in Washington and throughout the country, and have no semblance of systematic or responsible organization. All governmental labor activities must be placed under the direct authority and responsibility of the Secretary of Labor. Such labor bureaus as are not performing a substantial and definite service in the interest of labor must be abolished.

The Secretary of Labor should be a representative of Labor. The office of the Secretary of Labor was created under a Republican President, William Howard Taft. It was intended that a representative of labor should occupy this Cabinet office. The present administration is the first to disregard this intention.

The Republican Party accepts the purposes of the National Labor Relations Act, the Wages and Hours Act, the Social Security Act, and all other Federal statutes designed to promote and protect the welfare of American working men and women, and we promise a fair and just administration of these laws.

American well-being is indivisible. Any national program which injures the national economy inevitably injures the wage earner. The American labor movement and the Republican Party, while continuously striving for the betterment of labor's status, reject the communistic and New Deal concept that a single group can benefit while the general economy suffers.

AGRICULTURE

We commend the American farmers, their wives and families, for their magnificent job of wartime production and their contribution to the war effort, without which victory could not be assured. They have accomplished this in spite of labor shortages, a bungled and inexcusable machinery program, and confused, unreliable, impractical price and production administration.

Abundant production is the best security against inflation. Governmental policies in war and in peace must be practical and efficient with freedom from regimentation by an impractical Washington bureaucracy in order to assure independence of operation and bountiful production. fair and equitable market prices for farm products, and a sound program for conservation and use of our soil and natural resources. Educational progress and the social and economic stability and well-being of the farm family must be a prime national purpose.

For the establishment of such a program we propose the following:

1. A Department of Agriculture under practical and experienced administration free from regimentation and confusing Government manipulation and control of farm programs.

2. An American market price to the American farmer and the protection of such price by means of support prices, commodity loans or a combination thereof, together with such other economic means as will assure an income to agriculture that is fair and equitable in comparison with labor, business, and industry. We oppose subsidies as a substitute for fair markets.

3. Disposition of surplus war commodities in an orderly manner without destroying markets or continued production and without benefit to speculative profiteers.

4. The control and disposition of future surpluses by means of (a) new uses developed through constant research, (b) vigorous development of foreign markets, (c) efficient domestic distribution to meet all domestic requirements, and (d) arrangements which will enable farmers to make necessary adjustments in production of any given basic crop only if domestic surpluses should become abnormal and exceed manageable proportions.

5. Intensified research to discover new crops, and new and profitable uses for existing crops.

6. Support of the principle of bona fide farmer-owned and farmer-operated co-operatives.

7. Consolidation of all Government farm credit under a nonpartisan board.

8. To make life more attractive on the family-type farm through development of rural roads, sound extension of rural electrification service to the farm, and elimination of basic evils of tenancy wherever they exist.

9. Serious study of and search for a sound program of crop insurance with emphasis upon establishing a self-supporting program.

10. A comprehensive program of soil, forest, water, and wildlife conservation and development, and sound irrigation projects, administered as far as possible at State and regional levels.

BUSINESS AND INDUSTRY

We give assurance now to restore peacetime industry at the earliest possible time, using every care to avoid discrimination between different sections of the country, (a) by prompt settlement of war contracts with early payment of Government obligations and disposal of surplus inventories, and (b) by disposal of surplus Government plants, equipment and supplies, with due consideration to small buyers and with care to prevent monopoly and injury to existing agriculture and industry.

Small business is the basis of American enterprise. It must be preserved. If protected against discrimination and afforded equality of opportunity throughout the Nation, it will become the most potent factor in providing employment. It must also be aided by changes in taxation, by eliminating excessive and repressive regulation and Government competition, by the enforcement of laws against monopoly and unfair competition, and by providing simpler and cheaper methods for obtaining venture capital necessary for growth and expansion.

For the protection of the public, and for the security of millions of holders of policies of insurance in mutual and private companies, we insist upon strict and exclusive regulation and supervision of the business of insurance by the several States where local conditions are best known and where local needs can best be met.

We favor the re-establishment and maintenance, as early as military considerations will permit, of a sound and adequate American merchant marine under private ownership and management.

The Republican Party pledges itself to foster the development of such strong privately owned air-transportation systems and communications systems as will best serve the interests of the American people.

The Federal Government should plan a program for flood control, inland waterways and other economically justifiable public works, and prepare the necessary plans in advance so that construction may proceed rapidly in emergency and in times of reduced employment. We urge that States and local governments pursue the same policy with reference to highways and other public works within their jurisdiction.

TAXATION AND FINANCE

As soon as the war ends the present rates of taxation on individual incomes, on corporations, and on consumption should be reduced as far as is consistent with the payment of the normal expenditures of government in the postwar period. We reject the theory of restoring prosperity through government spending and deficit financing.

We shall eliminate from the budget all wasteful and unnecessary expenditures and exercise the most rigid economy.

It is essential that Federal and State tax structures be more effectively coordinated to the end that State tax sources be not unduly impaired.

We shall maintain the value of the American dollar and regard the payment of government debt as an obligation of honor which prohibits any policy leading to the depreciation of the currency. We shall reduce that debt as soon as economic conditions make such reduction possible.

Control of the currency must be restored to Congress by repeal of existing legislation which gives the President unnecessary and dangerous powers over our currency.

FOREIGN TRADE

We assure American farmers, livestock producers, workers and industry that we will establish and maintain a fair protective tariff on competitive products so that the standards of living of our people shall not be impaired through the importation of commodities produced abroad by labor or producers functioning upon lower standards than our own.

If the post-war world is to be properly organized, a great extension of world trade will be necessary to repair the wastes of war and build an enduring peace. The Republican Party, always remembering that its primary obligation, which must be fulfilled, is to our own workers, our own farmers and our own industry, pledges that it will join with others in leadership in every co-operative effort to remove unnecessary and destructive barriers to international trade. We will always bear in mind that the domestic market is America's greatest market and that tariffs which protect it against foreign competition should be modified only by reciprocal bilateral trade agreements approved by Congress.

RELIEF AND REHABILITATION

We favor the prompt extension of relief and emergency assistance to the peoples of the liberated countries without duplication and conflict between government agencies.

We favor immediate feeding of the starving children of our allies and friends in the Nazi-dominated countries and we condemn the New Deal Administration for its failure, in the face of humanitarian demands, to make any effort to do this.

We favor assistance by direct credits in reasonable amounts to liberated countries to enable them to buy from this country the goods necessary to revive their economic systems.

BUREAUCRACY

The national administration has become a sprawling, overlapping bureaucracy. It is undermined by executive abuse of power, confused lines of authority, duplication of effort, inadequate fiscal controls, loose personnel practices and an attitude of arrogance previously unknown in our history.

The times cry out for the restoration of harmony in Government, for a balance of legislative and executive responsibility, for efficiency and economy, for pruning and abolishing unnecessary agencies and personnel, for effective fiscal and personnel controls, and for an entirely new spirit in our Federal Government.

We pledge an administration wherein the President, acting in harmony with Congress, will effect these necessary reforms and raise the Federal service to a high level of efficiency and competence.

We insist that limitations must be placed upon spending by Government corporations of vast sums never appropriated by Congress but made available by directives, and that their accounts should be subject to audit by the General Accounting Office.

TWO-TERM LIMIT FOR PRESIDENT

We favor an amendment to the Constitution providing that no person shall be President of the United States for more than two terms of 4 years each.

EQUAL RIGHTS

We favor submission by Congress to the States of an amendment to the Constitution providing for equal rights for men and women. We favor job opportunities in the post-war world open to men and women alike without discrimination in rate of pay because of sex.

VETERANS

The Republican Party has always supported suitable measures to reflect the Nation's gratitude and to discharge its duty toward the veterans of all wars.

We approve, have supported and have aided in the enactment of laws which provide for re-employment of veterans of this war in their old positions, for mustering-out pay, for pensions for widows and orphans of such veterans killed or disabled, for rehabilitation of disabled veterans, for temporary unemployment benefits, for education and vocational training, and for assisting veterans in acquiring homes and farms and in establishing themselves in business.

We shall be diligent in remedying defects in veterans' legislation and shall insist upon efficient administration of all measures for the veteran's benefit.

RACIAL AND RELIGIOUS INTOLERANCE

We unreservedly condemn the injection into American life of appeals to racial or religious prejudice.

We pledge an immediate congressional inquiry to ascertain the extent to which mistreatment, segregation, and discrimination against Negroes who are in our armed forces are impairing morale and efficiency, and the adoption of corrective legislation.

We pledge the establishment by Federal legislation of a permanent Fair Employment Practice Commission.

ANTI-POLL TAX

The payment of any poll tax should not be a condition of voting in Federal elections and we favor immediate submission of a constitutional amendment for its abolition.

ANTI-LYNCHING

We favor legislation against lynching and pledge our sincere efforts in behalf of its early enactment.

INDIANS

We pledge an immediate, just, and final settlement of all Indian claims between the Government and the Indian citizenship of the Nation. We will take politics out of the administration of Indian affairs.

PROBLEMS OF THE WEST

We favor a comprehensive program of reclamation projects for our arid and semiarid States, with recognition and full protection of rights and interests of those States in the use and control of water for present and future irrigation and other beneficial consumptive uses.

We favor (a) exclusion from this country of livestock and fresh and chilled meat from countries harboring foot-and-mouth disease or Rinderpest; (b) full protection of our fisheries, whether by domestic regulation or treaties; (c) consistent with military needs, the prompt return to private ownership of lands acquired for war purposes; (d) withdrawal or acquisition of lands for establishment of national parks, monuments and wildlife refuges, only after due regard to local problems and under closer controls to be established by the Congress; (e) restoration of the long-established public-land policy which provides opportunity of ownership by citizens to promote the highest land use; (f) full development of our forests on the basis of cropping and sustained yield; co-operation with private owners for conservation and fire protection; (g) the prompt reopening of mines which can be operated by miners and workers not subject to military service and which have been closed by bureaucratic denial of labor or material; (h) adequate stock piling of war materials and metals for possible future emergencies; (i) continuance, for tax purposes, of adequate depletion allowances on oil, gas and minerals; (j) administration of laws relating to oil and gas on the public domain to encourage exploratory operations to meet the public need; (k) continuance of present Federal laws on mining claims on the public domain, good-faith administration thereof, and we state our opposition to the plans of the Secretary of the Interior to substitute a leasing system; and (l) larger representation in the Federal Government of men and women especially familiar with western problems.

HAWAII

Hawaii, which shares the Nation's obligations equally with the several States, is entitled to the fullest measure of home rule looking toward statehood; and to equality with the several States in the rights of her citizens and in the application of all our national laws.

ALASKA

Alaska is entitled to the fullest measure of home rule looking toward statehood.

PUERTO RICO

Statehood is a logical aspiration of the people of Puerto Rico who were made citizens of the United States by Congress in 1917; legislation affecting Puerto Rico, insofar as feasible, should be in harmony with the realization of that aspiration.

PALESTINE

In order to give refuge to millions of distressed Jewish men, women, and children driven from their homes by tyranny, we call for the opening of Palestine to their unrestricted immigration and land ownership, so that in accordance with the full intent and purpose of the Balfour Declaration of 1917 and the resolution of a Republican Congress in 1922, Palestine may be constituted as a free and democratic commonwealth. We condemn the failure of the President to insist that the mandatory of Palestine carry out the provision of the Balfour Declaration and of the Mandate while he pretends to support them.

FREE PRESS AND RADIO

In times like these, when whole peoples have found themselves shackled by governments which denied the truth, or, worse, dealt in half-truths or withheld the facts from the public, it is imperative to the maintenance of a free American that the press and radio be free and that full and complete information be available to Americans.   There must be no censorship except to the extent required by war necessity.

We insistently condemn any tendency to regard the press or the radio as instruments of the administration and the use of Government publicity agencies for partisan ends.   We need a new radio law which will define, in clear and unmistakable language, the role of the Federal Communications Commission.

All channels of news must be kept open with equality of access to information at the source.   If agreement can be achieved with foreign nations to establish the same principles, it will be a valuable contribution to future peace.

Vital facts must not be withheld.

We want no more Pearl Harbor reports.

GOOD FAITH

The acceptance of the nominations made by this convention carries with it, as a matter of private honor and public faith, an undertaking by each candidate to be true to the principles and program herein set forth.

CONCLUSION

The essential question at trial in this Nation is whether men can organize together in a highly industrialized society, succeed, and still be free.   That is the essential question at trial throughout the world today.

In this time of confusion and strife, when moral values are being crushed on every side, we pledge ourselves to uphold with all our strength the Bill of Rights, the Constitution, and the law of the land.   We so pledge ourselves that the American tradition may stand forever as the beacon light of civilization.

QUESTIONS AND PROBLEMS

CHAPTER 1

1. What is politics?

2. Can an adequate understanding of the nature of political power be gained from a study of the machinery of government?

3. Are there "right" solutions for all public questions?

4. What differentiates the political process in democracies and in dictatorships?

5. Is the seeking of political power and influence motivated by a desire for power and influence or by a desire for the ends that may result from the possession of power?

6. Are there any common elements in the politics of the United States, Soviet Russia, and an aboriginal tribe?

7. Could it be said that there is a "ruling class" in your community? If so, identify it.

8. Is the conception of politics presented in this chapter broad enough to include international politics?

9. Could it be contended that the study of political behavior is a branch of psychology?

10. Which deals with the more important type of question, political science or political philosophy?

CHAPTER 2

1. Account for the rise of the Granger movement.

2. What conditions stimulated the growth of the Farm Bureau Federation?

3. Contrast the general viewpoints of the chief national farm organizations.

4. Is there any essential difference in the motivation of agrarian, business, and labor attempts to influence the course of public policy?

5. Is the tendency toward more or less agrarian influence in national politics?

6. Examine the resolutions adopted by a recent annual convention of any state or national farmers' organization. To what extent do the resolutions represent the expression of the narrow vocational interests of farmers? To what extent do they reflect the broader interests of the farmer as a citizen?

7. What is the function of the process of rationalizing or reconciling public policies enacted for the benefit of one part of the people with the general welfare?

8. Through what stages does a typical political movement pass?

9. Observe closely some movement for legislation in your state. Are your observations in accord with your views on the preceding question?

10. What is meant by political equilibrium?

11. What sorts of factors set in motion movements that disturb the political equilibrium?

CHAPTER 3

1. Does the process of government in private associations have any relevance for the student of politics?

2. What are the causes and results of federalism within the A.F.L.?

3. In what respects has the attitude of labor toward government been like that of business? Is this similarity purely nominal or is it substantial?

4. Has organized labor in its opposition to the formation of a labor party followed a course of action wise from its own viewpoint?

5. Describe the methods used by labor to influence elections and legislation.

6. Ascertain the nature of recent activities of organized labor in the politics of your state or city.

7. Estimate and account for the degree of power exercised by labor in national politics.

8. Some labor leaders would like to be able to swing the vote of labor and thereby to determine the outcome of presidential elections. Would this state of affairs be desirable?

9. What is tradition? What is its importance or function in the political order?

10. Do the leaders of private groups necessarily reflect accurately the interests and views of the members of the group?

CHAPTER 4

1. What are the underlying objectives of the public-relations activities of business?

2. Outline the methods employed by business groups to influence public policy.

3. Determine (by reference to the *Census of Manufactures* and like sources) the chief types of business enterprise in your state. What sorts of governmental policy would each class of business probably seek to influence? Why?

4. Has business been primarily concerned with the initiation or the obstruction of new public policy? Why?

5. How does the nature of the composition of a business association influence the type of position it takes on public questions?

CHAPTER 5

1. Discuss the phrase of the constitution of the American Legion which states that the Legion "shall be absolutely nonpolitical."

2. How can the power of the Legion in dealing with Congress be accounted for?

3. "The settlement and conciliation of intergroup differences are often accomplished without the interposition of government." Discuss with special reference to the position of the Negro.

4. To what extent should the judgment of professional groups be accepted by legislators in determining public policy?

5. Under what conditions are private groups likely to be most influential in the administration of legislation affecting their members?

6. Relate the discussion, in this chapter, of the tendency toward guild control of governmental action to material in your courses in political theory concerning pluralism.

CHAPTER 6

1. What is meant by the term "sectionalism"?

2. It is sometimes proposed that a system of seven or eight great regions be substituted for the states. What might be the effects of such an arrangement?

3. What has been the effect, if any, of the rise of cities on the sectional pattern of American national politics?

4. What has been the chief economic basis of sectionalism in the United States?

5. Do political disputes in your state frequently assume the form of a sectional cleavage? (If so, a more exact idea of their nature may be gained by preparing maps showing the distribution over the state of votes in the legislature on intersectional issues. In some instances a map showing the percentage of the total vote polled by the winning candidate for governor in each county is illuminating. What are the underlying reasons for the pattern shown by your maps?)

6. What kinds of issues have generated intersectional friction in national politics in recent years?

7. Is it probable that diversification of economic activity will eliminate sectional groupings in national politics?

8. Do geographical factors positively influence political behavior?

9. Determine the relation, if any, of the geography of your state to its politics.

10. Could it be contended that a general national policy calculated to minimize intersectional friction is desirable? If so, why?

CHAPTER 8

1. Differentiate political parties and pressure groups.

2. What are the functions performed by political parties?

3. What factors have probably been important in conditioning the United States toward the two-party rather than the multiparty system?

4. If it is assumed to be desirable to minimize social conflict, what is the best type of party system? Why?

5. Do you believe that the discussion in this chapter underestimates the differences between the Republican and Democratic parties? If so, why?

6. What are the prospects for the continuation of the two-party system in the United States?

7. Ascertain how your state has voted at each of the last ten presidential elections. Can the results be reasonably attributed to a relationship between the predominant interests of the people of the state and the issues of each campaign?

8. Determine the percentage of the total presidential vote in your state polled by third-party candidates at each of the past ten elections. Consider the causes of the variations in the percentages polled by minor candidates.

9. Classify the conditions that may lead to the formation of minor parties.

10. In the promotion of a cause, what are the relative advantages of (a) working from within a major party, (b) organizing a minor party, and (c) forming a pressure group?

11. How has the direct primary affected the tendency to form minor parties?

12. If there are important minor parties concerned with state or local matters in your state or city, trace and explain their growth.

CHAPTER 9

1. Discuss the differences in general emphasis of legislative programs of Democratic and Republican Administrations since 1896.

2. It is often observed that the major American parties stand for nothing. Consider this popular belief in the light of the presidential campaigns since 1896.

3. Relate the issues in the presidential campaigns of 1936 and 1940 to the unlikeness in composition of the major parties at those times as presented in Chapter 8.

4. Discuss the nature of party cycles. Does consideration of the cycle phenomenon alter your conception of the nature of the popular decision in a presidential campaign.

5. Obtain from the *Public Opinion Quarterly* Gallup poll figures on the occupational distribution of party strength in 1948 comparable with those included in Table 10 in Chapter 8. Does consideration of shifts in party affiliations of occupational groups over the period 1936–1948 suggest an hypothesis about the nature of party cycles?

CHAPTER 10

1. What is meant by the term "organization"?

2. Determine from the statutes the legal structure of party organization in your state.

3. Interview a precinct captain with reference to his duties and methods of operation.

4. What are the functions of the national chairman of a party?

5. What is the nature of the control exercised by national party leaders over state organizations of their party?

6. How has our federal system of government influenced the character of our party organization?

7. Collect information on the nature of the dominant party organization in your community.

8. What are the methods by which the mass of party adherents control the party leaders, and how effective are they?

9. Defenders of the party machine argue that it lends stability to government and prevents the precipitous adoption of erratic policies. Do your observations of the party organization in your state support this contention?

CHAPTER 11

1. In what respects may the party machine be considered to be similar to a pressure group?

2. What was Andrew Jackson's theory about rotation in office?

3. What would be the probable consequences if American parties were deprived of patronage?

4. Trace the development of legislation to prevent partisan activity by federal civil servants.

5. Ascertain the nature of the laws and regulations with reference to political activity by civil servants of your state and city. How effective are these rules in practice?

6. Classify types of spoils other than jobs sought by party machines.

7. Which of the types of practices included in the preceding question prevail in your state or city?

8. How does the spoils system divert popular attention from social and economic issues?

CHAPTER 12

1. Account for the early assumption by legislative caucuses of the function of making nominations.

2. In what respects was the movement to abolish the legislative caucus mode of nominations similar to the later movement to abolish the convention system?

3. Does the evolution of the nominating process throw any light on the theory that groups tend to be controlled by oligarchies?

4. With what political movements was the rise of the direct primary associated?

5. In terms of effects on the outcome of the nominating process, what is the significance of the type of nominating procedure used?

6. Distinguish between the open and closed form of the direct primary.

7. It could be said that the evolution of the nominating process reflects the tendency toward increased democratization of American politics. Comment.

8. Ascertain the form and as much as you can about the actual practice of nominations in your state or city.

CHAPTER 13

1. What characteristics make a person "available" as a presidential candidate?

2. What are the specific objectives of a preconvention campaign?

3. Outline the history of the problem of the apportionment of delegates to the Republican national convention among the states.

4. Analyze the law and practice of selection of delegates to the national convention from your state.

5. What problems of strategy does the "favorite son" create for a leading aspirant for the presidential nomination?

6. What sorts of controversies occur over the report of the committee on permanent organization?

7. What is the importance of the action of the convention on the recommendations of the committee on credentials?

8. Convention interest tends to be concentrated on one or two planks of the platform. Why?

9. Why does not the winning party follow more closely the program laid down in its platform?

10. Examine the platforms (reprinted in the Appendix to this volume). Determine the differences. Compare the platform promises of the winning party with the subsequent action by the government.

11. What was the origin of the two-thirds rule in Democratic conventions? Why was it retained so long?

12. Can you devise any method other than the national convention to perform the functions of the convention?

CHAPTER 14

1. Outline the structure of the organization for conducting a presidential campaign.

2. What is "propaganda"?

3. Why is it essential for the propagandist to have an intimate knowledge of the cultural fixations of the group to which he directs his appeals?

4. Analyze a few campaign speeches in the light of the general discussion of propaganda in this chapter.

5. From your own observation of campaigns, what weight do you give to the theory that successful politicians tend to appear to be prototypes of their constituencies?

6. If possible, interview a politician of some prominence. Compare your firsthand impressions with your earlier impressions gained through the newspapers.

7. Discuss the problem of choice and emphasis among propaganda media in the conduct of political campaigns.

8. What are the chief recurring problems of campaign strategy?

CHAPTER 15

1. Examine and evaluate the corrupt practices act and related legislation of your state.

2. If the data are accessible, an instructive project for several students would be the analysis of the financial reports filed during a state or local campaign to determine total costs, total revenues, sources of revenues, and such other factors as might be possible to ascertain.

3. What are the principal purposes for which campaign expenditures are made?

4. What conclusions about the party loyalties of economic classes may be drawn from the analysis of contributions to the national committees?

5. With respect to the financing of campaigns, what advantages are enjoyed by the party in power?

6. Differentiate between bribes and campaign contributions.

7. Determine the prevalence of assessment of officeholders for campaign purposes in your community.

8. Classify the objectives of the regulation of party finance.

9. Would it be advisable to regulate expenditures designed to influence legislation?   In view of experience in the regulation of campaign finance, what kind of regulation would you suggest?

10. It is possible with simultaneous campaigns for federal and state office to limit effectively total campaign expenditures?

CHAPTER 16

1. What theory have you evolved in explanation of the broadening of the suffrage?

2. How do you reconcile the suffrage requirements of 1800 with the doctrines of the Declaration of Independence?

3. How did the treatment of the question of manhood suffrage differ in the seaboard states and the frontier states?

4. How did political struggles between economic classes among the whites in the South affect the question of Negro suffrage?

5. Trace the course of constitutional litigation with respect to the "white" primary.

6. What interests were involved in the dispute over women suffrage?

7. What are the lessons in the technique of political agitation of the later stages of the woman-suffrage movement?

8. Classify the rules embodied in state laws regulating the suffrage.

CHAPTER 17

1. Classify and define the types of registration systems.

2. Examine and summarize the laws of your state regulating the registration of voters.

3. Does a system of permanent registration assure more accurate lists than periodic registration? Why?

4. What influence may the form of the registration system have on the proportion of the potential electorate actually registered as voters?

5. Ascertain from the legislation the general structure of the election machinery in your community.

6. If practicable, observe the conduct of an election as a watcher.

7. What are the principal forms of election fraud?

8. What sorts of groups were active in bringing about the adoption of the Australian ballot? Why?

9. What are the principal forms of ballots?

10. What are the advantages, if any, of voting machines over paper ballots?

CHAPTER 18

1. On what principles are public-opinion polls based?

2. How do variations in electoral participation affect the problems of opinion polling?

3. How may the phrasing of questions influence the results of polls on issues?

4. Of what importance are polls for campaign managers?

5. Do the polls have a band-wagon effect?

6. Examine the results of a dozen recent polls on issues. (The current poll findings are available in the *Public Opinion Quarterly*.) What do you conclude about the wisdom of the judgment of the mass of the people?

7. What are the uses of public-opinion polling for the public administrator?

8. A useful class project to demonstrate the problems of sampling opinion could be devised if campus elections fortuitously fall at the right time.

CHAPTER 19

1. What are the chief differences in participation in voting among different classes of the population?

2. What significance, if any, do you attach to the variations in electoral participation among different groups?

3. Analyze the variations in electoral participation among wards of your city or among counties of your state. If you discover that variations prevail, what is the explanation?

4. If your state is a two-party state, an instructive class project would be to analyze the vote in your state by counties over a period of, say, twenty-five years, to determine the degree of consistency of party loyalty in each county. How can the variations be accounted for?

5. Can you reconcile the fact of a high degree of consistent party voting with the theory that voting is motivated by the interests of the voter?

6. From the data presented in this chapter plus your own observations, formulate a theory of the motivation of voting behavior.

7. To test in a crude way the relationship between changes in economic

status and electoral behavior, chart trends of the prices over a twenty-year period of the chief agricultural commodities produced in one of the agricultural counties of your state. Place alongside this a trend line showing the percentage of the total vote polled by one of the major parties at elections held during the period. Are the inferences from the data in accord with those of the studies cited in this chapter?

CHAPTER 20

1. What considerations indicate the relevance of a treatment of violence alongside discussions of parties and pressure groups?

2. Under what conditions does the resort to force in internal politics occur?

3. How significant do you believe the fear of revolution is in persuading dominant groups to make concessions to social reform groups?

4. Has the function of violence in the definition of the status of labor in American society been overestimated in the discussion in this chapter?

5. How do you account for the prevalence of violence in the relations of worker and employer?

6. What is the significance of violence in industrial relations in comparison with other methods of class warfare?

7. Differentiate the ordinary strike from the "political" strike.

8. Can power be maintained or disputes be settled by the use of force alone?

CHAPTER 21

1. Under what sort of conception of politics does the analysis of education become relevant in the study of politics?

2. Consider the relative political significance of the family and the school.

3. Define the political function of education.

4. By what methods is the political orthodoxy of American schools maintained?

5. Is the influence of education generally exerted for the maintenance of the *status quo* or in the direction of political change?

6. What is the significance for the political order of universal compulsory education?

7. What difficulties are encountered in the effectuation of proposals that the schools exert their power to remake the political order?

8. Reflect on your own education and its political effects in terms of the discussion in this chapter.

CHAPTER 22

1. What machinery has been developed by political parties for the guidance of the work of Congress?

2. What are the basic factors that make the maintenance of party unity in Congress difficult?

3. Read the debates on a bill as reported in the *Congressional Record*.

Note particularly the role of the party machinery in the conduct of the debate and the guidance of procedure.

4. Analyze several recent roll calls on important bills in the House or Senate to determine the degree to which party lines are followed in voting. (Stuart A. Rice's method, explained in the text, is the best method for measuring party cohesion.)

5. Follow the course of a current piece of legislation to determine, in the light of the discussion in this chapter, the nature and function of Presidential leadership in the legislative process.

6. What are the major consequences of the gerrymander for public policy?

CHAPTER 23

1. How has the development of the administrative services been associated with economic specialization?

2. Discuss the motivation of administrative efforts to influence the determination of public policy.

3. Is there any conflict between the general principles of our constitutional system and the view that administrative agencies should perform a representative function?

4. In what respects are the public-relations activities of administrative agencies similar to those of private pressure groups?

5. What is the function of the clearance of departmental legislative requests through the Bureau of the Budget?

6. Why are administrative agencies limited by law in their lobbying and promotional activities?

INDEX

Index